Civil Procedure in Focus

Focus Casebook Series

CIVIL PROCEDURE IN FOCUS

Jeremy Counseller and Eric Porterfield

 Wolters Kluwer

Published by Wolters Kluwer in New York.

Wolters Kluwer Legal & Regulatory U.S. serves customers worldwide with CCH, Aspen Publishers, and Kluwer Law International products. (www.WKLegaledu.com)

To contact Customer Service, e-mail customer.service@wolterskluwer.com, call 1-800-234-1660, fax 1-800-901-9075, or mail correspondence to:

Wolters Kluwer
Attn: Order Department
PO Box 990
Frederick, MD 21705

Printed in the United States of America.

2 3 4 5 6 7 8 9 0

ISBN 978-1-4548-7757-8

Library of Congress Cataloging-in-Publication Data

Names: Counseller, Jeremy, author. | Porterfield, Eric, author.
Title: Civil procedure in focus / Jeremy Counseller and Eric Porterfield.
Description: New York : Wolters Kluwer, [2017] | Series: Focus casebook series
Identifiers: LCCN 2017029446 | ISBN 9781454877578
Subjects: LCSH: Civil procedure — United States. | Civil procedure — United
  States — Cases. | LCGFT: Casebooks.
Classification: LCC KF8840 .C585 2017 | DDC 347.73/5 — dc23
LC record available at https://lccn.loc.gov/2017029446

MIX
Paper from
responsible sources
FSC® C008955
FSC
www.fsc.org

About Wolters Kluwer Legal & Regulatory U.S.

Wolters Kluwer Legal & Regulatory U.S. delivers expert content and solutions in the areas of law, corporate compliance, health compliance, reimbursement, and legal education. Its practical solutions help customers successfully navigate the demands of a changing environment to drive their daily activities, enhance decision quality, and inspire confident outcomes.

Serving customers worldwide, its legal and regulatory solutions portfolio includes products under the Aspen Publishers, CCH Incorporated, Kluwer Law International, ftwilliam.com, and MediRegs names. They are regarded as exceptional and trusted resources for general legal and practice-specific knowledge, compliance and risk management, dynamic workflow solutions, and expert commentary.

For my dad, who took an old book off the shelf and read it to his son.—JC

For my dearest wife, who encouraged me to follow my heart.—EP

Summary of Contents

Table of Contents

PART III   LEARNING ABOUT THE CASE 243

 **PART IV** **ADDING PARTIES AND CLAIMS 375**

PART VI APPEALING THE TRIAL COURT'S DECISION 521

Chapter 23: Appealing the Trial Court's Decisions   523

PART VII PRECLUDING FURTHER LITIGATION 547

PART VIII The *Erie* Problem 581

The Focus Casebook Series

Help students reach their full potential with the fresh approach of the
Focus Casebook Series. Instead of using the "hide the ball" approach,
selected cases illustrate key developments in the law and show how courts
develop and apply doctrine. The approachable manner of this series provides
a comfortable experiential environment that is instrumental to student success.

Students perform best when applying concepts to real-world scenarios.
With assessment features, such as Real Life Applications and Applying the
Concepts, the **Focus Casebook Series** offers many opportunities for students to
apply their knowledge.

Focus Casebook Features Include:

Case Previews and Post-Case Follow-Ups — To succeed, law students must know
how to deconstruct and analyze cases. Case Previews highlight the legal concepts
in a case before the student reads it. Post-Case Follow-Ups summarize the
important points.

Case Preview

Carden v. Arkoma Associates

As you read *Carden*, think about the answers to these
questions:

1. What does *Carden* say about how the citizenship of an
   unincorporated association must be determined?
2. Does a limited partnership take on the citizenship of both
   its limited and general partners, or only its general partners?
3. How, if at all, does a state's recognition of an unincorporated association as one
   of its citizens affect the citizenship analysis under the diversity statute?
4. Do you think the Co[...]
   and lower courts in d[...]
   so, what might those [...]

Post-Case Followup

The Court recognizes that basic considerations of fairness
might justify treating unincorporated entities like corporations
for purposes of the citizenship analysis and that its decision
might fairly be categorized as form over substance. However,
the Court takes the position that creating a test for the citizenship of unincorporated associations is best left to Congress.
Congress has after all included in the diversity statute a test
for corporate citizenship. It could do the same for unincorporated associations. In
fact, 28 U.S.C. section 1332(d) provides that in class actions unincorporated associations are citizens of their states of organization and the states in which they have
their principal place of business (like corporations), but this standard does not apply
in direct actions (i.e., non-class actions). In the nearly three decades since *Carden*,
Congress has not defined the citizenship of unincorporated associations in direct
actions and the Supreme Court has not changed the position it took in *Carden*.

Carden creates problems for lower courts and litigants alike. It may be difficult
to determine the identity — let alone the citizenship — of all the constituent members of an unincorporated association. As a result, the trial court may lack diversity
of citizenship jurisdiction, yet only discover that fact after expending significant
resources. For example, in *Hart v. Terminex Int'l*, the court of appeals dismissed the
case for lack of diversity subject matter jurisdiction after eight years of litigation.

The Focus Casebook Series

Real Life Applications —
Every case in a chapter is followed by Real Life Applications, which present a series of questions based on a scenario similar to the facts in the case. Real Life Applications challenge students to apply what they have learned in order to prepare them for real-world practice. Use Real Life Applications to spark class discussions or provide them as individual short-answer assignments.

Avitts v. Amoco Production Co.: Real Life Applications

1. John, a citizen of Texas, files suit for breach of warranty against Advanced Technologies, Inc., a citizen of California and Delaware, in Texas state court. John ordered a large supply of computer equipment from Advanced Technologies and claims that none of the equipment functions properly. John seeks $100,000 in damages, which is what he paid for the equipment.

   a. Advanced Technologies files a notice of removal in the appropriate federal district court immediately after receiving John's initial pleading in the Texas state court action. John files a motion to remand claiming the court lacks subject matter jurisdiction, and that therefore the case was improperly removed. How should the court rule?

   b. Assume Advanced Technologies chooses not to remove the case. Instead, Advanced Technologies claims that the Texas state court lacks subject matter jurisdiction and must dismiss the case because it falls within the federal district court's "original and removal jurisdiction." Does the Texas state court lack subject matter jurisdiction?

Applying the Concepts/Rules and Civil Procedure in Practice

These end-of-chapter exercises encourage students to synthesize the chapter material and apply relevant legal doctrine and code to real-world scenarios. Students can use these exercises for self-assessment or the professor can use them to promote class interaction.

Applying the Concepts

1. Are the following cases properly removed to federal district court?

   a. Blake files suit against Acorn Industries, his former employer, in state court for age discrimination in violation of the federal Age Discrimination in Employment Act.

   b. Claire and Alison are in a car wreck. Claire, a citizen of New Mexico, files a state law
   Arizona.
   the car w

   c. Justin fil
   against C

Civil Procedure in Practice

Reynaldo Garza and his son Julian Garza are seriously injured in a single vehicle accident in McAllen, Texas. Reynaldo, the driver, lost control of his sport utility vehicle ("SUV") after one of the tires failed. The SUV then rolled over several times. Believing that the accident was the result of design defect in the vehicle and the negligence of its designer or designers, Reynaldo and Julian file suit in the United States District Court for the Southern District of Texas on February 12, 2015. In their complaint, they plead negligence under Texas law in the design of the vehicle. Reynaldo and Julian name one defendant in their complaint — the designer and manufacturer of the vehicle, U.S. Autos, LLC. Their complaint seeks damages for each one of them "in an amount not less than $5 million," including compensation for medical expenses, lost wages, pain and suffering, and disfigurement. In addition to pleading simple negligence, the Garzas also plead another cause of action, pleading that "U.S. Autos' negligence consists of the failure to comply with federal regulations regarding the design of vehicles marketed for sale in the U.S."

Preface

Ensure student success with the Focus Casebook Series.

THE FOCUS APPROACH

In a law office, when a new associate attorney is being asked to assist a supervising attorney with a legal matter in which the associate has no prior experience, it is common for the supervising attorney to provide the associate with a recently closed case file involving the same legal issues so that the associate can see and learn from the closed file to assist more effectively with the new matter. This experiential approach is at the heart of the *Focus Casebook Series*.

Additional hands-on features, such as Real Life Applications, Applying the Concepts, and In Practice provide more opportunities for critical analysis and application of concepts covered in the chapters. Professors can assign problem-solving questions as well as exercises on drafting documents and preparing appropriate filings.

CONTENT SNAPSHOT

This book is designed to help you understand federal civil procedure by starting with the big picture and then delving into the details of each topic and concept. This book has eight parts with each part corresponding to one of the seven major topics that together make up the law of federal civil procedure. It makes sense here to provide an overview of the eight parts of this book to help you conceptualize the whole of the law of federal civil procedure.

Part I provides an introduction to federal civil procedure – the rules that govern how disputes are resolved in federal court. Part II is Choosing the Proper Court. There are thousands of courts, both state and federal, scattered all across the United States. But which of these thousands of courts is a proper forum for resolving a particular dispute? The answer to this question is important because a court that is distant or inconvenient or unfamiliar with the governing law is unlikely to reach a fair and just resolution. The chapters in Part II address federal subject matter jurisdiction, personal jurisdiction, and federal venue, which, taken together, determine which courts are proper and which are not.

Part III is Learning About the Case. How do the parties learn of each other's claims and defenses and the evidence that will be used to support or refute them? Part III answers this question with chapters on notice, pleadings, and discovery.

Part IV is Adding Parties and Claims. This part answers a simple question: How big can a civil action be? Can we have more than one plaintiff or more than one defendant? If so, under what circumstances? Can multiple different claims be asserted in a civil action, and, if so, under what circumstances? Part IV answers these questions with chapters on party joinder and claim joinder.

Part V is Pretrial and Trial. It addresses pretrial and trial procedure, including chapters on disposing of the case without trial, basic trial procedure, and judgment as a matter of law. Part VI is Appealing the Trial Court's Decision. It addresses when you may appeal the trial court's decision, how to properly argue the court committed an error, and whether that error requires the appellate court to reverse the trial court's judgment. Part VII is Precluding Further Litigation. It addresses the requirements you must establish before a court will use a prior court's decision in a case to preclude further litigation.

Part VIII is The *Erie* Problem. The *Erie* Problem addresses what law the court should use to resolve a civil action where subject matter jurisdiction is based on diversity of citizenship or possibly supplemental jurisdiction. Perhaps more precisely, it addresses which jurisdiction's law should apply in a given situation. All 50 states have their own tort law, contract law, and property law, just to name a few. Of course there is also federal law and sometimes the law of a foreign nation becomes relevant to a civil action. Part VIII addresses the principles courts use to determine whose law applies to resolve the issues in the case.

RESOURCES

Casebook: The casebook is structured around text, cases, and application exercises. Highlighted cases are introduced with a *Case Preview*, which sets up the issue and identifies key questions. *Post-Case Follow-Ups* expand on the holding in the case. *Real Life Applications* present opportunities to challenge students to apply concepts covered in the case to realistic hypothetical cases. *Application Exercises* offer a mix of problem solving and research activities to determine the law of the state where the student plans to practice. State law application exercises better prepare the student to actually handle cases. The *Applying the Concepts* and *Civil Procedure in Practice* features demand critical analysis and integration of concepts covered in the chapter.

Other resources to enrich your class include: *Examples & Explanations for Civil Procedure*, by Joseph W. Glannon. Ask your Wolters Kluwer sales representative or visit the Wolters Kluwer site at *wklegaledu.com* to learn more about building the product package that's right for you.

Acknowledgments

We thank our families, Jennifer, Jack, Brett, and Kate, and Elizabeth, Zack, Sara, and Mimi, for their love, support, and patience while we wrote a book they have no reason to read. We thank our colleagues at Baylor Law School and the University of North Texas at Dallas College of Law for their support of this project, and in particular Deans Brad Toben, Royal Furgeson, and Ellen Pryor. We are fortunate to have such wonderful colleagues. Without their support and encouragement, this project would not have been possible.

We are especially grateful to our editor, Jane Hosie-Bounar, whose insight, attention to detail, and patience made her a joy to work with. We thank David Herzig at Wolters Kluwer for getting us involved in this project and for his encouraging words early on. Thank you also to The Froebe Group and Joe Stern for their help in editing and producing this text.

We are indebted to the reviewers of early drafts of these chapters for their edits and suggestions and especially for their candid and constructive critiques.

An Introduction to Civil Procedure

An Introduction to Federal Civil Procedure

Attorneys play a central role in resolving disputes. Find a significant dispute and chances are you will also find attorneys trying to resolve it in favor of their clients. Many of these disputes find their way into an American court system, and, even those that never become the subject of a legal action, can only be resolved with a view to how they would be adjudicated in court. An attorney's effectiveness as an advisor and advocate is determined largely by the attorney's knowledge of the rules that govern the resolution of these disputes in court. The law of federal civil procedure is the body of law that governs the resolution of civil actions in federal court. Your command of this important subject area will help you become an effective attorney. This introductory chapter defines federal civil procedure, addresses why the subject is so important to your future, and provides you an overview of the information you need to get off to a good start in your study of federal civil procedure.

A. WHAT IS FEDERAL CIVIL PROCEDURE?

Federal civil procedure is the law that governs how civil actions are resolved in the federal court system. This simple definition has three components that warrant further discussion — (1) federal, (2) civil, and (3) procedure.

This book focuses on the methods and practices for resolving civil actions in *federal* court. Each state has its own courts with their own

Key Concepts

- The definition of federal civil procedure, including the terms federal, civil, and procedure
- Why the subject is important both to becoming and being a competent attorney
- The primary sources of procedural law and their hierarchical relationship
- The dual nature of the American court system and the key differences between state courts' and federal courts' authority to hear cases
- An overview of the civil litigation process

body of procedural law for resolving civil actions. As examples, the law of California Civil Procedure governs the resolution of disputes in California state courts, the law of Texas Civil Procedure governs disputes in Texas state courts, and so on. To be sure, many of the topics and concepts discussed in this book apply in both state and federal court, but this book does not attempt to address the idiosyncrasies of each state's procedural law comprehensively. Instead, it focuses on federal civil procedure; so, you will be studying federal case law, statutes, and rules almost exclusively, rather than state law. Although it might strike you as odd to study only federal civil procedure, the skills you acquire in reading cases and analyzing jurisdictional statutes will serve you well in a state court practice. Moreover, many states use similar or even identical rules to the federal ones you'll be studying in this course.

This book addresses how *civil* actions are resolved in federal court, rather than how criminal actions are resolved. A **civil action** is one brought to resolve a dispute between the litigants based on the breach of some duty the defendant is alleged to owe the plaintiff, rather than one brought to determine whether the defendant is guilty of a crime. A criminal action is prosecuted by the state or federal government, whereas civil actions may be brought by and against individuals, corporations, or other types of entities. A governmental entity may be and often is a party to a civil action, but it is treated for the most part like any other private party in a civil action. In a civil action, what is at stake is typically money damages for the redress of whatever injury the plaintiff alleges the defendant caused him. In a criminal action, the stakes can obviously be much higher, including imprisonment or even the death penalty in some states. As examples, actions for breach of contract, negligence, and workplace discrimination are all civil in nature. A body of law called *criminal* procedure governs how criminal actions are resolved, but this book does not address it. You'll take another course that covers that subject.

Procedure is perhaps the most important element of our definition. Procedural law stands in contrast to the substantive law. Not all laws fall neatly into one category or the other, but, as a rule of thumb, the substantive law governs our out-of-court conduct while procedural laws govern how we resolve disputes filed in court. Most of the other courses you are taking or will take during your 1L year — courses like Contracts, Property, and Torts — are substantive law courses. They focus on laws that govern our out-of-court conduct. Contract law is used to determine whether or not a contract has been formed and what the rights and obligations are of the parties to the contract. Property law determines what a person can or cannot do with property she owns or with a tenant to whom she has leased property. Tort law may deem a person negligent who crashes his car into another car after running a red light, and it also addresses many other duties of care we owe. The substantive law governs our conduct every day as we go about our lives.

Procedural law, on the other hand, governs how disputes arising out of the breach of some substantive law right are resolved in court. To put it simply, the law of procedure provides the rules of the game for resolving conflicts in a judicial proceeding. Contract law says you have a right to be paid under a contract when you have performed the services you promised, but what do you do when the other party refuses to pay you? Where do you file suit? What documents do you file to commence the action? What do you need to say in those documents? How do you notify the defendant that you have sued him? How do you go about obtaining evidence from the defendant to support your claim? If you're defending such a claim, where and when do you present your objections to the action? Can you challenge the plaintiff's choice of court (sometimes referred to as "the forum") in which he filed the action? If so, how? Procedural law answers all of these questions and many, many more. The substantive law is a big part of *what* we are fighting over in litigation, but the law of procedure governs *how* we fight over it.

B.   WHY IS CIVIL PROCEDURE IMPORTANT?

If you're like most law students, civil procedure played no role in inspiring you to become a lawyer. Prior to law school, curiosity about procedural matters such as how and where to file a lawsuit, who can be parties to that suit, or what body of law will govern the dispute is rare. On the other hand, many law students are understandably curious about the substantive law. Constitutional, contract, tort, and property law are cornerstones of American society worthy of your devoted study. But a substantive law right is only as good as the procedures in place that allow individuals to protect that right. Of what value is the right to the quiet enjoyment of your property if there is no procedure for ejecting a trespasser? How would you get paid pursuant to the terms of a contract if no procedures exist for enforcing that contract? Without an effective body of procedural law for protecting our rights, the substantive law is little more than a set of hollow promises. The law of procedure breathes life into the substantive law.

If you feel some trepidation about studying civil procedure, you are not alone. For many law students, civil procedure seems alien. Whether you know it or not, you gained experience with the other areas of law you will study this year before coming to law school. You encountered contract law when you signed a lease, took a job, or ordered dinner in a restaurant. You've owned, leased, and rented property. If you've ever been pulled over for speeding, you came face to face with the criminal law. Most everyone studies the Constitution at some point in their education, perhaps in a high school civics course or a political science course in college.

We acquire at least some familiarity with the substantive law in the routine course of our lives because we need to comply with it or else face consequences. The businessperson needs some understanding of contract law to effectively sell goods and services. The homeowner benefits from knowledge of property law. Knowledge of constitutional law makes us more effective citizens when we vote or go down to the courthouse for jury duty. Non-lawyers benefit from a basic understanding of the substantive law. The non-lawyer doesn't need to know much, if anything at all, about civil procedure. It doesn't make sense for a non-lawyer to familiarize herself with a body of law she will encounter rarely, if ever, and then in all likelihood only with legal assistance. Because by and large only lawyers concern themselves with civil procedure, this subject is likely a complete unknown to you, and we tend to fear the unknown.

It is this unique feature of civil procedure — that it is a body of law designed to govern principally lawyers, rather than the public — that ought to inspire you to dedicate yourself to its study. Civil procedure is law for lawyers. It is our thing. Knowledge of civil procedure distinguishes you as a lawyer. In a few short years, a client will call you with a problem she wants you to solve. Perhaps she tells you that she paid a contractor to repair the roof on her home but the contractor never did the work. Because of your knowledge of contract law, you will be able to engage in a lengthy explanation using legal terms your client has never heard of, telling her that she and the contractor formed a binding contract and that the contractor must do the work or return the money. Your client's reaction to this explanation is likely to be something along the lines of "No kidding, that's why I'm calling you." Your client already has enough knowledge of the law of contracts to spot the substantive law issue, at least with sufficient clarity to realize that she may have a right to repayment and ought to consult a lawyer. She is calling you because she needs you to do something about it. Civil procedure is a course on what you do about it.

Civil procedure is important for other, more practical reasons as well. Civil procedure is one of only seven subjects tested on what is called the Multistate Bar Exam, which is a significant part of nearly every state's bar exam. Depending on which state's bar exam you take, you may also find civil procedure tested with essay and short answer questions. Even after you pass the bar exam, civil procedure will be critically important to your law practice. If you become a litigator, the law of civil procedure will govern virtually every aspect of navigating the civil justice system on behalf of your client, from filing suit to trial and appeal. You simply won't be able to help your client reach a positive result in civil litigation without having a strong command of this subject. Even if you want to be a transactional lawyer, you cannot draft effective documents or close a good deal on behalf of your client unless you know how those documents or that deal might be litigated later. Understanding civil procedure will allow you to craft documents that give your client an advantage later in litigation or, better yet, avoid it altogether.

C. SOURCES OF PROCEDURAL LAW

Your study of the law of civil procedure will include reading and analyzing the primary sources of this body of law. Neither your instructor nor this book will simply tell you what the law is without showing the source material to you. Instead, you will study the law itself. You will read and analyze constitutional provisions, statutes, rules, and judicial opinions that make up the body of law we call federal civil procedure. It is important to understand at the outset what these primary sources are and their relationship to one another.

The study of civil procedure includes a study of a variety of different sources of law. You will study relevant U.S. constitutional provisions, including those that create the federal judiciary and set out the limits of disputes federal courts are permitted to resolve. The Constitution is the supreme law of the land. Any statute or rule that conflicts with the Constitution as interpreted by the United States Supreme Court is unconstitutional.

You will also study federal statutes, such as those that describe what cases may be brought in federal court and where within the United States you may bring suit. You can identify a reference to a federal statute in the text by the citation to the United States Code (or "U.S.C."). The citation begins with the title number of the U.S. Code in which the statute is found and ends with the statute's section. For example, the citation to the Diversity Jurisdiction statute you will study in the next chapter is 28 U.S.C. §1332. This means the diversity statute is section 1332 of Title 28 of the United States Code. Any reference to language that is preceded by or followed by a citation in this format is federal statutory language. Federal statutes may not conflict with a U.S. constitutional provision, but they supersede all other state or federal laws in conflict with them.

You will also study the Federal Rules of Civil Procedure. According to Federal Rule of Civil Procedure 1, their purpose is to "secure the just, speedy, and inexpensive determination of every action and proceeding" in a federal district court. The Federal Rules are numbered 1 to 86. You can recognize references to a particular federal rule with citations such as Federal Rule of Civil Procedure 1, or simply Federal Rule 1, or more simply still, Rule 1. The Rules govern a wide variety of procedural matters, including how to commence a civil action, provide notice to defendants, conduct discovery and trials, and much more. The Federal Rules are neither constitutional provisions nor statutes. Instead, Congress provided the Supreme Court rulemaking authority to create rules of practice and procedure to govern in federal courts. The Federal Rules may not conflict with federal constitutional provisions or statutes.

Rules

Judicial opinions are another important source of procedural law. You will spend more time studying judicial opinions, particularly those of the U.S. Supreme Court, than any other source. The United States Supreme Court has the final say as to the meaning of the language in a federal constitutional provision, statute, or rule. If there is a question about what the language requires of a party or parties to a dispute, the Court will issue an opinion that both answers the question and provides a rationale for its answer. The Court determines the meaning of these provisions and other issues in the case by adhering to a concept called **stare decisis**. Stare decisis is a concept courts use to guide their decisions in the case before them by referring to past cases (a/k/a precedent), which generally requires them to follow the court's own prior rulings of law and those of a higher court within the same court system. This means that a case with similar governing law and similar facts ordinarily ought to be resolved in much the same way as the previous case or cases were resolved. Sometimes, courts have to consider the differences between previous cases and the current case, and decide whether those differences should change the result in the case currently being decided. As a result, as you read a court opinion, you will often see references to the governing laws, the facts, the result, and the rationale for why the court resolved the case in the manner it did. You will also likely see the court refer to the governing laws, facts, results, and rationales from previous opinions to explain and justify the result in the current case. All of this will help you understand what the law is, why the law is what it is, and the facts that were key to the court's decision. Stare decisis is beneficial because it helps provide predictability to the law and allows judges to draw on the

Precedents

wisdom (and the mistakes) of all the judges who have ever decided similar cases. It also provides an important tool for you as a future lawyer. You can read prior cases and form your own opinion as to how a court will resolve a certain kind of dispute. You can then use this knowledge to advise your client on how to resolve her dispute or avoid disputes altogether.

The Supreme Court's interpretation of a constitutional provision becomes part of the Constitution for all practical purposes. Congress cannot overturn the Supreme Court's interpretation of a constitutional provision by passing a conflicting statute. The Constitution can only be changed through the cumbersome process of adopting an amendment. Congress can, however, amend a federal statute to overturn the Supreme Court's interpretation of that statute. The same holds true for the Supreme Court's interpretation of a Federal Rule. Congress could overturn the Court's interpretation of a rule by passing a conflicting federal statute. Exhibit 1.1 depicts the hierarchical relationship of the sources of procedural law.

EXHIBIT 1.1   **Hierarchy of Federal Procedural Law**

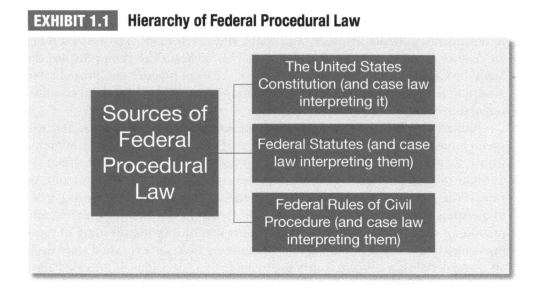

D. AN OVERVIEW OF THE AMERICAN COURT SYSTEM

American courts, both state and federal, apply the law of civil procedure to resolve the disputes pending before them. Although certainly not a perfect analogy, you might think of it this way, at least as a starting point: The law of civil procedure provides the rules of the game for resolving civil disputes, the parties are the players, our courts are where this game is played, and our judges are the referees. The first part of this book delves into the details of the structure of the court system and which court or courts may decide a particular case, but a brief overview here will help you understand the cases you will be reading early on in your study of civil procedure.

1. The Dual Nature of the American Court System

The United States has a dual court system consisting of both federal and state courts. Article III of the U.S. Constitution created the federal judiciary, but it is important to remember that the American colonies had their own court systems long before the Constitution was ratified. In other words, the Framers of the Constitution were not writing on a blank slate. Instead, the U.S. Constitution creates a federal system of government in which power is shared between the federal and state governments. Consistent with this power sharing arrangement, the federal judiciary exists side by side with 50 different state court systems.

The key distinction between state and federal courts lies in the kinds of cases they have the power to hear. **Subject matter jurisdiction** is a court's power to hear a type of case. State courts have what is called **general subject matter jurisdiction**. This means that state courts have the power to hear most any kind of case, regardless of what the case is about or who the parties are. This broad authority makes historical sense, because before the ratification of the federal constitution and the creation of the federal judiciary, state courts were the only courts in America. If they didn't decide the case, then no one else would. In contrast, federal courts are courts of **limited subject matter jurisdiction**. This means that federal courts only have the power to hear cases that meet certain requirements set out in the United States Constitution and federal statutes.

A relatively narrow class of cases may only be heard in federal court. Federal courts are said to have **exclusive jurisdiction** over these kinds of cases. Many other cases may be heard and decided by either a state or federal court. Federal and state courts are said to have **concurrent jurisdiction** over these kinds of cases. The next several chapters address the subject matter jurisdiction of the federal courts. These chapters will allow you to answer the important question of whether a particular case will be decided in state or federal court, or whether it could be decided in either court. The answers to these questions are critical because the judges, juries, and laws in state and federal court can vary widely and have important ramifications for how a dispute is resolved.

2. The Structure of the Court System

While their subject matter jurisdiction is different, the basic structure of the federal court system and most state court systems is similar. They typically consist of three different kinds of courts — (1) a trial court, (2) an intermediate appellate court, and (3) a "supreme" court. Each of these types of court has a different role to play in the resolution of civil disputes. Exhibit 1.2 depicts the basic structure of the federal court system.

A trial court exercises what is called **original jurisdiction**. To have original jurisdiction simply means that the trial court hears the case first, before either an intermediate appellate or a supreme court hears the case on appeal. So, a person commences a civil action by filing suit in a trial court, not by seeking review first in one of the appellate courts. As its name suggests, the trial court may conduct a trial to determine whether or not the parties' claims and defenses have merit. The trial court will hear

EXHIBIT 1.2   Basic Structure of the Federal Court System

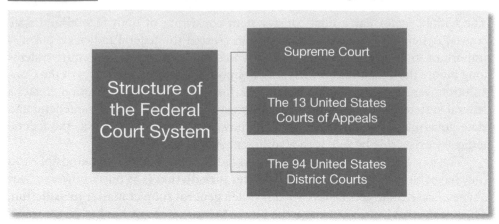

the evidence and make the initial determination of the legal issues arising in the case as well. The names of the trial courts in the state systems vary from state to state, but in the federal court system, the trial courts exercising original jurisdiction are the United States District Courts, also called informally the federal district courts.

Intermediate appellate courts exercise **appellate jurisdiction**, meaning they review the decisions of the trial court to determine if any errors require reversal of the trial court's judgment in the case. The 13 United States Courts of Appeals are the intermediate appellate courts in the federal system. The courts of appeals may affirm the judgment of the trial court, either because the trial court committed no error or because the error did not affect the propriety of the judgment, i.e., the error was harmless. If the court of appeals finds harmful error, the court of appeals will reverse the judgment of the trial court. Depending on the circumstances, the appellate court may either reverse and remand the case to the trial court for further proceedings or it will simply reverse and render judgment for the party that lost in the trial court. Most, but not all, state court systems also have intermediate appellate courts.

The court of last resort in the federal system is the Supreme Court of the United States. The court of last resort in most state systems is also typically referred to as the supreme court, e.g., the Supreme Court of California. These supreme courts hear appeals from the intermediate appellate courts. The U.S. Supreme Court and most state supreme courts are courts of **discretionary review**. This means that they may, but do not have to, hear appeals from the intermediate appellate courts. For example, the U.S. Supreme Court only hears and decides about 1 percent of the cases it is asked to review. In addition to hearing appeals from the U.S. Courts of Appeals, the U.S. Supreme Court may also review cases involving certain federal issues that have been decided by a state supreme court.

E. AN OVERVIEW OF THE CIVIL LITIGATION PROCESS

A brief overview of the civil litigation process will help you better understand the judicial opinions you will be reading early on in your civil procedure course, as well as those in your other 1L courses.

1. Commencing a Civil Action

Federal Rule 3 provides that a federal civil action is commenced by filing a complaint with the court. In virtually every federal civil action, the court in which the complaint is filed is one of the federal district courts, which is the court with original jurisdiction over most civil actions in the federal court system. The person or persons who file this complaint are called **plaintiffs**. The person or persons the plaintiffs name in the complaint as being responsible for their harm and against whom the plaintiffs seek judgment are called **defendants**. Suppose you hear someone say "John sued Ford in federal court," or "John filed suit against Ford in federal court." This means that John filed a complaint in federal district court naming himself as a plaintiff and Ford as a defendant.

The **complaint** commences a federal civil action and is the plaintiff's initial pleading to the court. In the complaint, the plaintiff will state his claim. This means that the plaintiff will provide both the factual and legal basis for the plaintiff's civil action. Typically, the complaint will tell the court the plaintiff's position on what happened (i.e., the factual basis for the suit) and why the law provides a remedy to the plaintiff under the circumstances (i.e., the legal basis for the suit). For example, suppose the plaintiff alleges the existence of a written agreement between himself and the defendant in which the plaintiff agreed to purchase manufacturing equipment from the defendant at a certain price, and the plaintiff further alleges that the defendant did not deliver the equipment even though the plaintiff paid the agreed upon price. These allegations would constitute the factual basis of the plaintiff's claim. It is not sufficient, however, to simply allege facts that sound unfair. The law must provide a remedy. Here, the plaintiff could allege that these facts constitute a breach of contract cause of action and that the plaintiff is entitled under governing contract law to the benefit of his bargain with the defendant. In this example, the plaintiff has stated a claim for breach of contract. In contrast, suppose your civil procedure instructor filed a federal civil action against you for cheating on the final examination. She might plead facts in her complaint to support the proposition that you cheated — she saw you glancing at your neighbor's paper, you did much better on the exam than she expected, etc. You might be furious at these allegations because you would never cheat on an exam. However, this case ought to be dismissed without you having to defend yourself against these factual allegations because the law simply does not provide a remedy to your instructor for any injuries caused by cheating students. Even if everything she alleges in her complaint is true, she is not entitled to judgment. In short, she has failed to state a claim.

In his complaint, the plaintiff must also state what relief he seeks from the court. This means the plaintiff must describe the remedy he seeks for his alleged injuries. In a civil action, the standard legal remedy is money damages. These may include compensatory damages designed to compensate the plaintiff for his injuries and may also include in certain cases (particularly tort cases) punitive (a/k/a exemplary) damages, which are designed to punish and deter similar conduct in the future. For example, if the plaintiff is injured in a car wreck with the defendant, the plaintiff may seek to recover his medical costs and lost wages as compensatory damages. He might also seek punitive damages against the defendant to deter him and others from engaging in the conduct that caused the plaintiff's injuries. Sometimes a plaintiff may seek injunctive relief in addition to or instead of money damages. An injunction is a court order telling a party to do or refrain from doing something. Suppose you find a notice posted on land you own that a construction company is going to begin building a shopping center there without your permission. You might seek an injunction ordering the construction company not to build the shopping center.

2. Providing Notice of the Action

Once the complaint is filed, the plaintiff must provide notice of the civil action to the defendant. The defendant has a right to defend himself and he cannot do this unless he is notified of the action against him. Rule 4 requires the plaintiff to provide the defendant two things: (1) a copy of his complaint and (2) the court's summons. The court will issue the summons upon the plaintiff's request. Among other things, the summons will identify the federal district court in which the complaint was filed and provide the defendant a deadline by which he must make an appearance. The summons will also tell the defendant that if he fails to respond to the action by the deadline, a default judgment may be entered against him. A **default judgment** is a judgment entered against a party based on the party's failure to defend the action. In other words, the summons informs the defendant that he must appear to defend or else the court will enter judgment in favor of the plaintiff. Put simply, the court's summons doesn't say only, "come to me," it says "come to me or else the plaintiff wins."

Together, the complaint and summons are called **process**. The plaintiff must serve process on the defendant. Depending on the circumstances, the plaintiff may serve process on the defendant by having a process server deliver it in person to the defendant, or the plaintiff may deliver it to someone of suitable age and discretion who lives with the defendant, or, sometimes, the plaintiff may be able to serve process by mail.

3. Responding to the Complaint

Service of process on the defendant triggers his obligation to respond to the action by presenting his defense or defenses. The defendant may present his defenses by filing an answer. The **answer** is the defendant's initial pleading to the court. In the answer, the defendant will admit or deny the various allegations in the plaintiff's complaint. The defendant's admission and denials help the court determine which issues are disputed and which are not. The defendant can also plead any other defenses to the action he believes he has.

There are a few defenses the defendant can raise without filing an answer to the complaint. If the defendant believes, for example, that the court is not a proper court for the resolution of the dispute or that he was not properly served, the defendant has the option to raise these defenses in a motion. Presenting these defenses by motion allows the defendant to delay or avoid altogether the obligation of having to respond to the merits of the plaintiff's claim with an answer. Suppose, for example, that a defendant in a breach of contract action believed that the federal court lacked subject matter jurisdiction and is therefore not a proper court. The defendant could raise this defense in his answer, but he could also raise it in a pre-answer motion objecting to lack of subject matter jurisdiction. If his motion is granted, the case will be dismissed without the defendant having had to respond to the merits of the plaintiff's breach of contract claim; i.e., he would not have to admit or deny the existence of a contract or whether or not he breached its terms. Parties often file pre-answer motions as an initial response, rather than answering the complaint.

4. Investigation and Discovery

The complaint and answer merely provide the parties' allegations — the things they *believe* they will be able to show. The court does not accept an allegation as true simply because one party has pled it. The parties must prove the allegations that support their claims and defenses. To prove them, they need evidence. Parties acquire the evidence they need through investigation and a more formal pretrial process called discovery. Informal investigation does not involve the assistance of the court. For example, an attorney's investigation would typically include an interview of his own client, obtaining records in his client's possession, or taking photographs of public areas relevant to the case. Discovery is a more formal pretrial process in which the court may become involved. The Federal Rules governing discovery allow a party to obtain the testimony of other parties and nonparty witnesses as well as documents, electronically stored information (e.g., emails), and other materials in the possession of other parties and even nonparties. If a party does not produce the requested material, the court may intervene to order production as appropriate. In other words, the court may assist the parties to ensure they obtain evidence relevant to the case. While discovery is conducted almost entirely between the parties themselves, outside of the view of the judge, the court's power to compel parties to provide information to each other underlies and shapes the parties' actions during discovery.

5. Pretrial Disposition

Investigation and discovery aren't the only things that happen pretrial. In fact, most cases are resolved pretrial without the court ever conducting a full trial on the merits of the parties' claims and defenses. Often, the parties are able to settle their dispute. The parties will memorialize the terms of their settlement in a written **settlement agreement**. A settlement agreement usually involves the defendant giving the plaintiff something of value (typically money) in exchange for the plaintiff's agreement to dismiss the lawsuit and release the defendant from any further liability related to the incident that is the subject of a pending or potential civil action. In most cases, the parties can choose to enter a settlement and jointly dismiss a case, without requiring approval from the court. The court can also resolve civil actions pretrial under certain circumstances. A court may dismiss a case because it is not a proper court for resolution of the action. For example, a federal court may dismiss a case because it lacks subject matter jurisdiction. The court may dismiss the case because the plaintiff's complaint does not state a claim that would entitle him to a judgment. Recall our cheating example above. In other cases, the court will grant summary judgment pretrial in favor of a party. **Summary judgment** is appropriately granted when the evidence does not raise a fact issue that could affect the proper judgment in the case. Trials are conducted to resolve disputed fact issues that could affect what judgment the court ultimately renders. If the evidence does not raise such a disputed fact issue, then summary judgment can be granted without the need for a trial.

6. Trial

A civil action proceeds to trial if not settled or resolved pretrial. Trials are conducted to resolve factual disputes as to the elements of the parties' claims and defenses. In a breach of contract action, for example, a trial might be conducted to determine whether or not the parties in fact had a contract and whether or not the defendant breached its terms. In a negligence action based on a car wreck, a trial could be used to determine whether or not the defendant breached his duty to the plaintiff under the governing tort law by running a red light and whether or not this caused the claimed injuries. In a workplace discrimination case, a trial could be used to determine if the plaintiff's race motivated the defendant to terminate the plaintiff's employment.

Some civil actions are tried to the judge while others are tried to a jury. A bench trial is a trial in which the judge determines the fact issues. A jury trial is a trial in which a jury of 6 to 12 citizens determines the fact issues. Based on the evidence presented at trial, the court instructs the jury as to the law it should apply, and the jury renders its verdict, deciding which party should prevail. Ordinarily, the court will enter judgment based on the jury's verdict, and we sometimes refer to such a judgment as a **judgment on a jury verdict**.

7. Judgment and Appeal

A party to a civil action, whether a plaintiff or defendant, seeks a judgment in his favor from the court. You have already in this introductory chapter encountered the terms **default judgment**, **summary judgment**, and **judgment on a jury verdict**. These terms describe *why* the judgment was rendered. A default judgment is rendered because the defendant did not appear to defend himself. A summary judgment is rendered because there was no disputed issue of material fact to be resolved. A judgment on a jury verdict is rendered consistent with the jury's verdict. The term "judgment" itself, however, has a precise meaning under the Federal Rules of Civil Procedure that has nothing whatsoever to do with why the judgment was rendered. Under the Federal Rules, a **judgment** is a court order from which an appeal lies. Generally speaking, a judgment is an order by which the district court finalizes its handling of the case. We'll discuss this concept in greater detail later, but for now understand that a district court's judgment resolves the parties' dispute (one way or the other) and indicates that the district court has no further matters to resolve. In short, the judgment indicates that the district court's work is done. If a party wishes to appeal the judgment and complain of an alleged error on the part of the district court, the judgment triggers the timetable for appealing to the appropriate court of appeals. The court of appeals will either affirm the judgment or reverse it. Once the court of appeals has made its decision, review may be sought in the Supreme Court, although the Court is under no obligation to actually hear the appeal. Once the appellate process is complete, the court system has fully and finally resolved the parties' dispute.

As a general rule, a trial court's final judgment precludes further litigation between the same parties arising out of the transaction or occurrence that was the subject of the litigation. For example, if the plaintiff loses in the federal district court, he cannot simply file another civil action against the defendant based on the same transaction or occurrence in an effort to get a different result in a different lawsuit. Similarly, if the plaintiff obtains a favorable judgment in district court, the defendant cannot simply file a new lawsuit in an effort to avoid liability, nor can the plaintiff file another lawsuit to add to his damages award. You will learn much more about the details and nuances of this doctrine in Chapter 24, which addresses the preclusive effect of a judgment. However, put simply, the judgment ensures that the winner remains the winner and the loser remains the loser. This result makes sense because otherwise civil litigation would never end. The losing party would continuously file new lawsuits based on the same dispute until he got the outcome he desired.

This introductory chapter only scratches the surface of the material you'll study in this course. By the time you complete the course, you will understand in some detail how civil actions are resolved in the federal court system. Most importantly, you will have a solid foundation for serving your future clients well.

Choosing the Proper Court

An Introduction to Subject Matter Jurisdiction

Subject matter jurisdiction plays an essential role in determining the proper court. Subject matter jurisdiction is about the kinds of cases courts have the power to hear. Different kinds of courts have the power to hear different kinds of cases. So subject matter jurisdiction answers this question: Does this court have the power to hear this type of dispute?

As a practical matter, subject matter jurisdiction tells us whether the case is one that is properly filed in state court, federal court, or either court. Federal courts are courts of limited jurisdiction. They may only hear cases that fall within the limits of their constitutional and statutory authority. In contrast, every state court system has at least one court of general jurisdiction. A state court of general jurisdiction can hear almost any kind of case. Even if a federal court has jurisdiction over a case, the state courts often do as well. For example, diversity and federal question cases are the two major categories of original federal subject matter jurisdiction, but state courts may also hear cases that meet the requirements of diversity and federal question jurisdiction. In such cases, the plaintiff has an initial choice between filing in a federal or state forum. The plaintiff's selection is an important one because it affects many aspects of the case, from who will decide the outcome to how it will be decided.

Key Concepts

- The constitutional source of federal judicial power and the objectives of the Framers in drafting it
- The meaning of limited, general, original, concurrent, and exclusive jurisdiction
- The two major categories of original federal subject matter jurisdiction
- How the choice of a federal or state forum affects the judge, jury, and law that will determine the case
- When an objection to lack of subject matter jurisdiction can be raised and who can raise it

A. THE CONSTITUTIONAL SOURCE OF FEDERAL COURT SUBJECT MATTER JURISDICTION: ARTICLE III, SECTION 2

While federal courts hear only a small fraction of the civil cases filed nationwide, they often handle the most important and far-reaching issues of constitutional and statutory law. The federal court system is a critical part of the constitutional framework of the United States, and is essential to our federal system wherein power is shared between the federal government and the states. Understanding what cases federal courts *can't* hear makes clear what civil actions will be heard in state court. Litigation strategy often involves choice of forum, and the choice between a federal or state court can fundamentally affect the outcome of the case.

1. The Constitutional Scope of Federal Judicial Power

Article III, Section 2 of the Constitution is the source of all federal court subject matter jurisdiction. The Framers were not writing on a blank slate when they drafted Article III of the Constitution. State courts already existed, and the Framers did not contemplate replacing state courts with the federal court system. Instead, state and federal court systems would exist side by side, with the state courts handling the majority of cases. The federal court system's subject matter jurisdiction would be limited, extending only to cases implicating certain national interests. The language of Article III, Section 2 reflects the Framers' intent regarding the role of the federal court system.

> The judicial power shall extend to all cases, in law and equity, arising under this Constitution, the laws of the United States, and treaties made, or which shall be made, under their authority; — to all cases affecting ambassadors, other public ministers and consuls; — to all cases of admiralty and maritime jurisdiction; — to controversies to which the United States shall be a party; — to controversies between two or more states; — between a state and citizens of another state; — between citizens of different states; — between citizens of the same state claiming lands under grants of different states, and between a state, or the citizens thereof, and foreign states, citizens or subjects.

This paragraph of just over 100 words creates all the judicial power Congress could ever authorize federal courts to exercise. It also reveals the objectives the Framers were trying to achieve by establishing a federal court system.

Providing Federal Courts the Ability to Interpret and Apply Federal Law

Article III, Section 2 creates federal judicial power over cases "arising under" federal law. This provision creates what is known as "arising under" or federal question jurisdiction. This "arising under" provision makes it possible for federal courts to have a say regarding the interpretation and application of federal law, rather than leaving such matters entirely to the state courts that might be hostile to the federal government and its laws.

Creating a Neutral Forum for Out-of-State Litigants

The Framers were concerned that state courts might favor their own citizens over citizens of other states, foreign citizens, and other state governments. For this reason, Article III, Section 2 allows federal courts to hear cases between citizens of different states and between citizens of a state and foreign citizens. This constitutional grant is known as diversity of citizenship jurisdiction.

Providing a Federal Forum for the Federal Government When It Is a Party

Article III, Section 2 creates federal judicial power over cases to which the United States is a party. This allows the federal government to vindicate its rights in its own court system, as opposed to a potentially hostile state court system.

Providing a Federal Forum for Certain Cases with an International Dimension

Article III, Section 2 also provides for federal judicial power in cases "affecting ambassadors or other public ministers and consuls," as well as in admiralty and maritime cases. These cases allow the federal government, through its court system, to handle cases that could impact its relationships with other nations. Article III, Section 2 also provides for federal judicial power in cases between U.S. states, and, in so doing, provides a neutral forum for such disputes, as opposed to a state litigating against another state in that state's own court system.

2. Federal Courts Are Courts of Limited Jurisdiction

If a case does not fall within the scope of Article III, Section 2, no federal court may hear it. Therefore, Article III, Section 2 makes clear that federal courts are courts of **limited jurisdiction**. In contrast, state court systems have at least one court of **general jurisdiction**. State courts can also hear most of the cases that can also be brought in federal court, except for those rare cases Congress selects for exclusive federal court jurisdiction, such as bankruptcy, admiralty, and patent infringement cases.

B. CONGRESSIONAL AUTHORIZATION TO EXERCISE JURISDICTION

1. The Requirement of Statutory Authorization to Exercise Jurisdiction

A federal court cannot exercise subject matter jurisdiction just because the case falls within the scope of Article III, Section 2. Despite stating that "the judicial power *shall* extend" to the cases it describes, Article III, Section 2 does not

----

"Jurisdiction Stripping" in Controversial Cases

Federal courts need congressional authorization to exercise the judicial power created in Article III, Section 2. If Congress has the authority to vest jurisdiction in federal courts, does it also have the power to strip federal courts of jurisdiction? Some members of Congress have taken that position. They have proposed legislation that would strip federal courts of jurisdiction to decide controversial cases involving (among other things) gay marriage, school prayer, and abortion rights. This legislation would have ensured that such cases would be decided only in state courts. None of these bills has become law.

automatically create jurisdiction directly in the federal courts. *Kline v. Burke Constr. Co.*, 260 U.S. 226 (1922). Instead, it gives Congress the power to vest jurisdiction in the federal courts by statute. In fact, the Constitution did not require Congress to create any lower federal courts at all, and only establishes the Supreme Court. But from the early days, Congress did create (and has continually expanded) the system of federal courts. However, because lower federal courts are not required at all as a constitutional matter, Congress has greater power to define and restrict the jurisdictional grant to the lower federal courts (for example, to limit diversity jurisdiction to cases over a certain amount in controversy).

Congress, however, cannot expand federal court jurisdiction beyond the limits in Article III, Section 2. Congress need not (and has not) authorized federal courts to exercise *all* of the judicial power in the Constitution. Therefore, Congress can limit a federal court's ability to exercise jurisdiction over particular cases, even though such cases fall within the scope of Article III, Section 2. Federal courts may exercise jurisdiction only when a case falls within the scope of Article III, Section 2 *and* meets the requirements of a congressional act that authorizes jurisdiction.

2. Concurrent Jurisdiction of State and Federal Courts

Article III, Section 2 describes the outer limits of cases over which federal courts could ever exercise judicial power. Notice, however, that it does not prohibit state courts from exercising jurisdiction over the same kinds of cases. Generally, state courts have jurisdiction over the same cases as federal courts. The jurisdiction of state and federal courts is said to be **concurrent** when both court systems have jurisdiction to hear the case.

For example, in the federal question statute, 28 U.S.C. §1331, Congress has authorized federal district courts to hear cases "arising under" federal law, but section 1331 doesn't grant federal courts exclusive jurisdiction over these cases; so, state courts may also hear cases involving federal claims and issues. The same is true of diversity of citizenship jurisdiction. Both state and federal courts may hear diversity cases. The practical effect of this concurrent jurisdiction is that a plaintiff seeking to file a federal question or diversity case may usually file in either state court or federal court.

Congress can elect to grant **exclusive jurisdiction** to the federal courts over a category of cases. In this situation, *only* the federal courts may hear and decide the case. For example, Congress has provided exclusive jurisdiction to federal courts in bankruptcy, admiralty, and patent cases. A grant of exclusive jurisdiction to the federal courts deprives state courts of subject matter jurisdiction. State courts, even state courts of general jurisdiction, have no jurisdiction over bankruptcy, patent infringement, and admiralty cases, for example.

3. The Role of Subject Matter Jurisdiction in Choosing the Proper Court

The subject matter jurisdiction analysis is an essential part of determining whether a court is a proper one in which to file the case, but it is not the only part. Even if a court has subject matter jurisdiction, it might not be a proper court in which to hear the case. A proper court must also have personal jurisdiction over the parties and be a proper venue. These topics are addressed in Chapters 6 through 12. The personal jurisdiction and venue analyses will tell us if the geographic location of the court is proper. It suffices to say for now that the federal question and diversity statutes do not answer this question. The subject matter jurisdiction analysis tells us whether we can file the case in state court, federal court, or either. For example, the subject matter jurisdiction analysis can tell us that we may (or must) file the case in some federal district court, but it will not tell us in which district court to file. Subject matter jurisdiction tells us nothing about whether to file in the United States District Court for the Eastern District of Texas or in the Southern District of New York. This is the work of personal jurisdiction and venue.

C. THE TWO MAJOR CATEGORIES OF ORIGINAL FEDERAL SUBJECT MATTER JURISDICTION: FEDERAL QUESTION AND DIVERSITY JURISDICTION

Like most first-year civil procedure courses, this book focuses on two categories of federal jurisdiction — federal question and diversity jurisdiction. In 28 U.S.C. §1331, Congress vested federal question jurisdiction in federal district courts over cases "arising under" federal law and, in 28 U.S.C. §1332, diversity jurisdiction over certain cases between citizens of different states or citizens of a state and foreign citizens. These two categories of cases account for the majority of civil cases filed in federal court. This book will also address supplemental subject matter jurisdiction. A court may exercise supplemental jurisdiction over certain additional claims if they are factually related to those over which it has original jurisdiction.

1. Original Jurisdiction

We will reserve the details of diversity of citizenship and federal question jurisdiction for Chapters 3 and 4 respectively. We address now a feature common to both the diversity and federal question statutes. Congress has granted federal district courts **original jurisdiction** over federal question and diversity cases. Having original jurisdiction means the federal district courts hear and decide the case before any other court. Original jurisdiction stands in contrast to appellate jurisdiction, which grants a court the power to review the decision of a court that has already decided the case. Federal district courts have original jurisdiction in diversity and federal question cases. This means plaintiffs may file their cases in federal district court, and the federal district court will serve as the trial court. The federal district court will conduct any trial and hear the witnesses and take evidence, while the appellate court simply considers the case on an appeal and reviews a paper record of the evidence taken in the district court.

2. Choosing State or Federal Court: What Difference Does It Make?

Plaintiffs may file federal question and diversity cases in either state or federal court. The differences between the state and federal court systems influence the plaintiff's choice.

The Jury Pools Are Different

Federal courts draw their jurors from a broader geographic area than state courts. State courts draw their jurors only from the county in which the court is located. Federal courts draw their jurors from their respective federal divisions, which consist of several counties, or sometimes even from the entire district, which consists of several divisions.

This geographic difference can result in a change in the overall makeup of the pool of potential jurors. Exhibit 2.1 is a map of the Southern District of Texas, including its constituent divisions and their constituent counties. Suppose a plaintiff wants to file her lawsuit in Houston, Texas and is deciding between state and federal court. The state court in Houston is the Harris County District Court. The federal court is the United States District Court for the Southern District of Texas, Houston Division. The Harris County District Court will draw its jurors only from Harris County, which is predominantly urban and suburban. The federal district court will draw its jurors from all the counties in the Houston Division, which include small towns and a great deal of rural farm and ranch land. The careers, attitudes, beliefs, and life experiences of the state and federal jury pools are likely to be vastly different. The plaintiff's choice of federal or state court has an impact on the kinds of people who may decide her case. Sometimes, a federal district court could summon potential jurors from throughout the district, rather than limiting the pool to its own division, which would further differentiate the federal jury pool, not to mention imposing a travel burden on jurors. Notice for example that the Southern District of Texas includes the Laredo, McAllen, and Brownsville Divisions, which lie on the U.S.-Mexico border more than 300 miles away from Houston.

The jury pools in state and federal court are different for another reason as well. Traditionally, federal district courts draw their jurors from voter registration records. State courts may draw them at least in part from driver's license records. The group of licensed drivers is a much larger and more racially and ethnically diverse group than registered voters.

EXHIBIT 2.1 **The Southern District of Texas**

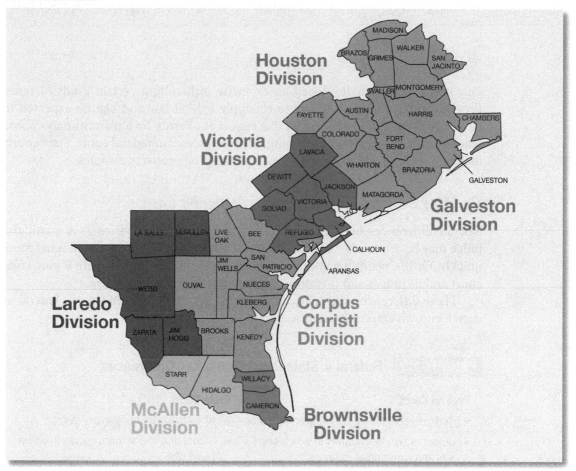

The Judges Are Different

Federal judges are appointed by the President and serve "during good behavior," usually for life. State judges may be elected or appointed, either for a certain term or for life, depending on the state. A federal judge holding a lifetime appointment might be less susceptible to local opinion and political pressures than an elected state court judge who must answer to the voters, including the lawyers who practice in his court. Out-of-state litigants often find this feature of the federal court system appealing, particularly when they are asking the judge to do something that will not be popular with the local electorate.

The Law Governing the Case Will Be Different

Federal courts will apply the Federal Rules of Evidence and Procedure. State courts often use the Federal Rules of Evidence and Procedure as a model for their own rules, but state rules can and often do differ from the Federal Rules in key respects.

The plaintiff's attorney may have more experience with one body of law or the other or believe there is some other advantage to having federal or state law applied to the case.

Their Areas of Expertise May Be Different

One court may have developed an expertise in handling certain kinds of cases. Federal courts, for example, routinely apply federal law and can be expected to have some skill and experience in that regard as a result. So a plaintiff may choose federal court in cases involving complex federal issues in federal court. State courts may have expertise in other areas, such as handling property disputes.

One May Be More Convenient in a Particular Case

Not all differences between state and federal court are systemic. A particular judge may have a smaller caseload that will allow the plaintiff to obtain relief more quickly. Or the plaintiff's attorney may simply be more familiar with a particular court and its judges and therefore more comfortable litigating there.

These differences, summarized in Exhibit 2.2, make the choice of a federal or state forum an extremely significant one.

EXHIBIT 2.2   **Federal v. State Court: Some Key Differences**

Federal Court	State Court
• Judges serve for life during good behavior	• In many states, judges are elected
• Jurors drawn from county in which court sits and surrounding counties	• Jurors drawn only from county in which court sits
• Jurors drawn from voter registration	• Jurors may be drawn from DMV records
• Federal Rules of Procedure and Evidence	• State Rules of Procedure and Evidence

---

3. When the Federal District Court Lacks Subject Matter Jurisdiction

The federal district court may not hear a case if it lacks original subject matter jurisdiction. Thus, a lack of subject matter jurisdiction is a defense to the action in federal court. The defense of lack of subject matter jurisdiction is different than most any other defense in two key respects. First, a party can raise a lack of subject matter jurisdiction at any time and cannot waive the objection due to the passage of time. Most defenses are waived if not raised in a timely fashion. Even the plaintiff who chose the federal forum in the first place can raise the issue. A party can raise a lack of subject matter jurisdiction long after the case is filed, even after trial. He may even raise it for the first time on appeal. Second, the federal district court is obligated to raise the issue *sua sponte*. This means the federal court must raise the jurisdictional issue on its own, even if no party has questioned the court's jurisdiction. This makes sense because the purpose of subject matter jurisdiction is not to protect any particular party. Instead, subject matter jurisdiction is about the distribution of power between the federal and state governments in our federal system. Federal courts will raise the issue on their own, therefore, to ensure they have not exceeded their authority.

Chapter Summary

- Subject matter jurisdiction is about the kinds of cases courts can hear. As a practical matter, subject matter jurisdiction tells us whether a case can be heard in state court, federal court, or either kind of court.
- Federal courts are courts of limited jurisdiction. They may only exercise jurisdiction when the case falls within the parameters of both Article III, Section 2 and a congressional act authorizing them to exercise jurisdiction.
- State courts systems all have at least one court of general jurisdiction. Such courts may hear almost any kind of case.
- The two major categories of federal jurisdiction authorized by Congress — accounting for the majority of cases filed in federal court — are federal question jurisdiction and diversity of citizenship jurisdiction.
- State courts may hear federal question and diversity cases as well. Thus, federal and state courts have concurrent jurisdiction over federal question and diversity cases.
- The choice of state or federal court affects the kind of judge, jurors, and law that will govern the case.

3

Diversity of Citizenship Jurisdiction

It might surprise you to learn that federal courts routinely hear state law claims, not just claims based on federal law. Federal courts have the authority to adjudicate certain state law claims for negligence and intentional torts, as well as state breach of contract and warranty claims and property disputes, among many others. Federal courts can hear these state law claims when the requirements of the diversity of citizenship jurisdiction statute are met. The traditional rationale for diversity jurisdiction is to provide a neutral forum in federal court in order to prevent local prejudice against out-of-state litigants in state court. The concern at the founding was that state courts might have been prejudiced against defendants from other states or against foreign citizens. Would a Georgia state court treat a Virginia defendant fairly? Would a Virginia state court treat a citizen of France fairly? Doubt about the answer to these questions led the Framers to include in Article III, Section 2 federal judicial power over cases "between Citizens of different States" and in cases between state citizens and foreign citizens. Whether or not this rationale was well founded at the time the Constitution was written — much less in the more than 200 years since — has long been the subject of debate. Despite this controversy, diversity of citizenship is still a valid basis for subject matter jurisdiction in the federal courts. In fact, tens of thousands of cases are heard in federal court on diversity grounds each year. The key point here is that diversity jurisdiction is based upon *who* the parties are, rather than what the claims are.

As discussed in the previous chapter, the language in Article III, Section 2, including the diversity language, does not vest jurisdiction in the federal courts. An Act

Key Concepts

- The meaning of the term complete diversity of citizenship
- When the federal district court has alienage jurisdiction
- How to determine the citizenship of individuals, corporations, and unincorporated entities and associations
- The amount in controversy requirement and how the amount in controversy is determined

of Congress is required. Because the constitutional language is not self-executing, Congress can and has limited federal court jurisdiction in important ways in the diversity statute — section 1332 of Title 28 of the United States Code. The diversity statute actually embraces two different types of subject matter jurisdiction: diversity jurisdiction (cases between citizens of different states), and alienage jurisdiction (cases between citizens of a state and citizens or subjects of a foreign state).

To understand the diversity statute, you must understand: (1) the meaning of the term "complete diversity"; (2) how a party's citizenship is determined; and (3) the amount in controversy requirement.

A. *COMPLETE* DIVERSITY OF CITIZENSHIP

The diversity statute requires complete diversity of citizenship. The term "complete diversity" is not found in the statutory language. Section 1332(a)(1), shown in Exhibit 3.1, says the case must be "between citizens of different States." The statutory language clearly calls for a difference in citizenship amongst the parties of some kind, but the statute is not clear about the difference it requires. What if the plaintiffs have the same citizenship? What if one defendant has the same citizenship as the plaintiff but the other defendant does not? The Supreme Court answered these questions over 200 years ago in *Strawbridge v. Curtiss*, 7 U.S. 267 (1806). In *Strawbridge*, the Court read the diversity statute to require *complete* diversity. **Complete diversity of citizenship** exists when no party on one side of the case has the same citizenship as any party on the other side of the case. Put simply, no plaintiff may share citizenship with any defendant. If *any* plaintiff has the same citizenship as *any* defendant, the federal district court lacks diversity jurisdiction under the statute. The diversity statute contemplates that a party may be either a citizen of a U.S. state or a foreign citizen or subject. This section of the chapter will address the meaning of "complete diversity," where only state citizens are parties, and then will address cases where foreign citizens or subjects are parties (so-called alienage jurisdiction cases).

1. State Citizenship

Section 1332(a)(1) requires a case between "citizens of different states," but we also know that *Strawbridge* requires complete diversity of citizenship. What does complete diversity look like in cases under 1332(a)(1)? Cases involving a single plaintiff

---

EXHIBIT 3.1   **28 U.S.C. §1332(a)(1)**

(a) The district courts shall have original jurisdiction of all civil actions where the matter in controversy exceeds the sum or value of $75,000 and is between —
    (1) citizens of different states. . . .

and a single defendant are relatively straightforward. Suppose that Bob is a citizen of Texas and files suit against John, a citizen of Oklahoma. The only plaintiff has a different citizenship than the only defendant. This example meets any definition of diversity. The analysis gets only slightly more complicated when dealing with multiple plaintiffs or multiple defendants. Assume Bob sues both John and Sheetrock, Inc., who are both citizens of Oklahoma. Now the case looks like this:

Bob (TX) ⟋ John (OK)
         ⟍ Sheetrock, Inc. (OK)

This is another example of complete diversity. Here, the only plaintiff is a Texas citizen and neither of the defendants is a Texas citizen. Complete diversity exists even if defendants have the same citizenship, as in this example, or if plaintiffs have the same citizenship.

But what if Sheetrock, Inc. was a citizen of Texas instead of Oklahoma? Now the case looks like this:

Bob (TX) ⟋ John (OK)
         ⟍ Sheetrock, Inc. (TX)

In this example, complete diversity does not exist. The plaintiff, Bob, and one of the defendants, Sheetrock, Inc., are both citizens of Texas. Remember, complete diversity is destroyed if *any* plaintiff shares citizenship with *any* defendant.

2. Alienage Jurisdiction

Foreign citizens, not just state citizens, frequently are parties to cases in federal district court. Section 1332(a)(2) of the diversity statute, shown in Exhibit 3.2 below, gives federal district courts what is called **alienage jurisdiction** over cases between citizens of a state and citizens or subjects of a foreign state. The purpose of alienage jurisdiction is to prevent discrimination in state court against foreign citizens.

Suppose Conchita, a citizen of Spain, files suit against Plum, Inc., a citizen of California, for $200,000. The case would look like this:

Conchita (Spain) ⟶ Plum, Inc. (CA)

EXHIBIT 3.2   **28 U.S.C. §1332(a)(2)**

> (a) The district courts shall have original jurisdiction of all civil actions where the matter in controversy exceeds the sum or value of $75,000 and is between —
> (2) citizens of a State and citizens or subjects of a foreign state. . . .

The federal district court could exercise alienage jurisdiction under 28 U.S.C. §1332(a)(2), because this example is a case between a citizen of a foreign state (Spain) and a citizen of a U.S. state (California). Alienage jurisdiction exists even if we add additional state citizens as defendants to this example. If Conchita sued Fig, Inc., a citizen of Oregon, as well as Plum, Inc., the case would look like this:

Conchita (Spain) ⟶ Plum, Inc. (CA)
⟶ Fig, Inc. (OR)

Alienage jurisdiction exists because this case is still one between a foreign citizen and citizens of a state under section 1332(a)(2).

An Exception to Alienage Jurisdiction Under §1332(a)(2)

Section 1332(a)(2) contains an important exception to alienage jurisdiction. District courts do *not* have original jurisdiction under subsection 1332(a)(2) where the case is between citizens of a state and citizens of a foreign state "who are lawfully admitted for permanent residence in the United States and are domiciled in the same State." Alienage jurisdiction under subsection 1332(a)(2) does not exist when a permanent legal resident alien of the United States is domiciled in a U.S. state and a party on the other side of the case is a citizen of that same state. **Domicile** is discussed in depth later in the chapter. For now, know that an individual is domiciled in the state where he resides with the intent to remain indefinitely. Without this exception, a permanent legal resident alien domiciled in a U.S. state could file suit in federal court against his neighbor on a state law claim, while an American citizen could not get into federal court on the same claim. This exception is also justified on the grounds that a permanent legal resident alien domiciled in a U.S. state who is a defendant may not need the same protection against local prejudice in state court as other foreign citizens.

To understand this exception, let's go back to our earlier example where Conchita, a citizen of Spain, sues Plum, Inc., a citizen of California. The case looks like this:

Conchita (Spain) ⟶ Plum, Inc. (CA)

Based on these facts alone, the exception does not apply. The district court would have alienage jurisdiction over this case because it is a case between a citizen of a U.S. state and a foreign citizen. But adding two additional facts implicates the exception. Assume that: (1) the federal government has admitted Conchita as a permanent legal resident of the United States; and (2) Conchita is domiciled in California (she lives there and has no present intention of moving away). Now, Conchita is a permanent legal resident alien of the United States ("PLRA"), who is domiciled in California, suing a California citizen. We can diagram the case this way:

Conchita (Spanish Citizen and PLRA Domiciled in CA) ⟶ Plum, Inc. (CA)

Under the exception in subsection 1332(a)(2), alienage jurisdiction does not exist here because this is a case between a citizen of a state, Plum, Inc., and a permanent legal resident alien domiciled in the same state, California. Alienage jurisdiction would also not exist if we flipped the plaintiff and defendant in this example.

Be careful not to read this exception too broadly. You need only concern yourself with the exception when dealing with foreign citizens who are humans. Only humans are admitted (or not) for permanent legal resident alien status, not corporations or other entities. Moreover, the exception probably only applies to foreign citizens admitted for *permanent* legal resident alien status. Many foreign citizens live in or visit the United States legally for extended periods of time without being admitted for *permanent* legal resident alien status. For example, they may have been admitted on a student visa or a temporary worker visa. Although the cases are not entirely consistent, these legally admitted foreign citizens probably do not implicate the "PLRA" exception to alienage jurisdiction in subsection 1332(a)(2).

EXHIBIT 3.3 **28 U.S.C. §1332(a)(3)**

(a) The district courts shall have original jurisdiction of all civil actions where the matter in controversy exceeds the sum or value of $75,000 and is between —

. . .

(3) citizens of different states and in which citizens or subjects of a foreign state are additional parties. . . .

Foreign Citizens as Additional Parties

Subsection 1332(a)(3), shown in Exhibit 3.3, authorizes alienage jurisdiction in cases between "citizens of different states and in which citizens or subjects of foreign states are additional parties. . . ." This subsection of the statute authorizes jurisdiction in cases where citizens of different states are on both sides of the case, and foreign citizens are also parties. For example, if Peach, Inc., a citizen of Georgia, files suit against Distributors, Inc., a citizen of California, and Transporters, S.A., a citizen of Mexico, jurisdiction under subsection 1332(a)(3) would exist. The case would look like this:

Peach, Inc. (GA) ⟶ Distributors, Inc. (CA)
Transporters, S.A. (Mexico)

Jurisdiction exists because this case is between diverse state citizens — a Georgia citizen as plaintiff and a California citizen as a defendant — with a foreign citizen as an additional party on one side of the case.

Jurisdiction under the diversity statute does *not* exist when the only parties to the case are foreign citizens. For example, if only Conchita, a citizen of Spain, filed suit only against Alice, a citizen of France, there is no alienage jurisdiction. The case looks like this:

Conchita (Spain) ——→ Alice (France)

This example is a case between foreign citizens. Note that it does not matter that the parties are citizens of different nations. Diversity jurisdiction does not exist because the plaintiff and defendant are both foreign citizens. Neither the diversity statute nor Article III, Section 2 permits jurisdiction in this case. Conchita would have to file this action in state court. Remember: State courts can hear virtually any kind of case. So, the lack of federal court jurisdiction does not deprive the plaintiff of a forum altogether, just a federal forum.

B. DETERMINING CITIZENSHIP

Now that we understand what complete diversity means and what citizenship combinations the diversity statute permits, we need to understand how to determine a party's citizenship. How a party's citizenship is determined depends upon the type of "person" the party is. All kinds of "persons" can be parties to a civil action. Humans, corporations, and other business and charitable entities are routinely parties to civil actions in federal court. The citizenship of individuals, corporations, and unincorporated associations are each determined differently. Once you have determined what kind of person you are dealing with, you will know what test to apply to that person in order to determine citizenship.

1. The Citizenship of Individuals (i.e., Humans)

Although we typically think of "citizenship" in terms of a person's affiliation with a nation or country, the term "citizen" has a special meaning under the diversity statute. Under the diversity statute, an individual might be either a citizen of a U.S. state or a foreign citizen. If a person is not a U.S. citizen, he is almost certainly a citizen or subject of a foreign state. For example, a citizen of France or Mexico is a foreign citizen under the diversity statute. Determining when an individual is a citizen of a U.S. state under the diversity statute is a bit more complicated. The *Mas v. Perry* case will help you understand how to determine citizenship for an individual.

Case Preview

Mas v. Perry

As you read *Mas v. Perry*, consider these questions:

1. What role does an individual's domicile play in the determination of his or her citizenship? How is a person's

domicile established? What impact, if any, can the domicile of the person's spouse have? What about the domicile of a minor child's parents?

2. What must a person do to change his domicile? Is it enough to simply reside in a different state? What if the person has not moved away from his state of domicile but intends to do so?

3. What impact, if any, does a party's change of domicile after the complaint is filed have on the court's diversity of citizenship jurisdiction?

4. Does the *Mas* court correctly apply the "indefinite intent" standard?

France

Mas v. Perry
489 F.2d 1396 (5th Cir. 1974)

AINSWORTH, Circuit Judge:

This case presents questions pertaining to federal diversity jurisdiction under 28 U.S.C. §1332, which, pursuant to article III, section II of the Constitution, provides for original jurisdiction in federal district courts of all civil actions that are between, inter alia, citizens of different States or citizens of a State and citizens of foreign states and in which the amount in controversy is more than $10,000.

Appellees Jean Paul Mas, a citizen of France, and Judy Mas were married at her home in Jackson, Mississippi. Prior to their marriage, Mr. and Mrs. Mas were graduate assistants, pursuing coursework as well as performing teaching duties, for approximately nine months and one year, respectively, at Louisiana State University in Baton Rouge, Louisiana. Shortly after their marriage, they returned to Baton Rouge to resume their duties as graduate assistants at LSU. They remained in Baton Rouge for approximately two more years, after which they moved to Park Ridge, Illinois. At the time of the trial in this case, it was their intention to return to Baton Rouge while Mr. Mas finished his studies for the degree of Doctor of Philosophy. Mr. and Mrs. Mas were undecided as to where they would reside after that.

moved

Upon their return to Baton Rouge after their marriage, appellees rented an apartment from appellant Oliver H. Perry, a citizen of Louisiana. This appeal arises from a final judgment entered on a jury verdict awarding $5,000 to Mr. Mas and $15,000 to Mrs. Mas for damages incurred by them as a result of the discovery that their bedroom and bathroom contained "two-way" mirrors and that they had been watched through them by the appellant during three of the first four months of their marriage.

Perry = LL

voyeur?

At the close of the appellees' case at trial, appellant made an oral motion to dismiss for lack of jurisdiction . . . the motion was denied by the district court. Before this Court, appellant challenges the final judgment below solely on jurisdictional grounds, contending that appellees failed to prove diversity of citizenship among the parties and that the requisite jurisdictional amount is lacking with respect to Mr. Mas. Finding no merit to these contentions, we affirm. Under section 1332(a)(2), the federal judicial power extends to the claim of Mr. Mas, a citizen of France, against the appellant, a citizen of Louisiana. Since we conclude that Mrs. Mas is a citizen of

Mississippi for diversity purposes, the district court also properly had jurisdiction under section 1332(a)(1) of her claim.

It has long been the general rule that complete diversity of parties is required in order that diversity jurisdiction obtain; that is, no party on one side may be a citizen of the same State as any party on the other side. Strawbridge v. Curtiss, 7 U.S. (3 Cranch) 267, 2 L. Ed. 435 (1806). This determination of one's State Citizenship for diversity purposes is controlled by federal law, not by the law of any State. As is the case in other areas of federal jurisdiction, the diverse citizenship among adverse parties must be present at the time the complaint is filed. Jurisdiction is unaffected by subsequent changes in the citizenship of the parties. . . . The burden of pleading the diverse citizenship is upon the party invoking federal jurisdiction, . . . and if the diversity jurisdiction is properly challenged, that party also bears the burden of proof. . . .

To be a citizen of a State within the meaning of section 1332, a natural person must be both a citizen of the United States . . . and a domiciliary of that State. . . . For diversity purposes, citizenship means domicile; mere residence in the State is not sufficient. . . .

A person's domicile is the place of "his true, fixed, and permanent home and principal establishment, and to which he has the intention of returning whenever he is absent therefrom. . . ." Stine v. Moore, 5 Cir., 1954, 213 F.2d 446, 448. A change of domicile may be effected only by a combination of two elements: (a) taking up residence in a different domicile with (b) the intention to remain there. . . .

It is clear that at the time of her marriage, Mrs. Mas was a domiciliary of the State of Mississippi. While it is generally the case that the domicile of the wife — and, consequently, her State citizenship for purposes of diversity jurisdiction — is deemed to be that of her husband, we find no precedent for extending this concept to the situation here, in which the husband is a citizen of a foreign state but resides in the United States. Indeed, such a fiction would work absurd results on the facts before us. If Mr. Mas were considered a domiciliary of France — as he would be since he had lived in Louisiana as a student-teaching assistant prior to filing this suit — then Mrs. Mas would also be deemed a domiciliary, and thus, fictionally at least, a citizen of France. She would not be a citizen of any State and could not sue in a federal court on that basis; nor could she invoke the alienage jurisdiction to bring her claim in federal court, since she is not an alien. On the other hand, if Mrs. Mas's domicile were Louisiana, she would become a Louisiana citizen for diversity purposes and could not bring suit with her husband against appellant, also a Louisiana citizen, on the basis of diversity jurisdiction. These are curious results under a rule arising from the theoretical identity of person and interest of the married couple.

An American woman is not deemed to have lost her United States citizenship solely by reason of her marriage to an alien. Similarly, we conclude that for diversity purposes a woman does not have her domicile or State Citizenship changed solely by reason of her marriage to an alien.

Mrs. Mas's Mississippi domicile was disturbed neither by her year in Louisiana prior to her marriage nor as a result of the time she and her husband spent at LSU after their marriage, since for both periods she was a graduate assistant at LSU. . . . Though she testified that after her marriage she had no intention of returning to her parents' home in Mississippi, Mrs. Mas did not effect a change of domicile since she and Mr. Mas were in Louisiana only as students and lacked the requisite intention to remain there. Until she acquires a new domicile, she remains a domiciliary, and thus a citizen, of Mississippi. . . .

Affirmed.

Post-Case Follow-Up

Mas holds that once a domicile is established — either by one's self or one's parents — the domicile changes only when the person does two things: (1) resides in a different state (2) with the intent to remain in that state indefinitely (or, in the words of *Mas*, with the intent to make the new state a "true, fixed, and *permanent* home"). Arguably, "permanence" expects too much. *Compare Gordon v. Steele*, 376 F. Supp. 575 (W.D. Pa. 1974) (holding that a student originally from Pennsylvania was domiciled in Idaho where she was attending school, though she testified she may move anywhere after graduation but had no definite plans to do so) *with Holmes v. Sopuch*, 639 F.2d 431 (8th Cir. 1981) (holding that a student was not domiciled in Ohio where he was attending graduate school when he testified that he intended to return to his previous job upon graduation, which was not in Ohio; thus, he had a definite plan to leave).

Note that the court concludes that Mrs. Mas is a domiciliary of Mississippi even though she did not intend to return to Mississippi. A person's domicile does not change simply because she resides elsewhere or simply because she no longer intends to remain in her state of domicile indefinitely. To change domicile, the person must both reside elsewhere and have the intent to remain in that state indefinitely. Thus, Mrs. Mas is a domiciliary of Mississippi until she both resides in another state and does so with the intent to remain there indefinitely.

Note that the court determined Mr. Mas to be a citizen of France without going into a discussion of his domicile. To be a citizen of a U.S. state, an individual *must* be a U.S. citizen. Even if Mr. Mas was domiciled in a U.S. state, he is a foreign citizen under the diversity statute because he is not a U.S. citizen.

Mas v. Perry and Domicile: Real Life Applications

1. Juan has lived in Texas since being admitted as a permanent legal resident alien 20 years ago. He is a citizen of Colombia. His primary residence is in Houston, Texas but he recently purchased a retirement home in Fredericksburg, Texas. Juan is injured when a car, driven by Alex, ran a stop sign and collided with Juan's car. Juan files suit against Alex seeking personal injury damages. Alex has

Not All "States" Are U.S. States

The United States consists of more than just the 50 states. It also includes territories, the District of Columbia, and the Commonwealth of Puerto Rico. 28 U.S.C. §1332(e) defines "States" to include U.S. territories, the District of Columbia, and Puerto Rico. Even though these districts and territories are not U.S. states, they are treated as "States" for section 1332 purposes.

resided in Oklahoma for over ten years and has no plans to ever leave, but Alex is a Canadian citizen who overstayed his student visa years ago. Assuming the amount in controversy requirement is met, does the federal district court in Texas have original subject matter jurisdiction under the diversity statute?

2. Chris is a U.S. citizen, born and raised on his family's farm outside Raleigh, North Carolina. Following his graduation from high school in North Carolina, Chris attended college in West Virginia. Throughout his time in college in West Virginia, Chris planned to return home to help run the family farm in North Carolina after he earned his four-year degree. As Chris neared the completion of his degree, his plans changed. Instead of returning to the family farm upon graduation, Chris joined the Peace Corps and agreed to live and serve in Bucharest, Romania for two years before returning to the United States to begin a career and start a family. While serving in the Peace Corps, Chris was offered teaching jobs at two different junior high schools in the United States — one located in New York and the other in New Jersey. While still living in Romania, Chris decided he would take one of the two jobs, but had not decided which one he would choose. Mary, a citizen of North Carolina who is in Romania, files suit against Chris in a federal district court in North Carolina on diversity of citizenship grounds. What is Chris's domicile at the time Mary files suit against Chris, who is living in Romania and serving in the Peace Corps? Is it North Carolina, Romania, New York, or New Jersey? Please explain.

   a. What effect would it have on Chris's domicile if, while living in Romania, Chris falls in love with a Romanian woman, marries her, and together they make plans to start a business and raise a family in Romania?

   b. What impact, if any, would Chris's Romanian domicile have on the federal district court's original subject matter jurisdiction under section 1332 in Mary's lawsuit against Chris?

The Domicile Determination

The judge, not the jury, determines a person's domicile. The judge must determine what the person's domicile was at the time the complaint was filed. Oftentimes, the domicile determination is easy. The person resides in the state and has absolutely no intention of ever leaving. Difficult cases arise when a person resides in a state but it is unclear whether or not the person intends to remain in that state indefinitely. In such cases, the inquiry is a fact-intensive one focusing on the person's intent. Evidence of a person's intent certainly includes what the person says about his intent to remain in the state. Does the individual say he intends to remain for a fixed period of time? — e.g., "I intend to move away from this state on July 1 of this year." Or, does his stated intent reveal an indefinite stay in the state? — e.g., "I don't plan to live in this state forever, but I'm not sure when I'll leave." This latter statement is key to understanding "indefinite intent." Even if he does not plan to stay forever, if he has no definite plan to leave, he likely has an indefinite intent to remain where he resides.

In making the domicile determination, the court is not limited only to the person's stated intent. The court may consider other evidence, such as the circumstances surrounding the person's stay in the state, which could either support or undermine the credibility of the person's stated intent. For example, the person whose domicile is at issue may say, "I don't intend to remain indefinitely in Ohio, I am moving to California in two months." The circumstances, however, might cut against this stated intent. For example, perhaps he has signed a six-month lease in Ohio, has a contractual obligation to work for another year in Ohio, and has made no travel or lodging arrangements in California. In cases such as these, the court must decide whether it finds the stated intent or the surrounding circumstances more credible and determine domicile accordingly.

U.S. Citizens Domiciled Abroad

Not all U.S. citizens are citizens of a U.S. state. U.S. citizens domiciled abroad, often referred to as American expatriates, are not citizens of any U.S. state because they are not domiciled in a U.S. state. By definition, an American expatriate does not qualify as a foreign citizen under the statute because they are U.S. citizens. Because they are neither state citizens nor foreign citizens, American expatriates simply slip through a crack in the diversity statute. Thus, an American expatriate cannot sue or be sued in federal court on diversity grounds.

No Waiver of an Objection to Subject Matter Jurisdiction

In *Mas*, the defendant Perry did not raise his objection to subject matter jurisdiction until the close of the plaintiffs' case. The district court and the parties had already expended a great deal of time and resources on the case before Perry raised his objection. Nevertheless, Perry's delay did not waive his objection. Unlike other defenses, an objection to lack of subject matter jurisdiction is not waived due to the passage of time. However, do you think Perry's delay helped or hurt his chances that the district court would find that Mrs. Mas was a citizen of Louisiana? If the court had found that it lacked subject matter jurisdiction, it would not be able to issue a valid judgment and much if not all of its work would have been for naught. When jurisdiction hinges on a judgment call — like whether or not Mrs. Mas was a citizen of Louisiana — a judge may resolve the doubt against a party who delayed her objection and in favor of preserving the work already completed.

EXHIBIT 3.4 **28 U.S.C. §1332(c)(1)**

(c) For the purposes of this section . . .
(1) a corporation shall be deemed to be a citizen of every state or foreign state where it has its principal place of business. . . .

2. The Citizenship of Corporations

The diversity statute defines the citizenship of a corporation. Under 28 U.S.C. §1332(c), shown in Exhibit 3.4 on the previous page, a corporation is deemed a citizen of every state and foreign state by which it is incorporated, and of the state or foreign state where it has its **principal place of business**, defined below. Therefore, a corporation often has dual citizenship. It is a citizen of *both* its state or nation of incorporation *and* of the state or nation where its principal place of business is located. For example, if Motorcars, Inc. is incorporated in Delaware and has its principal place of business in Michigan, Motorcars, Inc. is a citizen of both Delaware and Michigan. When the location of a corporation's headquarters and its state of incorporation are the same state, the corporation will not have dual citizenship. For example, if Motorcars, Inc. were incorporated in Michigan and had its principal place of business in Michigan as well, it would be a citizen only of Michigan.

Ordinarily, it is easy to determine a corporation's state or nation of incorporation. This fact is a matter of public record and not something corporations typically try or want to hide. It is, however, important to recognize that not all business entities are corporations. Corporations incorporated in a U.S. state are usually easily identified by the designation "Inc." or "Corp." following their trade name.

In addition to being a citizen of its state or nation of incorporation, the diversity statute tells us that a corporation is also a citizen of its principal place of business, but the statute does not define the term "principal place of business." Is a corporation's principal place of business the state or nation where it sells the most products? Where it has its primary production activities? Or is its principal place of business the state or nation where its activities are directed and controlled, no matter where those activities actually occur? For quite some time, the federal courts of appeals had different definitions of principal place of business. In *Hertz Corp. v. Friend*, the United States Supreme Court resolved this split in the courts of appeals.

Case Preview

Hertz Corp. v. Friend

As you read *Hertz Corp. v. Friend*, consider the following questions:

1. What test does the Supreme Court adopt for determining a corporation's principal place of business?
2. What advantages does the Court see to adopting this test?
3. What disadvantages does the Court see to adopting this test?

Hertz Corp. v. Friend
559 U.S. 77 (2010)

Justice BREYER delivered the opinion of the Court.

The federal diversity jurisdiction statute provides that "a corporation shall be deemed to be a citizen of any State by which it has been incorporated *and of the State where it has its principal place of business*." 28 U.S.C. §1332(c)(1) (emphasis added). We seek here to resolve different interpretations that the Circuits have given this phrase. In doing so, we place primary weight upon the need for judicial administration of a jurisdictional statute to remain as simple as possible. And we conclude that the phrase "principal place of business" refers to the place where the corporation's high level officers direct, control, and coordinate the corporation's activities. Lower federal courts have often metaphorically called that place the corporation's "nerve center." We believe that the "nerve center" will typically be found at a corporation's headquarters.

I

In September 2007, respondents Melinda Friend and John Nhieu, two California citizens, sued petitioner, the Hertz Corporation, in a California state court. They sought damages for what they claimed were violations of California's wage and hour laws. And they requested relief on behalf of a potential class composed of California citizens who had allegedly suffered similar harms.

Hertz filed a notice seeking removal to a federal court. Hertz claimed that the plaintiffs and the defendant were citizens of different States. Hence, the federal court possessed diversity-of-citizenship jurisdiction. Friend and Nhieu, however, claimed that the Hertz Corporation was a California citizen, like themselves, and that, hence, diversity jurisdiction was lacking.

To support its position, Hertz submitted a declaration by an employee relations manager that sought to show that Hertz's "principal place of business" was in New Jersey, not in California. The declaration stated, among other things, that Hertz operated facilities in 44 States; and that California — which had about 12% of the Nation's population — accounted for 273 of Hertz's 1,606 car rental locations; about 2,300 of its 11,230 full-time employees; about $811 million of its $4.371 billion in annual revenue; and about 3.8 million of its approximately 21 million annual transactions, i.e., rentals. The declaration also stated that the "leadership of Hertz and its domestic subsidiaries" is located at Hertz's "corporate headquarters" in Park Ridge, New Jersey; that its "core executive and administrative functions . . . are carried out" there and "to a lesser extent" in Oklahoma City, Oklahoma; and that its "major administrative operations . . . are found" at those two locations.

The District Court of the Northern District of California accepted Hertz's statement of the facts as undisputed. But it concluded that, given those facts, Hertz was a citizen of California. In reaching this conclusion, the court applied Ninth Circuit precedent, which instructs courts to identify a corporation's "principal place of business" by first determining the amount of a corporation's business activity State by State. If the amount of activity is "significantly larger" or "substantially predominates" in one State, then that State is the corporation's "principal place of business." If there is no such State, then the "principal place of business" is the corporation's "'nerve center,'" i.e., the place where "'the majority of its executive and administrative functions are performed.'" Friend v. Hertz, No. C–07–5222 MMC, 2008 WL 7071465 (N.D. Cal., Jan. 15, 2008), p. 3 (hereinafter Order); Tosco Corp. v. Communities for a Better Environment, 236 F.3d 495, 500–502 (C.A. 9 2001) (per curiam).

Applying this test, the District Court found that the "plurality of each of the relevant business activities" was in California, and that "the differential between the amount of those activities" in California and the amount in "the next closest state" was "significant." Order 4. Hence, Hertz's "principal place of business" was California, and diversity jurisdiction was thus lacking. The District Court consequently remanded the case to the state courts.

Hertz appealed the District Court's remand order. The Ninth Circuit affirmed in a brief memorandum opinion. Hertz filed a petition for certiorari. And, in light of differences among the Circuits in the application of the test for corporate citizenship, we granted the writ.

IV

The phrase "principal place of business" has proved more difficult to apply than its originators likely expected. . . . If a corporation's headquarters and executive offices were in the same State in which it did most of its business, the test seemed straightforward. The "principal place of business" was located in that State.

But suppose those corporate headquarters, including executive offices, are in one State, while the corporation's plants or other centers of business activity are located in other States? In 1959 a distinguished federal district judge, Edward Weinfeld, relied on the Second Circuit's interpretation of the Bankruptcy Act to answer this question in part:

> "Where a corporation is engaged in far-flung and varied activities which are carried on in different states, its principal place of business is the nerve center from which it radiates out to its constituent parts and from which its officers direct, control and coordinate all activities without regard to locale, in the furtherance of the corporate objective. The test applied by our Court of Appeals, is that place where the corporation has an 'office from which its business was directed and controlled' — the place where 'all of its business was under the supreme direction and control of its officers.'"

Numerous Circuits have since followed this rule, applying the "nerve center" test for corporations with "far-flung" business activities.

[This] analysis, however, did not go far enough. For it did not answer what courts should do when the operations of the corporation are not "far-flung" but rather limited to only a few States. When faced with this question, various courts have focused more heavily on where a corporation's actual business activities are located.

Perhaps because corporations come in many different forms, involve many different kinds of business activities, and locate offices and plants for different reasons in different ways in different regions, a general "business activities" approach has proved unusually difficult to apply. Courts must decide which factors are more

factors

important than others: for example, plant location, sales or servicing centers; transactions, payrolls, or revenue generation.

The number of factors grew as courts explicitly combined aspects of the "nerve center" and "business activity" tests to look to a corporation's "total activities," sometimes to try to determine what treatises have described as the corporation's "center of gravity." A major treatise confirms this growing complexity, listing Circuit by Circuit, cases that highlight different factors or emphasize similar factors differently, and reporting that the "federal courts of appeals have employed various tests" — tests which "tend to overlap" and which are sometimes described in "language" that "is imprecise."

This complexity may reflect an unmediated judicial effort to apply the statutory phrase "principal place of business" in light of the general purpose of diversity jurisdiction, i.e., an effort to find the State where a corporation is least likely to suffer out-of-state prejudice when it is sued in a local court. But, if so, that task seems doomed to failure. After all, the relevant purposive concern — prejudice against an out of state party — will often depend upon factors that courts cannot easily measure, for example, a corporation's image, its history, and its advertising, while the factors that courts can more easily measure, for example, its office or plant location, its sales, its employment, or the nature of the goods or services it supplies, will sometimes bear no more than a distant relation to the likelihood of prejudice. At the same time, this approach is at war with administrative simplicity. And it has failed to achieve a nationally uniform interpretation of federal law, an unfortunate consequence in a federal legal system.

V

A

In an effort to find a single, more uniform interpretation of the statutory phrase, we have reviewed the Courts of Appeals' divergent and increasingly complex interpretations. Having done so, we now return to, and expand, Judge Weinfeld's approach, as applied in the Seventh Circuit. See, e.g., Scot Typewriter Co., 170 F. Supp., at 865; Wisconsin Knife Works, 781 F.2d, at 1282. We conclude that "principal place of business" is best read as referring to the place where a corporation's officers direct, control, and coordinate the corporation's activities. It is the place that Courts of Appeals have called the corporation's "nerve center." And in practice it should normally be the place where the corporation maintains its headquarters — provided that the headquarters is the actual center of direction, control, and coordination, i.e., the "nerve center," and not simply an office where the corporation holds its board meetings (for example, attended by directors and officers who have traveled there for the occasion).

Three sets of considerations, taken together, convince us that this approach, while imperfect, is superior to other possibilities. First, the statute's language supports the approach. The statute's text deems a corporation a citizen of the "State where it has its principal place of business." 28 U.S.C. §1332(c)(1). The word "place" is in the singular, not the plural. The word "principal" requires us to pick out the "main, prominent" or "leading" place. 12 Oxford English Dictionary 495 (2d ed. 1989) (def.(A)(I)(2)). And

3 *considerations*

the fact that the word "place" follows the words "State where" means that the "place" is a place within a State. It is not the State itself.

A corporation's "nerve center," usually its main headquarters, is a single place. The public often (though not always) considers it the corporation's main place of business. And it is a place within a State. By contrast, the application of a more general business activities test has led some courts, as in the present case, to look, not at a particular place within a State, but incorrectly at the State itself, measuring the total amount of business activities that the corporation conducts there and determining whether they are "significantly larger" than in the next-ranking State.

This approach invites greater litigation and can lead to strange results, as the Ninth Circuit has since recognized. Namely, if a "corporation may be deemed a citizen of California on th[e] basis" of "activities [that] roughly reflect California's larger population . . . nearly every national retailer — no matter how far flung its operations — will be deemed a citizen of California for diversity purposes." But why award or decline diversity jurisdiction on the basis of a State's population, whether measured directly, indirectly (say proportionately), or with modifications?

Second, administrative simplicity is a major virtue in a jurisdictional statute. Complex jurisdictional tests complicate a case, eating up time and money as the parties litigate, not the merits of their claims, but which court is the right court to decide those claims. Complex tests produce appeals and reversals, encourage gamesmanship, and, again, diminish the likelihood that results and settlements will reflect a claim's legal and factual merits. Judicial resources too are at stake. Courts have an independent obligation to determine whether subject-matter jurisdiction exists, even when no party challenges it. So courts benefit from straightforward rules under which they can readily assure themselves of their power to hear a case.

Simple jurisdictional rules also promote greater predictability. Predictability is valuable to corporations making business and investment decisions. Predictability also benefits plaintiffs deciding whether to file suit in a state or federal court.

A "nerve center" approach, which ordinarily equates that "center" with a corporation's headquarters, is simple to apply comparatively speaking. The metaphor of a corporate "brain," while not precise, suggests a single location. By contrast, a corporation's general business activities more often lack a single principal place where they take place. That is to say, the corporation may have several plants, many sales locations, and employees located in many different places. If so, it will not be as easy to determine which of these different business locales is the "principal" or most important "place."

Third, the statute's legislative history, for those who accept it, offers a simplicity-related interpretive benchmark. The Judicial Conference provided an initial version of its proposal that suggested a numerical test. A corporation would be deemed a citizen of the State that accounted for more than half of its gross income. The Conference changed its mind in light of criticism that such a test would prove too complex and impractical to apply. That history suggests that the words "principal place of business" should be interpreted to be no more complex than the initial "half of gross income" test. A "nerve center" test offers such a possibility. A general business activities test does not.

B

We recognize that there may be no perfect test that satisfies all administrative and purposive criteria. We recognize as well that, under the "nerve center" test we adopt today, there will be hard cases. For example, in this era of telecommuting, some corporations may divide their command and coordinating functions among officers who work at several different locations, perhaps communicating over the Internet. That said, our test nonetheless points courts in a single direction, towards the center of overall direction, control, and coordination. Courts do not have to try to weigh corporate functions, assets, or revenues different in kind, one from the other. Our approach provides a sensible test that is relatively easier to apply, not a test that will, in all instances, automatically generate a result.

We also recognize that the use of a "nerve center" test may in some cases produce results that seem to cut against the basic rationale for 28 U.S.C. §1332. For example, if the bulk of a company's business activities visible to the public take place in New Jersey, while its top officers direct those activities just across the river in New York, the "principal place of business" is New York. One could argue that members of the public in New Jersey would be less likely to be prejudiced against the corporation than persons in New York — yet the corporation will still be entitled to remove a New Jersey state case to federal court. And note too that the same corporation would be unable to remove a New York state case to federal court, despite the New York public's presumed prejudice against the corporation.

We understand that such seeming anomalies will arise. However, in view of the necessity of having a clearer rule, we must accept them. Accepting occasionally counterintuitive results is the price the legal system must pay to avoid overly complex jurisdictional administration while producing the benefits that accompany a more uniform legal system.

VI

Petitioner's unchallenged declaration suggests that Hertz's center of direction, control, and coordination, its "nerve center," and its corporate headquarters are one and the same, and they are located in New Jersey, not in California. Because respondents should have a fair opportunity to litigate their case in light of our holding, however, we vacate the Ninth Circuit's judgment and remand the case for further proceedings consistent with this opinion.

It is so ordered.

Post-Case Follow-Up	The Court's decision in *Hertz* that principal place of business means the corporate **nerve center** is based in part on a desire to have relatively simple and predictable jurisdictional rules. What are the advantages of simple rules? Are there disadvantages? The Court's reference to "anomalies" that will arise as a result of its decision might help you answer these questions.

Dual Citizenship for Corporations

Corporations are citizens of both the state or nation under whose laws they are incorporated and the state or nation in which they have their principal place of business. But this has not always been the case. Until a 1958 amendment to section 1332, a corporation was a citizen only of its state of incorporation. Under this old rule, a corporation incorporated in State B doing most or all of its business in State A would be diverse from a citizen of State A. Recall that the purpose of diversity jurisdiction is to prevent local prejudice against an out of state defendant. A corporation with its principal place of business in the same state as an opposing party's citizenship is not meaningfully "out of state." Thus, section 1332 was amended to deem a corporation a citizen of the state or nation in which it has its principal place of business, as well as the state under whose laws it is incorporated.

Hertz Corp. v. Friend: Real Life Applications

1. Jane is injured when her toaster oven catches fire and burns her. She files suit in federal district court to recover personal injury damages against the corporation that manufactured and designed her toaster oven, Hotbox, Inc. Jane is a citizen of Ohio. Hotbox is incorporated under the laws of Delaware and has its principal place of business in Akron, Ohio. Assuming the amount in controversy requirement is met, does the federal district court have diversity of citizenship jurisdiction?

2. Cool, Inc. is in the business of manufacturing and selling ice chests. All of Cool's ice chests are manufactured at its production facility in Tamaulipas, Mexico. Although Cool sells ice chests to customers in every U.S. state as well as to customers in dozens of foreign markets, 52 percent of Cool's revenue is generated through sales to customers in California. Cool's president, vice-president, and other executives work at Cool's office in Houston, Texas. From Houston, these officers create the corporate budget; monitor sales, expenses, and production activities in Mexico; manage product marketing; and hire, evaluate, and fire employees. The corporation's board of directors meets twice per year at a resort and conference center on the Gulf Coast in Mississippi. Where is Cool's principal place of business and why?

3. Assume the same facts as in the previous question, except assume that Cool rents office space in Mississippi to hold its board meetings. Also assume that Cool names Mississippi as its corporate headquarters on its website as well as in court papers and in filings with various state offices and agencies. Does this change Cool's principal place of business under the diversity statute from Texas to Mississippi?

3. The Citizenship of Unincorporated Associations

We have fairly clear standards for determining the citizenship of individuals and corporations. However, some parties to a lawsuit are neither individuals nor corporations. Some are entities of various kinds, either for profit or not-for-profit, that are collectively referred to as unincorporated associations. Unincorporated associations include labor unions, unincorporated non-profit organizations, and state-created business entities, such as limited partnerships and limited liability companies, as well as traditional common law partnerships. None of these is an individual or a corporation, but all of them can wind up a party to a federal court lawsuit.

Unfortunately, neither the diversity statute nor the Supreme Court has provided a test for determining the citizenship of unincorporated associations like they did for corporations. Instead, courts have tended to treat these types of entities for citizenship purposes as a collection of individuals. Consequently, unincorporated associations take on the citizenship of all of their members. Take for instance a common law partnership with two partners — Jack and Jill — who are doing business as Jack & Jill Water Supply. Let's assume Jack & Jill Water Supply is sued in federal court on diversity grounds. In determining the citizenship of Jack & Jill Water Supply, we look to the citizenship of Jack and Jill, *not* to the partnership's principal place of business, like we would with a corporation. If Jack is a citizen of Texas and Jill is a citizen of Louisiana (based on their U.S. citizenship and domicile in those states), then Jack & Jill Water Supply is a citizen of both Texas and Louisiana under the diversity statute. Even if Jack & Jill Water Supply's principal place of business is in Arkansas, the partnership is a citizen only of Texas and Louisiana, not Arkansas. We look to the citizenship of the partners, not to the partnership's principal place of business. In this example, we are treating the partnership like a collection of individuals, rather than as a corporation.

The same rule holds true for other unincorporated associations. We look to the citizenship of their constituent members, not their principal place of business. A labor union is a citizen of every state of which its members are citizens. Similarly, limited partnerships share citizenship with both their general and limited partners. Limited liability companies take on the citizenships of all of their members.

Unincorporated state-created business entities, such as limited partnerships and limited liability companies, are organized under the laws of a state, like corporations, but they do not take on the citizenship of their states of organization. For example, a limited liability company organized under the laws of New Jersey with two members, both of whom are citizens of New York, is a citizen only of New York, not New Jersey. If this same limited liability company also had a member who was a citizen of New Jersey, it would be a citizen of New York and New Jersey, but this would be so because one of its *members* was a citizen of New Jersey, not because it was organized under the laws of New Jersey.

Complicating this analysis is the fact that some unincorporated business entities have members who are also unincorporated business entities. For example, a limited liability company may have a member that is also a limited liability company. Or it may have a member that is a limited partnership or some other unincorporated business entity. In cases such as these, one must determine the citizenship of the unincorporated member by looking at its membership, attribute that citizenship (or citizenships) to the member, and then attribute that citizenship to the unincorporated entity that is a party to the suit. There is no guarantee that the membership of the member does not also include other unincorporated entities whose membership's citizenships must also be considered. Very quickly, this analysis can come to resemble a spider web (or Alice's trip down the rabbit hole). Despite these difficulties, Congress and the Supreme Court have chosen not to treat unincorporated associations like corporations for citizenship purposes under section 1332(a) of the diversity statute. Another practical impact of this approach is that an unincorporated association may be a citizen of many, many states. *Carden v. Arkoma Associates* discusses some of the practical challenges of this approach and addresses the question of whether or not an unincorporated association takes on the citizenship of all of its partners, even if the partners are unequal in terms of their authority and responsibility.

Case Preview

Carden v. Arkoma Associates

As you read *Carden*, think about the answers to these questions:

1. What does *Carden* say about how the citizenship of an unincorporated association must be determined?
2. Does a limited partnership take on the citizenship of both its limited and general partners, or only its general partners?
3. How, if at all, does a state's recognition of an unincorporated association as one of its citizens affect the citizenship analysis under the diversity statute?
4. Do you think the Court's holding in *Carden* might cause problems for parties and lower courts in determining whether or not diversity jurisdiction exists? If so, what might those problems be?

Carden v. Arkoma Associates
489 U.S. 185 (1990)

Opinion
Justice SCALIA delivered the opinion of the Court.

The question presented in this case is whether, in a suit brought by a limited partnership, the citizenship of the limited partners must be taken into account to determine diversity of citizenship among the parties.

I

Respondent Arkoma Associates (Arkoma), a limited partnership organized under the laws of Arizona, brought suit on a contract dispute in the United States District Court for the Eastern District of Louisiana, relying upon diversity of citizenship for federal jurisdiction. The defendants, C. Tom Carden and Leonard L. Limes, citizens of Louisiana, moved to dismiss, contending that one of Arkoma's limited partners was also a citizen of Louisiana. The District Court denied the motion but certified the question for interlocutory appeal, which the Fifth Circuit declined. Thereafter Magee Drilling Company intervened in the suit and, together with the original defendants, counterclaimed against Arkoma under Texas law. Following a bench trial, the District Court awarded Arkoma a money judgment plus interest and attorney's fees; it dismissed Carden and Limes' counterclaim as well as Magee's intervention and counterclaim. Carden, Limes, and Magee (petitioners here) appealed, and the Fifth Circuit affirmed. With respect to petitioners' jurisdictional challenge, the Court of Appeals found complete diversity, reasoning that Arkoma's citizenship should be determined by reference to the citizenship of the general, but not the limited, partners. We granted certiorari.

II

Article III of the Constitution provides, in pertinent part, that "[t]he judicial Power shall extend to . . . Controversies . . . between Citizens of different States." Congress first authorized the federal courts to exercise diversity jurisdiction in the Judiciary Act of 1789. In its current form, the diversity statute provides that "[t]he district courts shall have original jurisdiction of all civil actions where the matter in controversy exceeds . . . $50,000 [Eds. — the diversity statute now requires the amount in controversy to exceed $75,000] . . . , and is between . . . citizens of different States. . . ." 28 U.S.C.A. §1332(a). Since its enactment, we have interpreted the diversity statute to require "complete diversity" of citizenship. See Strawbridge v. Curtiss, 3 Cranch 267, 2 L. Ed. 435 (1806). The District Court erred in finding complete diversity in this case unless (1) a limited partnership may be considered in its own right a "citizen" of the State that created it, or (2) a federal court must look to the citizenship of only its general, but not its limited, partners to determine whether there is complete diversity of citizenship. We consider these questions in turn.

A

We have often had to consider the status of artificial entities created by state law insofar as that bears upon the existence of federal diversity jurisdiction. The precise question posed under the terms of the diversity statute is whether such an entity may be considered a "citizen" of the State under whose laws it was created. A corporation is the paradigmatic artificial "person," and the Court has considered its proper characterization under the diversity statute on more than one occasion — not always reaching the same conclusion. Initially, we held that a corporation "is certainly not a citizen," so that to determine the existence of diversity jurisdiction the Court must "look to the character of the individuals who compose [it]." Bank of United States v. Deveaux, 5 Cranch 61, 86, 91–92, 3 L. Ed. 38 (1809). We overruled *Deveaux* 35 years later in Louisville, C. & C.R. Co. v. Letson, 2 How. 497, 558, 11 L. Ed. 353 (1844), which held that a corporation is "capable of being treated as a citizen of [the State which created it], as much as a natural person." Ten years later, we reaffirmed the result of *Letson*, though on the somewhat different theory that "those who use the corporate name, and exercise the faculties conferred by it," should be presumed conclusively to be citizens of the corporation's State of incorporation. Marshall v. Baltimore & Ohio R. Co., 16 How. 314, 329, 14 L. Ed. 953 (1854).

While the rule regarding the treatment of corporations as "citizens" has become firmly established, we have (with an exception to be discussed presently) just as firmly resisted extending that treatment to other entities. For example, in Chapman

v. Barney, 129 U.S. 677, 9 S. Ct. 426, 32 L. Ed. 800 (1889), a case involving an unincorporated "joint stock company," we raised the question of jurisdiction on our own motion, and found it to be lacking:

"On looking into the record we find no satisfactory showing as to the citizenship of the plaintiff. The allegation of the amended petition is, that the United States Express Company is a joint stock company organized under a law of the State of New York, and is a citizen of that State. But the express company cannot be a citizen of New York, within the meaning of the statutes regulating jurisdiction, unless it be a corporation. The allegation that the company was organized under the laws of New York is not an allegation that it is a corporation. In fact the allegation is, that the company is not a corporation, but a joint stock company—that is, a mere partnership." Id., at 682, 9 S. Ct., at 428.

Similarly, in Great Southern Fire Proof Hotel Co. v. Jones, 177 U.S. 449, 20 S. Ct. 690, 44 L. Ed. 842 (1900), we held that a "limited partnership association"—although possessing "some of the characteristics of a corporation" and deemed a "citizen" by the law creating it—may not be deemed a "citizen" under the jurisdictional rule established for corporations. Id., at 456, 20 S. Ct., at 693. "That rule must not be extended." Id., at 457, 20 S. Ct., at 693. As recently as 1965, our unanimous opinion in Steelworkers v. R.H. Bouligny, Inc., 382 U.S. 145, 86 S. Ct. 272, 15 L. Ed. 2d 217 reiterated that "the doctrinal wall of Chapman v. Barney," id., 129 U.S., at 151, 86 S. Ct., at 275, would not be breached.

The one exception to the admirable consistency of our jurisprudence on this matter is Puerto Rico v. Russell & Co., 288 U.S. 476, 53 S. Ct. 447, 77 L. Ed. 903 (1933), which held that the entity known as a sociedad en comandita, created under the civil law of Puerto Rico, could be treated as a citizen of Puerto Rico for purposes of determining federal-court jurisdiction. The sociedad's juridical personality, we said, "is so complete in contemplation of the law of Puerto Rico that we see no adequate reason for holding that the sociedad has a different status for purposes of federal jurisdiction than a corporation organized under that law." Id., at 482, 53 S. Ct., at 449. Arkoma fairly argues that this language, and the outcome of the case, "reflec[t] the Supreme Court's willingness to look beyond the incorporated/unincorporated dichotomy and to study the internal organization, state law requirements, management structure, and capacity or lack thereof to act and/or sue, to determine diversity of citizenship." Brief for Respondent 14. The problem with this argument lies not in its logic, but in the fact that the approach it espouses was proposed and specifically rejected in Bouligny. There, in reaffirming "the doctrinal wall of Chapman v. Barney," we explained Russell as a case resolving the distinctive problem "of fitting an exotic creation of the civil law . . . into a federal scheme which knew it not." 382 U.S., at 151, 86 S. Ct., at 275. There could be no doubt, after Bouligny, that at least common-law entities (and likely all entities beyond the Puerto Rican sociedad en comandita) would be treated for purposes of the diversity statute pursuant to what Russell called "[t]he tradition of the common law," which is "to treat as legal persons only incorporated groups and to assimilate all others to partnerships." 288 U.S., at 480, 53 S. Ct., at 448.

* * *

B

As an alternative ground for finding complete diversity, Arkoma asserts that the Fifth Circuit correctly determined its citizenship solely by reference to the citizenship of its general partners, without regard to the citizenship of its limited partners. Only the general partners, it points out, "manage the assets, control the litigation, and bear the risk of liability for the limited partnership's debts," and, more broadly, "have exclusive and complete management and control of the operations of the partnership." Brief for Respondent 30, 36. This approach of looking to the citizenship of only some of the members of the artificial entity finds even less support in our precedent than looking to the State of organization (for which one could at least point to Russell). We have never held that an artificial entity, suing or being sued in its own name, can invoke the diversity jurisdiction of the federal courts based on the citizenship of some but not all of its members. No doubt some members of the joint stock company in Chapman, the labor union in Bouligny, and the limited partnership association in Great Southern exercised greater control over their respective entities than other members. But such considerations have played no part in our decisions.

* * *

In sum, we reject the contention that to determine, for diversity purposes, the citizenship of an artificial entity, the court may consult the citizenship of less than all of the entity's members. We adhere to our oft-repeated rule that diversity jurisdiction in a suit by or against the entity depends on the citizenship of "all the members," Chapman, 129 U.S., at 682, 9 S. Ct., at 427, "the several persons composing such association," Great Southern, 177 U.S., at 456, 20 S. Ct., at 693, "each of its members," Bouligny, 382 U.S., at 146, 86 S. Ct., at 273.

C

The resolutions we have reached above can validly be characterized as technical, precedent-bound, and unresponsive to policy considerations raised by the changing realities of business organization. But, as must be evident from our earlier discussion, that has been the character of our jurisprudence in this field after Letson. See Currie, The Federal Courts and the American Law Institute, 36 U. Chi. L. Rev. 1, 35 (1968). Arkoma is undoubtedly correct that limited partnerships are functionally similar to "other types of organizations that have access to federal courts," and is perhaps correct that "[c]onsiderations of basic fairness and substance over form require that limited partnerships receive similar treatment." Brief for Respondent 33. Similar arguments were made in Bouligny. The District Court there had upheld removal because it could divine "'no common sense reason for treating an unincorporated national labor union differently from a corporation,'" 382 U.S., at 146, 86 S. Ct., at 273, and we recognized that that contention had "considerable merit," id., at 150, 86 S. Ct., at 274. We concluded, however, that "[w]hether unincorporated labor unions ought to be assimilated to the status of corporations for diversity purposes," id., at 153, 86 S. Ct., at 276, is "properly a matter for legislative consideration which cannot adequately or appropriately be dealt with by this Court," id., at 147, 86 S. Ct., at 273.

In other words, having entered the field of diversity policy with regard to artificial entities once (and forcefully) in Letson, we have left further adjustments to be made by Congress.

The judgment of the Court of Appeals is reversed, and the case is remanded for further proceedings consistent with this opinion.

It is so ordered.

Post-Case Follow-Up

The Court recognizes that basic considerations of fairness might justify treating unincorporated entities like corporations for purposes of the citizenship analysis and that its decision might fairly be categorized as form over substance. However, the Court takes the position that creating a test for the citizenship of unincorporated associations is best left to Congress. Congress has after all included in the diversity statute a test for corporate citizenship. It could do the same for unincorporated associations. In fact, 28 U.S.C. section 1332(d) provides that in class actions unincorporated associations are citizens of their states of organization and the states in which they have their principal place of business (like corporations), but this standard does not apply in direct actions (i.e., non-class actions). In the nearly three decades since *Carden*, Congress has not defined the citizenship of unincorporated associations in direct actions and the Supreme Court has not changed the position it took in *Carden*.

Carden creates problems for lower courts and litigants alike. It may be difficult to determine the identity — let alone the citizenship — of all the constituent members of an unincorporated association. As a result, the trial court may lack diversity of citizenship jurisdiction, yet only discover that fact after expending significant resources. For example, in *Hart v. Terminex Int'l*, the court of appeals dismissed the case for lack of diversity subject matter jurisdiction after eight years of litigation. 336 F.3d 541, 542 (7th Cir. 2003). Terminex was a limited partnership, in which one of the partners was itself another partnership. The second layer of partners included partners who were citizens of the same state as the plaintiffs. Thus, Terminex and the plaintiffs were citizens of the same state and complete diversity was lacking. Although neither side raised the issue, the court on its own determined that diversity was lacking and had no choice but to dismiss the action.

Carden v. Arkoma Associates: Real Life Applications

1. Bakers, Inc., a Delaware corporation with its principal place of business in New York, files suit against Flour, LLC for breach of a contract for the sale of goods in federal district court. Flour is a limited liability company organized under the law of Delaware. Flour's principal place of business is in New York. Flour has three members, all of whom are individuals and citizens of New Jersey. Assuming the amount in controversy requirement is met, does the district court have diversity of citizenship jurisdiction over this case?

2. Assume in the first example above that Flour, LLC has a fourth member, Mill-stone, Inc., and that Millstone is incorporated under the laws of Delaware and has its principal place of business in Connecticut. Does the district court have diversity of citizenship jurisdiction in Bakers' suit against Flour?

3. Assume once again that Flour, LLC has as members the three New Jersey individuals and Millstone, except assume now that Millstone is a limited liability company, rather than a corporation. Millstone has a single member, an individual who is a citizen of New York. Does the district court have diversity of citizenship jurisdiction in Bakers' suit against Flour?

---

4. Jurisdiction Is Determined at the Time the Complaint Is Filed

Jurisdiction is determined based on the facts at the time the complaint is filed. Thus, under section 1332, a post-complaint change in a party's citizenship does not affect the court's diversity jurisdiction. For example, suppose a Texas citizen files a $1 million tort suit against a citizen of California on May 1, 2017 in federal district court. On July 15, while the tort suit is still pending, the plaintiff becomes a California citizen. This change in the plaintiff's citizenship would not deprive the court of diversity jurisdiction because the change in citizenship came after the suit was filed. The same would be true if the parties were both citizens of California at the time of relevant events but one of them changed his citizenship (with a permanent move to Texas) before the suit was filed. The corollary to this rule is that the parties cannot create diversity jurisdiction by changing their citizenship after the complaint is filed. Suppose a Texas citizen files a $500,000 breach of contract action against a fellow Texas citizen on February 10, 2017. The federal district court could not exercise subject matter jurisdiction because the parties are not diverse on the day the complaint was filed. Even if the defendant changes his citizenship to Florida one day after the filing of the lawsuit, the court could not exercise diversity jurisdiction because it did not exist at the time of the filing of the complaint.

5. Dismissal to Perfect Diversity Jurisdiction

Jurisdiction is determined at the time the complaint is filed. Post-complaint changes in citizenship cannot destroy or create diversity jurisdiction. However, a court may dismiss a non-diverse defendant before rendering a final judgment in order to perfect its jurisdiction. *Caterpillar Inc. v. Lewis*, 519 U.S. 61 (1996). Dismissals to perfect jurisdiction typically take place when the jurisdictional defect was not discovered until late in the lawsuit. In *Caterpillar*, three years had passed in the federal district court proceeding before dismissal of the diversity-destroying defendant. In *Newman-Green, Inc. v. Alfonzo-Larrain*, 490 U.S. 826 (1989), the jurisdictional defect was first discovered on appeal by the court of appeals. Neither the district court nor the parties noticed that the parties were not diverse. The Supreme Court held that the district court (or the court of appeals) could dismiss the jurisdictional spoiler and thereby perfect its jurisdiction. However, it warned that the dismissals to perfect jurisdiction should be used "sparingly" and avoided when the remaining parties might be harmed by the dismissal of the jurisdictional spoiler.

The *Mas* court determined that Mrs. Mas was a Mississippi citizen and therefore diverse from Perry, a citizen of Louisiana. But what if the court in *Mas* had determined Mrs. Mas was a citizen of Louisiana? The holdings in *Newman-Green* and *Caterpillar* suggest that the district court (or the court of appeals) could have dismissed Mrs. Mas from the case and proceeded to judgment on Mr. Mas's claim against Perry. The case would then fall within the court's alienage jurisdiction in section 1332 because it would be a claim by a French citizen against a citizen of Louisiana. In this scenario, Mrs. Mas would have the option to file suit against the landlord defendant in state court.

6. The Probate and Domestic Relations Exceptions

Federal district courts will not exercise diversity jurisdiction in cases seeking divorce, child custody, or child support payments, or in cases seeking to probate an estate, even if the amount in controversy requirement is met and the parties are diverse. This exception is not contained in the diversity statute and is instead recognized in Supreme Court precedent. *See, e.g., Marshall v. Marshall*, 547 U.S. 293 (2006). Construe this exception narrowly. It does not prevent the court from exercising jurisdiction over all cases involving disputes between family members or involving the estate of a decedent. It applies only to cases in which a party is seeking a divorce, child custody, child support, or in which a party seeks to probate an estate.

C. THE AMOUNT IN CONTROVERSY REQUIREMENT

Complete diversity of citizenship is not the only requirement in the diversity statute. The diversity statute has always contained an **amount in controversy requirement** (although Article III, Section 2 does not). The purpose of the amount in controversy requirement is to prevent federal courts from spending time on "petty controversies." Congress has from time to time raised the amount in controversy requirement in the diversity statute. Back in 1789, the amount in controversy had to exceed $500. Today, the amount in controversy must exceed $75,000, exclusive of interest and costs. This section of the chapter addresses how the court determines whether the amount in controversy requirement is met.

1. Good Faith and Legal Certainty

Including an amount in controversy requirement in a jurisdictional statute raises a question — how can the federal court know what the true amount in controversy is without first determining the merits of the case? Ideally, the court determines whether or not it has diversity of citizenship jurisdiction at the beginning of the lawsuit. It makes no sense for the court to exhaust time and resources determining the merits only to learn later that it has no authority to make those determinations because it lacks subject matter jurisdiction.

The Supreme Court answered this conundrum in the case of *St. Paul Mercury Indemnity Co. v. Red Cab Co.*, 303 U.S. 283 (1938). The Court held that when determining the amount in controversy under the diversity statute, we do not look at the amount the plaintiff actually recovers. Instead, we look to the amount the plaintiff claims he should recover. The amount claimed by the plaintiff will be accepted if it appears to be made in good faith. The amount the plaintiff claims will be rejected only if it appears to a "legal certainty" that the plaintiff could never recover the jurisdictional amount. In other words, if it is possible for the plaintiff to recover the jurisdictional amount, the amount in controversy requirement is met, even if the court believes such an award is unlikely. The court will reject the plaintiff's claimed amount in controversy only if it believes recovery of the jurisdictional amount is not possible.

2. Amount in Controversy Is Determined Exclusive of Interest and Costs

The amount in controversy must exceed $75,000 exclusive of interest and costs. Interest on the plaintiff's claim does not count toward meeting the jurisdictional minimum. For example, if the plaintiff proves that the defendant breached a contract with him and has owed him $50,000 under the contract for three years, the plaintiff might recover interest for the three years' delay in payment, but that interest amount is not included in the amount in controversy determination. On the other hand, if interest is in the plaintiff's claim or part of the plaintiff's claim, that amount is included. For example, if a plaintiff sues the defendant on a promissory note claiming that the defendant owes $70,000 in principal and $6,000 in interest under the terms of the note, both the principal and interest amounts are added together to determine the amount in controversy. Court costs, including attorney fees generated in the litigation of the case, are not generally included in the calculation.

Case Preview

Diefenthal v. Civil Aeronautics

As you read *Diefenthal*, consider the following questions:

1. What is the general standard from *St. Paul Mercury* for determining whether or not the amount in controversy requirement is met?
2. What is the purpose of including an amount in controversy requirement in the diversity statute?
3. When might a plaintiff have to present more than a mere allegation that his claim meets the jurisdictional amount?
4. If a plaintiff honestly believes that his claim meets the jurisdictional amount, is it possible that the amount in controversy requirement is still not met?

Diefenthal v. Civil Aeronautics Board
681 F.2d 1039 (5th Cir. 1982)

CLARK, Chief Judge:

Stanley and Elka Diefenthal appeal from the district court's order dismissing their claims against the Civil Aeronautics Board (CAB) and Eastern Airlines. They also petition for review of a CAB order finding that regulating smoking was within the scope of its statutory authorization. We affirm.

I

The Diefenthals purchased first class tickets aboard a flight from New Orleans to Philadelphia on Eastern Airlines. They requested seats in the smoking section and confirmed that their request was granted prior to departure. After they boarded the flight, the Diefenthals were told that the smoking section in first class was filled and that they would have to sit in a no-smoking area if they wished to fly first class. The Diefenthals alleged that in informing them that they could not smoke the flight attendant treated them "brusquely," causing them extreme embarrassment, humiliation and emotional distress.

This relatively trivial incident has given rise to a spate of litigation. The Diefenthals brought suit in district court [and alleged among other theories] that Eastern had breached its contract with them by denying them first class seats in a smoking area and that it had tortiously embarrassed and humiliated them and deprived them of their right to smoke on board the plane. Eastern moved to dismiss the complaint for failure to state a claim on which relief could be granted. . . .

The district court dismissed the Diefenthals' contract and tort claims for lack of diversity jurisdiction. With respect to the contract claim, the district court found that even though the parties were diverse, it could not "conceive by the wildest stretch of the imagination how there could be $10,000.00 damage on the basis of what (the Diefenthals) allege."

With respect to the tort claim, it was developed that the Diefenthals' claim was based solely on Eastern's duty to follow its manual. The Diefenthals argued that if Eastern had correctly followed the seating procedures outlined in its manual, they would have been able to smoke on board the flight. The district court dismissed this theory apparently on the ground that it turned implicitly on the existence of a private right of action. However, it allowed the Diefenthals to amend their complaint to allege that the actions of Easterns' employees had tortiously humiliated and embarrassed them. The court expressly cautioned the Diefenthals that the jurisdictional amount would again be in question. The court stated, "you ought to do something to satisfy me of that (the jurisdictional amount) from the very beginning, because it's tough to conceive of the kind of damage you're talking about. . . ."

The amended complaint alleged that an unknown flight attendant "maliciously, and intentionally treated plaintiffs in a manner calculated to cause plaintiffs serious embarrassment and humiliation." Eastern moved to dismiss the complaint for lack of subject matter jurisdiction. At a hearing on Eastern's motion to dismiss, the district court noted that the Diefenthals had not alleged any physical or emotional damage or loss of reputation. Although the Diefenthals never stated exactly what the flight attendant had said, the court found that it could not "conceive how being told, no matter how abruptly, that you cannot smoke before the few passengers that are in the first class cabin of an airplane can possibly, in the absence of some (physical or emotional) damage . . . entitle (the Diefenthals) to $10,000.00."

* * *

The district court dismissed the Diefenthals' contract and tort claims against Eastern for lack of diversity jurisdiction. Even though the parties were diverse, the court found that it could not conceive how the inquiries alleged satisfied the requisite $10,000 limitation. See 28 U.S.C. §1332. The Diefenthals argue that because their request for $50,000 in damages was made in good faith the district court had jurisdiction. We disagree.

Before considering the merits of the Diefenthals' argument, it is important to review the allegations made in their complaint. The plaintiffs initially alleged only that the stewardess had "brusquely" informed them that there were no vacant seats in the first-class smoking section. Because of her manner, they claimed that they were "damaged, embarrassed, humiliated and were deprived of their right to smoke during said flight." During the first hearing on Eastern's motion to dismiss, the district court judge told the Diefenthals' counsel that he doubted highly that the damages alleged amounted to $10,000. When the judge allowed the Diefenthals to amend their complaint, he expressly advised their counsel that "you ought to do something to satisfy me of (the jurisdictional amount) from the very beginning, because it's tough to conceive of the kind of damage you're talking about. . . ."

The amended complaint alleged only that a flight attendant "maliciously and intentionally treated plaintiffs in a manner calculated to cause plaintiffs serious embarrassment and humiliation." No physical contact was asserted. The complaint did not allege that any physical or emotional impairment or loss of reputation resulted from the stewardess' actions, nor did it seek punitive damages. It simply alleged that the stewardess' remarks were brusque and intentional and that they had resulted in $50,000 worth of humiliation. When Eastern moved to dismiss for lack of jurisdiction, the Diefenthals did not attempt to support their complaint with affidavits which might have revealed some factual basis of their claim for damages. They simply rested on the unsupported allegation that the stewardess' actions humiliated them.

In *St. Paul Mercury Indemnity Co. v. Red Cab Co.*, 303 U.S. 283, 288, 58 S. Ct. 586, 590, 82 L. Ed. 845 (1938) (footnotes omitted), the Court stated:

> The rule governing dismissal for want of jurisdiction in cases brought in the federal court is that, unless the law gives a different rule, the sum claimed by the plaintiff controls if the claim is apparently made in good faith. It must appear to a legal certainty that the claim is really far [Eds. — The word "far" is a misquote; *St. Paul Mercury* uses the word "for"] less than the jurisdictional amount to justify dismissal.

The Court, however, also noted that the party invoking the court's jurisdiction bears the burden of "alleg(ing) with sufficient particularity the facts creating jurisdiction" and of "support(ing) the allegation" if challenged. In order to meet this burden, a party may amend the pleadings, as was done in this case, or may submit affidavits. This procedure provides a court with a basis for making a threshold determination as to whether the jurisdictional amount has been satisfied.

In establishing the jurisdictional amount, Congress intended to set a figure "not so high as to convert the Federal Courts into courts of big business nor so low as to fritter away their time in the trial of petty controversies." Sen. Rep. No. 1830, 85th Cong., 2d Sess., reprinted in 1958 U.S. Code Cong. & Ad. News 3099, 3101 (explaining the $10,000 threshold figure). While a federal court must of course give due credit to the good faith claims of the plaintiff, a court would be remiss in its obligations if it accepted every claim of damages at face value, no matter how trivial the underlying injury. This is especially so when, after jurisdiction has been challenged, a party has failed to specify the factual basis of his claims. Jurisdiction is not conferred by the stroke of a lawyer's pen. When challenged, it must be adequately founded in fact.

In the case at bar, the only specific factual incident alleged was that the stewardess had brusquely told the Diefenthals that there were no vacant seats left in the first-class smoking section. The amended complaint merely alleged that the stewardess had intended to humiliate the plaintiffs. It failed to demonstrate how the Diefenthals had suffered anything more than a trivial loss. Even though the Diefenthals were aware that both the court and Eastern questioned the factual basis of their damage claim, they wholly failed to specify that basis.

To a legal certainty, the brusque refusal by a stewardess to permit a passenger to sit in a particular smoking section, even a refusal the requesting passenger asserts was intended to "humiliate," will not justify a damage claim of $10,000.[15] This aspect of the suit is precisely the kind of "petty controversy" that Congress intended the jurisdictional amount to exclude from federal jurisdiction.

In sum, the party invoking the court's jurisdiction has the burden of establishing the factual basis of his claim by pleading or affidavit. This allows the court to test its jurisdiction without requiring the expense and burden of a full trial on the merits. The Diefenthals were put on notice both by the court's own statements and by Eastern's motion to dismiss for lack of jurisdiction, that they needed to show some basis for the amount of damages they claimed. They failed to do so and the district court properly dismissed their claims.

AFFIRMED.

---

[15]Each of the Diefenthals may aggregate his tort and contract claims in order to satisfy the $10,000 jurisdictional minimum. See Edwards v. Bates County, 163 U.S. 269, 16 S. Ct. 967, 41 L. Ed. 155 (1896). However, because the claims are separate and distinct as to each plaintiff, the two plaintiffs may not add their own individual claims together in order to reach the jurisdictional minimum. . . .

Post-Case Follow-Up

The court of appeals in *Diefenthal* determines that the amount in controversy requirement ($10,000 was the jurisdictional threshold at the time) was not met, despite the plaintiffs' contrary allegation. The burden of establishing jurisdiction is on the party invoking the court's jurisdiction. Since the plaintiffs filed their case in federal court, thereby invoking its jurisdiction, that burden fell to the plaintiffs. Once a question arose about the amount in controversy, the plaintiffs had the burden to show some basis for the amount of damages they claimed. Even after the court provided an opportunity to amend their pleadings, the plaintiffs alleged no new facts that showed anything other than a "trivial loss." The court says that this case is precisely the kind of "petty controversy" the amount in controversy requirement was designed to keep out of federal court. Even if a plaintiff subjectively believes his damages are sufficient to meet the requirement, a court can require him to allege facts or provide evidence that establishes there is a possibility of a recovery that meets the jurisdictional threshold requirement. The plaintiffs in *Diefenthal* failed to make that showing.

Diefenthal v. Civil Aeronautics Board: Real Life Applications

1. Joe files suit in federal district court on diversity grounds against Erectors, Inc. for personal injury damages. Joe was injured on a construction site when a piece of equipment suspended from a crane owned and operated by Erectors fell and crushed Joe's left thumb. Doctors had to amputate Joe's thumb at the hospital. Joe alleges damages of $250,000 in his complaint. The federal district judge is convinced to a legal certainty that Joe can never recover the $250,000 he alleges, and she believes it is possible but unlikely Joe will recover in excess of $75,000. Is the amount in controversy requirement met?

2. Assume that in the case of Joe v. Erectors, Inc., Joe specifically alleges that he seeks only $70,000 in damages. Is the amount in controversy requirement met?

3. Assume that instead of alleging only an amputated left thumb, Joe also alleges that the falling object paralyzed him from the neck down and that he will require lifelong medical treatment. Also assume that Joe never alleges a specific dollar amount of damages in his complaint. Is the amount in controversy requirement met?

4. Assume again that Joe sues Erectors for personal injury damages and alleges that the falling object paralyzed him. The jury determines that Erectors was not negligent and awards Joe no damages. The court renders a take-nothing judgment for Erectors. Does the jury's finding deprive the court of subject matter jurisdiction?

3. Aggregating Claims and Other Amount in Controversy Nuances

Aggregating Multiple Claims

A single plaintiff may aggregate (add together) the amounts in controversy in separate claims against the same defendant to meet the jurisdictional amount, even if the claims are factually unrelated. If John asserts a breach of contract claim of $50,000 and an unrelated personal injury claim of $30,000 against Tom, the amount in controversy requirement is met because the claims total $80,000, which exceeds $75,000.

Independently Meeting the Amount in Controversy Requirement

However, co-plaintiffs may not aggregate their claims to meet the jurisdictional amount. If John and Bob each assert a $40,000 breach of contract claim against Tom, the amount in controversy requirement is not met. Generally, each plaintiff must independently meet the amount in controversy requirement under the diversity statute.

An Exception to the General Rule

Despite the general rule that each plaintiff must independently meet the amount in controversy requirement, if one or more plaintiffs' claims meets the requirement, the fact that other plaintiffs do not independently meet the amount in controversy requirement will not deprive the court of subject matter jurisdiction. Let's modify the previous example. Assume that John and Bob both sue Tom for breach of contract, but John's claim is for $80,000 and Bob's claim is for $40,000. The fact that Bob does not independently meet the amount in controversy requirement will not deprive the court of subject matter jurisdiction because the other plaintiff, John, meets the requirement. In other words, Bob gets to "tag along" because John's claim independently meets the jurisdictional amount. We will explore this in greater detail under the topic of supplemental jurisdiction.

Multiple Plaintiffs Suing to Recover a Common Undivided Interest

Ordinarily, each plaintiff's claim is to recover a separate interest. In other words, we calculate each plaintiff's damage claim based on the injuries to the particular plaintiff. For example, if two plaintiffs are injured in the same car accident, they may file suit together to recover their own damages. The two plaintiffs' damages may be significantly different. One plaintiff might have broken a wrist while the other might have suffered a traumatic brain injury. Or maybe neither of the two plaintiffs was hurt severely. If each plaintiff in the car wreck case alleges only $50,000 in damages, the amount in controversy requirement is not met. Generally, each plaintiff must independently meet the amount in controversy requirement.

However, in rare cases, multiple plaintiffs may claim damages based on a common undivided interest in property, rather than based on their own separate interests. For example, two people who have an equal interest in a $1 million trust fund typically hold an undivided interest in the fund. Their interest in the fund is 50 percent each, but neither of them owns 100 percent of any particular dollar. They each own 50 percent of all the dollars (and all the pennies, for that matter). If these two beneficiaries file suit against the trustee alleging that his mismanagement depleted the fund by $100,000, the amount in controversy is $100,000, not $50,000 ($100,000 divided by the two plaintiffs). When the plaintiffs hold an undivided interest, we do not divide the amount in controversy by the number of plaintiffs.

Joint and Several Liability

Joint and several liability is a state tort law concept that permits multiple defendants to be held liable for the same event or act and allows the plaintiff to recover his damages from any one of them, all of them, or some combination of them. Assume Emilio sues Motorcars, Inc. and Airbags, Inc. under a product liability theory for personal injury damages he sustained in a car accident. If the jury awards Emilio $100,000 in damages, and under state tort law Motorcars and Airbags are jointly and severally liable, Emilio may recover $100,000 from Motorcars or $100,000 from Airbags, or he may recover some of the $100,000 from each of the defendants (e.g., $60,000 from Motorcars and $40,000 from Airbags). However, joint and several liability does not grant the plaintiff a windfall. Emilio could not recover more than a total of $100,000 from the defendants. For example, he could not recover $100,000 from Motorcars and then recover money from Airbags as well.

The possibility of multiple defendants being held jointly and severally liable affects the amount in controversy determination. When a plaintiff claims damages in excess of the jurisdictional amount against multiple defendants who may be held jointly and severally liable, he has satisfied the amount in controversy requirement. We do not divide the plaintiff's damages by the number of defendants who might be jointly and severally liable. Expanding on the example above, if Emilio alleges in good faith $100,000 in damages against Motorcars and Airbags and that Motorcars and Airbags are jointly and severally liable, the amount in controversy is $100,000, not $50,000 ($100,000 divided by the two defendants).

Counterclaims and Amount in Controversy

A **counterclaim** is a claim asserted by one party against an opposing party. The classic example of a counterclaim is the defendant asserting a claim back against the plaintiff. The value of a counterclaim cannot be added to the value of the plaintiff's claim to satisfy the amount in controversy requirement. If the plaintiff alleges $50,000 in damages and the defendant counterclaims for $50,000, the amount in controversy requirement is not met. We look to the amount the plaintiff claims in good faith, not to the amount of any counterclaim. Even if the counterclaim independently meets the jurisdictional amount, the amount in controversy requirement is not met. Thus, even if the defendant alleged a $90,000 counterclaim in the example above, the amount in controversy requirement is not met so as to give the court diversity jurisdiction over the plaintiff's action.

Injunctive Relief and the Amount in Controversy Requirement

Calculating the amount in controversy can be difficult in cases where the plaintiff seeks injunctive relief in addition to or instead of money damages. To seek injunctive relief is to ask the court to issue an **injunction**. An injunction is a court order requiring a party to do or refrain from doing something. The Supreme Court has not addressed this issue and the approach of lower courts has not been uniform. However, in a claim for injunctive relief the amount in controversy is probably met if either the cost to the defendant to comply with the injunction or the cost to the plaintiff if the injunction is not issued meets the jurisdictional amount. For example, if a plaintiff seeks to enjoin the construction of a cellphone tower on the defendant's adjacent property, the amount in controversy would be met if the plaintiff's property value would be diminished by the cellphone tower's presence by more than $75,000 or if the cost to the defendant of relocating the cellphone tower would be more than $75,000.

Chapter Summary

- Federal district courts have original jurisdiction over diversity cases under 28 U.S.C. section 1332. Diversity jurisdiction exists under section 1332 when there is complete diversity of citizenship and the amount in controversy exceeds $75,000 exclusive of interest and costs.
- Complete diversity of citizenship means that no party on one side of the case shares citizenship with any party on the other side of the case. This means that no plaintiff may share citizenship with any defendant.
- The citizenship of an individual is determined by looking first to his national citizenship. Foreign nationals are foreign citizens under the diversity statute and cannot be citizens of a U.S. state. A U.S. citizen is a citizen of the U.S. state in which he is domiciled. U.S. citizens domiciled abroad (American expatriates) are neither state nor foreign citizens and, thus, may not sue or be sued in federal court on diversity grounds.
- An individual establishes his domicile by residing in a state with the intention to remain there indefinitely. An individual can change his domicile only by residing elsewhere with the intention to remain indefinitely.
- Corporations are citizens of both their state or nation of incorporation and their principal place of business.
- Unincorporated associations take on the citizenship of all of their members. They do not take on the citizenship of their states of organization or their principal places of business.
- The amount in controversy in a diversity case must exceed $75,000, exclusive of interest and costs. In determining the amount in controversy, the amount claimed by the plaintiff in good faith controls, unless it appears to a legal certainty that the plaintiff could not recover the jurisdictional amount.

Applying the Concepts

1. Is there complete diversity of citizenship in the cases below?

   a. Lawrence, a citizen of New Mexico, files suit against Jerome, a citizen of Colorado. ✓

   b. Rey, a citizen of Delaware, files suit against Alto, Inc., a citizen of both New York and Delaware. ✗

   c. Thomas, a citizen of Texas, files suit against six different defendants. Five of them are citizens of Oklahoma. One defendant is a citizen of Texas. ✗

   d. Square, Inc., a citizen of North Dakota and Kansas, and Triangle, Inc., a citizen of Nebraska and Montana, file suit against Blue, LLC, a citizen of California and Oregon, and Red, LP, a citizen of Washington and Nebraska. ✗

2. Assuming the amount in controversy requirement is met, would there be alienage jurisdiction in the cases below?

   a. A citizen of Mexico files suit against a citizen of Mexico. ✗

   b. A citizen of Mexico files suit against a citizen of Canada. ✗

   c. A citizen of Canada files suit against a citizen of Texas. ✓

   d. A citizen of Texas files suit against a citizen of Canada. ✓

   e. A citizen of Texas files suit against a citizen of Canada and a citizen of Mississippi. ✓

3. Alejandro files a $100,000 breach of contract suit in federal district court against Doo-Dads, Inc., alleging that Doo-Dads failed to deliver multiple shipments of key chains and refrigerator magnets in accordance with a written contract between Alejandro and Doo-Dads. Alejandro is a U.S. citizen who has lived and run a business in Nevada for over 20 years. Doo-Dads, Inc. is incorporated under the laws of Delaware. Its top executives run the company from its headquarters in Reno, Nevada. Over 80 percent of Doo-Dads' sales revenue is generated through sales to customers in California, and most of Doo-Dads, employees are in California. Is this a proper diversity case?

4. Harper files a defamation action in federal district court against the publisher of a tabloid magazine, Smack-Talker, LP. Harper was born in and has always lived in California. Smack-Talker is a limited partnership organized under the laws of Georgia. Bob is Smack-Talker's only general partner and he runs the business from its headquarters in Florida. Smack-Talker's largest magazine circulation is in California. Smack-Talker has hundreds of limited partners who play no role in the operation of the business. They are Bob's silent partners, functioning only as investors. At the time Harper filed his suit, fewer than six of Smack-Talker's limited partners were U.S. citizens permanently residing in California. Is this a proper diversity case?

5. Assume in question 4 that Smack-Talker does not have any partners permanently residing in California. However, also assume that Whisper, LLC is a limited partner in Smack-Talker. Whisper is a limited liability company with three members. One of the members is a corporation organized under the laws of California with its principal place of business in Oregon. Would the federal district court have diversity of citizenship jurisdiction over Harper's suit on these facts?

6. Byron filed a $200,000 breach of contract action against Gulfport Shrimp, Inc. on May 1, 2016. Gulfport Shrimp is incorporated under the laws of Texas and has its principal place of business in Mississippi. Byron was born and raised in Louisiana and had lived there all his life, but he made a permanent move to Mississippi on December 10, 2016. Does the district court have diversity of citizenship jurisdiction over Byron's suit against Gulfport Shrimp?

7. Bonnie files a breach of contract action against BusCo, Inc. in federal district court. In her complaint Bonnie claims $50,000 in actual damages and $30,000 in punitive damages. Bonnie sincerely believes that punitive damages are warranted given the egregious nature of BusCo's conduct. The governing state contract law provides that punitive damages are not recoverable in breach of contract actions. Is the amount in controversy requirement met?

Civil Procedure in Practice

Reynaldo Garza and his son Julian Garza are seriously injured in a single vehicle accident in McAllen, Texas. Reynaldo, the driver, lost control of his sport utility vehicle ("SUV") after one of the tires failed. The SUV then rolled over several times. Believing that the accident was the result of design defect in the vehicle and the negligence of its designer or designers, Reynaldo and Julian file suit in the United States District Court for the Southern District of Texas on February 12, 2015. In their complaint, they plead negligence under Texas law in the design of the vehicle. Reynaldo and Julian name one defendant in their complaint—the designer and manufacturer of the vehicle, U.S. Autos, LLC. Their complaint seeks damages for each one of them "in an amount not less than $5 million," including compensation for medical expenses, lost wages, pain and suffering, and disfigurement.

Reynaldo is a citizen of Mexico, but he was legally admitted to the United States as a permanent resident alien 20 years ago and has lived in McAllen, Texas ever since. Julian was born in McAllen, Texas and has lived there all his life.

U.S. Autos, LLC is a limited liability company organized under the laws of Texas. Its administrative headquarters is located in Ohio, but its principal manufacturing facility is located in Monterrey, Mexico. As of February 12, 2015, U.S. Autos, LLC has only three members: (1) Tom Johnson, an American Citizen who had lived his entire life in California until he made a permanent move to Texas on March 1, 2015; (2) a corporation with its administrative headquarters in Arkansas and incorporated under the laws of New Jersey that has only five shareholders, all of whom are humans, American citizens, and longtime residents of Texas; and (3) a limited liability company organized under the laws of Texas and headquartered in Texas. This limited liability company has only one member, a corporation incorporated in and with its principal place of business in Oklahoma. On March 15, 2015, U.S. Autos, LLC adds a fourth member, Texas Holding Company, Inc., a corporation incorporated under the laws of Texas with its principal place of business in Dallas, Texas.

1. You are the law clerk for the United States District Judge in the Southern District of Texas to whom this case is assigned. Your judge expresses doubt about whether or not she has subject matter jurisdiction over this case. She asks you to tell her whether or not she does and to support your answer with the necessary legal analysis.

2. Assume the same facts as in question 1, except assume that Julian, although born in McAllen, Texas, lives and works in Matamoros, Mexico with no plans to move at the time the complaint is filed. Would the district court have diversity of citizenship jurisdiction over the case?

Federal Question Jurisdiction

4

This chapter addresses federal question jurisdiction, the second major category of federal court subject matter jurisdiction. Article III, Section 2 provides that the judicial power of federal courts includes cases "arising under" federal law. Because of this language, Congress can grant federal courts the power to interpret federal law and provide federal court access to plaintiffs seeking to vindicate federal rights. Without this provision of the Constitution, the interpretation and enforcement of federal law would be left largely to the whim of state courts that might be hostile to the federal government. Article III, Section 2 helps to ensure that federal courts have the final say about what federal law is.

Article III, Section 2 does not authorize federal district courts to exercise their power. Instead, Congress must grant federal courts jurisdiction by statute. In 28 U.S.C. §1331, the federal question statute, Congress has authorized federal district courts to exercise original subject matter jurisdiction over cases "arising under" federal law. Although the Constitution and the federal question statute use the same "arising under" language, a case must satisfy the requirements of the statute, not merely the Constitution, in order for a federal district court to exercise original federal question jurisdiction. This chapter will explain the meaning of "arising under," both under the Constitution and the statute. Courts have interpreted the phrase differently when interpreting the Constitution than when interpreting the statute.

Federal question jurisdiction is an independent basis for the exercise of subject matter jurisdiction, separate from diversity of citizenship jurisdiction. A federal

Key Concepts

- The "ingredient" a case must contain to fall within the constitutional scope of federal question jurisdiction
- The well-pleaded complaint rule and what it says about where within the case courts look to find a federal question
- The Creation Test and what it requires of a cause of action in order to be a federal question. The *Smith* exception and the circumstances in which a state-created cause of action "arises under" federal law

district court can exercise original subject matter jurisdiction if the requirements of either the diversity statute or the federal question statute are met. Also, federal district courts have original jurisdiction over federal question cases, but not exclusive jurisdiction; so, state courts may also hear these kinds of cases. The federal question statute requires an understanding of three key doctrines: (1) the well-pleaded complaint rule, (2) the Creation Test, and (3) and the *Smith* exception to the Creation Test.

A. THE CONSTITUTIONAL SCOPE OF FEDERAL QUESTION JURISDICTION

Article III, Section 2 allows Congress to confer jurisdiction on federal courts in "Cases, in Law and Equity, arising under this Constitution, the Laws of the United States, and Treaties made, or which shall be made, under their authority."

Courts have interpreted "arising under" in the Constitution broadly. In *Osborn v. Bank of the United States*, the Supreme Court interpreted "arising under" as used in the Constitution to require only that a federal issue be "an ingredient of the original cause." This language is even more expansive than it might seem. It allows Congress to confer jurisdiction on the federal courts in any case "that might call for the application of federal law." *Verlinden B.V. v. Central Bank of Nigeria*, 461 U.S. 480, 492 (1983). The possibility that a case may involve a federal issue — whether as part of a plaintiff's claim or a defendant's defense — is a case "arising under" federal law for purposes of Article III, Section 2.

Article III, Section 2 does not, however, vest federal question jurisdiction directly in the federal courts. The judicial power in the Constitution is not self-executing. Instead, Article III, Section 2 gives Congress the power to vest jurisdiction in the federal courts over cases "arising under" federal law. Congress need not (and has not) authorized federal courts to exercise all of the "arising under" power in Article III, Section 2, and Congress may not expand federal court jurisdiction beyond what the Constitution permits.

It is important to bear in mind the greater breadth of constitutional federal question jurisdiction. The federal question statute vests only *some* of the Article III, Section 2 "arising under" power in the federal district courts. Plenty of "arising under" power remains in Article III, Section 2 for Congress to vest in the federal courts. For example, drawing on Article III, Section 2, Congress has vested original and exclusive jurisdiction in the district courts over proceedings arising under federal patent law, 28 U.S.C. §1338, and under federal bankruptcy laws, 28 U.S.C. §1334. Moreover, Article III, Section 2 does not limit Congress to granting jurisdiction only to district courts. For instance, Congress has provided the Supreme Court the authority to review the decisions of the state supreme courts in cases involving certain federal issues. However, this chapter focuses on the scope of statutory federal question jurisdiction.

B. THE STATUTORY SCOPE OF FEDERAL QUESTION JURISDICTION—28 U.S.C. §1331

Federal courts cannot exercise "arising under" jurisdiction in Article III, Section 2 without congressional authorization. Congress provided federal district courts the authority to exercise federal question jurisdiction in 28 U.S.C. §1331. Under section 1331, federal district courts have original jurisdiction in cases "arising under the Constitution, laws, or treaties of the United States."

The language in the federal question statute is nearly identical to the consitutional language — both refer to cases "arising under" federal law — but the Supreme Court has held that the scope of federal question jurisdiction under section 1331 is much narrower than constitutional federal question jurisdiction. Congress could amend the federal question statute to expand (or contract) the federal district court's original jurisdiction, but it cannot expand it beyond the limits of Article III, Section 2.

A case must satisfy the stricter statutory requirements in order for a district court to exercise original federal question jurisdiction. Statutory federal questions are a smaller subset of constitutional federal questions. All statutory federal questions are constitutional federal questions under *Osborn*, but not all constitutional federal questions meet the narrower requirements of the federal question statute. Exhibit 4.1 is a diagram of this relationship.

The well-pleaded complaint rule and the Creation Test are the keys to a basic understanding of the federal question statute. Think of their respective functions this way: The well-pleaded complaint rule tells us *where* in the case we may look to find a federal question under section 1331 (as well as where we may not look) and the Creation Test tells us *what* we are looking to find.

1. The Well-Pleaded Complaint Rule

The **well-pleaded complaint rule** tells us where in the case we must look to find a statutory federal question. Under *Osborn*, the presence of a federal issue as an ingredient

EXHIBIT 4.1   **The Relationship Between Constitutional and Statutory Federal Questions**

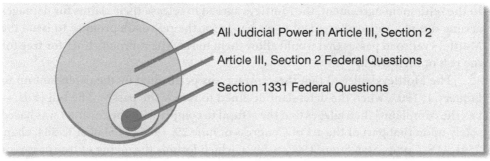

All Judicial Power in Article III, Section 2

Article III, Section 2 Federal Questions

Section 1331 Federal Questions

of a plaintiff's cause of action *or* a defendant's defense meets the constitutional test for federal question jurisdiction. However, as *Louisville & Nashville Railroad Co. v. Mottley* demonstrates, the federal question statute's requirements are stricter.

Case Preview

Louisville & Nashville Railroad Co. v. Mottley

The constitutional grant of federal question jurisdiction in Article III, Section 2 is satisfied when there is a federal "ingredient" anywhere in the case. The statute conferring federal question jurisdiction — 28 U.S.C. §1331 — is much narrower in scope. The well-pleaded complaint rule requires the court to look to the face of the plaintiff's complaint to determine whether or not there is a federal question under section 1331. But where in the complaint must we look? To the plaintiff's cause of action? His defenses? As you read *Mottley*, consider these questions:

1. We look to the plaintiff's complaint to determine the existence of a federal question under section 1331, but what precisely must "arise under" the Constitution, laws, or treaties of the United States? The plaintiff's cause of action? An anticipated defense referenced in the complaint? Either?
2. Does a defense raising a question of federal law present a federal question under section 1331?
3. Does an argument that a federal law defeats a defense present a federal question under section 1331?

Louisville & Nashville Railroad Co. v. Mottley
211 U.S. 149 (1908)

Statement by Mr. Justice MOODY:

[Eds. — The Mottleys, a married couple and Kentucky citizens, brought suit in federal court in Kentucky against the Louisville & Nashville Railroad Co., also a citizen of Kentucky. The Mottleys sought specific performance of a settlement agreement between the Mottleys and the railroad — essentially a state law contract claim. In the settlement agreement, the Mottleys agreed to release their claims for damages arising out of a railroad accident in exchange for the railroad's promise to issue the Mottleys railroad passes that would allow them to ride the railroad's lines for free for the rest of their lives.]

[The Mottleys] alleged that the contract was performed by the defendant up to January 1, 1907, when the defendant declined to renew the passes. The bill [Eds. — i.e., the complaint] then alleges that the refusal to comply with the contract was based solely upon that part of the act of Congress of June 29, 1906 (34 Stat. at L. 584, chap. 3591, U.S. Comp. Stat. Supp. 1907, p. 892), which forbids the giving of free passes or free transportation. The bill further alleges: First, that the act of Congress referred to does not prohibit the giving of passes under the circumstances of this case; and, second, that, if the law is to be construed as prohibiting such passes, it is in conflict with the 5th Amendment of the Constitution, because it deprives the plaintiffs of their property without due process of law. The defendant demurred to the bill. The judge of the circuit court overruled the demurrer, entered a decree for the relief prayed for, and the defendant appealed directly to this court.

Mr. Justice MOODY, after making the foregoing statement, delivered the opinion of the court:

Two questions of law were raised by the demurrer to the bill, were brought here by appeal, and have been argued before us. They are, first, whether that part of the act of Congress of June 29, 1906 . . . which forbids the giving of free passes or the *issue* collection of any different compensation for transportation of passengers than that specified in the tariff filed, makes it unlawful to perform a contract for transportation of persons who, in good faith, before the passage of the act, had accepted such contract in satisfaction of a valid cause of action against the railroad; and, second, whether the statute, if it should be construed to render such a contract unlawful, is in violation of the 5th Amendment of the Constitution of the United States. We do not deem it necessary, however, to consider either of these questions, because, in our opinion, the court below was without jurisdiction of the cause. Neither party has questioned that jurisdiction, but it is the duty of this court to see to it that the jurisdiction of the circuit court, which is defined and limited by statute, is not exceeded. This duty we have frequently performed of our own motion.

 There was no diversity of citizenship, and it is not and cannot be suggested that there was any ground of jurisdiction, except that the case was a 'suit . . . arising under the Constitution or laws of the United States.' . . . It is the settled interpretation of these words, as used in this statute, conferring jurisdiction, that a suit arises under the Constitution and laws of the United States only when the plaintiff's statement of his own cause of action shows that it is based upon those laws or that Constitution. It is not enough that the plaintiff alleges some anticipated defense to his cause of action, and asserts that the defense is invalidated by some provision of the Constitution of the United States. Although such allegations show that very likely, in the course of the litigation, a question under the Constitution would arise, they do not show that the suit, that is, the plaintiff's original cause of action, arises under the Constitution. In Tennessee v. Union & Planters' Bank, 152 U. S. 454, 38 L. Ed. 511, 14 Sup. Ct. Rep. 654, the plaintiff, the state of Tennessee, brought suit in the circuit court of the United States to recover from the defendant certain taxes alleged to be due under the laws of the state. The plaintiff alleged that the defendant claimed an immunity from the taxation by virtue of its charter, and that therefore the tax was void, because in violation of the provision of the Constitution of the United States, which forbids any state from passing a law impairing the obligation of contracts. The cause was held to be beyond the jurisdiction of the circuit court, the court saying, by Mr. Justice Gray (p. 464): 'A suggestion of one party, that the other will or may set up a claim under the Constitution or laws of the United States, does not make the suit one arising under that Constitution or those laws.' . . .

* * *

The application of this rule to the case at bar is decisive against the jurisdiction of the circuit court.

It is ordered that the judgment be reversed and the case remitted to the circuit court with instructions to dismiss the suit for want of jurisdiction.

Post-Case Follow-Up

Mottley sets out what has become known as the well-pleaded complaint rule: A federal question under section 1331 must appear on the face of the plaintiff's well-pleaded complaint in the statement of his own cause of action. A federal defense (or even a plaintiff's federal response to an anticipated defense) is not a federal question, even when that anticipated defense is mentioned in the complaint. The Mottleys' cause of action is pure state law — it doesn't even contain a federal ingredient — but federal issues were certain to arise in the Mottleys' case against the railroad. In fact, they were the central disputed issues in the case. The railroad could not credibly argue that it never had a contract with the Mottleys or that it was still issuing the passes. Instead, its defense was that federal law no longer allows it to honor its contractual obligation. Anticipated federal defenses and responses to defenses are not federal questions, even when, as in *Mottley*, everyone agrees that they will be the key to resolving the dispute.

Note that neither the Mottleys nor the railroad raised a question about the Court's subject matter jurisdiction. The Court raised the issue on its own, after the parties had already argued the merits of the federal statutory and constitutional issues. The fact that the Supreme Court would raise this issue on its own at such a late stage in the litigation should impress upon you how far federal courts will go to ensure they have subject matter jurisdiction over a case.

Louisville & Nashville Railroad Co. v. Mottley: Real Life Applications

1. Miguel suffers severe injuries when the brakes in his car fail. Miguel files suit in federal district court against Power Brakes, Inc., the manufacturer of the brakes. In his complaint, Miguel alleges that Power Brakes' negligence caused a design defect in the brakes which in turn caused the brake failure in Miguel's car. In his complaint, Miguel states that Power Brakes is likely to defend the suit, in part, on the ground that it is not liable because it designed the brakes in accordance with Federal Motor Vehicle Safety Standards and Regulations governing brake design. Does the federal district court have federal question jurisdiction over Miguel's case?

2. Suppose Miguel alleges $1 million in personal injury damages, he was born in California and has never lived anywhere else, and Power Brakes is incorporated under the laws of Delaware and has its principal place of business in Ohio. Does the federal district court have subject matter jurisdiction over Miguel's case?

Diversity Jur.

3. Miguel's case does not "arise under" federal law for purposes of section 1331. But does Miguel's case "arise under" federal law as that term is used in Article III, Section 2?

There must be "an ingredient"

2. The Holmes Creation Test

The well-pleaded complaint rule tells us *where* we must find a federal question — in the plaintiff's complaint in the statement of his own cause of action. Federal defenses and arguments that federal law defeats a defense do not give rise to federal question jurisdiction under section 1331. But clearly not all causes of action arise under federal law. The Mottleys' breach of contract cause of action didn't. Once we are properly focused on the plaintiff's cause of action, what are we looking for? More precisely, what kind of cause of action are we looking for?

In *American Well Works Co. v. Layne & Bowler Co.*, Justice Holmes provided a relatively straightforward test for determining the existence of a federal question. Writing for the majority, Holmes said, "[A] suit arises under the law that creates the cause of action." 241 U.S. 257 (1916). This language is what has become known as the Holmes test or the **Creation Test** for determining the existence of federal question jurisdiction.

Although the Creation Test is a century old, it still stands as the principal rule for determining if a cause of action is a federal question. A suit arises under the law that creates the cause of action. So, if federal law creates the cause of action, it arises under federal law and the district court may exercise original federal question jurisdiction under section 1331. If state law creates the cause of action, it does not arise under federal law and the court may not exercise original federal question jurisdiction. Put even more simply, federal causes of action are federal questions. Generally, state causes of action are not.

Consider how the well-pleaded complaint rule and the Creation Test apply to the Mottleys' lawsuit. Recall that the Mottleys claimed the railroad had breached their contract, and they also alleged that the railroad would raise a federal statute as a defense. The Mottleys alleged the statute did not prohibit the railroad from honoring their passes, but, even if it did, the statute violated the Due Process Clause of the Constitution. Under the well-pleaded complaint rule, we look only to the Mottleys' statement of their cause of action and ignore both the federal defense (the federal statute barring free passes) and their constitutional argument to defeat it (the statute would violate due process). Clearly, federal issues will be a critical part of the Mottleys' case against the railroad; in fact, they were the only disputed issues. But federal question jurisdiction must exist as part of the plaintiff's cause of action. Applying the Creation Test to the Mottleys' breach of contract cause of action — a suit arises under the law that creates the cause of action — we ask whether state law or federal law creates the Mottleys' breach of contract cause of action. State law creates breach of contract causes of action, not federal law. Thus, under the Creation Test, the Mottleys' suit does not arise under federal law.

The Creation Test provides clarity and certainty about the existence of federal question jurisdiction in most cases. Tort causes of action, such as negligence, assault, battery, trespass, and conversion, are all state-created causes of action and, therefore, do not arise under federal law. Breach of contract and warranty causes of action are also state-created, as are most causes of action asserted in property disputes, such as partition and quiet title actions.

Federal law creates a number of causes of action over which the federal district courts may exercise federal question jurisdiction. For example, Title VII of the federal civil rights act provides a cause of action to an employee who has suffered discrimination in the workplace on the basis of race, religion, sex, color, or national origin. The federal Age Discrimination in Employment Act provides a cause of action to employees who have suffered workplace discrimination based on age. The Americans with Disabilities Act creates a cause of action for discrimination based on disability. Federal law provides a cause of action to those whose civil rights have been violated by government officials. Federal law creates causes of action for patent and trademark infringement, as well as copyright violations, and it creates causes of action for securities fraud. This list is certainly not exhaustive of all federal causes of action. The point to remember is that, under the Creation Test, federal causes of action arise under federal law, and a federal court has federal question jurisdiction when a plaintiff pleads a federal cause of action.

3. The No-Counterclaim Rule

A federal district court may not exercise federal question jurisdiction over a plaintiff's case based on a counterclaim asserted in the action. Suppose a bank files suit to foreclose its mortgage on real property owned by the defendant. In his answer, the defendant asserts a counterclaim against the bank for violating the federal Truth in Lending Act. The federal court would not have federal question jurisdiction over the plaintiff's case.

Recall that the well-pleaded complaint rule requires a federal question to appear on the face of the *plaintiff's well-pleaded complaint* and the statement of his own cause of action. When a defendant asserts a counterclaim back against the plaintiff, the counterclaim allegations appear in the defendant's answer, not in the plaintiff's complaint. In *Holmes Group v. Vornado Air Circulation Systems, Inc.*, 535 U.S. 826 (2002), the Supreme Court refused to "transform the longstanding well-pleaded-complaint rule into the well-pleaded-complaint-or-counterclaim rule."

> Admittedly our prior cases . . . were decided on the principle that federal jurisdiction generally exists "only when a federal question is presented on the face of the plaintiff's properly pleaded complaint." . . . [W]hether a case arises under federal patent law "cannot depend upon the answer." Moreover, we have declined to adopt proposals that "the answer as well as the complaint . . . be consulted before a determination [is] made whether the case 'ar[ises] under' federal law. . . ." It follows that a counterclaim — which appears as part of the defendant's answer, not as part of the plaintiff's complaint — cannot serve as the basis for "arising under" jurisdiction.

535 U.S. at 831.

Applying the holding in *Holmes Group* to our example above, the defendant's federal Truth in Lending Act counterclaim against the bank does not give rise to federal question jurisdiction because it does not appear on the face of the plaintiff's well-pleaded complaint. It appears instead in the defendant's answer. In response to *Holmes Group*, in 2011 Congress amended 28 U.S.C. §1454. That statute permits a federal court to exercise removal jurisdiction over any claim by "any party" relating to "patents, plant variety protection, or copyrights," making such counterclaims a proper basis for removal.

4. Federal Question Jurisdiction in Declaratory Judgment Actions

The **Declaratory Judgment Act** allows federal courts to "declare the rights and other legal relations of any interested party seeking such declaration, whether or not further relief is or could be sought." 28 U.S.C. §2201(a). A plaintiff might bring a declaratory judgment action if she fears the defendant might later assert a claim against her. The plaintiff in the **declaratory judgment action** seeks a declaration of her rights so as to know whether or not she would be liable on the claim. A declaratory judgment action can prevent harm to the defendant (and liability of the plaintiff) because the court's declaration might discourage the plaintiff from harming the defendant in the first place.

Declaratory judgment actions resemble a case in reverse. The plaintiff in a declaratory judgment action is more like a defendant because her suit alleges that she is not liable, rather than demanding monetary or injunctive relief. Thus, the complaint in a declaratory judgment action might look more like an answer — alleging defenses to the claim the declaratory judgment plaintiff anticipates the declaratory judgment defendant might later assert. Given its nature, how does the well-pleaded complaint rule apply in declaratory judgment actions? In *Public Service Comm'n of Utah v. Wycoff Co., Inc.*, 344 U.S. 237 (1952), the Supreme Court explained its application:

> In this case, as in many actions for declaratory judgment, the realistic position of the parties is reversed. The plaintiff is seeking to establish a defense against a cause of action which the declaratory defendant may assert in the Utah courts. Respondent here has sought to ward off possible action of the petitioners by seeking a declaratory judgment to the effect that he will have a good defense when and if that cause of action is asserted. Where the complaint in an action for declaratory judgment seeks in essence to assert a defense to an impending or threatened state court action, it is the character of the threatened action, and not of the defense, which will determine whether there is federal-question jurisdiction in the District Court. If the cause of action, which the declaratory defendant threatens to assert, does not itself involve a claim under federal law, it is doubtful if a federal court may entertain an action for a declaratory judgment establishing a defense to that claim. This is dubious even though the declaratory complaint sets forth a claim of federal right, if that right is in reality in the nature of a defense to a threatened cause of action. Federal courts will not seize litigations from state courts merely because one, normally a defendant, goes to federal court to begin his federal-law defense before the state court begins the case under state law.

344 U.S. at 248.

The well-pleaded complaint rule is not applied to the declaratory judgment plaintiff's complaint. Instead, the court will imagine what the declaratory judgment defendant's complaint would look like in the threatened or anticipated action and apply the well-pleaded complaint rule to this hypothetical complaint. If the declaratory judgment plaintiff's claim in the declaratory judgment action would be a federal defense to a state law claim in the threatened action, federal question jurisdiction would not exist.

For example, if the railroad had brought a declaratory judgment action against the Mottleys, its complaint might allege something along the lines of "the railroad is not liable to the Mottleys for its failure to renew their passes, despite a contract that requires it to do so, because Congress has passed a law prohibiting the railroad from honoring such passes." We can see that the railroad's claim in the declaratory judgment action is based on a federal statute, but we must hypothesize about what the Mottleys' cause of action in the anticipated action would be. In this case, that would appear to be breach of contract under state law. The railroad's claim in the declaratory judgment action would be asserted only as a defense in the anticipated breach of contract action. We come to the same conclusion applying the well-pleaded complaint rule to the hypothetical complaint as we did applying it to the Mottleys' actual complaint — no federal question jurisdiction exists.

5. The Plaintiff as Master of His Complaint

A plaintiff is not required to assert a federal cause of action just because he has one available to him. He is the "master" of his complaint and is free to decide what law — state or federal — he will rely upon. A plaintiff who has both a federal and a state cause of action can assert one or the other or both. The existence of federal question jurisdiction will be determined based on what the plaintiff actually pled, not what he could have pled. The plaintiff does not allege a federal question when he relies exclusively upon state law.

For example, in *Caterpillar, Inc. v. Williams*, 482 U.S. 386 (1987), a group of former union workers filed suit against their former employer alleging that they had been terminated in violation of their employment contracts. The former employees were parties to a collective bargaining agreement. Section 301 of the federal Labor Management Relations Act (LMRA) provides a cause of action for breach of a collective bargaining agreement. The former employees also alleged that they were parties to individual employment contracts with their employer, which are governed by state law, not the LMRA. The plaintiffs alleged only breach of the individual contracts, not breach of the collective bargaining agreement. Because, as masters of their complaints, the plaintiffs chose to proceed only on their state law claims and to forgo their federal law claims, their case did not "arise under" federal law.

6. The Complete Preemption Rule: When the Plaintiff Is Not the Master

The plaintiff is not the master of his complaint only in one situation: when a federal claim completely preempts state law claims. Complete preemption occurs when federal law <u>not only provides</u> a cause of action but also preempts <u>state law causes of</u> <u>action</u> of the same sort. In essence, federal law provides a cause of action *and* federal law is the *only* cause of action for such cases. When a federal cause of action completely preempts state law, a plaintiff's cause of action "arises under" federal law even when it makes no mention of federal law and purports to rely exclusively on state law.

Very few federal statutes create a cause of action that completely preempts state causes of action, but one such statute is section 303 of the LMRA. Congress has provided a federal cause of action for breach of a collective bargaining agreement and it preempts all state causes of action for breach of such agreements. A plaintiff who pleads breach of any *collective* bargaining agreement has pled a case "arising under" federal law whether he mentions federal law or not.

Note that the *Caterpillar* case did not "arise under" federal law because the plaintiffs did not plead breach of a *collective bargaining agreement*. They pled breach of *individual employment contracts*. But had the plaintiffs pled "breach of a collective bargaining agreement in violation of state law," their case would have presented a federal question, despite not mentioning federal law and explicitly invoking state law.

The Creation Test: Real Life Applications

Assume the cases below are filed in federal district court. Does the court have original federal question jurisdiction?

1. Mary v. Mass Construction, LLC. In her complaint, Mary alleges that Mass Construction fired her because she is a woman, in violation of Title VII of the Federal Civil Rights Act. Title VII allows employees to seek damages resulting from sex discrimination by employers. *yes.*

2. Heartland National Bank v. Joe. In its complaint, Heartland claims that Joe has defaulted on a loan Heartland made to Joe for the purchase of a vehicle. Heartland seeks the principal and the interest owed on the loan. Heartland is chartered by the federal government, participates in the Federal Reserve System, and borrowed money from another participant system to fund Joe's loan. *yes?*

3. AT&E, Inc. v. Ted. AT&E alleges the tort of conversion, claiming that Ted, one of its former employees, took more than $10,000 of computer equipment *no.* belonging to AT&E. AT&E fired Ted on the day it discovered the missing equipment. In his answer, Ted counterclaims under the federal Age Discrimination in Employment Act, seeking damages on the ground that the true reason AT&E fired him was because of Ted's "advanced age."

4. Johnson v. Miracle Drug, Inc. Johnson's complaint claims that a drug for the treatment of joint pain manufactured by Miracle Drug caused his stroke after he took 15 of the pills in a single day. Johnson alleges that Miracle Drug was negligent per se under state tort law because the drug's packaging did not comply with federal regulations that require a label with proper daily dosages. *no.*

C. FEDERAL QUESTION JURISDICTION OVER CERTAIN STATE LAW CLAIMS

In rare cases, federal district courts may exercise federal question jurisdiction over certain state law claims. Under the Creation Test, a cause of action arises under the law that creates it. Therefore, a federal cause of action arises under federal law, and a state cause of action generally does not. The Supreme Court has described the Creation Test as a rule of inclusion rather than exclusion. The Creation Test makes all federally created causes of action federal questions, but it does not *exclude* all state-created causes of action. In particular, in rare cases, a state-created cause of action *might* arise under federal law when the state law claim necessarily raises a federal issue embedded in the state law claim. This type of federal question jurisdiction is sometimes referred to as the "*Smith* exception" to the Creation Test (after the Supreme Court case that recognized federal question jurisdiction over a state law claim).

1. The Well-Pleaded Complaint Rule and the *Smith* Exception

The *Smith* **exception** is an exception to the Creation Test, not the well-pleaded complaint rule. The federal issue embedded in the state law claim must still appear on the face of the plaintiff's complaint and in the plaintiff's statement of his cause of action. The exception does not find federal question jurisdiction based on defenses or counterclaims. Only state law claims with embedded federal issues can qualify as federal questions under the exception, and still only a fraction of these arise under federal law. A state law claim that does not necessarily raise a federal issue — i.e., a state cause of action without an embedded federal issue — is *never* a federal question. Exhibit 4.2 synthesizes all three of these rules to make clear when a case arises under federal law.

EXHIBIT 4.2   **28 U.S.C. §1331: Synthesizing the Well-Pleaded Complaint Rule, the Creation Test, and the *Smith* Exception**

1. A federally created cause of action alleged in the plaintiff's complaint *always* arises under federal law.
2. A state-created cause of action with an embedded federal issue *sometimes* arises under federal law.
3. A state-created cause of action without an embedded federal issue *never* arises under federal law.

---

2. Characteristics of the Rare State Law Claim that Arises Under Federal Law

Smith v. Kansas City Title & Trust Co. is the classic example of a state law claim arising under federal law. 255 U.S. 180 (1921). In *Smith*, a shareholder in a trust company filed suit to enjoin the trust company from investing funds in certain bonds. The bonds had been issued pursuant to the Federal Farm Loan Act. The trust company could invest funds only in legal securities. The shareholder argued that the bonds at issue were not legal securities because the Federal Farm Loan Act was unconstitutional. So, while the cause of action in *Smith* was state-created, it required resolution of a federal constitutional issue. To prevail on his state law claim, the shareholder had to prove the Farm Loan Act was unconstitutional in order to show that the bonds were not "legal securities." If the Federal Farm Loan Act were found constitutional, the shareholder's state law claim for injunction would fail. If it were found unconstitutional, he would prevail. The Supreme Court held that the shareholder's state law claim arose under federal law because it would be defeated by one interpretation of the Constitution and sustained by another. In other words, the shareholder's state law claim necessarily depended upon the resolution of a federal issue.

Even if a state-created cause of action depends upon the resolution of a federal issue, it does not necessarily arise under federal law. Sixty-five years after *Smith*, in *Merrell Dow Pharmaceuticals v. Thompson*, 478 U.S. 804 (1986), the Court held that a state negligence per se cause of action based on the violation of a federal statute did not arise under federal law. In *Merrell Dow*, the plaintiffs brought suit against a pharmaceutical company alleging that its drug taken during pregnancy caused birth defects in infants. Plaintiffs alleged a number of state-created causes of action, including negligence per se for violation of drug labeling standards set out in the federal Food Drug and Cosmetic Act (FDCA). Negligence per se is a state law claim based on the violation of some safety statute (or regulation) permitting a finding that the defendant's conduct was unreasonable under state law. In sum, the plaintiffs' negligence per se claim was that the defendant's conduct was negligent under state law because it violated the FDCA. The plaintiffs took the position that the FDCA did not create a federal cause of action for the misbranding of drugs. Instead, the plaintiffs alleged that the pharmaceutical company was negligent per se in violation of state tort law because it had not complied with FDCA labeling standards. Thus, the plaintiff's state law claim depended on the resolution of a federal issue because violation of the federal labeling standard was a necessary element of the negligence per se cause of action. Nevertheless, the Court held that the plaintiff's negligence per se cause of action did not arise under federal law, saying "the mere presence of a federal issue in a state cause of action does not automatically confer federal-question jurisdiction." The Court's sweeping conclusion in *Merrell Dow* — "a complaint alleging a violation of a federal statute as an element of a state cause of action . . . does not state a claim 'arising under the Constitution, laws, or treaties of the United States'" 478 U.S. at 818 — casts doubt on the continued viability of the *Smith* exception.

Grable & Sons Metal Products, Inc. v. Darue Engineering & Manufacturing dispelled the doubt created by *Merrell Dow* — *some* state-created causes of action that depend on the resolution of a federal issue do arise under federal law. *Grable* also provided guidance as to when these types of state law claims are a federal question and when they are not.

In *Grable*, the Internal Revenue Service (IRS) seized property belonging to Grable and sold it to Darue to satisfy Grable's federal tax delinquency. A federal statute required the IRS to provide Grable notice of the seizure, which it did by certified mail. Five years later, Grable brought a quiet title action (a state law claim) against Darue claiming that Darue's record title was invalid because the IRS had not provided him proper notice of the seizure. Grable argued that the federal notice statute required personal service, not service by certified mail. Grable's cause of action was state-created, but it depended upon the resolution of the federal notice issue. If the notice statute required personal service, Darue's title would be invalid and Grable would win his property back. If service by certified mail was adequate, Darue would have good title and Grable would lose.

The Court held that Grable's state-created cause of action arose under federal law. In reaching this conclusion, the Court identified the key characteristics of a state law claim that arises under federal law — (1) resolution of the federal issue must be necessary, (2) the federal issue must be actually disputed, (3) the issue must be substantial, and (4) resolution of the issue in federal court must be nondisruptive of the balance of cases in state and federal court. First, Grable's state law claim required resolution of the federal issue because it was an essential element of the claim. Grable's claim was such that the court could not decide the title issue without resolving the federal notice issue. Second, the parties "actually disputed" how the issue should be resolved. In fact, it appeared to be the only disputed issue in the case. Third, the federal notice issue was substantial because it indicated "a serious federal interest in claiming the advantages thought to be inherent in a federal forum" because the government has a strong interest in the collection of delinquent taxes.

Even if all three of these requirements are met, exercising federal question jurisdiction is subject to a "possible veto." State law claims with embedded federal issues — even substantial, contested federal issues — qualify as federal questions "only if federal jurisdiction is consistent with congressional judgment about the sound division of labor between state and federal courts. . . ." In other words, finding federal question jurisdiction must not disrupt the "Congressionally approved (or assumed)" federal-state balance of cases. Disrupting this balance was not a concern in *Grable* because so few quiet title claims involve federal issues that the effect on the federal-state division of labor would be "microscopic."

Grable makes clear that, even after *Merrell Dow*, some state law claims requiring resolution of a federal issue are federal questions. It also sets out the essential pieces of the analysis for identifying those that are, but it must be said that uncertainty about the precise contours of the *Smith* exception remains. The key takeaway here is that, while the vast majority of federal question cases involve federal causes of action, in rare cases a state law claim that necessarily depends on the resolution of an important federal issue *might* be a federal question.

D. *MOTTLEY II*—THE SEQUEL: REVISITING THE CONSTITUTIONAL SCOPE OF FEDERAL QUESTION JURISDICTION

In *Mottley*, the Supreme Court's decision that federal question jurisdiction did not exist apparently came as a surprise to both sides in the case. The Mottleys and the railroad had briefed and argued two points: (1) whether a federal statute prohibited the railroad from honoring the Mottleys' lifetime passes; and (2) if so, whether the statute violated the Due Process Clause of the Constitution. Neither party had raised the issue of a lack of subject matter jurisdiction. Recall this language from the Supreme Court's opinion:

> We do not deem it necessary, however, to consider either of these questions, because, in our opinion, the court below was without jurisdiction of the cause. Neither party has questioned that jurisdiction, but it is the duty of this court to see to it that the jurisdiction of the circuit court, which is defined and limited by statute, is not exceeded. This duty we have frequently performed of our own motion.

The Mottleys had pursued their claim all the way to the Supreme Court, only to be told that the Court would not answer the two disputed federal issues because the trial court never had jurisdiction in the first place. The Supreme Court's determination meant that all of the time and effort the parties and the lower court put into the case was for naught. The Supreme Court had everything it needed to decide the issues on appeal — the record and the merits briefs. Nevertheless, the Supreme Court refused to decide the issues. The *Mottley* case stands as an object lesson in what the Supreme Court is willing to sacrifice in order to police the limits of federal court jurisdiction.

If the Mottleys wanted the railroad to honor their lifetime passes, they would have to start all over in state court. And that's precisely what the Mottleys did. The Mottleys refiled their suit against the railroad for specific performance of the contract in a Kentucky state trial court. The Mottleys won in the trial court. The trial court's judgment required the railroad to issue the Mottleys free passes to ride the rail lines for the remainder of their lives. The railroad appealed the trial court's judgment to the Supreme Court of Kentucky. The Kentucky Supreme Court also sided with the Mottleys and affirmed the trial court decision. The Supreme Court had already determined that the case did not "arise under" federal law, despite the presence of federal issues. So, surely the U.S. Supreme Court could not deprive the Mottleys of their victory again. Right?

Wrong. The railroad sought review of the Kentucky Supreme Court's decision in the United States Supreme Court and review was granted. This time around, the Supreme Court did not determine that it lacked jurisdiction. It didn't even discuss subject matter jurisdiction, except to say that the grounds for its previous dismissal were "not important here." Instead, it held that the federal statute prohibited the railroad from honoring the Mottleys' passes and rejected the argument that the statute violated the Due Process Clause of the Constitution. After more than two additional years of litigation following the Supreme Court's dismissal of their federal court lawsuit, the Mottleys had lost, this time on the merits, and this time for good.

But how could the Supreme Court have possibly had subject matter jurisdiction in *Mottley II*? The answer lies in the difference between the meaning of "arising under" in Article III, Section 2 and in the federal question statute. To arise under federal law for purposes of the diversity statute, the federal question must appear in the plaintiff's statement of his cause of action and, generally, the cause of action must be a federally created one. A case "arising under" federal law for purposes of the Constitution is any case that might call for the application of federal law (recall *Osborn*). Thus, Congress can vest jurisdiction in federal courts to review cases involving a federal issue even if the case does not meet the requirements of the federal question statute.

Drawing on the "arising under" power in Article III, Section 2, Congress has authorized the United States Supreme Court to review by writ of certiorari the final judgments of state high courts in cases where the validity of a federal statute is drawn into question. 28 U.S.C. §1257. This jurisdictional statute clearly falls within the "arising under" power in Article III, Section 2 — a case questioning a federal statute certainly requires the application of federal law — and the *Mottley* suit meets the statutory requirements because they called into question the federal statute prohibiting the railroad from honoring their passes.

Chapter Summary

- Article III, Section 2 of the Constitution creates federal judicial power in cases "arising under" federal law. A constitutional federal question requires only the presence of a "federal ingredient" in the case. Any case that might require the application of federal law is, as a matter of constitutional law, a federal question.
- In order to exercise original federal question jurisdiction, a case must meet the stricter statutory requirements of 28 U.S.C. §1331.
- Under the well-pleaded complaint rule (adopted in *Mottley*), a statutory federal question under section 1331 exists when a federal question appears on the face of the plaintiff's complaint in his statement of his own cause of action. Federal question jurisdiction may not be premised on a federal defense or a federal response to a defense.
- The Creation Test (a/k/a the Holmes Test or Holmes Creation Test) describes the vast majority of federal questions. A suit arises under the law that creates the cause of action. A federally created cause of action is a federal question. A state-created cause of action is generally not.
- The *Smith* exception to the Creation Test describes a "slim category" of state created causes of action that "arise under" federal law.
- A state law claim with an embedded federal issue arises under federal law only if the federal issue is (1) necessarily raised, (2) actually disputed, (3) substantial, and (4) capable of resolution in federal court without disrupting the federal-state balance approved by Congress. A state law claim without an embedded federal issue never "arises under" federal law.

Applying the Concepts

1. Would a federal district court have federal question jurisdiction over the cases below?

   a. The plaintiff files a declaratory judgment action seeking a declaration from the court that a recent federal law excuses performance under the contract between the plaintiff and defendant.

   b. The plaintiff's complaint names his former employer as the defendant and alleges breach of contract under state law. The contract at issue is a collective bargaining agreement between the defendant and its union employees. Plaintiff was a union employee. The complaint explicitly "disavows and abandons any federal claims or causes of action the plaintiff may have against the defendant."

   c. The plaintiff's complaint alleges her employer discriminated against her on the basis of her race in violation of a state statute that provides a cause of action to employees against employers injured by workplace racial discrimination. Her complaint explicitly disavows and abandons any federal claims or causes of action the plaintiff may have against the defendant, including any and all claims provided by Title VII of the federal Civil Rights Act.

   d. Plaintiff's complaint alleges state tort causes of action. He also alleges that he anticipates the defendant will raise a federal statutory defense but that it is without merit.

   e. Plaintiff's complaint alleges the defendant violated her civil rights and asserts a cause of action under 42 U.S.C. §1983 of the Civil Rights Act of 1871.

2. Plaintiff files suit in New Jersey state court. Her complaint alleges a cause of action under the federal Americans with Disabilities Act. Six months after the lawsuit is filed, the defendant urges the New Jersey court to dismiss the case on the ground that it lacks subject matter jurisdiction. How should the court rule?

Civil Procedure in Practice

You represent Inventors, LLC. Inventors invented and patented a hand-held device it calls the Rejuvenator. The Rejuvenator regrows hair in men experiencing male-pattern baldness. Inventors discovers that Knockoffs, Inc. is manufacturing and selling the Rejuvenator without Inventors' permission. You file suit on behalf of Inventors against Knockoffs in federal district court. Both Inventors and Knockoffs are citizens of New Jersey. Your complaint alleges patent infringement under 35 U.S.C. §271, which authorizes a patent holder to seek damages against a party infringing on its patent. Three days before the case is set for trial, the federal district judge informs you and your opposing counsel that she believes jurisdiction is lack-ing because Knockoffs' infringement is so obvious the issue does not seem to be actually disputed or substantial.

a. Knockoffs' attorney argues that the court cannot dismiss the case for lack of subject matter jurisdiction for two independent reasons: (a) too much time has passed since the case was filed, and (b) neither party raised the objec-tion — the court did. Is Knockoffs correct that the court cannot dismiss the case for either of the reasons it offers?

b. Does your case on behalf of Inventors "arise under" federal law? If not, why not? If so, how would you answer the court's concerns about the lack of an actual dispute as to infringement and the substantiality of this federal issue?

Removal of Cases from State Courts

State and federal courts have concurrent jurisdiction over federal question and diversity cases. A plaintiff may often file a federal question or diversity case in either state or federal court. However, a plaintiff's decision to file a case in state court does not mean the case will remain in state court. The removal statutes allow a defendant to trump the plaintiff's choice of a state forum by substituting a federal forum for adjudication of the action. As a general rule, defendants may remove a case from state to federal court if the case is one over which the federal court has original jurisdiction. Since federal courts have original jurisdiction over federal question and diversity cases, such cases are routinely removed to federal court after plaintiffs file them in state court.

Recall that the purpose of diversity jurisdiction is to prevent local prejudice in state court against out-of-state defendants by providing them a federal forum. Federal question jurisdiction gives the federal court system the ability to interpret, apply, and enforce federal law. Without the removal statutes, plaintiffs could undermine these purposes simply by filing cases in state court.

Understanding the removal statutes requires you to understand new rules and concepts. You must understand (1) the general rule of removal; (2) the exceptions to the general rule; (3) the procedure for removal, including how a case is removed, who may remove a case, the deadline to remove, and to what federal court a case is removed; and (4) the procedure for remand to state court.

Key Concepts

- Which cases may be removed from state to federal court under the general rule of removal
- The Forum State Defendant Exception to Removal
- Who may remove a case, how they remove it, to where they remove it, and the deadline for removal
- How a plaintiff may secure remand to state court and the possible consequences of a delay in filing a motion to remand

A. AN OVERVIEW OF REMOVAL AND REMAND

A defendant has the option to remove certain cases filed in state court to federal court. A removal issue can only arise when the plaintiff files his case in state court. **Removal** plays no role in cases filed in federal court, and only the defendant has the option to remove a case to federal court. The defendant removes a case by filing a **notice of removal** in the federal court for the federal district and division in which the state court action is pending. Generally, a defendant may remove a case over which the federal district courts have original jurisdiction, including federal question and diversity cases. Following removal, the plaintiff can file a motion to **remand** with the federal court. The remand motion might seek remand on the grounds that the federal court lacks subject matter jurisdiction, or that the defendant failed to comply with proper removal procedures, or both. If the plaintiff's motion is granted, the federal court will remand the case to the state court in which the case was originally filed. Exhibit 5.1 provides an illustration of this process.

EXHIBIT 5.1   **An Overview of Removal and Remand**

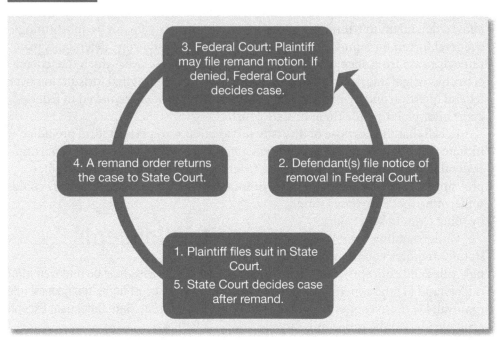

B. THE GENERAL RULE OF REMOVAL

28 U.S.C. §1441(a) describes cases that may be removed from state to federal court. The statute says that, as a general rule, a case may be removed from state to federal court if the case is one over which the district courts have original jurisdiction. So, if the federal court has original subject matter jurisdiction over the case, generally it may be removed from state to federal court. Put another way, if the case could have been filed in federal court in the first place, it is subject to removal if filed in state court.

Suppose Software, LLC, a citizen of Texas, files a $1 million breach of contract action against Hardware, Inc., a citizen of Maryland, in Texas state court. The case would look like this.

Software (TX) $1 million BOK ⟶   Hardware (MD)

Hardware could remove this case from state to federal court because the district court has original diversity of citizenship jurisdiction over the case. Software and Hardware are citizens of different states and the amount in controversy requirement is satisfied.

Federal question cases filed in state court can also be removed to federal court. Suppose Angela files suit in New York state court against her former employer, Greenleaf, Inc., and alleges that Greenleaf fired her because she is a woman, in violation of Title VII of the federal Civil Rights Act. Greenleaf could remove the case because the district court has original federal question jurisdiction over the case. Angela's federal sex discrimination cause of action satisfies both the well-pleaded complaint rule and the Creation Test for the existence of a federal question under 28 U.S.C. §1331.

State and federal courts have concurrent jurisdiction over diversity cases like Software's breach of contract action against Hardware and federal question cases like Angela's federal sex discrimination suit against Greenleaf. So, if Hardware and Greenleaf choose not to remove the cases, the state court can decide them. The removal statute gives defendants *the option* to remove cases over which the federal courts have original jurisdiction. The statute does not *require* defendants to remove them.

Importantly, the removal statutes do not expand the federal court's diversity of citizenship or federal question jurisdiction, as *Avitts v. Amoco Production Co.* demonstrates.

Case Preview

Avitts v. Amoco Production Co.

As you read *Avitts*, consider the following questions:

1. What forum did the plaintiffs choose? state dist.
2. A defendant may only remove a case if the district court has original subject matter jurisdiction over it. What did the defendants claim was the basis for the court's subject matter jurisdiction, and why didn't the court have subject matter jurisdiction on that basis? mention of fed. wasn't a cause of action.
3. The federal district court entered orders in the case. What did the court of appeals do to those orders and why? Vacate bc no s.m.j.
4. What did the court of appeals order the district court to do? Dismiss the case? Or something else? remand to state court.

Avitts v. Amoco Production Co.
53 F.3d 690 (5th Cir. 1995)

A Word on Per Curiam Opinions

Notice that *Avitts* is a per curiam opinion, which is Latin for "by the court." A **per curiam opinion** is one handed down by an appellate court without identifying the judge who wrote the opinion. BLACK'S LAW DICTIONARY 1201 (Bryan A. Garner ed., 9th ed. 2009). The use of per curiam opinions, particularly by the United States Supreme Court, has garnered criticism. Professor Robbins of American University Washington College of Law is one such critic. He said:

> Today, the per curiam is a misused practice that is at odds with the individualized nature of the American common law system, frustrating efforts to hold individual judges accountable and inhibiting the development of the law. . . . [T]he use of the per curiam in courts of last resort, including de facto courts of last resort such as the federal courts of appeals, should be limited to a very narrow class of opinions in which the use of formulaic, boilerplate language has already extinguished any sense of individuality. The per curiam is inappropriate, however, when the opinion begins to expound on the particular facts or law at issue.

Ira P. Robbins, *Hiding Behind the Cloak of Invisibility: The Supreme Court and Per Curiam Opinions*, 86 Tul. L. Rev. 1197, 1199 (2012) (internal citations omitted). Does *Avitts* fall into the "narrow class of cases" Professor Robbins believes are appropriate for per curiam opinions?

PER CURIAM:

This matter comes before the Court on a consolidated appeal from interim orders entered by the district court. . . . Appellants appeal from the entry of a preliminary injunction requiring them to complete a "phase II" environmental study. . . . Appellants appeal from an order requiring them to pay approximately $650,000 in interim costs and attorney's fees. We find that the district court lacks subject matter jurisdiction over this action, and therefore vacate the orders of the district court and remand with instructions to remand this action to the state court from which it was removed.

I. BACKGROUND

Appellees originally filed suit in Texas state district court to recover monetary damages for alleged injuries to their property caused by the defendants' oil and gas operations in the West Hastings Field. The matter was removed to the Southern District of Texas on the basis that Appellees' complaint stated,

> It is expected that the evidence will reflect that the damages caused by the Defendants are in violation of not only State law *but also Federal law.*

(emphasis supplied). Despite the nebulous referral to "federal law," the complaint stated no cause of action which could be read to confer federal question jurisdiction on the district court. In fact, in concert with their notice of removal, Appellants filed a Fed. R. Civ. P. 12(e) motion for a more definite statement, which inter alia stated,

> Plaintiffs claim Defendants violated "State law" and "Federal law" in allegedly causing these spills. However, Plaintiffs fail to specify which State or Federal laws Defendant allegedly violated. Consequently, Defendants cannot possibly formulate a response or know what defenses may apply.

Although the district court summarily denied Appellants' motion for a more definite statement, Appellees subsequently filed a first amended complaint, this time omitting all reference to federal law. Although the

Appellees' complaint has been amended several times during the pendency of this litigation, no federal question has ever been stated.

II. DISCUSSION

"Any civil action brought in a State court of which the district courts of the United States have original jurisdiction, may be removed by the defendant or the defendants, to the district court of the place where such action is pending." 28 U.S.C. §1441(a). Original jurisdiction over the subject matter is mandatory for the maintenance of an action in federal court. Subject matter jurisdiction may not be waived, and the district court "shall dismiss the action" whenever "it appears by suggestion of the parties or otherwise that the court lacks jurisdiction of the subject matter." Fed. R. Civ. P. 12(h)(3).

Original jurisdiction . . . lies where the conditions of 28 U.S.C. §§1331 or 1332 are satisfied. In the present action, the court claims original jurisdiction pursuant to §1331, also known as federal question jurisdiction. There is no dispute that original jurisdiction does not lie under §1332, diversity of citizenship, because complete diversity does not exist. Under 28 U.S.C. §1331, "[t]he district courts shall have original jurisdiction of all civil actions arising under the Constitution, laws, or treaties of the United States."

Plaintiff is generally considered the master of his complaint, and "whether a case arising . . . under a law of the United States is removable or not . . . is to be determined by the allegations of the complaint or petition and that if the case is not then removable it cannot be made removable by any statement in the petition for removal or in subsequent pleadings by the defendant." Great Northern Ry., Co. v. Alexander, 246 U.S. 276, 281, 38 S. Ct. 237, 239, 62 L. Ed. 713 (1918). . . . However, it is also plain that when both federal and state remedies are available, plaintiff's election to proceed exclusively under state law does not give rise to federal jurisdiction.

In the present case, there is no doubt that Appellees have chosen to pursue only state law causes of action. The only mention of federal law in any of Appellees' complaints was the above mentioned [sic] oblique reference to Appellants' violation of unspecified federal laws. No federal cause of action has ever been asserted, and it is plain that removal jurisdiction under 28 U.S.C. §1441 simply did not exist. The district court had no jurisdiction over the subject matter of the complaint, and the action should have been immediately remanded to state court. . . .

. . . Subject matter jurisdiction can be created only by pleading a cause of action within the district court's original jurisdiction. No such cause of action has ever been plead in this matter, and therefore subject matter jurisdiction is plainly absent.

III. CONCLUSION

The district court lacked subject matter jurisdiction over this action and was therefore without authority to enter its orders. The orders of the district court are vacated, and this matter is remanded to the district court with instructions to remand this action to the state court from which it was removed in accordance with 28 U.S.C. §1447(c).

VACATED and REMANDED.

Post-Case Follow-Up

Note that in *Avitts* the court of appeals vacated the orders of the district court because it lacked jurisdiction to enter them. Notice also that the court of appeals remanded the case to the federal district court with an order to remand the case to state court, not dismiss it. When a case is improperly removed, the federal district court remands the case to the state court in which it was originally filed rather than dismissing it, even when the remand is based on a lack of subject matter jurisdiction.

Avitts v. Amoco Production Co.: Real Life Applications

1. John, a citizen of Texas, files suit for breach of warranty against Advanced Technologies, Inc., a citizen of California and Delaware, in Texas state court. John ordered a large supply of computer equipment from Advanced Technologies and claims that none of the equipment functions properly. John seeks $100,000 in damages, which is what he paid for the equipment.

   a. Advanced Technologies files a notice of removal in the appropriate federal district court immediately after receiving John's initial pleading in the Texas state court action. John files a motion to remand claiming the court lacks subject matter jurisdiction, and that therefore the case was improperly removed. How should the court rule? *grant ~~motA~~ Advanced motion.*

   b. Assume Advanced Technologies chooses not to remove the case. Instead, Advanced Technologies claims that the Texas state court lacks subject matter jurisdiction and must dismiss the case because it falls within the federal district court's "original and removal jurisdiction." Does the Texas state court lack subject matter jurisdiction? *no, concurrent jurisdiction exists.*

2. Ruth, a citizen of North Carolina, files suit against Foodie, LLC, also a citizen of North Carolina and the owner of an oyster bar in Raleigh. Ruth files suit in North Carolina state court claiming she suffered severe food poisoning from consuming food at Foodie's oyster bar. Foodie's attorney removes the case to federal district court hoping to take advantage of what he perceives to be the federal court's more "sophisticated" jurors. Ruth files a motion to remand for lack of subject matter jurisdiction. The federal district court does not believe it has subject matter jurisdiction over the case but is also aware that the North Carolina state court has a congested docket and is unlikely to be able to handle this case expediently. The federal district court judge is considering overseeing discovery in the case, including issuing related orders, before remanding the case. You are the law clerk to the federal district court judge. What advice do you give him about his plan to conduct discovery before remand, and why? *no because our orders will be vacated due to lack of s.m.j.*

See Pg 212

NC v. NC
suit: NC SC

C. EXCEPTIONS TO THE GENERAL RULE OF REMOVAL

Some cases are not removable even though the district courts have original jurisdiction. This section discusses exceptions to the general rule of removal.

1. The Forum State (a/k/a In-State) Defendant Exception

Under 28 U.S.C. §1441(b)(2), a case may not be removed from state to federal court on diversity grounds if *any* defendant is a citizen of the forum state. This exception applies only to cases removed on diversity grounds, not federal question grounds. Because this is a point that often confuses students, it is worth clarifying at the outset. A case may be *filed* in federal district court on diversity grounds where a defendant is a citizen of the forum state. However, when first filed in state court, a case may not be *removed* on diversity grounds if any defendant is a citizen of the forum state.

This exception reflects the rationale for diversity jurisdiction. The purpose of diversity jurisdiction is to prevent local prejudice in state court against out-of-state defendants. A defendant who shares citizenship with the forum state does not implicate this concern. Moreover, Congress has determined that the concern about local prejudice does not warrant removal in cases with both in-state and out-of-state defendants. So, in a case with multiple defendants, the presence of a single forum state defendant precludes removal on diversity grounds.

Suppose Jack, a citizen of Oregon, wants to bring a negligence action in California against Kate, a California citizen, for $2 million of personal injury damages he sustained in a car accident with Kate. The case would look like this.

Jack (OR) $2 million ⟶   Kate (CA)

Jack's case is a diversity case. He and Kate do not share citizenship and the amount in controversy far exceeds $75,000. Consequently, Jack could file his case in federal district court in California on diversity grounds. However, if Jack chooses instead to file in a California state court, Kate may not remove the case to federal court — even though it has original diversity jurisdiction over the case — because she is a citizen of the forum state. Even if Jack also sued two citizens of Nevada along with Kate, none of the defendants could remove the case because one of them, Kate, is a citizen of the forum state. Defendants may not remove a case on diversity grounds if any one of them is a citizen of the forum state.

The **forum state defendant rule** is only an exception to the removal of diversity cases. Suppose Brett files a federal Age Discrimination in Employment (ADEA) action against Jennifer, a citizen of New York, in New York state court. Federal district courts have original jurisdiction over ADEA cases because they "arise under" federal law; so, this case is removable under the general rule. Moreover, Jennifer can remove this case even though she is a citizen of the forum state because the forum state defendant rule only limits the removability of diversity cases.

2. Removal and Fraudulent Joinder

28 U.S.C. §1441(b)(2) sets out the forum state defendant exception to removal of diversity cases. This provision provides that a diversity case is not removable if any party "properly joined and served" as a defendant is a citizen of the forum state. Sometimes a defendant will remove a case even though another defendant is a citizen of the forum or destroys diversity. The removing defendant alleges that the forum state or diversity-destroying defendant is not "properly joined and served," but is instead **fraudulently joined** to defeat removal. The dominant rule is that a defendant is fraudulently joined only if the plaintiff cannot state a claim for relief under the governing substantive law against the defendant. Put another way, if there is any reasonable possibility (or, as some courts have said, "plausibility") that the plaintiff could prevail against the defendant, the defendant is not fraudulently joined.

Suppose a California plaintiff files an action in Texas state court seeking $1 million in personal injury damages and alleging strict product liability against the Michigan manufacturer of his vehicle and the Texas dealership that sold him the car. At first blush, it would appear that this case is not removable to federal court because of the presence of a forum state defendant, the dealership. Suppose however that a Texas statute makes clear that an "innocent retailer" is not strictly liable for defective products it sells to consumers. Because the California plaintiff has alleged only strict liability against the dealership, he has failed to plead facts showing that recovery against the dealer is possible. Therefore, the defendants (or the car manufacturer alone) may remove the case based on the allegation that the dealership is fraudulently joined. If the federal court agrees, it will dismiss the dealership from the action and the case will proceed in federal court against the manufacturer.

3. Cases Made Non-Removable by Statute

28 U.S.C. §1445 makes non-removable certain cases over which the federal district courts have original jurisdiction. Under section 1445, actions in state court by railroad employees against railroads under the Federal Employers' Liability Act (FELA) are not removable. Section 1445 limits the removability of state court suits against a common carrier for delay, loss, or injury to shipments under the Interstate Commerce Act to cases where the amount in controversy exceeds $10,000. Cases brought under a state's workers' compensation laws for on-the-job injuries are not removable. Statutes may also make cases removable. Recall from Chapter 4 that 28 U.S.C. §1454 makes a claim by any party removable if it relates to "patents, plant variety protection, or copyrights."

D. PROCEDURE FOR REMOVAL

Now that you understand what cases are removable (and what cases are not), we turn to a discussion of the procedure for removal, which is governed principally by 28 U.S.C. §1446. Section 1446 answers basic questions about removal, including who may remove cases, when they must be removed, and to what federal court they are removed. Understanding this procedure is critical. A defendant's failure to comply with it may result in the remand to state court of an otherwise properly removed case and the loss of the defendant's desired federal forum.

1. Who May Remove

Only defendants may remove a case under section 1441, and the defendants can only remove a case based on the claims asserted against them. Defendants cannot remove cases based on claims they assert. For example, a defendant cannot remove a case based on his federal counterclaim. Third-party defendants may not remove a case. Third-party defendants are joined by defendants based on their responsibility to the defendant for all or part of the plaintiff's injuries. Third-party defendants often include persons the plaintiff could have but did not join as defendants. Nevertheless, they may not remove the case. Plaintiffs may not remove a case, even if a defendant asserts a counterclaim against them that is otherwise removable.

Section 1446(b)(2)(A), shown in Exhibit 5.2, sets out what is called the **unanimity of consent rule** for removal. In cases with more than one defendant, this unanimity of consent rule requires all defendants properly joined and served to consent to the removal in writing. If any such defendant objects to removal or fails to consent in writing, the case may not be removed, or, if already removed, must be remanded.

EXHIBIT 5.2   **§1446(b)(2)(A) Unanimity of Consent**

> (A) When a civil action is removed solely under section 1441(a), all defendants who have been properly joined and served must join in or consent to the removal of the action.

2. When the Case Must Be Removed: The Deadline

It makes sense to establish early on in the litigation whether the case will be adjudicated in a state or federal forum. Neither the parties nor the court would have much incentive to make progress toward a resolution of the dispute if they did not have some certainty that the current forum would remain the forum.

Consequently, section 1446(b), shown in Exhibit 5.3, requires the defendant to make the removal decision fairly quickly. Delay in removal can waive the defendant's right to remove. The defendant has 30 days after formal notice of the state court action to remove the case. Formal notice to the defendant can occur weeks or even months after the plaintiff files suit in state court. The 30-day deadline runs from the date of formal notice, not from the date the suit was filed. Suppose the plaintiff filed his state court complaint on July 1 but did not serve the defendant with process until July 20. The defendant's 30-day deadline to remove will run from July 20, not July 1.

EXHIBIT 5.3 §1446(b) The Deadline to Remove

b) Requirements; Generally.—

(1) The notice of removal of a civil action or proceeding shall be filed within 30 days after the receipt by the defendant, through service or otherwise, of a copy of the initial pleading setting forth the claim for relief upon which such action or proceeding is based, or within 30 days after the service of summons upon the defendant if such initial pleading has then been filed in court and is not required to be served on the defendant, whichever period is shorter.

(2)

(A) When a civil action is removed solely under section 1441(a), all defendants who have been properly joined and served must join in or consent to the removal of the action.

(B) Each defendant shall have 30 days after receipt by or service on that defendant of the initial pleading or summons described in paragraph (1) to file the notice of removal.

(C) If defendants are served at different times, and a later-served defendant files a notice of removal, any earlier-served defendant may consent to the removal even though that earlier-served defendant did not previously initiate or consent to removal.

(3) Except as provided in subsection (c), if the case stated by the initial pleading is not removable, a notice of removal may be filed within thirty days after receipt by the defendant, through service or otherwise, of a copy of an amended pleading, motion, order or other paper from which it may first be ascertained that the case is one which is or has become removable.

Procedure for Formal Notice Varies by State

How a defendant receives formal notice of the state court action varies by state. Many states require simultaneous service of both the summons and the initial state court pleading. In these states, the defendant's 30-day deadline is triggered at once by the simultaneous service of the initial pleading and summons. In other states, the initial pleading is filed with the court, but only the summons is served on the defendant. In such states, the 30-day deadline is triggered by service of the summons. The summons puts the defendant on notice to acquire a copy of the initial pleading to determine removability. In some states, the defendant may be served with the summons before the complaint has been filed, in which case the 30-day deadline begins to run when the complaint is filed or provided to the defendant.

The Deadline to Remove When Defendants Are Served at Different Times

Under 28 U.S.C. §1446(b), each defendant has 30 days from the date he was served to remove the case. This means that later-served defendants may remove cases even after the 30-day deadline has expired for earlier-served defendants. Suppose

Defendant 1 is served with a state court summons and complaint on July 1. Suppose Defendant 2 is served on August 15. Defendant 2 has 30 days from August 15 to remove the case, even though Defendant 1's deadline to remove has already passed. Moreover, Defendant 1 may join in this removal despite his failure to remove within 30 days of the day he was served.

A Non-Removable Case May Become Removable

Even if the case stated by the initial state court pleading is not removable, the case might become removable later. As examples, a plaintiff could make a case removable by alleging a federal question, voluntarily dismissing a nondiverse or forum state defendant, or increasing his damage claim to exceed the $75,000 jurisdictional threshold in diversity cases.

If the case stated by the initial pleading is not removable, a defendant may file a notice of removal within 30 days of receipt of the first pleading, motion, order, or "other paper" that allows the defendant to determine that the case has become removable. The term "other paper" includes responses to discovery requests, correspondence from the plaintiff to the defendants, and deposition transcripts.

Suppose Ted, a citizen of Ohio, files a product liability action in Indiana state court against Autos, Inc., a citizen of Michigan, and Tires, Inc., a citizen of Ohio, seeking $3 million in personal injury damages. The case stated in Ted's initial pleading in the Indiana state court looks like this.

Ted (OH)⸺ $3 million product liability claim ⟶ Autos (MI)

⟶ Tires (OH)

Ted's initial pleading does not state a case that is removable. The product liability claim is not a federal question, and Ted's case is not a diversity case because the plaintiff, Ted, shares Ohio citizenship with one of the defendants, Tires. But suppose that six months after filing his state court action Ted discovers that Tires is bankrupt and cannot pay a judgment. Ted wants the jury to focus on Autos' fault; so, he serves Autos with an amended pleading that drops Tires from the case. Ted's amended pleading states a case that looks like this.

Ted (OH) $3 million product liability claim ⟶   Autos (MI)

Ted's amended pleading now states a diversity case. The amount in controversy requirement is met because Ted alleges damages in excess of the jurisdictional threshold and the plaintiff and the defendant do not share citizenship. Autos has 30 days from the day it receives Ted's amended pleading to remove the case to federal court.

A defendant must remove the case within 30 days of receipt of the first paper that indicates the case has become removable. Subsequent papers that also indicate the case has become removable on the same ground do not restart the 30-day clock.

Suppose Autos does not remove Ted's case within 30 days of receiving his amended pleading, but 45 days after receipt of the amended pleading Autos receives a letter from Ted's attorney that says, "as you know, we have dropped Tires from our lawsuit." This paper does not revive Autos' ability to remove the case. Thirty days from receipt of the first paper indicating the case was removable — the amended pleading — has already passed and the letter indicates no new grounds for removal.

One-Year Limit on Removal of Diversity Cases

Generally, a case may not be removed on diversity grounds more than one year after the state court action was commenced. Section 1446(c)(1), shown in Exhibit 5.4, sets out this rule. For example, if Ted had amended his complaint to drop Tires from the case 15 months after filing his state court action, Autos could not remove the case.

This one-year outside limit on the removal of diversity actions does not apply if the federal court finds that the plaintiff acted in bad faith to prevent removal. Suppose a plaintiff consistently maintained in state court that he only sought $70,000 in damages and then one year and one day after the commencement of the action, he amends his pleadings to allege $150,000 in damages and for the first time produces evidence to the defendant supporting such a damages award. The defendant could remove the case despite the passage of one year, and the federal court could uphold the removal if it finds the plaintiff acted in bad faith by, for example, concealing evidence of the true amount of damages.

EXHIBIT 5.4   **§1446(c)(1) One-Year Limit on Removal of Diversity Actions**

> A case may not be removed under subsection (b)(3) on the basis of jurisdiction conferred by section 1332 more than 1 year after commencement of the action, unless the district court finds that the plaintiff has acted in bad faith in order to prevent a defendant from removing the action.

---

3. To What Federal Court Is a Case Removed?

A defendant cannot remove a case to the federal district court of his choosing. The purpose of the removal statutes is to permit defendants to change court systems, not to change geographic locations. Cases may be removed only to the federal court for the district and division where the state court in which the suit was filed is located. This requirement is sometimes referred to as **removal venue**. Exhibit 5.5 depicts the Southern District of Texas. It is composed of seven divisions, each of which are composed of several counties. For example, Harris County is located in the Houston Division. So, a case pending in state court in Harris County, Texas may only be removed to the Houston Division of the Southern District. The Harris

EXHIBIT 5.5   **Removal Venue**

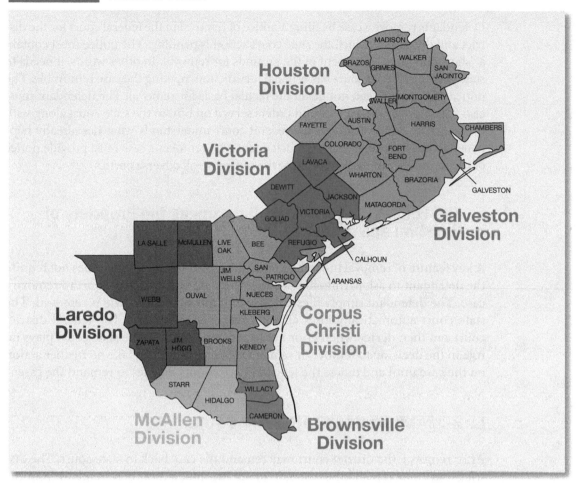

County state civil courthouse and the federal courthouse for the Houston Division
of Texas are both located in downtown Houston about a mile apart. This removal
changes the court system from state to federal court but has virtually no impact on
the forum's geographic location.

Changing the geographic location of the forum is not the purpose of the
removal statutes. Nevertheless, removal can have an impact on forum location.
Federal courthouses tend to be located in the larger cities within the division.
Plaintiffs who filed their cases in state courts in rural areas within the division can
find themselves with a significant change in geographic location after removal. For
example, Madison County, Texas is also located in the Houston Division; so, a case
pending in Madison County State District Court in Madisonville, Texas (with a
population of about 4,500 people) must be removed to the Houston Division. The
Madison County Courthouse and the federal courthouse in Houston are nearly 100
miles apart.

4. How Defendants Remove a Case

Defendants remove a case by filing a notice of removal in the federal court for the district and division in which the state court action is pending. The notice must contain a "short and plain" statement of the grounds for removal. In other words, it needs to state why the district court has original jurisdiction, making the case removable. The notice of removal need not detail the factual basis for removal. The defendant must also file all processes, papers, and orders served on him in the state court along with his notice of removal so that the federal court understands what has already happened in the state court action. A defendant who removes a case must provide notice of the removal "promptly after filing the notice" to all adverse parties.

5. The Federal District Court Determines the Propriety of Removal and Remand

A key feature of removal procedure under 28 U.S.C. §1446 is that it does not require the defendant to ask permission of either the state or the federal court to remove a case. The defendant simply files a notice of removal and the case is removed. The state court automatically loses all authority over the action. The federal district court can then decide whether or not to remand the case. The state court plays no role in the decision to remove or remand the case, and it can take no further action on the case until and unless the federal district court decides to remand the case.

E. REMAND OF CASES TO STATE COURT

After removal, the district court may remand the case back to state court. The district court may remand the case *sua sponte* (without a motion to remand from the plaintiff), but ordinarily the district court will do this only when it lacks subject matter jurisdiction. Typically, the plaintiff will file a motion to remand in the federal district court. If the federal district court grants the motion to remand, it may remand the case only to the state court from which it was removed. The plaintiff's motion to remand must provide the grounds for remand, and an untimely motion to remand may result in waiver of the grounds for remand.

1. Grounds

Grounds for remand fall into one of two categories: (1) a defect in removal procedure or (2) a lack of subject matter jurisdiction. Procedural defects occur when the defendant fails to comply with proper procedures for removing a case. Untimely removal, removal to the wrong district or division, and a lack of defendants' unanimous consent to remove are all procedural defects. The presence of a forum state defendant is also a procedural defect in removal. A plaintiff can also move to remand on the grounds that the district court lacks subject matter jurisdiction over the case. For example, a tort action between a Texas plaintiff and a Texas defendant removed to federal court should be remanded for lack of subject matter jurisdiction. Such a case is neither a federal question nor a diversity case.

2. Waiver of Procedural Defects

Recognizing whether a ground for removal is procedural or jurisdictional is important because procedural defects are waived if not raised in a timely manner. Under 28 U.S.C. §1447(c), shown in Exhibit 5.6, a motion to remand generally must be made within 30 days after the filing of the notice of removal. Failure to file a motion to remand within this time period waives all procedural defects in removal. In contrast, a motion to remand for lack of subject matter jurisdiction may be made at any time before final judgment (consistent with the rule that lack of subject matter jurisdiction is never waived).

Suppose Brian, a citizen of California, files a $500,000 negligence action in Texas state court against Powell, a citizen of Oklahoma, and Gail, a citizen of Texas. Powell timely removes the case. The district court has original jurisdiction over this case on diversity grounds. The plaintiff does not share citizenship with any defendant and the amount in controversy exceeds the $75,000 threshold. However, the case falls within the forum state defendant exception. Gail is a forum state defendant because she is a citizen of the forum state of Texas. If Brian's motion to remand is filed within 30 days of the filing of the notice of removal, the case should be remanded. However, if Brian files his motion to remand more than 30 days after the notice of removal, his remand motion will be denied. The presence of a forum state defendant is a procedural defect and, thus, is waived if the motion to remand is not timely.

EXHIBIT 5.6   §1447(c) Waiving Procedural Defects in Removal

> A motion to remand the case on the basis of any defect other than lack of subject matter jurisdiction must be made within 30 days after the filing of the notice of removal under section 1446(a). If at any time before final judgment it appears that the district court lacks subject matter jurisdiction, the case shall be remanded.

Chapter Summary

- Generally, a defendant or defendants may remove a case the plaintiff files in state court to federal court if the federal district court has original jurisdiction over the case. Because the federal court has original jurisdiction over federal question and diversity cases, as a general rule, they may be removed to federal court.
- A defendant may not remove a case to federal court on diversity grounds if *any* defendant is a citizen of the forum state. The citizenship of the defendants is irrelevant to removal on federal question grounds.
- Certain cases over which federal district courts have original jurisdiction are made non-removable by statute, including FELA claims by railroad workers

against railroads and workers' compensation cases. Suits against common carriers for damage to or loss of a shipment under the Interstate Commerce Act are not removable unless the amount in controversy exceeds $10,000.

■ Only defendants may remove a case. Plaintiffs and third-party defendants may not. A defendant may not remove a case based on a claim he asserts, such as a counterclaim, if the claim is otherwise within the original jurisdiction of the federal court.

■ Defendants remove a case by filing a notice of removal with the federal district court for the district and division where the state court action is pending. The unanimity rule requires all defendants to join in or consent to the notice of removal.

■ Each defendant has 30 days from formal notice of the state court action to remove the case. A later-served defendant may remove the case even after an earlier-served defendant's time to remove has run. An earlier-served defendant may consent to timely removal by a later-served defendant, even after his deadline to remove.

■ If the case stated by the initial pleading is not removable, the case can become removable later. Alleging additional damages to meet the amount in controversy requirement, adding a federal question to the suit, or dropping a diversity-destroying or forum state defendant are some of the most common ways to make a previously non-removable case removable. Defendants have 30 days from receipt of the first pleading, motion, order, or other paper that shows the case has become removable to remove the case.

■ A case may not be removed on diversity grounds more than one year from the commencement of the action unless the court finds the plaintiff acted in bad faith to prevent removal.

■ The plaintiff may seek remand by filing a motion to remand with the federal district court following removal. The federal district court may remand only to the state court from which the action was removed.

■ Procedural defects in removal and lack of subject matter jurisdiction are both proper grounds for remand. Procedural defects include removal to the wrong district or division, untimely removal, lack of unanimity amongst the defendants, and the presence of a forum state defendant.

■ The plaintiff's failure to file a motion to remand within 30 days of the filing of the notice of removal waives all procedural defects in removal. A motion to remand for lack of subject matter jurisdiction may be made at any time before final judgment.

Applying the Concepts

1. Are the following cases properly removed to federal district court?

   a. Blake files suit against Acorn Industries, his former employer, in state court for age discrimination in violation of the federal Age Discrimination in Employment Act.

b. Claire and Alison are in a car wreck. Claire, a citizen of New Mexico, files a state law negligence action in Arizona state court against Alison, a citizen of Arizona. Claire seeks $250,000 in personal injury damages she sustained in the car wreck.

c. Justin files a section 1983 federal civil rights action in New York state court against Officer Tom. Tom is a citizen of New York.

2. Saddles, Inc., a citizen of Texas, files suit in Texas state court in Victoria County, Texas against Dressage, LLC, a citizen of Massachusetts, seeking $100,000 for nonpayment under a contract for the supply of tack and saddles. Dressage is formally served with Saddles' initial pleading on November 3, 2017. Dressage wants to remove the case to federal court. Using Exhibit 5.7, answer the following questions.

a. Can Dressage remove the case on December 1, 2017? Why or why not?

b. What must Dressage file to remove the case, and in what federal district court and in which division must Dressage file it?

EXHIBIT 5.7   The Southern District of Texas

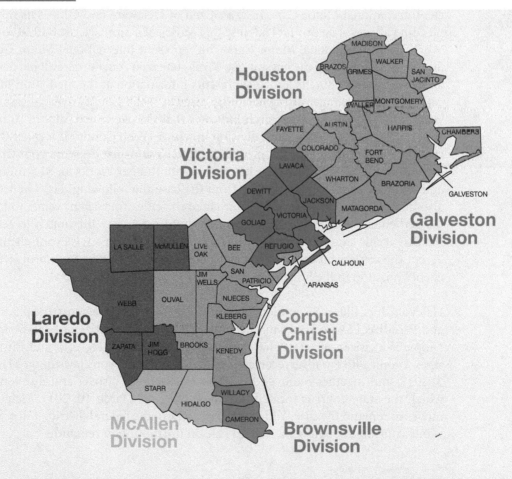

3. Should the federal district court order remand in the examples below?

   a. Californian v. Texan in Texas state court. The Texas defendant removed the California plaintiff's $1 million breach of contract action on December 15, 2017. The plaintiff moves to remand on January 25, 2018.

   b. Same case as in part a., except the plaintiff's remand motion is filed on December 20, 2017.

   c. Same case as in part a., except assume the California plaintiff sued both the Texas defendant and a California defendant in his Texas state court action. The plaintiff moves to remand in the middle of trial on September 10, 2018.

Civil Procedure in Practice

1. Butch was severely injured in a single vehicle accident. The accident occurred when the tread on his tire separated from the tire, causing the vehicle to swerve, and, in turn, to roll over. Butch is a citizen of New Mexico. He files suit in Texas state court in Webb County against the manufacturer of the tire, Rubber Works, Inc., a citizen of Texas and Delaware, and against the manufacturer of the vehicle, International Motor Cars, Inc., a citizen of Delaware and Ohio. His initial pleading alleges state product liability tort causes of action against both Rubber Works and International Motor Cars. You represent International Motor Cars. Six months after filing the lawsuit, the Texas state trial court orders all parties to attend mediation. Butch's attorney presents information at the mediation indicating that the average verdict in similar cases in Webb County over the last ten years is $5 million. Your research indicates that the average verdict in similar cases in the federal district and division in which Webb County is located is $2 million. Three hours into the mediation, Butch's attorney presents you with a letter drafted by him that says he has settled with Rubber Works for $1.5 million and will take steps to dismiss him from the case the following day. The letter also demands $3.5 million from your client to settle. Your client wants to take the settlement offer but also tells you it would never pay this much to settle the case if this case were pending in federal court. Do you advise your client to accept the settlement offer? If not, what steps might you take to improve your client's position in the litigation?

2. Halcyon, Inc. files a $5 million breach of contract action against Utopia, Inc. and Paradise, LLC in Louisiana state court. Halcyon is a citizen of Mississippi. Utopia is a citizen of Louisiana. Paradise is a citizen of New York and Mississippi. Utopia and Paradise received formal notice of Halcyon's lawsuit on March 3, 2017, and together removed the case to the federal district and division in which the state court is located one week later, on March 10, 2017. Halcyon moves to remand the case. You are the law clerk to the federal district judge. She wants your input on how she should rule on the motion to remand.

a. If the motion to remand is filed on April 13, 2017, should you advise the judge to grant or deny the motion to remand? If you advise her to deny the motion, what's your rationale? If you advise her to grant the motion, what ground or grounds exist to remand the case?

b. If the motion to remand is filed on March 20, 2017, should you advise the judge to grant or deny the motion to remand? If you advise her to deny the motion, what's your rationale? If you advise her to grant the motion, what ground or grounds exist to remand the case?

Introduction to Personal Jurisdiction

When a plaintiff brings a dispute to court, the court must have the authority to resolve the dispute. There are many limits on a court's authority to resolve disputes, and many of the chapters of this book explain those limits. One such limit is a limit on the court's authority to require a defendant to appear and personally defend himself. We call this limit **personal jurisdiction**. The plaintiff initially chooses the forum. We call this court the **forum court** and the state in which it is located the **forum state**. But the court may not have the authority to require the defendant to appear and defend himself because it lacks personal jurisdiction over the defendant. The Constitutition is the source of this limit on a court's personal jurisdiction. The Constitution guarantees that no person will be deprived of life, liberty, or property without due process of law. Due process creates a personal right of the defendant to challenge a court's authority to deprive him of property (usually money in a civil case). What does it mean for a defendant to have a due process right to contest the court's authority to lawfully render a binding judgment against him?

Think about this situation from the defendant's perspective. The United States is a large country comprised of 50 states, the District of Columbia, and several territories. The plaintiff may choose to file suit in a federal or state court located in a state with which the defendant has no connection. Though you will learn that due process has different meanings in different contexts, due process here is essentially concerned with fundamental fairness. Requiring a defendant to defend herself in a court located in a state where she does not live, where she has never been, and to which she has little or no connection seems fundamentally unfair. The doctrine of personal jurisdiction primarily attempts to protect defendants from this risk of funda-

Key Concepts

- The difference between personal jurisdiction and subject matter jurisdiction
- The definition of personal jurisdiction
- The limits of personal jurisdiction as defined by the Due Process Clauses in the Constitution
- The evolution of personal jurisdiction

mental unfairness. In so doing, the personal jurisdiction analysis determines in what state or states a lawsuit may be filed and prosecuted to a valid judgment that is binding on the parties.

More than a century ago, courts could only render valid judgments against defendants who were present in the forum state, unless the defendant voluntarily agreed to appear in court. This idea of presence was tied to a strict territorial view of personal jurisdiction. This view prevailed at a time when interstate travel (let alone international travel) was far less common than today. In essence, a state could not exercise its judicial power over defendants who were beyond its borders. As a result, a defendant had to be within a state's borders before courts located in that state could exercise personal jurisdiction over that defendant. Defendants who could be found inside the borders of the state and served with notice of the suit could be compelled to defend themselves in that state. It did not matter why the defendant was present in the state. Defendants who made their home in the state were also considered present. And defendants who voluntarily came into the state to defend themselves were present. Otherwise, a court could not validly render a judgment against an absent or nonresident defendant. As technology changed and mobility increased, this territorial, presence-based theory led to problems. What if someone just driving through your state harms you? Or what if you do business with a corporation in another state and the corporation refuses to live up to its end of the bargain? Must you go out of state and file suit where you know the defendant is present? Or hope that you can find a way to serve the defendant in the state where you want to sue?

At first, courts expanded the meaning of the concept of presence. By 1945, the Supreme Court abandoned the notion of personal jurisdiction based solely on presence or consent. In the *International Shoe* case, which you will read below, the Court modified the standard for personal jurisdiction to consider a defendant's contacts with the forum state. Chapters 7 and 8 will explain how courts now attempt to apply a primarily contacts-based doctrine to a world of international disputes and virtual interaction. Chapter 9 will explain how courts have kept many traditional bases for exercising personal jurisdiction. For example, courts may still require defendants to appear and defend themselves in their home state. Courts may also require individual defendants who are personally served with notice within the state's borders to appear and defend themselves in the forum state. And a defendant may always consent or waive his objection to personal jurisdiction.

A. PERSONAL JURISDICTION AND SUBJECT MATTER JURISDICTION: SIMILARITIES AND DIFFERENCES

Personal jurisdiction and subject matter jurisdiction share a common feature in addition to the fact that they are both limits on a court's authority. A court considers whether it has both types of jurisdiction *when the case is filed*. The time the complaint is filed is the relevant time to determine whether the court has personal jurisdiction and subject matter jurisdiction.

The two doctrines are different in one key respect. This book is concerned almost exclusively with the rules that apply in federal court. Subject matter jurisdiction is a good example. The book concentrates on what types of claims *federal* courts can resolve. State courts must also have subject matter jurisdiction over the claims they wish to resolve, but the rules vary from state to state. Unlike federal courts, which have limited subject matter jurisdiction, each state has at least one court of general subject matter jurisdiction that can hear almost any claim. Personal jurisdiction, however, is one of the relatively rare doctrines this book discusses that applies to both state and federal courts.

Personal jurisdiction is also different in other important respects when compared with subject matter jurisdiction. Though they are both limits on a court's authority, the limits are based on different portions of the Constitution. They focus on different aspects of a lawsuit, and an objection to personal jurisdiction (unlike an objection to subject matter jurisdiction) can be waived.

1. Personal Jurisdiction Focuses Primarily on the Defendant, While Subject Matter Jurisdiction Focuses on the Nature of the Dispute

Although both doctrines include the term "jurisdiction" and impose limits on a court's authority, personal jurisdiction and subject matter jurisdiction impose different kinds of limits. Personal jurisdiction focuses primarily on the defendant and her connection to the forum state. It is the defendant's right to object to personal jurisdiction, and she may waive that right or consent to personal jurisdiction. Subject matter jurisdiction, however, focuses on the nature of the dispute. No one can waive an objection to subject matter jurisdiction or otherwise create it by agreement — not even the court.

These two limitations are also independent of one another. To be a proper court, the court must have *both* personal *and* subject matter jurisdiction. A defendant may have a strong connection to the place where the lawsuit was filed. The connection may be such that it does not violate due process for a court to require the defendant to appear and defend herself against the claim. For example, the plaintiff may have chosen to file the lawsuit in the defendant's home state. The forum court, however, may be forbidden from hearing this particular *kind* of dispute because it lacks subject matter jurisdiction. Perhaps the dispute is simply too small or based on the wrong type of law for the court to hear. If the plaintiff has chosen to file in a federal court, the lawsuit must be one of the limited suits that federal courts are allowed to hear — even if the court could otherwise validly require the defendant to appear and defend herself.

2. The Constitutional Source of Personal Jurisdiction's Limits: Due Process

Two amendments to the U.S. Constitution provide the limits imposed by the doctrine of personal jurisdiction. The Fifth Amendment, which applies to the federal government, and the Fourteenth Amendment, which applies to the states, both prohibit the government from depriving a person of life, liberty, or property without due process of law. In other words, a court — an instrument of the government — cannot deprive a person of property (often money in a civil lawsuit) without using proper procedures. One of those procedures is to make sure the person has a sufficient connection to the place where the forum court is located. For reasons more fully explained in later chapters, personal jurisdiction often imposes the same limits on a court's exercise of authority over defendants in both federal and state courts.

3. Jurisdictional Limits Versus Jurisdictional Authorization: State Long Arm Statutes

Another feature common to both subject matter and personal jurisdiction is that the Constitution imposes limits on when courts may exercise each kind of jurisdiction. The Constitution, however, does not authorize or create either type of jurisdiction explained in this book. There must also be a separate statutory authorization that allows a court to exercise both jurisdiction over the subject matter of the claim and jurisdiction over the person. With respect to personal jurisdiction, each state has a **long arm statute** that permits courts in that state to exercise personal jurisdiction over out-of-state defendants. Many long arm statutes authorize a court to exercise personal jurisdiction over such defendants to the full extent allowed by due process. Such statutes are said to reach to the limits of due process. In other words, if the exercise of personal jurisdiction does not violate due process, then it is also permitted by the long arm statute. As a result, in many or even most cases, personal jurisdiction is essentially a one-step analysis: Does the court's exercise of personal jurisdiction satisfy due process? Chapter 10 will discuss the rarer occasion when a state has chosen to pass a long arm statute that is more restrictive than due process. In that case, you must ask two questions: You must ensure that the requirements of the long arm statute are satisfied and ensure that the exercise of personal jurisdiction under the long arm statute does not reach beyond the limits imposed by due process.

B. THE HISTORY AND EVOLUTION OF PERSONAL JURISDICTION

1. Presence or Consent as Bases for Personal Jurisdiction

Pennoyer v. Neff is an early, important United State Supreme Court case that sets the stage for modern day personal jurisdiction. Although the central holding of the case is no longer binding law, and many of the rules *Pennoyer* described are no longer correct statements of the law, some of the rules explained in *Pennoyer* remain good law. For example, personally serving an individual with notice of the lawsuit while she is present in the forum state is still sufficient to establish the court's personal jurisdiction over her. Also, a court may validly exercise personal jurisdiction over a nonresident defendant who consents or otherwise waives her objection to personal jurisdiction. In *Pennoyer*, these were the only valid bases to establish personal jurisdiction over a nonresident defendant (as opposed to jurisdiction over her property). Today, these methods remain sufficient, but they are not necessary. In other words, they are ways to establish personal jurisdiction, but they are not the only ways, as *Pennoyer* said they were. Later chapters will explain these concepts in more detail.

Pennoyer, decided in 1877, is a procedurally complex case. It actually describes two different lawsuits. In 1865, J.H. Mitchell sued Marcus Neff in Oregon state court. Mitchell claimed Neff (who was not present in Oregon at the time) owed Mitchell money for legal services Mitchell provided to Neff. As Oregon law permitted at the time, Mitchell published a notice in the newspaper in an attempt to notify Neff that the lawsuit was pending. Unsurprisingly, Neff never appeared in the first lawsuit in the Oregon state court. A notice in a newspaper is unlikely to provide actual notice to the defendant, and, in any event, Neff was illiterate, a fact Mitchell may have well known since he had provided legal representation to Neff.

As a result, the court entered a default judgment — a judgment in favor of Mitchell and against the defendant Neff for failing to appear and contest the claim. Following the default judgment, Neff purchased land in Oregon. Mitchell then used the default judgment to try and collect the money Neff owed him by obtaining a court order to auction off Neff's land to satisfy the default judgment. Mitchell himself bought the land at the auction and sold it to Pennoyer.

When Neff returned to Oregon, he discovered his property had been sold. Neff filed suit in federal court in Oregon, claiming that the original suit and the auction were invalid because the Oregon state court never obtained *personal* jurisdiction over Neff. The opinion describes the second suit, in which the Supreme Court held that the Oregon state court did not validly exercise jurisdiction. The Supreme Court's reasoning can be basically summed up from this language from the opinion:

> ## Mitchell's "Notice" to Neff
>
> This is the newspaper notice Mitchell had published in a local Oregon paper called the *Pacific Christian Advocate*. The notice ran for six weeks. Do you think Neff actually read the notice and ignored it? Do you think newspaper notices like this are likely to inform people like Neff that they have been sued?

> The authority of every tribunal is necessarily restricted by the territorial limits of the State in which it is established. . . . The force and effect of judgments rendered against non-residents without personal service of process upon them, or their voluntary appearance, have been the subject of frequent consideration in the courts of the United States and of the several States. . . . To give such proceedings any validity, there must be a tribunal competent by its constitution — that is, by the law of its creation — to pass upon the subject-matter of the suit; and, if that involves merely a determination of the personal liability of the defendant, he must be brought within its jurisdiction by service of process within the State, or his voluntary appearance.

Pennoyer v. Neff, 95 U.S. 714 (1877).

Pennoyer: More History and Complexity

Pennoyer can also be confusing because the case discusses two categories of jurisdiction known as jurisdiction *in rem* and *quasi in rem*. In sum, *in rem* jurisdiction permitted a court to exercise its authority over a *thing*; perhaps the most common example would be a piece of real property in the forum state. A court in the forum state could exercise jurisdiction *over the property* (technically not *over the person*), yet require the person to appear and defend himself. The property acted as a kind of leverage. The property was a way for the court to acquire jurisdiction, and the property served as a way to require a defendant to defend. The property also served as a resource to satisfy any judgment that resulted from the dispute.

Another complexity arises from the fact that Neff bought property in Oregon *after* Mitchell sued Neff. At the time of *Pennoyer*, if Mitchell had wanted to use Neff's property to obtain jurisdiction, Mitchell would have had to attach or seize the property *before* filing suit. Obviously, that was not possible. This helps explain *Pennoyer*'s extended discussion of *in rem* and *quasi in rem* jurisdiction when Mitchell had, in truth, attempted to acquire jurisdiction over Neff's person.

This passage contains three important points, the last of which is implied. Under *Pennoyer*, a court could only exercise personal jurisdiction over a defendant if (1) the defendant is served with process within the state, (2) the defendant voluntarily appears, or (3) the defendant is a resident of the state. This last point is implied by the court's statement that judgments rendered against "non-residents" without either in-state service or voluntary appearance means the proceedings lack "validity."

The Court has also since confirmed that individuals who are domiciled in a state are subject to personal jurisdiction in the state in which they are domiciled. *Milliken v. Meyer*, 311 U.S. 457 (1940) ("domicile in the state is alone sufficient" for a court to exercise personal jurisdiction over even an absent defendant).

Thus, under the doctrine of personal jurisdiction that existed in the late nineteenth century, in each case the defendant had to consent to personal jurisdiction or be somehow "present" within the "territorial limits of the State."

2. Expanding the Concepts of Presence and Consent

As technology and mobility evolved, the concept of presence posed new challenges. Particularly as interstate road travel increased, the problem of car accidents in which nonresidents injured forum state residents stretched the concepts of presence and consent. In *Hess v. Pawloski*, Hess (from Pennsylvania) collided with Pawloski (from Massachusetts) in Massachusetts. 274 U.S. 352 (1927). Hess returned to Pennsylvania and Pawloski sued him in a Massachusetts state court. Massachusetts state law provided that a person who operated a motor vehicle on a public road in Massachusetts automatically appointed the registrar (a Massachusetts state official) as his attorney for receiving service of process, just as if it had been served on the driver personally in the state. This statute essentially forced drivers to consent to personal jurisdiction in Massachusetts for any action involving a collision in return for the benefit of using Massachusetts' public roads. Of course, no one actually filled out any paperwork appointing an agent, granting consent, or otherwise waiving any objection to personal jurisdiction. Instead, the Massachusetts statute "deems" this to have taken place. Despite *Pennoyer*'s holding that "[a] personal judgment rendered against a nonresident, who has neither been served with process nor appeared in the suit, is without validity," the Court upheld the Massachusetts implied consent statute.

The Court in later cases explicitly admitted that the concept of consent had been stretched to meet the demands of a modern society:

> It is true that in order to ease the process by which new decisions are fitted into pre-existing modes of analysis there has been some fictive talk to the effect that the reason why a non-resident can be subjected to a state's jurisdiction is that the non-resident has "impliedly" consented to be sued there. In point of fact, however, jurisdiction in these cases does not rest on consent at all. . . . [T]o conclude . . . that the motorist, who never consented to anything and whose consent is altogether immaterial, has actually agreed to be sued . . . is surely to move in the world of Alice in Wonderland.

Olberding v. Ill. Cent. R. Co., Inc., 346 U.S. 338, 340-41 (1953).

This problem was not limited to individuals. Businesses, particularly corporations, presented problems for a doctrine based on presence or consent. Corporations are considered persons, though they are intangible. Even though they are not tangible, they can sue and be sued like individuals. They too increasingly did business in many states. But where is a corporation present? Is it only present where it has its headquarters? Is it present anywhere the corporation has any operations, like a manufacturing plant, warehouse, or satellite offices? Is it present anywhere it does any kind of business? And if the corporation can consent, how does an intangible entity like a corporation consent to personal jurisdiction? The Court wrestled with these questions in a number of cases throughout the early twentieth century.

Courts and state legislatures tried both approaches — presence and consent — to render corporations subject to personal jurisdiction in states where they allegedly should be subject to suit for some reason. One approach was consent-based; out-of-state corporations must appoint a registered agent to receive process in the state as a condition of doing business in the state. In other words, state law would require the corporation to appoint a person who consented on its behalf to personal jurisdiction. And, like in *Hess*, some states had "implied consent" statutes that did not require any actual appointment of an agent. The Court also expanded the concept of presence to find that a corporation was present in the state when "the corporation is . . . carrying on business in [the state in] such sense to manifest its presence within the state. . . ." *Int'l Harvester Co. v. Kentucky*, 234 U.S. 579, 589 (1914). But what does "carrying on business in the state" mean? Different courts decided this question differently, and personal jurisdiction was in a state of disarray. The Court then decided on a new approach — one based on a nonresident defendant's contacts with the forum state, where those contacts are sufficiently related to the lawsuit. In the next chapter we will explain what it means for a defendant to purposefully make contacts with the forum state such that courts located in that state may properly exercise personal jurisdiction over a defendant. Later chapters will explain how many of the traditional bases for personal jurisdiction (like consent, or personal service while voluntarily present in the state) remain valid alternatives to acquire personal jurisdiction over a defendant.

Chapter Summary

- Personal jurisdiction is a limit on a court's authority to require a defendant to defend himself in the forum state. The limit applies in both federal and state court and often applies the same way.

- Personal jurisdiction, like subject matter jurisdiction, is a constitutional limit. The Constitution does not authorize personal jurisdiction; a statute must do so, although many statutes reach to the full constitutional limit.

- Both types of jurisdiction must be evaluated at the time the lawsuit is filed. The time when the plaintiff files the complaint is the relevant time to determine whether the court has both subject matter jurisdiction and personal jurisdiction.

- Unlike subject matter jurisdiction, personal jurisdiction is a due process right of the defendant, who may consent to personal jurisdiction or waive any objection to personal jurisdiction by failing to properly object.

- Personal jurisdiction is a doctrine that has evolved significantly. The largest shift is that courts replaced the concept of a defendant's presence in the state with a defendant's contacts with the state. A defendant who has minimum contacts with the forum state, with a suit arising out of those contacts, is subject to personal jurisdiction in courts located in that state.

- Despite evolving significantly, some traditional bases for personal jurisdiction remain valid, as later chapters will explain. Consent, waiver, domicile, and in-state service while voluntarily present in the forum state remain permissible methods to establish personal jurisdiction.

Specific Personal Jurisdiction

Chapter 6 introduced personal jurisdiction as a limit on the court's authority to require a defendant to defend himself in the forum state. It also compared and contrasted jurisdiction over the subject matter of an action with jurisdiction over the defendant. Finally, it provided the basic history and evolution of the doctrine over time, moving from a strictly territorial view based on either consent or presence to the modern view that focuses on a defendant's contacts with the forum state.

As an initial matter, it is important to understand that modern personal jurisdiction law is subdivided into two distinct doctrines: **specific personal jurisdiction** and **general personal jurisdiction**. Specific personal jurisdiction requires a relationship between the defendant, the forum, and the litigation. In sum, the defendant's contacts with the forum state must bear a relationship to the claim: The claim must arise out of or be connected with the defendant's contacts with the state. This is why specific personal jurisdiction has its name — the exercise of jurisdiction is specific to the specific claim against the defendant. General jurisdiction, however, considers only the relationship between the defendant and the forum state; this relationship must be much stronger than simply contacts between the defendant and the forum state. Chapter 8 will address general personal jurisdiction. In this chapter, we will explain how the minimum contacts analysis is the key to understanding specific personal jurisdiction. This chapter will also address some problems courts encounter when trying to apply the minimum contacts analysis. We will consider how courts sometimes struggle to apply a contacts-based analysis to a world of international commerce, complex corporate structures, and virtual contacts via the Internet.

Key Concepts

- Specific personal jurisdiction and general personal jurisdiction
- Minimum contacts test for specific personal jurisdiction
- What qualifies as a contact for the valid exercise of specific personal jurisdiction
- When a claim arises out of a contact
- Special problems posed by "stream of commerce" cases and virtual contacts via the Internet

A. MINIMUM CONTACTS: THE STANDARD FOR SPECIFIC PERSONAL JURISDICTION

The following case, *International Shoe*, is the turning point in the doctrine of modern personal jurisdiction. The previous chapter explored the history of personal jurisdiction based exclusively on increasingly strained notions of consent or presence. This case introduces the concept, still at the core of specific personal jurisdiction today, that it is the nonresident defendant's conduct or activity directed at the forum state that justifies the exercise of personal jurisdiction over that out-of-state defendant. In other words, where a defendant has at least minimum contacts with the forum state and the claim is sufficiently related to the defendant's contacts, it will often be fair and reasonable to require the defendant to appear and defend himself in the forum state.

Case Preview

International Shoe Co. v. State of Washington

International Shoe is a good example of how courts struggled with how to apply personal jurisdiction rules based on presence or consent to business entities that might seem to be present in many places. The defendant company was incorporated in Delaware and had its corporate headquarters in Missouri, but it arguably did business in many states. Can the state of Washington require this out-of-state company to pay unemployment taxes because it employs about a dozen salesmen in Washington who take orders for shoes, which are eventually shipped to Washington? To decide whether a court can exercise personal jurisdiction over a defendant, courts historically focused on whether a defendant was present in the forum state. *International Shoe* provides a new standard based on contacts. As you read *International Shoe*, consider these questions:

1. What contacts with the state of Washington led the Court to hold that International Shoe Company was subject to personal jurisdiction in Washington's courts?
2. Why is a contacts-based analysis consistent with due process?
3. What if a defendant has no contacts with the state? What if the defendant has extensive contacts with the state? What is the new standard?

International Shoe Co. v. State of Washington
326 U.S. 310 (1945)

Mr. Chief Justice STONE delivered the opinion of the Court.

The questions for decision are (1) whether, within the limitations of the due process clause of the Fourteenth Amendment, appellant, a Delaware corporation, has by its activities in the State of Washington rendered itself amenable to proceedings in the courts of that state to recover unpaid contributions to the state unemployment compensation fund exacted by state statutes . . . , and (2) whether the state can exact those contributions consistently with the due process clause of the Fourteenth Amendment.

The statutes in question set up a comprehensive scheme of unemployment compensation, the costs of which are defrayed by contributions required to be made by employers to a state unemployment compensation fund. The contributions are a specified percentage of the wages payable annually by each employer for his employees' services in the state. The assessment and collection of the contributions and the fund are administered by respondents. Section 14(c) of the Act, . . . authorizes respondent Commissioner to issue an order and notice of assessment of delinquent contributions upon prescribed personal service of the notice upon the employer if found within the state, or, if not so found, by mailing the notice to the employer by registered mail at his last known address. . . .

In this case notice of assessment for the years in question was personally served upon a sales solicitor employed by appellant in the State of Washington, and a copy of the notice was mailed by registered mail to appellant at its address in St. Louis, Missouri. Appellant appeared specially before the office of unemployment and moved to set aside the order and notice of assessment on the ground that the service upon appellant's salesman was not proper service upon appellant; that appellant was not a corporation of the State of Washington and was not doing business within the state; that it had no agent within the state upon whom service could be made; and that appellant is not an employer and does not furnish employment within the meaning of the statute.

The motion was heard on evidence and a stipulation of facts by the appeal tribunal which denied the motion and ruled that respondent Commissioner was entitled to recover the unpaid contributions. That action was affirmed by the Commissioner; both the Superior Court and the Supreme Court [of Washington] affirmed. . . . Appellant in each of these courts assailed the statute as applied, as a violation of the due process clause of the Fourteenth Amendment, and as imposing a constitutionally prohibited burden on interstate commerce. The cause comes here on appeal . . . assigning as error that the challenged statutes as applied infringe the due process clause of the Fourteenth Amendment and the commerce clause.

The facts as found by the appeal tribunal and accepted by the state Superior Court and Supreme Court, are not in dispute. Appellant is a Delaware corporation, having its principal place of business in St. Louis, Missouri, and is engaged in the manufacture and sale of shoes and other footwear. It maintains places of business in several states, other than Washington, at which its manufacturing is carried on and from which its merchandise is distributed interstate through several sales units or branches located outside the State of Washington.

Appellant has no office in Washington and makes no contracts either for sale or purchase of merchandise there. It maintains no stock of merchandise in that state and makes there no deliveries of goods in intrastate commerce. During the years from 1937 to 1940, now in question, appellant employed eleven to thirteen salesmen under direct supervision and control of sales managers located in St. Louis. These salesmen resided in Washington; their principal activities were confined to that state; and they were compensated by commissions based upon the amount of their sales. The commissions for each year totaled more than $31,000. Appellant supplies its salesmen with a line of samples, each consisting of one shoe of a pair, which they display to prospective purchasers. On occasion they rent permanent sample rooms, for exhibiting samples, in business buildings, or rent rooms in hotels or business buildings temporarily for that purpose. The cost of such rentals is reimbursed by appellant.

The authority of the salesmen is limited to exhibiting their samples and soliciting orders from prospective buyers, at prices and on terms fixed by appellant. The salesmen transmit the orders to appellant's office in St. Louis for acceptance or rejection, and when accepted the merchandise for filling the orders is shipped f.o.b. from points outside Washington to the purchasers within the state. All the merchandise shipped into Washington is invoiced at the place of shipment from which collections are made. No salesman has authority to enter into contracts or to make collections.

The Supreme Court of Washington was of opinion that the regular and systematic solicitation of orders in the state by appellant's salesmen, resulting in a continuous flow of appellant's product into the state, was sufficient to constitute doing business in the state so as to make appellant amenable to suit in its courts. But it was also of opinion that there were sufficient additional activities shown to bring the case within the rule frequently stated, that solicitation within a state by the agents of a foreign corporation plus some additional activities there are sufficient to render the corporation amenable to suit brought in the courts of the state to enforce an obligation arising out of its activities there. . . . The court found such additional activities in the salesmen's display of samples sometimes in permanent display rooms, and the salesmen's residence within the state, continued over a period of years, all resulting in a substantial volume of merchandise regularly shipped by appellant to purchasers within the state. . . .

Appellant . . . insists that its activities within the state were not sufficient to manifest its 'presence' there and that in its absence the state courts were without jurisdiction, that consequently it was a denial of due process for the state to subject appellant to suit. It refers to those cases in which it was said that the mere solicitation of orders for the purchase of goods within a state, to be accepted without the state and filled by shipment of the purchased goods interstate, does not render the corporation seller amenable to suit within the state. . . . And appellant further argues that since it was not present within the state, it is a denial of due process to subject it to taxation or other money exaction. It thus denies the power of the state to lay the tax or to subject appellant to a suit for its collection.

Historically the jurisdiction of courts to render judgment in personam is grounded on their de facto power over the defendant's person. Hence his presence within the territorial jurisdiction of court was prerequisite to its rendition of a judgment personally binding him. Pennoyer v. Neff, 95 U.S. 714, 733 (1878). But now that the capias ad respondendum has given way to personal service of summons or other form of notice, due process requires only that in order to subject a defendant to a judgment in personam, if he be not present within the territory of the forum, he have certain minimum contacts with it such that the maintenance of the suit does not offend 'traditional notions of fair play and substantial justice.' . . .

Since the corporate personality is a fiction, although a fiction intended to be acted upon as though it were a fact, . . . it is clear that unlike an individual its 'presence' without, as well as within, the state of its origin can be manifested only by activities carried on in its behalf by those who are authorized to act for it. To say that the corporation is so far 'present' there as to satisfy due process requirements, for purposes of taxation or the maintenance of suits against it in the courts of the state, is to beg the question to be decided. For the terms 'present' or 'presence' are used merely to symbolize those activities of the corporation's agent within the state which courts will deem to be sufficient to satisfy the demands of due process. . . . Those demands may be met by such contacts of the corporation with the state of the forum as make it reasonable, in the context of our federal system of government, to require the corporation to defend the particular suit which is brought there. An 'estimate of the inconveniences' which would result to the corporation from a trial away from its 'home' or principal place of business is relevant in this connection. . . .

'Presence' in the state in this sense has never been doubted when the activities of the corporation there have not only been continuous and systematic, but also give rise to the liabilities sued on, even though no consent to be sued or authorization to an agent to accept service of process has been given. . . . Conversely it has been generally recognized that the casual presence of the corporate agent or even his conduct of single or isolated items of activities in a state in the corporation's behalf are not enough to subject it to suit on causes of action unconnected with the activities there. . . . To require the corporation in such circumstances to defend the suit away from its home or other jurisdiction where it carries on more substantial activities has been thought to lay too great and unreasonable a burden on the corporation to comport with due process.

While it has been held in cases on which appellant relies that continuous activity of some sorts within a state is not enough to support the demand that the corporation be amenable to suits unrelated to that activity, there have been instances in which the continuous corporate operations within a state were thought so substantial and of such a nature as to justify suit against it on causes of action arising from dealings entirely distinct from those activities. . . .

Finally, although the commission of some single or occasional acts of the corporate agent in a state sufficient to impose an obligation or liability on the corporation has not been thought to confer upon the state authority to enforce it, . . . other such acts, because of their nature and quality and the circumstances of their commission, may be deemed sufficient to render the corporation liable to suit. . . . True, some of the decisions holding the corporation amenable to suit have been supported by resort to the legal fiction that it has given its consent to service and suit, consent being implied from its presence in the state through the acts of its authorized agents. . . . But more realistically it may be said that those authorized acts were of such a nature as to justify the fiction. . . .

It is evident that the criteria by which we mark the boundary line between those activities which justify the subjection of a corporation to suit, and those which do not, cannot be simply mechanical or quantitative. The test is not merely, as has sometimes been suggested, whether the activity, which the corporation has seen fit to procure through its agents in another state, is a little more or a little less. . . . Whether due process is satisfied must depend rather upon the quality and nature of the activity in relation to the fair and orderly administration of the laws which it was the purpose of the due process clause to insure. That clause does not contemplate that a state may make binding a judgment in personam against an individual or corporate defendant with which the state has no contacts, ties, or relations.

But to the extent that a corporation exercises the privilege of conducting activities within a state, it enjoys the benefits and protection of the laws of that state. The exercise of that privilege may give rise to obligations; and, so far as those obligations arise out of or are connected with the activities within the state, a procedure which requires the corporation to respond to a suit brought to enforce them can, in most instances, hardly be said to be undue.

Applying these standards, the activities carried on in behalf of appellant in the State of Washington were neither irregular nor casual. They were systematic and continuous throughout the years in question. They resulted in a large volume of interstate business, in the course of which appellant received the benefits and protection of the laws of the state, including the right to resort to the courts for the enforcement of its rights. The obligation which is here sued upon arose out of those very activities. It is evident that these operations establish sufficient contacts or ties with the state of the forum to make it reasonable and just according to our traditional conception of fair play and substantial justice to permit the state to enforce the obligations which appellant has incurred there. Hence we cannot say that the maintenance of the present suit in the State of Washington involves an unreasonable or undue procedure. . . .

Appellant having rendered itself amenable to suit upon obligations arising out of the activities of its salesmen in Washington, the state may maintain the present suit in personam to collect the tax laid upon the exercise of the privilege of employing appellant's salesmen within the state. For Washington has made one of those activities, which taken together establish appellant's 'presence' there for purposes of suit, the taxable event by which the state brings appellant within the reach of its taxing power. The state thus has constitutional power to lay the tax and to subject appellant to a suit to recover it. The activities which establish its 'presence' subject it alike to taxation by the state and to suit to recover the tax.

Affirmed.

Post-Case Follow-Up

International Shoe sets out what is still commonly referred to as the "minimum contacts" standard for exercising personal jurisdiction: A nonresident defendant must have certain minimum contacts with the state such that maintenance of the suit does not offend traditional notions of fair play and substantial justice. International Shoe Company had several contacts with the state of Washington. It employed between 11 and 13 salesmen there. Its salesmen rented a variety of spaces in Washington to display International Shoe Company's shoe samples. It fulfilled orders by shipping shoes to customers in the state of Washington.

The idea that a defendant that makes contacts with a state should be subject to personal jurisdiction in courts located in that state makes sense. A defendant benefits from and is protected by a state's laws when it has contacts with that state. As a result, the defendant should be required to comply with that state's laws and the obligations those laws impose. And a defendant has at least some control over where it has contacts. It can direct its activities toward or away from certain states. Thus, it is fair to require the defendant to answer for alleged obligations, particularly if the contact or contacts with the state are the reason why the obligation exists.

If the defendant has no contacts with the state, the answer is simple: The court cannot exercise personal jurisdiction over the defendant. But once we have found at least one contact the defendant made with the forum state, the quantity and quality of those contacts are important and will be explored in the following cases and chapters.

International Shoe is also the beginning of the split of personal jurisdiction into two distinct doctrines: specific personal jurisdiction and general personal jurisdiction. Each doctrine will be explored in its own chapter. The first — specific personal jurisdiction — involves a scenario often similar to *International Shoe*. The very reason the state of Washington could sue the company in Washington is the same reason the company owed taxes to the state of Washington in the first place: It conducted sales activity in the state. It employed salesmen there who rented display space for shoe samples and took orders, which were fulfilled by shipments into Washington. Having sales employees conducting sales activity in Washington rendered International Shoe Company liable to the state for unemployment taxes and, similarly, constituted contacts with Washington that subjected the company to personal jurisdiction in Washington's courts to collect those taxes. Thus, International Shoe Company had more than "minimum contacts" with Washington and the suit clearly arose from those contacts.

The second type of jurisdiction — general personal jurisdiction — also has its roots in *International Shoe*. As explained in Chapter 8, it has diverged from a strictly contacts-based analysis. For many years, lawyers and judges relied on language from *International Shoe* suggesting that "continuous corporate operations within a state" or "systematic and continuous" contacts with a state could render the defendant subject to general personal jurisdiction. In other words, the defendant could be sued in the forum state for any claim, whether the claim bore any relation to the defendant's contacts with the state, because the defendant had some vague notion of continuous and substantial contacts with the state — a standard that is difficult to explain or apply quantitatively or qualitatively. As Chapter 8 will explain, the standard for general personal jurisdiction has evolved, requiring a very substantial connection between the defendant and the forum state. The defendant must be essentially at home. Chapter 8 will explain this further.

International Shoe Co. v. State of Washington: *Real Life Applications*

Use Exhibit 7.1 below to help answer these questions.

1. Recall *Hess v. Pawloski*, where Hess (from Pennsylvania) collided with Pawloski in Massachusetts. Assume the scenario in *Hess* occurred right after *International Shoe* was decided. Could Pawloski sue Hess in a court located in Massachusetts

consistent with due process? Does it matter whether Massachusetts has an implied consent statute? Does it matter whether Hess has been to Massachusetts only once — the occasion of the collision? Does it matter whether Hess was personally served with notice of the lawsuit in Massachusetts or Pennsylvania?

2. Now assume the only time Hess has ever had any contact with New York was when he drove through it to get to Massachusetts on the occasion when the collision occurred. What if Pawloski wants to sue Hess for the collision, but he wants to sue him in southern New York — halfway between the location of the collision (Massachusetts) and where Hess lives (Pennsylvania)? Does it matter if Hess thinks that sounds reasonable and agrees to have a court in New York hear the suit?

3. Now assume Hess drove around New York, through Canada, back into the U.S., and then collided with Pawloski in Massachusetts. What if Pawloski wants to sue Hess in New York but Hess has never had any contact with New York?

EXHIBIT 7.1

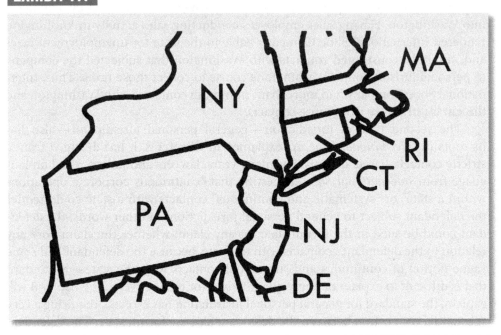

B. SPECIFIC PERSONAL JURISDICTION REQUIRES A RELATIONSHIP BETWEEN THE DEFENDANT, THE FORUM, AND THE LITIGATION

The minimum contacts test as it applies today requires a particular relationship between the defendant, the forum, and the litigation. As illustrated in Exhibit 7.2, the defendant must have at least one contact with the state in which the litigation

| EXHIBIT 7.2 | **Specific Personal Jurisdiction Relationships** |

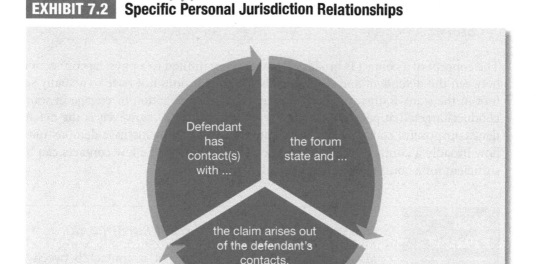

is pending, and the claim must arise out of or be connected with that contact or those contacts. And even if the defendant has contacts with the forum state and the claim is sufficiently connected to those contacts, the exercise of personal jurisdiction must still be fair and reasonable. A court will consider several factors to determine this last part of the test — whether the court's exercise of personal jurisdiction is fair and reasonable. Thus, a court must be convinced the answer is "yes" to all three questions before exercising personal jurisdiction over a defendant. First, did the defendant have contacts with the forum state? Second, did the claim against that defendant arise out of or is it connected to the defendant's contacts? Third, would it be fair and reasonable to require the defendant to defend himself in the forum state? To be able to answer these questions, you must become familiar with (1) what conduct or activities qualify as a contact, particularly a *defendant's* contact; (2) what relationship the claim must have to the contact for the claim to arise out of or be connected to the contact; and (3) what factors a court will consider to determine whether personal jurisdiction is fair in any particular case.

International Shoe — Arising Out of or Connected to?

International Shoe, Inc. "maintain[ed] places of business in several states, . . . from which its merchandise is distributed interstate through several sales units or branches located outside the State of Washington." As a result, it would appear that International Shoe had contacts with many states. Suppose that the state of Washington had tried to collect employment taxes from International Shoe by suing it in another state where International Shoe had sufficient contacts. Would that claim arise out of or be connected to International Shoe's activity in the forum state?

1. What Qualifies as a Defendant's Contact with the Forum State?

The concept of a contact is broad. A contact is not limited to a physical connection between the defendant and the state. The defendant does not have to actually set foot in the state. Rather, the defendant must take some action or engage in some conduct targeted at people or things in the state. The key, however, is the defendant's purposeful contacts with the forum state. The following case demonstrates how broadly a contact is defined and how even one or just a few contacts can be sufficient for a court to exercise personal jurisdiction.

Case Preview

McGee v. International Life Insurance Co.

McGee demonstrates the concept of a contact between a defendant and the forum state. It also demonstrates how few contacts are required for a court to validly exercise personal jurisdiction. As you read *McGee*, consider these questions:

1. Who is the defendant in the trial court? Was the defendant always based there?
2. What did the Court consider to be the defendant's contacts with the forum state? What was the most important contact, in terms of finding personal jurisdiction here? What role did the contract between the plaintiff and defendant play?
3. Did the Court focus only on the actions of the defendant? Is the case consistent with *International Shoe*?

McGee v. International Life Insurance Co.
355 U.S. 220 (1957)

Opinion of the Court by Mr. Justice BLACK, announced by Mr. Justice DOUGLAS.

Petitioner, Lulu B. McGee, recovered a judgment in a California state court against respondent, International Life Insurance Company, on a contract of insurance. Respondent was not served with process in California but by registered mail at its principal place of business in Texas. The California court based its jurisdiction on a state statute, which subjects foreign corporations to suit in California on insurance contracts with residents of that State even though such corporations cannot be served with process within its borders.

Unable to collect the judgment in California petitioner went to Texas where she filed suit on the judgment in a Texas court. But the Texas courts refused to enforce her judgment holding it was void under the Fourteenth Amendment because service of process outside California could not give the courts of that State jurisdiction over respondent. . . . Since the case raised important questions, not only to California but to other States which have similar laws, we granted certiorari. . . . It is not controverted that if the California court properly exercised jurisdiction over respondent the Texas courts erred in refusing to give its judgment full faith and credit. . . .

The material facts are relatively simple. In 1944, Lowell Franklin, a resident of California, purchased a life insurance policy from the Empire Mutual Insurance Company, an Arizona corporation. In 1948 the respondent agreed with Empire Mutual to assume its insurance obligations. Respondent then mailed a reinsurance certificate to Franklin in California offering to insure him in accordance with the terms of the policy he held with Empire Mutual. He accepted this offer and from that time until his death in 1950 paid premiums by mail from his California home to respondent's Texas office. Petitioner Franklin's mother, was the beneficiary under the policy. She sent proofs of his death to the respondent but it refused to pay claiming that he had committed suicide. It appears that neither Empire Mutual nor respondent has ever had any office or agent in California. And so far as the record before us shows, respondent has never solicited or done any insurance business in California apart from the policy involved here.

Since Pennoyer v. Neff, 95 U.S. 714, 24 L. Ed. 565, this Court has held that the Due Process Clause of the Fourteenth Amendment places some limit on the power of state courts to enter binding judgments against persons not served with process within their boundaries. But just where this line of limitation falls has been the subject of prolific controversy, particularly with respect to foreign corporations. In a continuing process of evolution this Court accepted and then abandoned 'consent,' 'doing business,' and 'presence' as the standard for measuring the extent of state judicial power over such corporations. . . . More recently in International Shoe Co. v. State of Washington, 326 U.S. 310, 66 S. Ct. 154, 90 L. Ed. 95, the Court decided that "due process requires only that in order to subject a defendant to a judgment in personam, if he be not present within the territory of the forum, he have certain minimum contacts with it such that the maintenance of the suit does not offend 'traditional notions of fair play and substantial justice.'" Id., 326 U.S. at page 316, 66 S. Ct. at page 158.

Looking back over this long history of litigation a trend is clearly discernible toward expanding the permissible scope of state jurisdiction over foreign corporations and other nonresidents. In part this is attributable to the fundamental transformation of our national economy over the years. Today many commercial transactions touch two or more States and may involve parties separated by the full continent. With this increasing nationalization of commerce has come a great increase in the amount of business conducted by mail across state lines. At the same time modern transportation and communication have made it much less burdensome for a party sued to defend himself in a State where he engages in economic activity.

Turning to this case we think it apparent that the Due Process Clause did not preclude the California court from entering a judgment binding on respondent. It is sufficient for purposes of due process that the suit was based on a contract which had substantial connection with that State. . . . The contract was delivered in California, the premiums were mailed from there and the insured was a resident of that State when he died. It cannot be denied that California has a manifest interest in providing effective means of redress for its residents when their insurers refuse to pay claims. These residents would be at a severe disadvantage if they were forced to follow the insurance company to a distant State in order to hold it legally accountable. When claims were small or moderate, individual claimants frequently could not afford the cost of bringing an action in a foreign forum — thus in effect making the company judgment proof. Often the crucial witnesses — as here on the company's defense of suicide — will be found in the insured's locality. Of course there may be inconvenience to the insurer if it is held amenable to suit in California where it had this contract but certainly nothing which amounts to a denial of due process. . . . There is no contention that respondent did not have adequate notice of the suit or sufficient time to prepare its defenses and appear. . . .

The judgment is reversed and the cause is remanded to the Court of Civil Appeals of the State of Texas, First Supreme Judicial District, for further proceedings not inconsistent with this opinion.

It is so ordered.

Post-Case Follow-Up

Note that the plaintiff, who lived in California, is suing for breach of an insurance policy that was purchased from Empire Mutual Insurance Company, an Arizona corporation. However, the defendant is International Life Insurance Company, a Texas corporation that assumed the obligations of Empire.

The Court focused on the fact that, after International Life assumed Empire's obligations, International Life "mailed a reinsurance certificate" to the policyholder in California. The Court also noted that the California policyholder mailed payments from California to the insurance company in Texas. However, the Court specifically mentioned that International Life "has never solicited or done any insurance business in California apart from the policy involved here." As a result, the Court could find only a single contact initiated by the Texas-based insurance company that targeted the California resident plaintiff. That contact resulted in a contract; indeed, it was the only contact the Court could find between the Texas-based insurance company and *anyone* in California.

The contract was relevant, but is not necessarily the defendant's *contact*. The important action or conduct here is something different. The relevant fact is that the defendant insurance company mailed the offer of reinsurance to the insured in California. The offer was accepted in California — creating an insurance contract — but the mere existence of a contract is not sufficient. As *Burger King v. Rudzewicz* describes below, the defendant's conduct leading up to a contract and the defendant's specific obligations under that contract may be purposeful availment, creating personal jurisdiction over the defendant. Here, however, the relevant contact is the defendant's action of mailing a document to someone in California. It is important to understand that contacts are broadly defined and do not require physical contact between the defendant and the forum state (using the mail, making phone calls, and sending other communications can all be contacts). It is also important to note how few contacts (arguably, just one) the defendant had with the forum state of California.

The Court also mentioned that the policyholder mailed payments from California to Texas. Under *International Shoe*, are these the *defendant's* contacts with the forum state? Did the defendant initiate the contacts? Can you characterize similar conduct such that it is the defendant's contact? What if the Texas insurance company withdrew money from a bank located in California?

McGee v. International Life Insurance Co.: Real Life Applications

1. Assume the same facts as in *McGee*. However, the policyholder/insured son died in California and his mother, the beneficiary, moved to Oregon shortly afterward. The plaintiff mother sues International Life Insurance Co. in state court in Oregon. Can the court in Oregon exercise personal jurisdiction over the insurance company? Why or why not?

2. Now assume the same facts as in *McGee*, except the policyholder/insured son did not die and stopped making payments on the insurance policy. Instead of cancelling the policy, International Life Insurance Co. sues the insured/son in state court in California for breach of contract. Can the court in California exercise personal jurisdiction over the insured? Why or why not?

3. Assume that a potential policyholder in California emailed Empire in Arizona and asked for a quote on a policy of insurance. Empire emailed the potential policyholder the requested quotes. The potential policyholder later called Empire back and the two parties came to an agreement over the phone. The policyholder/insured then dies and Empire refuses to pay the beneficiary in California. Can the court in California exercise personal jurisdiction over Empire? Does the contract between the parties create personal jurisdiction over Empire? Explain your answers.

Contracts as Contacts?

Contracts are relevant, but a mere contract with a person in the forum state is not a sufficient contact with the forum state. In *Burger King Corp. v. Rudzewicz*, the Court considered when a contractual relationship and the specific terms of that contact may be the basis for exericising personal jurisdiction over a defendant franchisee. Mr. Rudzewicz was a citizen of Michigan who wanted to open a Burger King franchise in Michigan. He started negotiations with Burger King's regional office in Michigan and later negotiated with its main office in Florida. The parties eventually came to an agreement, which required all payments to be made to Burger King's headquarters in Florida, although the Michigan office would oversee most of

Mr. Rudzewicz's operations of the restaurant. When Mr. Rudzewicz fell behind on franchise payments, Burger King sued him in federal court in Florida.

The Court made it clear that the contract alone was not the basis for holding that the court in Florida could exercise personal jurisdiction over the nonresident defendant, Mr. Rudzewicz:

> If the question is whether an individual's contract with an out-of-state party alone can automatically establish sufficient minimum contacts in the other party's home forum, we believe the answer clearly is that it cannot. . . . Instead, we have emphasized the need for a "highly realistic" approach that recognizes that a "contract" is "ordinarily but an intermediate step serving to tie up prior business negotiations with future consequences which themselves are the real object of the business transaction." It is these factors — prior negotiations and contemplated future consequences, along with the terms of the contract and the parties' actual course of dealing — that must be evaluated in determining whether the defendant purposefully established minimum contacts within the forum. . . .
>
> The contract documents themselves emphasize that Burger King's operations are conducted and supervised from the Miami headquarters, that all relevant notices and payments must be sent there, and that the agreements were made in and enforced from Miami. Moreover, the parties' actual course of dealing repeatedly confirmed that decisionmaking authority was vested in the Miami headquarters and that the district office served largely as an intermediate link between the headquarters and the franchisees. When problems arose over building design, site-development fees, rent computation, and the defaulted payments, Rudzewicz and [his business partner] learned that the Michigan office was powerless to resolve their disputes and could only channel their communications to Miami. Throughout these disputes, the Miami headquarters and the Michigan franchisees carried on a continuous course of direct communications by mail and by telephone, and it was the Miami headquarters that made the key negotiating decisions out of which the instant litigation arose.
>
> Moreover, we believe the Court of Appeals gave insufficient weight to provisions in the various franchise documents providing that all disputes would be governed by Florida law. The franchise agreement, for example, stated:
>
>> "This Agreement shall become valid when executed and accepted by BKC at Miami, Florida; it shall be deemed made and entered into in the State of Florida and shall be governed and construed under and in accordance with the laws of the State of Florida. The choice of law designation does not require that all suits concerning this Agreement be filed in Florida."

Burger King Corp. v. Rudzewicz, 471 U.S. 462, 478-81 (1985).

In other words, Mr. Rudzewicz had a number of contacts with Burger King in Florida, including specifically mail and phone communications in which he negotiated the contract. And the contract contained specific terms, like the place where payment was required (Florida) and the law that governs the interpretation of the agreement (also Florida). This last point becomes particularly important when we discuss whether it is fair and reasonable to require a nonresident defendant to defend himself in a far away court. The contract — although not irrelevant — was not the contact that justified personal jurisdiction over Mr. Rudzewicz in Florida. Rather, it was Mr. Rudzewicz's conduct during the course of negotiating the contract and the terms of the contract that also required his future contacts with the state of Florida that were jurisdictionally significant.

Expanding and Defining the Limits of What Qualifies as a Contact

The United States Supreme Court decided two cases on the same day involving libel claims — essentially claims that someone wrote and published an untrue statement that caused harm to the plaintiff's reputation. In the first case, *Keeton v. Hustler Magazine, Inc.*, the plaintiff, Keeton, was a resident of New York. She sued the defendant, Hustler, in New Hampshire because the statute of limitations had expired in every other state where the article had been published. Keeton sought damages for harm to her reputation for *every* publication, not just the harm from publications in New Hampshire. The facts relevant to Hustler's contacts with New Hampshire were straightforward:

> Hustler Magazine, Inc., is an Ohio corporation, with its principal place of business in California. [Hustler]'s contacts with New Hampshire consist of the sale of some 10 to 15,000 copies of Hustler magazine in that State each month. [Plaintiff] claims to have been libeled in five separate issues of [Hustler]'s magazine published between September, 1975, and May, 1976.

Keeton v. Hustler Magazine, Inc., 465 U.S. 770, 772 (1984).

Does it seem reasonable for the Court to hold that a New Hampshire court could properly exercise personal jurisdiction over Hustler? First, it may seem that Hustler's contacts were insufficient. Hustler's sales of the allegedly defamatory magazine paled in comparison to its sales in other states. Arguably, Hustler only had a strong connection to two states: Ohio and California. It may also seem unfair that Keeton was suing for harm that occurred mostly outside New Hampshire, especially when she had little or no connection to New Hampshire. She was a resident of New York. It may also seem unfair that the plaintiff was trying to circumvent statutes of limitations in other states and sue for harm that occurred in those other states by suing in the one state left open to her — New Hampshire.

You must focus on the relevant test. Did the defendant have minimum contacts with the forum state? Did the claim arise out of or was it connected to the defendant's contacts with the forum state? Here, Hustler had sufficient contacts with the state of New Hampshire, and the claim arose out of the publication in New Hampshire. Hustler's contacts with *other* states are not relevant for specific personal jurisdiction. It does not matter that the defendant may have more or stronger contacts with other states. Those other contacts may simply provide additional locations a plaintiff may file suit. Hustler may be subject to both specific and general personal jurisdiction in Ohio and California by virtue of its connection to those states, but that does not tell us whether Hustler had sufficient contacts with the *forum* state: New Hampshire. The plaintiff's contacts with the forum state are not relevant to determine whether the defendant has made purposeful contacts with the forum state. It is the defendant's contacts that matter. Although it may seem like gamesmanship, the plaintiff suffered at least some harm from the publications in New Hampshire, making it likely that the claim arose from Hustler's contacts — its sales of its magazine in New Hampshire. Similarly, whether she can recover for harm to her reputation felt all over the country is a matter for New Hampshire's substantive tort law. In other words, what does New Hampshire's libel law allow for damages? The statutes of limitations are also irrelevant. It may seem unfair to the defendant that New Hampshire's statute of limitations has not expired yet, but the sort of fairness that due process and personal jurisdiction are concerned with have to do with the burden and expense of making a nonresident defendant appear and defend itself in a distant forum — not whether the plaintiff seems to have taken advantage of New Hampshire's generous statute of limitations for libel. As the Court explained:

> The district court found that "[t]he general course of conduct in circulating magazines throughout the state was purposefully directed at New Hampshire, and inevitably affected persons in the state." Such regular monthly sales of thousands of magazines cannot by any stretch of the imagination be characterized as random, isolated, or fortuitous. It is, therefore, unquestionable that New Hampshire jurisdiction over a complaint based on those contacts would ordinarily satisfy the requirement of the Due Process Clause that a State's assertion of personal jurisdiction over a nonresident defendant be predicated on "minimum contacts" between the defendant and the State.

Keeton v. Hustler Magazine, Inc., 465 U.S. 770 (1984).

If *Keeton* seems like a straighforward case, *Calder*, decided the same day, presents a tougher question. Like *Keeton*, it involved a libel claim published in a magazine, the *National Enquirer*. The magazine did not challenge personal jurisdiction, which seems wise in light of the holding in *Keeton*. But two other defendants did: the writer and the editor of the allegedly defamatory article.

The writer and editor worked on the article in Florida. The article concerned actress Shirley Jones (of *Partridge Family* fame) and suggested she had a drinking problem. Jones sued the magazine, the writer, and the editor — all of whom were Florida-based. She sued them in California, where she lived and worked. The Court announced a rule that seemed to focus nearly as much on the plaintiff's connection to California as it did with the defendants' connection to California:

> The allegedly libelous story concerned the California activities of a California resident. It impugned the professionalism of an entertainer whose television career was centered in California. The article was drawn from California sources, and the brunt of the harm, in terms both of respondent's emotional distress and the injury to her professional reputation, was suffered in California. In sum, California is the focal point both of the story and of the harm suffered. Jurisdiction over [the writer and editor] is therefore proper in California based on the "effects" of their Florida conduct in California.
> [The writer and editor] argue that they are not responsible for the circulation of the article in California. A reporter and an editor, they claim, have no direct economic stake in their employer's sales in a distant State. Nor are ordinary employees able to control their employer's marketing activity. The mere fact that they can "foresee" that the article will be circulated and have an effect in California is not sufficient for an

assertion of jurisdiction. . . .

[The writer and editor] are not charged with mere untargeted negligence. Rather, their intentional, and allegedly tortious, actions were expressly aimed at California. [The writer] wrote and [the editor] edited an article that they knew would have a potentially devastating impact upon [Jones]. And they knew that the brunt of that injury would be felt by [Jones] in the State in which she lives and works and in which the National Enquirer has its largest circulation. Under the circumstances, [the writer and editor] must "reasonably anticipate being haled into court there" to answer for the truth of the statements made in their article. . . .

[The writer and editor] are correct that their contacts with California are not to be judged according to their employer's activities there. On the other hand, their status as employees does not somehow insulate them from jurisdiction. Each defendant's contacts with the forum State must be assessed individually. In this case, [they] are primary participants in an alleged wrongdoing intentionally directed at a California resident, and jurisdiction over them is proper on that basis.

Calder v. Jones, 465 U.S. 783, 788-90 (1984).

Calder is perhaps one of the (if not the most) expansive examples of what the Court will consider to be a defendant's contacts with the forum state. Conduct occurring in Florida that was intentionally targeted at California was sufficient to justify personal jurisdiction over the defendants in California. Often referred to as the "effects test," the Court expanded what can be considered a contact with the forum state.

Many courts limit the "effects test" to cases of intentional conduct occurring outside the forum state specifically aimed at the forum state. Normally, however, even making an unwitting or careless contact with the forum state is sufficient to be the kind of contact that justifies exercising personal jurisdiction. Do not be misled by terms you see in opinions like "deliberate conduct" or "purposeful availment" that seem to suggest that the defendant must consciously intend to direct activity at the forum state. For example, if you drive briefly through Rhode Island on your drive from New York to Massachusetts, you do not have to *plan* to take that route; you might deviate from your intended route, you might be unaware of where the actual border is, or you may simply have no idea that you are in Rhode Island. In each case, your drive through Rhode Island is a contact with the state of Rhode Island. Whether you intended to or not, you purposefully availed yourself of the privileges and benefits of Rhode Island law, and your conduct — your contact — was deliberate for personal jurisdiction purposes.

Similarly, do not be misled to think that all intentional or knowing conduct that affects a person in the forum state automatically confers personal jurisdiction over the defendant where the harm is felt. In other words, merely knowing your actions outside the forum state have consequences in the forum state is not enough.

In 2014, the Court decided *Walden v. Fiore*, which reaffirmed *Calder*, yet demonstrated the limits of an "effects" test. The plaintiffs were professional gamblers from Nevada who were flying home from Puerto Rico. While on a layover in Georgia, a DEA agent seized a large amount of cash from the gamblers. The agent then prepared an allegedly false affidavit for the purposes of starting a civil asset forfeiture action. The plaintiffs sued the agent in federal court in Nevada and claimed the court in Nevada could exercise personal jurisdiction over the Georgia DEA agent because the agent knew his actions caused the plaintiffs harm in Nevada. The Court unanimously rejected personal jurisdiction under these circumstances. Even when intentional torts are involved, jurisdiction must be based on "intentional conduct by the defendant that creates the necessary contacts with the forum," and "mere injury to a forum resident" is not sufficient.

The Court did not overrule *Calder*; it distinguished the two cases. The Court contrasted the writer and editor's conduct in *Calder* with the DEA agent's conduct:

> [In *Calder*,] [t]he defendants relied on phone calls to "California sources" for the information in their article; they wrote the story about the plaintiff's activities in California; they caused reputational injury in California by writing an allegedly libelous article that was widely circulated in the State; and the "brunt" of that injury was suffered by the plaintiff in that State. "In sum, California [wa]s the focal point both of the story and of the harm suffered." Jurisdiction over the defendants was "therefore proper in California based on the 'effects' of their Florida conduct in California." . . . "[T]he reputational injury caused by the defendants' story would not have occurred but for the fact that the defendants wrote an article for publication in California that was read by a large number of California citizens." Indeed, *because publication to third persons is a necessary element of libel, the defendants' intentional tort actually occurred in California.*

Walden v. Fiore, 134 S. Ct. 1115, 1123 (2014) (emphasis added). In contrast, the DEA agent:

> approached, questioned, and searched [the plaintiff gamblers], and seized the cash at issue, in the Atlanta airport. . . . [The agent] later helped draft a "false probable cause affidavit" in Georgia and forwarded that affidavit to a United States Attorney's Office in Georgia to support a potential action for forfeiture of the seized funds. [The agent] never traveled to, conducted activities within, contacted anyone in, or sent anything or anyone to Nevada. . . . Rather than assessing [the agent's] own contacts with Nevada, the [lower court] looked to [the agent]'s knowledge of [plaintiffs'] "strong forum connections." In the court's view, *that knowledge, combined with its conclusion that respondents suffered foreseeable harm in Nevada, satisfied the "minimum contacts" inquiry.* . . . Such reasoning improperly attributes a plaintiff's forum connections to the defendant and makes those connections "decisive" in the jurisdictional analysis. It also obscures the reality that none of [the agent]'s challenged conduct had anything to do with Nevada itself.

Id. (emphasis added). Foreseeing or even knowing that your actions outside the forum state will cause harm to persons in the forum state is not enough. Unlike *Calder*, the agent did not aim his conduct at the forum state, and the plaintiffs' connections to the forum state are not the proper focus. What might the agent have done to subject himself to personal jurisdiction in Nevada? What if he had forwarded the allegedly false affidavit to the U.S. Attorney's Office in Nevada to commence asset forfeiture proceedings in Nevada? What if the agent had called the plaintiffs in Nevada to interrogate them about the source of the funds? Unfortunately for the plaintiffs, all the calls to the agent in Georgia originated from the Nevada plaintiffs. These are the plaintiffs' contacts with Georgia, not the agent's contacts with Nevada. This important distinction is explained in the next section. Whose contact is it? When is activity a contact attributable to the defendant?

2. When Is a Contact the Defendant's Contact?

Although the definition of what counts as a contact is very broad, the contact must be the *defendant's* contact with the forum state. The contact you identify must be one that the defendant initiated. The following case considers what conduct is properly attributable to the defendant as the defendant's contact.

Case Preview

World-Wide Volkswagen Corp. v. Woodson

World-Wide Volkswagen reinforces the portion of the rule that each defendant's contacts must be judged independently. It also makes clear that the contact must be that particular *defendant's* contact. As you read *World-Wide Volkswagen*, consider these questions:

1. Which defendants challenged personal jurisdiction?
2. What contacts does the Court identify? Whose contacts are they?
3. How strong of a connection did the litigation have to the forum state of Oklahoma? Was that enough to justify personal jurisdiction over all of the defendants?
4. Does the Court introduce another step in the test for whether personal jurisdiction is consistent with due process?
5. Do you see references that remind you of a territorial view of personal jurisdiction as described in the previous chapter and in *Pennoyer*?

World-Wide Volkswagen Corp. v. Woodson
444 U.S. 286 (1980)

Mr. Justice WHITE delivered the opinion of the Court.

The issue before us is whether, consistently with the Due Process Clause of the Fourteenth Amendment, an Oklahoma court may exercise in personam jurisdiction over a nonresident automobile retailer and its wholesale distributor in a products-liability action, when the defendants' only connection with Oklahoma is the fact that an automobile sold in New York to New York residents became involved in an accident in Oklahoma.

I

Respondents Harry and Kay Robinson purchased a new Audi automobile from petitioner Seaway Volkswagen, Inc. (Seaway), in Massena, N.Y., in 1976. The following year the Robinson family, who resided in New York, left that State for a new home in Arizona. As they passed through the State of Oklahoma, another car struck their Audi in the rear, causing a fire which severely burned Kay Robinson and her two children.

The Robinsons subsequently brought a products-liability action in the District Court for Creek County, Okla., claiming that their injuries resulted from defective design and placement of the Audi's gas tank and fuel system. They joined as defendants the automobile's manufacturer, Audi NSU Auto Union Aktiengesellschaft (Audi); its importer Volkswagen of America, Inc. (Volkswagen); its regional distributor, petitioner World-Wide Volkswagen Corp. (World-Wide); and its retail dealer, petitioner Seaway. Seaway and World-Wide entered special appearances, claiming that Oklahoma's exercise of jurisdiction over them would offend the limitations on the State's jurisdiction imposed by the Due Process Clause of the Fourteenth Amendment.

The facts presented to the District Court showed that World-Wide is incorporated and has its business office in New York. It distributes vehicles, parts, and accessories, under contract with Volkswagen, to retail dealers in New York, New Jersey, and Connecticut. Seaway, one of these retail dealers, is incorporated and has its place of business in New York. Insofar as the record reveals, Seaway and World-Wide are fully independent corporations whose relations with each other and with Volkswagen and Audi are contractual only. Respondents adduced no evidence that either World-Wide or Seaway does any business in Oklahoma, ships or sells any products to or in that State, has an agent to receive process there, or purchases advertisements in any media calculated to reach Oklahoma. In fact, as respondents' counsel conceded at oral argument, there was no showing that any automobile sold by World-Wide or Seaway has ever entered Oklahoma with the single exception of the vehicle involved in the present case.

Despite the apparent paucity of contacts between petitioners and Oklahoma, the District Court rejected their constitutional claim and reaffirmed that ruling in denying petitioners' motion for reconsideration. Petitioners then sought a writ of prohibition in the Supreme Court of Oklahoma to restrain the District Judge, respondent Charles S. Woodson, from exercising in personam jurisdiction over them. They renewed their contention that, because they had no "minimal contacts" with the State of Oklahoma, the actions of the District Judge were in violation of their rights under the Due Process Clause.

The Supreme Court of Oklahoma denied the writ holding that personal jurisdiction over petitioners was authorized by Oklahoma's "long-arm" statute. Although the court noted that the proper approach was to test jurisdiction against both statutory and constitutional standards, its analysis did not distinguish these questions, probably because §1701.03(a)(4) has been interpreted as conferring jurisdiction to the limits permitted by the United States Constitution. The court's rationale was contained in the following paragraph, 585 P.2d, at 354:

"In the case before us, the product being sold and distributed by the petitioners is by its very design and purpose so mobile that petitioners can foresee its possible use in Oklahoma. This is especially true of the distributor, who has the exclusive right to distribute such automobile in New York, New Jersey and Connecticut. The evidence presented below demonstrated that goods sold and distributed by the petitioners were used in the State of Oklahoma, and under the facts we believe it reasonable to infer, given the retail value of the automobile, that the petitioners derive substantial income from automobiles which from time to time are used in the State of Oklahoma. This being the case, we hold that under the facts presented, the trial court was justified in concluding that the petitioners derive substantial revenue from goods used or consumed in this State."

We granted certiorari to consider an important constitutional question with respect to state-court jurisdiction and to resolve a conflict between the Supreme Court of Oklahoma and the highest courts of at least four other States. We reverse.

II

The Due Process Clause of the Fourteenth Amendment limits the power of a state court to render a valid personal judgment against a nonresident defendant. A judgment rendered in violation of due process is void in the rendering State and is not entitled to full faith and credit elsewhere. In the present case . . . the only question is whether these particular petitioners were subject to the jurisdiction of the Oklahoma courts.

As has long been settled, and as we reaffirm today, a state court may exercise personal jurisdiction over a nonresident defendant only so long as there exist "minimum contacts" between the defendant and the forum State. The concept of minimum contacts, in turn, can be seen to perform two related, but distinguishable, functions. It protects the defendant against the burdens of litigating in a distant or inconvenient forum. And it acts to ensure that the States through their courts, do not reach out beyond the limits imposed on them by their status as coequal sovereigns in a federal system.

The protection against inconvenient litigation is typically described in terms of "reasonableness" or "fairness." We have said that the defendant's contacts with the forum State must be such that maintenance of the suit "does not offend 'traditional notions of fair play and substantial justice.'" The relationship between the defendant and the forum must be such that it is "reasonable . . . to require the corporation to defend the particular suit which is brought there." Implicit in this emphasis on reasonableness is the understanding that the burden on the defendant, while always a primary concern, will in an appropriate case be considered in light of other relevant factors, including the forum State's interest in adjudicating the dispute; the plaintiff's interest in obtaining convenient and effective relief, at least when that interest is not adequately protected by the plaintiff's power to choose the forum; the interstate judicial system's interest in obtaining the most efficient resolution of controversies; and the shared interest of the several States in furthering fundamental substantive social policies.

The limits imposed on state jurisdiction by the Due Process Clause, in its role as a guarantor against inconvenient litigation, have been substantially relaxed over the years. As we noted in McGee v. International Life Ins. Co., this trend is largely attributable to a fundamental transformation in the American economy:

> "Today many commercial transactions touch two or more States and may involve parties separated by the full continent. With this increasing nationalization of commerce has come a great increase in the amount of business conducted by mail across state lines. At the same time modern transportation and communication have made it much less burdensome for a party sued to defend himself in a State where he engages in economic activity."

The historical developments noted in McGee, of course, have only accelerated in the generation since that case was decided.

Nevertheless, we have never accepted the proposition that state lines are irrelevant for jurisdictional purposes, nor could we, and remain faithful to the principles of interstate federalism embodied in the Constitution. The economic interdependence of the States was foreseen and desired by the Framers. In the Commerce Clause, they provided that the Nation was to be a common market, a "free trade unit" in which the States are debarred from acting as separable economic entities. But the Framers also intended that the States retain many essential attributes of sovereignty, including, in particular, the sovereign power to try causes in their courts. The sovereignty of each State, in turn, implied a limitation on the sovereignty of all of its sister States — a limitation express or implicit in both the original scheme of the Constitution and the Fourteenth Amendment.

Hence, even while abandoning the shibboleth that "[t]he authority of every tribunal is necessarily restricted by the territorial limits of the State in which it is established," we emphasized that the reasonableness of asserting jurisdiction over the defendant must be assessed "in the context of our federal system of government," and stressed that the Due Process Clause ensures not only fairness, but also the "orderly administration of the laws." As we noted in Hanson v. Denckla:

> "As technological progress has increased the flow of commerce between the States, the need for jurisdiction over nonresidents has undergone a similar increase. At the same time, progress in communications and transportation has made the defense of a suit in a foreign tribunal less burdensome. In response to these changes, the requirements for personal jurisdiction over nonresidents have evolved from the rigid rule of Pennoyer v. Neff, to the flexible standard of International Shoe Co. v. Washington. But it is a mistake to assume that this trend heralds the eventual demise of all restrictions on the personal jurisdiction of state courts. Those restrictions are more than a guarantee of immunity from inconvenient or distant litigation. They are a consequence of territorial limitations on the power of the respective States."

Thus, the Due Process Clause "does not contemplate that a state may make binding a judgment in personam against an individual or corporate defendant with which the state has no contacts, ties, or relations." Even if the defendant would suffer minimal or no inconvenience from being forced to litigate before the tribunals of another State; even if the forum State has a strong interest in applying its law to the controversy; even if the forum State is the most convenient location for litigation, the Due Process Clause, acting as an instrument of interstate federalism, may sometimes act to divest the State of its power to render a valid judgment.

III

Applying these principles to the case at hand, we find in the record before us a total absence of those affiliating circumstances that are a necessary predicate to any exercise of state-court jurisdiction. Petitioners carry on no activity whatsoever in Oklahoma. They close no sales and perform no services there. They avail themselves of none of the privileges and benefits of Oklahoma law. They solicit no business there either through salespersons or through advertising reasonably calculated to reach the State. Nor does the record show that they regularly sell cars at wholesale or retail to Oklahoma customers or residents or that they indirectly, through others, serve or seek to serve the Oklahoma market. In short, respondents seek to base jurisdiction on one, isolated occurrence and whatever inferences can be drawn therefrom: the fortuitous circumstance that a single Audi automobile, sold in New York to New York residents, happened to suffer an accident while passing through Oklahoma.

It is argued, however, that because an automobile is mobile by its very design and purpose it was "foreseeable" that the Robinsons' Audi would cause injury in Oklahoma. Yet "foreseeability" alone has never been a sufficient benchmark for personal jurisdiction under the Due Process Clause. In Hanson v. Denckla, supra, it was no doubt foreseeable that the settlor of a Delaware trust would subsequently move to Florida and seek to exercise a power of appointment there; yet we held that Florida courts could not constitutionally exercise jurisdiction over a Delaware trustee that had no other contacts with the forum State. In Kulko v. California Superior Court, it was surely "foreseeable" that a divorced wife would move to California from New York, the domicile of the marriage, and that a minor daughter would live with the mother. Yet we held that California could not exercise jurisdiction in a child-support action over the former husband who had remained in New York.

If foreseeability were the criterion, a local California tire retailer could be forced to defend in Pennsylvania when a blowout occurs there; a Wisconsin seller of a defective automobile jack could be haled before a distant court for damage caused in New Jersey; or a Florida soft-drink concessionaire could be summoned to Alaska to account for injuries happening there. Every seller of chattels would in effect appoint the chattel his agent for service of process. His amenability to suit would travel with the chattel. . . .

This is not to say, of course, that foreseeability is wholly irrelevant. But the foreseeability that is critical to due process analysis is not the mere likelihood that a product will find its way into the forum State. Rather, it is that the defendant's conduct and connection with the forum State are such that he should reasonably anticipate being haled into court there. The Due Process Clause, by ensuring the "orderly administration of the laws," gives a degree of predictability to the legal system that allows potential defendants to structure their primary conduct with some minimum assurance as to where that conduct will and will not render them liable to suit.

When a corporation "purposefully avails itself of the privilege of conducting activities within the forum State," it has clear notice that it is subject to suit there, and can act to alleviate the risk of burdensome litigation by procuring insurance, passing the expected costs on to customers, or, if the risks are too great, severing its connection with the State. Hence if the sale of a product of a manufacturer or distributor such as Audi or Volkswagen is not simply an isolated occurrence, but arises from the efforts of the manufacturer or distributor to serve directly or indirectly, the market for its product in other States, it is not unreasonable to subject it to suit in one of those States if its allegedly defective merchandise has there been the source of injury to its owner or to others. The forum State does not exceed its powers under the Due Process Clause if it asserts personal jurisdiction over a corporation that delivers its products into the stream of commerce with the expectation that they will be purchased by consumers in the forum State. Cf. Gray v. American Radiator & Standard Sanitary Corp., 22 Ill. 2d 432, 176 N.E.2d 761 (1961).

But there is no such or similar basis for Oklahoma jurisdiction over World-Wide or Seaway in this case. Seaway's sales are made in Massena, N.Y. World-Wide's market, although substantially larger, is limited to dealers in New York, New Jersey, and Connecticut. There is no evidence of record that any automobiles distributed by World-Wide are sold to retail customers outside this tristate area. It is foreseeable that the purchasers of automobiles sold by World-Wide and Seaway may take them to Oklahoma. But the mere "unilateral activity of those who claim some relationship with a nonresident defendant cannot satisfy the requirement of contact with the forum State."

In a variant on the previous argument, it is contended that jurisdiction can be supported by the fact that petitioners earn substantial revenue from goods used in Oklahoma. The Oklahoma Supreme Court so found, drawing the inference that because one automobile sold by petitioners had been used in Oklahoma, others might have been used there also. While this inference seems less than compelling on the facts of the instant case, we need not question the court's factual findings in order to reject its reasoning.

This argument seems to make the point that the purchase of automobiles in New York, from which the petitioners earn substantial revenue, would not occur but for the fact that the automobiles are capable of use in distant States like Oklahoma. Respondents observe that the very purpose of an automobile is to travel, and that travel of automobiles sold by petitioners is facilitated by an extensive chain of Volkswagen service centers throughout the country, including some in Oklahoma. However, financial benefits accruing to the defendant from a collateral relation to the forum State will not support jurisdiction if they do not stem from a constitutionally cognizable contact with that State. In our view, whatever marginal revenues petitioners may receive by virtue of the fact that their products are capable of use in Oklahoma is far too attenuated a contact to justify that State's exercise of in personam jurisdiction over them.

 Because we find that petitioners have no "contacts, ties, or relations" with the State of Oklahoma, the judgment of the Supreme Court of Oklahoma is

Reversed.

Mr. Justice MARSHALL, with whom Mr. Justice BLACKMUN joins, dissenting.

. . . This is a difficult case, and reasonable minds may differ as to whether respondents have alleged a sufficient "relationship among the defendant[s], the forum, and the litigation," to satisfy the requirements of International Shoe. I am concerned, however, that the majority has reached its result by taking an unnecessarily narrow view of petitioners' forum-related conduct. The majority asserts that "respondents seek to base jurisdiction on one, isolated occurrence and whatever inferences can be drawn therefrom: the fortuitous circumstance that a single Audi automobile, sold in New York to New York residents, happened to suffer an accident while passing through Oklahoma." If that were the case, I would readily agree that the minimum contacts necessary to sustain jurisdiction are not present. But the basis for the assertion of jurisdiction is not the happenstance that an individual over whom petitioner had no control made a unilateral decision to take a chattel with him to a distant State. Rather, jurisdiction is premised on the deliberate and purposeful actions of the defendants themselves in choosing to become part of a nationwide, indeed a global, network for marketing and servicing automobiles.

Petitioners are sellers of a product whose utility derives from its mobility. The unique importance of the automobile in today's society, which is discussed in Mr. Justice BLACKMUN's dissenting opinion, post, needs no further elaboration. Petitioners know that their customers buy cars not only to make short trips, but also to travel long distances. In fact, the nationwide service network with which they are affiliated was designed to facilitate and encourage such travel. Seaway would be unlikely to sell many cars if authorized service were available only in Massena, N.Y. Moreover, local dealers normally derive a substantial portion of their revenues from their service operations and thereby obtain a further economic benefit from the opportunity to service cars which were sold in other States. It is apparent that petitioners have not attempted to minimize the chance that their activities will have effects in other States; on the contrary, they have chosen to do business in a way that increases that chance, because it is to their economic advantage to do so.

To be sure, petitioners could not know in advance that this particular automobile would be driven to Oklahoma. They must have anticipated, however, that a substantial portion of the cars they sold would travel out of New York. Seaway, a local dealer in the second most populous State, and World-Wide, one of only seven regional Audi distributors in the entire country, would scarcely have been surprised to learn that a car sold by them had been driven in Oklahoma on Interstate 44, a heavily traveled transcontinental highway. In the case of the distributor, in particular, the probability that some of the cars it sells will be driven in every one of the contiguous States must amount to a virtual certainty. This knowledge should alert a reasonable businessman to the likelihood that a defect in the product might manifest itself in the forum State — not because of some unpredictable, aberrant, unilateral action by a single buyer, but in the normal course of the operation of the vehicles for their intended purpose.

It is misleading for the majority to characterize the argument in favor of jurisdiction as one of "'foreseeability' alone." As economic entities petitioners reach out from New York, knowingly causing effects in other States and receiving economic advantage both from the ability to cause such effects themselves and from the activities of dealers and distributors in other States. While they did not receive revenue from making direct sales in Oklahoma, they intentionally became part of an interstate economic network, which included dealerships in Oklahoma, for pecuniary gain. In light of this purposeful conduct I do not believe it can be said that petitioners "had no reason to expect to be haled before a[n Oklahoma] court."

The majority apparently acknowledges that if a product is purchased in the forum State by a consumer, that State may assert jurisdiction over everyone in the chain of distribution. With this I agree. But I cannot agree that jurisdiction is necessarily lacking if the product enters the State not through the channels of distribution but in the course of its intended use by the consumer. We have recognized the role played by the automobile in the expansion of our notions of personal jurisdiction. Unlike most other chattels, which may find their way into States far from where they were purchased because their owner takes them there, the intended use of the automobile is precisely as a means of traveling from one place to another. In such a case, it is highly artificial to restrict the concept of the "stream of commerce" to the chain of distribution from the manufacturer to the ultimate consumer.

I sympathize with the majority's concern that the persons ought to be able to structure their conduct so as not to be subject to suit in distant forums. But that may not always be possible. Some activities by their very nature may foreclose the option of conducting them in such a way as to avoid subjecting oneself to jurisdiction in multiple forums. This is by no means to say that all sellers of automobiles should be subject to suit everywhere; but a distributor of automobiles to a multistate market and a local automobile dealer who makes himself part of a nationwide network of dealerships can fairly expect that the cars they sell may cause injury in distant States and that they may be called on to defend a resulting lawsuit there. . . .

Manifestly, the "quality and nature" of commercial activity is different, for purposes of the International Shoe test, from actions from which a defendant obtains no economic advantage. Commercial activity is more likely to cause effects in a larger sphere, and the actor derives an economic benefit from the activity that makes it fair to require him to answer for his conduct where its effects are felt. The profits may be used to pay the costs of suit, and knowing that the activity is likely to have effects in other States the defendant can readily insure against the costs of those effects, thereby sparing himself much of the inconvenience of defending in a distant forum.

Of course, the Constitution forbids the exercise of jurisdiction if the defendant had no judicially cognizable contacts with the forum. But as the majority acknowledges, if such contacts are present the jurisdictional inquiry requires a balancing of various interests and policies. I believe such contacts are to be found here and that, considering all of the interests and policies at stake, requiring petitioners to defend this action in Oklahoma is not beyond the bounds of the Constitution. Accordingly, I dissent.

Post-Case Follow-Up

The case involved four defendants; only two challenged personal jurisdiction. The plaintiff, the Robinson family, sued (1) the designer and manufacturer of the Audi, Audi NSU Auto Union Aktiengesellschaft (Audi); (2) its importer, Volkswagen of America, Inc. (Volkswagen); (3) its regional distributor, World-Wide Volkswagen Corp. (World-Wide); and (4) its retail dealer, Seaway. Seaway and World-Wide objected to personal jurisdiction but Audi and Volkswagen did not pursue any objection before the Supreme Court. It is important to remember who challenged personal jurisdiction and who did not — the two entities with arguably the least connection to the state of Oklahoma (Seaway — the dealer — and World-Wide Volkswagen — the northeast regional distributor) objected and prevailed before the Supreme Court.

The Court identified a few simple contacts: World-Wide provided the Audi to Seaway in New York, Seaway sold the Audi to the Robinsons in New York, and the Audi was involved in a collision in Oklahoma. The lawsuit centered on the Oklahoma collision. The key for the Court was that the only contact between defendants World-Wide Volkswagen and Seaway on the one hand and the state of Oklahoma on the other hand was the fact that the Robinsons drove the Audi through Oklahoma. In other words, the *Robinsons* had contact with the state of Oklahoma — not the defendants.

Is this a seemingly narrow view of contacts? The dissent makes an arguable case for the fact that here, "jurisdiction is premised on the deliberate and purposeful actions of the defendants themselves in choosing to become part of a nationwide, indeed a global, network for marketing and servicing automobiles." As we will see with modern problems of the minimum contacts analysis, this is likely not enough to be a *defendant's* contacts with the forum state. Although what qualifies as a contact is still probably expansive even after *World-Wide Volkswagen*, what qualifies as the *defendant's* contact is narrower. This case is a good example of what courts will consider to be the defendant's actions rather than the plaintiff's actions.

The litigation had a very strong connection with Oklahoma. The collision was there, the allegedly defective product caused harm there, many important witnesses were there, and certainly a car dealer can foresee that the car it sells could end up in any state. These are all relevant facts. They are just not relevant to whether the defendant had contacts with the forum. The Court does remind us that there is a third step to the analysis: The exercise of jurisdiction must be fair and reasonable. Although the Court did not make its decision on this basis, after *World-Wide Volkswagen*, the Court has left us with a number of factors it will consider *even if* the defendant has contacts with the state and the claim arises out of those contacts:

> Implicit in this emphasis on reasonableness is the understanding that [1] the burden on the defendant, while always a primary concern, will in an appropriate case be considered in light of other relevant factors, including [2] the forum State's interest in adjudicating the dispute; [3] the plaintiff's interest in obtaining convenient and effective relief, at least when that interest is not adequately protected by the plaintiff's power to choose the forum; [4] the interstate judicial system's interest in obtaining the most efficient resolution of controversies; and [5] the shared interest of the several States in furthering fundamental substantive social policies.

These five factors have come to be known as the "fairness" or "reasonableness" factors that apply in the third step of the test.

The Court seems torn between the dual policies behind personal jurisdiction — the protection of the defendant from burdensome litigation, and the interstate system our nation is based on. The Court seems worried about protecting both defendants and state sovereignty. Do you find one policy more persuasive than the other? Think about these two rationales for *why* we have a due process limit on personal jurisdiction as you read personal jurisdiction cases, and whether one view seems to prevail over the other at different times.

World-Wide Volkswagen Corp. v. Woodson: Real Life Applications

1. What if the Robinsons told Seaway at the time they purchased the Audi in New York that they planned immediately to drive through Oklahoma during their move to Arizona? Suppose Seaway provided the Robinsons with a map showing all the service stations that are certified to work on Audi vehicles. Would Seaway be subject to specific personal jurisdiction in Oklahoma? What about World-Wide Volkswagen? Is there any difference between the dealer and regional distributor? Does it matter what the dealer knew at the time of the sale? If so, what part of the minimum contacts test might such facts be relevant to? Explain your answer.

2. What if the Robinsons had completed their move to Arizona and then became interested in purchasing an Audi? While surfing the Internet, the Robinsons shopped for Audis all over the country and found that Seaway was offering the best price. What if the Robinsons purchased the Audi via phone calls and emails and Seaway shipped the Audi to Arizona where the same kind of collision occurred? Could a court in Arizona subject Seaway to specific personal jurisdiction? What about the regional distributor? Explain your answer.

3. What if the Robinsons purchased the Audi from Seaway in New York and just completed packing for Arizona? Just as they crossed the border into New Jersey, they were involved in the same terrible collision. Both Seaway and World-Wide Volkswagen have sold and distributed many Audis in New Jersey. Could a court located in New Jersey exercise specific personal jurisdiction over Seaway and World-Wide Volkswagen? Why or why not?

Personal jurisdiction focuses on the defendant, not the plaintiff. Not only must a contact be the *defendant's* contact with the forum state, it does not matter whether the plaintiff has any contact with the forum state:

> But we have not to date required a plaintiff to have "minimum contacts" with the forum State before permitting that State to assert personal jurisdiction over a nonresident defendant. On the contrary, we have upheld the assertion of jurisdiction where such contacts were entirely lacking. . . .

Keeton v. Hustler Magazine, Inc., 465 U.S. 770, 779 (1984).

The plaintiff's connection to the forum state, however, remains relevant for the third part of the test — whether the exercise of jurisdiction is fair and reasonable:

> The plaintiff's residence is not, of course, completely irrelevant to the jurisdictional inquiry. As noted, that inquiry focuses on the relations among the defendant,

the forum and the litigation. Plaintiff's residence may well play an important role in determining the propriety of entertaining a suit against the defendant in the forum. That is, plaintiff's residence in the forum may, because of defendant's relationship with the plaintiff, enhance defendant's contacts with the forum. Plaintiff's residence may be the focus of the activities of the defendant out of which the suit arises. See Calder v. Jones; McGee v. International Life Ins. Co., 355 U.S. 220, 78 S. Ct. 199, 2 L. Ed. 2d 223 (1957). But plaintiff's residence in the forum State is not a separate requirement, and lack of residence will not defeat jurisdiction established on the basis of defendant's contacts.

Keeton v. Hustler Magazine, Inc., 465 U.S. 770, 780 (1984).

3. When Does a Claim Arise Out of or Connect to the Defendant's Contacts with the Forum State?

Recall that specific personal jurisdiction requires a relationship between the defendant, the forum, *and the litigation*. A court must consider each defendant's contacts individually *and* must determine whether the *claim* arises out of or is connected to those contacts. The facts of *Calder* provide a concrete example of a defendant's activity that may well be a contact with the forum state, yet bears no relation to the claim at issue. The Court summed up the writer's and editor's contacts with the forum state:

> [The writer] is a reporter employed by the Enquirer. He is a resident of Florida, though he frequently travels to California on business. [He] wrote the first draft of the challenged article, and his byline appeared on it. He did most of his research in Florida, relying on phone calls to sources in California for the information contained in the article. Shortly before publication, South called [Jones'] home and read to her husband a draft of the article so as to elicit his comments upon it. Aside from his frequent trips and phone calls, [the writer] has no other relevant contacts with California.

> [The editor] is also a Florida resident. He has been to California only twice — once, on a pleasure trip, prior to the publication of the article and once after to testify in an unrelated trial. Calder is president and editor of the Enquirer. He "oversee[s] just about every function of the Enquirer." He reviewed and approved the initial evaluation of the

---

Considering the Plaintiff's Connection to the Forum State

The injuries to the Robinson family were simply horrific:

> Kay, Sam, and Eva Robinson all received severe burns. . . . Both Sam and Eva were hospitalized for *six weeks* in Tulsa, and spent *many months* undergoing physical therapy and reconstructive surgery. Since Kay Robinson had been trapped in the burning car the longest, her burns were the most horrible of all. . . . Kay was in the intensive care unit for *seventy-seven days and was hospitalized in Tulsa for another several months*.

Charles W. Adams, *World-Wide Volkswagen v. Woodson: The Rest of the Story*, 72 Neb. L. Rev. 1122 (1993) (emphasis added).

The Robinsons were hospitalized in Oklahoma and unable to travel to New York for a significant period of time. Should the Court have considered these facts in deciding whether personal jurisdiction was appropriate in Oklahoma? Should a plaintiff's circumstances factor into the court's analysis at the contacts stage? Should the test balance the defendant's connections with the forum against the plaintiff's interests?

subject of the article and edited it in its final form. He also declined to print a retraction requested by respondent. [The editor] has no other relevant contacts with California.

Calder v. Jones, 465 U.S. 783, 785-86 (1984).

First, consider the writer. He frequently travels to California on business. This is unquestionably the writer's contact with the state of California. However, there is no suggestion that he interviewed sources or otherwise worked on the article in California. These contacts — even though frequent — appear to bear no relationship to the allegedly defamatory article. On the other hand, he made "phone calls to sources in California for the information contained in the article." Not only are the phone calls the writer's deliberate contacts with California, the claim arose out of those contacts because the article contained the information gathered through those phone calls. The last contact is a closer call. The writer called Jones' husband for comment on the article before it was published. There is nothing that suggests the husband made any comments or that they were included in the article. However, the call to the husband is certainly the writer's purposeful contact with California and does seem to bear some relationship to the claim. Simply applying the cases we have studied so far, the Court could have determined that the writer's phone calls to California sources were sufficient contacts with California and that the claim (the allegedly libelous story) arose out of those contacts.

Next, consider the editor. He has set foot in California twice — both times are certainly his purposeful contacts with California. But the facts make clear that one visit was for pleasure and the other for an explicitly "unrelated trial." Neither of these contacts seems to bear any relationship to the libel claim. The facts do suggest that he edited the allegedly libelous article and oversaw operations of the magazine from Florida. Thus, all of his conduct occurred in Florida. Given the cases that had come before *Calder*, it is not difficult to imagine a split decision: The writer had minimum contacts with the state of California and the claim arose from those contacts, yet the editor had some contacts with the state of California but those contacts were so unrelated that the claim did not arise from them nor was it even connected to them. As a result, the writer would be subject to personal jurisdiction and the editor would not.

Of course, the Court did not make this holding in *Calder*. Instead, it considered that even the editor's Florida-based activities were expressly aimed at California. Viewed in this light, the claim is at least connected to his intentional conduct aimed at California. But it is important to remember that you must separately analyze each contact's relationship to each claim and each defendant.

4. When Is Personal Jurisdiction Fair and Reasonable?

The third element of the minimum contacts test may be the hardest to apply. The Court in *Asahi* (in the next section) agreed that specific personal jurisdiction would be unfair under the circumstances of that case. However, no Supreme Court case has yet determined that the defendant had minimum contacts with the forum state, and the claim arose from those contacts, yet it would be unfair to require the defendant to defend himself in the forum state. In other words, if the Court has found that the claim arises out of the defendant's contacts with the state, it has also found it fair to exercise specific personal jurisdiction.

Three cases we have already studied provide good examples of how the Court tends to consider this third element: Is specific personal jurisdiction fair and reasonable?

In *Burger King*, the defendant franchisee operated his Burger King restaurant in Detroit, Michigan. He conducted the vast majority of his negotiations with the local Michigan office of Burger King, and the local office was his primary point of contact on a day-to-day basis. The local office also oversaw most of his activities. Consider the burden on the defendant—he was a small business owner who lived and worked in Detroit, Michigan and would have to defend himself in Miami, Florida, roughly 1,400 miles away. Consider also the disparity in terms of resources of the parties. Even more than 30 years ago when the case was decided, the Court described Burger King as "one of the world's largest restaurant organizations, with over 3,000 outlets in the 50 States, the Commonwealth of Puerto Rico, and 8 foreign nations." Certainly, Burger King would find it less burdensome to come to Detroit than Mr. Rudzewicz would find it to come to Miami. Even so, the Court never made it to the third step; the defendant had sufficient contacts such that he could reasonably expect to be sued there.

On the other hand, the defendant in *Keeton v. Hustler Magazine* made a fairness argument, but did not focus on the financial burden of Hustler defending itself in the forum state. The plaintiff had no connection to the forum state. She simply chose to sue there because it was her only available forum. The statute of limitations had expired on her claim everywhere else. Hustler was being sued for damages for nationwide publication and harm in a state that had a small proportion of Hustler's sales and, as a result, a small proportion of the harm suffered by the plaintiff. Again, the Court did not find it unfair for Hustler to defend itself when it circulated copies of the offending article in the forum state; thus, it could reasonably expect to be sued in New Hampshire despite the foregoing facts that might suggest jurisdiction would be unreasonable.

World-Wide Volkswagen presents the opposite problem: Even if specific personal jurisdiction seems fair and reasonable in the forum state, that is no substitute for the defendant's lack of contacts with the forum. The dissent makes a good point. The very nature of the car—an inherently mobile instrument often involved in lawsuits—makes it foreseeable to the seller that the seller could be sued anywhere where the car causes harm. And the point that some financial benefit likely flows to the defendants from participating in the world-wide distribution network may seem valid, particularly in an international world of modern commerce. But the defendants' lack of contacts trumps any fairness inquiry. In each case, the focus is on the defendant's contacts with the forum state *such that* it is fair and reasonable to subject the defendant to suit there. Without those contacts, fairness is a moot point. With those contacts, fairness is virtually a given.

With that in mind, the case that follows is the rare case that actually applies — and holds — that the fairness factors are not satisfied; thus, personal jurisdiction is lacking. As we will see in the next section, the Court reached and decided the fairness question even though it could not agree on whether the defendant had contacts with the forum state. The next section explains the recurring problem of finding contacts when the defendant arguably merely introduced a product into the so-called stream of commerce.

C. THE STREAM OF COMMERCE: WHEN MINIMUM CONTACTS ARE HARD TO FIND

Most cases are relatively straightforward applications of the rules we have learned so far. Does the defendant have contacts with the forum state? Does the claim arise out of or is it connected to those contacts? And is the exercise of personal jurisdiction fair and reasonable? However, even a flexible contacts-based doctrine has limitations. One recurring problem is known as the "stream of commerce" problem.

Two common fact scenarios often implicate a stream of commerce issue. Many modern products contain numerous component parts from all over the world. These components may have been designed, manufactured, and sold outside the U.S., yet end up in finished products sold here. What happens when that product injures someone? This scenario is depicted in Exhibit 7.3.

Similarly, the structures of modern business entities have become increasingly complicated. How do we determine whether a parent company is subject to personal jurisdiction when it provides a product or service through one or more intermediaries, and the parent company has no obvious contacts with the forum state? This scenario is depicted in Exhibit 7.4.

The following cases grapple with these difficult questions. The first case, *Asahi*, unfortunately results in a fractured opinion with no clear guidance on how to analyze whether a defendant has contacts with the forum state in these situations. The Court's recent attempt, *Nicastro*, fares no better; it does not make the outcome in these scenarios more predictable.

EXHIBIT 7.3   Common Stream of Commerce Scenario 1

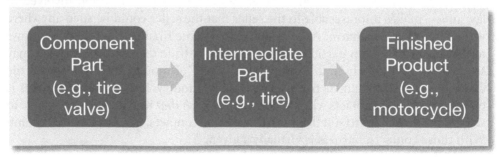

EXHIBIT 7.4   **Common Stream of Commerce Scenario 2**

Foreign Manufacturing Company

↓

Subsidiary Distributing Company

↓

Local Distributing Company

Case Preview

Asahi Metal Industry Co., Ltd. v. Superior Court of California, Solano County

Asahi addresses the problem of a nonresident defendant that supplies a component part of a larger product that injures someone in a state of the U.S. If there was a clear contact between the component part manufacturer and the forum state, the Court could just apply established rules and (hopefully) come up with a result that a majority of the Court agrees with. As you read *Asahi*, consider these questions:

1. Unless an opinion (or portion of an opinion) garners a majority of votes, that opinion is not the law. Sometimes you must "count noses" and determine who agreed with what part of an opinion and see whether that constitutes a majority. What part of the opinion garnered support of a majority of the Justices? What key fact or facts made it easy for the Court to agree on at least one part of the minimum contacts analysis?
2. Why did the Court reverse the California Supreme Court's decision?
3. After *Asahi*, how do lower courts approach problems like the one presented in *Asahi*? How would you advise a client in light of this opinion?

Asahi Metal Industry Co., Ltd. v. Superior Court of California, Solano County

480 U.S. 102 (1987)

handwritten margin notes:
I ʜᴀᴛ॥॥
IIA ॥॥
IIB ʜᴀ॥॥
III ॥॥

Opinion

Justice O'CONNOR announced the judgment of the Court and delivered the unanimous opinion of the Court with respect to Part I, the opinion of the Court with respect to Part II–B, in which THE CHIEF JUSTICE, Justice BRENNAN, Justice WHITE, Justice MARSHALL, Justice BLACKMUN, Justice POWELL, and Justice STEVENS join, and an opinion with respect to Parts II–A and III, in which THE CHIEF JUSTICE, Justice POWELL, and Justice SCALIA join.

This case presents the question whether the mere awareness on the part of a foreign defendant that the components it manufactured, sold, and delivered outside the United States would reach the forum State in the stream of commerce constitutes "minimum contacts" between the defendant and the forum State such that the exercise of jurisdiction "does not offend 'traditional notions of fair play and substantial justice.'"

I *binding*

On September 23, 1978, on Interstate Highway 80 in Solano County, California, Gary Zurcher lost control of his Honda motorcycle and collided with a tractor. Zurcher was severely injured, and his passenger and wife, Ruth Ann Moreno, was killed. In September 1979, Zurcher filed a product liability action in the Superior Court of the State of California in and for the County of Solano. Zurcher alleged that the 1978 accident was caused by a sudden loss of air and an explosion in the rear tire of the motorcycle, and alleged that the motorcycle tire, tube, and sealant were defective. Zurcher's complaint named, inter alia, Cheng Shin Rubber Industrial Co., Ltd. (Cheng Shin), the Taiwanese manufacturer of the tube. Cheng Shin in turn filed a cross-complaint seeking indemnification from its codefendants and from petitioner, Asahi Metal Industry Co., Ltd. (Asahi), the manufacturer of the tube's valve assembly. Zurcher's claims against Cheng Shin and the other defendants were eventually settled and dismissed, leaving only Cheng Shin's indemnity action against Asahi.

handwritten margin note: indemnity action = agree to pay legal damage incurred by the other party

California's long-arm statute authorizes the exercise of jurisdiction "on any basis not inconsistent with the Constitution of this state or of the United States." Asahi moved to quash Cheng Shin's service of summons, arguing the State could not exert jurisdiction over it consistent with the Due Process Clause of the Fourteenth Amendment.

In relation to the motion, the following information was submitted by Asahi and Cheng Shin. Asahi is a Japanese corporation. It manufactures tire valve assemblies in Japan and sells the assemblies to Cheng Shin, and to several other tire manufacturers, for use as components in finished tire tubes. Asahi's sales to Cheng Shin took place in Taiwan. The shipments from Asahi to Cheng Shin were sent from Japan to Taiwan. Cheng Shin bought and incorporated into its tire tubes 150,000 Asahi valve assemblies in 1978; 500,000 in 1979; 500,000 in 1980; 100,000 in 1981; and 100,000 in 1982. Sales to Cheng Shin accounted for 1.24 percent of Asahi's income in 1981 and 0.44 percent in 1982. Cheng Shin alleged that approximately 20 percent of its sales in the United States are in California. Cheng Shin purchases valve assemblies from other suppliers as well, and sells finished tubes throughout the world.

In 1983 an attorney for Cheng Shin conducted an informal examination of the valve stems of the tire tubes sold in one cycle store in Solano County. The attorney declared that of the approximately 115 tire tubes in the store, 97 were purportedly manufactured in Japan or Taiwan, and of those 97, 21 valve stems were marked with the circled letter "A," apparently Asahi's trademark. Of the 21 Asahi valve stems, 12 were incorporated into Cheng Shin tire tubes. The store contained 41 other Cheng Shin tubes that incorporated the valve assemblies of other manufacturers. An affidavit of a manager of Cheng Shin whose duties included the purchasing of component parts stated: "'In discussions with Asahi regarding the purchase of valve stem assemblies the fact that my Company sells tubes throughout the world and specifically the United States has been discussed. I am informed and believe that Asahi was fully aware that valve stem assemblies sold to my Company and to others would end up throughout the United States and in California.'" An affidavit of the president of Asahi, on the other hand, declared that Asahi "'has never contemplated that its limited sales of tire valves to Cheng Shin in Taiwan would subject it to lawsuits in California.'" The record does not include any contract between Cheng Shin and Asahi.

Primarily on the basis of the above information, the Superior Court denied the motion to quash summons, stating: "Asahi obviously does business on an international scale. It is not unreasonable that they defend claims of defect in their product on an international scale."

The Court of Appeal of the State of California issued a peremptory writ of mandate commanding the Superior Court to quash service of summons. The court concluded that "it would be unreasonable to require Asahi to respond in California solely on the basis of ultimately realized foreseeability that the product into which its component was embodied would be sold all over the world including California."

The Supreme Court of the State of California reversed and discharged the writ issued by the Court of Appeal. The court observed: "Asahi has no offices, property or agents in California. It solicits no business in California and has made no direct sales [in California]." Moreover, "Asahi did not design or control the system of distribution that carried its valve assemblies into California." Nevertheless, the court found the exercise of jurisdiction over Asahi to be consistent with the Due Process Clause. It concluded that Asahi knew that some of the valve assemblies sold to Cheng Shin would be incorporated into tire tubes sold in California, and that Asahi benefited indirectly from the sale in California of products incorporating its components. The court considered Asahi's intentional act of placing its components into the stream of commerce — that is, by delivering the components to Cheng Shin in Taiwan — coupled with Asahi's awareness that some of the components would eventually find their way into California, sufficient to form the basis for state court jurisdiction under the Due Process Clause.

We granted certiorari, and now reverse.

II

A *not binding*

The Due Process Clause of the Fourteenth Amendment limits the power of a state court to exert personal jurisdiction over a nonresident defendant. "[T]he constitutional touchstone" of the determination whether an exercise of personal jurisdiction comports with due process "remains whether the defendant purposefully established 'minimum contacts' in the forum State." Most recently we have reaffirmed the oft-quoted reasoning of Hanson v. Denckla, 357 U.S. 235, that minimum contacts must have a basis in "some act by which the defendant purposefully avails itself of the privilege of conducting activities within the forum State, thus invoking the benefits and protections of its laws." "Jurisdiction is proper . . . where the contacts proximately result from actions by the defendant himself that create a 'substantial connection' with the forum State."

Applying the principle that minimum contacts must be based on an act of the defendant, the Court in World-Wide Volkswagen Corp. v. Woodson, 444 U.S. 286, 100 S. Ct. 559, 62 L. Ed. 2d 490 (1980), rejected the assertion that a consumer's unilateral act of bringing the defendant's product into the forum State was a sufficient constitutional basis for personal jurisdiction over the defendant. It had been argued in World-Wide Volkswagen that because an automobile retailer and its wholesale distributor sold a product mobile by design and purpose, they could foresee being haled into court in the distant States into which their customers might drive. The Court rejected this concept of foreseeability as an insufficient basis for jurisdiction under the Due Process Clause. The Court disclaimed, however, the idea that "foreseeability is wholly irrelevant" to personal jurisdiction, concluding that "[t]he forum State does not exceed its powers under the Due Process Clause if it asserts personal jurisdiction over a corporation that delivers its products into the stream of commerce with the expectation that they will be purchased by consumers in the forum State." The Court reasoned:

> "When a corporation 'purposefully avails itself of the privilege of conducting activities within the forum State,' Hanson v. Denckla, 357 U.S. [235,] 253 [78 S. Ct. 1228, 1239, 2 L. Ed. 2d 1283 (1958)], it has clear notice that it is subject to suit there, and can act to alleviate the risk of burdensome litigation by procuring insurance, passing the expected costs on to customers, or, if the risks are too great, severing its connection with the State. Hence if the sale of a product of a manufacturer or distributor . . . is not simply an isolated occurrence, but arises from the efforts of the manufacturer or distributor to serve, directly or indirectly, the market for its product in other States, it is not unreasonable to subject it to suit in one of those States if its allegedly defective merchandise has there been the source of injury to its owners or to others." Id., at 297, 100 S. Ct., at 567.

In World-Wide Volkswagen itself, the state court sought to base jurisdiction not on any act of the defendant, but on the foreseeable unilateral actions of the consumer. Since World-Wide Volkswagen, lower courts have been confronted with cases in which the defendant acted by placing a product in the stream of commerce, and the stream eventually swept defendant's product into the forum State, but the defendant did nothing else to purposefully avail itself of the market in the forum State. Some courts have understood the Due Process Clause, as interpreted in World-Wide Volks-wagen, to allow an exercise of personal jurisdiction to be based on no more than the defendant's act of placing the product in the stream of commerce. Other courts have understood the Due Process Clause and the above-quoted language in World-Wide Volkswagen to require the action of the defendant to be more purposefully directed at the forum State than the mere act of placing a product in the stream of commerce.

The reasoning of the Supreme Court of California in the present case illustrates the former interpretation of World-Wide Volkswagen. The Supreme Court of California held that, because the stream of commerce eventually brought some valves Asahi sold Cheng Shin into California, Asahi's awareness that its valves would be sold in California was sufficient to permit California to exercise jurisdiction over Asahi consistent with the requirements of the Due Process Clause. The Supreme Court of California's position was consistent with those courts that have held that mere foreseeability or awareness was a constitutionally sufficient basis for personal jurisdiction if the defendant's product made its way into the forum State while still in the stream of commerce.

Other courts, however, have understood the Due Process Clause to require something more than that the defendant was aware of its product's entry into the forum State through the stream of commerce in order for the State to exert jurisdiction over the defendant. In the present case, for example, the State Court of Appeal did not read the Due Process Clause, as interpreted by World-Wide Volkswagen, to allow "mere foreseeability that the product will enter the forum state [to] be enough by itself to establish jurisdiction over the distributor and retailer." In Humble v. Toyota Motor Co., an injured car passenger brought suit against Arakawa Auto Body Company, a Japanese corporation that manufactured car seats for Toyota. Arakawa did no business in the United States; it had no office, affiliate, subsidiary, or agent in the United States; it manufactured its component parts outside the United States and delivered them to Toyota Motor Company in Japan. The Court of Appeals, adopting the reasoning of the District Court in that case, noted that although it "does not doubt that Arakawa could have foreseen that its product would find its way into the United States," it would be "manifestly unjust" to require Arakawa to defend itself in the United States.

We now find this latter position to be consonant with the requirements of due process. The "substantial connection," between the defendant and the forum State necessary for a finding of minimum contacts must come about by an action of the defendant purposefully directed toward the forum State. The placement of a product into the stream of commerce, without more, is not an act of the defendant purposefully directed toward the forum State. Additional conduct of the defendant may indicate an intent or purpose to serve the market in the forum State, for example, designing the product for the market in the forum State, advertising in the forum State, establishing channels for providing regular advice to customers in the forum State, or marketing the product through a distributor who has agreed to serve as the sales agent in the forum State. But a defendant's awareness that the stream of commerce may or will sweep the product into the forum State does not convert the mere act of placing the product into the stream into an act purposefully directed toward the forum State.

Assuming, arguendo, that respondents have established Asahi's awareness that some of the valves sold to Cheng Shin would be incorporated into tire tubes sold in California, respondents have not demonstrated any action by Asahi to purposefully avail itself of the California market. Asahi does not do business in California. It has no office, agents, employees, or property in California. It does not advertise or otherwise solicit business in California. It did not create, control, or employ the distribution system that brought its valves to California. There is no evidence that Asahi designed its product in anticipation of sales in California. On the basis of these facts, the exertion of personal jurisdiction over Asahi by the Superior Court of California exceeds the limits of due process.

B

The strictures of the Due Process Clause forbid a state court to exercise personal jurisdiction over Asahi under circumstances that would offend " 'traditional notions of fair play and substantial justice.' "

We have previously explained that the determination of the reasonableness of the exercise of jurisdiction in each case will depend on an evaluation of several factors. A court must consider the burden on the defendant, the interests of the forum State, and the plaintiff's interest in obtaining relief. It must also weigh in its determination "the interstate judicial system's interest in obtaining the most efficient resolution of controversies; and the shared interest of the several States in furthering fundamental substantive social policies."

A consideration of these factors in the present case clearly reveals the unreasonableness of the assertion of jurisdiction over Asahi, even apart from the question of the placement of goods in the stream of commerce.

Certainly the burden on the defendant in this case is severe. Asahi has been commanded by the Supreme Court of California not only to traverse the distance between Asahi's headquarters in Japan and the Superior Court of California in and for the County of Solano, but also to submit its dispute with Cheng Shin to a foreign nation's judicial system. The unique burdens placed upon one who must defend oneself in a foreign legal system should have significant weight in assessing the reasonableness of stretching the long arm of personal jurisdiction over national borders.

When minimum contacts have been established, often the interests of the plaintiff and the forum in the exercise of jurisdiction will justify even the serious burdens placed on the alien defendant. In the present case, however, the interests of the plaintiff and the forum in California's assertion of jurisdiction over Asahi are slight. All that remains is a claim for indemnification asserted by Cheng Shin, a Taiwanese corporation, against Asahi. The transaction on which the indemnification claim is based took place in Taiwan; Asahi's components were shipped from Japan to Taiwan. Cheng Shin has not demonstrated that it is more convenient for it to litigate its indemnification claim against Asahi in California rather than in Taiwan or Japan.

Because the plaintiff is not a California resident, California's legitimate interests in the dispute have considerably diminished. The Supreme Court of California argued that the State had an interest in "protecting its consumers by ensuring that foreign manufacturers comply with the state's safety standards." The State Supreme

Court's definition of California's interest, however, was overly broad. The dispute between Cheng Shin and Asahi is primarily about indemnification rather than safety standards. Moreover, it is not at all clear at this point that California law should govern the question whether a Japanese corporation should indemnify a Taiwanese corporation on the basis of a sale made in Taiwan and a shipment of goods from Japan to Taiwan. The possibility of being haled into a California court as a result of an accident involving Asahi's components undoubtedly creates an additional deterrent to the manufacture of unsafe components; however, similar pressures will be placed on Asahi by the purchasers of its components as long as those who use Asahi components in their final products, and sell those products in California, are subject to the application of California tort law.

World-Wide Volkswagen also admonished courts to take into consideration the interests of the "several States," in addition to the forum State, in the efficient judicial resolution of the dispute and the advancement of substantive policies. In the present case, this advice calls for a court to consider the procedural and substantive policies of other nations whose interests are affected by the assertion of jurisdiction by the California court. The procedural and substantive interests of other nations in a state court's assertion of jurisdiction over an alien defendant will differ from case to case. In every case, however, those interests, as well as the Federal interest in Government's foreign relations policies, will be best served by a careful inquiry into the reasonableness of the assertion of jurisdiction in the particular case, and an unwillingness to find the serious burdens on an alien defendant outweighed by minimal interests on the part of the plaintiff or the forum State. "Great care and reserve should be exercised when extending our notions of personal jurisdiction into the international field."

Considering the international context, the heavy burden on the alien defendant, and the slight interests of the plaintiff and the forum State, the exercise of personal jurisdiction by a California court over Asahi in this instance would be unreasonable and unfair.

III   *not binding*

Because the facts of this case do not establish minimum contacts such that the exercise of personal jurisdiction is consistent with fair play and substantial justice, the judgment of the Supreme Court of California is reversed, and the case is remanded for further proceedings not inconsistent with this opinion.

It is so ordered.

Justice BRENNAN, with whom Justice WHITE, Justice MARSHALL, and Justice BLACKMUN join, concurring in part and concurring in the judgment.

I do not agree with the interpretation in Part II–A of the stream-of-commerce theory, nor with the conclusion that Asahi did not "purposely avail itself of the California market." I do agree, however, with the Court's conclusion in Part II–B that the exercise of personal jurisdiction over Asahi in this case would not comport with "fair play and substantial justice." This is one of those rare cases in which "minimum requirements inherent in the concept of 'fair play and substantial justice' . . . defeat the reasonableness of jurisdiction even [though] the defendant has purposefully engaged in forum activities." I therefore join Parts I and II–B of the Court's opinion, and write separately to explain my disagreement with Part II–A.

Part II–A states that "a defendant's awareness that the stream of commerce may or will sweep the product into the forum State does not convert the mere act of placing the product into the stream into an act purposefully directed toward the forum State." Under this view, a plaintiff would be required to show "[a]dditional conduct" directed toward the forum before finding the exercise of jurisdiction over the defendant to be consistent with the Due Process Clause. I see no need for such a showing, however. The stream of commerce refers not to unpredictable currents or eddies, but to the regular and anticipated flow of products from manufacture to distribution to retail sale. As long as a participant in this process is aware that the final product is being marketed in the forum State, the possibility of a lawsuit there cannot come as a surprise. Nor will the litigation present a burden for which there is no corresponding benefit. A defendant who has placed goods in the stream of commerce benefits economically from the retail sale of the final product in the forum State, and indirectly benefits from the State's laws that regulate and facilitate commercial activity. These benefits accrue regardless of whether that participant directly conducts business in the forum State, or engages in additional conduct directed toward that State. Accordingly, most courts and commentators have found that jurisdiction premised on the placement of a product into the stream of commerce is consistent with the Due Process Clause, and have not required a showing of additional conduct.

The endorsement in Part II–A of what appears to be the minority view among Federal Courts of Appeals represents a marked retreat from the analysis in World-Wide Volkswagen v. Woodson, 444 U.S. 286. In that case, "respondents [sought] to base jurisdiction on one, isolated occurrence and whatever inferences can be drawn therefrom: the fortuitous circumstance that a single Audi automobile, sold in New York to New York residents, happened to suffer an accident while passing through Oklahoma." The Court held that the possibility of an accident in Oklahoma, while to some extent foreseeable in light of the inherent mobility of the automobile, was not enough to establish minimum contacts between the forum State and the retailer or distributor. The Court then carefully explained:

> "[T]his is not to say, of course, that foreseeability is wholly irrelevant. But the foreseeability that is critical to due process analysis is not the mere likelihood that a product will find its way into the forum State. Rather, it is that the defendant's conduct and connection with the forum State are such that he should reasonably anticipate being haled into Court there." Id., at 297, 100 S. Ct., at 567.

The Court reasoned that when a corporation may reasonably anticipate litigation in a particular forum, it cannot claim that such litigation is unjust or unfair, because it "can act to alleviate the risk of burdensome litigation by procuring insurance, passing the expected costs on to consumers, or, if the risks are too great, severing its connection with the State."

To illustrate the point, the Court contrasted the foreseeability of litigation in a State to which a consumer fortuitously transports a defendant's product (insufficient contacts) with the foreseeability of litigation in a State where the defendant's product was regularly sold (sufficient contacts). The Court stated:

> "Hence if the sale of a product of a manufacturer or distributor such as Audi or Volkswagen is not simply an isolated occurrence, but arises from the efforts of the manufacturer or distributor to serve, directly or indirectly, the market for its product in other States, it is not unreasonable to subject it to suit in one of those States if its allegedly defective merchandise has there been the source of injury to its owner or to others. The forum State does not exceed its powers under the Due Process Clause if it asserts personal jurisdiction over a corporation that delivers its products into the stream of commerce with the expectation that they will be purchased by consumers in the forum State." Id., at 297–298, 100 S. Ct., at 567 (emphasis added).

The Court concluded its illustration by referring to Gray v. American Radiator & Standard Sanitary Corp., 22 Ill. 2d 432, 176 N.E.2d 761 (1961), a well-known stream-of-commerce case in which the Illinois Supreme Court applied the theory to assert jurisdiction over a component-parts manufacturer that sold no components directly in Illinois, but did sell them to a manufacturer who incorporated them into a final product that was sold in Illinois. 444 U.S., at 297–298, 100 S. Ct., at 567.

The Court in World-Wide Volkswagen thus took great care to distinguish "between a case involving goods which reach a distant State through a chain of distribution and a case involving goods which reach the same State because a consumer . . . took them there." Id., at 306–307, 100 S. Ct., at 584 (BRENNAN, J., dissenting). The California Supreme Court took note of this distinction, and correctly concluded that our holding in World-Wide Volkswagen preserved the stream-of-commerce theory.

In this case, the facts found by the California Supreme Court support its finding of minimum contacts. The court found that "[a]lthough Asahi did not design or control the system of distribution that carried its valve assemblies into California, Asahi was aware of the distribution system's operation, and it knew that it would benefit economically from the sale in California of products incorporating its components." Accordingly, I cannot join the determination in Part II–A that Asahi's regular and extensive sales of component parts to a manufacturer it knew was making regular sales of the final product in California is insufficient to establish minimum contacts with California.

Justice STEVENS, with whom Justice WHITE and Justice BLACKMUN join, concurring in part and concurring in the judgment.

The judgment of the Supreme Court of California should be reversed for the reasons stated in Part II–B of the Court's opinion. While I join Parts I and II–B, I do not join Part II–A for two reasons. First, it is not necessary to the Court's decision. An examination of minimum contacts is not always necessary to determine whether a state court's assertion of personal jurisdiction is constitutional. Part II–B establishes, after considering the factors set forth in World-Wide Volkswagen Corp. v. Woodson, 444 U.S. 286, 292, that California's exercise of jurisdiction over Asahi in this case would be "unreasonable and unfair." This finding alone requires reversal; this case fits within the rule that "minimum requirements inherent in the concept of 'fair play and substantial justice' may defeat the reasonableness of jurisdiction even if the defendant has purposefully engaged in forum activities." Accordingly, I see no reason in this case for the plurality to articulate "purposeful direction" or any other test as the nexus between an act of a defendant and the forum State that is necessary to establish minimum contacts.

Second, even assuming that the test ought to be formulated here, Part II-A misapplies it to the facts of this case. The plurality seems to assume that an unwavering line can be drawn between "mere awareness" that a component will find its way into the forum State and "purposeful availment" of the forum's market. Over the course of its dealings with Cheng Shin, Asahi has arguably engaged in a higher quantum of conduct than "[t]he placement of a product into the stream of commerce, without more. . . ." Whether or not this conduct rises to the level of purposeful availment requires a constitutional determination that is affected by the volume, the value, and the hazardous character of the components. In most circumstances I would be inclined to conclude that a regular course of dealing that results in deliveries of over 100,000 units annually over a period of several years would constitute "purposeful availment" even though the item delivered to the forum State was a standard product marketed throughout the world.

Post-Case Follow-Up

This is an important point: Appellate courts often have odd numbers of judges to avoid ties. Even so, sometimes opinions do not garner a majority of the court.

The opinion is divided into several sections. In Part I, the Court unanimously agreed on the question to be answered, the basic facts, and the fact that the California Supreme Court's judgment must be reversed. But why must the judgment be reversed? That is the harder question. In Part II-B, eight Justices agreed that the fairness and reasonableness factors we learned about in *World-Wide Volkswagen* were not satisfied. In other words, it was not fair and reasonable to require Asahi, the Japanese tire valve manufacturer, to defend itself in a California court. A crucial fact was that the original California resident plaintiff had settled and was no longer a party. All that was left was a dispute between Asahi and Cheng Shin, the Taiwanese tire tube company. Without the California plaintiff involved in the suit, California did not have a strong interest in deciding this case.

What about minimum contacts? The Court could not agree on whether the defendant, Asahi, had contacts with the state of California. Certainly Asahi did not have any of the obvious contacts we look for first, like selling or shipping its products there.

After *Asahi*, lower courts have split into essentially three camps: Justice O'Connor's "stream of commerce plus" approach, Justice Brennan's "foreseeability" approach, and Justice Stevens' "volume" approach. Most courts have chosen to follow one of the first two approaches because they each represent the opinion of four Justices, while Justice Stevens wrote for only three. The three approaches are well summarized by the following language from the opinion:

J. O'Connor's "Stream of Commerce Plus"

The placement of a product into the stream of commerce, without more, is not an act of the defendant purposefully directed toward the forum State. Additional conduct of the defendant may indicate an intent or purpose to serve the market in the forum State, for example, designing the product for the market in the forum State, advertising in the forum State, establishing channels for providing regular advice to customers in the forum State, or marketing the product through a distributor who has agreed to serve as the sales agent in the forum State.

As a result, Justice O'Connor's approach, which garnered the vote of four Justices, would require some additional conduct that showed the defendant somehow targeted the forum state.

However, Justice Brennan's approach, which also garnered the support of four Justices, does not require any "plus" conduct.

J. Brennan's Stream of Commerce: Regularity, Awareness, and Economic Benefit

Under [Justice O'Connor's approach], a plaintiff would be required to show "[a]dditional conduct" directed toward the forum before finding the exercise of jurisdiction over the defendant to be consistent with the Due Process Clause. I see no need for such a showing, however. The stream of commerce refers not to unpredictable currents or eddies, but to the regular and anticipated flow of products from manufacture to distribution to retail sale. As long as a participant in this process is aware that the final product is being marketed in the forum State, the possibility of a lawsuit there cannot come as a surprise. Nor will the litigation present a burden for which there is no corresponding benefit. A defendant who has placed goods in the stream of commerce benefits economically from the retail sale of the final product in the forum State, and indirectly benefits from the State's laws that regulate and facilitate commercial activity. These benefits accrue regardless of whether that participant directly conducts business in the forum State, or engages in additional conduct directed toward that State.

J. Stevens' Stream of Commerce: Volume, Value, and Dangerous Nature of the Product

The plurality seems to assume that an unwavering line can be drawn between "mere awareness" that a component will find its way into the forum State and "purposeful availment" of the forum's market. Over the course of its dealings with Cheng Shin, Asahi has arguably engaged in a higher quantum of conduct than "[t]he placement of a product into the stream of commerce, without more. . . ." Whether or not this conduct rises to the level of purposeful availment requires a constitutional determination that is affected by the volume, the value, and the hazardous character of the components. In most circumstances I would be inclined to conclude that a regular course of dealing that results in deliveries of over 100,000 units annually over a period of several years would constitute "purposeful availment" even though the item delivered to the forum State was a standard product marketed throughout the world.

In short, all three approaches consider whether the defendant introduced the component product into the stream of commerce. But the first approach requires some further conduct aimed at the forum, the second focuses on the defendant's awareness that the product is being marketed in the forum state, and the third would consider the volume of sales, the value of those sales, and the nature of the product sold.

How do you advise clients in the face of ambiguity like this? If your client is a manufacturer or designer of component parts, you could advise your client to write its contracts and structure its business in a way that avoids any sales or other connections with any U.S. jurisdictions. That is probably not attractive, because it may cost your client lucrative business opportunities.

It seemed likely that the Court would remedy this problem in the recent case of *Nicastro*, described below. Unfortunately, things are no less complicated today than they were after *Asahi*.

Asahi Metal Industry Co., Ltd. v. Superior Court of California, Solano County: Real Life Applications

1. Assume that you are in a jurisdiction that follows the "stream of commerce plus" approach described in J. O'Connor's opinion in Part II-A. What if the valve manufacturer provided the tire manufacturer with valves that were specifically designed to comply with California's more stringent environmental regulations? Would a court applying the stream of commerce plus approach find that the defendant had contacts with California? What about the other elements of the minimum contacts analysis — would they be satisfied? Why or why not?

2. Assume now that you are in a jurisdiction that follows J. Brennan's approach. The valve manufacturer sells 5 million tire valves per year to three tire manufacturers in Japan, but does not make any direct sales in the United States. Ten percent of its valves end up in finished products in California, and the valve manufacturer can trace approximately 10 percent of its revenue from the tire sales the Japanese companies make in California. The valve in the tire that failed and injured the plaintiff, however, was originally sold in Ohio, and the plaintiff brought the motorcycle equipped with the tire to California when he moved there. Would a court applying J. Brennan's approach find that the defendant had contacts with California? Would J. Stevens' approach be satisfied? What about the other elements of the minimum contacts analysis — would they be satisfied? Why or why not?

3. The Court in *Asahi* agreed it was not fair and reasonable for the valve manufacturer to defend the indemnity suit (essentially a contract dispute between the Japanese valve manufacturer and the Taiwanese tire tube manufacturer) in a court located in California. What if the plaintiff had sued both Asahi and Cheng Shin for the allegedly defective tire, had not settled, and was still a party to the lawsuit? Would that change the Court's analysis of whether jurisdiction was fair and reasonable over Cheng Shin? If so, how?

In 2011, the Court decided *J. McIntyre Mach. Ltd. v. Nicastro. Nicastro* involved the other recurring situation, depicted in Exhibit 7.4, where a nonresident defendant distributes its products through one or more layers of independent companies, making it difficult to find contacts between the manufacturer and the forum state.

In *Nicastro*, the plaintiff Nicastro seriously injured his hand in a metal-shearing machine manufactured by defendant J. McIntyre in the United Kingdom. J. McIntyre sold the machine through an independent distributor throughout the United States. The machine that injured Nicastro was the only one sold in New Jersey. Once again, the Court was unable to fashion a majority opinion describing the limits of personal jurisdiction in stream of commerce cases.

Four members of the Court essentially endorsed Justice O'Connor's "stream of commerce plus" test, requiring additional conduct by the defendant that is purposefully directed at the forum state. Justice Kennedy, writing for the four-Justice plurality, focused specifically on J. McIntyre's conduct. Whether phrased as "purposeful availment," "activity directed at the sovereign," or "a course of conduct directed at the society or economy existing within the jurisdiction of a given sovereign," all phrases describe the same concept: the defendant's contacts with the forum state. The plurality stressed that "an independent company agreed to sell J. McIntyre's machines in the United States," and "J. McIntyre itself did not sell its machines to buyers in this country beyond the U.S. distributor...." Though Justice Kennedy acknowledged that selling through a distributor who serves the entire United States may demonstrate an intent to serve the U.S. as a whole, he emphasized that J. McIntyre did not advertise or market in, send or ship to, or otherwise target New Jersey.

The two concurring Justices declined (at least facially) to decide between the two competing tests. Instead, they focused on the fact that there was no "*stream of commerce*" to begin with — with only one machine sold in New Jersey, there was no regular flow of products into the forum state. The concurring Justices were persuaded that, whether foreseeability or additional conduct is required, a single sale in the forum state is not even a "stream" of commerce that can justify New Jersey's exercise of personal jurisdiction over the foreign manufacturer.

The dissent recognized the implications of the common ground between the plurality and concurring opinions: A foreign manufacturer that not only foresaw, but specifically intended that its products be sold in the United States, can "Pilate-like wash its hands of a product by having independent distributors market it." Essentially, the distributor, by making the actual sale, insulated J. McIntyre from the jurisdiction of the New Jersey court. Although all nine members of the Court apparently believed J. McIntyre at least "purposefully availed" itself of the entire United States market, no *state* would be able to exercise jurisdiction over J. McIntyre, the U.K. manufacturer.

As a result, we are essentially left where we were when *Asahi* was decided. First, look for contacts between the defendant and the forum state. Then, if you are faced with one of these paradigm situations, investigate what lower courts in your jurisdiction have said about *Asahi* and *Nicastro*, and be prepared to do your best to fashion an argument in favor of your client that tracks whichever approach your court follows.

D. CONTACTS AND THE INTERNET: ARE VIRTUAL CONTACTS DIFFERENT?

Does modern technology require a new set of rules when dealing with problems posed by the Internet? Changes in technology—particularly the automobile—made it untenable to require either presence or consent before the defendant is subject to personal jurisdiction. The Internet, social media, and other communication technologies pose new problems, but the minimum contacts doctrine can likely accommodate most situations.

The Supreme Court has not decided a case involving contacts via the Internet. Lower courts, however, have. The most influential opinion in this area remains an outdated federal district court opinion, *Zippo Manufacturing Company v. Zippo Dot Com, Incorporated*, decided in 1997. Courts, however, still often consider the *Zippo* factors when faced with personal jurisdiction over a defendant based on his Internet activities. In *Zippo*, the court had to decide whether a defendant's website justified personal jurisdiction over the defendant. The opinion identified a "sliding scale" of interactivity wherein the defendant targets the forum state. According to *Zippo*, websites fall along a continuum: At one extreme, a website may be purely passive, merely displaying information and not allowing any interactivity. In this situation, maintaining a passive website, without more, would not be sufficient for the court to exercise personal jurisdiction over the defendant. This category in particular is difficult to square with the modern reality of websites. Websites use cookies to gather information about a user's computer, target ads at website users based on a sometimes massive collection of data about the user, and typically have a contact portal or an interface to allow the user to leave comments. Whether these technological changes since 1997—or others that are sure to come—can establish personal jurisdiction over a defendant remains to be seen.

On the other hand, one comparatively rare example of a purely passive website that did not target a forum state is *Pavlovich v. Superior Court*, 58 P.3d 2, 9 (Cal. 2002). Pavlovich, the defendant, posted code on his website that could be used to decrypt the encryption software used to protect DVDs from illegal copying under copyright law. The defendant, however, did not target any state with his website. It was purely informational. In fact, he was unaware that the company that had developed the software was in California. The California court held that, even if he had been aware that harm would be felt in California, he had not purposefully directed any activity at the forum state of California. In other words, he had no California contacts. Without those contacts, the website could not properly form the basis for personal jurisdiction over Pavlovich.

At the other extreme, active websites permit business transactions, forming contracts, or transmitting files back and forth. Purchasing shoes over eBay or Amazon or media content from iTunes or Netflix are simply virtual transactions that can be analyzed using the existing framework. When a seller's or buyer's activities over the Internet suggest the defendant targets the forum state, the defendant has engaged in purposeful contact with the forum state virtually—through the Internet. In the middle of the spectrum are websites that allow the exchange of information, but do not necessarily suggest that the defendant has targeted the forum state. In each case the question is still the same: Has the defendant made purposeful contact with the forum state? In other words, the ultimate question should be the same. If a nonresident defendant engages in activities via the Internet, the court must still ultimately apply the minimum contacts analysis, evaluating whether such activities show that the defendant "purposefully availed" himself of the forum state.

The *Zippo* sliding scale test is a useful way to consider whether the defendant purposefully availed himself of conducting activities in the forum state. In other words, the sliding scale is most likely to tell us whether the defendant has contacts with the forum state. Active websites seem like the most likely scenario for a court to find such contacts; the most likely example would be by entering into contracts with the residents of that state and the interactions that go along with negotiating and forming those contacts, as we saw in *Burger King*. Recall that a defendant does not have to physically make contact with the state. These interactions would occur virtually. But such modern contacts do not seem conceptually different from "virtual" contacts that have existed for more than a century, such as telegraphs, phone calls, and mail correspondence.

Even "passive" websites, though probably not sufficient to justify personal jurisdiction, could be relevant contacts. Does the website act as advertising in the forum state, even if consumers cannot communicate or make a contract via the website? Interactive websites are more likely to involve activity that a court would deem to be a defendant's contact with the forum state. Even so, recall that the claim must arise out of or be connected to the defendant's contacts with the forum state. If those contacts are via the Internet or other modern technology, the contacts must still be related to the plaintiff's claim against that particular defendant. And the third step, whether the exercise of personal jurisdiction is fair and reasonable, remains part of the test. Given the especially global reach of the Internet, the fairness factors may have more weight in modern cases. Much like the stream of commerce cases, defendants may operate websites from all corners of the globe. And given the low cost of operating such websites, the defendant may be in an even more remote part of the world and not have the financial ability to travel long distances to defend himself in a distant country like the United States.

Courts have considered some common, recurring factors that suggest the website may not qualify as a contact with the forum state in the first instance. For example: (1) Does the website include language indicating it is intended for a certain, limited audience? (2) Does the website include only local phone numbers? (3) Does the website publish information targeted to, or only of use to, a limited audience? (4) Does the website include disclaimers that it is intended to provide information only? (5) Does it require any contracts or purchases to be completed outside the website? (6) Does the website include statements that suggest it is targeted at a particular state, region, or similarly limited geographic area? (7) Does the website exclude users in the forum state? In other words, does it permit interaction only with certain users outside the forum state? (8) Is there any evidence that residents of the forum state actually use or interact with the website? (9) Does the website require users to agree to forum-selection or choice-of-law provisions that specify another state as the proper place to litigate any disputes, or another state's law to govern any such disputes?

[handwritten margin note: not relevant (maybe) law]

Courts have also considered factors that suggest the defendant does have contacts with the forum state: (1) Does the website generate income for the defendant from residents of the forum state? (2) ~~Does the defendant know that the Internet activity will cause serious harm to the plaintiff in the forum state?~~ (3) Do residents of the forum state routinely access the website, generating a high number of "hits"? (4) Does the defendant respond to emails from forum state residents sent via the website? (5) Does the website content suggest it targets residents of the forum state? (6) Are the Internet service provider, servers, or other infrastructure located in the forum state?

Though lower courts do not present a uniform approach, the test remains the same: the minimum contacts test. The *Zippo* sliding scale and the factors mentioned above all attempt to answer the same question: Does the defendant have contacts with the forum state? If so, we must still ask whether the claim arises out of those contacts and whether exercising personal jurisdiction in this case would be fair and reasonable. In short, the Internet has not radically changed the minimum contacts analysis — at least not yet.

Chapter Summary

■ Specific personal jurisdiction requires a relationship between the defendant, the forum, and the litigation. This is summarized by the minimum contacts test: (1) a defendant must have minimum contacts with the forum state, (2) the claim must arise out of or be connected to the defendant's contacts with the forum state, and (3) the exercise of personal jurisdiction must be fair and reasonable.

■ A defendant must have minimum contacts with the forum state. However, a single contact can suffice if the other requirements are satisfied.

■ The contact must be the defendant's contact; the defendant — not the plaintiff — must have initiated the contact.

■ The claim must arise out of or be connected to the defendant's contact. The contact must be related to the claim against the specific defendant.

■ Even if the defendant has contacts with the forum state and the claim is sufficiently related to those contacts, the exercise of jurisdiction must be fair and reasonable.

■ A court will consider a number of factors to decide whether the exercise of jurisdiction is fair and reasonable: (1) the burden on the defendant, (2) the forum state's interest in adjudicating the dispute; (3) the plaintiff's interest in obtaining convenient and effective relief, at least when that interest is not adequately protected by the plaintiff's power to choose the forum; (4) the interstate judicial system's interest in obtaining the most efficient resolution of controversies; and (5) the shared interest of the several states in furthering fundamental substantive social policies.

■ If a court finds minimum contacts, and that the suit arises out of those contacts, the court is virtually certain to find that exercising jurisdiction is fair and reasonable.

■ When contacts between the defendant and the forum state are difficult to identify, and the defendant has placed a product into the stream of commerce, you must analyze whether personal jurisdiction is proper using the different approaches from *Asahi* and *Nicastro*, even though no approach garnered a majority opinion.

■ Even in cases where a product injures someone or the identifiable contacts are via the Internet, the minimum contacts analysis is still the ultimate test for whether personal jurisdiction satisfies due process.

Applying the Concepts

1. Patricia is crossing the street in Tulsa, Oklahoma when she is struck by a car driven by Damian. Damian is just driving through Oklahoma on his way to Texas; he has lived his entire life in Kansas. After Damian returns home to Kansas, Patricia sues Damian in federal court in Tulsa, Oklahoma. Can the Oklahoma federal court properly exercise specific personal jurisdiction over Damian? Why or why not?

2. An unemployed engineer living in Texas hears from his neighbor that a company in Oklahoma is looking for an engineer. The Oklahoma company has not advertised the job opening. The engineer emails the company a resume and cover letter. A week later, the engineer calls the company. During the phone call, the company hires the engineer. The engineer drives to Oklahoma and the two parties sign a six-month contract of employment. As soon as the engineer arrives at the job site to start work, the company fires the engineer. The engineer sues the company in state court in Texas for breach of contract. Can the Texas court properly exercise personal jurisdiction over the company? Why or why not?

3. A manufacturer of cigarette lighters has its only plant and offices in Oklahoma. The manufacturer employs 20 salespeople in Texas who sell the lighters that are shipped to them from Oklahoma. A raw materials supplier in Arkansas sues the manufacturer in state court in Texas for failing to pay for raw materials. The manufacturer ordered the raw materials from the supplier in Arkansas; payment for the materials was due and payable in Arkansas. The manufacturer picked up the raw materials in Arkansas. Can the Texas court properly exercise personal jurisdiction over the manufacturer? Why or why not?

4. Brakes, Inc. manufactures brake pads in China. Brakes, Inc. is a corporation formed under the laws of China and has its only offices and plant in China. Auto Manufacturer Corporation in Michigan sells a car equipped with Brakes, Inc.'s brake pads to a customer in California. While driving to work one day in California, the customer is injured in a crash when the brakes on his car fail. The customer sues Auto Manufacturer Corporation in state court in Michigan. Auto

Manufacturer Corporation settles with the customer and then files a separate suit against Brakes, Inc. in state court in Michigan, claiming that Brakes, Inc. is required to reimburse Auto Manufacturer Corporation under their contract. Brakes, Inc. has timely objected to personal jurisdiction. What additional information may satisfy J. O'Connor's approach to find personal jurisdiction over Brakes, Inc. in Michigan?

5. Brakes, Inc. manufactures brake pads in China. Brakes, Inc. is a corporation formed under the laws of China and has its only offices and plant in China. Auto Manufacturer Corporation in Michigan sells a car equipped with Brakes, Inc.'s brake pads to a customer in California. While driving to work one day in California, the customer is injured in a crash when the brakes on his car fail. The customer sues Auto Manufacturer Corporation and Brakes, Inc. in state court in California. Brakes, Inc. has timely objected to personal jurisdiction. What additional information may satisfy J. Brennan's approach to find personal jurisdiction over Brakes, Inc. in California?

6. Seller, Inc. advertises its water heaters on the Internet. Seller, Inc.'s website permits buyers in every state to make orders completely online and sells its water heaters to consumers in every state. The website also provides a toll-free phone number for orders. A buyer who lives in Pennsylvania calls the toll-free number and orders a water heater. The buyer drives to Seller, Inc.'s warehouse in New Jersey and picks up the water heater. The water heater explodes while the buyer attempts to install it at home in Pennsylvania. The buyer sues Seller, Inc. in federal court in Pennsylvania. Can the Pennsylvania federal court properly exercise personal jurisdiction over Seller, Inc.? Why or why not?

Civil Procedure in Practice

1. You are an associate at a law firm. Your client, Cars-a-lot, is a car dealer in Missouri. It sells a car to a customer named Peter in Louisiana, but Peter stops making payments on the car. Peter has always lived in Arkansas, but sometimes visits family in Missouri. Cars-a-lot wants to sue Peter for breach of contract, and its general counsel has asked you where Peter can be sued; more specifically, courts in which states could properly exercise specific personal jurisdiction over Peter? How would you advise Cars-a-lot?

2. Your next client comes into your office for advice about a contract he is negotiating. His company is based in Los Angeles, California and supplies ceramic heating elements for a new kind of clothes dryer. The heating element will be installed in a finished product manufactured in Canada and sold throughout the United States. Your client is concerned about the contract he is making with the Canadian company that is purchasing the heating elements. Your client

wants to make sure that, in the event of a dispute between his company and the Canadian company, he can sue the Canadian company for breach of contract in California. He is also concerned about being sued throughout the United States if a clothes dryer fails and injures someone. How would you advise him to structure his contract and his business to accomplish his goals?

General Personal Jurisdiction

Chapters 6 and 7 introduced personal jurisdiction — one of the three doctrines that help a lawyer choose the proper court. Chapter 6 introduced the concept of personal jurisdiction. Chapter 7 explained specific personal jurisdiction. This chapter explains a different, independent basis for personal jurisdiction known as general personal jurisdiction. In short, a court has general personal jurisdiction over a person or entity in the state where they are "essentially at home." A natural person (i.e., a human) is **essentially at home** where he or she is domiciled. Fortunately, the test for domicile is the same as the test explained in Chapter 3 dealing with diversity of citizenship and how to determine citizenship for individuals. Entities like corporations are at home in the state in which the entity was formed and the state in which it has its principal place of business. The rest of the chapter will further explain these terms.

Unlike specific jurisdiction, which requires a connection between the defendant, the forum state, and the litigation, general personal jurisdiction focuses only on the connection between the defendant and the forum state. In other words, a defendant that is "essentially at home" is subject to personal jurisdiction for any claim. This is true even if the claim is unrelated to the defendant's activities in her home state. Because there is often at least one state in which a defendant can be said to be at home, it is important for lawyers to understand this concept in choosing the proper court.

Key Concepts

- ▉ Know the difference between specific and general personal jurisdiction
- ▉ Understand where a corporation or other entity is "essentially at home" and subject to general personal jurisdiction
- ▉ Understand where a natural person is domiciled and subject to general personal jurisdiction

A. GENERAL PERSONAL JURISDICTION: HOW IS IT DIFFERENT THAN SPECIFIC PERSONAL JURISDICTION?

Unlike specific personal jurisdiction, general jurisdiction is, as the name suggests, not specific to any particular claim. General personal jurisdiction permits a plaintiff to sue a defendant where that defendant is considered to be at home, even if the claim has nothing to do with the defendant's activities in the state. Put another way, a defendant is subject to personal jurisdiction where the defendant is essentially at home for events that happened anywhere in the world. Similarly, when the person or entity is at home, the court does not ask whether it is fair and just to require the defendant to appear and defend the lawsuit. This makes sense. A defendant sued in the defendant's home state is probably not unduly burdened by defending a lawsuit in the defendant's home state. This approach is consistent with the idea that due process is concerned with avoiding fundamental unfairness to the defendant. Requiring a defendant to defend a lawsuit at home is also consistent with the historical basis of personal jurisdiction — that the state has the authority to exercise power over people and things within its boundaries. That includes the authority to make a person appear and defend a lawsuit in a court located within that person's home state.

Consider the difference between specific and general personal jurisdiction in the context of the specific personal jurisdiction case of *World-Wide Volkswagen v. Woodson* in Chapter 7. Imagine that the plaintiffs, the Robinson family, were injured in the collision in Oklahoma but, instead of suing in Oklahoma, they sued the seller Seaway Volkswagen, Inc. in New York. As the Court noted, Seaway was incorporated in New York and likely had its only place of business in New York. Rather than analyze whether the Robinson family's product defect lawsuit arises out of the sale of the car to the Robinsons in New York (which it did), a court would likely hold that a court in New York could exercise general personal jurisdiction over Seaway; thus, the Robinsons could sue Seaway in New York for any claim, regardless of whether it was related to Seaway's activity in New York. It would not matter whether the claim was for breaching a warranty Seaway made when it sold the car to the Robinsons in New York or whether it was a suit involving a collision halfway across the country in Oklahoma. The court would likely reason that Seaway was at home in New York in two ways: Seaway was incorporated or "formed" in New York and Seaway had its principal (and only) place of business in New York.

B. WHEN IS A DEFENDANT SUBJECT TO GENERAL PERSONAL JURISDICTION?

As you will see below, the Court has simplified the test for general personal jurisdiction. Also unlike specific personal jurisdiction, courts do not focus on the defendant's "contacts" with the forum state. Rather, the standard for personal jurisdiction is one that will be simpler to apply in most cases: If the person or entity is "essentially at home" in the forum state, then the courts of the forum state can exercise personal jurisdiction over that defendant for any claim. For entities like corporations and other companies, the entity will be "at home" in the state in which it was formed and in the state in which it has its **principal place of business**. Fortunately, the standard for where an entity has its principal place of business is the same for both the question of citizenship for diversity purposes and being "at home" for general personal jurisdiction. For persons, they are "at home" where they are domiciled. Fortunately, once again, the standard for where a person is domiciled is the same for both the question of citizenship for diversity purposes and being "at home" for general personal jurisdiction. The test, however, is whether the person or entity is "essentially at home." Although the Court has given lawyers considerable guidance about how to apply that test, some unanswered questions remain.

Case Preview

Daimler AG v. Bauman

As you read this case, consider these questions:

1. When is a defendant subject to general personal jurisdiction?
2. Did the Court overrule *Perkins*? Or did the Court leave open the possibility that *Perkins* would come out the same way today?
3. Will entities be subject to general personal jurisdiction in fewer or more states than under the old "continuous and systematic" contacts approach?
4. Why would the court not have specific personal jurisdiction over Daimler AG?

Daimler AG v. Bauman
134 S. Ct. 746 (2014)

Justice GINSBURG delivered the opinion of the Court.

This case concerns the authority of a court in the United States to entertain a claim brought by foreign plaintiffs against a foreign defendant based on events occurring entirely outside the United States. The litigation commenced in 2004, when twenty-two Argentinian

The History of General Personal Jurisdiction

Until 2011, general personal jurisdiction — like specific personal jurisdiction — focused on the defendant's contacts with the forum state. As you will see below, the test has been significantly simplified and streamlined, though some questions remain.

International Shoe — The Birth of an Idea. *International Shoe* created a framework for analyzing personal jurisdiction in terms of "contacts." For decades, lawyers and judges analyzed whether a defendant was subject to personal jurisdiction based on the defendant's contacts with the forum state. Even when considering general personal jurisdiction, the question was whether the defendant had "continuous and substantial" contacts with the forum state. If so, the defendant could be sued for any claim — regardless of whether the claim was related to the defendant's contacts with the state.

Perkins — The Idea Is Sustained. A Philippine mining company temporarily conducted substantially all of its business in Ohio while Japan occupied the Philippines during WWII. In a short opinion, the Court held that it would not violate due process for a court to require the mining company to appear and defend itself in courts located in Ohio under a theory of general personal jurisdiction.

Helicopteros — The Idea Is Further Sustained. After a helicopter crash in Peru, the plaintiffs sued the Colombian helicopter manufacturer in Texas. The manufacturer had several contacts with Texas, including negotiating contracts in Texas, buying equipment and supplies and accepting checks from Texas, and sending employees to Texas for training. The parties agreed that specific personal jurisdiction did not exist, so the plaintiffs were left to argue that the court had general personal jurisdiction over the foreign manufacturer. The Court, however, held that these regular contacts were not extensive enough to be considered "continuous and systematic" and held that general personal jurisdiction was not satisfied.

Goodyear v. Brown — *A New Idea*. In 2011, the Court announced a new test: A defendant is subject to general personal jurisdiction wherever that defendant is "essentially at home." The Court further explained the test in 2014 in *Daimler AG v. Bauman.*

residents filed a complaint in the United States District Court for the Northern District of California against DaimlerChrysler Aktiengesellschaft (Daimler), a German public stock company, headquartered in Stuttgart, that manufactures Mercedes-Benz vehicles in Germany. The complaint alleged that during Argentina's 1976–1983 "Dirty War," Daimler's Argentinian subsidiary, Mercedes-Benz Argentina (MB Argentina) collaborated with state security forces to kidnap, detain, torture, and kill certain MB Argentina workers, among them, plaintiffs or persons closely related to plaintiffs. Damages for the alleged human-rights violations were sought from Daimler under the laws of the United States, California, and Argentina. Jurisdiction over the lawsuit was predicated on the California contacts of Mercedes-Benz USA, LLC (MBUSA), a subsidiary of Daimler incorporated in Delaware with its principal place of business in New Jersey. MBUSA distributes Daimler-manufactured vehicles to independent dealerships throughout the United States, including California.

The question presented is whether the Due Process Clause of the Fourteenth Amendment precludes the District Court from exercising jurisdiction over Daimler in this case, given the absence of any California connection to the atrocities, perpetrators, or victims described in the complaint. Plaintiffs invoked the court's general or all-purpose jurisdiction. California, they urge, is a place where Daimler may be sued on any and all claims against it, wherever in the world the claims may arise. Exercises of personal jurisdiction so exorbitant, we hold, are barred by due process constraints on the assertion of adjudicatory authority.

In Goodyear Dunlop Tires Operations, S.A. v. Brown, we addressed the distinction between general or all-purpose jurisdiction, and specific or conduct-linked jurisdiction. As to the former, we held that a court may assert jurisdiction over a foreign corporation "to hear any and all claims against [it]" only when the corporation's affiliations with the State in which suit is brought are so constant and pervasive "as to render [it] essentially at home in the forum State." Instructed by Goodyear, we conclude Daimler is not "at home" in California, and cannot be sued there for injuries plaintiffs attribute to MB Argentina's conduct in Argentina.

Plaintiffs' operative complaint names only one corporate defendant: Daimler, the petitioner here. Plaintiffs seek to hold Daimler vicariously liable for MB Argentina's alleged malfeasance. Daimler is a German Aktiengesellschaft (public stock company) that manufactures Mercedes-Benz vehicles in Germany and has its headquarters in Stuttgart. At times relevant to this case, MB Argentina was a subsidiary wholly owned by Daimler's predecessor in interest.

Daimler moved to dismiss the action for want of personal jurisdiction. Opposing the motion, plaintiffs submitted declarations and exhibits purporting to demonstrate the presence of Daimler itself in California. Alternatively, plaintiffs maintained that jurisdiction over Daimler could be founded on the California contacts of MBUSA, a distinct corporate entity that, according to plaintiffs, should be treated as Daimler's agent for jurisdictional purposes.

MBUSA, an indirect subsidiary of Daimler, is a Delaware limited liability corporation. MBUSA serves as Daimler's exclusive importer and distributor in the United States, purchasing Mercedes-Benz automobiles from Daimler in Germany, then importing those vehicles, and ultimately distributing them to independent dealerships located throughout the Nation. Although MBUSA's principal place of business is in New Jersey, MBUSA has multiple California-based facilities, including a regional office in Costa Mesa, a Vehicle Preparation Center in Carson, and a Classic Center in Irvine. According to the record developed below, MBUSA is the largest supplier of luxury vehicles to the California market. In particular, over 10% of all sales of new vehicles in the United States take place in California, and MBUSA's California sales account for 2.4% of Daimler's worldwide sales.

We granted certiorari to decide whether, consistent with the Due Process Clause of the Fourteenth Amendment, Daimler is amenable to suit in California courts for claims involving only foreign plaintiffs and conduct occurring entirely abroad. . . .

[The Court's] 1952 decision in Perkins v. Benguet Consol. Mining Co. remains the textbook case of general jurisdiction appropriately exercised over a foreign corporation that has not consented to suit in the forum. The defendant in Perkins, Benguet, was a company incorporated under the laws of the Philippines, where it operated gold and silver mines. Benguet ceased its mining operations during the Japanese occupation of the Philippines in World War II; its president moved to Ohio, where he kept an office, maintained the company's files, and oversaw the company's activities. The plaintiff, an Ohio resident, sued Benguet on a claim that neither arose in Ohio nor related to the corporation's activities in that State. We held that the Ohio courts could exercise general jurisdiction over Benguet without offending due process. That was so, we later noted, because Ohio was the corporation's principal, if temporary, place of business. . . .

IV

With this background, we turn directly to the question whether Daimler's affiliations with California are sufficient to subject it to the general (all-purpose) personal jurisdiction of that State's courts. In the proceedings below, the parties agreed on, or failed to contest, certain points we now take as given. Plaintiffs have never attempted to fit this case into the specific jurisdiction category. Nor did plaintiffs challenge on appeal the District Court's holding that Daimler's own contacts with California were, by themselves, too sporadic to justify the exercise of general jurisdiction. While plaintiffs ultimately persuaded the Ninth Circuit to impute MBUSA's California contacts to Daimler on an agency theory, at no point have they maintained that MBUSA is an alter ego of Daimler. . . .

This Court has not yet addressed whether a foreign corporation may be subjected to a court's general jurisdiction based on the contacts of its in-state subsidiary. . . . But we need not pass judgment on invocation of an agency theory in the context of general jurisdiction, for in no event can the appeals court's analysis be sustained. . . .

agent at home ≠ [ome at home

MBUSA as an agent?
↓
SC: no.
not supported

B

Even if we were to assume that MBUSA is at home in California, and further to assume MBUSA's contacts are imputable to Daimler, there would still be no basis to subject Daimler to general jurisdiction in California, for Daimler's slim contacts with the State hardly render it at home there.

Goodyear made clear that only a limited set of affiliations with a forum will render a defendant amenable to all-purpose jurisdiction there. "For an individual, the paradigm forum for the exercise of general jurisdiction is the individual's domicile; for a corporation, it is an equivalent place, one in which the corporation is fairly regarded as at home." With respect to a corporation, the place of incorporation and principal place of business are "paradig[m] . . . bases for general jurisdiction." Those affiliations have the virtue of being unique — that is, each ordinarily indicates only one place — as well as easily ascertainable. These bases afford plaintiffs recourse to at least one clear and certain forum in which a corporate defendant may be sued on any and all claims.

Goodyear did not hold that a corporation may be subject to general jurisdiction only in a forum where it is incorporated or has its principal place of business; it simply typed those places paradigm all-purpose forums. Plaintiffs would have us look beyond the exemplar bases Goodyear identified, and approve the exercise of general jurisdiction in every State in which a corporation "engages in a substantial, continuous, and systematic course of business." That formulation, we hold, is unacceptably grasping.

[T]he words "continuous and systematic" were used in International Shoe to describe instances in which the exercise of specific jurisdiction would be appropriate.

Turning to all-purpose jurisdiction, in contrast, International Shoe speaks of "instances in which the continuous corporate operations within a state [are] so substantial and of such a nature as to justify suit . . . on causes of action arising from dealings entirely distinct from those activities."

Accordingly, the inquiry under Goodyear is not whether a foreign corporation's in-forum contacts can be said to be in some sense "continuous and systematic," it is whether that corporation's "affiliations with the State are so 'continuous and systematic' as to render [it] essentially at home in the forum State."[19]

Here, neither Daimler nor MBUSA is incorporated in California, nor does either entity have its principal place of business there. If Daimler's California activities sufficed to allow adjudication of this Argentina-rooted case in California, the same global reach would presumably be available in every other State in which MBUSA's sales are sizable. Such exorbitant exercises of all-purpose jurisdiction would scarcely permit out-of-state defendants "to structure their primary conduct with some minimum assurance as to where that conduct will and will not render them liable to suit."

For the reasons stated, the judgment of the United States Court of Appeals for the Ninth Circuit is

Reversed.

---

[19] We do not foreclose the possibility that in an exceptional case, see, e.g., Perkins . . . a corporation's operations in a forum other than its formal place of incorporation or principal place of business may be so substantial and of such a nature as to render the corporation at home in that State. But this case presents no occasion to explore that question, because Daimler's activities in California plainly do not approach that level. It is one thing to hold a corporation answerable for operations in the forum State . . . quite another to expose it to suit on claims having no connection whatever to the forum State.

Harder to sue corporations?

Post-Case Follow-Up

A court can exercise general personal jurisdiction over a defendant where the defendant is at home: "For an individual, the paradigm forum for the exercise of general jurisdiction is the individual's domicile; for a corporation, it is an equivalent place, one in which the corporation is fairly regarded as at home." *Bauman*, 134 S. Ct. at 760.

The Court did not overrule *Perkins*. The *Bauman* Court seems to say that corporations are essentially at home in their state of incorporation and the state in which they have their principal place of business. But notice footnote 19: "We do not foreclose the possibility that in an exceptional case, see, e.g., Perkins . . . a corporation's operations in a forum other than its formal place of incorporation or principal place of business may be so substantial and of such a nature as to render the corporation at home in that State." Remember, the test is whether the defendant corporation is essentially at home. Most often that will mean the corporation's state of incorporation and principal place of business. By expressly preserving *Perkins* as good law, the Court left room for the possibility that unusual circumstances could lead to a court finding general personal jurisdiction in a state other than these two paradigm bases.

"Essentially at home" is significantly narrower and will likely result in entities being subject to general personal jurisdiction in far fewer states than before *Bauman*. The old test, which considered whether the defendant had continuous and substantial contacts with the forum state, led to results where defendants could be subject to general personal jurisdiction in many states or even every state. Consider national chain stores like Wal-Mart or Target or chain restaurants like McDonald's or Starbucks. Could you make an argument that these entities have continuous and substantial contacts with any given state? The Court was likely considering the national impact of the test it was creating and the test it was significantly altering.

The Court would be very unlikely to hold that the trial court has specific personal jurisdiction over Daimler AG. Daimler had few if any contacts with California. Daimler AG is a German company that does business through independent distributors. The distributors arguably have contacts with California, not the parent company. The event that is the subject of the lawsuit occurred in Argentina. Even if Daimler AG had contacts with California, it is hard to see how the lawsuit would arise out those contacts.

Daimler AG v. Bauman: Real Life Applications

1. Under Texas law, general partnerships can be formed by an agreement of the partners. There is no filing requirement. Attorneys Robert Davis and his son, Robert Davis, Jr., decide to form a law firm called Davis & Davis. It is a general partnership under Texas law. Their main (and only) office is in Houston, Texas. Where is Davis & Davis subject to general personal jurisdiction? Explain your answer.

2. Assume that the facts of *Perkins v. Benguet Consolidated Mining Co.* described in *Bauman* occurred after the *Bauman* case was decided. Recall that the defendant

mining company was a Philippine corporation with all of its operations in the Philippines. After the Japanese invasion, the president relocated temporarily to Ohio and conducted there what little business the mining company had during World War II. What arguments could you make that the defendant mining company is subject to general personal jurisdiction in the state of Ohio, even after *Bauman*?

3. Paul has lived his entire life in Kansas. After graduating from college in Kansas, Paul joined an engineering firm in Kansas. After a couple of years, Paul decided to get a one-year master's degree from MIT to further his career. Paul packed his belongings in a moving van and drove to Boston, though he plans to return to Kansas after he graduates. Paul's former landlord in Kansas sues Paul in state court in Boston, claiming that Paul failed to pay his last month's rent when he moved to Boston. Does the court in Boston, Massachusetts have personal jurisdiction over Paul? Why or why not?

4. Aircraft Corp. builds airplanes and sells them to all the major airlines. Aircraft Corp. is incorporated in Washington, has its only manufacturing plant in Seattle, Washington, and has always had its corporate headquarters in Seattle. All of Aircraft Corp.'s corporate officers work in Seattle, Washington, where they make high-level decisions about Aircraft Corp.'s business. Aircraft Corp. decides to move its corporate headquarters to Chicago, Illinois and makes a press announcement to that effect, although the move will not happen for five years. Can a court in Washington exercise general personal jurisdiction over Aircraft Corp. before the move? Can a court in Illinois exercise general personal jurisdiction over Aircraft Corp. before the move? Does it matter if the claim is one regarding defective manufacturing of airplanes or one regarding corporate officer wrongdoing? Explain your answers.

---

1. Defendants Are Subject to General Personal Jurisdiction Where They Are Considered Essentially at Home

Natural persons and entities are subject to general personal jurisdiction where they are considered to be "at home." As the Court stated:

> "For an individual, the paradigm forum for the exercise of general jurisdiction is the individual's domicile; for a corporation, it is an equivalent place, one in which the corporation is fairly regarded as at home." With respect to a corporation, the place of incorporation and principal place of business are "paradig[m] . . . bases for general jurisdiction." Those affiliations have the virtue of being unique — that is, each ordinarily indicates only one place — as well as easily ascertainable. These bases afford plaintiffs recourse to at least one clear and certain forum in which a corporate defendant may be sued on any and all claims.
>
> Goodyear did not hold that a corporation may be subject to general jurisdiction only in a forum where it is incorporated or has its principal place of business; it simply typed those places paradigm all-purpose forums.

Bauman, 123 S. Ct. at 760.

Individuals Are at Home Where They Are Domiciled

For individuals, the test for whether an individual is "at home," in the general personal jurisdiction sense, turns on where the individual is domiciled. *See Milliken v. Meyer*, 311 U.S. 457, 462 (1940). The test for where an individual is domiciled is the same test from Chapter 3, which explained domicile of individuals for diversity of citizenship subject matter jurisdiction. Recall that a person is domiciled in the state in which he or she resides with the intent to remain indefinitely. The other details of the domicile rule from diversity subject matter jurisdiction apply as well: For example, a person can have only one domicile at a time, does not lose her domicile until she establishes a new one, and the person must both physically reside in the state and have the right kind of intent (to remain indefinitely) before a person is domiciled in the forum state.

In Most Cases, Entities Are Considered Essentially at Home in Their State of Formation and the State of Their Principal Place of Business

For entities, the question is a little more uncertain, although *Bauman* has substantially simplified nearly all general personal jurisdiction questions. The question for general personal jurisdiction over entities is: Where are they considered essentially at home? As we have also seen from diversity of citizenship subject matter jurisdiction, entities come in many varieties: corporations, LLCs (limited liability companies), partnerships, unions, and many others. Unlike in the diversity of citizenship subject matter jurisdiction context, corporations and unincorporated entities like LLCs are not treated differently. For general personal jurisdiction purposes, they are treated the same.[1] One of the places the Court considers a prime example of where an entity is considered essentially at home is the state under whose laws the entity was formed. Some types of entities have formation requirements under state law. For example, corporations must be incorporated, which often requires filing specific documents with the state and paying fees. LLCs are often similarly created by filing documents with the state and paying fees. Other entities may not have filing requirements. How do you determine whether an entity is one that requires formation documents? State law will answer that question. It will often be a simple matter to determine where an entity's formation documents have been filed — often the state's secretary of state's office. If the entity is required to file documents to come into existence, that fact will tell you at least one state in which the entity is subject to general personal jurisdiction.

---

[1] It is not immediately clear from the *Daimler* opinion that all entities — whether corporations or unincorporated associations — should be subject to the same test for being "essentially at home," particularly when they are treated differently for other purposes like subject matter jurisdiction. For a well-reasoned, extended discussion of why all types of entities are treated the same for purposes of general personal jurisdiction, see John P. Lenich, *A Simple Question That Isn't So Simple: Where Do Entities Reside for Federal Venue Purposes?*, 84 Miss. L.J. 253 (2015) ("The Court in *Daimler* held that MBUSA was not subject to general personal jurisdiction in California because it was not incorporated there and did not have its principal place of business there. MBUSA, however, is not a corporation. It is instead a Delaware limited liability company. The Court must have known that. At the beginning of its opinion, the Court stated the entity's name as 'Mercedes-Benz USA, LLC.' The Court also described the entity as a 'limited liability corporation' that was incorporated in Delaware").

The other prime example of where an entity is considered essentially at home is the state in which the entity has its principal place of business. Also like diversity of citizenship subject matter jurisdiction, the principal place of business test is the same. Where do the entity's decision-makers make high-level decisions directing and controlling the entity's affairs? Once again, it does not matter whether the entity is a corporation or an unincorporated association. Each entity, whether a corporation, LLC, partnership, union, or other type of entity will almost certainly have a principal place of business. This is a second state in which the entity is subject to general personal jurisdiction. As a result, unlike individuals, an entity may be subject to general personal jurisdiction in more than one state (much like how corporations may be citizens of more than one state for diversity of citizenship purposes). Of course, an entity may be formed under the laws of one state and have its principal place of business in that same state. Thus, it would be subject to general personal jurisdiction in that single state.

The Court left open the possibility that the connection between an entity defendant and the forum state is strong enough that the defendant should be considered "essentially at home" somewhere besides its state of formation and its principal place of business. At the same time, under the *Daimler* test, an entity will rarely if ever be "at home" in more than two states. *See BNSF Ry. Co. v. Tyrrell*, 137 S. Ct. 1549 (2017)("[I]t is virtually inconceivable that [large multistate or multinational corporations] will ever be subject to general jurisdiction in any location other than their principal places of business or of incorporation.")(SOTOMAYOR, J., dissenting). Consider, also, that the Supreme Court has found general personal jurisdiction to be satisfied in only one other case: *Perkins*. That case presented unusual circumstances. The fact that World War II caused mining operations to cease and the company president to flee to the United States certainly qualifies as extenuating circumstances. If the mining company conducted any business, it was in Ohio, despite the fact that the corporate headquarters of the company might ordinarily be considered to be in the Philippines. Thus, even after *Daimler*, the facts of *Perkins* likely result in an Ohio court properly exercising general personal jurisdiction over the mining company, because its principal place of business was in Ohio at the time the suit was filed.

Chapter Summary

- General personal jurisdiction does not require a connection between the claim and the defendant's activities in the forum state. Unlike specific personal jurisdiction, general personal jurisdiction focuses on the relationship between the defendant and the forum.

- General personal jurisdiction requires a very strong connection between the defendant and the forum. The defendant must be considered essentially at home in the forum state.

- Individuals are "essentially at home" and therefore subject to general personal jurisdiction in the state in which they are domiciled. The domicile test is the same for both diversity of citizenship subject matter jurisdiction and general personal jurisdiction.

■ Entities are subject to general personal jurisdiction where they are considered essentially at home. An entity is most likely subject to general personal jurisdiction in no more than two states: the state in which the entity was formed and the state in which the entity maintains its principal place of business. The principal place of business test is the same for diversity of citizenship subject matter jurisdiction and general personal jurisdiction. An entity's principal place of business is where the entity's decision-makers (e.g., officers, managers, partners, etc.) make high-level decisions about the entity's affairs.

Applying the Concepts

1. An individual, born and raised in Virginia, is still in high school and a minor. She has never been outside Virginia but she said she wants to move to California when she graduates in three months. She wants to pursue an acting career and has found an apartment in Hollywood and signed a lease, co-signed by her parents. Courts located in which state or states may properly exercise general personal jurisdiction over the high school student? Explain your answer.

2. An airplane manufactured by AirCo., a Delaware corporation with its manufacturing facilities and corporate headquarters in China, crashed in the Andes mountains in Chile. Three U.S. citizens on board were killed in the crash. The mother of one of the U.S. citizen victims wants to sue AirCo. in the United States for the death of her son because AirCo.'s plane was defectively manufactured. Can any court located in the United States properly exercise personal jurisdiction over AirCo.? If so, which state or states and why?

Civil Procedure in Practice

1. You are an associate at a New York law firm. Deutsche Products Aktiengesellschaft (DPAG), a company formed under the laws of Germany with its only offices in Munich, seeks your advice on how to structure its business affairs. It wants to sell industrial turbines to customers in the United States, but it is concerned with the tort liability system in the United States. DPAG's general counsel asks you whether it should form a separate corporation in the United States or a separate corporation in Germany to distribute its turbines. Assuming the general counsel is only worried about DPAG being sued in the United States for possible torts, how would you advise the general counsel?

2. You are a recent law graduate and you open your own practice in Houston, Texas. Your very first client walks in the door. He was crossing Main Street in

downtown Oklahoma City, Oklahoma when a driver hit him. The driver is life-long Texas resident who was just passing through Oklahoma on his way to Kansas. The pedestrian is a life-long Oklahoma resident, who just moved to Houston after the accident and has no plans to leave. Your client wants to sue the driver, but does not want to go back to Oklahoma to do so. How would you advise your very first client?

Physical Presence and Consent as Bases for Personal Jurisdiction

This chapter explains some alternative circumstances in which a court may be able to exercise personal jurisdiction over a defendant. Chapter 6 described the history of personal jurisdiction and how formerly a court could compel only those defendants who were present in the forum state to appear and defend themselves. Even after the revolution of *International Shoe*, one historical basis remains from the concept of presence described in *Pennoyer*: A court may exercise personal jurisdiction consistent with the Due Process Clause over a person who is personally served with notice of the lawsuit while voluntarily present in the forum state (even without any other connection to that state). Despite the evolution of personal jurisdiction toward a doctrine based on a defendant's contacts or connections to the forum state, this basis for personal jurisdiction remains viable. Chapter 6 also introduced the concept that personal jurisdiction is a personal right of the defendant that can be waived. The defendant may choose to consent to personal jurisdiction — either before or after a dispute arises. The defendant may also unintentionally waive an objection to personal jurisdiction. In short, all three of these bases, (1) in-state service, (2) consent, and (3) waiver, are valid alternatives to establish personal jurisdiction over a defendant. Importantly, if any of these alternative bases for personal jurisdiction is satisfied, the court will *not* engage in the minimum

Key Concepts

- Know that a person is subject to personal jurisdiction in the forum state when that person is served with the summons and complaint while voluntarily present in the forum state
- Know that a person can consent to personal jurisdiction either before or after a suit is filed or waive a valid objection to personal jurisdiction
- Know that establishing personal jurisdiction based on physical presence or consent is independent from the specific or general personal jurisdiction tests explained in Chapters 7 and 8

contacts analysis from Chapter 7 or the essentially-at-home analysis from Chapter 8. In other words, the three methods described in this chapter are independent alternatives to establish personal jurisdiction over a defendant.

A. WHAT IS LEFT FROM *PENNOYER*?

1. *In Rem* and *Quasi in Rem* Jurisdiction?

As Chapter 6 explained, *Pennoyer*'s central holding — that a state can exercise jurisdiction over only those persons and things within that state — is no longer good law. However, *International Shoe* did not resolve two categories of jurisdiction discussed in *Pennoyer*, both of which seemed to remain viable. The first category, briefly described in Chapter 6, focuses on a defendant's property as the basis for jurisdiction, generally classified as **in rem** (or **quasi in rem**) jurisdiction. Both types of *in rem* jurisdiction used property located within the forum state as the basis to require the person who owned the property to appear and defend the lawsuit. The property acted as a kind of leverage. The dispute did not necessarily have to center on ownership in the property. In fact, the dispute could be about a completely unrelated matter for *quasi in rem* jurisdiction. The property also served as a resource to satisfy any judgment that resulted from the dispute. The second question left open was whether a nonresident who was personally served with process while present in the forum state — even temporarily — could be properly subjected to the court's personal jurisdiction. The next two cases deal with these questions.

The Court's opinion in *Shaffer v. Heitner* answered the first question. The idea that a court could exercise jurisdiction over a person's property located in the state, but was not in reality exercising jurisdiction *over the person* who was required to defend the action in the forum state, was a fiction the Court could no longer overlook:

> The fiction that an assertion of jurisdiction over property is anything but an assertion of jurisdiction over the owner of the property supports an ancient form without substantial modern justification. Its continued acceptance would serve only to allow state-court jurisdiction that is fundamentally unfair to the defendant.
>
> We therefore conclude that *all assertions of state-court jurisdiction* must be evaluated according to the standards set forth in International Shoe and its progeny.

Shaffer v. Heitner, 433 U.S. 186, 212 (1977) (emphasis added). While owning property in the forum state certainly remains relevant (it is the property owner's contact with the forum state and might even be the property where the defendant is domiciled or "essentially at home" for general personal jurisdiction purposes), the Court no longer considered owning an interest in property in the forum state sufficient for exercising authority over the defendant. Just as *International Shoe* and the specific personal jurisdiction cases that follow it have repeatedly held, the defendant must have purposeful contacts with the forum state, the suit must arise out of or be connected with those contacts, and the exercise of jurisdiction must be fair and reasonable, using the factors detailed in *World-Wide Volkswagen* and *Asahi*.

2. Transient Presence, Also Known as "Tag" Jurisdiction?

This last statement from *Shaffer* is key: "We therefore conclude that all assertions of state-court jurisdiction must be evaluated according to the standards set forth in *International Shoe* and its progeny." It sets up the problem in the next case. When the Court said "all assertions" of personal jurisdiction must be evaluated using a minimum contacts analysis, did the Court truly mean "all"? The next case answers the question of when nonresident defendants who are only temporarily in the forum state may be subject to personal jurisdiction.

Case Preview

Burnham v. Superior Court of California, County of Marin

As you read *Burnham v. Superior Court of California, County of Marin*, consider the following questions:

1. Does Mr. Burnham's temporary presence in the forum state justify personal jurisdiction over him?
2. Can you count votes to get to a majority rule? If so, what is the rule and what is the rationale?
3. Why was Mr. Burnham in the forum state? Does it matter why he was there?
4. Given the contacts Mr. Burnham had with the forum state, would a court be able to exercise specific personal jurisdiction based on the minimum contacts test over Mr. Burnham? How does the Court deal with its decision in *Shaffer*?

Burnham v. Superior Court of California, County of Marin
495 U.S. 604 (1990)

Justice SCALIA announced the judgment of the Court and delivered an opinion in which THE CHIEF JUSTICE and Justice KENNEDY join, and in which Justice WHITE joins with respect to Parts I, II–A, II–B, and II–C.

The question presented is whether the Due Process Clause of the Fourteenth Amendment denies California courts jurisdiction over a nonresident, who was personally served with process while temporarily in that State, in a suit unrelated to his activities in the State.

I ᴌ

Petitioner Dennis Burnham married Francie Burnham in 1976 in West Virginia. In 1977 the couple moved to New Jersey, where their two children were born. In July 1987 the Burnhams decided to separate. They agreed that Mrs. Burnham, who intended to move to California, would take custody of the children. Shortly before

Mrs. Burnham departed for California that same month, she and petitioner agreed that she would file for divorce on grounds of "irreconcilable differences."

In October 1987, petitioner filed for divorce in New Jersey state court on grounds of "desertion." Petitioner did not, however, obtain an issuance of summons against his wife and did not attempt to serve her with process. Mrs. Burnham, after unsuccessfully demanding that petitioner adhere to their prior agreement to submit to an "irreconcilable differences" divorce, brought suit for divorce in California state court in early January 1988.

In late January, petitioner visited southern California on business, after which he went north to visit his children in the San Francisco Bay area, where his wife resided. He took the older child to San Francisco for the weekend. Upon returning the child to Mrs. Burnham's home on January 24, 1988, petitioner was served with a California court summons and a copy of Mrs. Burnham's divorce petition. He then returned to New Jersey.

Later that year, petitioner made a special appearance in the California Superior Court, moving to quash the service of process on the ground that the court lacked personal jurisdiction over him because his only contacts with California were a few short visits to the State for the purposes of conducting business and visiting his children. The Superior Court denied the motion, and the California Court of Appeal denied mandamus relief, rejecting petitioner's contention that the Due Process Clause prohibited California courts from asserting jurisdiction over him because he lacked "minimum contacts" with the State. The court held it to be "a valid jurisdictional predicate for in personam jurisdiction" that the "defendant [was] present in the forum state and personally served with process." We granted certiorari.

II

A

The proposition that the judgment of a court lacking jurisdiction is void traces back to the English Year Books. . . . In Pennoyer v. Neff, we announced that the judgment of a court lacking personal jurisdiction violated the Due Process Clause of the Fourteenth Amendment as well.

To determine whether the assertion of personal jurisdiction is consistent with due process, we have long relied on the principles traditionally followed by American courts in marking out the territorial limits of each State's authority. That criterion was first announced in Pennoyer v. Neff, supra, in which we stated that due process "mean[s] a course of legal proceedings according to those rules and principles which have been established in our systems of jurisprudence for the protection and enforcement of private rights," id., at 733, including the "well-established principles of public law respecting the jurisdiction of an independent State over persons and property," id., at 722. In what has become the classic expression of the criterion, we said in International Shoe Co. v. Washington, that a state court's assertion of personal jurisdiction satisfies the Due Process Clause if it does not violate " 'traditional notions of fair play and substantial justice.' " Id., at 316. Since International Shoe, we have only been called upon to decide whether these "traditional notions" permit States to exercise jurisdiction over absent defendants in a manner that deviates from the rules of jurisdiction applied in the 19th century. We have held such deviations permissible, but only with respect to suits arising out of the absent defendant's contacts with the State. The question we must decide today is whether due process requires a similar connection between the litigation and the defendant's contacts with the State in cases where the defendant is physically present in the State at the time process is served upon him.

B 4

Among the most firmly established principles of personal jurisdiction in American tradition is that the courts of a State have jurisdiction over nonresidents who are physically present in the State. The view developed early that each State had the power to hale before its courts any individual who could be found within its borders, and that once having acquired jurisdiction over such a person by properly serving him with process, the State could retain jurisdiction to enter judgment against him, no matter how fleeting his visit. . . .

[J]udging by the evidence of contemporaneous or near-contemporaneous decisions, one must conclude that [this long-standing view] was shared by American courts at the crucial time for present purposes: 1868, when the Fourteenth Amendment was adopted. . . .

This American jurisdictional practice is, moreover, not merely old; it is continuing. It remains the practice of, not only a substantial number of the States, but as far as we are aware all the States and the Federal Government — if one disregards (as one must for this purpose) the few opinions since 1978 that have erroneously said, on grounds similar to those that petitioner presses here, that this Court's due process decisions render the practice unconstitutional. We do not know of a single state or federal statute, or a single judicial decision resting upon state law, that has abandoned in-state service as a basis of jurisdiction. Many recent cases reaffirm it.

C 4

Despite this formidable body of precedent, petitioner contends, in reliance on our decisions applying the International Shoe standard, that in the absence of "continuous and systematic" contacts with the forum, see n.1, supra, a nonresident defendant can be subjected to judgment only as to matters that arise out of or relate to his contacts with the forum. This argument rests on a thorough misunderstanding of our cases.

The view of most courts in the 19th century was that a court simply could not exercise in personam jurisdiction over a nonresident who had not been personally served with process in the forum. Pennoyer v. Neff, while renowned for its statement of the principle that the Fourteenth Amendment prohibits such an exercise of jurisdiction, in fact set that forth only as dictum and decided the case (which involved a judgment rendered more than two years before the Fourteenth Amendment's ratification) under "well-established principles of public law." Those principles, embodied in the Due Process Clause, required (we said) that when proceedings "involv[e] merely a determination of the personal liability of the defendant, he must be brought within [the court's] jurisdiction by service of process within the State, or his voluntary appearance." Id., at 733. We invoked that rule in a series of subsequent cases, as either a matter of due process or a "fundamental principl[e] of jurisprudence."

* * *

Nothing in International Shoe or the cases that have followed it, however, offers support for the very different proposition petitioner seeks to establish today: that a defendant's presence in the forum is not only unnecessary to validate novel, nontraditional assertions of jurisdiction, but is itself no longer sufficient to establish jurisdiction. That proposition is unfaithful to both elementary logic and the foundations of our due process jurisprudence. . . .

The short of the matter is that jurisdiction based on physical presence alone constitutes due process because it is one of the continuing traditions of our legal system that define the due process standard of "traditional notions of fair play and substantial justice." That standard was developed by analogy to "physical presence," and it would be perverse to say it could now be turned against that touchstone of jurisdiction.

D

Petitioner's strongest argument, though we ultimately reject it, relies upon our decision in Shaffer v. Heitner. . . .

It goes too far to say, as petitioner contends, that Shaffer compels the conclusion that a State lacks jurisdiction over an individual unless the litigation arises out of his activities in the State. Shaffer, like International Shoe, involved jurisdiction over an absent defendant, and it stands for nothing more than the proposition that when the "minimum contact" that is a substitute for physical presence consists of property ownership it must, like other minimum contacts, be related to the litigation. Petitioner wrenches out of its context our statement in Shaffer that "all assertions of state-court jurisdiction must be evaluated according to the standards set forth in International Shoe and its progeny." When read together with the two sentences that preceded it, the meaning of this statement becomes clear:

> The fiction that an assertion of jurisdiction over property is anything but an assertion of jurisdiction over the owner of the property supports an ancient form without substantial modern justification. Its continued acceptance would serve only to allow state-court jurisdiction that is fundamentally unfair to the defendant.
>
> We therefore conclude that all assertions of state-court jurisdiction must be evaluated according to the standards set forth in International Shoe and its progeny.

Shaffer was saying, in other words, not that all bases for the assertion of in personam jurisdiction (including, presumably, in-state service) must be treated alike and subjected to the "minimum contacts" analysis of International Shoe; but rather that quasi in rem jurisdiction, that fictional "ancient form," and in personam jurisdiction, are really one and the same and must be treated alike — leading to the conclusion that quasi in rem jurisdiction, i.e., that form of in personam jurisdiction based upon a "property ownership" contact and by definition unaccompanied by personal, in-state service, must satisfy the litigation-relatedness requirement of International Shoe. . . .

III

A few words in response to Justice BRENNAN's opinion concurring in the judgment: It insists that we apply "contemporary notions of due process" to determine the constitutionality of California's assertion of jurisdiction. But our analysis today comports with that prescription, at least if we give it the only sense allowed by our precedents. The "contemporary notions of due process" applicable to personal jurisdiction are the enduring "traditional notions of fair play and substantial justice" established as the test by International Shoe. By its very language, that test is satisfied if a state court adheres to jurisdictional rules that are generally applied and have always been applied in the United States.

But the concurrence's proposed standard of "contemporary notions of due process" requires more: It measures state-court jurisdiction not only against traditional doctrines in this country, including current state-court practice, but also against each Justice's subjective assessment of what is fair and just. Authority for that seductive standard is not to be found in any of our personal jurisdiction cases. It is, indeed, an outright break with the test of "traditional notions of fair play and substantial justice," which would have to be reformulated "our notions of fair play and substantial justice."

The subjectivity, and hence inadequacy, of this approach becomes apparent when the concurrence tries to explain why the assertion of jurisdiction in the present case meets its standard of continuing-American-tradition-plus-innate-fairness. Justice BRENNAN lists the "benefits" Mr. Burnham derived from the State of California — the fact that, during the few days he was there, "[h]is health and safety [were] guaranteed by the State's police, fire, and emergency medical services; he [was] free to travel on the State's roads and waterways; he likely enjoy[ed] the fruits of the State's economy." Three days' worth of these benefits strike us as powerfully inadequate to establish, as an abstract matter, that it is "fair" for California to decree the ownership of all Mr. Burnham's worldly goods acquired during the 10 years of his marriage, and the custody over his children. We daresay a contractual exchange swapping those benefits for that power would not survive the "unconscionability" provision of the Uniform Commercial Code. Even less persuasive are the other "fairness" factors alluded to by Justice BRENNAN. It would create "an asymmetry," we are told, if Burnham were permitted (as he is) to appear in California courts as a plaintiff, but were not compelled to appear in California courts as defendant; and travel being as easy as it is nowadays, and modern procedural devices being so convenient, it is no great hardship to appear in California courts. The problem with these assertions is that they justify the exercise of jurisdiction over everyone, whether or not he ever comes to California. The only "fairness" elements setting Mr. Burnham apart from the rest of the world are the three days' "benefits" referred to above — and even those, do not set him apart from many other people who have enjoyed three days in the Golden State (savoring the fruits of its economy, the availability of its roads and police services) but who were fortunate enough not to be served with process while they were there and thus are not (simply by reason of that savoring) subject to the general jurisdiction of California's courts. In other words, even if one agreed with Justice BRENNAN's conception of an equitable bargain, the "benefits" we have been discussing would explain why it is "fair" to assert general jurisdiction over Burnham-returned-to-New-Jersey-after-service only at the expense of proving that it is also "fair" to assert general jurisdiction over Burnham-returned-to-New-Jersey-without-service — which we know does not conform with "contemporary notions of due process."

There is, we must acknowledge, one factor mentioned by Justice BRENNAN that both relates distinctively to the assertion of jurisdiction on the basis of personal in-state service and is fully persuasive — namely, the fact that a defendant voluntarily present in a particular State has a "reasonable expectatio[n]" that he is subject to suit there. By formulating it as a "reasonable expectation" Justice BRENNAN makes that seem like a "fairness" factor; but in reality, of course, it is just tradition masquerading as "fairness." The only reason for charging Mr. Burnham with the reasonable expectation of being subject to suit is that the States of the Union assert adjudicatory jurisdiction over the person, and have always asserted adjudicatory jurisdiction over the person, by serving him with process during his temporary physical presence in their territory. . . .

Nothing we say today prevents individual States from limiting or entirely abandoning the in-state-service basis of jurisdiction. And nothing prevents an overwhelming majority of them from doing so, with the consequence that the "traditional notions of fairness" that this Court applies may change. But the States have overwhelmingly declined to adopt such limitation or abandonment, evidently not considering it to be progress. . . .

Because the Due Process Clause does not prohibit the California courts from exercising jurisdiction over petitioner based on the fact of in-state service of process, the judgment is

Affirmed.

Justice WHITE, concurring in part and concurring in the judgment.

I join Parts I, II–A, II–B, and II–C of Justice SCALIA's opinion and concur in the judgment of affirmance. The rule allowing jurisdiction to be obtained over a nonresident by personal service in the forum State, without more, has been and is so widely accepted throughout this country that I could not possibly strike it down, either on its face or as applied in this case, on the ground that it denies due process of law guaranteed by the Fourteenth Amendment. Although the Court has the authority under the Amendment to examine even traditionally accepted procedures and declare them invalid, there has been no showing here or elsewhere that as a general proposition the rule is so arbitrary and lacking in common sense in so many instances that it should be held violative of due process in every case. . . . Here, personal service in California, without more, is enough, and I agree that the judgment should be affirmed.

Justice BRENNAN, with whom Justice MARSHALL, Justice BLACKMUN, and Justice O'CONNOR join, concurring in the judgment.

I agree with Justice SCALIA that the Due Process Clause of the Fourteenth Amendment generally permits a state court to exercise jurisdiction over a defendant if he is served with process while voluntarily present in the forum State. I do not perceive the need, however, to decide that a jurisdictional rule that "'has been immemorially the actual law of the land,'" automatically comports with due process simply by virtue of its "pedigree." Although I agree that history is an important factor in establishing whether a jurisdictional rule satisfies due process requirements, I cannot agree that it is the only factor such that all traditional rules of jurisdiction are, ipso facto, forever constitutional. Unlike Justice SCALIA, I would undertake an "independent inquiry into the . . . fairness of the prevailing in-state service rule." I therefore concur only in the judgment. . . .

I believe that the approach adopted by Justice SCALIA's opinion today — reliance solely on historical pedigree — is foreclosed by our decisions in International Shoe Co. v. Washington, and Shaffer v. Heitner. In International Shoe, we held that a state court's assertion of personal jurisdiction does not violate the Due Process Clause if it is consistent with "'traditional notions of fair play and substantial justice.'" In Shaffer, we stated that "all assertions of state-court jurisdiction must be evaluated according to the standards set forth in International Shoe and its progeny." The critical insight of Shaffer is that all rules of jurisdiction, even ancient ones, must satisfy contemporary notions of due process. No longer were we content to limit our jurisdictional analysis to pronouncements that "[t]he foundation of jurisdiction is physical power," McDonald v. Mabee, and that "every State possesses exclusive jurisdiction and sovereignty over persons and property within its territory." Pennoyer v. Neff. While acknowledging that "history must be considered as supporting the proposition that jurisdiction based solely on the presence of property satisfie[d] the demands of due process," we found that this factor could not be "decisive." We recognized that "'[t]raditional notions of fair play and substantial justice' can be as readily offended by the perpetuation of ancient forms that are no longer justified as by the adoption of new procedures that are inconsistent with the basic values of our constitutional heritage." Id. I agree with this approach and continue to believe that "the minimum-contacts analysis developed in International Shoe . . . represents a far more sensible construct for the exercise of state-court jurisdiction than the patchwork of legal and factual fictions that has been generated from the decision in Pennoyer v. Neff." Id.

* * *

II

Tradition, though alone not dispositive, is of course relevant to the question whether the rule of transient jurisdiction is consistent with due process. . . .

I find the historical background relevant because, however murky the jurisprudential origins of transient jurisdiction, the fact that American courts have announced the rule for perhaps a century (first in dicta, more recently in holdings) provides a defendant voluntarily present in a particular State today "clear notice that [he] is subject to suit" in the forum. World–Wide Volkswagen Corp. v. Woodson. . . . [O]ur common understanding now, fortified by a century of judicial practice, is that jurisdiction is often a function of geography. The transient rule is consistent with reasonable expectations and is entitled to a strong presumption that it comports with due process. "If I visit another State, . . . I knowingly assume some risk that the State will exercise its power over my property or my person while there. My contact with the State, though minimal, gives rise to predictable risks." Shaffer (STEVENS, J., concurring in judgment); see also Burger King Corp. v. Rudzewicz ("Territorial presence frequently will enhance a potential defendant's affiliation with a State and reinforce the reasonable foreseeability of suit there"). Thus, proposed revisions to the Restatement (Second) of Conflict of Laws §28, p. 39 (1986), provide that "[a] state has power to exercise judicial jurisdiction over an individual who is present within its territory unless the individual's relationship to the state is so attenuated as to make the exercise of such jurisdiction unreasonable."

By visiting the forum State, a transient defendant actually "avail[s]" himself, *Burger King*, of significant benefits provided by the State. His health and safety are guaranteed by the State's police, fire, and emergency medical services; he is free to travel on the State's roads and waterways; he likely enjoys the fruits of the State's economy as well. Moreover, the Privileges and Immunities Clause of Article IV prevents a state government from discriminating against a transient defendant by denying him the protections of its law or the right of access to its courts. Subject only to the doctrine of forum non conveniens, an out-of-state plaintiff may use state courts in all circumstances in which those courts would be available to state citizens. Without transient jurisdiction, an asymmetry would arise: A transient would have the full benefit of the power of the forum State's courts as a plaintiff while retaining immunity from their authority as a defendant.

The potential burdens on a transient defendant are slight. "'[M]odern transportation and communications have made it much less burdensome for a party sued to defend himself'" in a State outside his place of residence. *Burger King,* quoting McGee v. International Life Ins. Co. That the defendant has already journeyed at least once before to the forum—as evidenced by the fact that he was served with process there—is an indication that suit in the forum likely would not be prohibitively inconvenient. Finally, any burdens that do arise can be ameliorated by a variety of procedural devices. For these reasons, as a rule the exercise of personal jurisdiction over a defendant based on his voluntary presence in the forum will satisfy the requirements of due process.

In this case, it is undisputed that petitioner was served with process while voluntarily and knowingly in the State of California. I therefore concur in the judgment.

Justice STEVENS, concurring in the judgment.

As I explained in my separate writing, I did not join the Court's opinion in Shaffer v. Heitner, because I was concerned by its unnecessarily broad reach. The same concern prevents me from joining either Justice SCALIA's or Justice BRENNAN's opinion in this case. For me, it is sufficient to note that the historical evidence and consensus identified by Justice SCALIA, the considerations of fairness identified by Justice BRENNAN, and the common sense displayed by Justice WHITE, all combine to demonstrate that this is, indeed, a very easy case. Accordingly, I agree that the judgment should be affirmed.

Post-Case Follow-Up

Even Mr. Burnham's temporary visit to California was sufficient for the court to exercise personal jurisdiction over him. The key is that Mr. Burnham was personally served with notice of the lawsuit while he was voluntarily present in the forum state. This is the source of the terms **transient presence jurisdiction** or "**tag**" **jurisdiction.**

Somewhat like the opinion in *Asahi*, Justice Scalia is not writing for a majority of the Court. Note that his opinion garnered only three votes for most of the opinion; Justice White declined to join Part III. However, unlike *Asahi*, the Court is not as fractured. The four concurring Justices stated: "I agree with Justice SCALIA that the Due Process Clause of the Fourteenth Amendment *generally permits a state court to exercise jurisdiction over a defendant if he is served with process while voluntarily present in the forum State.*" Thus, eight Justices explicitly approved of the rule.

Justice Scalia's rationale seems to be that at the time the Fourteenth Amendment with its Due Process Clause was adopted, in-state service was the norm. As a result, the Fourteenth Amendment should be read to permit personal jurisdiction using this method. Justice Scalia also seems to believe that this mode of establishing personal jurisdiction is so well rooted in history that it is by its nature consistent with traditional notions of fair play and substantial justice. Thus, the Court need not analyze the fairness factors from Chapter 7, as laid out in *World-Wide Volkswagen* and *Asahi*.

The difference between Justice White's and Justice Brennan's concurrences on the one hand and Justice Scalia's opinion on the other seems to lie in this last point. The concurring Justices seem unwilling to say that the Court will never question the fairness of this rule, despite its historical roots. In practice, however, this method of service seems likely to survive. In the words of Justice Stevens, "this is, indeed, a very easy case."

Mr. Burnham was in the forum state for two reasons: He originally traveled there on business. Then he went to see his children, who lived there with their mother. He was served with process after returning his older child after a weekend trip. The Court does state that it matters why Mr. Burnham was in the state. Various opinions refer to the fact that the defendant must be *voluntarily* in the forum state. In other words, if Mr. Burnham had been lured or tricked into coming to California so that he could be served there, a court is likely to hold that personal jurisdiction is lacking.

Given Mr. Burnham's contacts with the forum state — a few trips for business and for visiting his children — the court would probably not have specific personal jurisdiction over Mr. Burnham. Recall that this was a suit for divorce. Although Mr. Burnham did have contacts with California, the divorce suit did not arise out of his contacts with California. His visits to his children bear some relationship to the lawsuit, but the suit would likely have been filed whether he visited California or not. This last point is an important one. In this respect, it does not matter why Mr. Burnham visited California. The court can exercise personal jurisdiction over him, even if his contacts — here, his presence — in the state have nothing to do with the lawsuit. It does not matter if the suit arises out of his contacts with California.

As for *Shaffer*, the Court dealt with the potential inconsistency by stating that there is no inconsistency. *Shaffer* simply called *in rem* jurisdiction what it actually was: exercising jurisdiction over property as a way of exercising jurisdiction over a nonresident (or "absent") defendant. *Burnham*, on the other hand, stands for the proposition that a defendant who is *present* is treated differently. If personally served while voluntarily present in the forum state, the Due Process Clause is satisfied and personal jurisdiction is proper.

Justice Antonin Scalia

Justice Scalia was appointed by President Ronald Reagan and served on the Court from 1986 until his death in 2016. He was known as one of the intellectual leaders of originalism, a theory that focuses on interpreting the Constitution in a way consistent with what the text meant when it was drafted and understood to mean by those who would have read it at the time it was adopted. This theory attempts to identify the original intent or meaning of the words used, which should control how the words are interpreted. Justice Scalia's belief that the Due Process Clause of the Fourteenth Amendment should be interpreted in light of what those words meant in 1868, when the amendment was adopted, is prevalent in *Burnham* and many other opinions he authored in his career.

Justice Antonin Scalia, Collection of the Supreme Court of the United States

Burnham v. Superior Court of California, County of Marin: Real Life Applications

1. You live in Ḳansas and are driving through Nebraska on your way to South Dakota to see Mount Rushmore. You stop for gas in Nebraska and while filling up your gas tank, a man walks up to you. He asks you your name and hands you some papers. When you open the papers, you discover that they consist of a complaint and summons, and the complaint names you as a defendant in a Nebraska state court. You have never been to Nebraska before. Can a court in Nebraska properly exercise personal jurisdiction over you? Why or why not?

2. You are flying from your home in Florida to California on vacation. While in the air over Texas at 30,000 feet, a man sitting next to you on the plane hands you papers and says "you have been served." The papers are a complaint and summons naming you as a defendant in a federal court in Texas. You have never set foot in Texas before. Can a court in Texas properly exercise personal jurisdiction over you? Compare your answer to *Grace v. MacArthur*, 170 F. Supp. 442 (E.D. Ark. 1959). Do you agree or disagree with the court? Why or why not?

3. Assume the same facts as in *Burnham*. This time, however, Mrs. Burnham called her husband and said that if he picked them up, Mr. Burnham could have custody of the children for the summer while they worked out how to get divorced. When Mr. Burnham steps off the plane, he is served in the airport. Can the court in California properly exercise personal jurisdiction over him? Why or why not?

Transient Presence Jurisdiction Does Not Apply to Most Entities

Serving a corporate executive while that executive is present in the forum state does not establish personal jurisdiction over the corporation. Just because an officer, employee, member, manager, or other representative of an entity is in the forum state does not mean *the entity* is present in the forum state. *James Dickinson Farm Mortgage Co. v. Harry*, 273 U.S. 119, 122 (1927) ("[j]urisdiction over a corporation of one state cannot be acquired in another state or district in which it has no place of business and is not found, merely by serving process upon an executive officer temporarily therein, even if he is there on business of the company"). This same rule would hold true for other entities like LLCs, LLPs, Professional Corporations, and others. Recall, however, that not all entities are the same. A general partnership usually does not require any special method of formation. As a general rule, general partnerships do not have an existence that is independent of the individual partners. In many cases, service on one of the partners may establish jurisdiction over the partnership. *See, e.g., First American Corp. v. Price Waterhouse LLP*, 154 F.3d 16, 19 (2d Cir. 1998). As Chapter 10 will explain, a state's long arm statute can act as a limit on this method; not all states authorize jurisdiction over a partnership by serving a partner. *See, e.g., Shank/Balfour Beatty, Inc. v. Int'l Brotherhood of Elec. Workers Local 99*, 497 F.3d 83, 94 (1st Cir. 2007).

B. CONSENT AND WAIVER ARE VALID BASES FOR PERSONAL JURISDICTION

1. A Defendant Can Affirmatively Consent to Personal Jurisdiction

A defendant can explicitly consent to personal jurisdiction. Recall that, unlike subject matter jurisdiction, personal jurisdiction is a limit on a court's authority that can be waived. As a result, a defendant may choose to raise the defense — or not — either before or after a dispute arises. A potential defendant can agree ahead of time that he will not object to personal jurisdiction in a particular court or courts. This is known as a **forum selection clause**, which is common in many contracts. The clause is often phrased like this: "The parties agree that any dispute related to this contract must be resolved in a court of competent jurisdiction in the state of California." These clauses are often specific to a particular forum state, but they need not be. The clause could simply state that the parties do not object to personal jurisdiction in a particular forum. These clauses are generally enforceable; a court will likely enforce a term in a contract where the parties have agreed to personal jurisdiction in a particular court or courts. *See, e.g., Carnival Cruise Lines, Inc. v. Shute*, 499 U.S. 585, 597 (1991) (holding that forum selection clause on cruise ship ticket was valid and enforceable). From airplane and cruise ship tickets to "click wrap" agreements on websites, you have likely consented to personal jurisdiction just buy buying a ticket or clicking a box on a website, even though you had no power to negotiate the terms of that clause. Note, however, that the parties cannot agree to resolve their dispute in a court that lacks subject matter jurisdiction.

Even after a dispute has arisen, a defendant can agree not to raise an objection. A defendant may use an otherwise valid personal jurisdiction objection as leverage. For example, a defendant may agree to not object to personal jurisdiction in exchange for the plaintiff choosing a particular court in the forum state. And regardless of whether the defendant has made an agreement, the defendant can simply decide not to raise the objection. He may want to litigate the dispute in the forum court, even if he could validly object.

2. A Defendant Can Impliedly Consent to Personal Jurisdiction

A defendant may also impliedly consent to personal jurisdiction in the forum state. *Hess v. Pawloski*, explained in Chapter 6, is an example of implied consent. In *Hess*, a Massachusetts statute made the registrar the agent to accept service of process for out-of-state drivers for any claims that arose from that person's in-state driving. This case has never been overruled. In fact, in the *Shaffer* case described above, the Court held that exercising jurisdiction over property (here, stock) ostensibly located in Delaware was insufficient to justify jurisdiction over the owner of the stock. As a result, Delaware passed a statute that stated that officers or directors of a Delaware corporation implicitly authorize the corporation's registered agent to accept service of process on the officer's or director's behalf.

3. A Defendant Can Waive His or Her Objection to Personal Jurisdiction

A defendant may also unintentionally waive a valid objection to personal jurisdiction. Courts do not raise objections to personal jurisdiction *sua sponte* (i.e., on their own). It is the defendant's objection to raise or waive. Both state and federal courts often have time limits and specific procedures for raising personal jurisdiction objections. If a defendant misses the deadline, the objection is waived. If a defendant fails to raise the objection properly, the objection is waived. In any event, whether the defendant chooses not to object, fails to object, or fails to object properly, the forum court can validly exercise personal jurisdiction over the defendant.

Finally, a defendant may be found subject to a court's personal jurisdiction as a litigation sanction. In *Insurance Corp. of Ireland v. Compagnie des Bauxites de Guinee*, 456 U.S. 694, 706 (1982), the defendant challenged personal jurisdiction. The court-ordered discovery focused on whether the defendant had contacts with the forum state. The defendant, however, refused to comply with the discovery orders. As a sanction, the court ruled that the defendant waived any personal jurisdiction defense. The Supreme Court affirmed the sanction, concluding that "[b]y submitting to the jurisdiction of the court for the limited purpose of challenging jurisdiction, the defendant agree[d] to abide by that court's determination on the issue of jurisdiction." *Id.*

Chapter Summary

■ A person who is served with process while voluntarily present in the forum state is subject to the forum court's personal jurisdiction. This is commonly referred to as transient presence or "tag" jurisdiction. It does not matter whether the suit is related to the reason the defendant is present in the forum state. The defendant, however, must be voluntarily present in the forum state. A defendant lured into the state for the purposes of service in the state is likely not subject to personal jurisdiction in the forum state.

■ Transient presence jurisdiction does not apply to entities that have a separate existence from their constituent members (e.g., corporations, LLCs, LLPs, etc.). One common exception is a general partnership, which often does not have a separate existence apart from the individual partners.

■ A defendant can consent to personal jurisdiction. Such consent can come before or after a dispute arises. The most common way to consent to personal jurisdiction before a dispute arises is a forum selection clause. Courts usually enforce forum selection clauses.

■ A defendant may impliedly consent to personal jurisdiction. State law may dictate that certain conduct or a certain status subjects a person to jurisdiction in courts located in the forum state.

■ A defendant can waive his objection to personal jurisdiction. A defendant could (1) fail to object before the proper deadline, (2) fail to follow the proper procedures for objecting, or (3) fail to comply with court orders, resulting in waiver of an objection to personal jurisdiction.

Applying the Concepts

1. A driver from Rhode Island intended to drive into Massachusetts, but got lost and ended up in New Hampshire. The driver never intended to travel to New Hampshire. The driver stops at a convenience store and asks for directions. While in the store, a process server serves the driver with notice of a lawsuit naming the driver as a defendant in a lawsuit pending in New Hampshire. Can the court in New Hampshire properly exercise personal jurisdiction over the driver? Does it matter that he was unintentionally in New Hampshire? Explain your answer.

2. The CEO of DrinkCo visited California on her vacation. The CEO lives and works in New York, where DrinkCo has its headquarters and is incorporated. While in California, the CEO is personally served with notice of a lawsuit by several shareholders of DrinkCo claiming she defrauded the company out of large sums of money. The complaint names both the CEO and DrinkCo as defendants. Both the CEO and DrinkCo move to dismiss for lack of personal jurisdiction. How should the court rule? Explain your answer.

3. ABC Co. is a large company that sells water heaters and is based in Pennsylvania. XYZ Co. is a small company that supplies inexpensive rubber O-rings to ABC Co. for use in the water heaters. XYZ Co. supplies all of the O-rings to the manufacturer, Interco, in New York. XYZ Co. has no contacts with or other connections to Pennsylvania. ABC Co. insists that the contract with XYZ Co. includes a forum selection clause stating that all disputes, if any, in connection with or related in any way to their contract must be decided in a court of competent jurisdiction located in Pennsylvania. ABC Co. claims that XYZ Co. supplied defective O-rings and sues XYZ Co. in a state court in Pennsylvania. Can a court in Pennsylvania exercise personal jurisdiction over XYZ Co.? Why or why not?

4. A man receives a summons and complaint naming him as a defendant in a case pending in a state he has no contact with, no connection to, and has never been to — even momentarily. The rules of civil procedure of the state court where the case is pending require that the defendant object to a lack of personal jurisdiction by motion filed within 30 days of service. The defendant answers the lawsuit on the 35th day and includes in his answer his objection to personal jurisdiction. What is the result of the defendant's actions? Explain your answer.

5. Assume the same facts as in question 4 above, except the defendant files a motion to dismiss for lack of personal jurisdiction 21 days after being served. The court orders the defendant to sit for a deposition so that the plaintiff can determine whether the defendant has any connection to the forum state. The defendant refuses and stands on his objection. May the court consider the defendant subject to personal jurisdiction? Why or why not?

Civil Procedure in Practice

1. You are a staffer to a U.S. Congressman. The Congressman is concerned about products imported from countries that do not have the same safety standards as the U.S. In many cases, these imported products come from companies with no direct contacts with the U.S. As a result, U.S. consumers who are harmed often cannot establish personal jurisdiction over the product manufacturer. The Congressman has asked for your help in drafting legislation that would make it possible to sue foreign companies whose products end up causing harm to consumers in the United States. What would your draft legislation look like?

2. You are a law clerk to a state trial court judge. The judge is faced with a motion to dismiss for lack of personal jurisdiction brought by a defendant who is in prison in Utah. The defendant was personally served with notice of the suit

while in prison in Utah. The suit names the defendant in a lawsuit pending in Utah. The defendant argues that he was domiciled in Oregon when he was sentenced and assigned to a prison and has no contacts or other connections to Utah, other than the fact he is incarcerated there. He argues that transient presence or "tag" jurisdiction does not apply because he is not voluntarily within the forum state. How would you advise your judge to decide the motion?

State Long Arm Statutes

This chapter explains state long arm statutes, another limit on a court's exercise of personal jurisdiction. Chapters 6 to 9 explained how the Constitution — specifically the Due Process Clauses of the Fifth and Fourteenth Amendments — sets limits on when a court may require a defendant to appear and defend himself in the forum court. This chapter explains a different kind of limit. Unlike the constitutional limits of due process, this chapter explains that a court must also have statutory authorization to exercise personal jurisdiction. The kinds of statutes legislating this authority are known as **long arm statutes**, because they permit a court to "reach out" and exercise personal jurisdiction over a defendant beyond the forum court's borders. This is an independent limit on personal jurisdiction. In other words, before a court can exercise personal jurisdiction over a defendant, the court must be convinced that the circumstances satisfy both the long arm statute *and* the due process limitations explained in Chapters 6 to 9.

A. STATE LONG ARM STATUTES ARE LIMITED BY DUE PROCESS

The forum court cannot exercise personal jurisdiction unless the forum state's long arm statute is satisfied. The reverse is not true. Just because the forum state's long arm statute is satisfied does not mean the court can exercise personal jurisdiction. State long arm statutes can authorize personal jurisdiction up to the limit of due process. Many long arm statutes do just that. When they do, they are said to reach to the "full limits of due process." State long arm statutes, however, cannot expand a court's ability to exercise personal jurisdiction beyond the limits of due process.

The relationship between long arm statutes and the Constitution for personal jurisdiction is similar to the relationship between the diversity or federal question statutes and the Constitution for subject matter

Key Concepts

- Statutes authorizing the exercise of personal jurisdiction (commonly called long arm statutes)
- When long arm statutes reach to the limit of due process and when they do not
- How to interpret and apply long arm statutes

EXHIBIT 10.1 **Constitutional Due Process and State Long Arm Statutes**

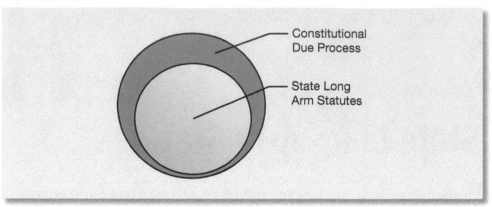

jurisdiction. The visual representation of this relationship shown in Exhibit 10.1 should look familiar. It is similar to the graphic relationship between federal subject matter jurisdiction statutes and the Constitution in Chapters 3 and 4.

The small circle represents the scope of a state long arm statute. The large circle represents the outer limits of when a court can exercise personal jurisdiction consistent with due process. A state is free to draft its long arm statute so that it allows personal jurisdiction any time the Constitution would not forbid it. In other words, the small circle can expand to be as big as — but no bigger than — the larger circle. If a state were to write a long arm statute in such a way that it expanded beyond the limits of due process, a court would either strike the statute down or interpret it to avoid the constitutional conflict.

1. Many State Long Arm Statutes Reach to the Full Limit of Due Process

More than half of the states have long arm statutes that reach to the full limit of due process. Although scholars may disagree as to the precise number, at the time of writing this book, somewhere between 27 and 32 states have adopted long arm statutes that reach to the limit of due process — either explicitly or because the state court has interpreted its state statute to reach to the limit of due process. *See* 4 Charles Alan Wright, Arthur R. Miller & Adam N. Steinman, Federal Practice and Procedure §1068 n.11 (4th ed. 2015) ("Alabama, Arkansas, California, Colorado, Georgia, Indiana, Iowa, Kansas, Kentucky, Louisiana, Maryland, Michigan, Minnesota, Missouri, Nevada, New Jersey, North Dakota, Oregon, Pennsylvania, Puerto Rico, South Carolina, South Dakota, Tennessee, Texas, Utah, Washington, and West Virginia also have enacted long-arm statutes that have been interpreted to assert maximum jurisdiction"); *see also* Douglas D. McFarland, *Dictum Run Wild: How Long-Arm Statutes Extended to the Limits of Due Process*, 84 B.U. L. Rev. 491,

524-31 (2004) (counting 32 states as having explicitly or implicitly extended the state long arm provision's reach to the full extent of due process).

Some states' long arm statutes reach to the limits of due process in a simple, straightforward way. For example, California's long arm statute states: "A court of this state may exercise jurisdiction on any basis not inconsistent with the Constitution of this state or of the United States." Cal. Civ. Proc. Code §410.10 (West 2010). However, even if the statute is more complex, a court may have interpreted the state statute to reach to the limit of due process. For example, Texas permits its courts to exercise personal jurisdiction over persons "doing business" in the state. Texas has several statutory sections that concern long arm jurisdiction. One of them expands on what "doing business" means:

ACTS CONSTITUTING BUSINESS IN THIS STATE

In addition to other acts that may constitute doing business, a nonresident does business in this state if the nonresident:

(1) contracts by mail or otherwise with a Texas resident and either party is to perform the contract in whole or in part in this state;

(2) commits a tort in whole or in part in this state; or

(3) recruits Texas residents, directly or through an intermediary located in this state, for employment inside or outside this state.

Tex. Civ. Prac. & Rem. Code §17.042 (West 2015). Though not as direct as California's approach, Texas has interpreted its long arm statute to reach to the full limit of due process. *See Moki Mac River Expeditions v. Drugg*, 221 S.W.3d 569, 574 (Tex. 2007). When a state's long arm statute reaches to the limits of due process, the two questions collapse into one: Does the court's exercise of personal jurisdiction over this defendant satisfy due process?

2. Some State Long Arm Statutes Do Not Reach to the Limit of Due Process

Some states, on the other hand, have long arm statutes that are more restrictive than due process. In other words, even if, as a constitutional matter, the defendant had sufficient contacts with the forum state, the claim arose from those contacts, and it would be consistent with traditional notions of fair play and substantial justice to require the defendant to appear and defend in the forum state, the state's long arm statute may not be satisfied. For example, New York's statute does not reach to the limits of due process. New York's long arm statute lists activities that can subject a nonresident defendant to personal jurisdiction in a court in New York:

PERSONAL JURISDICTION BY ACTS OF NON-DOMICILIARIES

(a) Acts which are the basis of jurisdiction. As to a cause of action arising from any of the acts enumerated in this section, a court may exercise personal jurisdiction over any non-domiciliary, or his executor or administrator, who in person or through an agent:

1. transacts any business within the state or contracts anywhere to supply goods or services in the state; or

2. commits a tortious act within the state, except as to a cause of action for defamation of character arising from the act; or

3. commits a tortious act without the state causing injury to person or property within the state, except as to a cause of action for defamation of character arising from the act, if he

(i) regularly does or solicits business, or engages in any other persistent course of conduct, or derives substantial revenue from goods used or consumed or services rendered, in the state, or

(ii) expects or should reasonably expect the act to have consequences in the state and derives substantial revenue from interstate or international commerce; or

4. owns, uses or possesses any real property situated within the state.

N.Y. C.P.L.R. §302 (McKinney). Courts often find that, while personal jurisdiction may comport with due process, the facts of the case do not fall within the listed activities in New York's long arm statute. For example, in *Ball v. Metallurgie Hoboken-Overpelt, S.A.*, 902 F.2d 194, 199 (2d Cir. 1990), the plaintiff claimed that the Belgian defendant company's product harmed him in New York. The plaintiff relied on section 302(a)(3)(i) as his basis for why the New York long arm statute was satisfied. The court, however, held that the plaintiff failed to prove the Belgian company regularly did business in the state or derived any revenue from goods used or consumed in New York. *Id.* As a result, the court did not even analyze whether the defendant had minimum contacts with New York; the long arm statute was not satisfied, so personal jurisdiction was improper. It did not matter that due process may have been satisfied.

3. Does a State's Long Arm Statute Apply to *All* Assertions of Personal Jurisdiction?

As a practical matter, long arm statutes often do not apply when a person is subject to general personal jurisdiction. All jurisdictions likely include some sort of statutory provision that permits courts to exercise personal jurisdiction over individuals who are domiciled in the forum state. States also likely have similar provisions that permit courts to exercise personal jurisdiction over entities under circumstances where they would be constitutionally considered "essentially at home" in the state. States often have statutes that require entities to appoint in-state agents as a mechanism to require consent to personal jurisdiction in exchange for doing business in the state. Remember that the purpose of a long arm statute is to reach out beyond a state's borders to exercise personal jurisdiction over those beyond its borders. As a result, long arm statutes are not at issue when personal jurisdiction is based on *general* personal jurisdiction.

What if the basis for exercising personal jurisdiction is one of those discussed in Chapter 9? What if personal jurisdiction is premised on service in the state (also called "tag" jurisdiction), consent, or waiver? Can a defendant waive an objection based on a state's long arm statute? The likely answer is that when personal jurisdiction is based on one of the historical bases from Chapter 9, the long arm statute is not at issue. *See, e.g., Lindley v. St. Louis-San Francisco Ry. Co.*, 407 F.2d 639, 640 (7th Cir. 1968) ("[W]e reject the contention that [the Illinois long arm statute] sets outer limits over all Illinois in personam jurisdiction over foreign corporations. It does not control Illinois common-law jurisdiction over persons and corporations who, although domiciled in foreign states, are considered residents of Illinois for purposes of in personam jurisdiction."); *Schinkel v. Maxi-Holding, Inc.*, 565 N.E.2d 1219, 1222-23 (Mass. App. Ct. 1991) ("There is no need to predicate jurisdiction over Cederberg on the long-arm statute. Jurisdiction over his person was conferred by service of process in Boston."); Kevin M. Clermont, *Principles of Civil Procedure* §4.2(B)(2)(a) (2d ed. 2009) ("[A] state court must be authorized by state statute to exercise the various bases of jurisdictional power except for the bases of presence and consent, which were recognized at common law"). Though this issue has not been squarely addressed by the U.S. Supreme Court, it is likely that the traditional bases explained in Chapter 9 do not require an independent inquiry into whether the state's long arm statute is satisfied.

4. In Most Cases, State Long Arm Statutes Also Apply in Federal Court

In most cases in federal court, Rule 4(k)(1)(A) requires the federal court to apply the state long arm statute of the state in which the federal court sits. Rule 4(k)(1)(A) acts as a back door through which the state statute is imported. The Rule provides that a court has personal jurisdiction over a defendant where the "defendant is subject to the [personal] jurisdiction of a court of general [subject matter] jurisdiction in the state where the district court is located." In other words, the analysis for most cases is the same whether the case is in federal court or state court. There are some notable exceptions with special federal long arm statutes, such as bankruptcy cases and some securities actions, but most of the time the federal court must apply the state's long arm statute.

Chapter Summary

■ A state court must have statutory authorization before it can exercise personal jurisdiction over an out-of-state defendant. The statutes legislating this authority are commonly known as long arm statutes. A court must also be satisfied that the exercise of personal jurisdiction does not exceed the limits of due process.

■ Some states have passed long arm statutes that authorize personal jurisdiction under any circumstances that would not violate constitutional due process. Such a statute is said to reach to the full limits of due process.

■ More than half of the states have long arm statutes that reach to the full limits of due process. In such cases, the statutory authorization and due process limit collapse into one question: Is the exercise of personal jurisdiction consistent with due process?

■ Some states have not passed long arm statutes that reach to the full limits of due process. In such cases, the court must ask two questions: (1) Does the state long arm statute authorize personal jurisdiction? and (2) even if the long arm statute authorizes personal jurisdiction, would exercising personal jurisdiction violate due process?

■ Long arm statutes can reach to the limits of due process, but not beyond. A state statute that attempted to authorize personal jurisdiction under circumstances that violated constitutional due process would be struck down or interpreted to reach no further than due process allowed.

■ Long arm statutes likely do not apply to every exercise of personal jurisdiction. Where personal jurisdiction is based on the defendant being "essentially at home" (i.e., subject to general personal jurisdiction), long arm statutes are likely automatically satisfied or not at issue. Where personal jurisdiction is based on in-state service (also known as "tag" jurisdiction), consent, or waiver, a state's long arm statute is likely irrelevant.

■ State long arm statutes apply to most cases in federal court. Rule 4(k)(1)(A) requires the federal court to apply the state long arm statute of the state in which the federal court sits. There are exceptions to this rule, so in practice you should research whether an exception applies.

Applying the Concepts

1. A vacationer is walking down the street in New York City when a cab collides with her. The cab's driver was born and raised in New York and has never lived anywhere else. The vacationer sues the cab driver in state court in New York. Assume the New York long arm statute quoted above in the text is New York's applicable long arm statute. Can the New York court exercise personal jurisdiction over the cab driver consistent with the New York long arm statute? Why or why not?

2. Assume the same facts from question 1. Can the New York court exercise personal jurisdiction over the cab driver consistent with due process? Is there any conflict between the New York long arm statute and the due process analysis? Explain your answer.

3. A Texas consumer buys an orange at a grocery store. A farmer in Florida grew the orange and the farmer has no connection to the state of Texas. The orange was sold to a produce distributor in Florida that ultimately sold it to the grocery store in Texas. Unfortunately, the orange had been sprayed with a dangerous chemical pesticide. After the consumer ate the orange, he fell ill and required serious medical attention. Assume that the Texas long arm statute quoted above in the text is Texas's applicable long arm statute. However, also assume that the Texas Supreme Court has never interpreted the long arm statute. The consumer wants to sue the farmer in Texas. What section of the Texas long arm statute would you rely on in arguing that the Florida farmer is subject to personal jurisdiction in Texas? Explain your answer.

4. Assume the same facts from question 3. Can the Texas court exercise personal jurisdiction over the Florida farmer consistent with due process? Is there any conflict between the Texas long arm statute analysis and the due process analysis? Explain your answer.

5. Assume the same facts from question 3. The consumer sues the farmer in state court in Texas. The farmer appears in the Texas court and files a motion challenging personal jurisdiction, arguing that the court cannot exercise personal jurisdiction over him consistent with due process. He makes no mention of the long arm statute. However, the farmer files his motion after the deadline and the court holds that the farmer has waived his objection to personal jurisdiction. May the farmer still object that personal jurisdiction violates the Texas long arm statute? Why or why not?

Civil Procedure in Practice

1. You are a staffer to a New York state legislator. The legislator wants to amend New York's long arm statute to permit courts in New York to exercise personal jurisdiction over anyone who causes harm to any person in New York. What advice would you give the legislator? What statute would you draft?

2. You are a law clerk to a state trial judge in New York. The judge has asked for your help in deciding a motion to dismiss for lack of personal jurisdiction that is based on New York's long arm statute. The New Jersey resident defendant is a hunter who shot at a deer in New Jersey but accidentally hit a New York resident. The plaintiff's response to the motion to dismiss cites section 302(a)(3)(i) (quoted in the text above) as the basis for satisfying the long arm statute. The

judge has asked you to look through the plaintiff's response to see if section 302(a)(3)(i) is satisfied. There is no dispute about the fact that the New Jersey hunter accidentally shot the New York resident. What further information would you look for in the plaintiff's response to decide whether 302(a)(3)(i) is satisfied?

The General Venue Statute

This chapter explains the basic statute that governs **venue,** the third requirement for choosing a proper court. Venue focuses on a specific geographical region called a federal judicial district. The general venue statute considers what relationship the litigation has to the specific federal judicial district the plaintiff has chosen. As we learned in Chapters 2 through 5, subject matter jurisdiction focuses on claims; i.e., the type of dispute the court is being asked to resolve. As we learned in Chapters 6 through 10, personal jurisdiction focuses on the defendant's relationship to the forum state. Like personal jurisdiction, venue is concerned with fairness and convenience. But venue takes into account a wider range of convenience factors, including the convenience of defendant(s), non party witnesses, and where the sources of evidence may be due to where the dispute originated.

All three doctrines limit which court may hear and resolve a dispute. Unless all three requirements — subject matter jurisdiction, personal jurisdiction, and venue — are met in a case, the court in which the case is pending is not a proper court, which is the focus of the first part of this book. If each doctrine is represented by a circle, the three circles must overlap in order for a particular court to be a proper court, as illustrated below in Exhibit 11.1.

Although each doctrine is a limitation, often these three circles will overlap in more than one court. In other words, plaintiffs will likely have more than one proper court to choose to resolve their disputes.

Venue is governed by statute. Unlike subject matter jurisdiction and personal jurisdiction, there is no constitutional component to venue. But like personal jurisdiction, venue is a defense to an action that can be waived. No one can create or agree to subject matter jurisdiction where it does not exist; however, a party can waive any objection it may have to personal jurisdiction or venue.

Key Concepts

- Concept of a federal judicial district
- Differences between venue, personal jurisdiction, and subject matter jurisdiction
- How to apply the general venue statute to determine which federal districts are proper venues and which are not

EXHIBIT 11.1   **Choosing the Proper Court**

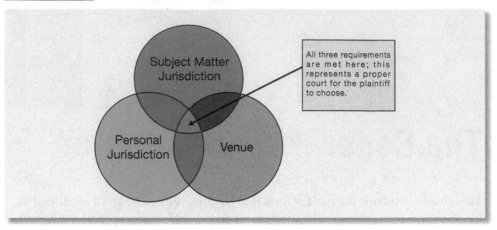

A. WHAT ARE FEDERAL JUDICIAL DISTRICTS?

To understand the role that venue plays, you must understand the concept of a **federal judicial district.** The United States federal court system is divided into 94 judicial districts. Some large or populous states have as many as four judicial districts. States with smaller populations often have a single district that encompasses the entire state. In other words, the borders of the judicial district and the state itself are the same. Exhibit 11.2 is a map depicting the borders of the 94 judicial districts in the United States, as well as the appellate circuits to which each state belongs:

EXHIBIT 11.2   **Borders of the 94 Judicial Districts**

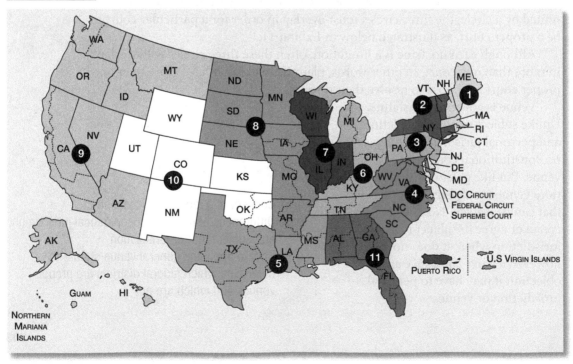

States like New York, Texas, and California have four judicial districts (they are the most populous states in the Union), while Rhode Island, Delaware, and even our geographically largest state — Alaska — have only one judicial district. As you think about and apply the venue statute, remember that not all states have more than one judicial district.

B. THE GENERAL VENUE STATUTE

Most claims in federal court are governed by the general venue statute, 28 U.S.C. §1391(b):

> (b) Venue in general. — A civil action may be brought in —
>   (1) a judicial district in which any defendant resides, if all defendants are residents of the State in which the district is located;
>   (2) a judicial district in which a substantial part of the events or omissions giving rise to the claim occurred, or a substantial part of property that is the subject of the action is situated; or
>   (3) if there is no district in which an action may otherwise be brought as provided in this section, any judicial district in which any defendant is subject to the court's personal jurisdiction with respect to such action.

Section 1391 is structured so that you must first determine whether (b)(1) or (b)(2) applies. Only if you cannot find *any* judicial district that is a proper venue under either (b)(1) or (b)(2) do you consider (b)(3).

1. When Does (b)(1) Apply?

An easily overlooked situation when (b)(1) provides a proper venue is when only one defendant is a party to the lawsuit and resides in a judicial district in the United States. In a single defendant case, 1391(b)(1) provides that venue is proper in the judicial district or districts in which that defendant resides. When there are multiple defendants, the analysis is only slightly more complicated. In multi-defendant cases, a district where any defendant resides is a proper venue so long as all the defendants reside in the state in which that district is located. Consider a state that is composed of a single federal district, like North Dakota. The venue is the District of North Dakota. If all the defendants reside in North Dakota, the District of North Dakota is a proper venue as to all defendants.

In a state that has multiple federal districts, subsection (b)(1) does not require that multiple defendants reside in the same *judicial district* within a state. Rather, if the defendants reside in the same state (even if the state has multiple districts and the defendants live in different districts within that state), venue is proper in a judicial district within that state where any one of the defendants resides. To determine proper venue in multi-defendant cases under subsection (b)(1) in multi-district states, ask two questions about the district: (1) Does at least one of the defendants reside in the district? and (2) Do all of the defendants reside in the state where the district is located? Consider a state like Texas, which has four judicial districts: the Northern, Eastern, Southern, and Western Districts. Suppose the plaintiff files suit against Tomás and ABC, Inc. Tomás resides in the Eastern District of Texas and ABC, Inc. resides in the Southern District of Texas. Venue is proper under subsection (b)(1) in the Eastern District of Texas because Tomás resides in that district and all defendants, both Tomás and ABC, Inc., reside in Texas. Venue is also proper in the Southern District of Texas because ABC, Inc. resides there and all defendants reside in Texas. However, venue is not proper in either the Western or Northern Districts of Texas because neither Tomás nor ABC, Inc. resides in those districts, even though both defendants reside in Texas.

A key takeaway from this discussion is that, in order for venue to be proper under subsection (b)(1), all defendants must reside in the state wherein the chosen judicial district is located. In short, for venue to be proper under subsection (b)(1), all defendants must reside in the same state. Let's modify this example to demonstrate the limits of proper venue under subsection (b)(1). Suppose Tomás resides in the Eastern District of Texas and ABC, Inc. resides only in the Eastern District of Oklahoma. Under these facts, subsection (b)(1) simply does not provide a proper venue because the defendants do not reside in the same state. Venue would not be proper in the Eastern District of Texas, even though Tomás resides there, because ABC, Inc. does not reside in Texas. Notice also that venue would not be proper under subsection (b)(1) in the Eastern District of Oklahoma, even though ABC, Inc. resides there, because Tomás does not reside in Oklahoma.

What Does It Mean to "Reside" in a State for Venue Purposes?

Subsection (b)(1) uses residency to determine proper venue. Therefore, determining proper venue under subsection (b)(1) requires an understanding of the term **residency** under the statute. The venue statute treats individuals differently than entities. The test for where a natural person resides should look familiar from general personal jurisdiction and diversity of citizenship original subject matter jurisdiction. The test is the same domicile test.

As explained more fully below, the test for where entities reside for venue purposes is a bit more complicated because it turns on whether the entity is subject to either or both specific and general personal jurisdiction in the district. It has also become a bit more unsettled because Congress amended section 1391 in 2011 and created a conflict that could make determining residency for some kinds of entities different than for others, making residency determinations even more complicated. So far, most courts have treated residency for all entities the same, despite the conflicting statutory language.

Residence for Individuals

Subsection (c)(1) governs residence for natural persons for venue purposes:

> (c) Residency. — For all venue purposes —
>
> (1) a natural person, including an alien lawfully admitted for permanent residence in the United States, shall be deemed to reside in the judicial district in which that person is domiciled. . . .

Domicile has the same meaning it does in the diversity of citizenship context explained in Chapter 3 and the general personal jurisdiction context explained in Chapter 8. A person is domiciled in the district in which he or she resides with the intent to remain indefinitely. The other features of domicile remain the same as well. A person can have only one domicile at a time, does not lose her domicile until she establishes a new one, and the person must both physically reside in the district and have the right kind of intent (e.g., to remain there indefinitely) before a person is domiciled in the district. Note that the venue statute is concerned about *the judicial district* in which the person is domiciled while general personal jurisdiction and the diversity statute concern themselves with *the state* in which the person is domiciled. Sometimes this distinction makes no difference. As you can see from the map in Exhibit 11.2, some states are single judicial districts, in which case the residency analysis is identical to the domicile analysis you already know. But some states contain multiple judicial districts. In states with multiple judicial districts, to determine residency you must determine where within the state (i.e., in what particular judicial district) the natural person is domiciled. For example, if a natural person is domiciled in Texas, he is subject to general personal jurisdiction in any court in Texas. But determining proper venues within Texas under subsection (b)(1) in a case with that same natural person as a defendant would require determining in what particular judicial district within Texas the natural person is domiciled.

Residence for Entities

Two subsections found in section 1391 seem to govern how to determine residency for entities. These two subsections are difficult to reconcile. As you read them, see if you can see the conflicts:

(c) Residency. — For all venue purposes —

* * *

(2) an entity with the capacity to sue and be sued in its common name under applicable law, whether or not incorporated, shall be deemed to reside, if a defendant, in any judicial district in which such defendant is subject to the court's personal jurisdiction with respect to the civil action in question and, if a plaintiff, only in the judicial district in which it maintains its principal place of business;

* * *

(d) Residency of corporations in States with multiple districts. — For purposes of venue under this chapter, in a State which has more than one judicial district and in which a defendant that is a corporation is subject to personal jurisdiction at the time an action is commenced, such corporation shall be deemed to reside in any district in that State within which its contacts would be sufficient to subject it to personal jurisdiction if that district were a separate State, and, if there is no such district, the corporation shall be deemed to reside in the district within which it has the most significant contacts.

Subsection (c)(2) seems to govern both incorporated and unincorporated entities, whether or not the state contains multiple districts, while subsection (d) seems to govern only corporations that reside in multi-district states. Rather than ironing out the differences and trying to harmonize these two subsections — neither of which can be given full effect as written — most courts have simply applied subsection (c)(2). At least so far, courts have treated all entities alike, whether incorporated or not. And courts so far have considered whether that entity would be subject to personal jurisdiction in the judicial district where venue is sought, if that district were treated as a state. *See* John P. Lenich, *A Simple Question That Isn't So Simple: Where Do Entities Reside for Venue Purposes?*, 84 Miss. L.J. 253, 255, n.9 (2015) (collecting cases).

Note also that the statutory definition of venue for entities incorporates the concept of "personal jurisdiction" as a key statutory test for determining residency of entities for venue purposes. This requires you to revisit the tests that you learned for applying personal jurisdiction in earlier chapters.

Recall that personal jurisdiction can be either specific or general. When analyzing residency for entities, you must examine both types. In which judicial district(s) would the entity be subject to specific jurisdiction if that district were treated as a state? And in which judicial district(s) would the entity be subject to general personal jurisdiction if that district were treated as a state? The results of that analysis will tell you the judicial districts in which the entity resides for purposes of venue. Often, that analysis will result in an entity residing in more than one judicial district.

For example, suppose plaintiff sues two defendants: ABC Corp. and XYZ LLC. Let's consider general personal jurisdiction first — Where is the entity's principal place of business and what is its state of formation (remembering that we focus on a federal district — not the state as a whole)? ABC Corp.'s corporate headquarters, where all the high-level officers make high-level decisions about the corporation, is in Sacramento, California. Sacramento is in the Eastern District of California. Thus, ABC Corp.'s principal place of business is in the Eastern District of California. Suppose also that ABC Corp. is incorporated in Delaware, a single district state. XYZ LLC was formed under the laws of North Dakota, a single district state, and has its corporate headquarters and principal place of business in Los Angeles, California, which is in the Central District of California. So far, the defendants are residents (for venue purposes) of the following judicial districts:

■ ABC Corp.: Eastern District of California and the District of Delaware
■ XYZ LLC: Central District of California and the District of North Dakota

Note that before we analyze specific personal jurisdiction, we can already determine that (b)(1) applies. The defendants are residents of the same state (California) and venue would be proper in any judicial district *in that state* in which any defendant resides. Thus, both the Eastern and Central Districts of California are already proper venues.

Now consider specific personal jurisdiction. Suppose also that the dispute between the plaintiff and the defendants is about a contract that all three parties negotiated in-person in San Diego, which is in the Southern District of California. The contract called for performance in San Diego and the plaintiff is suing because she claims the defendants materially failed to perform their obligations in San Diego. Thus, it appears that the defendants had minimum contacts with the Southern District of California (treating it as if it were a state) and that the claim arises out of those contacts. Under such circumstances, it certainly seems fair and reasonable to subject the defendants to specific personal jurisdiction there. Assuming we cannot find any other judicial district in a state with which either ABC Corp. or XYZ LLC had contacts for the purposes of specific jurisdiction, we now have another appropriate venue under (b)(1). ABC Corp. and XYZ LLC still reside in the same state, but now venue is proper in one more district *in that state* — namely, the Southern District of California, because the defendants would be subject to specific personal jurisdiction there and, as a result, reside there for venue purposes.

Let's change the situation slightly. Suppose that ABC Corp. had its principal place of business in Houston, Texas, which is in the Southern District of Texas. Recall that an entity can have only one principal place of business. Would that render (b)(1) inapplicable? No. XYZ LLC would be subject to general personal jurisdiction and thus reside in a judicial district located in California. ABC Corp. would be subject to *specific* personal jurisdiction and thus reside in a judicial district located in California. Both defendants would reside in California, so venue would be proper in any judicial district in California in which any defendant resides. As a result, venue under (b)(1) would be proper under this slightly altered scenario in either the Central or Southern Districts of California. Note also that the two defendants reside in more than one judicial district. For (b)(1) to apply, there need be only one state of overlap. However, it is also common to have more than one state of overlap. Many entities are incorporated or formed under the laws of the state of Delaware for many reasons. If both ABC Corp. and XYZ LLC had also been formed under the laws of the state of Delaware, the District of Delaware would be another proper venue under (b)(1) because the defendants would both reside in the same state (Delaware), making any district in that state in which any defendant resides (though Delaware has only one district) a proper venue under (b)(1). In that situation, venue would be proper under (b)(1) in the Central or Southern Districts of California as well as the District of Delaware.

2. When Does (b)(2) Apply?

As you read this section, note the significant overlap between the specific personal jurisdiction analysis you must do for (b)(1) and the analysis for (b)(2). The events or omissions that may justify personal jurisdiction (and thus residency in the district) and a substantial part of the events or omissions giving rise to the claim that would render venue proper under (b)(2) will likely rely on the same facts.

Case Preview

Uffner v. La Reunion Francaise

As you read *Uffner*, consider the following questions:

1. Does (b)(1) apply?
2. What districts would be proper venue(s)?
3. What does a "substantial part of the events or omissions giving rise to the claim" mean?

Uffner v. La Reunion Francaise
244 F.3d 38 (1st Cir. 2001)

TORRUELLA, Chief Judge.

Plaintiff-appellant Daniel L. Uffner, Jr. filed this diversity suit in federal district court in the District of Puerto Rico against his insurance issuer and underwriters for wrongful denial of an insurance claim. Defendants-appellees La Reunion Francaise, S.A. ("La Reunion"), T.L. Dallas & Co. Ltd. ("T.L. Dallas"), and Schaeffer & Associates, Inc. ("Schaeffer") filed motions to dismiss for lack of subject matter jurisdiction, failure to state a claim, and improper venue. The district court granted the motions based upon lack of personal jurisdiction and improper venue. For the reasons stated below, we vacate the district court's dismissal and remand the case for further proceedings.

BACKGROUND

La Reunion is a French insurance company which provides vessels with marine insurance coverage and has its principal place of business in Paris, France. T.L. Dallas, a marine underwriting manager based in Bradford, England, specializes in insuring yachts and represents La Reunion in the placement of marine insurance policies. Finally, Schaeffer is an underwriting agent located in the State of Georgia that places yacht policies in the United States (including Puerto Rico) for T.L. Dallas. Together, these three entities issued and underwrote a marine policy for Uffner's sailing yacht, La Mer, in a cover note dated March 18, 1997.

On June 14, 1997, Uffner departed from Fajardo, Puerto Rico on a voyage to St. Thomas, U.S. Virgin Islands. When he was positioned near Isla Palominos, a small island approximately one mile off the coast of Puerto Rico, a fire broke out in the engine room, forcing Uffner to abandon the vessel. The yacht subsequently sank in the same location. Shortly thereafter, Uffner contacted his insurance broker, International Marine Insurance Services ("IMIS") to file a claim for the loss of the boat. After a series of written communications and telephone calls between IMIS and appellees, the claim was denied due to the alleged absence of a "current out-of-water survey."

Uffner filed this suit on June 12, 1998, claiming damages for a bad-faith denial of an insurance claim. La Reunion and T.L. Dallas filed separate motions to dismiss based on lack of subject matter jurisdiction, failure to state a claim upon which relief can be granted, and improper venue. Schaeffer filed a motion joining these motions to dismiss on the same grounds. Uffner timely opposed all motions.

On September 20, 1999, the district court dismissed Uffner's complaint without prejudice, concluding that the court lacked personal jurisdiction over appellees and that venue did not lie in Puerto Rico. Uffner moved the court to reconsider its ruling and requested leave to amend the complaint in order to assert admiralty jurisdiction as an alternative basis for subject matter jurisdiction. The court denied both motions on December 10, 1999, and this appeal followed.

DISCUSSION

The district court dismissed appellant's complaint on two grounds. First, the court concluded that pursuant to the provisions of the Puerto Rico Long-Arm statute, appellees lacked sufficient minimum contacts with the forum to be subject to personal jurisdiction therein. In addition, the court determined that the suit involved a contract claim unrelated to the District of Puerto Rico, making it an improper forum for litigation. We review the court's legal conclusions supporting the dismissal de novo.

A. Personal Jurisdiction

In their motions to dismiss, appellees argued that the court lacked subject matter jurisdiction, Fed. R. Civ. P. 12(b)(1), that Uffner failed to state a claim for which relief could be granted, Fed. R. Civ. P. 12(b)(6), and that venue was improper, Fed. R. Civ. P. 12(b)(3). None of the parties raised any objection to personal jurisdiction. See Fed. R. Civ. P. 12(b)(2). Nevertheless, the court itself raised and disposed of the motion on this ground. In doing so, it overlooked the provisions of Fed. R. Civ. P. 12(g), which states that "[i]f a party makes a motion under this rule but omits therefrom any defense or objection then available to the party which this rule permits to be raised by motion, the party shall not thereafter make a motion based on the defense or objection so omitted. . . ." Rule 12(h)(1)(A) provides, in turn, that "[a] defense of lack of personal jurisdiction over the person is waived . . . if omitted from a motion in the circumstances described in subdivision (g). . . ." Fed. R. Civ. P. 12(h)(1)(A). By failing to include a 12(b)(2) argument in their motion to dismiss, appellees waived this defense in the district court.

Once a party has waived its defense of lack of personal jurisdiction, the court may not, sua sponte, raise the issue in its ruling on a motion to dismiss. This is so because, since personal jurisdiction may be acquired through voluntary appearance and the filing of responsive pleadings without objection, the court has no independent reason to visit the issue. Furthermore, such a prohibition avoids prejudicing the plaintiff, who has not had an opportunity to respond to the issue before the court, and promotes the purpose of Rules 12(g) and (h). There is no evidence here that the Rule 12(b)(2) defense was unavailable to appellees at the time they filed their answer. Nor is this merely a case of a litigant improperly characterizing a substantive argument for lack of personal jurisdiction under a different subsection. Rather, appellees simply failed to raise the issue in their motion to dismiss and thereby consented to the court's jurisdiction. Since the court was not at liberty to nullify appellees' consent, we conclude that the district court erred in dismissing the complaint for lack of personal jurisdiction.

B. Venue

Due to its focus on personal jurisdiction, the district court dealt only perfunctorily with the issue of whether venue was proper in the district of Puerto Rico. Specifically, the court found that the appellant's claim sounded in contract rather than tort. As such, the court observed, the claim was wholly unrelated to Puerto Rico: the "triggering event" was the denial of the claim and "[t]he issue at bar is the interpretation of the contract." The court also noted that the contract was neither negotiated nor formed in Puerto Rico. Finally, according to the court, the occurrence of the fire in Puerto Rican waters was "a tenuous connection at best."

To begin, the distinction between tort and contract is immaterial to the requirements for venue set forth in the general venue statute, 28 U.S.C. §1391(a). . . .

There is no dispute that §1391(a)(1) [now 1391(b)(1)] is inapplicable in this case. The question, then, is whether "a substantial part of the events . . . giving rise to the claim occurred" in Puerto Rico.

Prior to 1990, §1391(a) provided venue in "the judicial district . . . in which the claim arose." 28 U.S.C. §1391(a) (1988). Congress amended the statute to its current form because it found that the old language "led to wasteful litigation whenever several different forums were involved in the transaction leading up to the dispute." The pre-amendment statute also engendered a plethora of tests to determine the single venue in which the claim "arose." By contrast, many circuits have interpreted the legislative history of the 1990 amendment as evincing Congress's recognition that when the events underlying a claim have taken place in different places, venue may be proper in any number of districts. We look, therefore, not to a single "triggering event" prompting the action, but to the entire sequence of events underlying the claim.

In so doing, we consider the following acts: (1) appellant, a resident of the Virgin Islands, obtained an insurance policy for his yacht, La Mer; (2) the insured vessel caught fire and sank in Puerto Rican waters; (3) appellant filed a claim with appellees through his insurance broker demanding payment for this loss; and (4) the claim was ultimately denied because it was allegedly not covered by the policy. Though this is merely a skeletal outline of events leading to the claim, for purposes of this appeal, we need just establish that the sinking of La Mer was one part of the historical predicate for the instant suit. It is the only event, however, that occurred in Puerto Rico. For venue to be proper in that district, therefore, the loss of La Mer must be "substantial."

Appellees argue that Uffner's complaint alleges a bad faith denial of his insurance claim, not that the loss itself was due to their fault or negligence. Consequently, they reason, the sinking of the vessel cannot be considered "substantial." It is true, as the district court pointed out, that the legal question in the suit is "whether [an out-of-water survey] was necessary under the terms of the insurance contract." Resolving this issue does not require an investigation into how, when, or why the accident occurred. In this sense, the sinking of Uffner's yacht is not related to the principal question for decision.

However, an event need not be a point of dispute between the parties in order to constitute a substantial event giving rise to the claim. Cf. Woodke v. Dahm, 70 F.3d 983, 986 (8th Cir. 1995) (requiring that the event itself be "wrongful" in order to support venue). In this case, Uffner's bad faith denial claim alleges that the loss of his yacht was covered by the contract and the payment due to him wrongfully denied. Thus, although the sinking of La Mer is itself not in dispute, the event is connected to the claim inasmuch as Uffner's requested damages include recovery for the loss. We conclude that, in a suit against an insurance company to recover for losses resulting from a vessel casualty, the jurisdiction where that loss occurred is "substantial" for venue purposes.

We add that our conclusion does not thwart the general purpose of statutorily specified venue, which is "to protect the defendant against the risk that a plaintiff will select an unfair or inconvenient place of trial." Leroy v. Great W. United Corp., 443 U.S. 173 (1979). First, appellees have not alleged — either below or on appeal — that continuing the suit in the district of Puerto Rico would confer a tactical advantage to appellant or prejudice their own case in any way. We also highlight the absence of a forum-selection clause in the insurance policy indicating appellees' preferred forum for litigation. Finally, appellees conceded at oral argument that they would not object to litigating in the Virgin Islands, suggesting that traveling to the Caribbean would not be unduly burdensome. We therefore hold that venue properly lies in the district of Puerto Rico.

CONCLUSION

Appellees have suggested that venue is proper in the Virgin Islands or in Georgia. We do not address these possibilities since, as we have already noted, §1391 contemplates that venue may be proper in several districts. In this case, Puerto Rico is at least one of them.

The judgment of the district court is vacated and the case remanded for further proceedings.

Post-Case Follow-Up

The court is interpreting subsection (b)(2), particularly what it means for a "substantial part of the events or omissions" to have taken place in a given federal judicial district. Subsection (b)(1) would not have applied because the defendants did not all reside in the same state. In fact, they all resided in different countries: France, England, and the United States.

The court interprets "substantial part of the events or omissions" very broadly. The court states that as long as what happened in the forum was an important part of the "sequence of events" or "historical predicates" giving rise to the case, venue is proper in that forum. The court looks to the underlying facts of the event. Importantly, these facts need not be in dispute. No one argued that the plaintiff's boat sank or that it sank in Puerto Rican waters. The issue was who (if anyone) should pay for that harm. Even so, the sinking of the boat was an important part of the events giving rise to the litigation. That was sufficient to satisfy subsection (b)(2).

Uffner v. La Reunion Francaise: Real Life Applications

1. A Seller made a contract with a Buyer for the Buyer to purchase used cars at Seller's wholesale lot and sell them on Buyer's retail lot. The contract was signed in New Jersey, a single district state. The Buyer picks up the cars from the Seller's lot and sells them in the Buyer's retail lot, both of which are in New Jersey. The contract calls for all payments to be made in Rhode Island, where the Seller keeps a post office box. The Buyer misses a payment and the seller sues Buyer in federal court in Rhode Island. The Buyer claims he made the allegedly missed payment as required. Is the District of Rhode Island a proper venue? Why or why not?

2. Assume the same facts as in question 1 above. Now, however, the Buyer admits he failed to make the payment but claims the contract is unenforceable under the statute of frauds, requiring such contracts to be in writing. Does that change your answer to question 1? Why or why not?

3. Assume the same facts as in question 1 above. Now, however, the contract contains the following clause: "Any disputes concerning the contract between Seller and Buyer must be resolved by a court of competent jurisdiction in the state of Rhode Island." What effect, if any, does that contract term have on whether Rhode Island is a proper venue? Explain your answer.

---

3. How Do (b)(1) and (b)(2) Work Together?

Both subsections could provide the plaintiff with possible venues for her lawsuit. Consider the following hypothetical. A consumer is injured when he is in a crash in Manhattan, in the Southern District of New York, when his airbag does not deploy. The consumer wants to sue the other driver, the car company, and the airbag company. The other driver has always lived in Lansing, Michigan, in the Western District of Michigan. The car company is an LLC formed under the laws of Delaware, a single district state, and has its principal place of business in Detroit, in the Eastern District of Michigan. The airbag company is a Japanese corporation, with its principal place of business in Detroit. The car company sold the car to the consumer in Manhattan. The airbag company has no contacts with any state other than Michigan. Where is venue proper?

First, does (b)(1) apply? Are all of the defendants residents of the same state? Yes. There are three defendants: the other driver, the car company, and the airbag company. The other driver resides in Michigan, specifically in the Western District of Michigan (WDMI). He appears to be domiciled there because he physically resides there and the facts suggest no intent or plan to leave. He can have only one domicile. Whether or not he is subject to personal jurisdiction in a particular district is irrelevant for determining residency for venue purposes because he is a natural person.

The other two defendants are entities. Thus, they reside — for venue purposes — in each district in which they would be subject to any form of personal jurisdiction (specific or general) if that district were treated as a state. Because the car company is formed under the laws of Delaware and has its principal place of business in Detroit, it is subject to general personal jurisdiction in the District of

Delaware and in the Eastern District of Michigan (EDMI). The airbag company also has its principal place of business in Detroit, in the EDMI. The car company would also likely be subject to specific jurisdiction in New York City (Manhattan) in the Southern District of New York (SDNY), because the car company sold the car there and the claim arises out of that contact. Thus, the car company also resides in the SDNY. The airbag company may or may not be subject to specific personal jurisdiction in New York under the stream of commerce doctrine or another theory. However, it does not matter, because all three defendants reside in Michigan. Thus, venue under (b)(1) is proper in any district in Michigan in which any defendant resides. Here, those districts are the EDMI and the WDMI. Note that venue is not proper under (b)(1) in any federal district in New York because all of the defendants do not reside in the state of New York.

Second, under (b)(2), a substantial part of the events or omissions occurred in the SDNY. That is at least one other proper venue (recall, however, the stream of commerce doctrine: the airbag company is likely not subject to personal jurisdiction under this theory in the SDNY). Other important events may have occurred elsewhere, but the SDNY is clearly a place where venue is proper as to all defendants under (b)(2) because a substantial part of the events or omissions — namely the sale of the car — occurred in the SDNY. As a result, (b)(3) does not apply.

4. When Does (b)(3) Apply?

Subsection (b)(3) does not apply often. In order for it to apply, you would first have to determine that the defendant or defendants do not share a common state of residence and that no substantial part of the events or omissions occurred in a federal judicial district.

(c) Residency. — For all venue purposes —

* * *

(3) if there is no district in which an action may otherwise be brought as provided in this section, any judicial district in which any defendant is subject to the court's personal jurisdiction with respect to such action.

Though rare, this does happen. Suppose you are vacationing in Mexico and are in a three-car pileup. Coincidentally, the other two drivers are tourists too. You are a resident of Texas, the second driver is a resident of (and thus domiciled and subject to personal jurisdiction in) Arizona, and the third is a resident of (and thus domiciled and subject to personal jurisdiction in) New Mexico. The defendants do not share a state of residence and all the events or omissions appear to have happened in Mexico. Thus, under (b)(3), venue is proper in Arizona or New Mexico (both single district states). Personal jurisdiction is still an issue; the second driver may have no connection whatsoever with New Mexico and the third driver may have no connection whatsoever to Arizona. As a practical matter, you may have to file two suits to recover, one in Arizona and one in New Mexico. Even so, venue would be proper under (b)(3).

C. SPECIALIZED VENUE STATUTES

Some claims have their own specialized venue provisions that either replace or supplement the general venue statute. Some are found in Title 28 of the United States Code, like the general venue statute. For example, tort claims against the federal government can be brought where the plaintiff resides or where the incident at issue occurred. 28 U.S.C. §1402. Copyright and patent infringement claims also have specialized venue rules. 28 U.S.C. §§1400(a)-(b) (venue is proper "where the defendant resides, or where the defendant has committed acts of infringement and has a regular and established place of business").

Some claims have their own built-in venue provisions. The statute governing employment discrimination cases, commonly referred to as Title VII claims, contains a specialized venue rule. Venue in such cases is proper "in any judicial district . . . in which the unlawful employment practice is alleged to have been committed, in the judicial district in which the employment records relevant to such practice are maintained and administered, or in the judicial district in which the aggrieved person would have worked but for the alleged unlawful employment practice, but if the respondent is not found within any such district, such an action may be brought within the judicial district in which the respondent has his principal office. . . ." *See* 42 U.S.C. §2000e-5(f)(3).

D. REMOVAL VENUE

Venue in cases removed from state court to federal court is simple. There is one — and only one — proper venue to which a defendant may properly remove a case to federal court. The defendant must remove to the federal court for the district and division embracing the place where the state court sits. Given that directive, the removal statute, 28 U.S.C. §1441(a), is a sort of specialized venue statute. 28 U.S.C. §1391 applies to cases originally filed in federal court, not those removed from state to federal court. After removal, however, the defendant may have options. The next chapter, covering transfer of venue and dismissal for improper venue under certain circumstances, gives litigants options once they are in federal court. But as an initial matter, do not forget that there is only one proper venue to which a defendant may remove a removable case to federal court — the one specified in section 1441(a).

Chapter Summary

- Venue focuses on the relationship between the litigation and a federal judicial district, which is sometimes a smaller unit than a state.
- Venue is one of the three key elements to choosing a proper court. A court must be a proper venue in order to resolve the dispute before it. Like personal jurisdiction, an objection to venue can be waived. Thus, a court can hear a case based on consent or waiver of an objection to venue.

■ The general federal venue statute, 28 U.S.C. §1391, applies in most federal cases. More than one venue may be proper under 28 U.S.C. §1391.

■ Despite the contradiction in the statute as amended in 2011, courts currently determine where entities reside for purposes of subsection (b)(1), by considering §1391(c), which says that an entity resides in a district where it would be subject to personal jurisdiction if that district were treated as its own state.

■ Not all cases are governed by the general venue statute; some claims have specialized venue rules that supplant or supplement the general rule.

Applying the Concepts

1. Driver A is driving on I-35 in Oklahoma City, which is in the Western District of Oklahoma. Driver B collides with Driver C, who collides with Driver A.

Driver B resides in Dallas, which is in the Northern District of Texas. Driver C resides in Houston, which is in the Southern District of Texas. Driver A wants to sue Drivers B and C. Where is venue proper? Explain your answer.

2. Bus passengers on vacation in Rome were injured when the bus driver was texting while driving and crashed into an oncoming car. The bus passengers want to sue the bus driver in the United States. The bus driver resides in Rome and is an Italian citizen. The bus passengers learn that the bus driver will be visiting California and that the bus driver will have a layover at Newark International Airport in New Jersey, a single district state. The bus passengers arrange to have the bus driver served with process during his layover in Newark. Is venue proper in any judicial district in the United States? If so, which one(s)? Explain your answer.

Civil Procedure in Practice

You are a congressional staffer and the member for whom you work thinks venue is too complicated and that personal jurisdiction already protects defendants sufficiently. The member suggests redrafting the general venue statute to say "venue is proper in any judicial district in which any defendant is subject to personal jurisdiction." Could Congress amend the general venue statute in this way? What issues do you see if Congress amends the general venue statute in this manner? What would be the effect of amending the statute in this way—and is it consistent with the purpose of the general venue statute as it exists?

Challenging Venue: Dismissal and Transfer

This chapter explains how to challenge venue. Although a plaintiff chooses the venue when he files suit in federal court, the plaintiff's chosen venue is subject to challenge by the defendant. If the court grants the defendant's venue challenge, the court may either dismiss the case outright or transfer the case from one federal judicial district to another. In rare cases, venue is not proper in any judicial district in the United States. In that situation, the court must dismiss the case. In most cases, however, there is a proper venue and the court has considerable discretion to dismiss or transfer venue based on the doctrines this chapter explains.

Recall that, much like personal jurisdiction (and unlike subject matter jurisdiction), a party can waive its challenge to venue either before or after suit is filed. Even if the plaintiff files suit in an improper venue, if the defendant does not object (or does not do so properly), the defendant has waived any objection to venue and the court may still hear the case. Also, like personal jurisdiction, the parties may agree to a particular venue before a dispute arises or after a suit is filed.

A. INTRODUCTION

There are three basic doctrines that parties use to challenge venue: Two are statutory provisions; the third is a longstanding common law doctrine known as *forum non conveniens*. Some challenges to venue result in the court dismissing the case in its entirety because venue is not proper in any judicial district in the United States, or would be more appropriate in a foreign jurisdiction. Yet other challenges result in transfer of the case from an

Key Concepts

- Understand the three doctrines that allow a party to challenge venue
- Determine when a court is most likely to dismiss a case for improper venue or transfer a case to a proper venue

improper venue to a proper venue in the United States. Finally, some challenges result in a court transferring a case from a proper venue to another proper venue that is more convenient to the parties and witnesses.

At the outset it is important to understand that courts cannot transfer venue from one court system to another. A federal court cannot transfer a case to a state court or vice versa. Recall, however, the doctrine of removal, when a defendant removes a case filed in state court to a particular, statutorily specified federal judicial district court. Similarly, a federal court may remand a removed case back to the specific state court from which it was removed. Neither of these situations is a challenge to venue. State courts of one state also cannot transfer cases to courts of another state. State courts have their own rules for when and how to dismiss or transfer cases among their own courts when a party makes a challenge to venue. Similarly, courts in the United States cannot transfer a case to a court in another nation. When a court located in a foreign country may be a more appropriate venue, a party may move to dismiss the case under the common law doctrine of *forum non conveniens* with the idea being that the plaintiff should refile her lawsuit in the proper foreign court.

As Exhibit 12.1 demonstrates, the law a party would use to challenge venue in a federal court depends on whether the case was filed in a proper venue in the first place and whether the party seeks dismissal or transfer of the case:

EXHIBIT 12.1   **Dismissal or Transfer**

	Moving to Dismiss?	Moving to Transfer?
The case was filed in an improper venue.	28 U.S.C. §1406	28 U.S.C. §1406
The case was filed in a proper venue.	*Forum non conveniens*	28 U.S.C. §1404

We start with the statutory doctrines: 28 U.S.C. §§1406 and 1404.

B. VENUE DISMISSAL OR TRANSFER STATUTES

Most people would rather sue or be sued in a place that is convenient for them (if they must be sued at all). A defendant may want to **transfer venue** for more than mere convenience, however. Changing venue could result in a whole host of changes that a defendant believes is favorable. For example, the decision-maker will change. If the litigation goes to trial — regardless of whether the trial is a bench trial or a jury trial — there will either be a new judge or new jury deciding the case. If the trial is by jury, the composition of the jury pool will change, which can sometimes radically change the outcome due to the views of the local population. Additionally, because the general venue statute described in Chapter 11 sometimes makes it unclear whether a particular judicial district is a proper venue, and often makes more than one judicial district a proper venue, motions to dismiss or transfer venue are common.

1. Cases Filed in an Improper Venue: §1406 Dismissal or Transfer

Two statutes govern most motions to dismiss or transfer venue in federal court. The applicable statute depends on whether the case was filed in a proper venue or an improper venue. The first involves a situation where the case was filed in an improper venue and a party (virtually always the defendant) wants to dismiss the case:

---

28 U.S.C. §1406. CURE OR WAIVER OF DEFECTS

(a) The district court of a district in which is filed a case laying venue in the wrong division or district shall dismiss, or if it be in the interest of justice, transfer such case to any district or division in which it could have been brought.

Notice the wording of the statute. If a case is filed "laying venue in the wrong . . . district [the court] *shall* dismiss. . . ." (emphasis added). If the statute ended there, the remedy would be simple: If venue is improper, the court must dismiss the case. The statute, however, goes on to say that if it is "in the interest of justice," a court may transfer a case to a district "in which it could have been brought" (i.e., a district that is a proper venue and in which the defendants are subject to personal jurisdiction). If there is no district that would be a proper venue, then the result is straightforward: The court must dismiss.

If there is some other district that would be a proper venue, a court is likely to decide it is in the "interests of justice" to transfer the case to that district rather than dismiss. *Goldlawr, Inc. v. Heiman*, 369 U.S. 463, 467 (1962). Transferring the case is less costly, quicker, and simpler. The plaintiff will not have to pay another filing fee. The plaintiff will not have to pay for a process server to properly serve the defendant. The court can simply send the existing case file to the court to which the case is transferred. The transfer also avoids the possibility that the plaintiff's claims will be barred by the statute of limitations, because a transferred case is treated as filed when originally filed in the court that orders transfer. In other words, if the statute of limitations expired while the case was pending in the first court, or limitations would have likely expired between the time the case was dismissed and refiled in a proper venue, the transfer avoids that possible injustice.

2. Cases Filed in a Proper Venue: §1404 Transfer of Venue

The second statute involves a situation where the case was filed in a proper venue, but a party (usually the defendant, but not necessarily) wants **transfer of venue**:

---

28 U.S.C. §1404. CHANGE OF VENUE

(a) For the convenience of parties and witnesses, in the interest of justice, a district court may transfer any civil action to any other district or division where it might have been brought or to any district or division to which all parties have consented.

Notice that the statute does not restrict transfers of venue to defendants. A plaintiff who later learns that litigation would be more convenient in another venue may move to transfer venue herself.

Section 1404 is also the mechanism to transfer cases within judicial districts. About half of the states are comprised of only one judicial district — but within that district are separate divisions. If venue would be more convenient in a different *division* within a *district*, the court will analyze whether the case should be transferred.

A concrete example may help demonstrate this. Many large, yet sparsely populated states have only one judicial district but several divisions within that district. Even large states with more than one district may have districts covering wide swaths of geography. Texas is perhaps one of the most extreme examples.

Suppose the plaintiff's venue analysis suggests that venue is proper in the Northern District of Texas and he files suit in the Dallas Division of the Northern District of Texas. Suppose also, however, that the event that is the focal point of the suit happened in Amarillo. The map in Exhibit 12.2 visibly demonstrates the

EXHIBIT 12.2 **Division Within the Northern District of Texas**

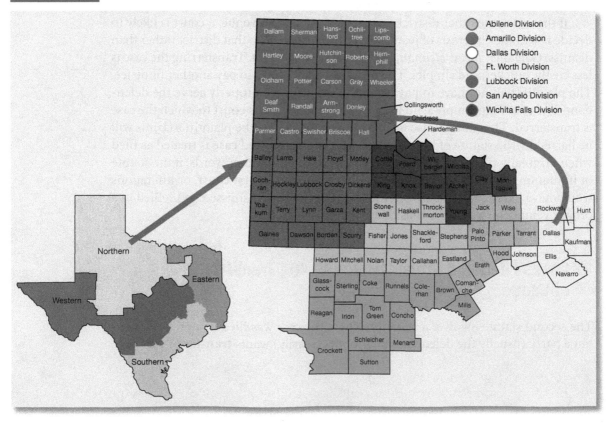

problem of when large judicial districts contain many divisions. The map on the left in Exhibit 12.2 depicts all four judicial districts in Texas: Northern, Southern, Eastern, and Western. The map on the right is an enlargement of the 100 counties that comprise the 7 divisions within the Northern District of Texas.

The curved arrow on the right depicts the distance as the crow flies between Dallas and Amarillo, two of the divisions within the Northern District of Texas — more than 300 miles. By way of comparison, Rhode Island is approximately 50 miles from north to south. This is a simple example of when a party may want to transfer divisions *within a district* for convenience. When a party wants such a transfer, the party uses section 1404.

Consent as a Valid Basis for Venue

Note also that the statute explicitly provides that the court may transfer a case to a venue "to which all parties have consented." Thus, the parties can consent to venue in a particular district court, even if that venue would not otherwise be proper under the general venue statute explained in Chapter 11.

Challenges to Venue Can Be Waived

Much like personal jurisdiction, a party can waive its objection to venue by failing to timely object. *See* Rules 12(g)-(h). Courts are unlikely to dismiss sua sponte for these waivable defenses. *Buchanan v. Manley*, 145 F.3d 386, 387-88 (D.C. Cir. 1998) (holding that sua sponte dismissal on venue grounds was an error); *see also Uffner v. La Reunion Francaise*, 244 F.3d 38, 38 (1st Cir. 2001) ("Once a party has waived its defense of lack of personal jurisdiction, the court may not, *sua sponte*, raise the issue in its ruling on a motion to dismiss").

Pre-dispute consent to venue has become common in the setting of consumer contracts and interactions. For quite a while, many sophisticated contracts have included clauses making venue mandatory in a certain place. These pre-dispute consents to venue are often referred to as **forum selection clauses**. In other words, the parties have decided, even before any dispute has arisen, that disputes between them must be resolved in certain courts. Today, even the most routine transactions likely require parties to consent to a particular venue if a dispute between the parties arises. For example, in Google's Terms of Service, the following language appears:

> The laws of California, U.S.A., excluding California's conflict of laws rules, will apply to any disputes arising out of or relating to these terms or the Services. All claims arising out of or relating to these terms or the Services will be litigated exclusively in the federal or state courts of Santa Clara County, California, USA, and you and Google consent to personal jurisdiction in those courts.

Note the language that all claims "will be litigated exclusively in the federal or state courts of Santa Clara County, California, USA." While that still leaves a couple of possible venues, the number of proper venues has become considerably smaller.

These provisions requiring venue in a particular court or district are generally valid. *See Carnival Cruise Lines, Inc. v. Shute*, 499 U.S. 585, 591 (1991) (enforcing a forum selection clause contained on a ticket for passage on a cruise ship).

Parties may also agree to transfer venue to another judicial district after the suit has commenced. If the parties agree to a transfer, a court is likely to grant the parties' agreed motion. Often, however, a party perceives an advantage in transferring the lawsuit to another judicial district. Thus, courts must have some framework for deciding whether to transfer the case.

Discretionary Transfers

Section 1404 gives some guidance — the court should consider convenience and justice. But just what does that mean?

Case Preview

MacMunn v. Eli Lilly Co.

The following case deals with a motion to transfer venue from one proper venue to another. As you read the case, consider the following questions:

1. How does the court analyze whether to transfer venue? What steps does it take, and in what order?
2. What factors does the court consider in deciding whether to transfer venue?
3. Does the court categorize the factors in any way? Does the court consider any factor or factors more important than others?
4. Does the court decide to transfer? If so, why?

MacMunn v. Eli Lilly Co.
559 F. Supp. 2d 58 (D.D.C. 2008)

RICARDO M. URBINA, District Judge.

I. INTRODUCTION

Before the court is the defendant's motion to transfer this products liability case to Massachusetts. The defendant, Eli Lilly & Co., argues that both private and public interests favor transfer primarily because the case has little if any ties to this District. The plaintiffs, Judith MacMunn and her husband Michael MacMunn, oppose transfer citing numerous cases involving the same defendant and subject matter that have been resolved in this District. Because the contacts relevant to this dispute are overwhelmingly focused in Massachusetts and because this case is still in its nascent stages, the court grants the defendant's motion to transfer.

II. FACTUAL AND PROCEDURAL BACKGROUND

Plaintiff Judith MacMunn alleges that her mother ingested Diethylstilbestrol ("DES") while pregnant with her in 1962. The exposure to DES in utero purportedly resulted in uterine and cervical malformations, infertility, physical and mental pain and medical expenses and treatment. On September 14, 2007, the plaintiff and her husband, Michael MacMunn filed a 7-count complaint in D.C. Superior Court, claiming negligence, strict liability, breach of warranty, misrepresentation and loss of consortium. Collectively, the plaintiffs seek 3 million dollars in compensatory damages and 3 million dollars in punitive damages. On November 2, 2007, the defendant removed the case to this court based on diversity of citizenship.... Four months after the initial status conference, the defendant filed a motion to transfer this case to the District of Massachusetts....

III. ANALYSIS

A. *Legal Standard for Venue Under 28 U.S.C. §1391(a) and Transfer Pursuant to 28 U.S.C. §1404(a)*

When federal jurisdiction is premised solely on diversity, 28 U.S.C. §1391(a) controls venue....

In an action where venue is proper, 28 U.S.C. §1404(a) nonetheless authorizes a court to transfer a civil action to any other district where it could have been brought "for the convenience of parties and witnesses, in the interest of justice[.]" 28 U.S.C. §1404(a). Section 1404(a) vests "discretion in the district court to adjudicate motions to transfer according to [an] individualized, case-by-case consideration of convenience and fairness." *Stewart Org., Inc. v. Ricoh Corp.*, 487 U.S. 22, 27 (1988).... Under this statute, the moving party bears the burden of establishing that transfer is proper.

Accordingly, the defendant must make two showings to justify transfer. First, the defendant must establish that the plaintiff originally could have brought the action in the proposed transferee district. Second, the defendant must demonstrate that considerations of convenience and the interest of justice weigh in favor of transfer to that district. As to the second showing, the statute calls on the court to weigh a number of case-specific private and public-interest factors. The private-interest con- *non-exhaustive list.* siderations include: (1) the plaintiff's choice of forum, unless the balance of convenience is strongly in favor of the defendants; (2) the defendant's choice of forum; (3) whether the claim arose elsewhere; (4) the convenience of the parties; (5) the convenience of the witnesses; and (6) the ease of access to sources of proof. The public-interest considerations include: (1) the transferee's familiarity with the governing laws; (2) the relative congestion of the calendars of the potential transferee and transferor courts; and (3) the local interest in deciding local controversies at home.

B. *The Court Grants the Defendant's Motion to Transfer*

1. The Private Interests Favor Transfer

Surveying the private interest factors, the defendant concludes, based on the plaintiffs' responses to interrogatories, that "all of the potential witnesses and sources of proof concerning the injuries alleged in this case are located in the District of Massachusetts." Specifically, the defendant recounts that the plaintiff's mother (the principal witness for the issue of exposure) resides in Massachusetts; the medical records regarding the plaintiff's mother's pregnancy are likely in Massachusetts; any still-living physicians who prescribed the plaintiff's mother medicine during her pregnancy would likely reside in Massachusetts (outside the scope of the District of Columbia's subpoena power); the pharmacists and pharmacy records regarding the manufacturer of the DES that the plaintiff's mother allegedly ingested would be located in Massachusetts; and the physicians and medical records related to injuries allegedly caused by DES would all be in Massachusetts. The plaintiffs counter that the defendant has not met its burden to demonstrate that any of the witnesses will be unavailable for trial and, lacking that, the court should assume that the witnesses will voluntarily appear.

Although the plaintiffs are correct in stating that the defendant has not demonstrated, or even argued, that the nonparty witnesses would be unavailable at trial, the fact that almost all of the nonparty, nonexpert witnesses reside in Massachusetts clearly weighs in favor of transfer. 15 Wright, Miller & Cooper, Fed. Prac. & Proc. §3851 (noting that "courts weigh more heavily the residence of important nonparty witnesses, who may be within the subpoena power of one district but not the other"). Furthermore, the plaintiffs do not dispute that all the sources of relevant medical records are located in Massachusetts. Accordingly, both the convenience of the witnesses and the ease of access to sources of proof both weigh in favor of transfer.

This typically is not enough to overcome the plaintiffs' choice of forum, however. *See Piper Aircraft*, 454 U.S. at 255 (stating that "there is ordinarily a strong presumption in favor of the plaintiff's choice of forum, which may be overcome only when the private and public interest factors clearly point towards trial in the alternative forum"). It is enough in this case though because the District has no meaningful ties to the controversy and because the plaintiffs reside in Massachusetts. And the plaintiffs' suggestion that "an army of lobbyists and salespeople familiar with the marketing strategies and communications regarding DES" are located in the D.C. does not "tip the balance in favor of maintaining this case in the District of Columbia." Moreover, the operative facts giving rise to the plaintiffs' claim arose in Massachusetts. These circumstances coupled with the defendant's choice of forum, asserted before the parties have engaged in significant discovery, lead the court to conclude that the private interest factors favor transfer.

2. The Public Interests Favor Transfer

The defendant contends that Massachusetts has a strong interest "in seeing that the product liability claims of Massachusetts citizens are tried fairly and effectively." Furthermore, under D.C. choice of law provisions, Massachusetts law is likely to apply, and "there is no reason that the District of Massachusetts cannot adequately resolve this case." The plaintiffs do not dispute, and the court has little reason to doubt, the applicability of Massachusetts law in this case; rather, the plaintiffs contend that the District's law applies to the statute of limitations, which is an important issue in DES cases. In addition, the plaintiffs respond by noting that the history of

DES litigation in the District is sufficient to prevent transfer. Although this District is familiar with DES litigation, "[t]here is an appropriateness . . . in having the trial of a diversity case in a forum that is at home with the state law that must govern the case." Gulf Oil Corp. v. Gilbert, 330 U.S. 501, 509 (1947). Familiarity with DES litigation does not counterbalance this interest; accordingly, this factor points toward Massachusetts.

The plaintiffs next contend that "there is nothing uniquely local about DES litigation." There are, however, local harms that one community may have a stronger interest in resolving over another. Here, plaintiff Judith MacMunn's mother allegedly ingested DES in Massachusetts; the plaintiffs allegedly suffered the ill-effects from this ingestion in Massachusetts; and these individuals all currently reside in Massachusetts. The District, while its contacts with the case are not "legally insignificant," does not derive as great an interest from those contacts as Massachusetts does from its interest in redressing the harms of its citizens. The fact that DES litigation involves nationwide marketing practices does not upend this local interest. Thus, this factor, too, favors transfer. The court turns at last to the relative congestion of the courts. As the defendant notes, this District has a more congested docket than the District of Massachusetts. The plaintiffs do not dispute this fact but protest that Magistrate Judge Kay is experienced in settling DES cases, which would likely result in a speedy resolution to this case. The defendant responds that the District of Massachusetts has a similarly experienced magistrate judge whom both parties have requested to mediate other DES cases. While not striking definitively for or against transfer, the factor shades nearer to transfer. On balance then, both the private and the public interest factors support transferring the case to the District of Massachusetts, and the court, therefore, grants the defendant's motion.

IV. CONCLUSION

For the foregoing reasons the court grants the defendant's motion to transfer.

Post-Case Follow-Up

Recall the general venue statute from Chapter 11. Section 1404 applies when a party moves to transfer venue from a proper venue to another proper venue. Thus, the first step is to determine whether the venue in which the case is pending is proper and that the venue to which the case would be transferred would itself be a proper venue under 28 U.S.C. §1391.

Assuming the transferee venue would be appropriate under federal law, the court applies a set of factors. The factors break down into two types: private interest factors and public interest factors.

The private interest factors include: (1) the plaintiff's choice of forum, unless the balance of convenience is strongly in favor of the defendants; (2) the defendant's choice of forum; (3) whether the claim arose elsewhere; (4) the convenience of the parties; (5) the convenience of the witnesses; and (6) the ease of access to sources of proof.

The public interest considerations include: (1) the transferee's familiarity with the governing laws; (2) the relative congestion of the calendars of the potential transferee and transferor courts; and (3) the local interest in deciding local controversies at home.

Although each factor is just that—a factor—the plaintiff's choice of forum is the most important. Here, however, the plaintiff's choice was substantially outweighed by the other factors. It did not help the plaintiff's case that the plaintiff did not reside in the venue she chose.

MacMunn v. Eli Lilly Co.: Real Life Applications

1. The plaintiff filed suit in the Northern District of California where the defendant resides. The car accident that is the subject of the lawsuit occurred in the Southern District of California. The plaintiff, the eyewitnesses to the accident, the physicians who treated the plaintiff, and the police officers who investigated the accident also all reside in the Southern District of California. Who is likely to be a witness in a case like this? Does the court consider the convenience of some witnesses more important than others? If so, which ones and why? Is there a factor the court generally considers the most important? If so, which one? If you had to choose a second most important factor, what would it be and why?

2. Assume the same facts as above. Is the court likely to transfer the case to the Southern District of California? What statutory provision should the defendant rely upon—section 1406 or 1404? Now assume the plaintiff is the one who moves to transfer venue to the Southern District of California. Is the plaintiff permitted to do so? Would this make the court more or less likely to grant transfer? Why or why not?

3. A plaintiff sues a Canadian pharmaceutical company and a Canadian doctor in the federal court for the Northern District of California for providing him a drug without warning the plaintiff of its serious side effects. All of the treatment occurred in Canada. While the doctor was on vacation in California, the plaintiff arranged to have a process server serve the doctor with the summons and complaint in the pending federal action. Focusing only on challenging venue, what statutory provision should the defendants rely upon—section 1406 or 1404? Is the court likely to dismiss or transfer the case based on a challenge to venue? Why or why not?

When Do I Use Section 1406 or 1404?

Exhibit 12.1 lays out when each of the three doctrines—including *forum non conveniens*—is the appropriate tool to challenge venue. But how do you decide whether section 1406 or 1404 is the appropriate vehicle in seeking a transfer of venue for a given federal case? Exhibit 12.3 should help you decide.

EXHIBIT 12.3	**When to Use Section 1406 or 1404**	
	Transferor Court:	**Transferee Court:**
28 U.S.C. §1406	Improper venue	Proper venue
28 U.S.C. §1404	Proper, but less convenient than another proper venue	Proper and more convenient

C. COMMON LAW VENUE DISMISSALS: *FORUM NON CONVENIENS*

The common law doctrine of *forum non conveniens* fills a gap. It is the mechanism to dismiss, rather than transfer, a case on venue grounds when the case was originally brought in a proper venue. Although this comes up most often in situations where the moving party thinks a more appropriate venue lies in a foreign nation, it is available to parties to use when the case has been filed in a proper venue but the court lacks the authority to transfer the case to the different legal system. Recall the earlier discussion on the ban on intersystem transfers; federal courts cannot transfer cases to other jurisdictions, whether they are other states or foreign countries. And state courts cannot transfer cases from one state court to another.

Case Preview

Piper Aircraft Co. v. Reyno

Before you read *Piper*, consider the procedural history. This will help you to understand exactly what the Court is deciding — and what it is not. The case was initially filed in California state court. The defendant then removed the case to federal court in California. After removal, the defendants moved to transfer venue to another federal court in Pennsylvania and the court transferred the case to that court under section 1404. The defendants then moved to dismiss the case on *forum non conveniens* grounds and the Pennsylvania district court granted the motion and dismissed the case. The court of appeals reversed that decision, holding that dismissal was improper. In the case below, the United States Supreme Court is analyzing whether the court of appeals considered the right factors and whether it gave too much or too little weight to certain factors.

As you read *Piper*, consider the following questions:

1. What is the standard for dismissing a case on *forum non conveniens* grounds? How does the analysis compare to transfers of venue under section 1404?
2. What was the main reason the court of appeals reversed the trial court? In other words, why did the court of appeals decide that the trial court should not have dismissed the case on *forum non conveniens* grounds?

3. What does the Court say about the main reason the court of appeals reversed the trial court? Can a court consider such a reason in deciding a motion to dismiss on *forum non conveniens* grounds? If so, when and to what extent?

Piper Aircraft Co. v. Reyno
454 U.S. 235 (1981)

Justice MARSHALL delivered the opinion of the Court.

These cases arise out of an air crash that took place in Scotland. Respondent, acting as representative of the estates of several Scottish citizens killed in the accident, brought wrongful-death actions against petitioners that were ultimately transferred to the United States District Court for the Middle District of Pennsylvania. Petitioners moved to dismiss on the ground of forum non conveniens. After noting that an alternative forum existed in Scotland, the District Court granted their motions. The United States Court of Appeals for the Third Circuit reversed. The Court of Appeals based its decision, at least in part, on the ground that dismissal is automatically barred where the law of the alternative forum is less favorable to the plaintiff than the law of the forum chosen by the plaintiff. Because we conclude that the possibility of an unfavorable change in law should not, by itself, bar dismissal, and because we conclude that the District Court did not otherwise abuse its discretion, we reverse.

I

A

In July 1976, a small commercial aircraft crashed in the Scottish highlands during the course of a charter flight from Blackpool to Perth. The pilot and five passengers were killed instantly. The decedents were all Scottish subjects and residents, as are their heirs and next of kin. There were no eyewitnesses to the accident. At the time of the crash the plane was subject to Scottish air traffic control.

The aircraft, a twin-engine Piper Aztec, was manufactured in Pennsylvania by petitioner Piper Aircraft Co. (Piper). The propellers were manufactured in Ohio by petitioner Hartzell Propeller, Inc. (Hartzell). At the time of the crash the aircraft was registered in Great Britain and was owned and maintained by Air Navigation and Trading Co., Ltd. (Air Navigation). It was operated by McDonald Aviation, Ltd. (McDonald), a Scottish air taxi service. Both Air Navigation and McDonald were organized in the United Kingdom. The wreckage of the plane is now in a hangar in Farnsborough, England.

The British Department of Trade investigated the accident shortly after it occurred. A preliminary report found that the plane crashed after developing a spin, and suggested that mechanical failure in the plane or the propeller was responsible. At Hartzell's request, this report was reviewed by a three-member Review Board, which held a 9-day adversary hearing attended by all interested parties. The Review Board found no evidence of defective equipment and indicated that pilot error may have contributed to the accident. The pilot, who had obtained his commercial pilot's license only three months earlier, was flying over high ground at an altitude considerably lower than the minimum height required by his company's operations manual.

In July 1977, a California probate court appointed respondent Gaynell Reyno administratrix of the estates of the five passengers. Reyno is not related to and does not know any of the decedents or their survivors; she was a legal secretary to the attorney who filed this lawsuit. Several days after her appointment, Reyno commenced separate wrongful-death actions against Piper and Hartzell in the Superior Court of California, claiming negligence and strict liability. Air Navigation, McDonald, and the estate of the pilot are not parties to this litigation. The survivors of the five passengers whose estates are represented by Reyno filed a separate action in the United Kingdom against Air Navigation, McDonald, and the pilot's estate. Reyno candidly admits that the action against Piper and Hartzell was filed in the United States because its laws regarding liability, capacity to sue, and damages are more favorable to her position than are those of Scotland. Scottish law does not recognize strict liability in tort. Moreover, it permits wrongful-death actions only when brought by a decedent's relatives. The relatives may sue only for "loss of support and society."

On petitioners' motion, the suit was removed to the United States District Court for the Central District of California. Piper then moved for transfer to the United States District Court for the Middle District of Pennsylvania, pursuant to 28 U.S.C. §1404(a). Hartzell moved to dismiss for lack of personal jurisdiction, or in the alternative, to transfer. In December 1977, the District Court quashed service on Hartzell and transferred the case to the Middle District of Pennsylvania. Respondent then properly served process on Hartzell.

B

In May 1978, after the suit had been transferred, both Hartzell and Piper moved to dismiss the action on the ground of forum non conveniens. The District Court granted these motions in October 1979. It relied on the balancing test set forth by this Court . . . . The Court stated that a plaintiff's choice of forum should rarely be disturbed. However, when an alternative forum has jurisdiction to hear the case, and when trial in the chosen forum would "establish . . . oppressiveness and vexation to a defendant . . . out of all proportion to plaintiff's convenience," or when the "chosen forum [is] inappropriate because of considerations affecting the court's own administrative and legal problems," the court may, in the exercise of its sound discretion, dismiss the case. To guide trial court discretion, the Court provided a list of "private interest factors" affecting the convenience of the litigants, and a list of "public interest factors" affecting the convenience of the forum.

After describing [the balancing test], the District Court analyzed the facts of these cases. It began by observing that an alternative forum existed in Scotland; Piper and Hartzell had agreed to submit to the jurisdiction of the Scottish courts and to waive any statute of limitations defense that might be available. It then stated that plaintiff's choice of forum was entitled to little weight. The court recognized that a plaintiff's choice ordinarily deserves substantial deference. It noted, however, that Reyno "is a representative of foreign citizens and residents seeking a forum in the

United States because of the more liberal rules concerning products liability law," and that "the courts have been less solicitous when the plaintiff is not an American citizen or resident, and particularly when the foreign citizens seek to benefit from the more liberal tort rules provided for the protection of citizens and residents of the United States."

The District Court next examined several factors relating to the private interests of the litigants, and determined that these factors strongly pointed towards Scotland as the appropriate forum. Although evidence concerning the design, manufacture, and testing of the plane and propeller is located in the United States, the connections with Scotland are otherwise "overwhelming." The real parties in interest are citizens of Scotland, as were all the decedents. Witnesses who could testify regarding the maintenance of the aircraft, the training of the pilot, and the investigation of the accident — all essential to the defense — are in Great Britain. Moreover, all witnesses to damages are located in Scotland. Trial would be aided by familiarity with Scottish topography, and by easy access to the wreckage.

The District Court reasoned that because crucial witnesses and evidence were beyond the reach of compulsory process, and because the defendants would not be able to implead potential Scottish third-party defendants, it would be "unfair to make Piper and Hartzell proceed to trial in this forum." The survivors had brought separate actions in Scotland against the pilot, McDonald, and Air Navigation. "[I]t would be fairer to all parties and less costly if the entire case was presented to one jury with available testimony from all relevant witnesses." Ibid. Although the court recognized that if trial were held in the United States, Piper and Hartzell could file indemnity or contribution actions against the Scottish defendants, it believed that there was a significant risk of inconsistent verdicts.

The District Court concluded that the relevant public interests also pointed strongly towards dismissal. The court determined that Pennsylvania law would apply to Piper and Scottish law to Hartzell if the case were tried in the Middle District of Pennsylvania. As a result, "trial in this forum would be hopelessly complex and confusing for a jury." Id., at 734. In addition, the court noted that it was unfamiliar with Scottish law and thus would have to rely upon experts from that country. The court also found that the trial would be enormously costly and time-consuming; that it would be unfair to burden citizens with jury duty when the Middle District of Pennsylvania has little connection with the controversy; and that Scotland has a substantial interest in the outcome of the litigation.

In opposing the motions to dismiss, respondent contended that dismissal would be unfair because Scottish law was less favorable. The District Court explicitly rejected this claim. It reasoned that the possibility that dismissal might lead to an unfavorable change in the law did not deserve significant weight; any deficiency in the foreign law was a "matter to be dealt with in the foreign forum." Id., at 738.

C

On appeal, the United States Court of Appeals for the Third Circuit reversed and remanded for trial. The decision to reverse appears to be based on two alternative grounds. First, the Court held that the District Court abused its discretion in conducting the Gilbert analysis. Second, the Court held that dismissal is never appropriate where the law of the alternative forum is less favorable to the plaintiff.

The Court of Appeals began its review of the District Court's Gilbert analysis by noting that the plaintiff's choice of forum deserved substantial weight, even though the real parties in interest are nonresidents. It then rejected the District Court's balancing of the private interests. It found that Piper and Hartzell had failed adequately to support their claim that key witnesses would be unavailable if trial were held in the United States: they had never specified the witnesses they would call and the testimony these witnesses would provide. The Court of Appeals gave little weight to the fact that Piper and Hartzell would not be able to implead potential Scottish third-party defendants, reasoning that this difficulty would be "burdensome" but not "unfair," 639 F.2d, at 162. Finally, the court stated that resolution of the suit would not be significantly aided by familiarity with Scottish topography, or by viewing the wreckage.

The Court of Appeals also rejected the District Court's analysis of the public interest factors. It found that the District Court gave undue emphasis to the application of Scottish law: "'the mere fact that the court is called upon to determine and apply foreign law does not present a legal problem of the sort which would justify the dismissal of a case otherwise properly before the court.'" Id., at 163. In any event, it believed that Scottish law need not be applied. After conducting its own choice-of-law analysis, the Court of Appeals determined that American law would govern the actions against both Piper and Hartzell. The same choice-of-law analysis apparently led it to conclude that Pennsylvania and Ohio, rather than Scotland, are the jurisdictions with the greatest policy interests in the dispute, and that all other public interest factors favored trial in the United States.

In any event, it appears that the Court of Appeals would have reversed even if the District Court had properly balanced the public and private interests. The court stated:

> "[I]t is apparent that the dismissal would work a change in the applicable law so that the plaintiff's strict liability claim would be eliminated from the case. But . . . a dismissal for forum non conveniens, like a statutory transfer, 'should not, despite its convenience, result in a change in the applicable law.' Only when American law is not applicable, or when the foreign jurisdiction would, as a matter of its own choice of law, give the plaintiff the benefit of the claim to which she is entitled here, would dismissal be justified." 630 F.2d, at 163–164.

In other words, the court decided that dismissal is automatically barred if it would lead to a change in the applicable law unfavorable to the plaintiff.

We granted certiorari in these cases to consider the questions they raise concerning the proper application of the doctrine of forum non conveniens.

II

The Court of Appeals erred in holding that plaintiffs may defeat a motion to dismiss on the ground of forum non conveniens merely by showing that the substantive law that would be applied in the alternative forum is less favorable to the plaintiffs than that of the present forum. The possibility of a change in substantive law should ordinarily not be given conclusive or even substantial weight in the forum non conveniens inquiry.

We expressly rejected the position adopted by the Court of Appeals in our decision in Canada Malting Co. v. Paterson Steamships, Ltd., 285 U.S. 413, 52 S. Ct. 413, 76 L. Ed. 837 (1932). That case arose out of a collision between two vessels in American waters. The Canadian owners of cargo lost in the accident sued the Canadian owners of one of the vessels in Federal District Court. The cargo owners chose an American court in large part because the relevant American liability rules were more favorable than the Canadian rules. The District Court dismissed on grounds of forum non conveniens. The plaintiffs argued that dismissal was inappropriate because Canadian laws were less favorable to them.

This Court nonetheless affirmed:

> "We have no occasion to enquire by what law the rights of the parties are governed, as we are of the opinion that, under any view of that question, it lay within the discretion of the District Court to decline to assume jurisdiction over the controversy.... '[T]he court will not take cognizance of the case if justice would be as well done by remitting the parties to their home forum.'" Id., at 419–420, 52 S. Ct., at 414, quoting Charter Shipping Co. v. Bowring, Jones & Tidy, 281 U.S. 515, 517, 50 S. Ct. 400, 414, 74 L. Ed. 1008 (1930). The Court further stated that "[t]here was no basis for the contention that the District Court abused its discretion." 285 U.S., at 423, 52 S. Ct., at 415–16.

It is true that . . . the doctrine of forum non conveniens was not fully crystallized until our decision in that case. However, . . . the central focus of the forum non conveniens inquiry is convenience, [and] dismissal may not be barred solely because of the possibility of an unfavorable change in law. . . . [D]ismissal will ordinarily be appropriate where trial in the plaintiff's chosen forum imposes a heavy burden on the defendant or the court, and where the plaintiff is unable to offer any specific reasons of convenience supporting his choice. If substantial weight were given to the possibility of an unfavorable change in law, however, dismissal might be barred even where trial in the chosen forum was plainly inconvenient.

The Court of Appeals' decision is inconsistent with this Court's earlier forum non conveniens decisions in another respect. Those decisions have repeatedly emphasized the need to retain flexibility. . . . [T]he Court refused to identify specific circumstances "which will justify or require either grant or denial of remedy." 330 U.S., at 508, 67 S. Ct., at 843. Similarly, . . . the Court rejected the contention that where a trial would involve inquiry into the internal affairs of a foreign corporation, dismissal was always appropriate. "That is one, but only one, factor which may show convenience." 330 U.S., at 527, 67 S. Ct., at 833. And . . . we [have] stated that we would not lay down a rigid rule to govern discretion, and that "[e]ach case turns on its facts." If central emphasis were placed on any one factor, the forum non conveniens doctrine would lose much of the very flexibility that makes it so valuable.

In fact, if conclusive or substantial weight were given to the possibility of a change in law, the forum non conveniens doctrine would become virtually useless. Jurisdiction and venue requirements are often easily satisfied. As a result, many plaintiffs are able to choose from among several forums. Ordinarily, these plaintiffs will select that forum whose choice-of-law rules are most advantageous. Thus, if the possibility of an unfavorable change in substantive law is given substantial weight in the forum non conveniens inquiry, dismissal would rarely be proper.

* * *

The Court of Appeals' approach is not only inconsistent with the purpose of the forum non conveniens doctrine, but also poses substantial practical problems. If the possibility of a change in law were given substantial weight, deciding motions to dismiss on the ground of forum non conveniens would become quite difficult. Choice-of-law analysis would become extremely important, and the courts would frequently be required to interpret the law of foreign jurisdictions. First, the trial court would have to determine what law would apply if the case were tried in the chosen forum, and what law would apply if the case were tried in the alternative forum. It would then have to compare the rights, remedies, and procedures available under the law that would be applied in each forum. Dismissal would be appropriate only if the court concluded that the law applied by the alternative forum is as favorable to the plaintiff as that of the chosen forum. The doctrine of forum non conveniens, however, is designed in part to help courts avoid conducting complex exercises in comparative law. . . .

Upholding the decision of the Court of Appeals would result in other practical problems. At least where the foreign plaintiff named an American manufacturer as a defendant, a court could not dismiss the case on grounds of forum non conveniens where dismissal might lead to an unfavorable change in law. The American courts, which are already extremely attractive to foreign plaintiffs, would become even more attractive. The flow of litigation into the United States would increase and further congest already crowded courts.

The Court of Appeals based its decision, at least in part, on an analogy between dismissals on grounds of forum non conveniens and transfers between federal courts pursuant to §1404(a). . . . [T]his Court ruled that a §1404(a) transfer should not result in a change in the applicable law. Relying on dictum in an earlier Third Circuit opinion . . . the court below held that that principle is also applicable to a dismissal on forum non conveniens grounds. However, §1404(a) transfers are different than dismissals on the ground of forum non conveniens. . . .

Congress enacted §1404(a) to permit change of venue between federal courts. Although the statute was drafted in accordance with the doctrine of forum non conveniens, . . . , it was intended to be a revision rather than a codification of the common law. . . . District courts were given more discretion to transfer under §1404(a) than they had to dismiss on grounds of forum non conveniens. . . .

The statute was designed as a "federal housekeeping measure," allowing easy change of venue within a unified federal system. . . . The Court feared that if a change in venue were accompanied by a change in law, forum-shopping parties would take unfair advantage of the relaxed standards for transfer. The rule was necessary to ensure the just and efficient operation of the statute.

We do not hold that the possibility of an unfavorable change in law should never be a relevant consideration in a forum non conveniens inquiry. Of course, if the remedy provided by the alternative forum is so clearly inadequate or unsatisfactory that it is no remedy at all, the unfavorable change in law may be given substantial weight;

the district court may conclude that dismissal would not be in the interests of justice. In these cases, however, the remedies that would be provided by the Scottish courts do not fall within this category. Although the relatives of the decedents may not be able to rely on a strict liability theory, and although their potential damages award may be smaller, there is no danger that they will be deprived of any remedy or treated unfairly.

III

The Court of Appeals also erred in rejecting the District Court's . . . analysis. The Court of Appeals stated that more weight should have been given to the plaintiff's choice of forum, and criticized the District Court's analysis of the private and public interests. However, the District Court's decision regarding the deference due plaintiff's choice of forum was appropriate. Furthermore, we do not believe that the District Court abused its discretion in weighing the private and public interests.

A

The District Court acknowledged that there is ordinarily a strong presumption in favor of the plaintiff's choice of forum, which may be overcome only when the private and public interest factors clearly point towards trial in the alternative forum. It held, however, that the presumption applies with less force when the plaintiff or real parties in interest are foreign.

The District Court's distinction between resident or citizen plaintiffs and foreign plaintiffs is fully justified. [This] Court [has] indicated that a plaintiff's choice of forum is entitled to greater deference when the plaintiff has chosen the home forum. . . . When the home forum has been chosen, it is reasonable to assume that this choice is convenient. When the plaintiff is foreign, however, this assumption is much less reasonable. Because the central purpose of any forum non conveniens inquiry is to ensure that the trial is convenient, a foreign plaintiff's choice deserves less deference.

B

The forum non conveniens determination is committed to the sound discretion of the trial court. It may be reversed only when there has been a clear abuse of discretion; where the court has considered all relevant public and private interest factors, and where its balancing of these factors is reasonable, its decision deserves substantial deference. . . . Here, the Court of Appeals expressly acknowledged that the standard of review was one of abuse of discretion. In examining the District Court's analysis of the public and private interests, however, the Court of Appeals seems to have lost sight of this rule, and substituted its own judgment for that of the District Court.

(1)

In analyzing the private interest factors, the District Court stated that the connections with Scotland are "overwhelming." 479 F. Supp., at 732. This characterization may be somewhat exaggerated. Particularly with respect to the question of relative ease of access to sources of proof, the private interests point in both directions. As respondent emphasizes, records concerning the design, manufacture, and testing of the propeller and plane are located in the United States. She would have greater access to sources of proof relevant to her strict liability and negligence theories if trial were held here. However, the District Court did not act unreasonably in concluding that fewer evidentiary problems would be posed if the trial were held in Scotland. A large proportion of the relevant evidence is located in Great Britain.

The Court of Appeals found that the problems of proof could not be given any weight because Piper and Hartzell failed to describe with specificity the evidence they would not be able to obtain if trial were held in the United States. It suggested that defendants seeking forum non conveniens dismissal must submit affidavits identifying the witnesses they would call and the testimony these witnesses would provide if the trial were held in the alternative forum. Such detail is not necessary. Piper and Hartzell have moved for dismissal precisely because many crucial wit nesses are located beyond the reach of compulsory process, and thus are difficult to identify or interview. Requiring extensive investigation would defeat the purpose of their motion. Of course, defendants must provide enough information to enable the District Court to balance the parties' interests. Our examination of the record convinces us that sufficient information was provided here. Both Piper and Hartzell submitted affidavits describing the evidentiary problems they would face if the trial were held in the United States.

The District Court correctly concluded that the problems posed by the inability to implead potential third-party defendants clearly supported holding the trial in Scotland. Joinder of the pilot's estate, Air Navigation, and McDonald is crucial to the presentation of petitioners' defense. If Piper and Hartzell can show that the acci dent was caused not by a design defect, but rather by the negligence of the pilot, the plane's owners, or the charter company, they will be relieved of all liability. It is true, of course, that if Hartzell and Piper were found liable after a trial in the United States, they could institute an action for indemnity or contribution against these parties in Scotland. It would be far more convenient, however, to resolve all claims in one trial. The Court of Appeals rejected this argument. Forcing petitioners to rely on actions for indemnity or contributions would be "burdensome" but not "unfair." 630 F.2d, at 162. Finding that trial in the plaintiff's chosen forum would be burdensome, how ever, is sufficient to support dismissal on grounds of forum non conveniens.

(2)

The District Court's review of the factors relating to the public interest was also reasonable. On the basis of its choice-of-law analysis, it concluded that if the case were tried in the Middle District of Pennsylvania, Pennsylvania law would apply to Piper and Scottish law to Hartzell. It stated that a trial involving two sets of laws would be confusing to the jury. It also noted its own lack of familiarity with Scot tish law. Consideration of these problems was clearly appropriate. . . . The Court of Appeals found that the District Court's choice-of-law analysis was incorrect, and that American law would apply to both Hartzell and Piper. Thus, lack of familiarity with foreign law would not be a problem. Even if the Court of Appeals' conclusion is correct, however, all other public interest factors favored trial in Scotland.

Scotland has a very strong interest in this litigation. The accident occurred in its airspace. All of the decedents were Scottish. Apart from Piper and Hartzell, all potential plaintiffs and defendants are either Scottish or English. . . . [T]here is "a local interest in having localized controversies decided at home." 330 U.S., at 509, 67 S. Ct., at 843. Respondent argues that American citizens have an interest in ensuring that American manufacturers are deterred from producing defective products, and that additional deterrence might be obtained if Piper and Hartzell were tried in the United States, where they could be sued on the basis of both negligence and strict liability. However, the incremental deterrence that would be gained if this trial were held in an American court is likely to be insignificant. The American interest in this accident is simply not sufficient to justify the enormous commitment of judicial time and resources that would inevitably be required if the case were to be tried here.

IV

The Court of Appeals erred in holding that the possibility of an unfavorable change in law bars dismissal on the ground of forum non conveniens. It also erred . . . [because] [t]he District Court properly decided that the presumption in favor of the respondent's forum choice applied with less than maximum force because the real parties in interest are foreign. It did not act unreasonably in deciding that the private interests pointed towards trial in Scotland. Nor did it act unreasonably in deciding that the public interests favored trial in Scotland. Thus, the judgment of the Court of Appeals is

Reversed.

Post-Case Follow-Up

The Court engages in an analysis that is very similar to section 1404 transfers. Note the strong similarity between the factors the Court considers in determining whether to transfer and whether to dismiss.

The Court decided *Piper* and reversed the court of appeals on two basic grounds. One ground is that the court of appeals failed to give proper deference to the trial court's application of the private and public interest factors. More importantly, the Court reversed the court of appeals because it set up a per se rule inconsistent with prior Supreme Court doctrine and the purpose of *forum non conveniens*. The court of appeals erroneously held that if the more appropriate venue (here, Scotland) would provide less appealing relief, the district court can never dismiss on *forum non conveniens* grounds. That rule flies in the face of the flexibility that the doctrine is intended to provide.

The Court did not say that if the laws of the foreign jurisdiction would provide less or no relief, such a fact would be irrelevant. In fact, the Court reinforced the idea that the doctrine is intended to be flexible — and whether the plaintiff would be effectively denied relief if a *forum non conveniens* dismissal is granted is relevant. In some cases, it may be determinative; the Court suggested that a district court may properly refuse to dismiss a case on *forum non conveniens* grounds if a dismissal would result in the plaintiff having no remedy at all. Given the posture of *Piper*, a plaintiff would likely have to convince the court that dismissal would be tantamount to being deprived of any opportunity for a meaningful remedy.

Piper Aircraft Co. v. Reyno: Real Life Applications

1. A plaintiff had his fingers cut off in a metal shearing machine while working in a New Jersey scrap yard. The machine was made in the U.K. by a company that regularly does business in New Jersey, selling hundreds of machines to scrapyards throughout New Jersey. The plaintiff sued the U.K. company in New Jersey federal court and his claim is a design defect claim. The design documents and product witnesses are all located in the U.K. and the New Jersey court believes U.K. law would apply and would limit the damages the plaintiff is permitted to recover. What doctrine should the U.K. company use to challenge venue? Should it seek dismissal or transfer? Is the U.K. company's motion likely to be granted? Why or why not?

2. A helicopter crashed in Brazil killing a U.S. citizen on board. The representative of the estate of the deceased U.S. citizen sued the helicopter manufacturer for manufacturing a defective helicopter and the pilot for negligence in the federal court in the Northern District of Texas. The helicopter was manufactured in the Northern District of Texas and the pilot, who survived, is a Brazilian citizen. Brazil has a complex state-sponsored insurance scheme to compensate injured people that applies only to its citizens. Brazil does not recognize negligence or product defect claims. The pilot and helicopter manufacturer move to dismiss on *forum non conveniens* grounds. How is the court likely to rule? What factors is the court likely to consider — or not consider — and why?

Chapter Summary

- Section 1406 applies if a case is filed in an improper venue. Although a court may have to dismiss a case if there is no proper venue in any federal judicial district, more often there is at least one proper venue under the general venue statute explained in Chapter 11. When that is the case, federal courts typically transfer the case in the interest of justice to the venue where the case could have been filed.

- Section 1404 applies to cases that are filed in a proper venue. It authorizes a federal court to transfer venue to another federal court that is also a proper venue. A court will weigh a number of private and public interest factors. The private interest factors include: (1) the plaintiff's choice of forum, unless the balance of convenience is strongly in favor of the defendants; (2) the defendant's choice of forum; (3) whether the claim arose elsewhere; (4) the convenience of the parties;

(5) the convenience of the witnesses; and (6) the ease of access to sources of proof. The public interest considerations include: (1) the transferee's familiarity with the governing laws; (2) the relative congestion of the calendars of the potential transferee and transferor courts; and (3) the local interest in deciding local controversies at home.

▪ Federal district courts can transfer cases to other federal districts, but not to state courts or to courts in other countries. Cases can also be transferred from one division to another division within a federal judicial district.

▪ Parties can waive the issue of venue and usually can consent by agreement to litigate in a particular venue in the event that a dispute arises.

▪ Federal courts use the common law doctrine of *forum non conveniens* to dismiss a case that was filed in a proper venue in favor of a foreign forum that can provide an adequate remedy to a plaintiff. The factors a court considers in deciding such a motion are the same factors described above in deciding whether to transfer under section 1404. In general, however, courts are more reluctant to grant a *forum non conveniens* dismissal than to grant a motion to transfer.

Applying the Concepts

1. During an apparent terrorist attack on a German hotel, a U.S. citizen was killed in the hotel while staying at the hotel on vacation. The administrator of the U.S. citizen's estate sued the German hotel for its lack of proper security as well as suing the hotel's parent company, which is a corporation formed under Delaware law, with its only place of business in Germany. The suit is filed in the federal district court in Delaware, a single district state. Is the hotel likely to be able to dismiss the case for improper venue? If so, under what doctrine? Would the fact that the hotel offered in its motion to agree to submit to the personal jurisdiction of the courts in Germany affect your analysis? If so, how? Explain your answer.

2. Swiss Watch, Inc. (SWI) is a corporation formed under Swiss law with its principal place of business in Switzerland. China Watch Corp. (CWC) is a corporation formed under Chinese law with its principal place of business in China. SWI filed suit against CWC in federal court in the Southern District of New York and claims CWC sold SWI-branded watches in Manhattan, in the Southern District of New York, in violation of U.S. trademark law. Your research indicates that Chinese courts would not recognize or enforce U.S. trademark laws and that Chinese courts take about as long to resolve cases as federal courts in New York. What doctrine should CWC rely upon to have the case dismissed for improper venue? What is the best argument CWC should make to have the case dismissed on venue grounds? What is its weakest argument?

Civil Procedure in Practice

You are a lawyer representing a new client, UGS. UGS's general counsel tells you that it does not want to litigate in Texas; it would rather litigate in Michigan where it is well known and respected. The UGS general counsel provides you a summary of the pending case and asks if you think you can get the case transferred from Texas to Michigan. Here are the facts he has given you:

Plaintiff Weinstein filed claims against UGS. Mr. Weinstein has been a citizen and resident of Michigan at all relevant times. UGS is a Delaware corporation with its principal place of business in Plano, Texas, but with offices in Livonia, Michigan.

While employed by UGS in Michigan, Mr. Derringer struck and killed Judith, Alexander, and Samuel Weinstein while driving under the influence of alcohol after leaving UGS's offices in Livonia, Michigan. Mr. Derringer had apparently been drinking on the job. Mr. Derringer was tried and convicted of second degree murder and was sentenced to 19 years in prison in the Michigan Department of Corrections, where he currently resides. Mr. Weinstein alleges that UGS is liable both vicariously and independently for Mr. Derringer's negligence.

There has been a significant amount of litigation related to this accident. Mr. Derringer's insurer filed suit against him in Oakland County, Michigan claiming that his automobile insurance lapsed by the time of the accident. In that lawsuit, several of UGS's employees were subpoenaed and noticed for deposition. The witness lists in that litigation included multiple individuals located in Michigan, including UGS employees. Mr. Derringer's employment records and their relation to Mr. Derringer's job performance and mental state before the collision were at issue in another Oakland County lawsuit.

Probate proceedings are currently pending in the Oakland County Probate Court. Previously, Mr. Weinstein settled wrongful death claims against other defendants. The Oakland Country Probate Court had to approve that settlement just as it must approve this settlement. The vast majority of likely witnesses in this litigation are located in Michigan. Substantially all of the events that give rise to this lawsuit occurred in Michigan.

The general counsel has asked you to prepare a memo. As you conduct your analysis, apply the factors methodically — factor by factor. Focus on one factor at a time and decide whether each specific factor favors transfer, disfavors transfer, or is neutral. Then, provide your opinion overall as to whether the court will grant a motion to transfer venue under section 1404.

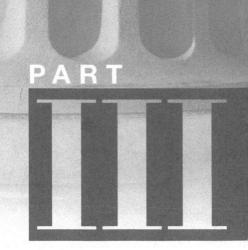

Learning About the Case

Notice: Methods of Service of Process and the Constitutional Requirement of Notice

This chapter explains **service of process**, the vehicle a plaintiff uses to inform the defendant that he has been sued. The chapter begins by explaining the various service of process methods. However, even if a particular rule permits a party to use a given method, that method must also satisfy due process. The party serving the defendant with process must not only comply with the rule authorizing the method of service, but the method of service must be one that is reasonably likely to inform the defendant that an action is pending against her and give her the opportunity to defend herself. Regardless of the method the plaintiff uses, the method must satisfy both the requirements of the rule itself and the minimum standards of constitutional due process.

Just as with personal jurisdiction described in Chapters 6 through 10, the Constitution contains two Due Process Clauses: one in the Fifth Amendment that applies to the federal government and one in the Fourteenth Amendment that applies to the states. To give **notice** that satisfies constitutional due process, a plaintiff must use a method reasonably calculated under all the circumstances to inform the defendant that he has been sued and give him an opportunity to defend himself. When the plaintiff uses an established method and follows the requirements of

Key Concepts

- The rules that govern service of process
- The requirements the Constitution imposes upon a plaintiff to inform a defendant that he has been sued and to give him an opportunity to defend himself
- The requirement that the plaintiff must both use a permissible method of service *and* ensure that the method satisfies constitutional due process

Complaint vs. Summons

As you will learn in Chapters 14 through 17, the complaint is the document that lays out the plaintiff's allegations against the defendant and the remedy the plaintiff seeks. The **summons** is the court document that informs the defendant of her legal obligation to respond to the complaint and the consequences of the failure to do so in a timely manner. Fed. R. Civ. P. 4(a), (c)(1).

the service rule, the plaintiff has likely provided notice that also satisfies constitutional due process. However, as we will see later in the chapter, that is not always the case; sometimes a rule permitting a type of service — even if followed to the letter — does not satisfy due process. And sometimes, particularly when the defendant is hard to identify or locate, some rules permit the court to fashion an alternative method of service. In this type of scenario, the parties and the court should be careful to ensure that the method satisfies the defendant's constitutional due process rights.

A. THE WHO, WHAT, AND WHEN OF SERVICE

Although the civil action begins when the plaintiff files his complaint, the defendant's obligations as to the pending action do not begin until the defendant is served with **process**. Process refers to two documents that must be served on the defendant: the summons and the complaint. Before we begin with methods of service and due process, we should define what **service of process** is; it is the formal procedure by which the defendant is served with the summons and complaint, notifying him that he has been sued, providing basic notice of the claims against him, and informing him of his obligation to respond. The plaintiff must serve both on the defendant. Otherwise, service is improper and the defendant may object to improper process.

In fact, the plaintiff cannot serve the defendant until after he files his complaint. *See* Rule 4(b). If a plaintiff violates that rule, that is also defective service. But the plaintiff does have a ticking clock once the complaint is filed; Rule 4(m) was recently amended to provide that the plaintiff must serve the defendant within just 90 days of filing the complaint. *See* Exhibit 13.1. The plaintiff can request more time but must show good cause for the delay. Otherwise, the court may dismiss the action.

Finally, the plaintiff himself is actually not allowed to serve the defendant. This rule makes good sense. If the situation has come to the point that the plaintiff is suing the defendant, it is fair to assume the relationship between them is not a

---

EXHIBIT 13.1   **Rule 4(m) Time Limit for Service**

> If a defendant is not served within ~~120~~ 90 days after the complaint is filed, the court—on motion or on its own after notice to the plaintiff—must dismiss the action without prejudice against that defendant or order that service be made within a specified time. But if the plaintiff shows good cause for the failure, the court must extend the time for service for an appropriate period.

good one. To alleviate the possibilities of unnecessary friction between the parties, Rule 4(c)(2) states that "[a]ny person who is at least 18 years old and not a party may serve a summons and complaint." This often requires hiring a private process server. Occasionally, a law enforcement officer is authorized to execute service, but if a rule permits service by mail or a similar method, the lawyer herself will likely perform the act of service of process.

Suppose you represent a defendant in a dispute between neighbors over a fence *hypo* your client just built. The plaintiff is upset because he believes the defendant built the fence on the plaintiff's property. The plaintiff does not obtain a lawyer and handwrites the complaint himself. On the way to the courthouse to file the complaint, the plaintiff hands a copy of the complaint to your client and says, "You've been served. I'm taking this all the way to the Supreme Court!" Fortunately, no violence ensues. The defendant brings the document the plaintiff handed him and tells you his story. Is service of process proper under this scenario? No. There are many defects in the form of service under this scenario. First, the plaintiff attempted to serve the defendant before the complaint was filed. The facts also do not mention that the plaintiff served the defendant with a summons; this makes sense because the summons would be issued by the court upon filing the complaint. Next, the plaintiff himself — not a process server — attempted to serve the defendant. Finally, the plaintiff had better realize his errors quickly and correct them quickly — recall that he has only 90 days to perfect service on the defendant under Rule 4(m) or risk dismissal.

B. METHODS OF SERVICE

The Federal Rules of Civil Procedure provide a great deal of flexibility when it comes to serving defendants with process. The method of service depends, however, on the type of defendant the plaintiff wishes to serve. The type of defendant is crucial. There are different rules for serving: (1) individuals inside the U.S. and outside the U.S.; (2) minors and incompetents; (3) non-governmental entities and associations of any type; and (4) the U.S. government and its agencies, corporations, officers, and employees, in either an individual capacity or an official capacity. This section, however, focuses on the two most common types of service you are likely to encounter and use in practice: (1) service on individuals in the U.S., and (2) service on corporations and unincorporated associations.

1. Service on Individuals in the U.S.

A plaintiff has several options in Rule 4(e)(2)(A), (B), and (C) for serving individuals who are to be served in the U.S. *See* Exhibit 13.2. First, the process server may deliver the papers to the defendant personally, often called **"in-hand" service,** wherever she can find the defendant. Second, the process server may leave the summons and complaint at the defendant's "dwelling or usual place of abode with someone of suitable age and discretion who resides there." Third, the process server may deliver the summons and complaint to an agent of the defendant authorized by appointment or by law to receive service of process.

| EXHIBIT 13.2 | **Rule 4(e) Serving an Individual Within a Judicial District of the United States** |

> Unless federal law provides otherwise, an individual—other than a minor, an incompetent person, or a person whose waiver has been filed—may be served in a judicial district of the United States by:
>
> (1) following state law for serving a summons in an action brought in courts of general jurisdiction in the state where the district court is located or where service is made; or
>
> (2) doing any of the following:
>
> (A) delivering a copy of the summons and of the complaint to the individual personally;
>
> (B) leaving a copy of each at the individual's dwelling or usual place of abode with someone of suitable age and discretion who resides there; or
>
> (C) delivering a copy of each to an agent authorized by appointment or by law to receive service of process.

Rule 4(e)(1) creates even more flexibility. The process server may use any method permitted by the state in which the federal suit is pending. The process server may also use any method permitted by the state where process is to be made. Fed. R. Civ. P. 4(e)(1). This last provision gives a plaintiff several alternatives to the three methods specified in Rule 4(e)(2) above. Suppose Johann sues George in federal court in Massachusetts following a car wreck that happened in Massachusetts. George, however, has always lived in Connecticut but is subject to personal jurisdiction in Massachusetts because of his contacts with that state by virtue of the car wreck there. George is back at home in Connecticut by the time Johann's lawyer files the suit. Johann's lawyer is now considering his options for how to properly serve George with process. He has many options. The first is to simply have a process server serve George wherever he can be found by personally delivering ("in hand") the summons and complaint. This is often called the gold standard for serving an individual. George could also have a process server leave a copy of the summons and complaint at George's "dwelling or usual place of abode with someone of suitable age and discretion who resides there." This should seem a bit risky. First, the lawyer needs to be sure it is actually George's dwelling. More problematic is whether the person who is served is of suitable age and discretion. Does a 14-year-old qualify? That appears to be the low range for an acceptable age. Another problem is whether the person who is served resides there. An uncle just visiting or the housekeeping service cannot validly accept service. That leaves service on an agent. It seems unlikely that George would have an agent appointed to accept service in matters like these. Fortunately, Johann's lawyer can resort to the service rules of either Massachusetts or Connecticut. Many states include a method of service like certified mail, return receipt requested. This is likely the easiest method (Johann's lawyer can complete all the paperwork) and he will have proof as to whether George received the summons and complaint thanks to the return receipt.

Lawyers must beware, however, to strictly comply with whatever service rule they choose. In *Hulkill v. Oklahoma Native American Violence Coalition*, the plaintiff filed suit in federal court but elected to use Oklahoma's service of process methods. 542 F.3d 794 (10th Cir. 2008). This is permissible because this is a method of serving process under the law of the state where the federal court case is pending. Rule 4(e)(1). Do not forget that this same rule also allows a plaintiff to resort to the service methods permitted by the state where service is to be made. In *Hulkill*, the relevant Oklahoma service method provided that "[s]ervice by mail shall be accomplished by mailing a copy of the summons and petition by certified mail, return receipt requested and delivery restricted to the addressee." The plaintiff served the defendants by certified mail, return receipt requested, but the return receipt came back with a signature of someone other than the defendants. Apparently, the plaintiff forgot to check the box on the post office form that restricted delivery to the addressee (here, the defendants). Interestingly, Oklahoma law provided that substantial compliance with service rules is sufficient to satisfy Oklahoma's service methods. However, Oklahoma state precedent provided that this kind of error is not substantial compliance. As a result, the court held that neither defendant had been properly served. Thus, there are two lessons from this case. First, if plaintiffs serve using state law service methods, the federal court will look to any state court interpretations of those methods in determining whether service was proper. And second, even in a state that defines proper service as "substantial compliance," plaintiffs should strictly comply with service methods they choose — federal or state.

2. Service on Corporations and Other Entities

A plaintiff also has several options in Rule 4(h) for serving a "corporation, partnership or association." *See* Exhibit 13.3. Associations include labor unions, church groups, political groups, and other unincorporated entities. First, a process server may deliver a copy of the summons and complaint to an officer, a managing agent, or a general agent of the entity. Next, the process server may deliver the papers to an agent authorized by law or by appointment to receive service of process. This, however, does not refer to a general business agent such as a regular employee. Rather, the agent must be one specifically granted the authority to receive service. For example, many states have statutes authorizing service of process on the state's secretary of state for actions against corporations doing business within the state. *See, e.g.,* Tex. Civ. Prac. & Rem. Code §17.044 (2015) (requiring entities doing business in Texas to appoint an agent for service of process and making the Texas Secretary of State the default agent if the entity fails to properly designate such an agent).

Last but not least, a process server may serve process under state rules for serving corporations, in either the state where the federal court suit is pending or in the state where service is made. Although Rule 4(h)(1)(A) provides that service may be made "in the manner prescribed by Rule 4(e)(1) for serving an individual,"

EXHIBIT 13.3 **Rule 4(h) Serving a Corporation, Partnership, or Association**

Unless federal law provides otherwise or the defendant's waiver has been filed, a domestic or foreign corporation, or a partnership or other unincorporated association that is subject to suit under a common name, must be served:
(1) in a judicial district of the United States:
(A) in the manner prescribed by Rule 4(e)(1) for serving an individual; or
(B) by delivering a copy of the summons and of the complaint to an officer, a managing or general agent, or any other agent authorized by appointment or by law to receive service of process and — if the agent is one authorized by statute and the statute so requires — by also mailing a copy of each to the defendant; or
(2) at a place not within any judicial district of the United States, in any manner prescribed by Rule 4(f) for serving an individual, except personal delivery under (f)(2)(C)(i).

this actually means that that the plaintiff may use state service rules for serving a corporation. *See Duckworth v. GMAC Ins.*, 2010 WL 1529392 (N.D. Miss., April 14, 2010) ("Rule 4(e)(1), however, also allows for service pursuant to state law. The court, therefore, must review state law regarding proper service of process on a corporation.").

3. Waiving Service

An easier way to accomplish service in many federal cases is to make use of the provision that enables the plaintiff to ask the defendant to "waive" service by following certain steps. The waiver rule contains both a carrot and a stick: A defendant who agrees to waive any objections to service gets additional time to respond to the complaint, and a defendant who refuses to agree can face a court order requiring him to pay the plaintiff's costs of service. Most defendants have a duty to avoid the costs of formal service unless they can show "good cause" for refusing to do so. If they do not return the waiver, they must pay the costs of formal service, including the attorneys' fees for any motion to collect those costs. Only defendants located in the U.S., however, may be sanctioned for failing to waive formal service. Failing to prove "good cause" for refusing to waive service is difficult; for example, a valid reason would be that the defendant does not read English. An invalid reason would be because the defendant simply wants to force the plaintiff to go through the hassle and expense of service. Fortunately, under Rule 4(d), a defendant may easily waive service of process. The procedure is simple: The plaintiff requests the defendant to waive formal service. The plaintiff sends the defendant a notice of the action with two copies of the waiver form, the complaint, and a prepaid envelope for returning the waiver via first class mail or another reliable means. As noted, the Rule also offers further incentive for a defendant to waive service by giving the defendant additional time to answer or otherwise respond to the complaint. When a defendant waives service, the defendant has 60 days to act rather than the default 21. By encouraging defendants to accept service, this rule serves the courts' interest in minimizing disputes over service in cases in which the defendant is actually aware of the case that has been filed (which is the ultimate goal).

4. Dodging Service

Service becomes more problematic when a defendant avoids service. Suppose that the plaintiff has exhausted all her options — the list provided in Rule 4 and all available state law options, both in the state where the suit is pending and where the defendant seems likely to be found. But the plaintiff has been unable to serve the defendant using any method listed by or incorporated in Rule 4. Does the plaintiff have any other options? If the plaintiff clearly proves to the court that all prior multiple, diligent attempts available to her have failed, the court may authorize **notice by publication** or other means. Rule 4 does not explicitly authorize such an order. However, many state rules include a fallback provision allowing plaintiffs to request that the court authorize an alternative means of service. *See, e.g., Webster Industries, Inc. v. Northwood Doors, Inc.,* 244 F. Supp. 2d 998 (N.D. Iowa 2003) (describing methods for service by publication under both Minnesota and Iowa rules of civil procedure); *see also* N.Y. C.P.L.R. §308(5) (similar rule). In cases where the plaintiff has tried every available method multiple times and the court is convinced no other method is likely to be successful, a court might order service by publication in a newspaper in the county where the case is pending and perhaps where the defendant was last known to reside, together with mail notice to the defendant's last known address.

Notice by publication, however, is problematic. It may be the only way to try and give notice to those who are entitled to know about a pending action. But notice by publication hardly seems likely to provide actual notice. When was the last time you opened your local paper, turned to the classified ads and obituaries, and looked to see if a notice was there informing you that you had been sued? As an example, look at the notice in Exhibit 13.4 below. How likely do you think it is that this notice, which was buried in a local paper, will successfully give notice of the lawsuit pending several states away to its intended target? This problem, and others like it, has inspired the Court to set a standard — a floor — for giving interested persons notice of an action that may detrimentally affect their rights and obligations if they do not appear and defend themselves.

C. CONSTITUTIONAL DUE PROCESS STANDARD FOR NOTICE

As you learned in Chapters 6 through 10 with respect to personal jurisdiction, the Constitution contains two Due Process Clauses — one in the Fifth Amendment applicable to the federal government and one in the Fourteenth Amendment applicable to state governments. While those chapters were concerned with one aspect of due process — the territorial limits on a state court's power to exercise jurisdiction over out-of-state defendants — this chapter focuses on another aspect of the same constitutional guarantee, known as procedural due process. Due process

EXHIBIT 13.4 **Notice by Publication**

NOTICE TO MEAGAN RENEE BROWN THE STATE OF TENNESSEE
NOTICE TO MEAGAN RENEE BROWN

The State of Tennessee, Department of Children's Services, has filed a petition against you regarding the termination of your parental rights as to the minor child, Crisean Marcel Brown. It appears that ordinary process of law cannot be served upon you because your whereabouts are unknown. You are hereby **ORDERED** to appear in the Juvenile Court of Williamson County, located at 408 Century Court, Franklin, Tennessee 37064 for the final hearing on the Department of Children's Services' Petition for Termination of Parental Rights set to be heard on the **18th day of July, 2016 at 9:00 a.m.** to personally answer the Petition for Termination of Parental Rights or serve upon Sarah Grey McCroskey, Assistant General counsel, Department of Children's Services, 1810 Columbia Avenue, Suite 18 Franklin, TN 37064 an answer to said petition within 30 days of the last date of publication of this notice. Failure to appear for the final hearing on this date and time, without good cause, pursuant to Rule 39(c)(3) of the Tennessee Rules of Juvenile Procedure and the Tennessee Rules of Civil Procedure will result in a loss of your right to contest the petition to terminate your parental rights to the above mentioned child. You may view and obtain a copy of the Petition and any other subsequently filed legal documents at the Juvenile Court located at 408 Century Court, Franklin, Tennessee 37064.

ENTERED this, the 28th day of April 2016

SHARON GUFFEE
JUVENILE COURT JUDGE

APPROVED FOR ENTRY:
Sarah Grey McCroskey, BPR# 33427
Assistant General Counsel
Tennessee Department of Children's Services
1810 Columbia Avenue, Suite 18
Franklin, TN 37064
(615) 790-5965

means the government may not deprive a person of life, liberty, or property without due process of law. Due process, at its most basic level, requires notice and an opportunity to be heard. *Mullane v. Central Hanover Bank & Trust Co.* deals with the Constitution's standard for notice that all methods of service must be judged against. In other words, just because you follow one or more of the methods of service permitted by law does not mean that method satisfies due process.

Case Preview

Mullane v. Central Hanover Bank & Trust Co.

As you read *Mullane*, consider these questions:

1. What methods did the bank use to attempt to notify those who may have had an interest in the trusts?
2. Did the Court hold that the bank was required to give the same kind of notice to all persons with an interest in the trust?
3. Did the Court approve notice by publication? Why or why not?
4. What is the "classic" method for providing notice to a defendant?

Mullane v. Central Hanover Bank & Trust Co.
339 U.S. 306 (1950)

Mr. Justice JACKSON delivered the opinion of the Court. This controversy questions the constitutional sufficiency of notice to beneficiaries on judicial settlement of accounts by the trustee of a common trust fund established under the New York Banking Law. . . .

[Eds. — Some background on common trusts should help you understand this case. Banks are often popular choices to act as trustees to administer trusts. Banks are likely to be familiar with the procedures and obligations of administering trusts. Put simply, a trust is a device for administering assets. The common trust fund law was aimed at administering trusts that were so small that it would not be financially viable for a bank to administer them. As a result, New York law permitted banks to pool the assets of small trusts in a "common trust fund." This allowed banks to invest the assets of many small trusts in a single fund to achieve economies of scale and reduce expenses. New York law provided that banks had to provide regular accountings to the court and get court approval in order to ensure the bank was administering the common trust fund properly. But if the court approved the accountings, the bank was insulated from liability; no one could sue the bank for mismanaging the common trust. However, providing actual notice of the court proceeding to everyone with a possible interest in the common trust would be nearly impossible. Each small trust likely contained different terms. One might call for payment of trust income to Person A, then to Person B if A dies, and perhaps require distributing the trust's assets to Person C when she turns 18, or dividing the trust's assets among various beneficiaries in the future. In short, many people might have an interest in the income and/or principal of each pooled trust at any given time. Considering that fact, the bank estimated that perhaps 5,000 people could have interests in these commingled common trusts, and deciphering who may be entitled to what and providing notice to all of them would be so time consuming and expensive that it would destroy the utility of the common fund device.]

Statutory authorization for the establishment of such common trust funds is provided in the New York Banking Law. Under this Act a trust company may, with approval of the State Banking Board, establish a common fund and, within prescribed limits, invest therein the assets of an unlimited number of estates, trusts or other funds of which it is trustee. Each participating trust shares ratably in the common fund, but exclusive management and control is in the trust company as trustee, and neither a fiduciary nor any beneficiary of a participating trust is deemed to have ownership in any particular asset or investment of this common fund. The trust company must keep fund assets separate from its own, and in its fiduciary capacity may not deal with itself or any affiliate. Provisions are made for accountings twelve to fifteen months after the establishment of a fund and triennially thereafter. The decree in each such judicial settlement of accounts is made binding and conclusive as to any matter set forth in the account upon everyone having any interest in the common fund or in any participating estate, trust or fund.

In January, 1946, Central Hanover Bank and Trust Company established a common trust fund in accordance with these provisions, and in March, 1947, it petitioned the Surrogate's Court for settlement of its first account as common trustee. During the accounting period a total of 113 trusts, approximately half inter vivos and half testamentary, participated in the common trust fund, the gross capital of which was nearly three million dollars. The record does not show the number or residence of the beneficiaries, but they were many and it is clear that some of them were not residents of the State of New York.

[Eds. — The New York statute required the bank to provide notice of the account settlement procedure to those with an interest in the fund. Note how the bank gave notice of the settlement action to the specific beneficiaries who are complaining of inadequate notice.]

The only notice given beneficiaries of this specific application was by publication in a local newspaper in strict compliance with the minimum requirements of N.Y. Banking Law §100-c(12): "After filing such petition [for judicial settlement of its account] the petitioner shall cause to be issued by the court in which the petition is filed and shall publish not less than once in each week for four successive weeks in a newspaper to be designated by the court a notice or citation addressed generally without naming them to all parties interested in such common trust fund and in such estates, trusts or funds mentioned in the petition, all of which may be described in the notice or citation only in the manner set forth in said petition and without setting forth the residence of any such decedent or donor of any such estate, trust or fund." Thus the only notice required, and the only one given, was by newspaper publication setting forth merely the name and address of the trust company, the name and the date of establishment of the common trust fund, and a list of all participating estates, trusts or funds.

At the time the first investment in the common fund was made on behalf of each participating estate, however, the trust company, pursuant to the requirements of §100-c(9), had notified by mail each person of full age and sound mind whose name and address was then known to it and who was "entitled to share in the income therefrom . . . [or] . . . who would be entitled to share in the principal if the event upon which such estate, trust or fund will become distributable should have occurred at the time of sending such notice." Included in the notice was a copy of those provisions of the Act relating to the sending of the notice itself and to the judicial settlement of common trust fund accounts.

[Under New York law, the court appointed a] special guardian and attorney for all persons known or unknown not otherwise appearing who had or might thereafter have any interest in the income of the common trust fund; and appellee Vaughan was appointed to represent those similarly interested in the principal. There were no other appearances on behalf of anyone interested in either interest or principal.

Appellant appeared specially, objecting that notice and the statutory provisions for notice to beneficiaries were inadequate to afford due process under the Fourteenth Amendment, and therefore that the court was without jurisdiction to render a final and binding decree. Appellant's objections were entertained and overruled, the Surrogate holding that the notice required and given was sufficient. A final decree accepting the accounts has been entered, affirmed by the Appellate Division of the Supreme Court, and by the Court of Appeals of the State of New York.

The effect of this decree, as held below, is to settle "all questions respecting the management of the common fund." We understand that every right which beneficiaries would otherwise have against the trust company, either as trustee of the common fund or as trustee of any individual trust, for improper management of the common trust fund during the period covered by the accounting is sealed and wholly terminated by the decree.

[Eds. — The court-appointed attorney, Mullane, argued for those persons with an actual or potential interest in the common trust who had not appeared. He argued that the bank's attempt to give notice of an action that would cut off their rights to sue the bank without first giving them proper notice violated due process.]

* * *

It is sufficient to observe that, whatever the technical definition of its chosen procedure, the interest of each state in providing means to close trusts that exist by the grace of its laws and are administered under the supervision of its courts is so insistent and rooted in custom as to establish beyond doubt the right of its courts to determine the interests of all claimants, resident or nonresident, provided its procedure accords full opportunity to appear and be heard.

Quite different from the question of a state's power to discharge trustees is that of the opportunity it must give beneficiaries to contest. Many controversies have raged about the cryptic and abstract words of the Due Process Clause but there can be no doubt that at a minimum they require that deprivation of life, liberty or property by adjudication be preceded by notice and opportunity for hearing appropriate to the nature of the case.

In two ways this proceeding does or may deprive beneficiaries of property. It may cut off their rights to have the trustee answer for negligent or illegal impairments of their interests. Also, their interests are presumably subject to diminution in the proceeding by allowance of fees and expenses to one who, in their names but without their knowledge, may conduct a fruitless or uncompensatory contest. Certainly the proceeding is one in which they may be deprived of property rights and hence notice and hearing must measure up to the standards of due process.

[Eds. — The Court now resolves the conflict between the state's power to administer trusts and the due process rights of persons with actual and potential interests in the trust to notice and an opportunity to be heard before the state's approval of the trust potentially deprives them of property.]

Personal service [i.e., in-hand delivery] of written notice within the jurisdiction is the classic form of notice always adequate in any type of proceeding. But the vital interest of the State in bringing any issues as to its fiduciaries to a final settlement can be served only if interests or claims of individuals who are outside of the State can somehow be determined. A construction of the Due Process Clause which would place impossible or impractical obstacles in the way could not be justified.

Against this interest of the State we must balance the individual interest sought to be protected by the Fourteenth Amendment. This is defined by our holding that "The fundamental requisite of due process of law is the opportunity to be heard." Grannis v. Ordean, 234 U.S. 385, 394. This right to be heard has little reality or worth unless one is informed that the matter is pending and can choose for himself whether to appear or default, acquiesce or contest.

The Court has not committed itself to any formula achieving a balance between these interests in a particular proceeding or determining when constructive notice may be utilized or what test it must meet. Personal service has not in all circumstances been regarded as indispensable to the process due to residents, and it has more often been held unnecessary as to nonresidents. We disturb none of the established rules on these subjects. No decision constitutes a controlling or even a very illuminating precedent for the case before us. But a few general principles stand out in the books.

An elementary and fundamental requirement of due process in any proceeding which is to be accorded finality is notice reasonably calculated, under all the circumstances, to apprise interested parties of the pendency of the action and afford them an opportunity to present their objections. Milliken v. Meyer, 311 U.S. 457. The notice must be of such nature as reasonably to convey the required information, and it must afford a reasonable time for those interested to make their appearance. But if with due regard for the practicalities and peculiarities of the case these conditions are reasonably met the constitutional requirements are satisfied. "The criterion is not the possibility of conceivable injury, but the just and reasonable character of the requirements, having reference to the subject with which the statute deals." American Land Co. v. Zeiss, 219 U.S. 47.

But when notice is a person's due, process which is a mere gesture is not due process. The means employed must be such as one desirous of actually informing the absentee might reasonably adopt to accomplish it. The reasonableness and hence the constitutional validity of any chosen method may be defended on the ground that it is in itself reasonably certain to inform those affected, or, where conditions do not reasonably permit such notice, that the form chosen is not substantially less likely to bring home notice than other of the feasible and customary substitutes.

It would be idle to pretend that publication alone as prescribed here, is a reliable means of acquainting interested parties of the fact that their rights are before the courts. It is not an accident that the greater number of cases reaching this Court on the question of adequacy of notice have been concerned with actions founded on process constructively served through local newspapers. Chance alone brings to the attention of even a local resident an advertisement in small type inserted in the back pages of a newspaper, and if he makes his home outside the area of the newspaper's normal circulation the odds that the information will never reach him are large indeed. The chance of actual notice is further reduced when as here the notice required does not even name those whose attention it is supposed to attract, and does not inform acquaintances who might call it to attention. In weighing its sufficiency on the basis of equivalence with actual notice we are unable to regard this as more than a feint.

Nor is publication here reinforced by steps likely to attract the parties' attention to the proceeding. It is true that publication traditionally has been acceptable as notification supplemental to other action which in itself may reasonably be expected to convey a warning. The ways of an owner with tangible property are such that he usually arranges means to learn of any direct attack upon his possessory or proprietary rights. Hence, libel of a ship, attachment of a chattel or entry upon real estate in the name of law may reasonably be expected to come promptly to the owner's attention. When the state within which the owner has located such property seizes it for some reason, publication or posting affords an additional measure of notification.

A state may indulge the assumption that one who has left tangible property in the state either has abandoned it, in which case proceedings against it deprive him of nothing, or that he has left some caretaker under a duty to let him know that it is being jeopardized. . . . In the case before us there is, of course, no abandonment. On the other hand these beneficiaries do have a resident fiduciary as caretaker of their interest in this property. But it is their caretaker who in the accounting becomes their adversary. Their trustee is released from giving notice of jeopardy, and no one else is expected to do so. Not even the special guardian is required or apparently expected to communicate with his ward and client, and, of course, if such a duty were merely transferred from the trustee to the guardian, economy would not be served and more likely the cost would be increased.

This Court has not hesitated to approve of resort to publication as a customary substitute in another class of cases where it is not reasonably possible or practicable to give more adequate warning. Thus it has been recognized that, in the case of persons missing or unknown, employment of an indirect and even a probably futile means of notification is all that the situation permits and creates no constitutional bar to a final decree foreclosing their rights.

Those beneficiaries represented by appellant whose interests or whereabouts could not with due diligence be ascertained come clearly within this category. As to them the statutory notice [by publication] is sufficient. However great the odds that publication will never reach the eyes of such unknown parties, it is not in the typical case much more likely to fail than any of the choices open to legislators endeavoring to prescribe the best notice practicable.

Nor do we consider it unreasonable for the State to dispense with more certain notice to those beneficiaries whose interests are either conjectural or future or, although they could be discovered upon investigation, do not in due course of business come to knowledge of the common trustee. Whatever searches might be required in another situation under ordinary standards of diligence, in view of the character of the proceedings and the nature of the interests here involved we think them unnecessary. We recognize the practical difficulties and costs that would be attendant on frequent investigations into the status of great numbers of beneficiaries, many of whose interests in the common fund are so remote as to be ephemeral; and we have no doubt that such impracticable and extended searches are not required in the name of due process. The expense of keeping informed from day to day of substitutions among even current income beneficiaries and presumptive remaindermen, to say nothing of the far greater number of contingent beneficiaries, would impose a severe burden on the plan, and would likely dissipate its advantages. These are practical matters in which we should be reluctant to disturb the judgment of the state authorities.

Accordingly we overrule appellant's constitutional objections to published notice insofar as they are urged on behalf of any beneficiaries whose interests or addresses are unknown to the trustee.

As to known present beneficiaries of known place of residence, however, notice by publication stands on a different footing. Exceptions in the name of necessity do not sweep away the rule that within the limits of practicability notice must be such as is reasonably calculated to reach interested parties. Where the names and post office addresses of those affected by a proceeding are at hand, the reasons disappear for resort to means less likely than the mails to apprise them of its pendency.

The trustee has on its books the names and addresses of the income beneficiaries represented by appellant, and we find no tenable ground for dispensing with a serious effort to inform them personally of the accounting, at least by ordinary mail to the record addresses. Certainly sending them a copy of the statute months and perhaps years in advance does not answer this purpose. The trustee periodically remits their income to them, and we think that they might reasonably expect that with or apart from their remittances word might come to them personally that steps were being taken affecting their interests.

We need not weigh contentions that a requirement of personal service of citation on even the large number of known resident or nonresident beneficiaries would, by reasons of delay if not of expense, seriously interfere with the proper administration of the fund. Of course personal service even without the jurisdiction of the issuing authority serves the end of actual and personal notice, whatever power of compulsion it might lack. However, no such service is required under the circumstances. This type of trust presupposes a large number of small interests. The individual interest does not stand alone but is identical with that of a class. The rights of each in the integrity of the fund and the fidelity of the trustee are shared by many other beneficiaries. Therefore notice reasonably certain to reach most of those interested in objecting is likely to safeguard the interests of all, since any objections sustained would inure to the benefit of all. We think that under such circumstances reasonable risks that notice might not actually reach every beneficiary are justifiable. "Now and then an extraordinary case may turn up, but constitutional law, like other mortal contrivances, has to take some chances, and in the great majority of instances, no doubt, justice will be done." Blinn v. Nelson, supra, 222 U.S. at page 7.

The statutory notice to known beneficiaries is inadequate, not because in fact it fails to reach everyone, but because under the circumstances it is not reasonably calculated to reach those who could easily be informed by other means at hand. However it may have been in former times, the mails today are recognized as an efficient and inexpensive means of communication.

Justice Robert Jackson

Justice Robert Jackson (1892-1954) had an amazing legal career, yet never went to college or graduated from law school. He apprenticed in a law office and passed the New York bar at the age of 21. He was United States Solicitor General (1938-1940), United States Attorney General (1940-1941), and an Associate Justice of the United States Supreme Court (1941-1954) — the only person to have held all three offices. He also served as the chief prosecutor at the Nuremberg trials, prosecuting Nazi high officials for war crimes during World War II. He is also remembered for quotes such as these: "[A]ny lawyer worth his salt will tell the suspect in no uncertain terms to make no statement to the police under any circumstances" and, when describing the Supreme Court, "We are not final because we are infallible, but we are infallible only because we are final."

Moreover, the fact that the trust company has been able to give mailed notice to known beneficiaries at the time the common trust fund was established is persuasive that postal notification at the time of accounting would not seriously burden the plan.

In some situations the law requires greater precautions in its proceedings than the business world accepts for its own purposes. In few, if any, will it be satisfied with less. Certainly it is instructive, in determining the reasonableness of the impersonal broadcast notification here used, to ask whether it would satisfy a prudent man of business, counting his pennies but finding it in his interest to convey information to many persons whose names and addresses are in his files. We are not satisfied that it would. Publication may theoretically be available for all the world to see, but it is too much in our day to suppose that each or any individual beneficiary does or could examine all that is published to see if something may be tucked away in it that affects his property interests. We have before indicated in reference to notice by publication that, "Great caution should be used not to let fiction deny the fair play that can be secured only by a pretty close adhesion to fact." McDonald v. Mabee, 243 U.S. 90, 91.

We hold the notice of judicial settlement of accounts required by the New York Banking Law §100-c(12) is incompatible with the requirements of the Fourteenth Amendment as a basis for adjudication depriving known persons whose whereabouts are also known of substantial property rights. Accordingly the judgment is reversed and the cause remanded for further proceedings not inconsistent with this opinion.

Reversed.

Post-Case Follow-Up

The Court is attempting to strike a balance here. *Mullane* is probably best known for the following quote: "An elementary and fundamental requirement of due process in any proceeding which is to be accorded finality is *notice reasonably calculated, under all the circumstances, to apprise interested parties of the pendency of the action and afford them an opportunity to present their objections.*" The Court also noted that "[h]owever it may have been in former times, the mails today are recognized as an efficient and inexpensive means of communication."

Of course, the gold standard of service — the method the Court identified as the "classic" method of service — is virtually certain to suffice. When a process server personally hands the required documents to the person to be served, that is certain to qualify both as a permissible method under federal or state law (as described in the previous section) and satisfy due process. Most problems arise when that is either impossible or impractical.

The Court did not approve notice by publication, nor did it forbid such notice. When is notice by publication proper? The answer is fact-specific: It depends. For the trust beneficiaries the bank could readily determine, something more was required. But how much more and what method suffices? These are questions you must resolve when attempting to serve interested parties.

How would you apply *Mullane* to today's modern world? How does service by publication compare with service via email? Is email more or less reliable than the mail? Note that *Mullane* was decided in 1950 and in the quote above seems to bless service via mail. What about service via modern social media? Does notifying a defendant through the defendant's social media account like Facebook, Twitter, LinkedIn, or other similar modern communication methods meet the constitutional standard under *Mullane*?

Courts are struggling with these questions. For two competing examples, compare *In re Adoption of K.P.M.A.*, 341 P.3d 38, 51, *reh'g denied* (Okla. Nov. 16, 2014) (holding alternative service unreliable via Facebook "if the accountholder does not check it regularly or have it configured in such a way as to provide notification of unread messages by some other means") *with WhosHere, Inc. v. Orun*, No. 1:13-cv-00526-AJT-TRJ, 2014 U.S. Dist. LEXIS 22084 (E.D. Va. Feb. 20, 2014) (holding alternative service sufficient via two email addresses, Facebook, and LinkedIn where the plaintiff proved a communication trail via email and sufficient corroboration that the email addresses and social media accounts actually belonged to the defendants).

Mullane v. Central Hanover Bank & Trust Co: Real Life Applications

1. State law provides that abandoned property in the possession of the state may be sold if it is unclaimed after one year. The same state law provides that if the state has information suggesting the last known owner's identity and whereabouts, the state must provide notice via certified mail, return receipt requested, to such person before it may sell the property. The state sends first class mail notice to all persons for whom it has identity and location information, informing the person that the property at issue will be sold at auction at the state capitol building if it goes unclaimed five days after the date the notice was mailed. Would such notice be proper? Why or why not?

2. Suppose the same statute from question 1 also provides that if the state does not have information on the identity or location of potential owners of abandoned property, it may sell the property if it is unclaimed after one year. The statute provides that the state must publish notice in a newspaper of general circulation in the county in which the property was abandoned every day for three months. The content of the notice must describe the property in reasonable detail and state that the property will be sold at auction at the state capitol building if it goes unclaimed after the notice period. Would such notice be proper? Why or why not?

3. Now suppose that the statute from question 1 simply states that the state must provide notice to potential owners of abandoned property in a manner reasonably calculated to apprise the potential owners of the state's intent to sell the abandoned property. What methods do you think would satisfy this standard? Is the standard consistent with due process? Why or why not?

1. How Much Effort Does *Mullane* Require?

In a fairly recent case, *Jones v. Flowers*, a property owner failed to pay his taxes and the property was to be auctioned off to satisfy the tax debt. 547 U.S. 220 (2006). State law provided that notice in a tax sale was proper if executed by certified mail to the owner and, if returned unclaimed, notice by publication. The Supreme Court applied *Mullane* and held that this notice was insufficient; it violated the property owner's due process rights. The Court explained "that someone who actually wanted to alert Jones [the property owner] that he was in danger of losing his house would do more when the attempted notice letter was returned unclaimed, and there was more that reasonably could be done." *Id.* at 238. Just as *Mullane* advises to consider the circumstances, the Court considered that the tax sale of the property is a serious deprivation of property. The Court also considered what other steps the state could take to inform the property owner under the circumstances. The Court specifically noted that certified mail can be returned unclaimed, and suggested that the state could have provided regular, first class mail notice to the property owner. The Court also suggested combining this effort with posting a notice on the property itself. This is one of the major lessons from *Mullane*. If you want to serve someone by publication, use as many alternative methods as possible. In other words, how much effort is important, but how many efforts (particularly varying efforts) is also important.

2. Is Notice by Publication Ever Sufficient?

Mullane does stand for the proposition that if nothing else has worked or will work to notify interested parties, alternative service by publication may satisfy due process. This, however, is an absolute last resort and the wise litigant should consider other alternative service methods in conjunction with service by publication. For example, in *Gaeth v. Deacon*, the plaintiff's counsel was far more than merely diligent in attempting to locate and serve the defendant. 964 A.2d 621 (Me. 2009). He searched using a variety of computer programs, mailed the papers to an address he found for the defendant, and had the sheriff attempt service on the defendant. He then applied for an order of substitute service by publication. The trial court granted his request but the Supreme Court of Maine reversed. It suggested that the plaintiff's counsel could have done more. He could have hired an Internet web searching service, published notice in the area where the defendant had last resided, or used college records to try to locate members of the defendant's family in an effort to locate the defendant. So publication may theoretically satisfy due process in just the right case, but be sure that you leave no stone unturned before you rely on such substituted service, and use other available methods in conjunction with publication. This is where creativity in using modern communication like text messaging, email, social media and other methods may mean the difference between proper and improper service.

Chapter Summary

▪ Service of process is the means by which a defendant is notified of an action pending against him, and service must include both the complaint and the summons.

▪ Federal courts provide plaintiffs with many permissible methods for executing service process, including specific methods listed in Rule 4 as well as permitting service under the state rules of either where the federal court sits or where process is to be served. This provides even greater flexibility when you consider that most state court rules also permit you to request a court order permitting an alternative method of service than the listed methods.

▪ Properly following the method of service, however, is not sufficient. The method must be reasonably calculated under all the circumstances to inform interested parties of the pending action and provide them an opportunity to defend themselves.

▪ Under *Mullane*, service by publication alone is rarely sufficient. Courts will require sometimes extreme efforts to notify interested persons before they will order alternative service by publication; moreover, even if a court permits service by publication, it will likely order service via other, sometimes creative, methods as well.

▪ Personal delivery is virtually always sufficient, and mail service is considered reliable, although consider the circumstances before relying exclusively on mail service.

▪ A court does not necessarily acquire personal jurisdiction over the defendant, even if the defendant is properly served. The converse is also true. Just because the court has a valid basis for exercising personal jurisdiction over the defendant does not mean service is proper. These are two separate concepts. You must analyze each issue separately.

▪ When serving papers *other than* initial service of process, court rules or statutes specify other means of serving these later papers in the action, often in a much simpler manner.

Applying the Concepts

1. A plaintiff sued her former employer, a pizza restaurant, in federal court for gender discrimination. The plaintiff, representing herself, filed the complaint and the clerk issued a summons. The plaintiff walked into the restaurant and handed the summons and complaint to the hostess and told the hostess to give the documents to the manager. The hostess was busy and misplaced the documents but told the manager that the plaintiff was suing the restaurant. The restaurant's lawyer filed a motion to dismiss for improper service. What grounds should the lawyer include in his motion to dismiss? Explain your answer.

2. Plaintiff's car was illegally parked and ticketed. The ticket consisted of a summons and complaint and warned that failure to respond within 30 days would result in immobilization of the vehicle. The ticket was placed under the car's windshield wiper and an exact copy of the ticket was also mailed by first class mail to the address to which the car was registered. Plaintiff, however, had moved and never updated his registration. Plaintiff never saw or received the ticket and parked illegally again. This time, plaintiff's car was immobilized by attaching a large metal clamp known as a "boot" to one of the front wheels of plaintiff's vehicle. A notice placed under the windshield wiper on the vehicle explained that to have the boot removed, plaintiff would have to pay a civil fine, plus a boot removal fee. Plaintiff sued the city, claiming that the city violated the Due Process Clause by failing to provide adequate notice before immobilizing the vehicle. Was the method used to notify the plaintiff constitutionally adequate? Why or why not?

Civil Procedure in Practice

1. You represent a car dealership that provides financing for the cars it sells. One of its customers has failed to make payments on the car he purchased from your client for three months. You file a breach of contract action in state court, whose service rules provide that you may serve a person by personal service, certified mail, fax, or by any method approved by the court for good cause shown. You do not have a fax number for the customer and have tried six times to serve him by personal service but you cannot find him. You have been able to find the car parked outside his residence, but he never answers the door. You have also sent certified mail three times and each time it is returned to you unclaimed. Your client does not want to repossess the car because state law could create liability for your client for improper repossession. What are your options for attempting to notify the defendant customer? What would you do to best ensure that you satisfy both state law and due process?

2. A new client walks in your door and says he just read a notice in his local newspaper that the county has filed suit for permission to auction land in the county. The notice names the last known owner of the property as the client's father and lists a date a week from now for a hearing for all those who may claim an interest in the property. The client's father is deceased and the client has no other information about who may own the property. How would you advise your client to proceed?

3. Your client walks in the door and says she has just been evicted. The applicable state law permits service of process in an eviction action by posting the eviction papers on the tenant's door. Your client says she never saw any notice and that she lives in a busy apartment building where lots of children are playing. She also thinks her neighbor is out to get her. What challenge could you make to service in this case? What would be your argument?

The Complaint

The **complaint** is the plaintiff's initial pleading. A plaintiff commences a civil action in federal court by filing a complaint. Ordinarily, the plaintiff will attempt to set out his basic factual and legal theory for why he is entitled to relief from the court. He will tell the court what he alleges happened, i.e., his factual theory of the case, and why it matters legally, i.e., his legal theory. In other words, he is attempting to state a claim showing that he is entitled to relief. A plaintiff can't just complain about facts that seem unfortunate or even unjust. He needs to show the court that the facts, if true, legally entitle him to a remedy. The complaint also serves a notice function because it provides the defendant information he needs to present his defenses. How can a defendant present a defense if he doesn't know what claim he's defending? The complaint also tells the court the relief the plaintiff wants and helps it identify the issues it will have to resolve in order to determine if relief is appropriate. In some cases, the complaint alone may reveal that the case is not one that should be allowed to proceed further. The plaintiff has failed to state a claim, in which case the court can grant a defendant's motion to dismiss (covered in more detail in the next chapter). The standard the court uses to rule on such motions is a bit confusing, and is still evolving. Even as plaintiffs try to avoid dismissal, they have to ensure that they exercise care in pleading so as to avoid sanctions for improper pleadings.

A. THE PURPOSES OF THE COMPLAINT

The complaint serves a number of different purposes. Rule 8 requires only a "short and plain" statement of the claim. A good lawyer will often allege far more than just a short and plain statement of his claim in the complaint, particularly if he has a strong case. He will take the

Key Concepts

- The purposes of the complaint
- Rule 8(a)'s three requirements for any pleading, including a complaint, that states a claim for relief
- The plausibility pleading standard and best practices for attempting to satisfy it
- The certifications a party makes under Rule 11 when signing, filing, or advocating a pleading
- The process for imposing sanctions for a violation of Rule 11

opportunity to tell his client's story in a compelling way so as to begin the process of persuading the judge that his case has merit, laying the groundwork for both favorable rulings and a favorable settlement with the defendant. In other words, the complaint can provide an early opportunity for effective advocacy by the plaintiff. However, Rule 8 is concerned with the complaint's other purposes. One such purpose is to provide notice to the defendant of the claims against him. Recall the constitutional standard for adequate notice. It requires notice reasonably calculated to inform the defendant that an action is pending and to afford him an opportunity to present his objections to it. For a defendant to have a meaningful opportunity to present his objections, he must have notice of the claims. Without the complaint, the defendant would have only the summons after service, and its message to the defendant is essentially "you've been sued." Without more, the defendant would have no idea what objections or defenses he should present. Importantly, the complaint is preliminary in nature because it contains only allegations, not *proof* of the allegations. The complaint gives notice to the defendant so he can present his defenses, and then tells the defendant and plaintiff what information must be developed in discovery in order to prove the case at a later stage. Consider what the defendant would learn from just this portion of the complaint in the fictional case of *Sturmer v. Awesome Gadgets, Inc.*, shown in Exhibit 14.1.

EXHIBIT 14.1 **Complaint**

UNITED STATES DISTRICT COURT
SOUTHERN DISTRICT OF TEXAS

Bill Sturmer)
)
v.) No. 4:13CV003X1
)
Awesome Gadgets, Inc.)

COMPLAINT

NOW COMES the Plaintiff, Bill Sturmer, by and through his attorneys. . . .

* * *

ALLEGATIONS COMMON TO ALL COUNTS

2. Plaintiff was shopping in the Awesome Gadgets store (Store #TX0014) on the afternoon of Saturday, July 9, 2016 in Humble, Texas.

3. Defendant Awesome Gadgets owns and operates over 300 retail outlets throughout the United States including the Awesome Gadgets Store #TX0014 Plaintiff visited on July 9, 2016 in Humble, Texas.

EXHIBIT 14.1 **Complaint (Continued)**

4. In these Awesome Gadgets Stores, including the location in Humble, Texas, Defendant sells a wide variety of electronic devices and accessories, including televisions, computers, smart phones and tablets, console video games, stereo equipment and accessories.

5. On July 9, 2016, Plaintiff was present in the Humble, Texas store #TX0014 shopping for a DVD Player capable of playing high resolution video discs.

6. Approximately 20 minutes after entering the store, Plaintiff was approached by a man claiming to be "security for the store." He wore an Awesome Gadgets polo and had a walkie-talkie on his hip. The man later identified himself as Buck Stone. He demanded that Plaintiff come with him to discuss a "security matter" in the administrative offices at the back of the store.

7. Plaintiff politely asked for the man to elaborate on the need to accompany him to the rear of the store. Mr. Stone refused to do so. Instead, he grabbed Plaintiff by the arm and forcibly pulled him to the administrative offices at the back of the store. Mr. Stone did not release his grip on Plaintiff for approximately 3 minutes. Plaintiff incurred pain and bruising as a result.

8. Specifically, Mr. Stone pulled him into a windowless office, shut the door behind him, and ordered Plaintiff to sit down in a chair, which Plaintiff did because he felt he had no choice but to comply. Mr. Stone sat in another chair, positioned between Plaintiff and the only door providing entrance or exit to the office, blocking Plaintiff's route to exit the room.

9. Mr. Stone explained that he believed Plaintiff was a shoplifter. He said he had personally witnessed Plaintiff remove a small package from a wire rack on a store shelf and place the package in his front right pocket.

10. Mr. Stone asked Plaintiff if he could search his person to "confirm" that the item was in his pocket.

11. Plaintiff immediately stood up from his chair and voluntarily pulled the liners out of his front right and left pockets, which revealed that his pockets contained only his car keys.

12. Despite the fact that at this point it was clear that Plaintiff did not have any store items in his front pockets, Mr. Stone stood and conducted a full body frisk of Plaintiff. Plaintiff protested vigorously but Mr. Stone did not stop the frisk. This frisk did not uncover any stolen items.

13. Mr. Stone left the office, but locked the door behind him so that Plaintiff could not leave the room. There were no other means of leaving the office other than the locked door.

14. Plaintiff remained locked in the office for two hours, unable to speak to anyone. After two hours, Mr. Stone returned to the office and told Plaintiff that he was able to leave.

From these allegations alone, Awesome Gadgets knows where and when the alleged event occurred, a key witness from whom it can gather additional information (Buck Stone), and the basic facts of the case, at least as the plaintiff alleges them. These allegations will go a long way to help Awesome Gadgets present its defenses and objections to Mr. Sturmer's complaint.

The complaint is also important to the trial court. It informs the court that there is a dispute and that the plaintiff is seeking a resolution from the court. The complaint also plays a role in helping the court understand what issues it must resolve and which are undisputed. By comparing the allegations in the complaint to the defendant's answer, discussed in Chapter 15, the trial court can determine which of the allegations in the complaint are disputed and which are not. This comparison allows the court to narrow the issues it must resolve and thereby conserve the court's and the parties' time and resources. For example, if the plaintiff alleges that a fact is true in his complaint and the defendant admits it is true in his answer, the court need not spend any time or effort resolving the allegation. In Mr. Sturmer's case, Awesome Gadgets is likely to admit the allegations that it operates stores around the country, including the one in Humble, Texas, and sells electronic equipment and accessories. It might also admit that there was an encounter of some sort between Mr. Stone and Mr. Sturmer, and disagree only with Mr. Sturmer's characterization of the event. This process narrows considerably the allegations the court will have to determine, and it also helps the parties narrow their focus in discovery by narrowing the issues the parties must prove or disprove.

The complaint will also guide the court in admitting evidence at trial because the claims in the complaint help the court determine what evidence is relevant. The complaint will also guide the court in charging the jury, i.e., determining what questions to ask the jury about disputed fact issues. For example, the court should not admit evidence relevant only to a negligence claim or ask the jury if the defendant was negligent if the plaintiff did not plead a negligence claim in his complaint.

The complaint may also provide the court an opportunity to resolve the case very early in the litigation process. If the allegations in the complaint, even if true, would not permit the plaintiff to recover, there is no point in allowing the case to proceed.

B. FORM OF PLEADINGS

Rule 10 governs the form of pleadings. Rule 10(a) requires that all pleadings contain a caption (e.g., *Sturmer v. Awesome Gadgets, Inc.*) and a file number generated by the court in the case (which you can see in Sturmer's complaint at the top along the right side), so that the court and the clerk can keep track of all the papers filed by the parties. Rule 10(b) requires that the pleading contain a Rule 7(a) designation. Rule 7(a) sets out a list of pleadings permitted in federal court. All pleadings must be designated as one of the permitted pleadings. One such permitted pleading is the complaint. Notice that Sturmer's pleading meets this requirement because it contains the word "Complaint" just below the caption. Rule 10(b) requires numbered paragraphs, each one limited to the extent practicable to a single set of circumstances. Notice the numbered paragraphs in Sturmer's complaint, and that each paragraph is telling the story one small bite at a time.

Rule 10(b) also requires that each claim be stated in a separate count. Rule 10(c) allows a party to adopt earlier allegations by reference later in the same pleading, or even in a different pleading or motion. The example below shows how the separate counts requirement and the ability to adopt by reference might work in Sturmer's complaint.

EXHIBIT 14.2 **Counts**

COUNT I
BATTERY

20. Plaintiff repeats and realleges the allegations in paragraphs 2-7 as if fully set forth herein.

21. Mr. Stone committed battery because he intentionally and without justification touched Plaintiff's person and this touching was reasonably harmful and offensive.

22. Mr. Stone touched Plaintiff when he grabbed Plaintiff's arm. The fact that he dragged and pulled Mr. Stone toward the offices at the rear of the store, never releasing him from his grip, demonstrates that this touching was intentional.

23. The touching was reasonably harmful or offensive because . . . .

COUNT II
FALSE IMPRISONMENT

24. Plaintiff repeats and realleges the allegations in paragraphs 2-14 as if fully set forth herein.

25. Mr. Stone falsely imprisoned Plaintiff because . . . .

Rule 10(c) also allows a party to attach a "copy of a written instrument" to the pleading as an exhibit. An exhibit to the pleading is a part of the pleading for all purposes. So, for example, a party suing for breach of a written contract could attach a copy of the contract as an exhibit to the complaint.

C. STATING A CLAIM FOR RELIEF: RULE 8'S PLEADING REQUIREMENTS

In any pleading in which a party states a claim for relief, the party must satisfy the three requirements in Rule 8(a), set out in Exhibit 14.3. Of course, a party is attempting to state a claim for relief in a complaint, but recognize that Rule 8(a)'s requirements also apply to third-party complaints and other pleadings, such as answers if they assert crossclaims or counterclaims. Rule 8(a) requires a complaint

EXHIBIT 14.3   **Rule 8(a)**

> (a) Claim for Relief. A pleading that states a claim for relief must contain:
>   (1) a short and plain statement of the grounds for the court's jurisdiction, unless the court already has jurisdiction and the claim needs no new jurisdictional support;
>   (2) a short and plain statement of the claim showing that the pleader is entitled to relief; and
>   (3) a demand for the relief sought, which may include relief in the alternative or different types of relief.

to contain: (1) a short and plain statement of the grounds for the court's jurisdiction, (2) a short and plain statement of the claim showing that the pleader is entitled to relief, and (3) a demand for the relief sought. This section will discuss the most complex of these requirements first — the short and plain statement of the claim showing that the pleader is entitled to relief — and will then address the two other requirements.

1. A Short and Plain Statement of the Claim Showing that the Pleader Is Entitled to Relief

Litigation can be expensive and stressful, and it distracts the parties from their ordinary affairs. Sometimes the complaint reveals that the case is not one that belongs in the litigation stream at all, and thus these costs can largely be avoided through early resolution of the dispute based only on the pleadings. Suppose that the allegations in the complaint, even if true, would not permit the plaintiff to recover a judgment. Why should the court allow the case to proceed further? In this situation, the court may grant a motion to dismiss for failure to state a claim under Rule 12(b)(6). To avoid this result, the plaintiff's complaint must meet the standard set forth in Rule 8(a)(2) — the complaint must contain a "short and plain statement of the claim showing that the pleader is entitled to relief."

A Brief History of Pleading Standards

Rule 8(a)(2) requires the statement of the claim to be short and plain. This requirement may seem obvious to the law student — why wouldn't someone write in plain language? — but a bit of pleading history reveals that this language in Rule 8 is quite revolutionary.

Under English common law pleading rules, pleadings had to conform to a certain "form of action." Ejectment, trespass, and assumpsit are examples of early forms of action under the common law. The form of action determined the court that heard the action, the evidence needed to prove the action, and the pleadings required to proceed further. The common law pleading rules required the parties to say particular things, in a particular way, and in a particular place to have any hope of prevailing. Fitting all of the nuances that arise in disputes between complex human beings into a rigid form of action often proved difficult. The common law pleading rules valued form over substance, often resulting in adjudications based on a party's failure to comply with hyper-technical rules rather than the underlying merits.

The American colonies inherited the common law pleading rules, but by the mid-nineteenth century the states were abandoning the common law in favor of the Field Code's rules for pleading. The Field Code is named after a New York lawyer named David Dudley Field II, who was the principal drafter of the Code. The Field Code was adopted by New York and eventually by nearly two dozen other states. The Field Code imposed a **fact pleading** standard. The Field Code abandoned the forms of action, N.Y. Code Civ. Proc. §69 (1848) ("The distinction between actions at law and suits in equity, and the forms of all such actions and suits, heretofore existing are abolished . . ."), and instead required a "statement of the facts constituting the cause of action, in ordinary and concise language, without repetition, and in such manner as to enable a person of common understanding to know what is intended." *Id.* §142. The Field Code abandoned much of the formalism of the common law pleading rules by calling for pleadings in "ordinary and concise language." But the Field Code created other problems.

The Field Code required a "statement of the facts constituting the cause of action." Where precisely is the line between facts and causes of action? Suppose a plaintiff pleads facts but never names the cause of action. For example, the plaintiff pleads "I saw the defendant approach me and then he intentionally punched me in the nose, which both frightened and injured me," but he never says anything about the punch constituting the tort of battery. Is this an adequate pleading under the Code? And, even if the plaintiff mentions battery, has the plaintiff also stated a cause of action for assault (the apprehension of a battery) because the facts pled constitute assault? And what about the use of the word "intentionally"? Is that a statement of fact or a legal conclusion or both? Over time, the difficulty in drawing these lines led to formalistic rules that made the Field Code start to resemble the common law pleading rules. Additional reform was needed. Enter Federal Rule 8.

Rule 8 and the Plausibility Pleading Standard

Rule 8 preserves much of the Field Code's innovation. It requires pleadings to be "simple, concise, and direct," and says that "[n]o technical form is required." Rule 8(d)(1). Rule 8 abandons, however, the Field Code's fact pleading for what is called **notice pleading**. The plaintiff need only provide the defendant fair notice of his claim. The case of *Dioguardi v. Durning*, 139 F.2d 774 (2d Cir. 1944), demonstrates just how relatively relaxed Rule 8's pleading standard is. Dioguardi was an Italian immigrant proceeding *pro se* (i.e., he was not represented by an attorney) against a customs official in the Port of New York. His action was dismissed by the district court for failure to state a claim, but the court granted him permission to amend his complaint in an effort to state a claim. In short, Dioguardi alleged that the customs official sold his shipment of "tonics" to someone else, but he never mentioned any cause of action or otherwise explained why the facts entitled him to relief.

The district court dismissed his amended complaint. The Second Circuit Court of Appeals reversed the district court's judgment holding that Dioguardi had done enough to survive a motion to dismiss for failure to state a claim.

[P]laintiff filed an amended complaint, wherein, with an obviously heightened conviction that he was being unjustly treated, he vigorously reiterates his claims, including those quoted above and now stated as that his "medicinal extracts" were given to the Springdale Distilling Company "with my betting [bidding?] price of $110: and not their price of $120," and "It isn't so easy to do away with two cases with 37 bottles of one quart. Being protected, they can take this chance." An earlier paragraph suggests that defendant had explained the loss of the two cases by "saying that they had leaked, which could never be true in the manner they were bottled." On defendant's motion for dismissal on the same ground as before, the court made a final judgment dismissing the complaint, and plaintiff now comes to us with increased volubility, if not clarity.

It would seem, however, that he has stated enough to withstand a mere formal motion, directed only to the face of the complaint, and that here is another instance of judicial haste which in the long run makes waste. Under the new rules of civil procedure, there is no pleading requirement of stating "facts sufficient to constitute a cause of action," but only that there be "a short and plain statement of the claim showing that the pleader is entitled to relief," Federal Rules of Civil Procedure, rule 8(a), 28 U.S.C.A. following section 723c; and the motion for dismissal under Rule 12(b) is for failure to state "a claim upon which relief can be granted." The District Court does not state why it concluded that the complaints showed no claim upon which relief could be granted; and the United States Attorney's brief before us does not help us, for it is limited to the prognostication — unfortunately ill founded so far as we are concerned — that "the most cursory examination" of them will show the correctness of the District Court's action.

We think that, however inartistically they may be stated, the plaintiff has disclosed his claims that the collector has converted or otherwise done away with two of his cases of medicinal tonics and has sold the rest in a manner incompatible with the public auction he had announced — and, indeed, required by 19 U.S.C.A. §1491, above cited, and the Treasury Regulations promulgated under it, formerly 19 CFR 18.7-18.12, now 19 CFR 20.5, 8 Fed. Reg. 8407, 8408, June 19, 1943.

Dioguardi v. Durning, 139 F.2d 774, 775 (2d Cir. 1944).

Dioguardi was upset that a customs official had sold his tonics to someone else. He had an understanding of the facts, but he was not able to say "and these facts constitute the tort of conversion" and/or "these facts constitute a violation of Treasury regulations." In short, he was not able to say why the facts mattered legally. But the court of appeals could tell that his allegations might entitle him to relief because they might constitute conversion or a violation of treasury regulations. Thus, his allegations were sufficient to survive a motion to dismiss.

The Supreme Court cited *Dioguardi* with approval in *Conley v. Gibson*, 355 U.S. 41 (1957), saying that under Rule 8(a)(2) a plaintiff need only provide the defendant fair notice of what the claim is and the grounds upon which it rests. In *Conley*, the Court explained that a motion to dismiss for failure to state a claim should not be granted "unless it appears beyond doubt that the plaintiff can prove no set of facts in support of his claim which would entitle him to relief." Taking

Conley literally, the plaintiff didn't so much need to plead facts showing that he was entitled to relief. Instead, he needed to avoid pleading facts that showed that he could never recover. The relaxed *Conley* standard governed rulings on motions to dismiss for half a century. While it is still true that a motion to dismiss is properly granted if the plaintiff pleads facts showing that he can never recover, avoiding such allegations is no longer enough. After *Bell Atlantic Corp. v. Twombly*, satisfying *Conley* is necessary but not sufficient to survive a motion to dismiss for failure to state a claim.

Case Preview

Bell Atlantic Corp. v. Twombly

As you read *Bell Atlantic Corp. v. Twombly*, consider the following:

1. Apply the *Conley* standard to the complaint. Do the defendants have notice of the claim against them? Is there a set of facts the plaintiffs could prove that would entitle them to recover? If so, what is that set of facts?
2. What additional facts, if pled by the plaintiffs, might have made their claim plausible and avoided dismissal? Are plaintiffs in a Sherman Act case likely to have these kinds of additional facts? Why or why not?
3. What advantages, if any, do you see in the Court's interpretation of Rule 8(a)(2) compared to the *Conley* standard? Do you see any disadvantages?

Bell Atlantic Corp. v. Twombly
550 U.S. 544 (2007)

Justice SOUTER delivered the opinion of the Court.

[Eds. — From 1984 to 1996, a group of companies called Incumbent Local Exchange Carriers (ILECs) held congressionally approved regional monopolies over local telephone services. In the 1996 federal Telecommunications Act, Congress withdrew its approval of the ILECs' monopolies and required them to share their networks with other phone service providers. The new entrants into this market were called Competitive Local Exchange Carriers (CLECs). The plaintiffs in the case represented a putative class of phone and high-speed internet service subscribers against the ILECs and alleged violations of the Sherman Act's prohibition on agreements to restrain trade or commerce (i.e., competition). The key allegation in their complaint was: "based on information and belief . . . [the ILECs] have entered into a contract, combination or conspiracy to prevent [the CLECs from entering] their respective local telephone and/or high speed internet services markets and have agreed not to compete with one another and otherwise allocated customers and markets to one another." Importantly, a Sherman Act violation requires proof of an agreement to restrain trade or commerce. The plaintiffs did not allege a factual context for this agreement, such as when, where, or which persons reached it, but instead inferred that such an agreement must exist based on the "parallel conduct" of the ILECs.]

I.

Liability under §1 of the Sherman Act, 15 U.S.C. §1, requires a "contract, combination . . . , or conspiracy, in restraint of trade or commerce." The question in this putative class action is whether a §1 complaint can survive a motion to dismiss when it alleges that major telecommunications providers engaged in certain parallel conduct unfavorable to competition, absent some factual context suggesting agreement, as distinct from identical, independent action. We hold that such a complaint should be dismissed.

* * *

II

A

Because §1 of the Sherman Act "does not prohibit [all] unreasonable restraints of trade . . . but only restraints effected by a contract, combination, or conspiracy," . . . "[t]he crucial question" is whether the challenged anticompetitive conduct "stem[s] from independent decision or from an agreement, tacit or express." . . . While a showing of parallel "business behavior is admissible circumstantial evidence from which the fact finder may infer agreement," it falls short of "conclusively establish[ing] agreement or . . . itself constitut[ing] a Sherman Act offense." . . . Even "conscious parallelism," a common reaction of "firms in a concentrated market [that] recogniz[e] their shared economic interests and their interdependence with respect to price and output decisions" is "not in itself unlawful." . . .

The inadequacy of showing parallel conduct or interdependence, without more, mirrors the ambiguity of the behavior: consistent with conspiracy, but just as much in line with a wide swath of rational and competitive business strategy unilaterally prompted by common perceptions of the market. . . . Accordingly, we have previously hedged against false inferences from identical behavior at a number of points in the trial sequence. An antitrust conspiracy plaintiff with evidence showing nothing beyond parallel conduct is not entitled to a directed verdict. . . .

B

This case presents the antecedent question of what a plaintiff must plead in order to state a claim under §1 of the Sherman Act. Federal Rule of Civil Procedure 8(a)(2) requires only "a short and plain statement of the claim showing that the pleader is entitled to relief," in order to "give the defendant fair notice of what the . . . claim is and the grounds upon which it rests," Conley v. Gibson, 355 U.S. 41, 47, 78 S. Ct. 99, 2 L. Ed. 2d 80 (1957). While a complaint attacked by a Rule 12(b)(6) motion to dismiss does not need detailed factual allegations . . . a plaintiff's obligation to provide the "grounds" of his "entitle[ment] to relief" requires more than labels and conclusions, and a formulaic recitation of the elements of a cause of action will not do. . . . Factual allegations must be enough to raise a right to relief above the speculative level. . . .

In applying these general standards to a §1 claim, we hold that stating such a claim requires a complaint with enough factual matter (taken as true) to suggest that an agreement was made. Asking for plausible grounds to infer an agreement does not impose a probability requirement at the pleading stage; it simply calls for enough fact to raise a reasonable expectation that discovery will reveal evidence of illegal agreement. And, of course, a well-pleaded complaint may proceed even if it strikes a savvy judge that actual proof of those facts is improbable, and "that a recovery is very remote and unlikely." In identifying facts that are suggestive enough to render a §1 conspiracy plausible, we have the benefit of the prior rulings and considered views of leading commentators, already quoted, that lawful parallel conduct fails to bespeak unlawful agreement. It makes sense to say, therefore, that an allegation of parallel conduct and a bare assertion of conspiracy will not suffice. Without more, parallel conduct does not suggest conspiracy, and a conclusory allegation of agreement at some unidentified point does not supply facts adequate to show illegality. Hence, when allegations of parallel conduct are set out in order to make a §1 claim, they must be placed in a context that raises a suggestion of a preceding agreement, not merely parallel conduct that could just as well be independent action.

The need at the pleading stage for allegations plausibly suggesting (not merely consistent with) agreement reflects the threshold requirement of Rule 8(a)(2) that the "plain statement" possess enough heft to "sho[w]" that the pleader is entitled to relief." A statement of parallel conduct, even conduct consciously undertaken, needs some setting suggesting the agreement necessary to make out a §1 claim; without that further circumstance pointing toward a meeting of the minds, an account of a defendant's commercial efforts stays in neutral territory. An allegation of parallel conduct is thus much like a naked assertion of conspiracy in a §1 complaint: it gets the complaint close to stating a claim, but without some further factual enhancement it stops short of the line between possibility and plausibility of "entitle[ment] to relief." . . .

It is no answer to say that a claim just shy of a plausible entitlement to relief can, if groundless, be weeded out early in the discovery process through "careful case management," post, at 1975, given the common lament that the success of judicial supervision in checking discovery abuse has been on the modest side. . . . And it is self-evident that the problem of discovery abuse cannot be solved by "careful scrutiny of evidence at the summary judgment stage," much less "lucid instructions to juries," post, at 1975; the threat of discovery expense will push cost-conscious defendants to settle even anemic cases before reaching those proceedings. Probably, then, it is only by taking care to require allegations that reach the level suggesting conspiracy that we can hope to avoid the potentially enormous expense of discovery in cases with no " 'reasonably founded hope that the [discovery] process will reveal relevant evidence' " to support a §1 claim. . . .

Plaintiffs do not, of course, dispute the requirement of plausibility and the need for something more than merely parallel behavior explained in Theatre Enterprises, Monsanto, and Matsushita, and their main argument against the plausibility standard at the pleading stage is its ostensible conflict with an early statement of ours construing Rule 8. Justice Black's opinion for the Court in Conley v. Gibson spoke not only of the need for fair notice of the grounds for entitlement to relief but of "the accepted rule that a complaint should not be dismissed for failure to state a claim unless it appears beyond doubt that the plaintiff can prove no set of facts in support of his claim which would entitle him to relief." 355 U.S., at 45–46, 78 S. Ct. 99. This "no set of facts" language can be read in isolation as saying that any statement revealing the theory of the claim will suffice unless its factual impossibility may be shown from the face of the pleadings; and the Court of Appeals appears to have read Conley in some such way when formulating its understanding of the proper pleading standard, see 425 F.3d, at 106, 114 (invoking Conley's "no set of facts" language in describing the standard for dismissal).

On such a focused and literal reading of Conley's "no set of facts," a wholly conclusory statement of a claim would survive a motion to dismiss whenever the pleadings left open the possibility that a plaintiff might later establish some "set of [undisclosed] facts" to support recovery. . . .

Seeing this, a good many judges and commentators have balked at taking the literal terms of the Conley passage as a pleading standard. See, e.g., Car Carriers, 745 F.2d, at 1106 ("Conley has never been interpreted literally" and, "[i]n practice, a complaint . . . must contain either direct or inferential allegations respecting all the material elements necessary to sustain recovery under some viable legal theory." . . .)

The complaint leaves no doubt that plaintiffs rest their §1 claim on descriptions of parallel conduct and not on any independent allegation of actual agreement among the ILECs. Supra, at 1962–1963. Although in form a few stray statements speak directly of agreement, on fair reading these are merely legal conclusions resting on the prior allegations. Thus, the complaint first takes account of the alleged "absence of any meaningful competition between [the ILECs] in one another's markets," "the parallel course of conduct that each [ILEC] engaged in to prevent competition from CLECs," "and the other facts and market circumstances alleged [earlier]"; "in light of" these, the complaint concludes "that [the ILECs] have entered into a contract, combination or conspiracy to prevent competitive entry into their . . . markets and have agreed not to compete with one another." Complaint ¶51, App. 27.10 The nub of the complaint, then, is the ILECs' parallel behavior, consisting of steps to keep the CLECs out and manifest disinterest in becoming CLECs themselves, and its sufficiency turns on the suggestions raised by this conduct when viewed in light of common economic experience.

We think that nothing contained in the complaint invests either the action or inaction alleged with a plausible suggestion of conspiracy. As to the ILECs' supposed agreement to disobey the 1996 Act and thwart the CLECs' attempts to compete, we agree with the District Court that nothing in the complaint intimates that the resistance to the upstarts was anything more than the natural, unilateral reaction of each ILEC intent on keeping its regional dominance. The 1996 Act did more than just subject the ILECs to competition; it obliged them to subsidize their competitors with their own equipment at wholesale rates. The economic incentive to resist was powerful, but resisting competition is routine market conduct, and even if the ILECs flouted the 1996 Act in all the ways the plaintiffs allege . . . there is no reason to infer that the companies had agreed among themselves to do what was only natural anyway; so natural, in fact, that if alleging parallel decisions to resist competition were enough to imply an antitrust conspiracy, pleading a §1 violation against almost any group of competing businesses would be a sure thing.

The complaint makes its closest pass at a predicate for conspiracy with the claim that collusion was necessary because success by even one CLEC in an ILEC's territory "would have revealed the degree to which competitive entry by CLECs would have been successful in the other territories." . . . But, its logic aside, this general premise still fails to answer the point that there was just no need for joint encouragement to resist the 1996 Act; as the District Court said, "each ILEC has reason to want to avoid dealing with CLECs" and "each ILEC would attempt to keep CLECs out, regardless of the actions of the other ILECs." . . .

Plaintiffs' second conspiracy theory rests on the competitive reticence among the ILECs themselves in the wake of the 1996 Act, which was supposedly passed in the "'hop[e] that the large incumbent local monopoly companies . . . might attack their neighbors' service areas, as they are the best situated to do so.' . . . Contrary to hope, the ILECs declined "'to enter each other's service territories in any significant way,'" Complaint ¶38, App. 20, and the local telephone and high-speed Internet market remains highly compartmentalized geographically, with minimal competition. Based on this state of affairs, and perceiving the ILECs to be blessed with "especially attractive business opportunities" in surrounding markets dominated by other ILECs, the plaintiffs assert that the ILECs' parallel conduct was "strongly suggestive of conspiracy." . . .

But it was not suggestive of conspiracy, not if history teaches anything. In a traditionally unregulated industry with low barriers to entry, sparse competition among large firms dominating separate geographical segments of the market could very well signify illegal agreement, but here we have an obvious alternative explanation. In the decade preceding the 1996 Act and well before that, monopoly was the norm in telecommunications, not the exception. . . . The ILECs were born in that world, doubtless liked the world the way it was, and surely knew the adage about him who lives by the sword. Hence, a natural explanation for the noncompetition alleged is that the former Government-sanctioned monopolists were sitting tight, expecting their neighbors to do the same thing.

In fact, the complaint itself gives reasons to believe that the ILECs would see their best interests in keeping to their old turf. Although the complaint says generally that the ILECs passed up "especially attractive business opportunit[ies]" by declining to compete as CLECs against other ILECs . . . it does not allege that competition as CLECs was potentially any more lucrative than other opportunities being pursued by the ILECs during the same period, and the complaint is replete with indications that any CLEC faced nearly insurmountable barriers to profitability owing to the ILECs' flagrant resistance to the network sharing requirements of the 1996 Act. . . . Not only that, but even without a monopolistic tradition and the peculiar difficulty of mandating shared networks, "[f]irms do not expand without limit and none of them enters every market that an outside observer might regard as profitable, or even a small portion of such markets." . . . The upshot is that Congress may have expected some ILECs to become CLECs in the legacy territories of other ILECs, but the disappointment does not make conspiracy plausible. We agree with the District Court's assessment that antitrust conspiracy was not suggested by the facts adduced under either theory of the complaint, which thus fails to state a valid §1 claim.

* * *

The judgment of the Court of Appeals for the Second Circuit is reversed, and the case is remanded for further proceedings consistent with this opinion.

Post-Case Follow-Up

Twombly's interpretation of Rule 8(a)(2) is difficult to pin down, and not just for law students. It's difficult for lawyers and judges too. Some had hoped that *Twombly* might be limited to antitrust disputes, but two years after *Twombly*, the Court decided *Ashcroft v. Iqbal,* and made clear that the **plausibility pleading standard** applies to all civil actions in federal district courts. 556 U.S. 662 (2009). In *Iqbal*, a Pakistani citizen filed suit against officials of the federal government alleging that he had been arrested following the 9/11 attacks and was being detained in violation of his constitutional rights. *Iqbal* did attempt to clarify the plausibility pleading standard by setting out "two working principles" that underlie the *Twombly* decision. First, the Court accepts as true all factual allegations in the complaint but it does not accept legal conclusions as true. Thus, "threadbare recitals of the elements of a cause of action" will not state a claim. Second, the Court explained that "only a complaint that states a plausible claim for relief survives a motion to dismiss." Legal conclusions may provide the framework for a complaint, but these conclusions must be supported by factual allegations. The court will assume the truth of these factual allegations and then, using its experience and common sense, determine whether "they plausibly give rise to an entitlement to relief." These two "working principles" should make you think of two questions: (1) What is the difference between a fact and a legal conclusion? and (2) What does "plausible" mean? You may also wonder whether what is plausible to one person is plausible to another.

Bell Atlantic Corp. v. Twombly: Real Life Applications

1. Plaintiff's complaint alleges: "Defendant's negligent operation of his motor vehicle caused Plaintiff's injuries." Does this allegation state a claim for negligence?

2. Plaintiff alleges discrimination under the federal Age Discrimination in Employment Act, which provides employees and former employees over the age of 40 a cause of action against their employers for age discrimination in the workplace. In her complaint, Plaintiff states each element of the cause of action and supports each element with detailed factual allegations, including an allegation that Plaintiff is 37 years of age. Defendant moves to dismiss for failure to state a claim. How should the court rule on the motion?

3. Plaintiff fails to mention any of the elements of the tort of battery (e.g., a touching that was intentional, reasonably harmful, or offensive), nor does Plaintiff even mention the word battery in her complaint. Instead, Plaintiff alleges, "After shouting 'I'm going to kill you,' Defendant struck Plaintiff on the arm with a baseball bat, shattering Plaintiff's ulna and radius bones." Defendant moves to dismiss for failure to state a claim. How should the court rule on the motion?

Satisfying the Plausibility Pleading Standard

Twombly and *Iqbal* have been subjects of significant criticism, but it seems the plausibility pleading standard is here to stay. So, rather than complaining, plaintiff's lawyers have a practical concern — how to draft a complaint to avoid dismissal.

First, the complaint should recite the material elements of the cause of action. Recitation of the elements, alone, will not state a plausible claim, but the plausibility of the claim is measured against the elements that must be proved; so, the elements serve as a standard for measuring plausibility. Consider the claims in *Twombly* and *Iqbal*. *Twombly* involved allegations of a nationwide scheme to violate antitrust laws. *Iqbal* involved claims of violations of constitutional rights against some of our highest government officials. These are complex claims — much more complex than a typical negligence or breach of contract claim. The elements of these claims provide a structure to organize the complaint and the supporting factual allegations. Second, plead the facts that support the truth of each element of the cause of action. Appellate court opinions addressing what evidence is legally sufficient to support a judgment on a jury verdict in such cases can help identify the facts that will state a plausible claim.

A practical consequence of pleading more facts in the complaint may be that in certain cases, plaintiffs' lawyers will sometimes have to do more informal discovery pre-suit than they might have done before *Twombly*. The *Twombly* Court would view this additional burden as a positive, given its lack of faith in the ability of district courts to weed out implausible claims early on through "careful case management," and its concern about the abuses of formal discovery. Often the facts will be readily accessible through the attorney's client, like in simple breach of contract or negligence actions. The client has the information that can be placed in the complaint to survive a motion to dismiss. *Twombly* will pitch few of these simple cases out of the litigation stream. *Twombly*'s impact will likely be felt in a minority of cases that are either meritless or appear to be so because the necessary information is in possession of the defendant. For example, if the ILECs in *Twombly* had agreed to engage in conduct to restrain trade or commerce, their conduct would have been illegal, and they would therefore keep this information to themselves.

Finally, it is important to recognize that not all facts give support to a plausible claim. Suppose the plaintiff pleads negligence based on a car wreck, and after stating the breach element of his negligence cause of action, he pleads that the defendant's breach of duty consisted of running a red light at the intersection where the collision occurred. The allegation that the defendant ran the red light supports a plausible claim because running a red light is at least negligent under most any circumstance. Consider on the other hand the key factual allegation in the *Twombly* complaint — parallel conduct amongst the defendants. Parallel conduct does not necessarily mean the defendants had done anything illegal. One may infer from this allegation either that the defendants had agreed to engage in parallel conduct, which is illegal, or, as the Court points out, one may infer that the defendants were simply responding similarly to shared market forces, which is not illegal. When relying upon an inference from the facts, the complaint should plead additional facts that support the inference needed. Pleading, for example, that key decision-makers amongst the *Twombly* defendants had meetings or correspondence (rather than just opportunities for them as the *Twombly* plaintiffs alleged) that preceded a parallel change in conduct might move the needle toward the needed inference that the parallel conduct was the result of an agreement.

D. ALLEGING JURISDICTION AND A DEMAND FOR RELIEF

Rule 8(a)(1) requires the complaint to contain a short and plain statement of the grounds for the court's jurisdiction. Rule 8(a)(1) refers only to subject matter jurisdiction. It does not require allegations regarding personal jurisdiction or venue. Recall that federal courts are courts of limited jurisdiction, and so it makes sense that the plaintiff needs to invoke the jurisdiction of the court through the allegations in his complaint. No particular words are required, but the plaintiff should be careful to plead facts that conform to the statutory requirements for federal jurisdiction. Stating that the plaintiff alleges a federal claim, for example, invokes federal question jurisdiction under 28 U.S.C. §1331. To invoke the court's diversity jurisdiction, the plaintiff's allegations should address the citizenship of the parties in a way that shows that no plaintiff shares citizenship with any defendant and the amount in controversy requirement is satisfied. Exhibit 14.4 provides examples of a short and plain statement of diversity and federal question jurisdiction.

Rule 8(a)(3) requires the complaint to contain a demand for the relief sought, and explicitly allows relief in the alternative and different types of relief. A plaintiff files suit because he wants the court's help to fix a problem, so it makes sense that the plaintiff should tell the court what relief he wants. If the plaintiff wants money damages, he must demand it. If he wants injunctive relief, he must demand it. Exhibit 14.5 provides examples of demands for relief. Bear in mind that the plaintiff may ask for more than one form of relief, and can demand relief in the alternative, e.g., if not injunctive relief, then money damages. Sometimes the damages are of such a nature that calculating them at the pleadings stage is not possible. Damages for disfigurement and pain and suffering in a personal injury or wrongful death

---

EXHIBIT 14.4 **Short and Plain Statement of the Grounds for Jurisdiction**

Diversity of Citizenship

Plaintiff is a citizen of Alabama and defendant is a corporation incorporated under the laws of Delaware with its principal place of business in Georgia. The matter in controversy exceeds, exclusive of interest and costs, the sum specified by 28 U.S.C. §1332.

Federal Question

This action arises under the Americans with Disabilities Act, 42 U.S.C. §1201 et seq.

Adapted from Form 7, Fed. R. Civ. P. (Abrogated).

EXHIBIT 14.5   **Demands for Relief**

Money Damages

Plaintiff demands judgment against the defendant for $250,000, plus costs.

Relief in the Alternative

Plaintiff demands the defendant be required to specifically perform the contract or, if not ordered to specifically perform, pay damages in the amount of $100,000, plus interest and costs.

Injunctive Relief

A preliminary and continuing injunction against defendant's patent infringement.

From Forms 15, 17, and 18, respectively, Fed. R. Civ. P. (Abrogated).

case are examples. In this situation, rather than a sum certain, the plaintiff may demand "an amount of damages to be proved at trial."

E. HEIGHTENED PLEADING STANDARDS

Rule 9(b) applies a heightened pleading standard to allegations of fraud and mistake. There are a number of justifications for treating fraud and mistake allegations differently. Accusing someone of fraud is to call them a liar, and the accusation alone may damage the defendant's reputation. Rule 9(b) attempts to prevent such accusations from being made lightly. Also, allegations of fraud and mistake are often pled in an attempt to undo a completed transaction, perhaps because the plaintiff is upset that the deal was not as favorable to him as he had hoped. More than a bare assertion of fraud or mistake in the course of the transaction is necessary for the court to assess whether the alleged wrongdoing is worth potentially undoing the transaction. A heightened pleading standard also helps to prevent plaintiffs from using allegations of fraud and mistake to obtain a nuisance value settlement or gaining easy access to formal discovery in order to find other wrongdoing by the defendant.

For this and other reasons, Rule 9(b) requires that "the circumstances constituting fraud or mistake" be stated with particularity. Mistake is an allegation that one or both parties to a transaction were mistaken about a basic assumption upon which the contract was made at the time of contracting. To allege mistake with particularity, the plaintiff must provide the facts showing what the assumption was and why one or both parties were mistaken in that assumption.

In order to plead fraud with particularity, federal courts have required the complaint to name the person who made the allegedly fraudulent statement, the time it was made, the person to whom it was made, where it was made, and explain why the statement was fraudulent, i.e., that the defendant knew it was false when making it. In addition to Rule 9(b), the Private Securities Litigation Reform Act (PSLRA) applies to allegations of securities fraud and requires that the facts alleged must give rise to a "strong inference" of **scienter** (i.e., intent or knowledge of wrongdoing on the part of the defendant). 15 U.S.C. §78u-4(b)(2)(A). The PSLRA stays discovery until the trial court rules on a motion to dismiss for failure to state a claim. 15 U.S.C. §78u-4(b)(3)(B).

F. RULE 11: SUBSTANTIALITY OF PLEADINGS

How much support, if any, must a factual or legal contention in a complaint have before it may be included in a pleading? Knowing that they had to prove the existence of an agreement between the defendants, why didn't the plaintiffs in *Twombly* simply allege that the defendants reached such an agreement at a particular time and place? If your reaction to that question is something along the lines of "It would be wrong for them to allege those facts if they had no reason to believe they are true," good! In addition to an attorney's inherent sense of right and wrong, rules of professional conduct and Rule 11 prevent parties and attorneys from making baseless accusations in pleadings. For example, ABA Model Rule of Professional Conduct 3.3(a)(1) provides that a lawyer must not knowingly "make a false statement of fact or law to a tribunal or fail to correct a false statement of material fact or law previously made to the tribunal by the lawyer." Violation of this rule might get the attorney disciplined by the state bar for making false statements in a pleading. In addition, Rule 11 gives the court the power to impose sanctions for making unsubstantiated allegations in a pleading.

1. Rule 11 Certifications to the Court

Rule 11(a) requires pleadings like the complaint to be signed by the attorney, and Rule 11(b) says that by signing, filing, or advocating a pleading, motion, or other paper, the attorney is certifying to the court that the factual and legal contentions are substantiated, rather than baseless. *See* Exhibit 14.6. Importantly, Rule 11 does not govern discovery instruments or discovery disputes. Rules 37 and 26(g), not Rule 11, govern incomplete, unanswered, or evasive answers to discovery as well as other discovery abuses. As the Advisory Committee Note to Rule 11 says, the purpose of the Rule is to make attorneys "stop and think" before including a contention in their pleadings. Note also that the Rule does not apply to oral motions made in court. Rule 11 doesn't require the lawyer to explicitly make certain promises to the court. The Rule does not, for example, require the lawyer to say "I promise I have some evidentiary support for the factual contentions in my complaint." Instead, he makes certain assurances about his pleadings or other documents filed with the court, like motions, simply by virtue of having signed, filed, or advocated it. The

EXHIBIT 14.6   Rule 11(a)-(b)

(a) Signature. Every pleading, written motion, and other paper must be signed by at least one attorney of record in the attorney's name — or by a party personally if the party is unrepresented. The paper must state the signer's address, e-mail address, and telephone number. Unless a rule or statute specifically states otherwise, a pleading need not be verified or accompanied by an affidavit. The court must strike an unsigned paper unless the omission is promptly corrected after being called to the attorney's or party's attention.

(b) Representations to the Court. By presenting to the court a pleading, written motion, or other paper — whether by signing, filing, submitting, or later advocating it — an attorney or unrepresented party certifies that to the best of the person's knowledge, information, and belief, formed after an inquiry reasonable under the circumstances:

(1) it is not being presented for any improper purpose, such as to harass, cause unnecessary delay, or needlessly increase the cost of litigation;

(2) the claims, defenses, and other legal contentions are warranted by existing law or by a nonfrivolous argument for extending, modifying, or reversing existing law or for establishing new law;

(3) the factual contentions have evidentiary support or, if specifically so identified, will likely have evidentiary support after a reasonable opportunity for further investigation or discovery; and

(4) the denials of factual contentions are warranted on the evidence or, if specifically so identified, are reasonably based on belief or a lack of information.

court may impose sanctions on a party, his attorney, and the law firm for violations of Rule 11.

Reasonable Inquiry into Factual and Legal Contentions

In *Thomas v. Capital Security Services, Inc.*, 812 F.2d 984 (5th Cir. 1987), the Fifth Circuit Court of Appeals held that Rule 11 imposes three affirmative duties on an attorney:

(1) that the attorney has conducted a reasonable inquiry into the facts which support the document;

(2) that the attorney has conducted a reasonable inquiry into the law such that the document embodies existing legal principles or a good faith argument "for the extension, modification, or reversal of existing law;" and

(3) that the motion is not interposed for purposes of delay, harassment, or increasing costs of litigation.

The case of *Hays v. Sony Corp. of America* is an example of how an attorney can violate the duties imposed by Rule 11 in his complaint.

**Case
Preview**

Hays v. Sony Corp. of America

As you read *Hays v. Sony Corp. of America*, consider the
following:

1. Identify the Rule 11 duties the plaintiffs' attorney
   violated.
2. What effect, if any, does a lawyer's lack of experience in a particular area have on
   the analysis under Rule 11?
3. Rule 11 requires an inquiry into the facts and law supporting the contentions
   that is "reasonable under the circumstances." What circumstances might affect
   the level of inquiry required by Rule 11?

Hays v. Sony Corp. of America
847 F.2d 412 (1988)

POSNER, Circuit Judge.

The appeal in this copyright suit brings before us a medley of questions involving jurisdiction, copyright, and sanctions. The plaintiffs, Stephanie Hays and Gail MacDonald, teach business courses at a public high school in Des Plaines, Illinois. In 1982 or 1983 they prepared a manual for their students on how to operate the school's DEC word processors, and distributed copies to students and to other faculty members. In 1984 the school district, having bought word processors from Sony Corporation of America (the defendant in this suit), gave Sony the plaintiffs' manual and asked Sony to modify it so that it could be used with Sony's word processors. This Sony proceeded to do, resulting in a manual very similar to — in many places a verbatim copy of — the plaintiff's manual. Sony did not charge the school district anything for preparing the manual, which was delivered to the school district in December 1984 and, sometime afterward, distributed to the students. Nor is there any evidence that Sony has sold or disseminated the manual elsewhere.

In February 1985 the plaintiffs, presumably spurred by knowledge of Sony's manual, registered their own manual with the Copyright Office, and in July they filed this lawsuit in federal district court. Count I charges a violation of common law (i.e., state) copyright, Count II a violation of statutory (i.e., federal) copyright. The complaint alleges that Sony "has made large profits by reason of appropriating to its own use Plaintiffs' workbook," and demands compensatory and punitive damages, an accounting for profits, an injunction, attorney's fees, and other relief.

On October 31, 1986, the district judge dismissed the action on the ground that the plaintiffs had failed to state a claim. Sony had already filed several motions for sanctions under Rule 11 of the Federal Rules of Civil Procedure, seeking reimbursement of some $47,000 in attorney's fees and related expenses, and the district judge had heard, but not decided, the motions several days before he dismissed the action. Several months later, on February 18, 1987, the judge awarded Sony $14,895.46 in sanctions against the plaintiffs' counsel, Emmanuel F. Guyon, but not against the plaintiffs. Within ten days Guyon filed a motion to vacate the judgment, and the judge denied the motion on September 8. On October 8, a notice of appeal was filed in the district court, stating "that STEPHANIE HAYS and GAIL McDONALD [sic], Plaintiffs above named, hereby appeals [sic] to the United States Court of Appeals for the Seventh Circuit from the Final Judgment entered September 8, 1987, and prior Orders entered October 29, 1986 and February 19, 1987."

* * *

The suit is a mixture of the frivolous and the nonfrivolous. The claim of infringement of a common law copyright is frivolous. Until the Copyright Act of 1976, this country had a dual system of property rights in expression. Until published, a work was protected by state common law principles; the author had a common law copyright. Upon publication, the author's common law copyright terminated; to preserve his property right, he had to obtain a federal copyright. In order to simplify the law without diminishing the rights of authors, the 1976 Act abolished common law copyright as of January 1, 1978, see §301(a), but made federal copyright attach at the moment of creation, not publication, of any work within the scope of the statute. See 17 U.S.C. §302(a). Hays and MacDonald wrote their manual long after the abolition of common law copyright.

Guyon argues (for the first time on appeal, and in the face of his clients' contrary affidavits) that though not actually written until 1982, the manual incorporated materials created in the early 1970s, not published, and therefore covered by common law copyright. This argument is irrelevant, as well as untimely and factually unsupported. The statute explicitly abolishes common law copyright as of January 1, 1978, whether the work was created before or after that date. See §301(a). It is true that "any cause of action arising from undertakings commenced before January 1, 1978," survives, §301(b)(2), but this means only that if Sony had violated the plaintiffs' common law rights before 1978 their cause of action would have survived. E.g., *Mention v. Gessell*, 714 F.2d 87, 90 (9th Cir. 1983). By the time Sony commenced the activities that are alleged to have infringed the plaintiffs' common law copyright, the plaintiffs no longer had any common law copyright.

Although, as we shall see, the plaintiffs' claim that their statutory copyright was infringed is not frivolous, most of their requests for relief against that alleged infringement are frivolous. The plaintiffs could not obtain statutory damages or attorney's fees, because they did not register their copyright within three months after first publishing the manual (in the special meaning that "publication" bears in the Copyright Act, see 17 U.S.C. §101) and before Sony published its allegedly infringing manual. See 17 U.S.C. §412(2). They could not obtain an accounting for profits, because, according to Sony's uncontradicted affidavit, Sony never obtained any profits from the sale or distribution of the manual — indeed, never sold it. Sony may have earned goodwill or repeat sales by complying with the school district's request to modify the plaintiffs' manual, but the plaintiffs did not seek profits on that theory.

The plaintiffs could not obtain actual damages either. Although in the sanctions hearing Guyon told the judge that the plaintiffs had put out some (unsuccessful) feelers to publishers, he had presented no evidence in the suit itself that his clients had any plans or prospects for publishing their manual or otherwise obtaining a monetary return on it. And of course there is no evidence that Sony killed their market by distributing its version of the manual. Finally, the plaintiffs could not obtain punitive damages. Although authority on the question is surprisingly sparse, it appears to be accepted that punitive damages are not recoverable in federal copyright suits. See *Roy Export Co. v. Columbia Broadcasting System, Inc.*, 672 F.2d 1095, 1106 (2d Cir. 1982); *Kamakazi Music Corp. v. Robbins Music Corp.*, 534 F. Supp. 69, 78 (S.D.N.Y. 1982); 3 Nimmer on Copyright §14.02[B], at pp. 14–18 to 14–19 (1987). If there is any reason to doubt this conclusion, Guyon has not indicated to us what it might be. A willful infringer can be required to pay statutory damages of up to $50,000 instead of the usual maximum of $10,000, see 17 U.S.C. §504(c)(2), but, as already pointed out, the plaintiffs in this case are not eligible for statutory damages. And they have never suggested that Sony was acting willfully. It appears that Sony either believed that the manual it was asked to modify was not copyrighted or believed that the school district owned the copyright. Either belief would have been reasonable; the manual contained no copyright notice or other attempted reservation of rights.

Every request that the plaintiffs made for monetary relief thus was frivolous, yet they might have been entitled to an injunction, for they may have had a valid statutory copyright that was infringed. . . .

. . . The presence of a nonfrivolous claim would create a serious problem if the district judge had based his award of sanctions on a belief that the lawsuit was entirely frivolous, for while we have upheld sanctions against plaintiffs or their attorneys for bringing suits frivolous only in part . . . an award of sanctions that was premised on a seriously exaggerated view of the frivolousness of the suit could not stand. But that was not the nature of Judge Mihm's award. Realizing that the claim of statutory infringement had not been negligible, he made clear in awarding sanctions that the problem was not that the complaint had been frivolous but that the suit had not been pursued effectively. He therefore awarded Sony the following percentages of the attorney's fees that it had incurred in defending against the suit: 10 percent of the fees incurred between the filing of the suit in July 1985 and April 1, 1986, by which time it should have been obvious to Guyon, the district judge thought, that the suit was hopeless; 50 percent of the fees incurred after April 1; and 75 percent of the fees incurred in successfully moving to strike materials filed by Guyon in June 1986, after the close of the record on summary judgment, in a futile effort to stave off dismissal.

This method of calculation was lenient. The common law copyright claim and the requests for monetary relief showed that Guyon had not conducted the reasonable precomplaint inquiry into fact and law required by Rule 11, for that inquiry would have shown that he had no basis for these aspects of the suit. His argument that he didn't know how to find out whether Sony was selling its manual rings hollow, when he did not so much as write Sony (before suing it) to explain his clients' position and to inquire whether Sony was distributing the manual or planning to do so. Of course Sony might not have answered such a letter but at least Guyon would have discharged his duty of inquiring to the extent feasible to do. Copyright law makes it easy for the copyright holder to prove an entitlement to monetary relief (even if he is ineligible for statutory damages, which require no proof of injury), by allowing him to prove and recover either his actual damages or the infringer's profits, whichever is larger, and to presume profits from the gross revenues obtained by the infringer from the infringing work. See 17 U.S.C. §§504(a), (b); *Taylor v. Meirick,* 712 F.2d 1112, 1120–22 (7th Cir. 1983). It should not have been difficult for Guyon to obtain the minimal facts necessary to decide whether there was a basis for seeking monetary as well as injunctive relief; anyway Guyon didn't try. Certainly more than 10 percent of Sony's attorney's fees before April 1 were incurred in opposing the frivolous aspects of the suit, and by April 1 it should have been plain to Guyon that his clients' only hope was to obtain an injunction for infringement of a statutory copyright — but he continued to press his frivolous claims with undiminished enthusiasm.

In requiring reasonable inquiry before the filing of any pleading in a civil case in federal district court, Rule 11 demands "an objective determination of whether a sanctioned party's conduct was reasonable under the circumstances." *Brown v. Federation of State Medical Boards,* 830 F.2d 1429, 1435 (7th Cir. 1987). See also *In re Ronco, Inc.,* 838 F.2d 212, 217 (7th Cir. 1988). In effect it imposes a negligence standard, cf. *Pantry Queen Foods, Inc. v. Lifschultz Fast Freight, Inc.,* 809 F.2d 451, 453 (7th Cir. 1987); *Classic Components Supply, Inc. v. Mitsubishi Electronics America, Inc.,* 841 F.2d 163, 165 (7th Cir. 1988); *Gaiardo v. Ethyl Corp.,* 835 F.2d 479, 482 (3d Cir. 1987), for negligence is a failure to use reasonable care. The equation between negligence and failure to conduct a reasonable precomplaint inquiry is transparent in *Szabo Food Service, Inc. v. Canteen Corp.,* 823 F.2d 1073, 1083 (7th Cir. 1987), where we said that "the amount of investigation required by Rule 11 depends on both the time available to investigate and on the probability that more investigation will turn up important evidence; the Rule does not require steps that are not cost-justified." See also *Fred A. Smith Lumber Co. v. Edidin,* 845 F.2d 750, 751–52 (7th Cir. 1988).

Restating the standard in negligence terms helps one to see that Rule 11 defines a new form of legal malpractice, and there is thus no more reason for a competent attorney to fear being sanctioned under Rule 11 than to fear being punished for any other form of malpractice. The difference is merely in the victim. In the ordinary case of legal malpractice the victim is the lawyer's client, though there are exceptions, illustrated by our decision in *Greycas, Inc. v. Proud,* 826 F.2d 1560 (7th Cir. 1987). In the Rule 11 setting the victims are the lawyer's adversary, other litigants in the court's queue, and the court itself. By asserting claims without first inquiring whether they have a plausible grounding in law and fact, a lawyer can impose on an adversary and on the judicial system substantial costs that would have been — and should have been — avoided by a reasonable prepleading inquiry.

From his papers in both the district court and this court it is apparent that Mr. Guyon is not a specialist either in copyright law or in federal litigation. As a solo practitioner in the town of Streator, Illinois — population 14,000 — Mr. Guyon is not to be criticized for having failed to acquire expertness in an esoteric field of federal law and in the niceties of federal procedure. But the Rule 11 standard, like the negligence standard in tort law, is an objective standard, as we have said. It makes no allowance for the particular circumstances of particular practitioners. Cf. *Thornton v. Wahl,* 787 F.2d 1151, 1154 (7th Cir. 1986). There is no "locality rule" in legal malpractice, see Restatement (Second) of Torts, §299A, comment g (1965), and while a legal specialist may be held to an even higher standard of care than a generalist, see

Sparks v. NLRB, 835 F.2d 705, 707 (7th Cir. 1987); cf. Prosser and Keeton on the Law of Torts 185 (5th ed. 1984), the generalist acts at his peril if he brings a suit in a field or forum with which he is unacquainted. A lawyer who lacks relevant expertise must either associate with him a lawyer who has it, or must bone up on the relevant law at every step in the way in recognition that his lack of experience makes him prone to error. . . . He must litigate very carefully, just as a new driver must drive very carefully. Mr. Guyon failed to heed this precept, booting what may have been a meritorious though modest claim by pressing frivolous claims. . . .

. . . The award of Rule 11 sanctions against Mr. Guyon is affirmed. . . .

Post-Case Follow-Up

Rule 11 does not require that a legal contention always be supported by existing law. If that were the requirement, new law could not be developed because lawyers would be prohibited from raising the issue for the court's decision. A legal contention must be supported by existing law or "by a nonfrivolous argument for extending, modifying, or reversing existing law or for establishing new law." Certainly if the same argument for a change in the law was recently rejected in a similar case in the same jurisdiction, the pleader is in danger of being sanctioned. Support for a change in the law in other jurisdictions or academic literature helps avoid such sanctions.

Rule 11 requires an inquiry reasonable under the circumstances. Perhaps the most important circumstance in determining reasonableness is the amount of time available to the lawyer to conduct the inquiry. If the client approaches the lawyer for the first time only days before the expiration of the limitations period, the level of inquiry that constitutes reasonableness is lower than if the lawyer had six months to file suit. Another important factor is the extent to which any supporting evidence is accessible to the lawyer. If the lawyer can find the information easily, but doesn't, that cuts against reasonableness. If, on the other hand, most of the evidence is in the possession or control of potential opposing parties, a reasonable inquiry may consist only of information provided by the client or that is publicly available. As to legal contentions, the reasonableness of the inquiry will turn largely on the complexity of the law in the area. Notice, however, that Rule 11 applies, not only when a pleading is signed or filed, but also when an attorney later advocates the pleading. An attorney who advocates a contention in a pleading that is no longer warranted by the facts or law may be sanctioned, even if the factual and legal contentions were warranted when first made.

Hays v. Sony Corp. of America: Real Life Applications

1. Omar represents Trina. Omar files a complaint alleging that Trina was in a car accident with Phil, Trina was pregnant at the time of the accident, and that damages should be awarded on behalf of her stillborn child. The governing state substantive law includes the Born Alive Rule, which prohibits a claim for damages

based on injury to a fetus unless the fetus is born alive. Omar researches the law in the jurisdiction and determines that the Born Alive Rule was set down by the state's supreme court, but the court has not issued an opinion on the continued validity of the rule in over 20 years. Omar also determines that other jurisdictions have recently abrogated their version of the rule. Phil's attorney moves for sanctions on the grounds that Trina and Omar's claim violates Rule 11. How should the court rule and why?

2. Attorney Ignacio meets with Alexis with an eye to representing her in a personal injury action. Alexis tells Ignacio that she was injured by falling construction equipment while walking near a construction site two years earlier. She provides him the name of the construction company, High Tower Construction, Inc., the location of the accident, and the medical records indicating that she was treated for injuries to her head and back. Ignacio determines that the following day is the last day to file suit under the governing statute of limitations. Before filing the complaint, Ignacio learns from online news sources that falling equipment at a High Tower construction site had indeed injured several people at the time and place Alexis reported. A few months after filing the complaint, Ignacio learns that Alexis was out of state visiting family at the time of the incident at the construction site and that the medical treatment Alexis received was connected to a car accident, not a result of falling equipment at a construction site. Nevertheless, in response to a motion to dismiss for failure to state a claim, Ignacio cites his allegations about the construction site accident and Alexis' injuries and urges the court to deny the motion. Did Ignacio violate Rule 11? If so, when?

3. Tamara has been retained to file a breach of contract action on behalf of Tinker, LLC against Blinker, Inc. Her draft of the complaint alleges the existence of a contract between Tinker and Blinker. Her pre-suit investigation has uncovered conflicting evidence as to the existence of a contract. Some of the information she has supports the existence of a contract, while other information indicates Tinker and Blinker never reached an agreement. If Tamara signs and files her complaint, will she have violated Rule 11?

Improper Purpose

Rule 11 authorizes sanctions if the pleading is "presented for any improper purpose, such as to harass, cause unnecessary delay, or needlessly increase the cost of litigation." This standard is an objective one. The court's focus is not the parties' subjective intent (e.g., they did not mean to harass or cause delay), but rather whether the pleading or motion did *in fact* cause unnecessary delay, harassment, or needlessly increase the cost of litigation, regardless of what the parties intended. *See Sussman v. Bank of Israel*, 56 F.3d 450, 458 (2d Cir. 1995) (citing Schwarzer, *Sanctions Under the New Federal Rule 11 — A Closer Look*, 104 F.R.D. 181, 195-96 (1985)).

Often, attorneys and parties have more than one purpose in presenting a pleading or motion. If the party presents a pleading with both an improper and a proper purpose, sanctions under Rule 11 are not generally appropriate. The Second Circuit explained in *Sussman v. Bank of Israel*:

> The district court held that the filing of the complaint with a view to exerting pressure on defendants through the generation of adverse and economically disadvantageous publicity reflected an improper purpose. To the extent that a complaint is not held to lack foundation in law or fact, we disagree. It is not the role of Rule 11 to safeguard a defendant from public criticism that may result from the assertion of nonfrivolous claims. Further, unless such measures are needed to protect the integrity of the judicial system or a criminal defendant's right to a fair trial, a court's steps to deter attorneys from, or to punish them for, speaking to the press have serious First Amendment implications. Mere warnings by a party of its intention to assert nonfrivolous claims, with predictions of those claims' likely public reception, are not improper.

56 F.3d 450, 459 (2d Cir. 1995).

Inconsistent Pleadings

Rule 8(d)(3) allows parties to plead as many separate claims as they have, even if they are not consistent with one another. This means that a party's complaint can be factually inconsistent, i.e., one claim may be based on facts that conflict with the facts underlying another claim in the same complaint. How do inconsistent pleadings square with Rule 11's requirements? Rule 11 is not violated so long as there is evidentiary support for both factual theories. Rule 11 does not require that contentions be undergirded by conclusive evidence, but rather that *some* evidence supports them. It's possible that there is evidence supporting entirely inconsistent claims. For example, suppose that a lawyer representing a plaintiff in a car accident case has a statement the defendant made to the responding police officer that he accidentally drove his car into the plaintiff when he was distracted by an incoming text on his cell phone. Suppose the attorney also has information from a witness who claims that the defendant confessed to him that he ran into the plaintiff's car on purpose because she had cut him off while changing lanes. The evidence on the defendant's state of mind is conflicting and supports both an allegation of negligence and an allegation of battery, even though both cannot be true at the same time.

2. Sanctions Procedure

A party may make a motion for sanctions if it believes another party has violated Rule 11. However, Rule 11(c)(2) provides a "safe harbor" provision that provides a potential violator an opportunity to correct the problem. A motion for sanctions is served but is not filed or presented to the court if the challenged pleading is withdrawn or appropriately corrected within 21 days after service. Only if the pleading is not withdrawn or appropriately corrected may the motion for sanctions be filed with the court, at which point the court will determine if Rule 11 has been violated. Even if no party files a motion for sanctions, the court may issue an order for a party, attorney, or law firm to "show cause" why conduct described in the order does not violate Rule 11. Notice that whether the sanctions process is initiated by a party's motion or by a court's show cause order, the party who filed the pleading has an opportunity to be heard as to the propriety of issuing sanctions.

Rule 11(c) gives the court the authority to impose sanctions on the party, the attorney, and/or the law firm. However, a court may not sanction a represented party for frivolous legal contentions. That responsibility is more appropriately imposed on the attorney. Ordinarily, the law firm is held jointly responsible for any sanctions imposed on one of its attorneys. So, if you violate Rule 11, your law firm may have to pay any monetary sanctions on your behalf, even if the sanctions were not imposed directly on the firm. The purpose of the sanctions is to deter the conduct, not to punish the lawyer, party, or firm, and so should be limited to what suffices to deter similar conduct. Sanctions may include monetary sanctions paid either to the court or the opposing party. They may also include directives, such as to attend professionalism courses or training.

3. The Court's Inherent Power to Impose Sanctions

Apart from Rule 11, a federal court has an inherent power to impose sanctions for bad faith conduct, such as harassing conduct, delay, and other improper conduct that does not fall into Rule 11, or some other statutory or rule authorization for imposing sanctions. Federal courts should draw on their inherent power sparingly and only when sanctions are not appropriate under another rule or statute, such as Rule 11 or Rule 37 for discovery abuses. The court's inherent power ensures that the court can control its proceedings and deter an attorney whose conduct does not fall neatly into a rule or statute authorizing sanctions.

Chapter Summary

- The filing of a complaint in federal court commences a civil action.
- The complaint is served on the defendant along with the court's summons, and the allegations in the complaint help the defendant know what objections and defenses to present.
- The form of the complaint must adhere to the requirements in Rule 10, including containing a caption and a file number, and must be designated as a complaint. The complaint must consist of numbered paragraphs, and multiple claims generally should be set out in separate counts.
- For any pleading that states a claim for relief, including a complaint, the pleading must contain a short and plain statement of the grounds for the court's subject matter jurisdiction, a short and plain statement of the claim showing that the pleader is entitled to relief, and a demand for the relief sought.
- To state a claim for relief, the allegations in the complaint must show that recovery is plausible. The court accepts factual allegations as true, but will ignore legal conclusions in making this determination.

■ A pleading that fails to meet the plausibility pleading standard is subject to dismissal upon a Rule 12(b)(6) motion to dismiss for failure to state a claim.

■ Rule 11 requires a reasonable inquiry into the factual and legal contentions in the complaint to ensure they are not groundless or brought for an improper purpose. The court may impose sanctions on the party, the attorney, or the law firm for violation of Rule 11. In addition, the court has inherent power to impose sanctions for behavior that is in bad faith.

Applying the Concepts

1. Tripod, LLC is preparing a complaint naming Bipod, Inc. as the defendant and alleging that Bipod breached a written contract it had with Tripod. Tripod's attorney believes that Bipod will make a 12(b)(6) motion to dismiss for failure to state a claim. Tripod's attorney wants to make sure that the court can consider all the terms of the written contract when ruling on the motion. What can Tripod's attorney do to ensure the contract terms are considered?

2. Jimmy is deer hunting in Davy Crockett National Forest when he suffers a single gunshot wound from a rifle fired by another hunter who apparently mistook Jimmy for a deer. Only two other hunters were within range of Jimmy at the time he was shot, Marcus and Rogelio. Jimmy files suit against both Marcus and Rogelio. Jimmy alleges that either Marcus or Rogelio shot him and supports his contention with allegations that both were within rifle range, both were carrying rifles, and both of their rifles fired bullets matching the caliber of the bullet removed from Jimmy's body. Marcus moves for sanctions under Rule 11 because Jimmy has failed to conduct ballistic tests to match the bullet taken from his body to one of their rifles and because his allegations that Marcus and Rogelio shot him are contradictory given that he was only shot one time. How should the court rule on the motion?

Civil Procedure in Practice

Gretchen claims that her former employer, Sterling, LLP, fired her because she is a woman. Terminating employment based on sex violates Title VII of the Federal Civil Rights Act of 1964. The act will require Gretchen to prove discriminatory intent on the part of Sterling — i.e., that Sterling was motivated to fire her because she is a woman. Gretchen believes she could find internal memos revealing this discriminatory intent during discovery, but she is not currently aware of any such memos or their content. The only memo she has in her possession is one from Sterling stating that Gretchen was fired because of "poor performance." She does have information that Sterling terminated 7 of its 12 female employees, including

Gretchen, in a six-month time period, and fired only 2 of its 65 male employees during the same period. You represent Gretchen in her Title VII action against Sterling. You send a letter to Sterling requesting a pre-suit mediation and requesting Gretchen's human resources file and any other documentation as to why Gretchen's employment was terminated. Sterling does not respond to the letter. You also attempt to arrange interviews with the six other women who were fired during the same time period. Only one agrees to meet with you and she does not believe she was fired because she is a woman.

1. Two months after sending the letter, you file a complaint on behalf of Gretchen. Your complaint alleges that "Sterling fired Gretchen because she is a woman in violation of Title VII." In support of this allegation, you cite in your complaint the employment data and decisions made over the six-month time period. Sterling moves to dismiss the complaint for failure to state a claim. What is the standard the court should apply to determine the motion, and how should the court rule?

2. Sterling also moves for sanctions under Rule 11 on the grounds that you have failed to make a reasonable inquiry to ensure that the factual allegations have evidentiary support. Was your inquiry reasonable under the circumstances, and does your allegation of sex discrimination have sufficient evidentiary support to satisfy Rule 11?

Responding to the Complaint

We saw in the last chapter how a plaintiff states a claim for relief in his complaint. Now we turn to the defendant's response to the complaint. Just as the plaintiff must state his claim in the complaint, the defendant must assert his defenses in his response (or responses) to the complaint. How the defendant responds to the complaint will answer important questions about the scope of the litigation. Does the defendant object to the plaintiff's chosen forum? Is there some other defect that might prevent the court from reaching the merits of the plaintiff's allegations? Which of the plaintiff's factual contentions does the defendant dispute, and which of them does he admit? Does the defendant have other defenses based on facts outside the plaintiff's complaint that might eliminate or reduce liability? The defendant's initial response to the plaintiff's complaint can come in one of two forms — a Rule 12 motion or an answer. Responding by motion delays the need to file an answer and, if the motion is granted, may eliminate the need to file an answer altogether. Only a handful of defenses may be presented by pre-answer motion. These defenses allege that some defect prevents the court from reaching the merits of the plaintiff's allega-

tions. The advantage of filing a Rule 12 motion is that the defendant need not file an answer until and unless his motion is denied. The defendant's other option is to file an answer. The defendant may raise any and all defenses he has to the complaint in the answer, including the defenses that may also be raised by Rule 12 motion. If the defendant does make a Rule 12 motion and it is denied, the defendant typically will then file an answer raising other defenses he has to

Key Concepts

- The defenses that may be presented by motion and those that may be presented in the answer
- The defenses that are waived if not made in the defendant's first Rule 12 response
- The process of admitting and denying the allegations in the complaint and the effect of failing to properly deny those allegations
- Affirmative defenses and the obligation to affirmatively plead them
- The deadline to make a Rule 12 response and the consequences of failing to meet the deadline

the complaint. If the defendant does not respond at all to the complaint, a default judgment will be entered against him. This chapter discusses these response options and the consequences of failing to timely respond to the complaint.

A. RESPONDING BY MOTION

Under Rule 12(b), the defendant may raise only certain defenses by motion. This characteristic of a Rule 12 motion stands in juxtaposition to the answer. The answer is the pleading that responds to the complaint. Any and all defenses to the complaint may be asserted in the answer. This warrants emphasis. Any defense under the sun may be asserted in the answer. Contract defenses like failure of consideration and statute of frauds, tort defenses like contributory negligence and assumption of the risk, and defenses challenging the forum such as lack of personal and subject matter jurisdiction and improper venue may all be asserted in the answer. Moreover, most defenses *must* be asserted in the answer. There is simply no other proper way to present them. But a handful of defenses may instead be asserted by motion, and there is a possible advantage to the defendant of doing so.

1. Defenses Properly Raised by Motion

The defenses that may be presented by motion all have something in common. All are based on the idea the defendant should not have to answer the merits of the plaintiff's claim either in this court or under these circumstances. Unlike the answer, a motion is not a pleading. Instead, a motion is a request for a court order. Of course, the defenses that may be asserted by motion may instead be asserted in the answer. All defenses may be asserted in the answer. However, the advantage to asserting them by motion is that the defendant does not have to file an answer addressing the merits of the plaintiff's claim until and unless the court denies the motion. This makes sense, because the thrust of these defenses is that the defendant should not have to respond to the merits. If the court grants the motion, the defendant may not ever have to respond to the merits. Thus, asserting a proper defense by motion at a minimum delays the need to respond to the merits in an answer and may avoid it altogether.

Rule 12(b)(1)-(7) Defenses

Rule 12(b)(1)-(7) lists defenses that may be raised by motion. The list reads like an outline of a first-year civil procedure course. Notice what all seven defenses have in common. They each present a reason the defendant should not have to answer the merits of the plaintiff's claim. The defenses in 12(b)(1)-(3) — lack of subject matter jurisdiction, lack of personal jurisdiction, and improper venue, respectively — are objections to the propriety of the forum. They each argue that the defendant should not have to answer the merits *in this court*. The remainder of the defenses — 12(b)(4)-(7),

EXHIBIT 15.1   **Rule 12(b) Defenses and Objections**

> (b) How to Present Defenses. Every defense to a claim for relief in any pleading must be asserted in the responsive pleading if one is required. But a party may assert the following defenses by motion:
>
> (1) lack of subject-matter jurisdiction;
> (2) lack of personal jurisdiction;
> (3) improper venue;
> (4) insufficient process;
> (5) insufficient service of process;
> (6) failure to state a claim upon which relief can be granted; and
> (7) failure to join a party under Rule 19.
>
> A motion asserting any of these defenses must be made before pleading if a responsive pleading is allowed. If a pleading sets out a claim for relief that does not require a responsive pleading, an opposing party may assert at trial any defense to that claim. No defense or objection is waived by joining it with one or more other defenses or objections in a responsive pleading or in a motion.

listed in Table 15.1 — are based on the notion that the defendant should not have to answer the merits *under these circumstances*. In other words, each defense reflects an impediment to proceeding to the merits of the case.

Rule 12(e) Motion for More Definite Statement

Rule 12(e) allows a party to move for a more definite statement if the complaint is "so vague or ambiguous that the party cannot reasonably prepare a response." The

TABLE 15.1   **Summary of Rule 12(b)(4)-(7) Defenses**

The Defense	Impediment to Reaching the Merits
12(b)(4) Insufficient Process	What the defendant was served (process) was defective under Rule 4. *See* Chapter 13.
(5) Insufficient Service of Process	The way the defendant was served was wrong under Rule 4. *See* Chapter 13.
(6) Failure to State a Claim	Even if what the plaintiff alleges in the complaint is true, recovery is not plausible under Rule 8(a)(2). *See* Chapter 14.
(7) Failure to Join an Indispensable Party	Rule 19 requires a non-party (i.e., an absentee) to be made a party to the case in order to proceed. *See* Chapter 19.

motion must be made before filing an answer, and it must point out the defects complained of — i.e., the vague or ambiguous portions of the complaint — and the details desired. The non-movant has 14 days after notice of the court's order granting the motion to amend his complaint to fix the defect. A defendant may not use Rule 12(e) to require the plaintiff to identify and describe the evidence supporting his allegations. Instead, the defendant should use the motion, if at all, only when the complaint is so vague he cannot prepare a Rule 12 response. Notice the limited utility of the Rule 12(e) motion. If the motion is granted, the case is not dismissed. Instead, the plaintiff has an opportunity to fix the problem — not exactly cause for celebration. Also, don't forget about the plausibility pleading standard. After *Twombly*, the plaintiff's complaint must state a claim showing that the pleader is entitled to relief, which means showing that recovery is plausible. How can the complaint show recovery is plausible if the pleading is so vague that preparing a response is not possible?

Rule 12(f) Motion to Strike

A motion to strike has two purposes. It is used to strike from a pleading, including the complaint, "any redundant, immaterial, impertinent, or scandalous matter." And it is also used to strike an insufficient defense from an answer. Motions to strike are not favored by federal courts, because they are often used only to delay the proceedings and, thus, should be used sparingly. 5C Charles Alan Wright & Arthur R. Miller, Federal Practice and Procedure §1380 (3d ed. 2004 & Supp. 2017). Motions to strike are usually granted only when "the allegations being challenged are so unrelated to the plaintiff's claims as to be unworthy of any consideration as a defense and that their presence in the pleading throughout the proceeding will be prejudicial to the moving party." *Id.*

2. Waiver of Defenses

Although they are not actually highlighted in the official text, we have highlighted defenses (2) through (5) in Exhibit 15.2 because they share a unique characteristic and warrant special attention. Rule 12(h)(1) requires these defenses to be asserted in the defendant's first Rule 12 response — either motion or answer — or else they are waived. While this rule can be harsh, because it sometimes results in the loss of valid defenses, it serves an important purpose. It requires that the defendant present all of the defenses in Rule 12(b)(2)-(5) at the beginning of the litigation. Without this rule, a defendant could file a motion to dismiss for lack of personal jurisdiction that takes six months to resolve and, if it is denied, file a 12(b)(3) motion for improper venue that might take another six months to resolve. After a year, the court still has not reached the merits of the case. In fact, in this scenario, the defendant hasn't even responded to the merits of the case.

Waiver by Filing a Rule 12 Motion

Let's explore this trap for the unwary in a bit more depth. Remember that the defenses listed in Rule 12(b)(2)-(5) must be raised in the defendant's first Rule

EXHIBIT 15.2 Rule 12(b) Defenses and Objections

* * *

(b) How to Present Defenses. Every defense to a claim for relief in any pleading must be asserted in the responsive pleading if one is required. But a party may assert the following defenses by motion:

(1) lack of subject-matter jurisdiction;

(2) lack of personal jurisdiction;

(3) improper venue;

(4) insufficient process;

(5) insufficient service of process;

(6) failure to state a claim upon which relief can be granted; and

(7) failure to join a party under Rule 19.

12 response. However, Rule 12(b) allows a defendant to join multiple defenses together in a consolidated response filed at the same time without waiving any of the defenses included in the response. Suppose instead of filing an answer the defendant files a Rule 12(b)(6) motion to dismiss for failure to state a claim. The motion is denied and then the defendant files a 12(b)(2) motion to dismiss for lack of personal jurisdiction. The motion objecting to lack of personal jurisdiction will be denied, because the defendant waived this objection the moment he filed a motion to dismiss for failure to state a claim without also simultaneously objecting to lack of personal jurisdiction.

Defenses Not Waived by Filing a Motion

Let's reverse the order. Suppose the defendant first files a motion to dismiss for lack of personal jurisdiction, which is denied, and then files a motion to dismiss for failure to state a claim. The defendant has not waived his 12(b)(6) motion, because failure to state a claim is not one of the defenses listed in Rule 12(b)(2)-(5). The defenses of failure to state a claim and failure to join an indispensable party may be made either pretrial or at trial. *See* Rule 12(h)(2). A motion to dismiss for lack of subject matter jurisdiction may be made at any time, even after trial or on appeal. *See* Rule 12(h)(3).

Raising the Defenses in Rule 12(b)(1)-(7) in the Answer

Suppose a defendant doesn't make any motions at all. Instead, he files an answer. The defenses in Rule 12(b)(2)-(5) are waived if not included in the answer or in an amended answer under Rule 15(c)(1). Rule 15(c)(1) permits a defendant to amend his answer once as a matter of course within 21 days of serving it. So, if no Rule 12 motion is made, a defendant who fails to include one of the waivable defenses in his answer can avoid waiver by including it in an amended answer within 21 days of serving his original answer. Note that the amended answer can only prevent waiver if no Rule 12 motion was made. If a motion was made, the excluded 12(b)(2)-(5) defenses were waived at the time the motion was made.

Application Exercise

Try to determine if waiver has occurred in these examples.

1. The defendant's first response to the complaint is to file an answer. The answer includes an objection to both improper venue and insufficient service of process. The defendant then files a motion to dismiss for lack of personal jurisdiction. Which of these three defenses, if any, has the defendant waived?
2. The defendant's first response to the complaint is a motion to dismiss for lack of personal jurisdiction. A month later he files a motion to dismiss for failure to join an indispensable party. Has he waived either defense?
3. The defendant's first response to the complaint is an answer that includes an objection to venue. Seven days later, the defendant files an amended answer that includes both the original objection to improper venue and a new objection to lack of personal jurisdiction. Has either defense been waived?
4. The defendant's first response to the complaint is to file a motion to dismiss for lack of subject matter jurisdiction. A month later, the defendant files an answer that also includes an objection to subject matter jurisdiction. Ten days after filing his answer, the defendant files an amended answer that includes both the objection to subject matter jurisdiction and an objection to insufficient service of process. Has the defendant waived the objection to service of process?

B. THE ANSWER

The answer is the defendant's responsive pleading to the complaint. In the answer the defendant may assert any defense he has to the claim the plaintiff asserts in the complaint. Rule 8(b) requires the defendant's answer to admit or deny the allegations asserted in the complaint and state "in short and plain terms its defenses to each claim asserted against it." The admissions and denials will, hopefully, narrow the disputed issues for the court's determination and highlight the disputed allegations the court must resolve. The defendant may also state any other defenses he has, including those that may also be asserted by motion, and must affirmatively plead any affirmative defenses he has to the plaintiff's claim.

1. Admitting or Denying the Allegations in the Complaint

Rule 8(b)(1) requires the defendant in the answer to admit or deny the allegations in the complaint. This means that the defendant must go paragraph by paragraph in the complaint and either admit or deny the allegations in his answer.

The Effect of Admissions and Denials

If an allegation is denied, the plaintiff will have to prove the allegation at trial, and the defendant will be permitted to offer evidence that the allegation is not true. If, on the other hand, the defendant admits the allegation or fails to deny it, the plaintiff will not have to prove it, and the defendant will not be permitted to offer evidence of its untruth. The allegation is a fact for purposes of the action. Why waste time adjudicating an allegation the plaintiff has pled and the defendant has admitted (or failed to deny)?

Lack of Knowledge and Information

Often the defendant may not know whether an allegation in the complaint is true or false. In such a situation, Rule 8(b)(4) permits a defendant to state that he "lacks knowledge and information sufficient to form a belief about the truth of the allegation." This response has the same effect as a denial. The plaintiff will have to prove the allegation and the defendant can contest it with contradictory evidence. Note that using this language is only appropriate if the defendant both does not know if the allegation is true or false *and* has no information from which he can form a belief about its truth or falsity. If, for example, the answer is contained in documents within the defendant's possession, he must consult the documents to find the answer.

Admitting and Denying Allegations: Some Examples

Recall the fictional case from Chapter 14, *Sturmer v. Awesome Gadgets, Inc.* Plaintiff Sturmer pled battery and false imprisonment based on the allegation that an Awesome Gadget's security guard, Mr. Stone, had grabbed and detained him inside an office for two hours at the defendant's retail store. Suppose you represent Awesome Gadgets. In preparation for filing an answer on behalf of Awesome Gadgets, you speak with Mr. Stone. He tells you that he did approach Mr. Sturmer about 20 minutes after he saw Sturmer enter the store on the day alleged in the complaint. He identified himself as a security guard for Awesome Gadgets and wore a red polo embroidered with the Awesome Gadgets logo and had a radio on his hip. He approached Mr. Sturmer because he believed he saw Mr. Sturmer remove a phone charging cord from a rack and place it in his front right pocket. He also tells you he never grabbed Mr. Sturmer by the arm, but he did insist that Mr. Sturmer accompany him to his office to discuss a security matter. In his office, Mr. Stone introduced himself by name to Mr. Sturmer and less than ten minutes after their initial contact told Mr. Sturmer he was free to leave. This was immediately after Mr. Sturmer emptied his pockets revealing that they did not contain any store items. He flatly denies having frisked or even touched Mr. Sturmer.

Given this information from Mr. Stone, let's consider how to respond in the answer to these allegations from Paragraph 6 of Sturmer's Complaint:

> 6. Approximately 20 minutes after entering the store, Plaintiff was approached by a man claiming to be "security for the store." He wore an Awesome Gadgets polo and

had a walkie-talkie on his hip. The man later identified himself as Buck Stone. He demanded that Plaintiff come with him to discuss a "security matter" in the administrative offices at the back of the store.

Given the information from Mr. Stone, could you take issue with any of the facts in Paragraph 6? If not, then the response in the answer to Paragraph 6 is simple—"Defendant admits the allegations in Paragraph 6." How would you respond to Paragraph 12 of Sturmer's Complaint?

> 12. Despite the fact that at this point it was clear that Plaintiff did not have any store items in his front pockets, Mr. Stone stood and conducted a full body frisk of Plaintiff. Plaintiff protested vigorously but Mr. Stone did not stop the frisk. This frisk did not uncover any stolen items.

Stone denied that he frisked Sturmer at all, much less that it was a "full body" frisk or that Sturmer protested the frisk. The response in the answer to these allegations would likely be simply: "Defendant denies the allegations in Paragraph 12."

Denying Part of an Allegation

But what if the paragraph contains allegations that are true and others that aren't? Rule 8(b)(4) says, "a party that intends in good faith to deny only part of an allegation must admit the part that is true and deny the rest." *Zielinski v. Philadelphia Piers, Inc.* demonstrates the impact of a party denying an entire paragraph that contained both true and false allegations.

Case Preview

Zielinski v. Philadelphia Piers, Inc.

As you read *Zielinski v. Philadelphia Piers, Inc.*, consider the following:

1. What is the allegation in the complaint at the center of this dispute?
2. How did the defendant respond to this allegation? How should it have responded and why?
3. Is the instruction the jury will receive factually accurate? If not, can you justify providing such an instruction to a jury under these circumstances?

Zielinski v. Philadelphia Piers, Inc.
139 F. Supp. 408 (E.D. Pa. 1956)

VAN DUSEN, District Judge

Plaintiff requests a ruling that, for the purposes of this case, the motor-driven fork lift operated by Sandy Johnson on February 9, 1953, was owned by defendant and that Sandy Johnson was its agent acting in the course of his employment on that date. The following facts are established by the pleadings, interrogatories, depositions and uncontradicted portions of affidavits:

1. Plaintiff filed his complaint on April 28, 1953, for personal injuries received on February 9, 1953, while working on Pier 96, Philadelphia, for J. A. McCarthy, as a result of a collision of two motor-driven fork lifts.

2. Paragraph 5 of this complaint stated that 'a motor-driven vehicle known as a fork lift or chisel, owned, operated and controlled by the defendant, its agents, servants and employees, was so negligently and carelessly managed . . . that the same . . . did come into contact with the plaintiff causing him to sustain the injuries more fully hereinafter set forth.'

3. The 'First Defense' of the Answer stated 'Defendant . . . denies the averments of paragraph 5 . . . .'

Inappropriate response

4. The motor-driven vehicle known as a fork lift or chisel, which collided with the McCarthy fork lift on which plaintiff was riding, had on it the initials 'P.P.I.'

5. On February 10, 1953, Carload Contractors, Inc. made a report of this accident to its insurance company, whose policy No. CL 3964 insured Carload Contractors, Inc. against potential liability for the negligence of its employees contributing to a collision of the type described in paragraph 2 above.

6. By letter of April 29, 1953, the complaint served on defendant was forwarded to the above-mentioned insurance company. This letter read as follows:

'Gentlemen:

'As per telephone conversation today with your office, we attach hereto "Complaint in Trespass" as brought against Philadelphia Piers, Inc. by one Frank Zielinski for supposed injuries sustained by him on February 9, 1953.

'We find that a fork lift truck operated by an employee of Carload Contractors, Inc. also insured by yourselves was involved in an accident with another chisel truck, which, was alleged, did cause injury to Frank Zielinski, and same was reported to you by Carload Contractors, Inc. at the time, and you assigned Claim Number OL 0153-94 to this claim.

'Should not this Complaint in Trespass be issued against Carload Contractors, Inc. and not Philadelphia Piers, Inc.?

'We forward for your handling.'

7. Interrogatories 1 to 5 and the answers thereto, which were sworn to by defendant's General Manager on June 12, 1953, and filed on June 22, 1953, read as follows:

'1. State whether you have received any information of an injury sustained by the plaintiff on February 9, 1953, South Wharves. If so, state when and from whom you first received notice of such injury. *A. We were first notified of this accident on or about February 9, 1953 by Thomas Wilson.*

'2. State whether you caused an investigation to be made of the circumstances of said injury and if so, state who made such investigation and when it was made. *A. We made a very brief investigation on February 9, 1953 and turned the matter over to (our insurance company) for further investigation.*

'3. Give the names and addresses of all persons disclosed by such investigation to have been witnesses to the aforesaid occurrence. A. *The witnesses whose names we have obtained so far are:*

'*Victor Marzo, 2005 E. Hart Lane, Philadelphia*

'*Thomas Wilson, 6115 Reinhardt St., Philadelphia*

'*Sandy Johnson, 1236 S. 16th Street, Philadelphia*

'4. State whether you have obtained any written statements from such witnesses and if so, identify such statements and state when and by whom they were taken. If in writing, attach copies of same hereto. A. *We have obtained written statements from Victor Marzo, Thomas Wilson and Sandy Johnson and these statements are in the possession of our counsel . . . , who advises that copies need not be attached unless we are ordered by the court to do so.*

'5. Set forth the facts disclosed by such statements and investigation concerning the manner in which the accident happened. A. *Sandy Johnson was moving boxes on Pier 96 and had stopped his towmotor when a towmotor operated by an employe[e] of McCarthy Stevedoring Company with a person on the back, apparently the plaintiff, backed into the standing towmotor, injuring the plaintiff.*'

8. At a deposition taken August 18, 1953, Sandy Johnson testified that he was the employee of defendant on February 9, 1953, and had been their employee for approximately fifteen years.

9. At a pre-trial conference held on September 27, 1955, plaintiff first learned that over a year before February 9, 1953, the business of moving freight on piers in Philadelphia, formerly conducted by defendant, had been sold by it to Carload Contractors, Inc. and Sandy Johnson had been transferred to the payroll of this corporation without apparently realizing it, since the nature or location of his work had not changed.

* * *

Under these circumstances, and for the purposes of this action, it is ordered that the following shall be stated to the jury at the trial:

'It is admitted that, on February 9, 1953, the towmotor or fork lift bearing the initials 'P.P.I.' was owned by defendant and that Sandy Johnson was a servant in the employ of defendant and doing its work on that date.'

This ruling is based on the following principles:

1. Under the circumstances of this case, the answer contains an ineffective denial of that part of paragraph 5 of the complaint which alleges that 'a motor driven vehicle known as a fork lift or chisel (was) owned, operated and controlled by the defendant, its agents, servants and employees.'
F.R. Civ. P. 8(b), 28 U.S.C. provides:

'A party shall state in short and plain terms his defenses to each claim asserted and shall admit or deny the averments upon which the adverse party relies. . . . Denials shall fairly meet the substance of the averments denied. When a pleader intends in good faith to deny only a part or a qualification of an averment, he shall specify so much of it as is true and material and shall deny only the remainder.'

For example, it is quite clear that defendant does not deny the averment in paragraph 5 that the fork lift came into contact with plaintiff, since it admits, in the answers to interrogatories, that an investigation of an occurrence of the accident had been made and that a report dated February 10, 1953, was sent to its insurance company stating 'While Frank Zielinski was riding on bumper of chisel and holding rope to secure cargo, the chisel truck collided with another chisel truck operated by Sandy Johnson causing injuries to Frank Zielinski's legs and hurt head of Sandy Johnson.' Compliance with the above-mentioned rule required that defendant file a more specific answer than a general denial. A specific denial of parts of this paragraph and specific admission of other parts would have warned plaintiff that he had sued the wrong defendant.

Paragraph 8.23 of Moore's Federal Practice (2nd Edition) Vol. II, p. 1680, says: 'In such a case, the defendant should make clear just what he is denying and what he is admitting.' See, Kirby v. Turner-Day & Woolworth Handle Co., D.C.E.D. Tenn. 1943, 50 F. Supp. 469. This answer to paragraph 5 does not make clear to plaintiff the defenses he must be prepared to meet. . . .

* * *

2. Under the circumstances of this case, principles of equity require that defendant be estopped from denying agency because, otherwise, its inaccurate statements and statements in the record, which it knew (or had the means of knowing within its control) were inaccurate, will have deprived plaintiff of his right of action. . . .

Post-Case Follow-Up

The instruction to the jury makes the forklift operator an employee of the defendant "for purposes of this action," even though he wasn't actually an employee of the defendant at the time of the accident. This instruction is important for the plaintiff because under the tort theory of *respondeat superior* an employer is responsible for the negligence of its employees while acting within the course and scope of employment. What interests of a plaintiff may justify an instruction to the jury that is contrary to the actual facts? What about the interests of the court? It's a worthwhile exercise for you to draft a proper response to the allegations in Paragraph 5 of the plaintiff's complaint in *Zielinski*. Drafting it correctly would have avoided the possibility of liability for the defendant. When admitting or denying allegations in the complaint, a defendant does well to be as precise as possible.

Zielinski v. Philadelphia Piers, Inc.: Real Life Applications

1. Paragraph 9 of Plaintiff's complaint alleges: "Plaintiff and Defendant entered into a valid, written contract whereby Defendant agreed to purchase 10,000 widgets at price of $1 per widget. Plaintiff delivered the 10,000 widgets to Defendant. Defendant failed to pay the $10,000 owed under the contract." In

A

his answer, Defendant responds to this allegation by saying only: "Deny that Defendant failed to pay the $10,000 owed under the contract." At trial, Defendant proposes to offer evidence that Plaintiff and Defendant never reached an agreement regarding the purchase and sale of widgets and that Plaintiff never delivered the widgets to Defendant. Should the court admit the evidence?

2. Plaintiff's complaint alleges Plaintiff and Defendant were involved in a car accident as a result of Defendant's negligent driving. Plaintiff alleges that Defendant's negligence consisted, in part, of running the stop sign at the intersection where the wreck occurred. Defendant answers this allegation by saying, "Plaintiff has no proof Defendant ran the stop sign." What is the effect of Defendant's response?

3. Plaintiff's complaint alleges that a product designed and manufactured by Defendant injured Plaintiff. Paragraph 8 of Plaintiff's complaint alleges: "As a result of Plaintiff's physical injuries, Plaintiff is in constant and severe physical pain." Defendant does not know whether or not this allegation is true and is not able to access information to confirm or deny it. How should the defendant respond to this allegation in his answer? What is the effect of this response?

Rule 11 and Denials

In Chapter 14, we saw that a plaintiff cannot make baseless factual contentions in the complaint. Similarly, a defendant cannot make baseless denials of factual contentions in the answer. Under Rule 11(b)(4), by signing, filing, or advocating an answer, a defendant is certifying to the court that "the denials are warranted on the evidence, or, if specifically so identified, are reasonably based on belief or a lack of information." Recall that the certifications under Rule 11 are continuing rather than one-time certifications. If a defendant later discovers that the denial is no longer warranted, he should not continue to maintain the denial.

2. Affirmative Defenses

Rule 8(c) requires the defendant in the answer to "affirmatively state any avoidance or affirmative defense. . . ." Affirmative defenses must be pled by the defendant or they are lost. Without a supporting pleading, a defendant may not prove an affirmative defense at trial or rely on it in a pretrial or post-trial dispositive motion.

The Burden to Plead an Affirmative Defense

An **affirmative defense** is not raised by a defendant's denial of the plaintiff's allegations. A defendant who wishes to assert an affirmative defense will lose his ability to defend himself on that ground if all he does is deny the plaintiff's allegations. Instead, the defendant must separately state the defense. In doing so, his pleading, like those of the plaintiff in the complaint, must be "simple, concise, and direct," and defenses need not be consistent with one another; i.e., it is not necessary that it be possible for them to be true at the same time. Alleging the affirmative defense of statute of limitations in a tort action seeking personal injury damages might look like this.

FIRST DEFENSE

The applicable statute of limitations bars Plaintiff's action. The events set out in the Plaintiff's complaint occurred more than two years before this action was commenced. The governing statute of limitations bars this action because it requires that tort actions for the recovery of personal injury damages such as Plaintiff's action must be brought within two years.

Rule 8(c) sets out a laundry list of some of the most commonly encountered affirmative defenses. The defenses in 8(c) must be affirmatively pled or they are lost. Failure to plead them means the defendant cannot produce evidence to support them at trial, and the jury will not be asked a question about the defense in the court's charge. Notice, however, the use of the word "including" that precedes the list, meaning that Rule 8(c) is not an exhaustive list of affirmative defenses. If the defense is contained in Rule 8(c)'s list, the defendant must plead it. However, if the defense constitutes one in "confession and avoidance," it must be pled even though not on the list.

The nature of a confession and avoidance defense is that the defendant could confess the truth of the plaintiff's allegations and yet avoid or reduce liability because a separate set of facts constituting the defense is true. Consider the nature of the statute of limitations defense, for example. Even if the plaintiff's allegations are true, the defendant will avoid liability if the plaintiff did not file his action within the time proscribed by the applicable statute of limitations. To plead an affirmative defense, the defendant need not admit the truth of the plaintiff's allegations; but if he *could* and yet still avoid or reduce liability based on the defense, the defense is an affirmative defense and must be pled, even if not listed in Rule 8(c). If you're not sure that a defense is an affirmative defense, it is better to be safe than sorry. Plead it!

C. FAILING TO RESPOND

The defendant must make a timely Rule 12 response or the plaintiff will be able to obtain a default judgment for the relief he demands in his complaint. This section discusses the defendant's deadline to respond to the complaint and the consequences for his failure to meet that deadline.

1. Deadline to Respond

How long the defendant has to respond to the complaint differs depending upon whether or not he agreed to waive service. His decision to initially respond to the complaint with a Rule 12 motion can affect his deadline to answer the complaint if his motion is denied. And there is a separate answer deadline for cases removed from state to federal court.

Deadline to File the Defendant's First Rule 12 Response

Rule 12(a)(1) provides that the defendant must file an answer within 21 days of the day he was served with process. If, however, the defendant agreed to waive service under Rule 4(d), the defendant has 60 days from the date the waiver request was sent to file an answer. The additional time to file an answer is an incentive to waive service. If the waiver request was sent to a defendant outside the United States, the defendant has 90 days from the day the waiver request was sent to file an answer. If a defendant chooses a Rule 12 motion as his first response, he must file that motion within the deadline to file an answer.

Effect of a Rule 12 Motion on the Answer Deadline

Under Rule 12(a)(4), responding to the complaint with a motion alters the deadline to file an answer. If the motion is granted, the defendant may not have to answer at all. For example, if the court grants a motion to dismiss for lack of subject matter jurisdiction or personal jurisdiction, the defendant will not have to file an answer because the case has been dismissed. If, however, the court denies the Rule 12 motion, or decides to postpone its decision on the motion until trial, the defendant has 14 days after the court's order to file his answer.

Deadline to Answer in Cases Removed from State to Federal Court

When a case is removed from state to federal court, the defendant may have already filed an answer in state court. If so, Rule 81 provides that "repleading is unnecessary unless the court orders it." So, the court may order the defendant to file an answer that comports with federal pleading standards rather than state ones, but doing so is not necessary simply because the case was removed. Often, the defendant removes the case before he has filed an answer in state court. In this scenario, Rule 81 provides that the defendant has 21 days from the date he was formally served in state court or 7 days from the date of the notice of removal, whichever is longer, to file his first Rule 12 response — either motion or answer — in federal court.

2. Default and Default Judgment

A defendant is served under Rule 4 with the court's summons. The summons does what its name says — it summons the defendant to appear by either filing an answer or a motion under Rule 12. But the summons doesn't just demand an appearance. It tells the defendant to appear *or else he loses automatically*. The summons says "If you fail to appear, judgment by default will be entered against you for the relief demanded in the complaint." Obtaining a default judgment is a two-step process.

First, the plaintiff must have the clerk enter default, then the defendant must obtain a default judgment.

Entry of Default

If the defendant fails to respond to the complaint within the appropriate deadline either by filing an answer or a Rule 12 motion, Rule 55(a) provides that the entry of **default** is appropriate. The clerk's entry of default on the docket precludes the defendant from filing an answer or Rule 12 motion. However, the entry of default does not happen automatically after the defendant's deadline to respond passes. The plaintiff must make a motion for entry of default and demonstrate, typically with affidavits, that the court has subject matter jurisdiction and that entry of default is appropriate, i.e., that the time to respond has passed. If the plaintiff fails to seek entry of default, the defendant may file a Rule 12 response, even though his deadline to do so has passed, and thereafter entry of default is not appropriate.

Default Judgment by the Clerk

Entry of default does not entitle the plaintiff to recover. After entry of default, the plaintiff must obtain a **default** *judgment.* Rule 55(b)(1) provides that the clerk may enter the default judgment "[i]f the plaintiff's claim is for a sum certain or a sum that can be made certain by computation." A "sum certain" exists when the plaintiff pleads a precise amount in his complaint and the damages can be accurately calculated with mathematical precision. For example, in *Thorpe v. Thorpe*, the plaintiff filed suit alleging she was entitled to at least half of the proceeds of a check that the defendant had cashed. The clerk entered default judgment for the plaintiff. The court explained that entry of default judgment by the clerk, rather than the court, was proper.

> Here the plaintiff's complaint demanded judgment for $63,308.16, the full amount of the check in question, or $31,654.08, exactly one-half the amount of the check. Although there was an alternative demand in the complaint, this did not preclude the Clerk from validly entering a default judgment, at the request of appellee, for the smaller of the two specific amounts set forth in the complaint as constituting a 'claim . . . for a sum certain.'

Thorpe v. Thorpe, 364 F.2d 692, 694 (D.C. Cir. 1966).

Even if the "sum certain" requirement is met, the clerk may not enter default judgment if the defendant is a minor or incompetent person.

Default Judgment by the Court

In all other cases, the court must enter default judgment. Liability issues are conclusively established against the defendant, and the plaintiff will have to present evidence to the court on the amount of damages. A plaintiff may not be awarded relief that he did not demand in his complaint. If he asked for compensatory damages only, for example, the default judgment may not award punitive damages or injective relief. A court may enter default judgment against a minor or incompetent person, but only if represented by a guardian or similar person who has a fiduciary obligation to the minor or incompetent person.

Setting Aside Default and Default Judgments

Default judgments are not a favored way of disposing of cases. They dispose of cases because a defendant did not respond in time, rather than on the merits of the plaintiff's claim. Consequently, defaults and default judgments are often set aside. Rule 50(c) permits a court to set aside an entry of default "for good cause shown." To set aside a default judgment, the defendant must move under Rule 60(b), which allows a court to relieve a party from a final default judgment for "mistake, inadvertence, surprise, or excusable neglect." In addition, the defendant will have to show a viable defense. Why bother undoing the default judgment if it ultimately won't change the outcome?

Chapter Summary

- A defendant's initial response to the complaint may be a motion or an answer.
- In the answer, a defendant may assert any and all defenses he has. An initial response by motion may present the defenses enumerated in Rule 12(b)(1)-(7), a motion for more definite statement of a vague or ambiguous complaint, and a motion to strike immaterial or scandalous matters in the complaint.
- The defenses of lack of personal jurisdiction, improper venue, insufficient process, and insufficient service of process must be presented in the defendant's first Rule 12 response — either motion or answer — or they are waived.
- The defendant must admit or deny the allegations in the plaintiff's complaint. A failure to deny the allegation means that the allegation is a fact for purposes of the action.
- The defenses listed in Rule 8(c) and any others that constitute defenses in confession and avoidance must be affirmatively pled in the answer or they are lost.
- The defendant must file his Rule 12 response within 21 days of being served. If the defendant agreed to waive service, he has 60 days from the time the waiver was sent to file his response, unless he was located outside the United States, in which case he has 90 days to respond.
- A failure to timely file a Rule 12 response will, upon the request of the plaintiff, result in an entry of default, which precludes the defendant from filing a Rule 12 response. The plaintiff may then obtain a default judgment awarding him the relief demanded in the complaint.

Applying the Concepts

1. Yvonne's complaint names Altima, LLC as a defendant. Altima files no Rule 12 motions. Instead, Altima files an answer that states lack of personal jurisdiction as a defense. Yvonne argues that Altima waived this defense by failing to file a motion objecting to lack of personal jurisdiction. Is Yvonne correct? Why or why not?

2. Jaylen is named as a defendant in a federal court complaint. He files a motion objecting to lack of personal jurisdiction and two days later, an answer stating that venue is improper. Has Jaylen waived either defense?

3. Angus files suit against BLS, Inc. in federal court. Paragraph 10 of Angus' complaint alleges: "Plaintiff Angus was an employee of BLS, Inc. until BLS terminated Angus' employment on August 5, 2016 due to his age." BLS's answer responds to this allegation by saying, "BLS denies that it terminated Angus on the basis of his age." At trial, BLS proposes to offer evidence that Angus resigned his position at BLS. Can you think of a better way to phrase the denial given what BLS plans to prove at trial?

4. Abner files suit against Bullseye, LLP in federal court. Bullseye files only a motion to dismiss for improper venue in response to the complaint. The court denies the motion. Three weeks after the court issues the order denying the motion, Bullseye has filed no other Rule 12 response. What should Abner do?

Civil Procedure in Practice

Jada Bell files suit in in the United States District Court for the Southern District of New York against New Jersey Capital, LLC. You represent New Jersey Capital. You meet with a team of executives at New Jersey Capital who are serving as the decision-makers with respect to the litigation on behalf of the company. They provide you with a copy of the complaint with which they have been served. In pertinent part, the complaint reads:

> 5. Plaintiff Jada Bell was an employee of New Jersey Capital from December 1, 2003 to June 15, 2016.
>
> 6. Ms. Bell's supervisor at the time her employment ended was Alexander Nash. Mr. Nash notified Ms. Bell that her employment would be terminated on June 15, 2016 in a letter, signed by Mr. Nash, dated May 15, 2016. The letter provided no explanation for this employment decision.

7. Ms. Bell asked Mr. Nash to explain the reason she was being fired. Mr. Bell responded by saying that New Jersey Capital was "realigning its investment in human resources to provide more sophisticated customer service."

* * *

10. Ms. Bell is an African-American and was one of only 3 African-American employees of New Jersey Capital at the time she was fired. At the time of the termination of her employment, New Jersey Capital had more than 100 employees, more than 80 percent of whom were white.

11. Two weeks after terminating Ms. Bell's employment, New Jersey Capital filled her position with a white man who had both less formal education than Ms. Bell and less experience in the industry. . . .

* * *

COUNT ONE

20. Plaintiff Jada Bell adopts paragraphs 5-19 of this complaint and reasserts and realleges them as if fully set forth here.

* * *

21. New Jersey Capital's decision to terminate Ms. Bell's employment constituted racial discrimination in the work place in violation of Title VII of the federal Civil Rights Act, which prohibits an adverse employment decision based on race.

From your meeting with the executive team, you learn that New Jersey Capital has a single office in Newark, New Jersey, and that it is organized under the laws of New Jersey. Its lone office is where Jada Bell worked throughout the time of her employment with New Jersey Capital. You also learn from this meeting that all of the events alleged in her complaint occurred, if at all, at the New Jersey office.

1. Based on this information, what defense or defenses do you raise, how do you raise them, and when do you raise them?

2. A month after your meeting with the New Jersey Capital executive team, you learn that an associate you supervise has filed an answer on behalf of your client. The answer is the only response filed so far, and it contains only admissions to and denials of the allegations in the complaint. The answer was filed seven days earlier. What, if anything, can you do to assert the defenses you identified in question 1?

3. The case proceeds and you are obligated to respond to the allegations in the complaint. The executive team tells you that none of the members of the team has any knowledge about precisely how many employees New Jersey Capital had at the time Ms. Bell's employment ended or what the racial composition of the work force was. However, you learn from the team that such information is kept

by the director of human resources, but she is not a member of the team. Can you respond to the allegations in Paragraph 10 based on what you've learned? If so, what is that response? If not, what should you do?

4. How would you assert the following defenses on behalf of New Jersey Capital?

   a. New Jersey Capital fired Ms. Bell but not because of her race.
   b. Ms. Bell's allegations, even if true, do not constitute racial discrimination in violation of Title VII of the federal Civil Rights Act.
   c. New Jersey Capital was not properly served under Rule 4.
   d. Ms. Bell did not first pursue her administrative remedies with the Equal Employment Opportunity Commission, as required by law, which may defeat her lawsuit.

Amended and Supplemental Pleadings

The two preceding chapters addressed the plaintiff's initial pleading — the complaint — and the defendant's responsive pleading — the answer. In these pleadings, the parties allege their claims and defenses along with the factual allegations that support them. But the allegations made in pleadings are not written in stone. A party may want to change his pleading to allege new facts, claims, or defenses, or to add new parties. A party may also want to delete facts or drop claims, defenses, or parties. A party's desire to change his pleadings may be based on newly discovered evidence or legal theories or to correct a mistake in the original pleading. Parties change or add to their pleadings by filing amended pleadings and, on rarer occasions, supplemental pleadings. This chapter concerns when and under what circumstances a party may file an amended pleading and the effect of an amended pleading. It concludes with a discussion of supplemental pleadings.

A. AMENDED PLEADINGS

Rule 15 governs amended pleadings. Its liberal approach to permitting amendment of pleadings is a departure from the practice under the common law pleading rules. Rule 15 gives a party a right to amend his pleading as "a matter of course" under limited circumstances and strongly encourages courts to permit amendments, even during or after trial. But Rule 15 does not give a party a right to amend pleadings under all circumstances. This section discusses the purpose and effect of an amended pleading, as well as the effect Rule 15(c)'s relation back doctrine can have on the operation of the statute of limitations.

Key Concepts

- When a party may amend "as a matter of course"
- The reasons that might prevent a court from "freely" granting leave to amend
- Trial amendments, trying an issue by express or implied consent, and how to avoid it
- The "relation back" of amended complaints asserting a new claim or changing defendants
- The function of a supplemental pleading

1. The (Now Rejected) Common Law Pleading Rules

Under common law pleading rules, the ability to amend pleadings was extremely limited, and, if the evidence at trial varied from the allegations in the pleading, the consequences could be harsh. For example, in *Spangler v. Pugh*, 21 Ill. 85 (1859), the plaintiff filed suit to recover on a promissory note. His pleading alleged that he was owed $2,579.57. The evidence at trial proved he was owed half a penny more than alleged in his pleading; so, the trial court rendered judgment for the plaintiff in the amount $2,579.57-1/2. The Supreme Court of Illinois reversed the judgment in favor of the plaintiff because the evidence at trial was at variance with the plaintiff's pleading. By half a cent! By proving at trial that he was entitled to half a cent more than he requested in his pleading, he wound up with nothing.

This mechanical, form-over-substance approach has been rejected by the Federal Rules. Rule 15 governs the amended and supplemental pleadings in federal court, and it takes a far more liberal approach than the common law to permitting the amendment of pleadings both before, during, and after trial, so that claims are decided on their merits rather than on "procedural technicalities." 6 Charles Alan Wright, Arthur R. Miller & Mary Kay Kane, Federal Practice and Procedure §1471 (3d ed. 2010). Today, under Rule 15, the trial court could have permitted the plaintiff in *Spangler* to amend his pleadings, either before, during, or after trial, to conform to the evidence.

The amended pleading supersedes the prior pleading and, therefore, must be complete in itself. The party is not simply adding the new allegations in the amendment. The party must be sure to restate all of the claims, defenses, parties, and supporting allegations the party intends to continue to pursue after amendment.

Despite the liberal approach to amendment of pleadings embodied in Rule 15, there must be limits on a party's ability to alter his factual and legal theory of the case. An unfettered ability to amend pleadings at any time would cause prejudice to the opposing party, who would have been preparing to prosecute or defend one case only to find that his opponent's theory of the case has changed. Rule 15 attempts to strike a balance between ensuring that claims are decided on the merits rather than procedural technicalities, on the one hand, and avoiding prejudice to opposing parties, on the other.

2. Pretrial Amendment of Pleadings Under Rule 15(a)

Rule 15(a), set out in Exhibit 16.1, governs amendments of pleadings made before trial. The rule divides pretrial amendments into two categories — amendments as a matter of course under 15(a)(1) and "Other Amendments" under 15(a)(2). A party may make an amendment "as a matter of course" without seeking the permission of the court or the opposing parties. All other amendments require permission of either the court or the opposing parties.

EXHIBIT 16.1 **Rule 15(a)**

(a) Amendments Before Trial.
(1) Amending as a Matter of Course. A party may amend its pleading once as a matter of course within:
(A) 21 days after serving it, or
(B) if the pleading is one to which a responsive pleading is required, 21 days after service of a responsive pleading or 21 days after service of a motion under Rule 12(b), (e), or (f), whichever is earlier.
(2) Other Amendments. In all other cases, a party may amend its pleading only with the opposing party's written consent or the court's leave. The court should freely give leave when justice so requires.

Amendments as a Matter of Course

Rule 15(a)(1) allows a party to amend its pleading one time without permission of the court or the opposing parties within a relatively short window of opportunity at the beginning of the action. If asked to grant leave to amend, the court would almost certainly grant it at such an early point in the case; so, the Rule saves the court's time by simply allowing parties to amend without permission.

An amendment of the answer as a matter of course must occur within 21 days of service of the original answer. An amendment of the complaint as a matter of course must occur within 21 days after service of the defendant's first Rule 12 response. Amendments outside of this time period or subsequent amendments within it require the court's or the opposing parties' permission. For example, if the defendant files an amended answer within 21 days of his original answer, a second amended answer would require permission of the court or the opposing parties even if it occurred within 21 days of the original answer. Suppose a plaintiff seeks to amend his complaint for the first time 30 days after the defendant serves his answer. The plaintiff would have to seek leave to amend even though it is his first amendment, because the amendment comes outside of the 21-day window after the defendant made his first Rule 12 response.

An amendment of the complaint as a matter of course must be made within 21 days of the defendant's first Rule 12 response. The defendant's first Rule 12 response could be either an answer or a Rule 12 motion, which would include any Rule 12(b) motion, a motion for more definite statement under Rule 12(e), or a motion to strike under Rule 12(f). The first of these Rule 12 responses triggers the running of the 21-day deadline for the plaintiff to amend his complaint once without permission. Allowing the plaintiff to amend as a matter of course after receipt of the defendant's first Rule 12 response serves an important function. As the Advisory Committee Note to Rule 15 explains:

> This provision will force the pleader to consider carefully and promptly the wisdom of amending to meet the arguments in the motion. A responsive amendment may avoid the need to decide the motion or reduce the number of issues to be decided, and will

expedite determination of issues that otherwise might be raised seriatim. It also should advance other pretrial proceedings.

Rule 15 provides a plaintiff only one window to amend as a matter of course, even if the defendant files a Rule 12 motion and later files an answer. Suppose a defendant's first Rule 12 response is a motion to dismiss for lack of personal jurisdiction, but the court denies the defendant's motion three months later. The defendant then files an answer. The plaintiff's 21-day opportunity to amend once as a matter of course ran from service of the motion to dismiss. The filing of the answer does not create a second opportunity to amend as a matter of course. However, the defendant's decision to file a motion as his initial response to the complaint does not deprive him of his opportunity to amend his later answer once as a matter of course within 21 days of serving his answer.

Other Pretrial Amendments

All other amendments require permission. If the amendment does not qualify as one permitted "as a matter of course" under Rule 15(a)(1), permission from the court or the opposing parties to file an amended pleading is required. Rule 15(a)(2) directs the district court to "freely give" leave to amend "when justice so requires." Although this language demands a liberal approach to amending pleadings, it does not require the court to grant leave to amend in all cases. *Foman v. Davis* sets out a number of reasons for denying leave to amend despite Rule 15's declaration that leave should be "freely given when justice so requires."

Case Preview

Foman v. Davis

As you read the short *Foman v. Davis* case, consider the following:

1. What prompted the plaintiff (designated the petitioner in the opinion) to seek leave to amend her complaint?
2. What factors should a district court consider in determining whether or not to grant leave to amend?

Foman v. Davis
371 U.S. 178 (1962)

Opinion

Mr. Justice GOLDBERG delivered the opinion of the Court.

Petitioner filed a complaint in the District Court alleging that, in exchange for petitioner's promise to care for and support her mother, petitioner's father had agreed not to make a will, thereby assuring petitioner of an intestate share of the father's estate; it was further alleged that petitioner had fully performed her obligations under the oral agreement, but that contrary thereto the father had devised his property to respondent, his second wife and executrix. Petitioner sought recovery of what would have been her intestate share of the father's estate. Respondent moved to dismiss the complaint on the ground that the oral agreement was unenforceable under the applicable state statute of frauds [Eds. — The statute of frauds is a contract doctrine that requires certain agreements to be in writing in order to be enforceable]. Accepting respondent's contention, the District Court entered judgment on December 19, 1960, dismissing petitioner's complaint for failure to state a claim upon which relief might be granted. On December 20, 1960, petitioner filed motions to vacate the judgment and to amend the complaint to assert a right of recovery in *quantum meruit* for performance of the obligations which were the consideration for the assertedly unenforceable oral contract. [Eds. — *Quantum meruit* is an equitable doctrine that permits a person to receive the value of services provided, even in the absence of an enforceable agreement.] On January 17, 1961, petitioner filed a notice of appeal from the judgment of December 19, 1960. On January 23, 1961, the District Court denied petitioner's motions to vacate the judgment and to amend the complaint. On January 26, 1961, petitioner filed a notice of appeal from denial of the motions.

On appeal, the parties briefed and argued the merits of dismissal of the complaint and denial of petitioner's motions by the District Court. Notwithstanding, the Court of Appeals of its own accord dismissed the appeal insofar as taken from the District Court judgment of December 19, 1960, and affirmed the orders of the District Court. . . . This Court granted certiorari. 368 U.S. 951, 82 S. Ct. 396, 7 L. Ed. 2d 385.

* * *

The Court of Appeals also erred in affirming the District Court's denial of petitioner's motion to vacate the judgment in order to allow amendment of the complaint. As appears from the record, the amendment would have done no more than state an alternative theory for recovery.

Rule 15(a) declares that leave to amend 'shall be freely given when justice so requires'; this mandate is to be heeded. . . . If the underlying facts or circumstances relied upon by a plaintiff may be a proper subject of relief, he ought to be afforded an opportunity to test his claim on the merits. In the absence of any apparent or declared reason — such as undue delay, bad faith or dilatory motive on the part of the movant, repeated failure to cure deficiencies by amendments previously allowed, undue prejudice to the opposing party by virtue of allowance of the amendment, futility of amendment, etc. — the leave sought should, as the rules require, be 'freely given.' Of course, the grant or denial of an opportunity to amend is within the discretion of the District Court, but outright refusal to grant the leave without any justifying reason appearing for the denial is not an exercise of discretion; it is merely abuse of that discretion and inconsistent with the spirit of the Federal Rules.

The judgment is reversed and the cause is remanded to the Court of Appeals for further proceedings consistent with this opinion. It is so ordered.

Post-Case Follow-Up

Foman confirms that Rule 15 is a striking departure from the common law pleading rules exemplified in *Spangler v. Pugh*. Rule 15 provides that a trial court should "freely give leave [to amend] when justice so requires." The trial court has discretion to grant or deny leave to amend, but to deny leave to amend without explanation is "not an exercise of discretion."

Notice that the Court provides a number of reasons why a trial court may deny leave to amend: (1) undue delay in requesting the amendment, (2) a bad faith desire to delay proceedings on the part of the movant, (3) repeated failure to cure deficiencies by previous amendments, (4) the amendment would cause undue prejudice to the opposing party, and (5) futility of amendment. Would any of these have been grounds to deny leave to the plaintiff in *Foman*? What if the plaintiff had asked for leave to amend to allege an additional oral promise? Or to provide additional detail about the services she provided?

Foman v. Davis: Real Life Applications

1. Plaintiff pleads the tort of battery in her complaint and alleges "the defendant swung a baseball bat at Plaintiff's head and, although the bat did not strike the Plaintiff, Plaintiff believed the bat would strike her head and the attack terrified her." The defendant makes a pre-answer motion to dismiss for failure to state a claim, arguing "battery requires a 'touching' of the plaintiff and because the bat did not touch the plaintiff no battery could have occurred." The court grants the motion to dismiss one month after it was made. The plaintiff seeks leave to amend her complaint to allege the tort of assault, which is "the apprehension of a battery." The court issues an order that states only "Plaintiff's motion for leave to amend is denied." Did the court properly deny the motion for leave to amend? Why or why not?

2. Plaintiff's complaint alleges age discrimination in violation of the federal Age Discrimination in Employment Act (ADEA). The ADEA prohibits discrimination on the basis of age in the workplace, but only protects employees 40 years of age or older at the time of the alleged discrimination. Plaintiff's complaint alleges "shortly after Plaintiff turned 35 years old, Defendant passed her over for a promotion in favor of a younger worker." The court grants the defendant's motion to dismiss for failure to state a claim. The plaintiff moves for leave to amend the allegations supporting her ADEA claim. How should the court rule and why?

3. Asea's complaint names Charlie as the defendant and alleges that Charlie trespassed on Asea's property on October 1, 2016. Asea discovered in a pretrial deposition six months ago that he may have also entered her property without permission on a second occasion. Trial is scheduled to begin in less than two weeks. Asea seeks leave to amend her complaint to allege this second act of trespass. How should the court rule on the motion and why?

More on Denying Leave to Amend

If the plaintiff has already been given leave to amend to cure a problem with his pleading but has repeatedly failed to do so, the court may refuse additional leave to amend. Also, if amendment of the pleading would be a futile attempt to cure the defect, leave to amend is not required. For example, if the plaintiff pled a fact that shows he can never recover, permitting an amendment to change or delete that fact is likely futile. Recall the plaintiff in the Real Life Applications section above who pled that she was not over 40 at the time of the alleged workplace age discrimination, even though federal law requires her to be over 40 in order to prevail. Permitting amendment to her pleading is futile because she has shown she can never recover regardless of what additional facts she pleads.

Perhaps the most important and most common reason to disallow an amendment is because it will cause prejudice to an opposing party. In a sense, all amendments help the party making it and thereby prejudice opposing parties. If not, why bother amending? The prejudice that might prevent amendment is narrower than this. It is not enough for a party to show that he would have won the case if the amendment had been disallowed or lost the cause because it was allowed. Instead, he must show that the amendment prejudiced him in terms of preparing his case, and that allowing the amendment would cause him a "grave injustice." *Patton v. Guyer*, 443 F.2d 79, 86 (10th Cir. 1971). This kind of prejudice — **preparation prejudice** — may exist when crucial evidence needed to prove or disprove a claim or defense sought to be included in an amendment is no longer available. But preparation prejudice is most likely to exist when the requested amendment alters the legal theory asserted, or injects a new legal theory into the case, particularly when the new legal theory would require proof of new facts. Preparation prejudice may also exist when the amendment is requested close to trial and after a great deal of discovery has already occurred, particularly when the party requesting amendment should have known to request the amendment earlier. Consider the example of *Suehle v. Markem Machine Co.*, wherein the court denied the plaintiff's motion to amend his complaint alleging breach of contract to add an antitrust claim.

> Rule 15(a) of the Federal Rules of Civil Procedure provides that: ". . . [a] party may amend his pleading . . . by leave of court or by written consent of the adverse party; and leave shall be freely given when justice so requires. . . ."
>
> In the circumstances, we think that justice does not require grant of leave to amend. The action was instituted on March 15, 1962, and has been at issue since August of that year, when plaintiff's answer to defendant's counterclaim was filed. The case is now ready for pre-trial conference and shortly thereafter will be listed and called for trial.
>
> Plaintiff's former counsel indicated to defendant's counsel at a deposition hearing in August 1962, a probable disposition to amend the complaint to include an antitrust count. Some months later, plaintiff's former counsel did send a copy of a proposed amended and supplemental complaint to defendant's attorney, who refused to agree to the amendments. No motion to amend was then filed.
>
> The present motion to amend was not filed until February 11, 1965. Plaintiff attempts to excuse the delay by the statement that "plaintiff was struggling to establish a new business in the face of the difficulties created by defendant's interference with his

tape business and could not during that period undertake the expense of preparation in preparing an antitrust claim." Whatever such expense may have been, the cost of filing a timely application for leave to amend would have been minimal.

We are persuaded that plaintiff's delay was without justification, and that the grant of leave to amend would be highly prejudicial to defendant. Defendant is entitled to a trial of its counterclaim. The action is a simple breach of contract suit with a counterclaim; the issues are relatively uncomplicated, and a trial should be comparatively short. To add a claim under the antitrust laws now, necessarily involving lengthy, extensive discovery proceedings, would unduly complicate the issues, result in unnecessary confusion and unjustifiably delay defendant in the trial of its counterclaim.

38 F.R.D. 69, 70-71 (E.D. Pa. 1965).

Suehle presents the prototypical example of a request for leave to amend that should be denied. The plaintiff's amendment would cause prejudice to the defendant because it injects an entirely new claim into the case that the defendant was not prepared to defend. Moreover, the plaintiff's request was close to the time scheduled for trial and was made months after the plaintiff first realized the need to assert an antitrust claim. In cases such as this, prejudice exists and a trial court acts well within its discretion to deny leave to amend.

Procedure for Obtaining Leave to Amend

Except for amendments as a matter of course, a party must obtain permission to amend either from the court or the opposing parties. A party obtains permission from the court by filing a motion for leave to amend. However, a party should ask opposing parties for permission to amend before filing a motion with the court. This may seem counterintuitive given that the amendment is designed to help the party seeking it and harm opposing parties. However, an opposing party may agree to the amendment because he knows that the court will grant leave to amend. No lawyer wants the court to admonish him with a question like "Why are you wasting time opposing this motion for leave when you know I'll grant it under these circumstances?" Conversely, if the party moves for leave to amend without first asking permission from opposing parties he may find the court saying "Why are you wasting my time with this motion when you don't even know if the opposing party opposes it?" If instead the party desiring to amend asks his opponents if they will permit an amendment, even if permission is not granted by his opponents, at least he can say to the court he had no choice but to file a motion for leave to amend. In fact, some courts have local rules that require a party to confer with opposing parties before filing certain motions to ensure that the motion is opposed. *See, e.g.,* Local Civil Rule for the Northern District of Texas 7.1(b) ("Each motion for which a conference is required must include a certificate of conference indicating that the motion is unopposed or opposed"). An opposing party might also agree to allow an amendment because he wants something in return, such as an agreement to extend a discovery deadline or delay a deposition.

3. Amendments During and After Trial

The evidence offered at trial should conform to the pleadings. When it doesn't, it is said that the evidence is "at variance" with the pleadings. As we discussed in Chapters 14 and 15, one of the functions of pleadings is to provide other parties notice of the claims and defenses, and another is to guide the trial court in admitting evidence and in deciding what questions to ask the jury in the court's charge. These important functions of the pleadings are undermined if a party has an unfettered ability to prove a claim or defense he never pled. On the other hand, sometimes an amendment to the pleadings during or after trial is appropriate. Recall the plaintiff in *Spangler v. Pugh*. The fact that the plaintiff proved a half cent more in damages at trial than he pled was fatal to his judgment. Rule 15(b), shown in Exhibit 16.2, governs amendments during and after trial, and attempts to strike a balance between these two extremes.

Issues Tried by Consent

Suppose the plaintiff in *Suehle*, who you'll recall sought but was denied leave to amend his complaint alleging breach of contract to add an antitrust claim, offered evidence at trial proving an antitrust claim, even though he had no pleading to support such a claim. Such evidence would be at variance with the pleadings. How the court addresses a variance under Rule 15(b) depends upon whether or not the issue is tried by consent. An issue may be tried by the express or implied consent of the parties even though there is no pleading to support the issue.

The defendant in our modified version of *Suehle*, for example, might expressly consent to the trial of the antitrust claim by stipulation, or his consent might be reflected in a pretrial order. A defendant might impliedly consent to the trial by failing to object to evidence offered to support the antitrust claim, or by offering his own evidence contesting the antitrust claim, or by arguing to the jury that no such violations occurred. When an issue is tried by consent, Rule 15(b) provides

EXHIBIT 16.2   **Amendments During and After Trial**

(b) Amendments During and After Trial.

(1) *Based on an Objection at Trial.* If, at trial, a party objects that evidence is not within the issues raised in the pleadings, the court may permit the pleadings to be amended. The court should freely permit an amendment when doing so will aid in presenting the merits and the objecting party fails to satisfy the court that the evidence would prejudice that party's action or defense on the merits. The court may grant a continuance to enable the objecting party to meet the evidence.

(2) *For Issues Tried by Consent.* When an issue not raised by the pleadings is tried by the parties' express or implied consent, it must be treated in all respects as if raised in the pleadings. A party may move—at any time, even after judgment—to amend the pleadings to conform them to the evidence and to raise an unpleaded issue. But failure to amend does not affect the result of the trial of that issue.

that the issue "be treated in all respects as if raised in the pleadings." A party may then move at any time, even after judgment, to amend the pleadings to conform to the evidence offered and the issues tried.

Suppose, for example, that the defendant in *Suehle* failed to object during trial to the plaintiff's evidence proving an antitrust claim, and the plaintiff asks the court to submit questions to the jury regarding an antitrust violation and also seeks leave to amend the pleadings. Alternatively, he could seek leave to amend after trial or even after judgment. In either case, the court would allow the plaintiff to amend his pleading to include the antitrust claim. Or suppose that the defendant impliedly consented to trial of the antitrust claim, but the judgment is for the defendant. The defendant may move to amend the pleadings after trial to allege an antitrust claim in order to make clear that the judgment disposes of the antitrust claim and bars a future antitrust action under *res judicata* principles, discussed in Chapter 24. The court would also grant the defendant such leave to amend.

Trial Amendments

If the issue is not tried by consent because there is an objection to the evidence at variance with the pleadings, the court may allow a trial amendment to the pleadings. Rule 15(b)(1) provides that the court should "freely permit an amendment when doing so will aid in presenting the merits and the objecting party fails to satisfy the court that the evidence would prejudice that party's action or defense on the merits." Under this standard, to prevent a trial amendment from being freely given, the objecting party must show that allowing the amendment will prejudice its action or its defense. This standard is similar to the prejudice standard discussed for pretrial amendments, except that there is even less time to prepare to meet the new allegation because the case has now proceeded to trial. Most frequently, the objecting party will meet this standard when a wholly new legal theory is injected into the case and the defendant is surprised by it and unprepared to meet the new theory. Rule 15(b)(1) permits a court to grant a continuance "to enable the objecting party to meet the evidence." If the objecting party fails to request a continuance or refuses the court's offer of a continuance, he may not complain on appeal about his inability to meet the new theory.

4. Relation Back of Amendments

Rule 15(a) addresses when an amendment is permitted. Rule 15(c) addresses the effect of this amendment. In particular, Rule 15(c), shown in Exhibit 16.3, addresses the relation back of amended pleadings. Here's the issue Rule 15(c) answers: When does an amended pleading relate back to the date the pleading to be amended was filed? Put even more simply, when do we get to pretend that the amended pleading was filed on the day the original pleading was filed? Relation back is important for determining whether new claims or claims against new defendants are barred by the applicable statute of limitation.

EXHIBIT 16.3   **Rule 15(c)**

(c) Relation Back of Amendments.

(1) When an Amendment Relates Back. An amendment to a pleading relates back to the date of the original pleading when:

(A) the law that provides the applicable statute of limitations allows relation back;

(B) the amendment asserts a claim or defense that arose out of the conduct, transaction, or occurrence set out—or attempted to be set out—in the original pleading; or

(C) the amendment changes the party or the naming of the party against whom a claim is asserted, if Rule 15(c)(1)(B) is satisfied and if, within the period provided by Rule 4(m) for serving the summons and complaint, the party to be brought in by amendment:

[handwritten margin note: 96 days after com filed]

(i) received such notice of the action that it will not be prejudiced in defending on the merits; and

(ii) knew or should have known that the action would have been brought against it, but for a mistake concerning the proper party's identity.

Relationship Between Rule 15(a) and 15(c)

Leave to amend under subsection (a) and relation back under subsection (c) are related, but conceptually distinct. Even though a claim may "relate back" under subsection (c), a court will first assess a motion to amend under subsection (a) based upon the factors described above. Recall that leave to amend will be denied if the amendment would be "futile." With amendments that would add claims otherwise barred by limitations, the "futility" question is answered by the "relation back" question. It is futile to permit an amendment to add a claim that is barred by the statute of limitations. On the other hand, if the standard for relation back is satisfied, then limitations would not be a valid defense. Thus, the amendment would not be futile and the court should ordinarily grant leave to amend. Even if the amendment would not be futile because it would relate back, the court may deny leave to amend for another reason. For example, perhaps the movant has unduly delayed in seeking leave to amend and/or the opposing party would suffer preparation prejudice.

An Amendment Asserting a New Claim

Suppose Chiyu brings suit against the manufacturer of a toaster oven that she claims caused her injury when, due to a defect in the heating element, the toaster oven caught fire in her kitchen on June 15, 2015 and burned her arms and face. The applicable statute of limitations requires Chiyu to bring all her claims arising out of the toaster oven fire within two years of the date of injury. So June 15, 2017 is the last day to file her claims. Chiyu files her original complaint on May 1, 2017 and alleges that the defect in the toaster oven was the result of the defendant's negligence. Should the court grant her leave to amend her complaint to add the additional tort theory of strict product liability on July 10, 2017? The strict liability theory will allow Chiyu to recover if a defect in the product caused her injuries, even if the defect was not the result of any negligence on the part of the defendant. Because she won't have to prove fault on the part of the defendant manufacturer, the strict liability claim increases Chiyu's likelihood of success. A timeline may help to understand the issue:

The original complaint alleging negligence was filed a month and a half before the expiration of the limitations period. The strict liability claim alleged in the amended complaint was not brought within the two-year statute of limitations. But it will be timely if the relation back doctrine allows us to pretend it was filed at the time of the original complaint.

Rule 15(c)(1)(B) provides that an amended pleading that sets out a claim or defense that arises out of the same transaction or occurrence as that set forth in the original pleading relates back to the date of the original pleading. In our example, Chiyu's strict liability claim is based on the toaster oven fire in her kitchen that occurred on June 15, 2014, which is the same occurrence she alleged in her original complaint. So, Chiyu's amended complaint relates back to the date of the original complaint and her strict liability claim will not be barred by the statute of limitations.

The Same Transaction or Occurrence Standard

An amendment does not relate back unless the claim or defense it sets out arises out of the same conduct, transaction, or occurrence as that set out in the original pleading. The precise scope of the same transaction or occurrence standard is elusive, but also important because it appears in a number of different Federal Rules, particularly those dealing with party and claim joinder (addressed in Chapter 18). The Supreme Court addressed this standard for relation back in *Tiller v. Atlantic Coast Line R. Co.*, 323 U.S. 574 (1945). In *Tiller*, the plaintiff brought suit against the defendant railroad alleging that its negligence had caused the death of her husband. In her original complaint, she alleged the railroad failed to provide a proper lookout and warning and failed to keep the head car properly lighted. In her amended complaint, she alleged for the first time that the railroad's negligence consisted of the failure to keep the locomotive properly lighted. The Supreme Court held that the original and amended complaints set out the same conduct, transaction, or occurrence, explaining:

> The cause of action now, as it was in the beginning, is the same — it is a suit to recover damages for the alleged wrongful death of the deceased. "The effect of the amendment here was to facilitate a fair trial of the existing issues between plaintiff and defendant." . . . There is no reason to apply a statute of limitations when, as here, the respondent has had notice from the beginning that petitioner was trying to enforce a claim against it because of the events leading up to the death of the deceased in the respondent's yard.

The claim asserted in the amended complaint in *Tiller* — negligence based on the failure to properly light the locomotive — arose out of the same occurrence as that set forth in the original complaint — the death of plaintiff's husband in the railroad yard. Different conduct may be alleged in the amended complaint, but the transaction or occurrence from which the claim arose is the same. Rule 15(c) requires only that the claim in the amended complaint arise from the same conduct, transaction, *or* occurrence. The Court based its decision in large part on the fact that the defendant had notice from the original complaint of the nature of the claim. This is important because it means the defendant is unlikely to suffer much if any prejudice in maintaining a defense against the new allegation.

ASARCO, LLC v. Goodwin provides a contrasting example. 756 F.3d 191 (2d Cir. 2014). In *Goodwin*, the plaintiff sought a judgment requiring the defendant to contribute to the cost of cleaning up contaminated property. The plaintiff's amended complaint dealt with contamination of a facility in Snohomish County, Washington, whereas the original complaint had addressed only contamination of a different property in Everett, Washington. The court held that the amended complaint did not relate back. Unlike the original complaint in *Tiller*, the original complaint in *Goodwin* provided no notice to the defendant that the action would involve conduct and events at the Snohomish County facility. The defendant had no reason to gather evidence or interview witnesses related to its activities there and, therefore, was likely to suffer prejudice in maintaining a defense against the new allegation.

An Amendment Changing the Defendants

Rule 15(c)(1)(C) governs the relation back of amended complaints that change defendants or the naming of defendants. In addition, this provision in Rule 15(c) governs amended third-party complaints and other amended pleadings asserting a claim for relief that change the defending party or how he is named. As a threshold matter, it is important to understand what a "change" in defendants means. Rule 15(c)(1)(C) governs the relation back of an amendment that "changes the party or the naming of the party against whom a claim is asserted." A change in the party typically involves joining a new defendant to the action. The changing of the naming of the party occurs when the plaintiff has served the correct defendant with process but has called the defendant by the wrong name.

An amended complaint that names the newly joined defendant or renames a previously served defendant relates back if all of the following are true: (1) the amendment asserts a claim that arises out of the same transaction or occurrence as set forth in the original complaint, and within the Rule 4(m) period for service of process (within 90 days of the filing the complaint) the defendant both (2) received notice of the action so that it will not be prejudiced in defending the action and (3) knew or should have known that but for a mistake concerning his identify, the action would have been brought against him in the first place. The first requirement is the same as that for amendments that assert new claims. But the second and third requirements raise the bar for relation back of amendments that change defendants or how they are named.

Misnomer

Despite these requirements, some cases are fairly simple and straightforward. A **misnomer** occurs when the plaintiff has served process on the defendant but has called him by the wrong name in the complaint. Amendments to correct misnomers ordinarily relate back to the date of the original complaint. Suppose the plaintiff properly serves the registered agent for Precision Casings, LLC 10 days after filing the complaint, but his complaint names the defendant Precision Casings, Inc. After the statute of limitations passes, the plaintiff amends his complaint only to change the naming of the defendant from Precision Casings, Inc. to Precision Casings, LLC. The amended complaint relates back to the date of the original complaint in this example. The amended complaint asserts the same claim as what was set forth in the original complaint because the only change was to Precision Casings' name. Precision Casings had notice of the action within 90 days of the filing of the complaint because it was served with the complaint 10 days after it was filed, and Precision Casings almost certainly knew that but for a mistake in calling it a corporation rather than a limited liability company, it would have been named properly in the first place.

Misidentification

More difficult cases are those of **misidentification**. Misidentification occurs when the defendant named in the amended complaint was not served with process. Suppose in our previous example the plaintiff's mistake was naming and serving Precision *Carvings*, LLC rather than Precision Casings, LLC. Four months after filing the complaint and after the limitations period has passed, the plaintiff discovers his mistake and files an amended complaint naming Precision Casings as a defendant. This complaint will almost certainly not relate back because the newly named defendant is unlikely to have received notice of the action within 90 days of the filing of the complaint. Sometimes the amended complaint will relate back despite a misidentification. Suppose the plaintiff names related businesses entities in the original and amended complaints. For example, he names a subsidiary in his original complaint and the parent of this subsidiary in his amended complaint. Because of the relationship between the two defendants, the parent company may have had notice of the action within 90 days of filing the complaint such that the amended pleading will relate back.

Consider another example. The plaintiff's complaint names and serves Hobson General Contractors, LLC and Lobson Subcontractors, LLC, alleging that both defendants damaged plaintiff's home while attempting to repair its foundation. After the statute of limitations expires and 100 days after the complaint was filed, the plaintiff discovers that Lobson Subcontractors played no role whatsoever in the work on his home. Instead, it was Jobson Contractors, PC. The plaintiff amends his complaint to name Jobson Contractors and has process served on Jobson Contractors. On these facts alone, it would seem that relation back is not appropriate because Jobson Contractors did not receive formal notice of the action until 100 days after the complaint was filed. But bear in mind that Rule 15 does not require *formal* notice of the action within 90 days of the filing of the complaint, just notice of the action of some sort. Suppose the other defendant, General Contractors, LLC, had forwarded the complaint to Jobson Contractors shortly after the complaint was filed and that Jobson Contractors was aware that the conduct described and initially attributed to Lobson Contractors in the complaint was actually its conduct. In this scenario, the amended complaint would relate back to the date of the original complaint.

More on the Mistake Requirement

Rule 15(c)(1)(C) requires a mistake in order for an amended complaint changing the parties or the naming of the parties to relate back. As we've seen, a mistake may occur when a plaintiff misnames a defendant or names the wrong defendant. But what if the original complaint alleges a lack of knowledge about the identity of the proper defendants? *Worthington v. Wilson* addresses this question.

Case Preview

Worthington v. Wilson

As you read *Worthington v. Wilson*, consider the following questions:

1. The court notes that Rule 15(c) was amended in 1991. What did this amendment change about the relation back doctrine now set out in Rule 15(c)(1)(C), and how did this amendment affect the court's analysis?
2. How does the court define "mistake" in Rule 15(c)(1)(C)?
3. What, if anything, could Worthington have done differently to avoid losing his claim because of the statute of limitations?

Worthington v. Wilson
8 F.3d 1253 (7th Cir. 1993)

MANION, Circuit Judge.

In his 42 U.S.C. §1983 complaint, Richard Worthington claimed that while being arrested the arresting officers purposely injured him. When he filed suit on the day the statute of limitations expired, he named "three unknown named police officers" as defendants. Worthington later sought to amend the complaint to substitute police officers Dave Wilson and Jeff Wall for the unknown officers. The district court concluded that the relation back doctrine of Fed. R. Civ. P. 15(c) did not apply, and dismissed the amended complaint. *Worthington v. Wilson*, 790 F. Supp. 829 (C.D. Ill. 1992). We affirm.

I.

On February 25, 1989, Richard Worthington was arrested by a police officer in the Peoria Heights Police Department. At the time of his arrest, Worthington had an injured left hand, and he advised the arresting officer of his injury. According to Worthington's complaint, the arresting officer responded by grabbing Worthington's injured hand and twisting it, prompting Worthington to push the officer away and tell him to "take it easy." A second police officer arrived at the scene, and Worthington was wrestled to the ground and handcuffed. The police officers then hoisted Worthington from the ground by the handcuffs, which caused him to suffer broken bones in his left hand.

Exactly two years later, on February 25, 1991, Worthington filed a five-count complaint in the Circuit Court of Peoria County, Illinois, against the Village of Peoria Heights and "three unknown named police officers," stating the above facts and alleging that he was deprived of his constitutional rights in violation of 42 U.S.C. §1983. Counts one through three of the complaint named the police officers in their personal and official capacities, and alleged a variety of damages. Counts four and five named the Village of Peoria Heights, and alleged that it was liable for the police officers' conduct based on the doctrine of respondeat superior.

The Village removed the action to federal court and sought dismissal under Fed. R. Civ. P. 12(b)(6) for the reason that respondeat superior was not a valid basis for imposing liability against it under §1983. At a hearing on the motion to dismiss, Worthington voluntarily dismissed his claims against the Village and obtained leave to file an amended complaint. . . .

On June 17, 1991, Worthington filed an amended complaint in which he substituted as the defendants Dave Wilson and Jeff Wall, two of the twelve or so members of the Peoria Heights Police Department, for the "unknown named police officers" who arrested him on February 25, 1989. Wilson and Wall moved to dismiss the amended complaint primarily on grounds that Illinois' two-year statute of limitations expired . . . and that the amendment did not relate back to the filing of the original complaint under Rule 15(c). . . .

* * *

On April 27, 1992, the district judge granted Wilson's and Wall's motion to dismiss the amended complaint under revised Rule 15(c). . . .

II.

Rule 15(c) was amended to provide broader "relation back" of pleadings when a plaintiff seeks to amend his complaint to change defendants. . . .

* * *

Prior to this amendment, the standard for relation back under Rule 15(c) was set out in *Schiavone v. Fortune*, 477 U.S. 21, 106 S. Ct. 2379, 91 L. Ed. 2d 18 (1986):

The four prerequisites to a 'relation back' amendment under Rule 15(c) are: (1) the basic claim must have arisen out of the conduct set forth in the original pleading;

(2) the party to be brought in must have received such notice that it will not be prejudiced in maintaining its defense; (3) that party must or should have known that, but for a mistake concerning identity, the action would have been brought against it; and (4) the second and third requirements must have been fulfilled within the proscribed limitations period.

Id. at 29, 106 S. Ct. at 2384.

The Advisory Committee Notes to amended Rule 15(c) indicate that the amendment repudiates the holding in *Schiavone* that notice of a lawsuit's pendency must be given within the applicable statute of limitations period. The Advisory Committee stated:

> An intended defendant who is notified of an action within the period allowed by [Rule 4(j)] [Eds. — This time period is now set out in Rule 4(m)] for service of a summons and complaint may not under the revised rule defeat the action on account of a defect in the pleading with respect to the defendant's name, provided that the requirements of clauses (A) and (B) have been met. If the notice requirement is met within the . . . period, a complaint may be amended at any time to correct a formal defect such as a misnomer or misidentification.

Fed. R. Civ. P. 15(c), Advisory Committee Notes (1991 Amendment).

In the order amending Rule 15(c), the Supreme Court expressed its intention that "insofar as just and practicable," the amendment governs cases pending in the district courts on December 1, 1991. Order Adopting Amendments to Federal Rules of Civil Procedure, 111 S. Ct. 813 (Apr. 30, 1991).

In this case, Wilson and Wall did not know of Worthington's action before the limitations period expired, as was required by *Schiavone,* but they were aware of its pendency within the extra 120 days [Eds. — Now 90 days] provided by new Rule 15(c). *Worthington,* 790 F. Supp. at 833. Since the amendment was decisive to the issue of "notice," the district judge retroactively applied new Rule 15(c), finding it "just and practicable" to do so. *Id.* at 833–34. We have no need to consider the retroactivity of amended Rule 15(c) as it might apply in this case because Worthington's amended complaint did not relate back under either the old or new version of Rule 15(c).

Both versions of Rule 15(c) require that the new defendants "knew or should have known that, but for a mistake concerning the identity of the proper party, the action would have been brought against the party." In *Wood v. Worachek,* 618 F.2d 1225 (7th Cir. 1980), we construed the "mistake" requirement of Rule 15(c):

> A plaintiff may usually amend his complaint under Rule 15(c) to change the theory or statute under which recovery is sought; or to correct a misnomer of plaintiff where the proper party plaintiff is in court; or to change the capacity in which the plaintiff sues; or to substitute or add as plaintiff the real party interest; or to add additional plaintiffs where the action, as originally brought, was a class action. Thus, amendment with relation back is generally permitted in order to correct a misnomer of a defendant where the proper defendant is already before the court and the effect is merely to correct the name under which he is sued. But a new defendant cannot normally be substituted or added by amendment after the statute of limitations has run.

* * *

Correcting
the name, not the Party

> [Rule 15(c)(1)(C)] permits an amendment to relate back only where there has been an error made concerning the identity of the proper party and where that party is chargeable with knowledge of the mistake, but it does not permit relation back where, as here, there is a lack of knowledge of the proper party. Thus, in the absence of a mistake in the identification of the proper party, it is irrelevant for the purposes of [15(c)(1)(C)] whether or not the purported substitute party knew or should have known that the action would have been brought against him.

Id. at 1229 & 1230 (citation omitted). . . . The record shows that there was no mistake concerning the identity of the police officers. At oral argument, counsel for Worthington indicated that he did not decide to file suit until one or two days before the statute of limitations had expired. At that point, neither Worthington nor his counsel knew the names of the two police officers who allegedly committed the offense. Thus, the complaint was filed against "unknown police officers." Because Worthington's failure to name Wilson and Wall was due to a lack of knowledge as to their identity, and not a mistake in their names, Worthington was prevented from availing himself of the relation back doctrine of Rule 15(c).

Worthington argues that the amended complaint should relate back based on the district judge's proposed reading of Rule 15(c) as not having a separate "mistake" requirement. The district judge construed the word "mistake" to mean "change the party or the naming of the party." *Worthington,* 790 F. Supp. at 835. This construction, however, ignores the continuing vitality of *Wood*'s holding which interprets the "mistake" requirement under the old version of Rule 15(c). That holding remains unaffected by the 1991 amendment to Rule 15(c).

* * *

We conclude that the amendment adding Wilson and Wall failed to satisfy the "mistake" requirement of Rule 15(c). As a result, relation back was precluded, and Worthington's complaint was time-barred under Illinois law. Furthermore, Rule 11 did not authorize sanctions against Worthington's counsel for his state court pleadings in a removed case.

AFFIRMED.

Post-Case Follow-Up

Most courts of appeals have held that lack of knowledge is not a mistake under Rule 15(c). Fair enough. Saying you do not know is not the same as saying something that is wrong. But the holding in *Worthington* can put plaintiffs in a bind, particularly when the attorney first learns of the case on the eve of the expiration of the statute of limitations. What could Worthington's attorney have done differently? Could he have obtained the police report of the incident, which likely would have included the names of the arresting officers? Would the city's attorney have provided him the names if he called and asked? Alternatively, Worthington could have avoided a statute of limitations problem and a relation back issue altogether by naming all 12 officers in the police department. But this approach trades one problem for another. He would almost certainly be violating Rule

11 because he has no evidentiary support for believing all 12 officers were responsible for his injury. Following *Worthington*, some plaintiffs' attorneys began naming John and Jane Doe defendants in their complaint, rather than "unknown" defendants as Worthington did, so that if they needed to name other defendants they could argue mistake. It is of course a fiction to argue "I mistakenly thought the defendant was John Doe, but it turns out it was Officer Smith." A few courts allow the fiction, *see, e.g., Trautman v. Lagalski*, 28 F. Supp. 2d 327 (W.D. Pa. 1998) (amendment substituting the name of a correctional officer for "John Doe" related back), but the majority do not. *Garrett v. Fleming*, 362 F.3d 692, 696-97 (10th Cir. 2004) (noting that it was joining a majority of circuits to have decided the issue in holding that "[a] plaintiff's designation of an unknown defendant as 'John Doe' in the original complaint is not a formal defect of the type Rule 15(c)(3) was meant to address").

A fairly recent Supreme Court case seems to take a broader view of "mistake." In *Krupski v. Costa Crociere, S.p.A*, the Court held that "relation back under Rule 15(c)(1)(C) depends on what the party to be added knew or should have known, not on the amending party's knowledge or its timeliness in seeking to amend the pleading." 560 U.S. 538, 541 (2010). Moreover, the Court cited a dictionary's definition of mistake, which included errors based on inadequate information (e.g., a lack of knowledge like that present in *Worthington v. Wilson*). *Krupski v. Costa Crociere, S.p.A*, 560 U.S. 538, 548-49 (2010) (citing the definition of "mistake" from Webster's Third New International Dictionary 1446 (2002) to include "a wrong action or statement proceeding from faulty judgment, *inadequate knowledge*, or inattention"(emphasis added)). *Krupski* does not directly resolve the question of whether a lack of knowledge constitutes a mistake under Rule 15(c). However, plaintiffs faced with the challenge in *Worthington v. Wilson* have a good argument after *Krupski* that a "mistake" includes a lack of knowledge, and that relation back should be allowed when defendants, like Officers Wilson and Wall, knew or should have known that but for that lack of knowledge they would have been named defendants in the first place. For the time being, the prudent course for plaintiffs is to assume that a lack of knowledge is not a mistake and gather all the information they can to avoid "unnamed" or Jane/John Doe defendants. But plaintiffs should be prepared to make and defendants should be prepared to meet the argument that post-*Krupski*, a lack of knowledge is a mistake under Rule 15.

Rule 15(c) and Worthington v. Wilson: Real Life Applications

Gabriela's federal court complaint names United Autos, Inc., the manufacturer of her vehicle, as the defendant and alleges that United Autos' negligence in the manufacture and design of her vehicle caused a defect in the airbag system which in turn caused Gabriela to suffer severe physical injuries. Gabriela filed her complaint 15 days before the expiration of the applicable statute of limitations and served United Autos' registered agent one week later.

1. Five months after filing her complaint, Gabriela is granted leave to amend her complaint to allege that United Autos was grossly negligent in the design and

manufacture of her vehicle and airbag system and to demand punitive damages. United Autos moves to dismiss the claim on the ground that it is barred by the applicable statute of limitations, but Gabriela argues that her amended complaint relates back to the date of her original complaint. How should the court rule on the motion to dismiss?

2. Gabriela learns that the airbag system in her car was designed and manufactured by one of United Autos' suppliers, Automotive Safety Products, LLC. She is granted leave to amend her complaint to name Automotive Safety Products as a defendant, and has it served with the amended complaint 75 days after having filed her original complaint. Automotive Safety Products moves to dismiss on statute of limitation grounds. Gabriela argues the motion should be denied because her amendment relates back. How should the court rule?

3. A year after Gabriela filed her complaint, United Autos moves for summary judgment on statute of limitations grounds. United Autos acknowledges that it was served with complaint, but demonstrates that it is named United Autos, LLC, not United Autos, Inc., as stated in Gabriela's complaint. Gabriela is granted leave to amend her complaint and in her amended complaint she replaces all references to United Autos, Inc. with United Autos, LLC. In response to the motion for summary judgment, she argues that her amended complaint relates back. How should the court rule on the motion?

Relation Back Under State Law

Even if the federal relation back doctrine set out in Rule 15(c) does not permit relation back, a state law relation back doctrine might. Rule 15(c)(1)(A) provides that relation back is permitted if "the law that provides the applicable statute of limitations allows relation back." State law provides the applicable statute of limitations for all state law claims litigated in federal court, and even for some federal law claims (e.g., state statutes of limitations govern section 1983 claims like the one in *Worthington*). The state doctrine might provide a more relaxed standard for relation back than Rule 15(c)'s provisions and, if so, relation back is permitted. For example, where the applicable state law permits relation back of amendments substituting defendants for "John Doe" defendants, relation back is permitted even though not permitted under that particular federal jurisdiction's interpretation of Rule 15(c)(1)(C). *Lindley v. Gen. Elec. Co.*, 780 F.2d 797 (9th Cir. 1986).

B. SUPPLEMENTAL PLEADINGS

Rule 15(d), set out in Exhibit 16.4, permits a party to file a supplemental pleading that sets out "any transaction, occurrence, or event that happened after the date of the pleading to be supplemented." Like an amended pleading, a supplemental pleading may be used to add new claims, defenses, or parties along with supporting factual contentions, but it differs from an amended pleading in important ways.

EXHIBIT 16.4 **Rule 15(d)**

> (d) Supplemental Pleadings. On motion and reasonable notice, the court may, on just terms, permit a party to serve a supplemental pleading setting out any transaction, occurrence, or event that happened after the date of the pleading to be supplemented. The court may permit supplementation even though the original pleading is defective in stating a claim or defense. The court may order that the opposing party plead to the supplemental pleading within a specified time.

1. A Supplemental Pleading Alleges New Events

A supplemental pleading should only be used to allege matters that happened since the pleading to be supplemented. In other words, it alleges new events, not newly discovered or newly conceived matters. For example, suppose the complaint alleges the plaintiff suffered severe personal injuries and, after the filing of the complaint, the plaintiff dies as a result of the injuries; a supplemental complaint could allege the death and assert a wrongful death claim, and add any additional parties needed to assert or defend the new claim. A supplemental pleading is appropriate because the death occurred after the complaint to be supplemented. If, on the other hand, the death happened before the complaint was filed and the plaintiff simply forgot to allege a wrongful death claim, she should correct her error in an amended complaint.

2. A Supplemental Pleading Adds to the Pleading Supplemented

A supplemental pleading adds to but does not supersede the pleading to be supplemented. To see all that the pleader has alleged, one would have to look at both the supplemental pleading and the pleading it supplements. In the wrongful death example above, the defendant would have to read both the complaint and the supplemental complaint to understand that the plaintiff has alleged both wrongful death and a survival action for personal injuries. In contrast, an amended complaint supersedes the prior pleading and must be complete in itself. The amended complaint standing alone contains all of the plaintiff's live allegations.

3. Permission to File Is Always Required

An amendment as a matter of course may be filed without the permission of the court or opposing parties. Filing a supplemental pleading always requires leave of court. There is no supplemental pleading "as a matter of course" permitted under Rule 15.

Chapter Summary

- Rule 15 reflects a liberal approach to permitting amendments to pleadings. An amended pleading may be used to add or delete facts or to add or drop claims, defenses, and parties.
- A defendant may amend his answer once "as a matter of course" without the permission of either the court or opposing parties within 21 days of serving it, and the plaintiff may amend his complaint as a matter of course within 21 days of the defendant's first Rule 12 response.
- Other amendments require the permission of either the court or opposing parties, but leave should be freely given unless there are overriding concerns such as undue delay, futility of amendment, and, most importantly, prejudice to an opposing party in maintaining his action or defense.
- The evidence at trial should conform to the pleadings. If the evidence at trial varies from the pleadings and opposing party does not object, the issue will have been tried by consent and an amendment to the pleadings is appropriate at any time, even after judgment. Upon objection to the variance, the court will grant leave unless the objecting party can show prejudice.
- An amended pleading asserting a new claim or defense relates back to the date of the original pleading if it arises out of the same transaction or occurrence set forth in the original pleading.
- An amended pleading changing defendants or the naming of defendants relates back to the date of the original pleading if: (1) the claim against the defendant arises out of the same transaction or occurrence; (2) the defendant received notice of the action either within the statute of limitations or within the 90-day window for serving the complaint, whichever comes first; (3) the defendant will not be prejudiced in maintaining a defense; and (4) the defendant knew that but for a mistake he would have been named initially.
- A supplemental pleading is used to allege transactions, occurrences, or events that happened since the date of the pleading to be supplemented.

Applying the Concepts

1. Arthur filed an answer in response to Nancy's complaint on October 10. Nancy plans to file an amended complaint on October 25. Does she need to seek Arthur's or the court's permission to do so?

2. Nia's complaint names Sune as the defendant and alleges only the tort of assault. At trial, Nia offers evidence relevant only to battery. Sune has not prepared to defend a battery claim and can show that it involves different elements, different evidence, and that none of Nia's discovery responses or correspondence indicated she would pursue a battery claim at trial. How should Sune respond to Nia's offer of the battery evidence? What should Nia do in an effort to prove the battery claim? How should the court rule?

3. Alfred's complaint alleges breach of contract against Bo's Tavern, alleging that the Tavern failed to pay Alfred for liquor Alfred supplied it. Bo's Tavern is actually the trade name for Bodacious Industries, LLC, whose agent for service of process was served Alfred's complaint one month after it was filed. When Alfred learns that the proper party is Bodacious Industries, Inc., he amends his complaint with leave of court to substitute Bodacious Industries, Inc. for Bo's Tavern, but the amendment comes after the statute of limitations has expired, and Bodacious Industries, Inc. moves for summary judgment on this ground. How should the court rule on the motion?

Civil Procedure in Practice

You represent Alton. Alton was arrested by the police nearly two years ago and believes his arrest violated his federal civil rights. Alton claims that two police officers severely beat him with their batons, but he does not know the names of the officers. You obtain a copy of the police report related to Alton's arrest, which names the arresting officers as "Daryl Hansen" and "Jon Smith." You draft and file a complaint alleging a violation of section 1983 of the federal Civil Rights Act based on the beating Alton described, and naming as defendants "Officer Daryl Hansen, Officer John Smith, Officer John Doe, and Officer Jane Doe." You serve process on Officers Hansen and Smith within a month of filing the complaint.

You decide to amend the complaint to add claims for assault and battery against the officers based on their alleged beating of Alton. These claims are governed by a two-year state statute of limitations, which has expired since the filing of the complaint. The defendants filed only answers in response to the complaint six weeks ago. No discovery has yet taken place nor have any pretrial motions been made. The state relation back doctrine is identical to Rule 15(c).

1. Must you seek permission to file your amended complaint? If permission is required and the defendants oppose your motion for leave, how is the court likely to rule on the motion?

2. Assuming you are able to file the amended complaint alleging assault and battery, will it relate back to the date of the complaint? Why or why not?

3. During discovery, you send a request for admission to Officer John Smith that asks him to admit or deny he was one of the officers who arrested Alton on the date in question. Officer John Smith denies this allegation. You send a follow-up interrogatory asking John Smith to explain this given that he was named in the police report. Officer John Smith explains that the arresting officer was Jon Smith (no "h"), another officer in the same police department. Separately, you

learn that all officers in the department were notified of your lawsuit during a roll call six weeks after you filed the complaint. With leave of court, you amend your complaint to name Jon Smith (no "h") in place of John Smith as a defendant. Jon Smith appears and moves to dismiss the case on statute of limitation grounds. How should the court rule?

Discovery

The dramatic moment in a film or TV legal drama is often when a surprise witness takes the stand or a shocking document is produced for the first time at trial. The plucky hero is forced to recover from the trap the villain set by concealing the evidence until trial, or sometimes it is the hero who reveals the key, previously unknown or undisclosed evidence just in time to save the day for his client. Once upon a time, trial by ambush was not unheard of in American courts, but today such trials, particularly in civil actions, are largely limited to television and film. Instead, the parties learn about each other's claims and defenses and the evidence that will be used to support them before trial through a process called discovery.

Understanding discovery and the rules that govern it is particularly important for the aspiring civil litigator. If you choose this practice area, you will spend a great deal of time drafting and responding to discovery requests, taking and defending depositions (pretrial witness testimony), and arguing discovery-related motions early on and throughout your career.

For parties, discovery can be a time-consuming and costly process. They pay attorneys to conduct discovery, and often they or their employees spend a great deal of time responding to discovery rather than conducting their ordinary affairs. Many attorneys regard the discovery process as a burden that often involves conflict. Attorneys tend to make broad requests for information from their opponents,

Key Concepts

- The information that can be acquired through informal investigation without invoking the assistance of the court
- The scope of formal discovery and its limits, i.e., what can and cannot be discovered
- The information that must be disclosed in the required initial disclosures and pretrial disclosures without a request to produce it
- The discovery devices that may be used to obtain other information not disclosed in the required disclosures
- The parties' duties in discovery, including the duty to preserve evidence, cooperate in discovery, avoid unreasonable requests, and provide complete and accurate responses

but they tend to respond to requests narrowly or resist responding altogether. This push and pull can quickly devolve into frustrating litigation over the proper scope of disclosure. Such conflicts inspired few if any of us to go to law school or become a litigator. But discovery can also involve strategic thinking, cutting edge technology, and lots of opportunities for written and oral courtroom advocacy. This chapter attempts to provide you an overview of the rules that govern discovery and some practical advice on how you might use these rules effectively for the benefit of your future clients.

A. INFORMAL INVESTIGATION: LEARNING ABOUT THE CASE WITHOUT INVOKING THE FEDERAL RULES

Suppose Anthony is in an automobile accident with a delivery truck owned and operated by Big Box, Inc., a national retail chain. Anthony suffers injuries that prevent him from working his job with a construction company. Anthony plans to file a civil action against Big Box to recover his medical expenses and lost wages. Anthony's and Big Box's attorneys advise them (separately) that the federal discovery rules authorize a party to obtain information relevant to the case, and that a court can order production of this information even if an opposing party refuses to produce it. Anthony is concerned that the financial costs associated with this formal discovery process will reduce his recovery below what he needs. Big Box is not particularly concerned with the direct financial costs of discovery, but it is concerned that discovery will be time-consuming and distract its employees from its regular business.

Anthony's and Big Box's concerns are not unfounded. Formal discovery can often require parties to expend significant resources, both financial and human. Parties have to pay attorneys to take and defend depositions, prepare and respond to discovery requests, and attend hearings to resolve discovery disputes. Formal discovery can also distract a party from its regular affairs. A business may find itself assigning employees to address litigation matters, such as answering interrogatories or gathering documents and electronically stored information, rather than conducting the organization's business.

Fortunately for Anthony and Big Box, often a party can learn a great deal about a case through informal investigation without invoking the Federal Rules or court assistance. Informal investigation tends to be relatively simple and inexpensive, because it involves acquiring information that is readily accessible. Although informal investigation will rarely replace formal discovery altogether, it can narrow the issues on which formal discovery is needed. A party can determine who the parties should be, the nature and extent of the damages, the theory of liability, and any defense that may be asserted. Additionally, informal discovery can assist claimants in gathering sufficient facts to state a plausible claim in their pleadings before formal discovery even begins. Perhaps most importantly, informal investigation is necessary before filing a civil action in or filing a response to that civil action in order for the attorneys to comply with their ethical and professional obligations. An attorney must have an evidentiary basis for the allegations she makes and any denials she asserts. An informal investigation is necessary to satisfy this requirement.

1. Matters Within Your Client's Possession, Custody, or Control

Suppose you represent Anthony in his case against Big Box. Anthony has knowledge of both the accident and his injuries. Moreover, he is likely to have in his possession documents and other items that will be important evidence in his action against Big Box. You won't need to serve Anthony with a formal request under the discovery rules or acquire a court order to obtain this information from Anthony. You just ask him for it. Consider the kinds of things you could acquire from Anthony this way. You could interview Anthony to find out how the car wreck occurred, the nature of his injuries, and how they have affected him. You can even photograph his injuries. Anthony can probably give you pay stubs, W-2s, and even his tax returns to show what his earnings were before he lost his job. He can give you his medical bills from the hospital and other healthcare providers. Anthony can also give you access to his wrecked vehicle and you can inspect and photograph it. From this easily and inexpensively obtained information alone, you have acquired information about both the cause of the accident and the injuries it caused Anthony, and you are well on your way to having the evidence you need to prove Anthony's claim. If you're Big Box's lawyer, you can acquire similar information from Big Box without the need for a formal request or court order. You can interview the driver of the delivery truck and get his version of how the accident happened, inspect and photograph the delivery truck, and obtain any relevant records in Big Box's possession.

Interviews of Nonparty Witnesses

Suppose again that you represent Anthony and have interviewed him about what happened. The interview (and the other information you get from him) is likely to generate some leads you need to follow up on. In particular, you may learn the identities of potential witnesses who have knowledge of relevant facts. If these witnesses are not parties to the case (e.g., not Big Box employees), you can speak to them without a court order, formal discovery request, or notifying opposing parties. Such persons aren't obligated to speak to you during the informal investigation phase, but, if they are willing to, you can interview them. Of course, Big Box's attorneys can also contact and interview these nonparty witnesses as well.

Consider what an abundant source of information these nonparty witnesses can be. His treating physician can give you details about the nature and extent of his injuries (although the physician will want Anthony's permission to speak with you). Police officers who responded to the scene of the accident can give you an unbiased view of what may have caused the accident. Other drivers and pedestrians who witnessed the accident might also be able to give you an unbiased account of the accident and its cause. The construction foreman at Anthony's old job can talk to you about Anthony's lost wages and why he isn't physically able to perform his job duties anymore. These people are all potentially important witnesses in the case, and what they say will often be more credible to the fact-finder at trial because these witnesses don't have a stake in the outcome of the case. Unlike Anthony and Big Box, they don't stand to gain or lose anything based on the outcome of the case.

Importantly, attorneys have an ethical obligation to be candid with these non-party witnesses about their role in the case. Rule 4.1 of the ABA Model Rules of Professional Conduct prohibits an attorney from knowingly making a false statement of fact or law to an unrepresented person. Rule 4.3 prohibits the attorney from stating or implying to unrepresented persons that the attorney is disinterested, and if the attorney knows or should know that the person misunderstands the attorney's role in the case, he must take steps to correct that misunderstanding. In short, don't lie to nonparty witnesses or mislead them about who you represent.

Publicly Available Information

Information available to the public generally is an important source of information in an informal investigation. For example, you could photograph the scene of Anthony's car wreck so long as it occurred on a public road. The Internet is also an important source of information. You may find online official government regulations and standards regarding the appropriate load weight for the delivery truck involved in the accident, appropriate rest and recuperation times for truck drivers between hauls, and training and certification requirements for truck drivers. Such information can provide you a standard by which you, and ultimately the fact-finder, can judge the delivery truck driver's behavior on the day of the wreck. If the government has the information but has not published it, a freedom of information act request to the appropriate government agency can also uncover important information. In Anthony's case against Big Box, for example, the police likely responded to the scene of the accident and made a report that describes the event, names witnesses, and summarizes their statements. Both Anthony and Big Box would be able to acquire this report during their investigation of the case.

2. Limits on Informal Investigation

Informal investigation is principally limited to uncovering information from the attorney's client or a nonparty witness, or information that is publicly available. An attorney who seeks to use these informal methods to obtain information from other parties or their employees is treading on dangerous ground. Rule 4.2 of the ABA Model Rules of Professional Conduct prohibits attorneys from speaking to a person the attorney knows is represented by counsel in the matter without the permission of the other lawyer. An attorney should ordinarily use the formal discovery devices the Federal Rules make available to acquire information held by represented parties — including parties, potential parties, and their employees. For example, suppose you send Big Box a settlement demand letter on behalf of Anthony. This demand letter makes it clear to Big Box that Anthony is represented by an attorney in the matter. Big Box's attorneys would violate their ethical obligations by contacting Anthony to interview him about the car wreck without your permission.

B. REQUIRED DISCLOSURES: DISCLOSING MATTERS WITHOUT A REQUEST

Through informal investigation, both Anthony and Big Box have already acquired a lot of the information they will use to support their claims and defenses. As we transition now into our discussion of formal discovery, it's important to recognize that, although both sides have a lot of relevant information, they haven't had to share it with each other yet. If you're Anthony's attorney, you probably already know you are going to use Anthony's pay stubs and W-2s to help you prove his lost wages claim at trial. If you're Big Box's attorney, and your delivery driver's interview revealed that the accident may not have been his fault, you probably already know that you'll use his testimony at trial to support your defense. Given that the rules of discovery want to eliminate surprises at trial and avoid needless expense and delay, the federal discovery rules require the parties to exchange this kind of information without awaiting a formal request. This approach ensures that Big Box isn't surprised at trial by the evidence Anthony uses to support his claim, and that Anthony isn't surprised by the evidence Big Box uses to support its defense. It also saves time and resources because neither Anthony nor Big Box has to use a series of discovery requests to guess at what that information might be.

Federal Rule of Civil Procedure 26(a) requires parties to make certain disclosures to all other parties without awaiting a formal discovery request. These are the so-called self-executing disclosures. They must be made because a person is a party to the suit, not because anyone asked for the information. Rule 26(a) sets out three different required disclosures: (1) **initial disclosures,** (2) **required disclosures of expert witnesses,** and (3) **pretrial disclosures.** Initial disclosures are made at the beginning of the lawsuit. Pretrial and expert disclosures are made nearer the trial date. Each category of required disclosure is discussed below.

1. Initial Disclosures

Rule 26(a)(1)(A), shown in Exhibit 17.1, requires parties to disclose certain matters at the beginning of the litigation without awaiting a court order or a request from another party. These disclosures are called initial disclosures. The rule allows parties to receive the basic information they will need for further discovery or trial early in the litigation while eliminating the paper work (e.g., formal requests) previously needed to obtain the same information. The initial disclosures also allow parties to better and earlier assess the merits of their claims and defenses, which, in turn, could facilitate settlement and obviate the need for more complex, time-consuming,

EXHIBIT 17.1   Rule 26(a)(1)(A) Initial Disclosures

(1) Initial Disclosure.

(A) In General. Except as exempted by Rule 26(a)(1)(B) or as otherwise stipulated or ordered by the court, a party must, without awaiting a discovery request, provide to the other parties:

(i) the name and, if known, the address and telephone number of each individual likely to have discoverable information — along with the subjects of that information — that the disclosing party may use to support its claims or defenses, unless the use would be solely for impeachment;

(ii) a copy — or a description by category and location — of all documents, electronically stored information, and tangible things that the disclosing party has in its possession, custody, or control and may use to support its claims or defenses, unless the use would be solely for impeachment;

(iii) a computation of each category of damages claimed by the disclosing party — who must also make available for inspection and copying as under Rule 34 the documents or other evidentiary material, unless privileged or protected from disclosure, on which each computation is based, including materials bearing on the nature and extent of injuries suffered; and

(iv) for inspection and copying as under Rule 34, any insurance agreement under which an insurance business may be liable to satisfy all or part of a possible judgment in the action or to indemnify or reimburse for payments made to satisfy the judgment.

and expensive discovery procedures. Rule 26(a)'s disclosure requirements can be modified or eliminated altogether by agreement of all the parties. The court can also modify these disclosure requirements by order. In some federal venues, Rule 26(a) has been modified by **local rule**. A local rule is a rule of a particular court that supplements the Federal Rules of Civil Procedure. A particular court can use its local rules to create a standing order that modifies the Rule 26(a) disclosure requirements. The careful practitioner will always consult the local rules for modifications to Rule 26(a)'s disclosure requirements. Thus, Rule 26(a) should be read as providing a default set of disclosure requirements that apply in the absence of a court order, local rule, or an agreement between the parties modifying them.

What Must Be Disclosed in the Initial Disclosures

Rule 26(a) requires a party to disclose as part of the party's initial disclosure both: (1) the names of individuals the party may use to support the party's claims or defenses, along with the subjects on which the individuals have knowledge and, if known, the individuals' addresses and phone numbers; and (2) a copy (or a description and location) of all documents, electronically stored information, and tangible things the party has in its possession, custody, or control and may use to support the party's claims or defenses. A party need not provide witnesses or documents it intends to use solely for impeaching the credibility of witnesses. A few key points about the initial disclosures warrant emphasis.

A party need only provide information and materials it may use to support its claims or defenses.

A party need not initially disclose information or materials that refute its claims or defenses. Rule 26(a)(1) requires disclosure of "all documents, electronically stored information, and tangible things that the disclosing party has in its possession, custody, or control and may use *to support* its claims or defenses." Matters that refute a party's claims or defenses may have to be disclosed in response to a later request for such materials, but they are not part of the required initial disclosures. Suppose Anthony files suit against Big Box to recover personal injury and property damages. Anthony would have to disclose, for example, his W-2s (showing his earnings) if he plans to use them to support his lost wages claim. On the other hand, suppose Big Box has an internal memo showing that its driver has a very poor driving record. Big Box would not have to disclose this document as part of its initial disclosures because it would not use it to support its defense. If, however, Anthony had obtained a copy of this internal memo, he would have to disclose it because he would use it to support his claim.

A party's initial disclosure obligation extends only to documents, electronically stored information, and tangible things that are within its possession, custody, or control.

A party has no obligation to provide or identify documents, electronically stored information (ESI), and tangible things that are, for example, in the possession, custody, or control of someone else, even if the party is aware of their existence. Suppose Anthony's friend, Tara, came to the scene of the accident shortly after the collision. She observed and took photos of the damage to the vehicles and Anthony's injuries. Anthony is aware of the existence of the photos but he does not have them. Anthony would have to disclose Tara as a person he may use to support his claims, but he does not need to disclose the photos she took because they are not within his possession, custody, or control.

The initial disclosure obligation extends to electronically stored information.

The Federal Rules do not define electronically stored information, but the Advisory Committee (the drafters of the Rules) authored interpretive notes that have made clear that the term should be broadly defined to include "any type of information stored electronically." Fed. R. Civ. P. 34, advisory committee note, 2006 amendment, subdivision (a). Electronically stored information includes most anything stored electronically, including spreadsheets, word processing documents, emails, instant messages, text messages, and the whole host of ever-evolving social media. Thus, a party cannot refuse to disclose a document because it exists only in electronic rather than tangible form. Suppose Anthony took photos of his wrecked car using the camera app on his phone and plans to use them to support his claim. He must disclose the photos even though they exist only in electronic format.

The initial disclosure obligation does not extend to evidence a party intends to use solely for impeachment.

A party need not disclose the names of individuals, documents, electronically stored information, or tangible items it intends to use solely for impeachment. Impeaching a witness means to attack the credibility (i.e., the believability) of the witness. Suppose Big Box has obtained a record of Anthony's friend Tara's conviction for fraud and will use it to show her testimony should not be believed if she testifies at trial. Big Box would not have to disclose the record of conviction in its initial disclosures.

Computation of Damages; Insuring Agreements

In addition to identifying individuals and documents the party may use to support its claims or defenses, a party who asserts a claim for damages (i.e., most plaintiffs) must also provide a computation of each category of damages the party claims as part of its initial disclosures. Along with this computation, the party asserting a claim for damages must also make available for inspection and copying all documents or other evidence on which the computations are based. A party defending a claim (e.g., defendants) must provide any insuring agreements under which an insurance company might have to satisfy all or part of a judgment.

Deadline for the Initial Disclosure

The deadline for parties to make initial disclosures is tied to the timing of another event, the Rule 26(f) conference. Rule 26(f) requires the parties to "meet and confer" early on in the litigation in order to discuss a variety of issues, including the possibility of settlement and the development of a discovery plan. The initial disclosures are due no later than 14 days after the Rule 26(f) meet and confer. The court can modify this deadline by order and the parties can agree to modify it by stipulation (i.e., by agreement). Parties who are joined after the Rule 26(f) meet and confer have 30 days from the date they are served with summons, unless a court order or stipulation provides a different deadline.

When Initial Disclosures Are Not Required

There are a number of situations in which Rule 26 does not require the parties to make the required initial disclosures. Rule 26(a) provides authority to the court and the parties to eliminate the required disclosures. The court may issue an order or the parties may enter into a stipulation eliminating the requirement of initial disclosures. Also, Rule 26(a)(1)(B) lists a number of types of cases in which initial disclosures are not required, including actions brought by the United States to collect on a student loan guaranteed by the federal government, actions for review on an administrative record, petitions for habeas corpus to challenge a criminal conviction or sentence, and actions to enforce an arbitration award.

2. Required Disclosure of Expert Witnesses

Under Rule 26, a party must disclose to all other parties the identity of any person the party may use at trial to give expert testimony. A party need only disclose the identity of experts who may testify at trial. Parties may consult with experts to aid in the preparation of their case rather than to testify at trial. Rule 26 does not require disclosure of these consulting-only experts. Only experts who may testify at trial must be disclosed.

Deadline to Disclose Expert Witnesses

In the absence of a court order or stipulation setting a different deadline, the parties' deadline for disclosing expert witnesses is no later than 90 days before the trial date. Experts whose testimony will be used at trial solely to rebut or contradict the testimony of another party's expert must be disclosed no later than 30 days after the disclosure of the expert whose testimony is to be rebutted or contradicted. These deadlines for the disclosure of expert witnesses applies in the absence of a court order setting different deadlines. In most cases, the federal court will issue a scheduling order that will include, among other things, a deadline for the disclosure of expert witnesses. The parties should comply with the deadlines in the scheduling order even if they conflict with the default deadlines set out in Rule 26.

Content of Expert Witness Disclosure: The Expert Report

If the expert witness is one who is retained to provide expert testimony, or an employee of the disclosing party whose duties regularly involve giving expert testimony, the disclosure of the expert must be accompanied by a written report prepared and signed by the expert witness. This expert report must contain:

- A complete statement of all the opinions the witness will express and the basis and reasons for them;
- The facts or data considered by the witness in forming her opinions;
- The witness's qualifications, including a list of publications authored in the last ten years;
- A list of all other cases in which the witness has testified as an expert at trial or in a deposition in the previous four years; and
- A statement of the amount of compensation the expert will be paid for the study and testimony in the case.

Only those experts employed or retained by the party to provide expert testimony need to provide a written report. Experts not retained or employed by the party to give expert testimony need not provide a written report. For example, the physician who treated the plaintiff's injuries in a personal injury case generally does not need to provide an expert report, even though the physician may provide expert testimony at trial. If the witness is not required to provide a written report, the disclosing party need only disclose the subject matter on which the witness will testify and a summary of the facts and opinions on which the witness is expected to testify.

3. Pretrial Disclosures

Pretrial disclosures under 26(a)(3) are mandatory disclosures made on the eve of trial designed to inform the court and the parties of the exhibits and witnesses that will or may be presented at trial. In short, the parties must disclose their witness and exhibit lists. The pretrial disclosures avoid surprises to the parties and allow the court to rule on objections to the admissibility of evidence before the trial begins. Specifically, Rule 26(a)(3) requires the parties to file and serve on all other parties: (1) the name of each witness the party will call at trial, (2) the name of the witnesses the party may call if the need arises, (3) the witnesses the party may present by deposition, (4) a list of documents or other items the party expects to offer as exhibits, and (5) those documents or items it may offer as exhibits if the need arises. Unless the court orders otherwise, the pretrial disclosures must be made at least 30 days before trial.

C. WHAT CAN BE DISCOVERED WITH A FORMAL REQUEST?

As we've already seen, Anthony and Big Box have learned a great deal about their own claims and defenses through informal investigation, and each will have to disclose to the other the information and witnesses they'll use to support those claims or defenses at trial. Notice that neither of the topics we've addressed so far — informal investigation and required disclosures — involves one party requesting information from the other. During informal investigation, Anthony and Big Box acquired information for themselves, but did not share it with each other. The mandatory disclosure rules required them to disclose information and witnesses they would be using to *support* their claims or defenses, and to do so without a request. Now we turn to the information and materials parties like Anthony and Big Box may obtain from other parties through a formal discovery request, even if the responding party will not use it to support a claim or defense at trial. This means that discovery requests can be used to obtain information that is *damaging* to the responding party's case. For example, Anthony can request any information Big Box has about poor driving on the part of its delivery driver, and Big Box can seek information indicating whether Anthony might have been injured in a separate accident. As you might imagine, parties are reluctant to turn over information that is harmful to their case. Consequently, it is important to understand the scope of the information that may be discovered with a request. The parties may issue specific discovery requests seeking information from the other parties, or from witnesses, that will be helpful in pursuing or defending the suit, but will not have been turned over as a required matter. In this area, a party will only get (if at all) material that it specifically requests. Consequently, the drafting of discovery requests is something of an art.

1. Matters Relevant to a Party's Claim or Defense

A primary purpose of discovery is to collect evidence that might be offered at trial. For this reason, Rule 26(b), shown in Exhibit 17.2, limits discovery to matters that are *relevant* to any party's claim or defense. Information is relevant if it has *any*

EXHIBIT 17.2   **Rule 26(b)(1) The Scope of Discovery**

> Unless otherwise limited by court order, the scope of discovery is as follows: Parties may obtain discovery regarding any non-privileged matter that is relevant to any party's claim or defense and proportional to the needs of the case, considering the importance of the issues at stake in the action, the amount in controversy, the parties relative access to relevant information, the parties' resources, the importance of the discovery in resolving the issues, and whether the burden or expense of the proposed discovery outweighs its likely benefit.

tendency to make a claim or defense more or less likely *to any degree whatsoever*. The information sought, standing alone, need not conclusively prove or disprove the claim or defense. The Federal Rules of Evidence say two things that help us understand the scope of discovery: (1) irrelevant evidence is never admissible, and (2) relevant evidence is generally admissible, subject to a number of exceptions. Thus, it makes sense to use the concept of relevance as a starting point to outline the scope of discovery. If the information sought is not relevant, it is not discoverable. Why bother with the time and expense of discovering a matter that could never be used at trial? If, on the other hand, the information is relevant, it is generally discoverable, even if it would not be admissible at trial. Rule 26(b) explicitly states that "information within this scope of discovery need not be admissible in evidence to be discoverable." Admissibility is determined at trial, not during discovery. Suppose for example that Anthony has a copy of the police report about his accident in which the police officer quotes a witness to the accident as saying that Anthony "showed signs of intoxication at the scene." This statement is hearsay (double hearsay, actually), but it is relevant to Anthony's claim (and Big Box's defense); so, it is discoverable even though it might not be admissible at trial.

2. The Various Forms of Discoverable Information

The information and materials that fall within the scope of discovery may take many forms. Of course, hard copies of documents (i.e., paper) fall within the scope of discovery, but other types of materials are also discoverable. Relevant electronically stored information is discoverable. Tangible items relevant to a claim or defense are also discoverable. For example, the product the plaintiff alleges to be defective in a product liability case falls within the scope of discovery and would have to be made available to the other parties for inspection and possible testing. A party would have to disclose the location of relevant real property and, if under its custody or control, make it available to other parties for inspection. The identities of persons with relevant knowledge are discoverable, as previously discussed, but a party may also learn what these people know through the discovery process by, for example, having them give sworn pretrial testimony in a deposition.

3. Proportionality and Other Limits on the Discovery of Relevant Information

Suppose Anthony alleges that Big Box's negligence consisted of poorly training its delivery truck drivers. Anthony requests from Big Box all driver training manuals, training logs, and instructional videos it has used to train delivery truck drivers for the last 20 years. Big Box does not want to turn these materials over because to find them all it would have to search through millions of pages of documents and other materials at an offsite storage facility. Even though the materials Anthony has requested are relevant to his negligence claim (they have *some* tendency to show whether or not Big Box negligently trained its drivers), he may not be able to obtain them. A fairly recent amendment to Rule 26(b)(1) limits discovery to matters "proportional to the needs of the case." Exhibit 17.3 lists the factors from Rule 26(b) the court will consider in determining proportionality. So, in ruling on Anthony's request, the court can consider the amount of Anthony's claim, how much time and money Big Box would have to spend to acquire the information, how badly Anthony needs the information (Does he really need manuals going back 20 years? Does he need training manuals used for drivers other than the one involved in his accident?), and whether there is other evidence more easily accessible that Anthony could use.

Suppose the training materials Anthony requested are not stored in physical form in a warehouse somewhere as in the earlier example. Assume instead they exist only in electronic form and are stored either on long-obsolete floppy discs or have been copied over with more recent files and can only be recovered at great expense. Discovery of electronically stored information poses distinct challenges. Such information may live forever on a storage device, but accessing it can become increasingly difficult over time as the original storage devices become obsolete or files are overwritten (yet still capable of being recovered at great expense and effort). Rule 26(b)(2) directly addresses this challenge. The Rule provides that the responding party may assert that the requested electronically stored information is not "reasonably accessible." If the court agrees that it is not, it may deny discovery of the information. Alternatively, even if the court determines that the information is not reasonably accessible, it may nevertheless order production of the information, but may specify certain conditions for its production. For example, the court could order production conditioned on the requesting party paying for all or part

---

EXHIBIT 17.3   Factors Applied to Determine Proportionality Under Rule 26(b)

1. the importance of the issues at stake in the action;
2. the amount in controversy;
3. the parties' relative access to relevant information;
4. the parties' resources;
5. the importance of the discovery in resolving the issues; and
6. whether the burden or expense of the proposed discovery outweighs its likely benefit.

of the cost of production. So, in our example, Anthony may be able to obtain the information he has requested, even if it is not reasonably accessible, but he may have to pay the costs associated with recovering the deleted files and those from the old discs. As a practical matter, Anthony may reassess his need for the information once he learns how much it may cost to recover it.

The court's power to limit discovery of all kinds of matters is broad. Rule 26(c) permits a court to forbid discovery when: (1) it is duplicative of other information already produced; (2) it could be obtained from another more convenient, less burdensome, or less expensive source; (3) the party seeking discovery has already had ample opportunity to obtain the information earlier in the litigation; or (4) the burden and expense of the proposed discovery outweighs its benefits to resolving the dispute. Rather than forbidding discovery altogether, a court can set limits on discovery. Common examples of such limits include: (1) changing the timing or sequence of discovery, (2) limiting the matters a party may inquire about, and (3) altering the default rule that the responding party pays the costs of production and making the requesting party pay instead. A person who receives a discovery request can seek to limit or avoid production of the requested information by filing a motion for a protective order, or the court can impose such limits on its own. Protective orders may also be used to protect confidential information from disclosure. For example, suppose the plaintiff subpoenas the defendant's former employee to appear at a deposition, and the defendant fears that the former employee may reveal privileged information or information that constitutes a trade secret of the defendant. The defendant may move for a protective order to preclude or limit the scope of the deposition.

D. PRIVILEGES IN THE CONTEXT OF DISCOVERY

Suppose Big Box's attorney requests that Anthony disclose what he told his attorney about the accident. Or suppose Big Box asks Anthony to produce the notes his attorney made during Anthony's initial interview about the accident. Both requests seek discovery of relevant information. Indeed, the requests target matters that might prove highly significant or even dispositive. Moreover, it is not difficult to access or produce this information; so, these requests seem proportional to the needs of the case. Nevertheless, these matters do not fall within the scope of discovery because they are privileged. Rule 26(b) only permits discovery of *non-privileged* matters, and here, Big Box has requested information protected by the lawyer-client privilege (a/k/a the attorney-client privilege) and protected trial preparation materials (a/k/a the work product privilege). Although other privileges might arise during discovery, these two privileges are the most commonly encountered, and the litigator must understand how to protect privileged materials from disclosure.

1. The Lawyer-Client Privilege

The lawyer-client privilege protects from disclosure confidential communications between a lawyer and her client or either's representatives when the communications were made to facilitate the provision of legal services. This privilege applies only to communications between lawyer and client or either's representative. The privilege does not protect physical evidence or the underlying facts. Suppose Big Box alleges that Anthony caused the accident when he ran a red light because he was distracted by speaking on his cell phone. In a private meeting with his attorney, Anthony tells his attorney that he did in fact run the red light while talking on his cell phone. He also hands his cell phone over to his attorney for later inspection. Assume that in a pretrial deposition Big Box's attorney asks Anthony: (1) What did you tell your attorney about running the red light or talking on a cell phone? and (2) Did you run the red light while talking on your cell phone? Question 1 seeks privileged information. The privilege protects what Anthony told his attorney about running the red light and talking on his cell phone, because it is a confidential communication between Anthony and his lawyer in furtherance of legal services to Anthony. However, question 2 does not seek privileged information. The privilege does not protect the underlying facts, even if Anthony disclosed the facts to his attorney. A client cannot privilege the underlying facts by disclosing them to his attorney. Here, the privilege does not protect the color of the light or what Anthony was doing when he entered the intersection. Now assume Big Box's attorney requests production of the cell phone Anthony handed over to his attorney. The cell phone is not privileged, because the privilege applies only to communications, not to physical evidence like the cell phone, even when it is handed over to the attorney.

The communication must be between lawyer and client or their representatives. Communications by the lawyer to the client or by the client to the lawyer are clearly communications between the lawyer and client. Anthony's communications to his lawyer in the example above clearly meet this element of the privilege. Likewise, what Anthony's lawyer might have said to Anthony in the same meeting would meet this element. The privilege can also apply to communications between the representatives of the lawyer and client. For example, if Anthony had made his admission about running the red light while speaking to his lawyer's legal assistant, this element of the privilege would be satisfied. For a corporate client, communications between a lawyer and corporate employees who can act on legal advice — the so-called control group of employees — are privileged, as are communications between the lawyer and employees about matters within the scope of the employee's duties. In either case, the communication most likely is privileged. *See Upjohn Co. v. United States*, 449 U.S. 383 (1981). So, communications by the corporation's attorney to its senior executives may be privileged, because these are the people who may act on the advice. Likewise, communications to lower level employees whose conduct may be the basis of the suit may also be privileged. Confidential communications between an attorney and his representative in order to provide legal services to the client are also privileged. For example, if Anthony's attorney communicates information about the case to his legal assistant so that he can prepare a memo to the file, the communications would be privileged.

The communication must be confidential. A communication is not privileged if the client did not intend confidentiality. A communication is not confidential if it is disclosed to someone other than the client, the attorney, or their representatives.

When disclosure is made outside of these designated persons, the privilege is waived. Suppose for example that Anthony consults with his attorney while his friend Tara is present. No privilege will attach to these communications.

The purpose of the communication must be to facilitate the rendition of legal services. For example, the privilege does not apply to business or social advice a lawyer provides to a client. For example, a general counsel to a business might be both a lawyer for the business and be involved in making business decisions. The legal advice the lawyer provides may be privileged; the business advice is not.

2. Other Communications Privileges

The lawyer-client privilege is not the only privilege provided by state or federal law. Other commonly recognized privileges are the priest-penitent privilege (protecting confidential communications between a person and a spiritual adviser), the spousal communications privilege (protecting confidential communications between spouses during marriage), and the physician-patient privilege (protecting confidential communications between doctor and patient). During discovery, a party may withhold information by asserting that it is protected by one of these privileges.

3. Trial Preparation Materials (a/k/a Work Product)

As a general rule, a party need not disclose the party's trial preparation materials, also known as "work product," in discovery. Trial preparation materials are documents and tangible things that are prepared by a party or its representative, including an attorney, in anticipation of litigation. An attorney's notes about trial strategy, an investigator's report summarizing witness statements, drafts of demonstrative aids for trial, and research memos are common examples of trial preparation materials. *Hickman v. Taylor*—the Supreme Court case from which the doctrine originates—outlines the contours of this doctrine, its rationale, and its limited discoverability. Today, the doctrine that originated in *Hickman* is codified in Rule 26(b)(3), shown in Exhibit 17.4.

EXHIBIT 17.4   Rule 26(b)(3) Trial Preparation Materials

> Ordinarily, a party may not discover documents and tangible things that are prepared in anticipation of litigation or for trial by or for another party or its representative (including the other party's attorney, consultant, surety, indemnitor, insurer, or agent). But, subject to Rule 26(b)(4), those materials may be discovered if:
>   (i) they are otherwise discoverable under Rule 26(b)(1); and
>   (ii) the party shows that it has substantial need for the materials to prepare its case and cannot, without undue hardship, obtain their substantial equivalent by other means.

Case Preview

Hickman v. Taylor

As you read *Hickman*, consider the following questions:

1. What information did the plaintiffs request that defense counsel claimed was protected from disclosure?
2. Why wasn't this information protected by the attorney-client privilege?
3. What information does the Court say is generally protected from disclosure? Is there an exception to this general rule? If so, what is it?
4. What is the underlying rationale for the Court's rule limiting discovery?

Hickman v. Taylor
329 U.S. 495 (1947)

Mr. Justice MURPHY delivered the opinion of the Court.

This case presents an important problem under the Federal Rules of Civil Procedure . . . as to the extent to which a party may inquire into oral and written statements of witnesses, or other information, secured by an adverse party's counsel in the course of preparation for possible litigation after a claim has arisen. Examination into a person's files and records, including those resulting from the professional activities of an attorney, must be judged with care. It is not without reason that various safeguards have been established to preclude unwarranted excursions into the privacy of a man's work. At the same time, public policy supports reasonable and necessary inquiries. Properly to balance these competing interests is a delicate and difficult task.

On February 7, 1943, the tug "J. M. Taylor" sank while engaged in helping to tow a car float of the Baltimore & Ohio Railroad across the Delaware River at Philadelphia. The accident was apparently unusual in nature, the cause of it still being unknown. Five of the nine crew members were drowned. Three days later the tug owners and the underwriters employed a law firm, of which respondent Fortenbaugh is a member, to defend them against potential suits by representatives of the deceased crew members and to sue the railroad for damages to the tug.

A public hearing was held on March 4, 1943, before the United States Steamboat Inspectors, at which the four survivors were examined. This testimony was recorded and made available to all interested parties. Shortly thereafter, Fortenbaugh privately interviewed the survivors and took statements from them with an eye toward the anticipated litigation; the survivors signed these statements on March 29. Fortenbaugh also interviewed other persons believed to have some information relating to the accident and in some cases he made memoranda of what they told him. At the time when Fortenbaugh secured the statements of the survivors, representatives of two of the deceased crew members had been in communication with him. Ultimately claims were presented by representatives of all five of the deceased;

four of the claims, however, were settled without litigation. The fifth claimant, petitioner herein, brought suit in a federal court under the Jones Act on November 26, 1943, naming as defendants the two tug owners, individually and as partners, and the railroad. One year later, petitioner filed 39 interrogatories directed to the tug owners. The 38th interrogatory read: "State whether any statements of the members of the crews of the Tugs 'J. M. Taylor' and 'Philadelphia' or of any other vessel were taken in connection with the towing of the car float and the sinking of the Tug 'John M. Taylor'. Attach hereto exact copies of all such statements if in writing, and if oral, set forth in detail the exact provisions of any such oral statements or reports."

w. fress / statements

Supplemental interrogatories asked whether any oral or written statements, records, reports or other memoranda had been made concerning any matter relative to the towing operation, the sinking of the tug, the salvaging and repair of the tug, and the death of the deceased. If the answer was in the affirmative, the tug owners were then requested to set forth the nature of all such records, reports, statements or other memoranda.

The tug owners, through Fortenbaugh, answered all of the interrogatories except No. 38 and the supplemental ones just described. While admitting that statements of the survivors had been taken, they declined to summarize or set forth the contents. They did so on the ground that such requests called "for privileged matter obtained in preparation for litigation" and constituted "an attempt to obtain indirectly counsel's private files." It was claimed that answering these requests "would involve practically turning over not only the complete files, but also the telephone records and, almost, the thoughts of counsel."

* * *

In urging that he has a right to inquire into the materials secured and prepared by Fortenbaugh, petitioner emphasizes that the deposition-discovery portions of the Federal Rules of Civil Procedure are designed to enable the parties to discover the true facts and to compel their disclosure wherever they may be found. It is said that inquiry may be made under these rules . . . as to any relevant matter which is not privileged; and since the discovery provisions are to be applied as broadly and liberally as possible, the privilege limitation must be restricted to its narrowest bounds. On the premise that the attorney-client privilege is the one involved in this case, petitioner argues that it must be strictly confined to confidential communications made by a client to his attorney. And since the materials here in issue were secured by Fortenbaugh from third persons rather than from his clients, the tug owners, the conclusion is reached that these materials are proper subjects for discovery under Rule 26.

They want it for Discovery

* * *

We also agree that the memoranda, statements and mental impressions in issue in this case fall outside the scope of the attorney-client privilege and hence are not protected from discovery on that basis. It is unnecessary here to delineate the content and scope of that privilege as recognized in the federal courts. For present purposes, it suffices to note that the protective cloak of this privilege does not extend to information which an attorney secures from a witness while acting for his client in anticipation of litigation. Nor does this privilege concern the memoranda, briefs, communications and other writings prepared by counsel for his own use in prosecuting his client's case; and it is equally unrelated to writings which reflect an attorney's mental impressions, conclusions, opinions or legal theories.

But the impropriety of invoking that privilege does not provide an answer to the problem before us. Petitioner has made more than an ordinary request for relevant, non-privileged facts in the possession of his adversaries or their counsel. He has sought discovery as of right of oral and written statements of witnesses whose identity is well known and whose availability to petitioner appears unimpaired. He has sought production of these matters after making the most searching inquiries of his opponents as to the circumstances surrounding the fatal accident, which inquiries were sworn to have been answered to the best of their information and belief. Interrogatories were directed toward all the events prior to, during and subsequent to the sinking of the tug. Full and honest answers to such broad inquiries would necessarily have included all pertinent information gleaned by Fortenbaugh through his interviews with the witnesses. Petitioner makes no suggestion, and we cannot assume, that the tug owners or Fortenbaugh were incomplete or dishonest in the framing of their answers. In addition, petitioner was free to examine the public testimony of the witnesses taken before the United States Steamboat Inspectors. We are thus dealing with an attempt to secure the production of written statements and mental impressions contained in the files and the mind of the attorney Fortenbaugh without any showing of necessity or any indication or claim that denial of such production would unduly prejudice the preparation of petitioner's case or cause him any hardship or injustice. For aught that appears, the essence of what petitioner seeks either has been revealed to him already through the interrogatories or is readily available to him direct from the witnesses for the asking.

The District Court, after hearing objections to petitioner's request, commanded Fortenbaugh to produce all written statements of witnesses and to state in substance any facts learned through oral statements of witnesses to him. Fortenbaugh was to submit any memoranda he had made of the oral statements so that the court might determine what portions should be revealed to petitioner. All of this was ordered without any showing by petitioner, or any requirement that he make a proper showing, of the necessity for the production of any of this material or any demonstration that denial of production would cause hardship or injustice. The court simply ordered production on the theory that the facts sought were material and were not privileged as constituting attorney-client communications.

In our opinion, [no] rule dealing with discovery contemplates production under such circumstances. That is not because the subject matter is privileged or irrelevant, as those concepts are used in these rules. Here is simply an attempt, without purported necessity or justification, to secure written statements, private memoranda and personal recollections prepared or formed by an adverse party's counsel in the course of his legal duties. As such, it falls outside the arena of discovery and contravenes the public policy underlying the orderly prosecution and defense of legal claims. Not even the most liberal of discovery theories can justify unwarranted inquiries into the files and the mental impressions of an attorney.

Historically, a lawyer is an officer of the court and is bound to work for the advancement of justice while faithfully protecting the rightful interests of his clients. In performing his various duties, however, it is essential that a lawyer work with a certain degree of privacy, free from unnecessary intrusion by opposing parties and their counsel. Proper preparation of a client's case demands that he assemble information, sift what he considers to be the relevant from the irrelevant facts, prepare his legal theories and plan his strategy without undue and needless interference. That is the historical and the necessary way in which lawyers act within the framework of our system of jurisprudence to promote justice and to protect their clients' interests. This work is reflected, of course, in interviews, statements, memoranda, correspondence, briefs, mental impressions, personal beliefs, and countless other tangible and intangible ways — aptly though roughly termed by the Circuit Court of Appeals in this case . . . as the "Work product of the lawyer." Were such materials open to opposing counsel on mere demand, much of what is now put down in writing would remain unwritten. An attorney's thoughts, heretofore inviolate, would not be his own. Inefficiency, unfairness and sharp practices would inevitably develop in the giving of legal advice and in the preparation of cases for trial. The effect on the legal profession would be demoralizing. And the interests of the clients and the cause of justice would be poorly served.

We do not mean to say that all written materials obtained or prepared by an adversary's counsel with an eye toward litigation are necessarily free from discovery in all cases. Where relevant and non-privileged facts remain hidden in an attorney's file and where production of those facts is essential to the preparation of one's case, discovery may properly be had. Such written statements and documents might, under certain circumstances, be admissible in evidence or give clues as to the existence or location of relevant facts. Or they might be useful for purposes of impeachment or corroboration. And production might be justified where the witnesses are no longer available or can be reached only with difficulty. Were production of written statements and documents to be precluded under such circumstances, the liberal ideals of the deposition-discovery portions of the Federal Rules of Civil Procedure would be stripped of much of their meaning. But the general policy against invading the privacy of an attorney's course of preparation is so well recognized and so essential to an orderly working of our system of legal procedure that a burden rests on the one who would invade that privacy to establish adequate reasons to justify production through a subpoena or court order. That burden, we believe, is necessarily implicit in the rules as now constituted.

Rule 30(b), as presently written, gives the trial judge the requisite discretion to make a judgment as to whether discovery should be allowed as to written statements secured from witnesses. But in the instant case there was no room for that discretion to operate in favor of the petitioner. No attempt was made to establish any reason why Fortenbaugh should be forced to produce the written statements. There was only a naked, general demand for these materials as of right and a finding by the District Court that no recognizable privilege was involved. That was insufficient to justify discovery under these circumstances and the court should have sustained the refusal of the tug owners and Fortenbaugh to produce.

But as to oral statements made by witnesses to Fortenbaugh, whether presently in the form of his mental impressions or memoranda, we do not believe that any showing of necessity can be made under the circumstances of this case so as to justify production. Under ordinary conditions, forcing an attorney to repeat or write out all that witnesses have told him and to deliver the account to his adversary gives rise to grave dangers of inaccuracy and untrustworthiness. No legitimate purpose is served by such production. The practice forces the attorney to testify as to what he remembers or what he saw fit to write down regarding witnesses' remarks. Such testimony could not qualify as evidence; and to use it for impeachment or corroborative purposes would make the attorney much less an officer of the court and much more an ordinary witness. The standards of the profession would thereby suffer.

Denial of production of this nature does not mean that any material, non-privileged facts can be hidden from the petitioner in this case. He need not be unduly hindered in the preparation of his case, in the discovery of facts or in his anticipation of his opponents' position. Searching interrogatories directed to Fortenbaugh and the tug owners, production of written documents and statements upon a proper showing and direct interviews with the witnesses themselves all serve to reveal the facts in Fortenbaugh's possession to the fullest possible extent consistent with public policy. Petitioner's counsel frankly admits that he wants the oral statements only to help prepare himself to examine witnesses and to make sure that he has overlooked nothing. That is insufficient under the circumstances to permit him an exception to the policy underlying the privacy of Fortenbaugh's professional activities. If there should be a rare situation justifying production of these matters, petitioner's case is not of that type.

We fully appreciate the wide-spread controversy among the members of the legal profession over the problem raised by this case. It is a problem that rests on what has been one of the most hazy frontiers of the discovery process. But until some rule or statute definitely prescribes otherwise, we are not justified in permitting discovery in a situation of this nature as a matter of unqualified right. When Rule 26 and the other discovery rules were adopted, this Court and the members of the bar in general certainly did not believe or contemplate that all the files and mental processes of lawyers were thereby opened to the free scrutiny of their adversaries. And we refuse to interpret the rules at this time so as to reach so harsh and unwarranted a result.

We therefore affirm the judgment of the Circuit Court of Appeals.

Affirmed.

Post-Case Follow-Up

Rule 26(b)(3), set out in Exhibit 17.4, codifies the rule from *Hickman* and also answers a number of questions regarding the scope of the doctrine that the Court did not squarely address in its opinion. Rather than using the term "work product of an attorney," Rule 26(b)(3) uses the term "trial preparation materials." This term certainly encompasses *Hickman*'s work product, but the term also includes documents and tangible things prepared by a party or a party's representative, not just materials prepared by an attorney. So, a party, its employees, or the attorney's paralegal or secretary can create trial preparation materials that are generally protected from disclosure. The key is that the material must be prepared in anticipation of litigation or for trial.

This element of the Rule often presents difficult questions. "Litigation" includes proceedings in court as well as administrative proceedings and arbitrations. But when does a party *anticipate* litigation? Today, one can probably safely anticipate the prospect of litigation following any event resulting in harm or alleged harm. Though not dispositive, the involvement of an attorney or the labeling of the document as "privileged" or "work product" are circumstances indicating the party or his representative anticipated litigation. Consequently, attorneys tend to be quick and careful to add this label to documents.

Easier cases are those in which the document or tangible thing was created for trial. For example, an attorney's outline of his direct or cross examination of a trial witness is protected because it was created for use at trial. Also, materials created *solely because of* the prospect of litigation are relatively straightforward. If, for example, Big Box's attorney asks its driver to draw a diagram of the scene of the accident so that she can better understand the accident, the diagram is protected work product. In contrast, when the purpose of creating the material was unconnected to the prospect of litigation, the material is not protected from disclosure. Suppose Big Box routinely generates documents detailing driving performance for the purposes of deciding pay raises and promotions. Even if such documents are useful in litigation, they are not protected, because they were not made *because of* litigation. Instead, they were made in the ordinary course of business; thus, they are discoverable.

So-called dual-purpose materials present difficult cases. These are materials produced both for routine business purposes and also in anticipation of litigation. Suppose Big Box issued a report to its insurer after making a claim for the damage done to its truck in the wreck. This report has both a routine business purpose — recovering insurance proceeds — and a potential litigation purpose: to document facts relevant to the litigation. With such dual-purpose materials, the inquiry focuses on the principal purpose of the material's creation. If the principal purpose was because of the prospect of litigation, the material is protected. If the principal purpose was a routine business purpose, the material is not protected.

If a document or tangible thing meets the test for work product (is a document or tangible thing prepared in anticipation of litigation or for trial by or for a party), a party may properly refuse to disclose that item and withhold it, even though it is responsive to a discovery request. To assert this protection, the party would withhold the item and disclose this to the requesting party by providing a privilege log laying out a basic description of the item and noting the ground on which it was withheld. Unlike the lawyer-client privilege, the protection afforded to trial preparation or work product is qualified. That is, this protection can be overcome, and the item ordered to be disclosed, if a proper showing is made. Once the party that requested the discovery reviews the privilege log, that party can decide whether to go to the court to seek to challenge and overcome the work product claim. Table 17.1 compares the lawyer-client privilege and protection for trial preparation materials.

TABLE 17.1 Lawyer-Client Privilege and Trial Preparation Materials Compared	
Lawyer-Client Privilege	**Trial Preparation Materials**
Applies only to communications	Applies to certain communications but also tangible things
Applies to communications between lawyer and client or their representatives	May apply to certain communications to third parties
Communication's purpose was to facilitate legal services, but not necessarily in anticipation of litigation	Must have been made in anticipation of litigation
Party need not disclose regardless of requesting party's need for privilege information	"Opinion Work Product" is absolutely protected. Other trial preparation materials may be disclosed upon a showing of "substantial need" and inability to acquire the equivalent without undue burden.

Hickman v. Taylor and Rule 26(b)(3): Real Life Applications

1. Javier represents Chandlers, Inc., the owner and operator of a chain of grocery stores. Chandlers sends Javier a settlement demand from Jerry, who claims to have been injured in a slip and fall accident in a Chandlers grocery store. Before Jerry files suit, but after receiving the demand letter, Javier identifies a nonparty witness to Javier's fall and interviews the witness. Javier took handwritten notes about what the witness told him and also how effective Javier thought the witness would be at trial. After filing suit, Jerry demands production of any notes from witness interviews. Javier asserts the work product privilege in response to the request and provides a log to Jerry's attorney that provides the date on which he created the notes. Jerry's attorney moves to compel production of the notes on the grounds that they are not work product because no suit had been filed at the time Javier created the notes. How should the court rule?

2. Murphy's, LLC owns and operates a bar in Waco, Texas. Murphy's hires attorney Chang to make a presentation to the Waco City Council and argue against a proposed ordinance that would ban cigarette smoking in all bars and restaurants within Waco city limits. In preparation for the presentation, Chang creates an outline of the presentation, which includes the reasons Chang thinks the smoking ban is a bad idea. One year later, former Murphy's employees file suit against Murphy's for injuries they alleged they suffered as a result of inhaling cigarette smoke at Murphy's. The attorney for the former employees moves to compel production of the outline. Murphy's claims it is protected attorney work product. How should the court rule on the claim of work product?

3. Ahmed is injured in a car wreck with Sujeet. Ahmed files suit against Sujeet and alleges that Sujeet was intoxicated at the time of the collision. Sujeet hires

Howard to represent him in Ahmed's lawsuit. In a private meeting, Sujeet admits to Howard that he was intoxicated at the time of the accident. In a pre-trial deposition of Sujeet, Ahmed's attorney asks Sujeet what he told his attorney about being intoxicated at the time of the accident. Howard instructs Sujeet not to answer the question. Ahmed's attorney asks Howard to reveal the grounds for his instruction to Sujeet. What ground(s) should Howard provide? Is the ground valid?

Limited Discovery of Trial Preparation Materials

An attorney or party's mental impressions, opinions, and conclusions are referred to as "opinion work product," or sometimes "core work product," and are absolutely protected from disclosure. A party may overcome another party's claim of privilege as to other trial preparation materials. Other trial preparation materials enjoy only a qualified privilege from disclosure. A party may discover certain trial preparation materials by showing that the material is essential to the preparation of his case, and even if essential, the court will not order production if the party can acquire substantially similar information by other means. Suppose shortly after the accident involving Anthony, Big Box hires a private investigator and an attorney because it anticipates a lawsuit by Anthony. The investigator interviews witnesses and turns over his summary of the witness comments to Big Box's attorney. The attorney reads over the investigator's report and takes notes on his notepad about his impressions of the various witnesses. Anthony seeks to obtain a copy of both the investigator's summary and the attorney's notes. Anthony may be able to obtain the investigator's summary if he can prove it is essential to his preparation of the case and that he cannot obtain the information through other means. But the attorney's notes containing his mental impressions of the witnesses are absolutely protected and are not discoverable regardless of how much Anthony might need them.

Experts and Limitations on Discovery

Experts who may testify at trial must be disclosed as part of a party's initial disclosures. Expert *witnesses* must be disclosed, but not all experts are hired or retained to testify at trial. Some are hired only as consultants in order to help a party prepare for trial. Perhaps the trial involves complicated scientific or technical matters about which the typical attorney knows very little. Having an expert consultant help prepare for such a trial can be crucial. The facts known to and the opinions held by these consulting-only experts are not discoverable except under "exceptional circumstances," when it is impossible or impracticable for other parties to obtain by other means the facts or opinions the consultant holds.

The discovery rules also protect from disclosure certain matters related to an expert *who will testify at trial*. Communications between a party's attorney and an expert retained or employed to provide testimony at trial generally are not discoverable. However, such communications are discoverable if they relate to the expert's compensation or if they identify facts, data, or assumptions that the party's attorney provided and the expert considered or relied on in forming opinions. For example, suppose an expert testifies that his opinion was based on a fact he only knows because the attorney told him the fact. The expert cannot refuse to disclose that fact. As previously discussed, experts retained or employed by a party to provide trial testimony must provide to the other parties a report regarding his opinions and the basis for them. Earlier drafts of these reports are not discoverable.

Protecting Privileged and Trial Preparation Materials from Disclosure

In order to withhold otherwise discoverable information on the grounds that it is privileged or trial preparation material, the party must expressly assert the privilege. Typically, the party will make this assertion in response to the discovery request. Rather than providing the communication, information, document, or item in response to the request, the party will respond that the material is privileged or constitutes trial preparation material. In addition, the responding party must provide a privilege log to the requesting party. The privilege log is a document that must, without revealing the privileged or protected material, describe the nature of the material not produced so that the other parties are able to assess whether the privilege or protection applies.

E. DISCOVERY TOOLS: HOW INFORMATION IS OBTAINED

Now that we understand *what* can be discovered (i.e., what matters fall within the scope of discovery), we turn to the very practical question of *how* a party goes about discovering these matters. In this section, we'll talk about the various tools a party may use to obtain documents, electronically stored information, tangible things, and the testimony of witnesses. One important issue is whether a discovery tool can be used to obtain information from both parties and nonparties. Table 17.2 provides the answer to this question for each discovery tool.

TABLE 17.2   **Obtaining Discovery from Parties and Nonparties:** *Some discovery tools may be used to obtain information only from parties. Others can be used on both parties and nonparties.*

Parties Only	Parties and Nonparties
Requests for Admission	Requests for Production and Inspection
Mental and Physical Examinations	Depositions
Interrogatories	

1. Oral Depositions

Anthony has filed suit against Big Box; so, it's understandable that Big Box wants to understand what Anthony knows about the cause of the accident and the injuries Anthony alleges he has sustained. Big Box doesn't have to wait until trial to have Anthony's testimony on these matters. Big Box can take Anthony's oral deposition pretrial. An **oral deposition** is a witness's out-of-court testimony provided under oath and in response to questions from the examining attorneys. The **deponent** is the term used for the witness at the deposition. Attorneys do not take depositions in a courtroom. Depositions can be conducted in a variety of places, such as in a conference room in a law office or in a hotel meeting room. The deponent's testimony is typically recorded by a court reporter who creates a verbatim transcript of the testimony. Depositions are often videotaped as well. So, Big Box can take Anthony's deposition at Anthony's lawyer's office or at some other agreed upon location, and both Big Box's and Anthony's attorneys will attend. Depositions may be taken of both party and nonparty witnesses.

In order to compel Anthony's attendance at the deposition, Big Box needs to provide Anthony's attorney with a notice of deposition naming Anthony as the deponent. In a case with multiple parties, the deposition notice must be provided to all parties so that they may attend the deposition if they wish.

Compelling Attendance at a Deposition

Compelling the attendance of party witnesses, like Anthony, is simple — you just serve them with a deposition notice. This makes sense since the court already has jurisdiction over the parties. However, a party can also take the depositions of nonparty witnesses, but compelling their attendance is a bit more complicated. Suppose for example that Big Box wants to depose Alicia, who is not a party to the case but who witnessed the accident. Big Box will subpoena Alicia, rather than serving her only with a deposition notice, because a subpoena is required to compel a nonparty's attendance at a deposition. A **subpoena** is a writ issued by the court that compels the presence of the witness at a particular time and place.

Now suppose that Anthony wants to depose the delivery truck driver involved in the accident who is employed by Big Box. The delivery truck driver is not a party but he is employed by a party. Anthony can compel his attendance with a deposition notice alone (and without a subpoena) because a deposition notice compels the attendance of both parties and someone under the control of a party, such as a party's employee.

Deposing an Organization

Often, rather than having a particular individual in mind, a party will want to depose an organization on certain matters. In our example, Big Box is a corporation, a kind of fictional person that can only speak through its authorized agents and employees. Rule 30(b)(6), shown in Exhibit 17.5, authorizes a party to take the

EXHIBIT 17.5   **Rule 30(b)(6) Notice or Subpoena Directed to an Organization**

> In its notice or subpoena, a party may name as the deponent a public or private corporation, a partnership, an association, a governmental agency, or other entity and must describe with reasonable particularity the matters for examination. The named organization must then designate one or more officers, directors, or managing agents, or designate other persons who consent to testify on its behalf; and it may set out the matters on which each person designated will testify. A subpoena must advise a nonparty organization of its duty to make this designation. The persons designated must testify about information known or reasonably available to the organization. This paragraph (6) does not preclude a deposition by any other procedure allowed by these rules.

deposition of an organization on matters described in the notice. Suppose Anthony suspects that a cause of his accident was that the delivery truck driver had been driving without sufficient rest in violation of certain Big Box policies limiting the number of hours drivers can spend behind the wheel. Anthony wants to take the deposition of the Big Box employee responsible for monitoring compliance with these policies. If Anthony knows the identity of this person at Big Box, Anthony can simply notice the deposition of this employee by name. Suppose, however, that Anthony does not know the identity of this person. In this situation, instead of noticing the deposition of an individual, Anthony can notice the deposition of the organization itself and describe in the notice the matters on which he intends to depose the organization. So, here, Anthony would serve a notice that names Big Box as the deponent and states that he wants to depose Big Box on its policies regarding limitations on driving times and monitoring compliance with them. Big Box must then produce a witness with knowledge of these matters at the deposition.

Limitations on Depositions

Generally, parties may depose witnesses without court permission, and ideally the parties are able to arrange and conduct them without troubling the court with disputes over who may be deposed or when or where the deposition may take place. However, the Rules impose certain default limitations on the number and length of depositions that may not be exceeded without court permission or the agreement of the parties. A deposition may only last a single day of no more than seven hours in length. And a party may take no more than ten depositions in a case. Exceeding these limits requires a court order or the agreement of the parties.

2. Interrogatories to Parties

Interrogatories to parties are, as their name suggests, written questions directed to a party that must be answered under oath. Interrogatories may only be used against parties. Interrogatories are not an appropriate method to acquire information from nonparties. The party must answer each interrogatory, unless the party asserts an objection or privilege. The party has 30 days from the date served with the interrogatories to answer them, unless a different time is ordered by the court or agreed to by the parties. Interrogatories may be used at trial as evidence against the party that answered them. For example, the plaintiff may offer the defendant's answers, but the plaintiff may not, as a general rule, offer his own answers to the interrogatories. To do so would violate the hearsay rule.

An interrogatory must be answered by the person to whom it is directed. Interrogatories may be directed to a party that is an organization. The organization designates a person to answer the interrogatories on behalf of the organization. The designated person must answer the questions based on information available to the party, not just information the designee happens to know. Suppose Anthony serves Big Box with interrogatories. Big Box designates Lamar, one of its senior vice-presidents, to answer the interrogatories. One of the interrogatories asks for the vehicle identification number (VIN) for the Big Box delivery truck involved in the accident. Lamar does not know the answer, but he knows that Big Box's shipping manager knows. Lamar cannot respond to the interrogatory by saying he does not know the answer. Because the VIN is information available to Big Box, even if unknown to Lamar, he must acquire the information and provide it in the answer to the interrogatory.

3. Requests for Production

What May Be Requested

A party may serve on another party a request to produce for inspection, copying, testing, or sampling any designated documents, electronically stored information, or tangible things that are in the possession, custody, or control of the responding party. The **request for production** allows a party to obtain a wide variety of items so long as they are within the scope of discovery. Such items include writings, drawings, photographs, sound and video recordings, and data compilations (e.g., a spreadsheet with relevant financial data). A request for production would also require production of relevant tangible things, such as the allegedly defective product in a product liability case. This request may also be used to obtain materials from nonparties, but must be accompanied by a subpoena.

The requesting party may also serve on another party a request to enter designated land or other property owned or controlled by the responding party that is relevant to the case. A request to enter land or property may also be served on a nonparty but must be accompanied by a subpoena. The requesting party may inspect, measure, survey, photograph, test or sample the property or any designated object or operation on it. For example, in a case alleging soil contamination, the parties could request entry on the land to inspect and photograph the property and test the soil.

Response to the Request: Deadline

The responding party must respond to the request within 30 days of being served with it, unless a different time is ordered by the court or agreed to by the parties.

The responding party must state that the request will be permitted or state an objection to the request, specifying the particular request to which the objection is directed, the basis for the objection, and whether any documents are being withheld on the basis of that objection. If the objection is directed to only part of a request, the responding party must permit inspection of the remaining material. Documents must be produced either as they are kept in the usual course of business, or the responding party must organize and label them to correspond to the categories in the request.

Responding to a Request for Electronically Stored Information

The party requesting production of electronically stored information may state in the request the form in which the information is to be produced. The responding party may object to the form and state the form that it intends to use in its response. For example, if the requesting party asks for production of electronically stored information on a portable thumb drive, the responding party could object to the request and state that it intends to produce the information by granting the requesting party access to a secure cloud-based server.

The designated form of production must be in a reasonably usable form. Parties routinely disagree over the format in which the electronically stored information is produced. Should electronically stored documents be produced in PDF, TIF, or native format? Such disputes often boil down to whether or not the requesting party should have access to the metadata. Metadata is data that describes other data. In the context of electronically stored information, the metadata might provide information about who accessed and modified the document, when that access or modification occurred, and how long it took. Consider the difference between receiving a budget spreadsheet in PDF format versus in an Excel format. The PDF format would reveal entries such as revenue and expenses for each line of the budget, but the Excel format would also reveal the formulas used to calculate these numbers in each cell. If the requesting party wants the metadata for the spreadsheet, it would ask for the budget in Excel format. The responding party can object to the request and state that it intends to produce the budget in PDF format. The court would then rule on the objection.

4. Requests for Admission

A **request for admission** is a written request that a party admit the truth of a fact, a legal conclusion, or an opinion about either. For example, Big Box could serve the following request for admission on Anthony: "Admit that you were intoxicated at the time of the collision that is the subject of this action." The responding party has 30 days from the date served with the request to admit or deny the matters in the request, unless a different time is ordered by the court or agreed to by the parties.

Importantly, failure to timely respond to a request for admission results in a deemed admission. So, if in the example above Anthony failed to timely deny that he was intoxicated, he would be deemed to have admitted it. An admitted matter, including a matter deemed admitted, is conclusively established for purposes of the lawsuit. After all, why waste time litigating matters that have been admitted? A party may withdraw an admission only with court permission and only if the court concludes that allowing withdrawal would aid the presentation of the merits and not prejudice the requesting party.

5. Physical and Mental Examinations

The court may order the **physical or mental examination** of a party whose mental or physical condition is in controversy. For example, Anthony's physical condition is in controversy because he is suing for personal injury damages. The court, upon motion, could order an examination of Anthony by a licensed physician. In the absence of a stipulation of the parties, a court order is required in order to compel a physical or mental examination. Suppose Anthony alleges that he suffered back injuries in the collision. Big Box may want a doctor to examine the plaintiff to determine the true extent of his back injuries. Big Box cannot compel a physical examination of Anthony simply by requesting it. Instead, Big Box must secure Anthony's agreement or request and obtain an order from the court to compel the examination.

F. RESISTING AND COMPELLING DISCOVERY

Parties often disagree on what information must be produced in discovery or when or in what form it must be produced. Discovery can involve such time and expense that parties may be tempted to use this fact as a weapon against an opponent by making an unreasonable, unduly burdensome, or expensive request. Similarly, the responding party may be tempted to hide damaging evidence by refusing to disclose it. *Chudasama v. Mazda Motor Corp.* presents an extreme example of unreasonable discovery requests. 123 F.3d 1353 (11th Cir. 1997). The Chudasamas filed suit for compensatory and punitive damages against Mazda Motor Corp., alleging that defects in their Mazda MPV minivan caused them physical injury. The court described the case as a "drawn-out discovery battle" in which "both sides initially adopted extreme and unreasonable positions; the plaintiffs asked for almost every tangible piece of information or property possessed by the defendants, and the defendants offered next to nothing. . . ." The court detailed the improper requests, but a few examples are particularly instructive here. The court described the Chudasamas as seeking:

> 1. "production of nearly every document ever made that would list or assist in finding every person that ever had anything to do with any component of any year model of the MPV minivan 'and all vehicles similar'; and
>
> 2. "every document related to any form of advertising anywhere in the world of any year Mazda MPV minivan and 'all vehicles similar' *and* all components thereof."

When faced with vague and overbroad requests like the ones the Chudasamas sent Mazda, what should the responding party do? The answer involves a multi-step process for asserting and resolving disputes as the appropriate scope of a discovery request.

1. **Assert an Objection:** The first step is often to object in writing to the discovery within the time provided for a response and to serve the objection on the requesting party. An objection not made in writing and in a timely fashion is waived, unless the court finds good cause for the failure.
2. **Meet and Confer:** The second step is for the parties to meet and confer in an effort to resolve the dispute. Parties must attempt to resolve discovery disputes on their own before involving the court. The parties' meeting may avoid the need for court intervention altogether or, at a minimum, narrow the issues for the court to decide.
3. **Motion to Compel or for Protective Order:** If the parties cannot resolve the dispute on their own, the requesting party may move to compel the requested discovery. Alternatively, the responding party can move for a protective order that requests that the court preclude or limit discovery. Whether the issue is brought to the court's attention by a motion for protective order or motion to compel, the court has the authority to forbid or limit the extent of discovery on the matter or matters.

Not all efforts to resist discovery are based on the irrelevance, vagueness, burdensomeness, or breadth of the request. A party may resist responding even to a narrowly tailored request for critical evidence on the grounds that disclosure would threaten a trade secret or confidential research, development, or commercial information. In this situation, the responding party should move for a protective order, and if granted, the court can, in addition to forbidding or limiting discovery, order that production be made in a certain way (e.g., on a secure database that logs who accesses it) or only to certain persons so as to protect the trade secret or confidential information.

G. DUTIES IN DISCOVERY AND SANCTIONS

The discovery procedures we've seen for acquiring information cannot work effectively if the parties do not preserve relevant evidence or are otherwise unwilling to cooperate in the process. A request for production is of little value if a party can simply destroy the evidence. Interrogatory and deposition answers may be unreliable if a party has no obligation to correct an answer that is false or misleading. For this reason, the discovery rules impose an obligation on parties to preserve evidence, cooperate in discovery, and supplement their responses.

1. The Duty to Preserve Evidence

Parties have a duty to preserve evidence in pending or reasonably foreseeable litigation. Receipt of a demand letter or a letter demanding preservation of evidence indicates that a lawsuit may be forthcoming, and ordinarily triggers a duty to preserve evidence; but even if no such letter has been sent, a party has an obligation to preserve evidence if it can reasonably foresee litigation. **Spoliation** is a party's failure to preserve evidence, either by destroying it or by materially altering it. A party who burns or shreds documents with the intent to prevent their disclosure or use as evidence has certainly committed spoliation, but not all spoliation is quite so sinister. Spoliation can occur when a party fails to prevent the routine destruction of materials. For example, Big Box may have a policy of retaining documents for three years, after which they are deleted from servers or, if printed, shredded. However, Anthony's lawsuit would require Big Box to preserve relevant material even if the three-year mark is reached during the pendency of the action.

The penalty for spoliation depends upon the intent of the party. Under Rule 37(e), if the party destroyed or altered electronically stored information with the intent to deprive another party of the information, the court may instruct the jury that it may presume that the evidence would have been unfavorable to the party, dismiss the action, or enter a default judgment. If the evidence was destroyed without the intent to deprive another party of it — for example, if it was destroyed or altered negligently — the court should order measures "no greater than necessary" to cure the prejudice to other parties. This order might include making other evidence inadmissible in order to cure the prejudice caused by the spoliation. Similar penalties can be imposed for the spoliation of non-ESI, including an instruction to the jury that they may infer that the destroyed or altered evidence would have been unfavorable to the party that destroyed or altered it.

2. Duty to Cooperate in Discovery

Federal Rule 37 authorizes a court to impose sanctions against parties who resist discovery without justification. Rule 37 authorizes the court to impose sanctions for a party's failure to participate in good faith in the development of the proposed discovery plan required by Rule 26. The court could, for example, require the uncooperative party to pay the attorneys' fees and other expenses incurred in bringing the motion for sanctions and/or unnecessarily incurred in working to develop a plan without the party's cooperation.

Also, under Rule 37, a party who provides evasive or incomplete responses to a proper request may be ordered to pay the expenses incurred, including attorney's fees, in moving to compel a complete disclosure. A complete failure to answer discovery or to attend a deposition will result in disallowing the offending party to use the undisclosed information or witness to support a motion, at a hearing, or at trial. A failure to disclose may also result in other, harsher sanctions, including the striking of claims or defenses, or a finding that certain designated facts be taken as true. For example, the complete refusal to respond to discovery requests related to an objection to personal jurisdiction, even after ordered to respond by the court, might result in the court overruling the objection. *Ins. Corp. of Ireland, Ltd. v. Compagnie des Bauxites de Guinee*, 456 U.S. 694 (1982) (holding that the defendant was subject to the court's personal jurisdiction as a sanction for refusing to respond to discovery requesting information relevant to whether the defendant was subject to personal jurisdiction).

3. Duty to Avoid Unreasonable and Unduly Burdensome Requests

Rule 26(g) provides that discovery requests *and* responses must be signed by the attorney. This signature is a certification to the court that the response is complete and correct and that the request is not made for an improper purpose, such as to harass or delay. In addition, the signature is a certification that the requests are "neither unreasonable nor unduly burdensome, considering the needs of the case, prior discovery in the case, the amount in controversy, and the importance of the issues at stake in the action." In other words, the request must be proportional to the needs of the case. At some point, a party may commit abuses that are so egregious that the court may refer the attorneys to the state bar for discipline of ethical violations.

Recall the Chudasamas' discovery requests. They likely violated this rule by making requests that were unreasonable and unduly burdensome, especially in light of how insignificant much of what they requested was to the existence of a defect in their particular vehicle or any other issue in the case. What is unreasonable or unduly burdensome varies from case to case. Requesting production of large amounts of electronically stored information may be reasonable in a $100 million case, but not in a case with a $50,000 amount in controversy. Rule 26 authorizes the court to impose sanctions on the attorney, the party, or both for violations of this rule. Sanctions may include the reasonable expenses, including attorneys' fees, of violating the Rule. For example, the sanction might require the party making the request to pay the expenses incurred by the responding party in moving for a protective order.

4. Duty to Supplement Responses

Suppose Big Box serves Anthony with an interrogatory asking what future medical treatments his injuries will require. At the time he answered the interrogatory, Anthony had just been advised by his doctor that he would need back surgery; so, Anthony provides that information to Big Box in his answer to the interrogatory. Several months later, Anthony's doctor tells him that he will not require surgery after all. What obligation, if any, does Anthony's attorney have with respect to correcting or supplementing the interrogatory answer? Rule 26 imposes a duty on a party to make disclosures that are complete and correct as of the time the disclosure is made. Anthony did not violate this rule when he answered the interrogatory. Anthony's response was complete and correct based on the information he had at the time he answered it. However, even a complete and correct disclosure may become incomplete or incorrect based on additional information. A party has an ongoing duty to supplement its responses to written discovery to ensure they are complete and correct. So, Anthony needs to supplement his interrogatory answer with the statement that he may no longer require back surgery because, even though complete and correct at the time it was made, it is no longer complete and correct.

Chapter Summary

- Through informal investigation an attorney may obtain information without invoking the federal discovery rules and without the aid of the court. Generally, the information uncovered in informal investigation is information in the possession of the attorney's client or a nonparty witness, or that is publicly available.
- Required disclosures are initial disclosures, expert witness disclosures, and pretrial disclosures. The required disclosures must be made by all parties without a request.
- The federal discovery rules authorize discovery of information that is not privileged, relevant to any party's claim or defense, and proportional to the needs of the case. A matter need not be admissible in evidence to be discoverable.
- Privileged information is not discoverable. Trial preparation materials are ordinarily not discoverable. Trial preparation materials created in anticipation of litigation or for trial by a party or his representative are not generally discoverable.
- Oral depositions, interrogatories, requests for production and admission, and physical and mental examinations are discovery tools the Rules authorize a party to employ in order to obtain discoverable information.
- Parties may object to improper discovery requests in writing and move for a protective order to limit or preclude discovery. A party may move to compel production of information improperly withheld.
- Parties have a duty to preserve evidence, make complete and accurate responses to proper discovery requests, and supplement responses to ensure that they remain complete and accurate.

Applying the Concepts

Plaintiff files suit against her former employer, Pacer, Inc., alleging it fired her because of her race. The defendant has a memo from the plaintiff's former supervisor indicating that race did play in role in the termination of her employment.

1. Must the defendant disclose this memo in its required initial disclosures?

2. If the plaintiff has this same memo in her possession, must she disclose it in her initial disclosures?

3. Must the defendant produce this memo for inspection and copying in response to a request for production from the plaintiff seeking "any memos written by her former supervisor describing the reason or reasons for plaintiff's termination"?

4. Could the defendant refuse to produce the memo on the grounds that it only exists in the form of a word processing document on a hard drive?

5. Plaintiff wants to depose her former supervisor about the reasons for her termination. How does the plaintiff require the supervisor's attendance at the deposition? Can the plaintiff require the supervisor to produce the memo and other relevant documents at the deposition? If so, how?

6. Plaintiff wants to depose Pacer, Inc. regarding its policies and processes for reviewing employee performance and making employment decisions. Plaintiff does not know which Pacer employee can speak to these issues. How can Plaintiff require Pacer to produce the appropriate person for deposition?

7. Plaintiff serves Pacer with a request for production of "all documents of any kind whatsoever related to the hiring, promotion, or dismissal of any Pacer employee within the last 15 years." Pacer believes the request includes information that is beyond the scope of discovery, overbroad, and unduly burdensome. Can Pacer simply refuse to respond to the discovery? What steps should Pacer take to preclude or limit discovery?

Civil Procedure in Practice

Lorenzo files suit against Advance, Inc. alleging that Advance manufactured sheetrock containing asbestos to which Lorenzo was exposed while working as a plasterer from 1990 to 2000. Lorenzo alleges that exposure to Advance's asbestos-laden sheetrock caused him to develop terminal cancer six months ago.

1. Lorenzo seeks more than $3 million in damages. Lorenzo requests production of certain documents from the late 1980s that detail the extent of Advance's knowledge that its product contained asbestos and the danger it posed to plasterers like Lorenzo who installed the product. The documents exist only on backup tapes that are stored in an offsite storage facility, and to locate the documents and convert them to a readable form will likely cost more than $100,000.

   a. You represent Advance. What grounds might you assert to preclude or limit discovery of the documents Lorenzo has requested, and what steps must you take to do so?

   b. You represent Advance. Can the court order discovery even if the court believes that the documents are not reasonably accessible to your client? If so, what if any steps can the court take to reduce the burden and expense on your client, Advance?

2. Advance sends Lorenzo a set of ten interrogatories and ten requests for admission. Lorenzo fails to respond at all to either the interrogatories or the requests.

   a. As Advance's attorney, what should you do in response to Lorenzo's failure?

   b. Now assume you represent Lorenzo. What are the possible consequences to Lorenzo for his failure to respond, and how might you help Lorenzo avoid them?

Adding Parties
and Claims

18

Basic Party and Claim Joinder

This chapter addresses the basic party and claim joinder rules. Put simply, the issue addressed in this chapter is: How big can a civil action get? Put another way, how many parties and how many different claims can be properly brought in the action? These issues are governed by the joinder rules in the Federal Rules of Civil Procedure. Generally, the joinder rules provide the parties, and especially the plaintiff, wide latitude to control the size of the litigation. This latitude provides the parties with a number of tactical decisions. At the same time, the court may intervene to address concerns about efficiency, confusion, or fairness brought about by parties' use of this discretion. This chapter addresses the most commonly used joinder rules, rather than special procedures for more complex actions — like class actions — which will be addressed in the next chapter.

A. PERMISSIVE PARTY JOINDER: ADDING PARTIES TO THE SUIT

Let's begin our discussion of party joinder with a relatively simple idea. Courts resolve cases, and a case requires at least one plaintiff and one defendant. The party joinder rules do not directly address adding a single plaintiff or a single defendant. Instead, the rules take for granted that all cases will have at least one plaintiff and one defendant. Consequently, the permissive party joinder rules focus on the joinder of multiple plaintiffs and multiple defendants, and on third-party defendants (parties joined by

Key Concepts

- The "same transaction or occurrence" rule for joining multiple plaintiffs and defendants
- Third-party joinder, called "impleading," where a defendant adds a third-party defendant who may be liable to the defendant for the plaintiff's claim against the defendant
- Recognizing a counterclaim, and the difference between compulsory and permissive counterclaims
- Recognizing a crossclaim, and its "same transaction or occurrence" requirement.

defendants because they were not parties to the original action). It is also important to know that the permissive party joinder rules permit but do not require the joinder of any particular party. In other words, the rules speak in terms of what *may* be done, not what *must* be done. So, this section will first address when multiple plaintiffs and multiple defendants may be joined (governed by Rule 20), and then it will address when third parties may be joined via impleader (governed by Rule 14).

1. Joining Plaintiffs and Defendants

Suppose Linh, Gayatri, and Alice were passengers on a commercial bus and suffered injuries, along with dozens of other passengers, when the bus crashed. They want compensation from the bus company for the bodily injuries they sustained. Must Linh, Gayatri, and Alice each file separate actions? Can they join together in a single action? Do they have to get all the other injured passengers to join in an action with them before they may proceed? What if they think both the bus company and a defect caused by the bus manufacturer contributed to their injuries? Can they name both the bus company and the manufacturer in a single action? Rule 20 answers these questions and provides the plaintiffs a great deal of flexibility regarding who may be plaintiffs and defendants.

Permissive Joinder Under Rule 20

Rule 20(a), set out in Exhibit 18.1, governs the permissive joinder of multiple plaintiffs and defendants. Rule 20 provides that multiple persons may join in one action as plaintiffs if they all assert a claim that arises out of "the same transaction, occurrence, or series of transactions or occurrences; and any question of law or fact common to all plaintiffs will arise in the action." The rule for joining multiple defendants is the mirror image of the rule for joining multiple plaintiffs. Multiple persons may all be joined as defendants if claims are asserted *against* each of

EXHIBIT 18.1 **Rule 20(a)**

(a) Persons Who May Join or Be Joined.
  (1) *Plaintiffs.* Persons may join in one action as plaintiffs if:
      (A) they assert any right to relief jointly, severally, or in the alternative with respect to or arising out of the same transaction, occurrence, or series of transactions or occurrences; and
      (B) any question of law or fact common to all plaintiffs will arise in the action.
  (2) *Defendants.* Persons—as well as a vessel, cargo, or other property subject to admiralty process in rem—may be joined in one action as defendants if:
      (A) any right to relief is asserted against them jointly, severally, or in the alternative with respect to or arising out of the same transaction, occurrence, or series of transactions or occurrences; and
      (B) any question of law or fact common to all defendants will arise in the action.

them that arise out of "the same transaction, occurrence, or series of transactions or occurrences; and any question of law or fact common to all defendants will arise in the action." Ordinarily, if the same transaction or occurrence standard is met, so too is the common question of law or fact standard. This is so because when claims arise out of the same transaction, a party can generally identify at least one fact or legal issue that will have to be addressed for both claims to be resolved. Thus, to determine if multiple plaintiffs are properly joined, the first question to ask is whether or not they all assert a claim that arises out of the same transaction or occurrence. For multiple defendants, ask first whether or not claims asserted against each arise out of the same transaction or occurrence. If the answer to this first question is yes, the answer to the second question in the analysis — are there questions of law or fact common to both claims? — is also likely to be yes.

Think back to the example at the beginning of this section. Under Rule 20, Linh, Gayatri, and Alice may join as plaintiffs in a single action against the bus company because each of them will assert a claim for personal injury damages against the bus company that arises out of the same occurrence, the bus crash. The plaintiffs' claims will share common questions of fact; e.g., what caused the bus crash? And likely common questions of law; e.g., is the bus company liable for the driver's negligence? This example likely involves a number of common questions of both law *and* fact, but note that the second part of the joinder inquiry requires only a common question of law *or* fact. Also note that Rule 20 doesn't require all the questions arising as part of the plaintiffs' claims to be common. These plaintiffs are properly joined even though there are likely to be questions unique to each of them, such as the nature and extent of their injuries.

Now suppose that the plaintiffs believe that a defect in the bus's fuel line contributed to their injuries. Linh, Gayatri, and Alice could sue both the bus company and the manufacturer of the bus's fuel line in a single action because their claims against both defendants arise out of the same occurrence, the bus crash. Again, there would also be questions of law or fact common to the claims against both defendants. Notice that these defendants are properly joined, even though the legal theories pressed against the defendants are probably quite different. The theory against the bus company is likely to be simple negligence, while the claim against the manufacturer will be a product liability theory. The joinder inquiry focuses on whether both claims arise from the same transaction or occurrence and whether there are common questions, not on the legal theories asserted.

Remember, Rule 20 allows Linh, Gayatri, and Alice to join as plaintiffs in a single suit and to join both the bus company and the bus manufacturer as defendants in that suit, but Rule 20 doesn't require them to do so. Linh, Gayatri, and Alice could each file their own suits against the bus company and the bus manufacturer. Or they could each file two suits (for a total of six), one against the bus company and one against the bus manufacturer. To be sure, there are good reasons not to proceed this way — inefficiency being one — but Rule 20 doesn't require them to join together as plaintiffs, nor does it require them to join all persons as defendants who might be responsible for their harm. Recall also that Linh, Gayatri, and Alice weren't the only passengers injured in the bus crash. They could but don't need to invite other passengers to join the action as plaintiffs.

Practical and Strategic Considerations

It bears repeating: Like most joinder rules, Rule 20 speaks in terms of what the plaintiffs *may* do, not what they *must* do. Both practical and strategic considerations play an enormous role in how plaintiffs actually choose to use Rule 20. Multiple plaintiffs may choose to join in one action rather than filing individual ones in order to reduce the costs of litigation. Joining together might make it easier for the plaintiffs to share attorneys and expert witnesses. They may join multiple defendants in a single action so that the defendants blame each other for the plaintiff's harm. This puts the plaintiff in the enviable position of being able to tell the judge and jury, "The defendants agree they wronged me; they just don't agree which one of them wronged me." In contrast, suing them separately allows each defendant to blame the other, but the plaintiff can't recover in one action from a defendant that is named in a separate action. If the plaintiff sues the defendants in separate actions, he might wind up losing both, even though each defendant blamed the other in both actions! Sometimes a plaintiff may prefer a federal forum and will choose not to name a diversity-destroying defendant or other diversity-destroying plaintiffs.

The same transaction, occurrence, or series of transactions or occurrences standard is the key to permissive joinder of plaintiffs and defendants. *Hohlbein v. Heritage Mutual Insurance Company* explores the breadth and scope of this standard.

Case Preview

Hohlbein v. Heritage Mutual Insurance Company

As you read *Hohlbein*, consider the following questions:

1. How did the defendants raise the joinder issue, and what is the relief the defendants seek? Dismissal of certain plaintiffs? Or something else?
2. Why might the plaintiffs want to proceed together in a single action, and why might the defendants prefer four separate actions?
3. What are the advantages and disadvantages of permitting the plaintiffs to proceed in a single action?

Hohlbein v. Heritage Mutual Insurance Company
106 F.R.D. 73 (E.D. Wis. 1985)

MEMORANDUM AND ORDER

WARREN, District Judge

BACKGROUND

This action was initiated on January 31, 1985, when the plaintiffs, all individual residents of states other than Wisconsin, filed their complaint against the corporate defendant, which maintains its principal office in Sheboygan, Wisconsin. . . .

Although the complaint is framed in twelve discrete counts, each of the four individual plaintiffs articulates three, independent causes of action under parallel theories of false or reckless misrepresentation, fraud, and breach of promise. The factual basis common to the claims of all four plaintiffs is that each was purportedly contacted and interviewed by the defendant's representatives in connection with executive employment positions; that the defendant made material misrepresentations of fact and failed to disclose other material information with respect to those executive positions during the course of the respective interviews; and, specifically, that the plaintiffs were not advised that their employment with the corporate defendant would be subject to a probationary period.

At the same time, the particular circumstances under which each of the four plaintiffs was allegedly misled to his damage are unmistakably different. Plaintiff Norbert Hohlbein was purportedly interviewed by the defendant's representatives on various occasions in February of 1982 for the position of Vice President of Sales. Despite its apparent initial decision not to fill that position, the defendant allegedly renewed negotiations with this plaintiff from October through December of 1982, during which it made material misrepresentations of fact with respect to, among other things, the present performance of the duties of the Vice President of Sales; the nature and scope of the authority vested in the individual hired to fill that position; its intention regarding the promotion of that employee to the President's post; and the financial assistance to be provided to the prospective employee to facilitate his relocation to the State of Wisconsin — all representations made knowingly or with reckless disregard for the truth, or so the complaint charges. This plaintiff further claims that the defendant failed to disclose that his employment would be subject to a period of probation during which he could presumably be terminated at will — a failure of disclosure purposely undertaken to induce the plaintiff to accept the job offer.

Although this plaintiff apparently began his employment with the defendant on December 6, 1982, he resigned some two months later, on February 10, 1983, principally because he "was not given the duties and authority the defendant represented he would have and . . . was not provided the relocation assistance defendant represented would be provided. . . ." Plaintiffs' *Complaint* at 5 (January 31, 1985). Based on these claims, this plaintiff seeks $211,634.00 in actual damages, together with punitive damages in an amount not less than five times that sum.

By his discrete claims in the complaint, plaintiff Winston Howell states that he, too, was interviewed by the defendant for the position of Vice President of Sales, although on various occasions in April of 1981. During the course of those negotiations, the defendant's representatives allegedly made material misrepresentations with respect to both the authority and responsibility attendant upon the sales position and the corporation's expectations for the promotion and future responsibilities of the individual selected to fill that spot. This plaintiff claims that, in reliance on the defendant's representations, he began his employment on or about June 1, 1981, only to terminate some two months later, on or about August 6, 1981, upon discovering that the duties and authority of the sales vice presidency were not as the defendant's representatives had stated.

Like all of his co-plaintiffs, this party claims to have "sustained substantial damages . . . including but not limited to, loss of income, loss of future income, damage to his professional reputation, inconvenience, and emotional distress" all as direct and proximate result of the defendant's material misrepresentations and omissions. Plaintiffs' *Complaint* at 13 (January 31, 1985). Pursuant to his three counts of false or reckless misrepresentation, fraud, and breach of promise, he seeks actual damages in the amount of $104,070.00 and punitive damages totaling a sum not less than five times that figure.

Plaintiff James R. Beckey alleges that he applied for the position of Regional Claims Manager for the defendant and was interviewed for that job on various occasions in August and September of 1983. The material misrepresentations purportedly made to him during the course of his discussions with the defendant's representatives included certain guarantees with respect to the manager's responsibilities for overall claims administration and a promise that he would be paid temporary living expenses during the period of his relocation to Wisconsin. Like the others, he also charges that he was not notified that the conditions of his employment included an initial, probationary period.

Relying on the defendant's material misrepresentations and omissions, this plaintiff purportedly accepted the employment offer on or about October 3, 1983, and was thereafter advised that he would not be provided with the temporary living and pre-employment interview expenses to the extent previously indicated. He also charges that he was not accorded the duties and responsibilities of the position as described to him during the course of employment negotiations. Characterizing the defendant's material misrepresentations and omissions as willful, malicious, and in complete disregard for his rights, this plaintiff seeks actual damages totaling $102,500.00, together with punitive damages in a sum not less than five times that amount.

Finally, it is the principal allegation of plaintiff Edward White that he, too, was materially misled during interviews with the defendant, in his case, for the position of Training and Educational Specialist, conducted in the month of March of 1982. Among other things, those material misrepresentations allegedly included a promise that he would be responsible for supervising all of the defendant corporation's training activities when it moved to a new home office. Paralleling the charges of his co-plaintiffs, this party avers that his reliance on the defendant's various promises and concomitant failure to disclose the probationary nature of the employment relationship led him to accept the offered position in June of 1982. However, upon his entry of service, he was purportedly not given the position of Training Manager but was instead terminated some three months later, in September of 1982.

As a direct and proximate result of the defendant's material misrepresentations and omissions regarding the job, this plaintiff claims to have suffered damages, including losses attendant upon his move and sale of his previous home in New York, all in the amount of $143,750.00. In addition, he seeks punitive damages totaling not less than five times that figure. Collectively, the four plaintiffs also request the costs and disbursements of prosecuting this case and such other relief as the Court deems just and equitable.

By its answer of March 13, 1985, the defendant admits several of the principal jurisdictional and factual averments in the complaint but denies all material allegations of false or reckless misrepresentation, fraud, and breach of promise with respect to its employment of any of the four plaintiffs. . . .

Presently before the Court is the motion of the defendant, pursuant to Rule 20(a) and Rule 21 of the Federal Rules of Civil Procedure, to sever this action into four discrete lawsuits, one by each party-plaintiff. In support of its petition, the defendant recites the factual averments upon which the complaint is premised and concludes that none of the four plaintiffs' claims arise "out of the same transaction, occurrence, or series of transactions or occurrences," as prescribed by Rule 20(a). It also suggests, in the language of Rule 20(a) that there is no "question of law or fact common to all of these persons," as follows:

> . . . [N]one of the Plaintiffs were concurrently employed by Defendant. Moreover, with the exception of the Plaintiffs Hohlbein and Howell, both of whom served as Vice President of Sales, the positions held by the Plaintiffs were highly dissimilar. Indeed, it is manifest from Plaintiffs' Complaint that the only common aspect of these four men's lives is that each was employed, albeit briefly, by the Defendant. . . . [T]hat commonality is not sufficient to allow these four individuals to ban together as plaintiffs in a single action against Defendant.
>
> . . . Plaintiffs have not alleged any common transactions or occurrences which touch upon their separate claims. Instead, the only commonalities of Plaintiffs' claims are the legal theories upon which they allege a right to recovery, and the fact that all are proceeding against the same defendant. These commonalities, however, are wholly insufficient to support joinder.

Defendant's *Memorandum in Support of Motion to Sever* at 3 & 5 (March 22, 1985).

Invoking relevant authority on the circumstances under which joinder and severance are proper under Rule 20(a) and Rule 21, respectively, the movant also suggests that no legitimate interest in the promotion of judicial economy would be served if the action is prosecuted in its present form and, in fact, that the considerable likelihood of jury confusion strongly underscores the impropriety of trying the plaintiffs' discrete claims in one, consolidated proceeding.

Predictably, the plaintiffs take strong exception to the defendant's assertion that there does not exist sufficient commonality to permit consolidation of all of their claims in one action. The plaintiffs direct the Court's attention to these factual similarities between their discrete claims:

> Each of the plaintiffs are insurance executives. Each of the plaintiffs was contacted and interviewed by representatives of Defendant in connection with executive positions with the defendant company. Each of the plaintiffs allege that in connection with their interview and offers of employment representatives of the defendant made material misrepresentations of fact to each plaintiff and failed to disclose material facts to the plaintiffs; more specifically, each of the plaintiffs allege that notwithstanding the representations made by the representatives of defendant, the plaintiffs were not told that their employment with defendant company would be subject to a probationary period during which the defendant would determine whether the plaintiff was indeed the individual the defendant wished to employ.

Plaintiffs' *Memorandum in Opposition to Motion to Sever* at 1–2 (April 5, 1985).

Admitting to some factual dissimilarities between their discrete causes of action, the plaintiffs nonetheless maintain that the defendant-employer's treatment of each of them constitutes a "course of conduct" and an "on-going policy of material misrepresentations and fraud." Plaintiffs' *Memorandum in Opposition to Motion to Sever* at 2 (April 5, 1985). In further support of this position, the plaintiffs discuss numerous cases, principally in the area of employment discrimination, in which federal trial courts have ruled that the joinder of claims is appropriate, notwithstanding certain individual peculiarities of the plaintiffs' factual averments. Where, as here, the discrete causes of action all spring from a consistent pattern or practice of employment behavior on the part of a single defendant, the action is properly prosecuted and defended in a consolidated format, or so the plaintiffs conclude.

As demonstrated by the Court's discussion of this pending matter, it has carefully reviewed the plaintiffs' complaint and has considered at some length the opposing arguments articulated by the parties in support of and in opposition to the present motion. Although the Court opines that the question is a close one, it concludes, for the reasons set forth below, that the motion to sever the plaintiffs' claims should be denied.

RULE 20(a), RULE 21, AND THE DEFENDANT'S MOTION TO SEVER

As the parties to this action recognize, Rule 20(a) of the Federal Rules of Civil Procedure plainly establishes the right of all persons to "join in one action as plaintiffs if they assert any right to relief jointly, [severally], or in the alternative in respect of or arising out of the same transaction, occurrence, or series of transactions or occurrences and if any question of law or fact common to all these persons will arise in the action." The unmistakable purpose for the Rule is to promote trial convenience through the avoidance of multiple lawsuits, extra expense to the parties, and loss of time to the Court and the litigants appearing before it. *Anderson v. Frances I. duPont & Company,* 291 F. Supp. 705, 711 (D. Minn. 1968). Indeed, it is generally held that Rule 20(a) should be liberally interpreted and applied in practice when consistent with convenience in the disposition of litigation. *Kerr v. Enoch Pratt Free Library of Baltimore City,* 54 F. Supp. 514, 516 (D. Md. 1944), *reversed on other grounds,* 149 F.2d 212 (4th Cir.), *cert. denied,* 326 U.S. 721, 66 S. Ct. 26, 90 L. Ed. 427 (1946).

The Rule regarding permissive joinder of parties is wholly procedural in nature and does not create nor alter the substantive rights of the parties. *Fitch v. Firestone,* 173 F. Supp. 131, 133 (D.R.I. 1969). At the same time, there are two fundamental prerequisites for joinder under Rule 20(a) — namely, that the right to relief be asserted by each plaintiff relating to or arising out of the same transaction or occurrence or series of transactions or occurrences and that some question of law or fact common to all of the parties arise in the action. *Mosley v. General Motors Corporation,* 497 F.2d 1330, 1333 (8th Cir. 1974).

As the present movant accurately notes, the remedy for improper joinder is prescribed by Rule 21 of the Federal Rules of Civil Procedure, plainly establishing that "[a]ny claim against a party may be severed and proceeded with separately." Under this provision of the Rule, the determination of a motion to sever is committed to the broad discretion of the trial judge. *Bolling v. Mississippi Paper Company,* 86 F.R.D. 6, 8 (N.D. Miss. 1979). In fact, the powers of the trial court to sever unrelated claims and afford them separate treatment when to do so would promote the legitimate interests of some of the parties is well established. *American Fidelity Fire Insurance*

Company v. Construcciones Werl, Inc., 407 F. Supp. 164, 190 (D.V.I. 1975). The practical effect of severance of previously-joined claims is the creation of two or more separate actions. *Hess v. Gray,* 85 F.R.D. 15, 22 (N.D. Ill. 1979).

Applying these general standards to the circumstances of the present lawsuit, the Court opines that resolution of the parties' various claims would best be promoted if the action is litigated as it is now fashioned. Admittedly, there are several, material dissimilarities between the substantive allegations of the four plaintiffs; most notably, each was employed by the defendant at a different time and — with the exception of plaintiffs Hohlbein and Howell — occupied different positions in its corporate structure. Moreover, each accepted the defendant's employment offer based on discrete application and interview processes; subsequently, each was terminated — either voluntarily or involuntarily — at a different time and for what appears to be a different reason.

Nonetheless, the Court finds persuasive the plaintiffs' characterization of the defendant's actions as demonstrative of a continuing pattern or practice with respect to its employment of admittedly unrelated individuals. All of the developments upon which this consolidated action is premised took place within a two and one-half year period between April of 1981, when plaintiff Howell first interviewed for the position of Vice President of Sales, and October of 1983, when plaintiff Beckey accepted employment for what he thought would be the position of Regional Claims Manager. The particular circumstances under which each of the four plaintiffs interviewed for, began, and ultimately terminated employment with the defendant are, in the Court's view, sufficiently similar to overcome the peculiar temporal and factual dissimilarities that might otherwise justify severance.

Furthermore, each plaintiff alleges that the defendant's representatives failed to disclose the employer's policy requiring any newly-hired executive to complete a probationary period. The Court also notes that all plaintiffs claim to have sustained similar damages, including, in at least three cases, those losses attendant upon relocation to the State of Wisconsin. All of these factors together convince the Court that the present complaint does, indeed, arise out of the same series of transactions or occurrences and implicates questions of law or fact common to each of the named plaintiffs. The Court finds some precedential support for this conclusion in the authority advanced by the plaintiffs in opposition to the pending severance request. *See, e.g., King v. Ralston Purina Company,* 97 F.R.D. 477, 480–481 (W.D.N.C. 1983) (finding that, although the three plaintiffs worked in different places and in different divisions of the defendant company, their actions against that employer could be joined together in a single action where they each alleged a company-wide policy of age discrimination); *Mosley v. General Motors Corporation,* 497 F.2d 1330, 1333–1334 (8th Cir. 1974) (reversing trial court's severance order upon a finding that each of the ten plaintiffs had alleged like injuries as a result of the defendant-employer's purported policy of racial discrimination).

Finally, the Court feels strongly that any burden imposed upon the defendant in the consolidated trial of each of the plaintiffs' causes of action is far outweighed by the practical benefits likely to accrue to all players in the conservation of judicial, prosecutorial, and defensive resources. Likewise, the Court is unable to conclude, at this stage in the proceedings, that the specter of jury confusion is sufficiently ominous to justify wholesale severance of this matter into four, discrete lawsuits. As the case proceeds toward trial, the Court may find it appropriate to enter such pretrial orders as necessary to ensure that the several claims of the plaintiffs are presented to the jury in the clearest and most even-handed manner possible; to the extent that the Court shares with the parties this interest in developing an unobscure and transparent trial record, it will surely enlist the assistance of counsel in identifying the litigable issues and sharpening the presentations of their respective positions.

For the present, however, the Court simply cannot conclude that the interests of justice would be disserved if the action is permitted to proceed in its consolidated form. Rather, for the reasons stated above, the Court finds that severance of this matter into four, separate causes of action would, in the end, prove both unjustified and unwise. Accordingly, it will deny the defendant's motion for severance. . . .

Post-Case Follow-Up

Note that what's at issue in *Hohlbein* is whether or not to sever the action into separate actions. Rule 21 provides that "[m]isjoinder of parties is not a ground for dismissing an action." The proper remedy is to sever if the parties are not properly joined, or to add or drop parties as appropriate. The purpose of Rule 20 is to promote efficiency by avoiding a multiplicity of lawsuits, thereby conserving the resources of both the parties and the court. On the other hand, multiple parties to a single action whose claims have a number of factual dissimilarities raises a risk of confusing the jury. The decision to grant a motion to sever is striking a balance between efficiency on the one hand and avoiding confusion on the other. Even if claims and parties are properly joined, the court does not have to adjudicate them all together. And even if parties file multiple lawsuits based on a single event, this doesn't necessarily mean that all of the actions will be adjudicated separately. As you continue to study this chapter, be on the lookout for the tools a court has at its disposal to correct for the inefficiencies and confusion the joinder rules allow.

The "Shadow Rules of Joinder"

Does Rule 20 allow joinder too liberally? Does it always make sense to require no more than that the claims by multiple plaintiffs or against multiple defendants arise out of the same transaction or occurrence and share common questions? Even when this standard is met, the questions unique to each plaintiff or defendant might be the most complex and difficult. Suppose ten people file suit based on injuries and damages sustained in a plant explosion. Some of the plaintiffs suffered severe injuries, while others' injuries were minor, and still others incurred only property damage. The Rule 20 joinder standard is satisfied, but the individual questions as to the nature and extent of damages may predominate.

Professor Robin J. Effron has noted that some courts have

Hohlbein v. Heritage Mutual Insurance Company: *Real Life Applications*

Bajo, Inc. owns and operates deep injection wells around the country, including a deep injection well in West Texas, and charges other businesses in the petroleum industry a fee to dispose of liquid waste byproducts of oil and gas production by injecting them into a porous rock formation deep below the surface. The deep injection well is designed to trap the waste into the rock formation and allow it to spread laterally, but not up or down, as more waste is injected into the formation. Bajo has contracted with a separate company, HT Maintenance, LLC, to monitor the well's performance and to perform any necessary maintenance or repairs. More than 30 landowners who own separate parcels of land above the rock formation into which Bajo has injected waste over the years were concerned that the waste had escaped from the rock formation and had contaminated surface water on their properties (e.g., ponds, lakes, and stock tanks) and/or the water table on which they rely for residential drinking water and agricultural purposes. The landowners hired experts to test the water table and the surface water on their properties. The results of the testing revealed that all 30 landowners' properties may be contaminated with waste from the injection well. Three of the 30 landowners bring suit against Bajo and HT Maintenance seeking compensation for the damage to their property.

1. Bajo moves to dismiss the case because the three plaintiffs have not joined together with the other 27 landowners whose property may also have been contaminated. How should the court rule on the motion and why?

2. Of the three plaintiffs, one is a rancher who complains only about contamination to the water table he uses to provide drinking water to his cattle, one is a homeowner who complains about contamination to the water he pumps to the surface and uses for drinking and bathing in his home, and the third alleges contamination to his fishing pond located on his "weekend getaway ranch." Bajo's deep injection well in West Texas has been in operation for nearly ten years, and it appears that any contamination reached the three plaintiffs' properties at vastly different times. Bajo moves to sever the plaintiffs' action into three separate actions. What arguments should Bajo make in support of its motion? What argument should the plaintiffs make in response?

3. The plaintiffs' allegations against Bajo state that Bajo failed to properly assess whether or not the rock formation into which they drilled the well could trap the waste. Their allegations against HT Maintenance state that it failed to properly maintain and repair the well. HT Maintenance moves to sever on the ground that the defendants are improperly joined because "the plaintiffs' allegations against the defendants are based on entirely different conduct that occurred at different times." Should the court grant the motion to sever? Why or why not?

---

developed "shadow rules" to require more than mere "same transaction or occurrence" and "commonality." She writes:

> Implied predominance is a shadow rule used to interpret the rules containing the "common question of law or fact" standard for commonality. It occurs when courts recognize the presence of both common and uncommon issues between a set of claims or parties but require that the common issues outweigh or predominate over the uncommon issues.

Robin J. Effron, *The Shadow Rules of Joinder*, 100 Geo. L.J. 759, 789 (2012) (internal citations omitted).

Can you see benefits of bringing this rule out of the shadows and adding it to Rule 20? Is there a downside? Would it be more appropriately applied to some kinds of cases and not others? If so, to what kind of cases should the Rule be applied?

2. Joining Third-Party Defendants

Rule 20 does not authorize defendants to add anyone as a party. Rule 14, however, does under certain circumstances. Rule 14 governs the joinder of third-party defendants. Under Rule 14(a)(1), set out in Exhibit 18.2, a **third-party defendant** is a person who is or may be liable to a defending party (often but not always a defendant) for all or part of the claim against the defending party. Suppose in our bus crash example that Linh, Gayatri, and Alice join as plaintiffs in a single action, but they name only the bus company as a defendant, not the manufacturer of the bus, even though its fuel line may have contributed to their injuries. Recall that Rule 20 allows but does not require the plaintiffs to join both the bus company and the manufacturer in a single lawsuit. So Linh, Gayatri, and Alice have not violated any joinder rule by not joining the bus manufacturer as a defendant. However, as the only defendant, the bus company is facing the possibility of paying damages for which the bus manufacturer may share responsibility. As a result, the bus company may join the manufacturer as a third-party defendant, because it may be liable for all or part of the plaintiffs' claims against the bus company. **Impleader** is another name for joining a third-party defendant. To implead the bus manufacturer, the bus company will serve a third-party complaint and summons on the bus manufacturer. The bus company now wears two hats: It is both a defendant as to the passengers and a third-party plaintiff as to the manufacturer, who is now called a third-party defendant.

Joinder of a third-party defendant must be based on a claim that the third-party defendant is liable to the third-party plaintiff *for all or part of the claim against the third-party plaintiff*. The third-party defendant's liability is contingent upon resolution of the claim against the defending party/third-party plaintiff. In federal court, it is proper to bring a third-party defendant into the case only when the defending party can pass on or share its own liability with the third-party defendant. By filing a third-party complaint, the defendant is saying, in essence, "If I have to pay the plaintiff in this case, this third-party defendant should have to pay me back or share my costs." A defending party can't implead a third-party defendant by claiming that the third-party defendant is the one who should pay the plaintiff instead of the defendant. Put simply, the defending party can't say, "It's the third-party plaintiff's responsibility to pay the plaintiff, not mine." In our bus crash example, this standard is met because the manufacturer may be liable to the bus company if the

EXHIBIT 18.2   Rule 14(a)(1)

> (a) When a Defending Party May Bring in a Third Party.
>   (1) *Timing of the Summons and Complaint.* A defending party may, as third-party plaintiff, serve a summons and complaint on a nonparty who is or may be liable to it for all or part of the claim against it. But the third-party plaintiff must, by motion, obtain the court's leave if it files the third-party complaint more than 14 days after serving its original answer.

bus company is liable to the plaintiffs. The two most common scenarios involving impleader are contribution and indemnity. In most states, a defendant has a right to **contribution** from other people who may have helped cause or contributed to the harm. **Indemnification** is a situation in which a defendant is entitled to be fully reimbursed for any damages it has to pay (for example, based on a written indemnity agreement or from an insurance company).

If, however, the defending party tries to assert a claim that is separate and independent from the claim against the defending party, impleader is improper. The most common example of this is when the defendant impleads a party in order to recover only for his own injuries. Suppose instead that the bus company sought to implead a gas company for overcharging it for fuel for the trip (a claim that has no bearing on the accident or injury involving the plaintiff). Impleader would not be proper based on this claim because it is separate and independent from the plaintiffs' claims against the bus company. The gas company's liability for this claim does not depend on how the court resolves the plaintiffs' action for personal injuries. The bus company could file a separate action against the gas company asserting this claim, but joining the manufacturer as a third-party defendant is not proper on this basis.

Consider another example. Suppose Carlos, Brenna, and Albert are involved in a car wreck when Carlos rear-ends Brenna's car, which in turn pushes Brenna's car into Albert's car. Both Brenna and Albert's cars are damaged. Below is a diagram of the car wreck.

Carlos   Brenna   Albert

Assume Albert sues only Brenna for the damage to his car. Brenna could implead Carlos based on a claim that Carlos is responsible for all or part of Albert's claim against Brenna; i.e., that he caused the damage to Albert's car when he collided with Brenna and pushed her car into Albert's car (so Carlos must pay Brenna if she has to pay Albert). However, Brenna could not implead Carlos solely on a claim that Carlos was responsible only for the damage to Brenna's car. This claim is not dependent upon the resolution of Albert's claim against Brenna. She is trying to recover only for her own injuries.

B. CLAIM JOINDER: ADDING CLAIMS TO THE SUIT

The first section of this chapter addressed the permissive party joinder rules and explained how plaintiffs, defendants, and third-party defendants become parties to the action. This section addresses the claim joinder rules. It focuses on the claims that persons who are already parties to the suit may assert against one another. Understanding claim joinder requires an understanding of counterclaims and crossclaims under Rule 13, and joining multiple claims under Rule 18.

1. Joining Counterclaims

A **counterclaim** is a claim against an opposing party. A party asserting a counterclaim is a counter-plaintiff (and is sometimes referred to as a counterclaimant), and the party against whom the claim is asserted is a counter-defendant. The most common example of a counterclaim is a defendant asserting a claim against a plaintiff. Suppose two cars collide in an intersection and the drivers of both cars are injured. Each blames the other for the car accident and the injury. The driver who becomes the plaintiff in the action is the one who wins the race to the courthouse and files suit first. The defendant driver could then assert a counterclaim against the plaintiff driver to recover his own damages. The black arrow in the diagram below identifies the counterclaim.

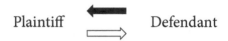

Plaintiff   Defendant

Although a defendant asserting a claim against a plaintiff is the classic example of a counterclaim, it is not the only example of a counterclaim. A party asserts a counterclaim any time he asserts a claim against a party who has already asserted a claim against him.

In contrast, a **crossclaim** is a claim by a party against another party who has not already asserted a claim against that party. Suppose that three cars collide in an intersection and all three drivers blame each other for their injuries. Driver 1 files suit against Drivers 2 and 3, making Driver 1 a plaintiff and Drivers 2 and 3 both defendants. Driver 2 could assert a counterclaim against Driver 1 seeking recovery of his damages, and he could also (as we'll discuss shortly) assert a crossclaim against Driver 3. If Driver 3 then asserts a claim for his damages against Driver 2, that claim is a counterclaim, not a crossclaim, because Driver 3 is asserting a claim against someone who has already asserted a claim against him. This distinction in terms may seem technical, but it is important to understand because the test that governs when counterclaims may be asserted and the test for when a crossclaim is proper are different in ways that can matter. The green arrow identifies the crossclaim and the black arrows identify both counterclaims in the diagram below.

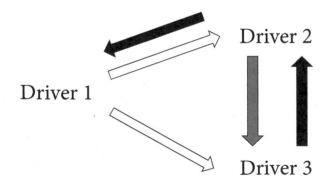

Driver 2

Driver 1

Driver 3

Compulsory and Permissive Counterclaims

There are two types of counterclaims — compulsory counterclaims under Rule 13(a) (that must be asserted or they are lost) and permissive counterclaims under Rule 13(b) (that may be asserted, but could also be asserted in a separate action). Rules 13(a) and (b) are set out in Exhibit 18.3. Compulsory counterclaims arise out of the same transaction or occurrence as the claim against the counterclaimant. Permissive counterclaims do not arise out of the same transaction or occurrence as the claim against the counterclaimant. Thus, all counterclaims may properly be joined under Rule 13. In other words, a party may assert any claim it has against an opposing party, even if it is wholly unrelated to the claim against the counterclaimant. So in our three car collision example diagramed above, Driver 2 could assert a counterclaim against Driver 1 arising out of the car wreck, or he could assert an unrelated breach of contract claim against Driver 1, or he could assert both claims. Both counterclaims could be properly joined as part of this case. The same principle applies to Driver 3's counterclaims against Driver 2.

The distinction between permissive and compulsory counterclaims, however, remains important. Both compulsory and permissive counterclaims are properly joined, but compulsory counterclaims generally *must* be asserted in the action, subject to some exceptions set out in Rule 13(a)(2), while permissive counterclaims *may but need not* be asserted in the action. Consider again Driver 2's counterclaim against Driver 1 arising out the car wreck that is the subject of Driver 1's claim against Driver 2. Driver 2 *must* assert his counterclaim arising out of the car wreck because it is a compulsory counterclaim. If he fails to assert this compulsory counterclaim, he will be prohibited from asserting that claim in a separate lawsuit. Driver 2 may assert any other claims he has against Driver 1 that do not arise out of the car wreck, but he does not have to do so. He has the option to assert them in separate lawsuits because they are permissive counterclaims.

EXHIBIT 18.3   Rule 13(a) and (b)

(a) Compulsory Counterclaim.
   (1) *In General.* A pleading must state as a counterclaim any claim that — at the time of its service — the pleader has against an opposing party if the claim:
      (A) arises out of the transaction or occurrence that is the subject matter of the opposing party's claim; and
      (B) does not require adding another party over whom the court cannot acquire jurisdiction.
   (2) *Exceptions.* The pleader need not state the claim if:
      (A) when the action was commenced, the claim was the subject of another pending action; or
      (B) the opposing party sued on its claim by attachment or other process that did not establish personal jurisdiction over the pleader on that claim, and the pleader does not assert any counterclaim under this rule.
(b) Permissive Counterclaim. A pleading may state as a counterclaim against an opposing party any claim that is not compulsory.

Note that Rule 13(a)(1) defines a counterclaim as compulsory only so long as it does not require adding another party over whom the court cannot acquire jurisdiction. Required parties are discussed in the next chapter, but for now understand that if the adjudication of the counterclaim requires an additional party that the court cannot compel to become a party (i.e., has personal jurisdiction over), then the counterclaim is not compulsory and can be brought in a separate action. Rule 13(a)(2) also provides that a compulsory counterclaim need not be asserted if it has already been asserted in a separate action.

2. Joining Crossclaims

Rule 13(g), set out in Exhibit 18.4, governs the assertion of crossclaims. A **crossclaim** is a claim by one party against a co-party who has not asserted a claim against the crossclaimant. A crossclaim must arise out of the transaction or occurrence that is the subject of the original action (filed by the plaintiff or plaintiffs) or of a counterclaim asserted in the action. Perhaps the most common example of a crossclaim is a defendant asserting a claim against a codefendant. But there are other examples of a crossclaim as well. Suppose a defendant, acting as a third-party plaintiff, joins two third-party defendants. A claim by one third-party defendant against the other would also be a crossclaim under Rule 13(g), and must arise out of the same transaction or occurrence as the original action by the plaintiff. Rule 13(g) provides that a crossclaim may assert that the co-party is or may be liable for all or part of the claim against the crossclaimant. This standard should sound familiar, because it is the same standard for joining a third-party defendant. The difference is that there is no need for the defendant to join the person as a third-party defendant, because the plaintiff has already made the person a party as a defendant. As is true for third-party claims, crossclaims may be used to assert a claim for indemnification or contribution against a co-party.

Suppose that Hakeem is injured when a chemical plant near his home explodes. Hakeem files suit against both ChemStor, Inc., the owner of the chemical plant that exploded, and against ChemGen, LLC, the original manufacturer of the chemicals that may have caused the explosion due to a defect in the composition of the chemicals. Under Rule 13(g), ChemStor could assert a crossclaim against ChemGen for the property damage to its chemical plant because that claim arises out of the same occurrence as Hakeem's claim, the explosion at the chemical plant. Rule 13(g) also allows ChemStor to assert as a crossclaim a claim that ChemGen is responsible

EXHIBIT 18.4 **Rule 13(g)**

> (g) Crossclaim Against a Coparty. A pleading may state as a crossclaim any claim by one party against a coparty if the claim arises out of the transaction or occurrence that is the subject matter of the original action or of a counterclaim, or if the claim relates to any property that is the subject matter of the original action. . . .

for all or part of Hakeem's claim against ChemStor because its defective chemical caused the explosion that injured Hakeem. Thus, Rule 13(g) allows the crossclaimant to recover both for his own damages and for all or part of the damages for which he may be adjudged otherwise responsible in the original action.

3. Claims Between Plaintiffs and Third-Party Defendants

When a third-party defendant has been added to a lawsuit, the question often arises as to what claims that third-party defendant may assert, and what claims may be asserted against this new party by parties other than the defending party who joined the third-party defendant. Rule 14(a) authorizes the joinder of certain claims between plaintiffs and third-party defendants. Under Rule 14(a), a third-party defendant may assert any claim against the plaintiff that arises out of the same transaction or occurrence as the plaintiff's claim against the third-party plaintiff (a/k/a the defendant). Rule 14(a) also authorizes the plaintiff to assert any claim against the third-party defendant that arises out of the same transaction or occurrence as the plaintiff's claim against the third-party plaintiff. This standard is similar to Rule 13(g)'s standard for joining crossclaims, but unlike Rule 13(g), it does not permit joinder of a claim that arises out of the same transaction or occurrence as a counterclaim asserted in the action.

Suppose that in the chemical plant explosion example, Hakeem files suit seeking compensation for his injuries, but he names only ChemStor as a defendant. ChemStor impleads ChemGen as a third-party defendant claiming that ChemGen is responsible for all or part of Hakeem's injuries. Hakeem could then assert a claim for his personal injury damages against ChemGen under Rule 14(a) because his claim against ChemGen (the third-party defendant) arises out of the same occurrence (the explosion) as his claim against ChemStor (the third-party plaintiff who impleaded ChemGen).

4. Joining Multiple Claims Against an Opposing Party

Rule 18, set out in Exhibit 18.5, governs the joinder of multiple claims against an opposing party. In particular, it explains when a party asserting a claim (of whatever type) against another party may assert, alongside that claim, other claims the party may have against the same opposing party. The Rule provides that "[a] party

---

EXHIBIT 18.5   **Rule 18(a) Joinder of "Tag Along" Claims**

(a) In General. A party asserting a claim, counterclaim, crossclaim, or third-party claim may join, as independent or alternative claims, as many claims as it has against an opposing party.

asserting a claim, counterclaim, crossclaim, or third-party claim may join, as independent or alternate claims, as many claims as it has against an opposing party." In other words, under Rule 18, if a party is making a properly joined claim under one of the Rules discussed above, he may also join any other claims he has against the opposing party, even if wholly unrelated to the other claims asserted. Importantly, joinder of claims under Rule 18 is permissive, not compulsory. Parties may assert them in the current lawsuit or a separate suit.

Students sometimes read Rule 18 as dispensing with all of the party and claim joinder rules this chapter has already addressed. Rule 18 is broad, but not quite that broad. Rule 18 must be understood to work alongside the other party and claim joinder rules. It authorizes a party asserting a properly joined claim, counterclaim, crossclaim, or third-party claim to also join along with it *any other claim* the party has against the opposing party. But Rule 18 requires at least one claim between the parties that is properly joined under another rule. An example will help illustrate this limitation.

Suppose Jones, Ortiz, and Chen are involved in a car accident. Jones files suit against both Ortiz and Chen seeking compensation for the bodily injuries he sustained in the wreck. Also suppose that Ortiz asserts a claim against Chen for the injuries he sustained in the same car wreck. The case looks like this.

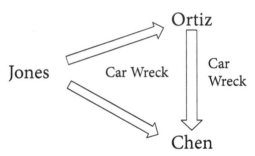

The claim by Ortiz against Chen is properly joined. It is a crossclaim because it is a claim against a co-party who has not asserted a claim against the crossclaimant. As a crossclaim, it must arise out of the same transaction or occurrence that is the subject of the original action. Here that standard is met because both the original action and the crossclaim arise out of the same car wreck.

Now suppose Ortiz has known Chen for a long time and that Chen owes Ortiz money under a written contract for the sale of some office furniture. Ortiz wants to recover the money Chen owes him; so, he asserts another claim for breach of contract against Chen. Now the case looks like this.

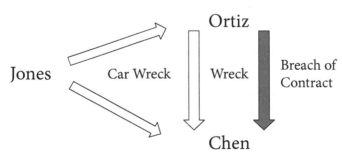

Ortiz's breach of contract claim is properly joined under Rule 18. Because he is also asserting a properly joined crossclaim, Rule 18 permits him to join any other claims he has against Chen, even if the claim is wholly unrelated to the original action and the crossclaim. Rule 18 allows unrelated claims to "tag along" with other properly joined claims, counterclaims, crossclaims, and third-party claims.

Importantly, Ortiz could not assert *only* the breach of contract claim against Chen. The breach of contract claim isn't a properly joined crossclaim (as it does not arise out of the same transaction or occurrence as the original action, the car wreck) and it would not be tagging along with a properly joined claim.

Recall our earlier three-car accident example from the discussion of impleading third-party defendants, wherein Carlos rear-ends Brenna's car, which in turn pushes Brenna's car into Albert's car. Both Brenna and Albert's cars are damaged. Albert filed suit only against Brenna. What we said earlier remains true. Brenna could implead Carlos based on a claim that Carlos is responsible for all or part of Albert's claim against Brenna, but Brenna could not implead Carlos solely on a claim that Carlos was responsible only for the damage to Brenna's car. However, if Brenna impleads Carlos based on a claim that Carlos is responsible for all or part of Albert's claim against Brenna, Rule 18 would allow Brenna to join with it a claim for her own damages as well. She cannot bring the claim for her own damages by itself, but it can tag along with the proper third-party claim.

Consider another example. Suppose in our earlier plant explosion example that Hakeem again sues both ChemStor and ChemGen for recovery of personal injury damages caused by the explosion. Now suppose that ChemStor asserts a claim in the action against ChemGen for trademark infringement, alleging that ChemGen's tradename and logo is too similar to ChemStor's. This claim is not properly joined under Rule 13(g), because it is a crossclaim but does not arise out of the same transaction or occurrence as Hakeem's claim based on the plant explosion. But if ChemStor instead asserted a claim against ChemGen for the property damage the chemicals caused, this would be a properly joined crossclaim, and under Rule 18, ChemStor could assert any other claim it has against ChemGen, including the trademark infringement claim.

Suppose instead that Hakeem names only ChemStor as a defendant. ChemStor could not implead ChemGen based on the trademark infringement claim (since this is an independent claim that ChemStor is asserting, and not an attempt to pass on liability that ChemStor may face in Hakeem's personal injury suit). ChemStor could, however, implead ChemGen claiming it was responsible for all or part of Hakeem's claim against ChemStor, and could also assert, under Rule 18, the trademark infringement claim.

One effect of Rule 18 is that a single plaintiff can join as many claims as he has against a single defendant, even if the claims do not arise out of the same transaction or occurrence. Rule 18 does not however displace Rule 20's requirement for the joinder of multiple plaintiffs and defendants. Under Rule 20, for two people to join as plaintiffs, they must both assert a claim that arises out of the same transaction or occurrence. For example, if two plaintiffs were to join together to bring one suit against a defendant, but one plaintiff asserted only a claim for personal injury damages against him and the other plaintiff asserted only a claim for breach of contract against him based on unrelated facts, the plaintiffs would be improperly joined under Rule 20. Rule 18 does not change that result. On the other hand, suppose instead that both plaintiffs suing the defendant were each asserting a claim for personal injury damages arising out of the same car wreck. Here, the plaintiffs are properly joined. In the second example, moreover, Rule 18 would allow both of them to assert any other claims they have against the defendant, even if wholly unrelated to the car wreck.

As these examples make clear, Rule 18's liberal approach to joining claims — which permits the parties who are properly in litigation to use that suit to resolve all existing disputes between them — comes into play only when there is, within a given case, actually a proper dispute between any given set of parties in the case. The impetus, in the Federal Rules, toward broad joinder of claims is thus not unlimited, though it is quite broad (and can, in some ways, seem arbitrary in some applications). Remember as well that a court always has the power, even when unrelated claims are properly joined, to sequence or separate them for trial or discovery purposes as further discussed below.

5. Misjoinder of Parties and Claims

Misjoinder means a party or claim is not properly joined. When misjoinder occurs, the court does not dismiss the action. Instead, Rule 21 authorizes the court to drop parties from the action who are not properly joined. The court, however, will continue to adjudicate the remainder of the action. If a claim is not properly joined, Rule 21 authorizes a court to sever from the action the improperly joined claim and proceed with the rest of the action.

6. Addressing Inefficiency and Confusion: Consolidation, Joint Hearings, Severance, and Separate Trials

 "Killing two birds with one stone" is a way of saying that a single action is efficient because it solves two disputes at the same time. The joinder rules can certainly allow courts to kill two (or more) birds with a single stone, such as when multiple plaintiffs join together in a single action to assert claims arising out of the same transaction or occurrence. On the other hand, because joinder is rarely compulsory, the parties' use of the joinder rules can also put courts in the position of having to throw multiple stones at a single bird, such as when multiple lawsuits arising out of a single event are filed. Rule 42(a) provides district courts with tools to correct for the inefficiencies that might arise from how parties choose to use the joinder rules. The district court can order consolidation of separate civil actions that share common questions of law or fact. A **consolidation order** consolidates two or more civil actions into a single action. Alternatively, a court can order **joint hearings or trials** when multiple civil actions share a common question of law or fact. An order requiring joint hearings or trials preserves the civil actions as separate actions, but it allows the court to hold hearings or trials for all the actions at the same time. For example, the court could order that all pretrial discovery hearings for the related cases will be conducted jointly. So the court has tools it can use to correct for inefficiencies, but inefficiency is not the only problem the parties' use of the joinder rules can cause.

The joinder rules can also allow parties to assert unrelated claims in a single case — permissive counterclaims and some Rule 18 claims, for example — but trying unrelated claims together may cause prejudice to one or more parties or confusion to the jury. Just because the parties join multiple claims in a single action does not guarantee that these claims will all be decided in a single trial. Rule 42(b) gives the district court broad discretion to order separate trials of one or more separate issues, claims, crossclaims, counterclaims, or third-party claims. Separate trials would avoid requiring a jury to simultaneously decide, for example, both a personal injury claim and a wholly unrelated breach of contract counterclaim. Separate trials can also avoid prejudice to a party by ensuring that evidence relevant to one claim that might be highly inflammatory is not introduced against the party when resolving another claim to which the evidence is irrelevant.

Chapter Summary

- Plaintiffs may join in a single action if each of them asserts a claim arising out of the same transaction or occurrence or series of transactions or occurrences, and any question of law or fact common to all plaintiffs will arise in the action. Defendants may be joined in one action if a claim is asserted against each one of them that satisfies the transaction or occurrence and common question requirements.
- A defending party may implead a person and bring that person into the case as a third-party defendant when the person may be liable for at least part of the claim against the defending party.
- Counterclaims are claims against opposing parties and are properly joined, whether or not related to the opposing party's claim. Compulsory counterclaims — those arising out of the same transaction or occurrence as the claim against the counterclaimant — generally must be joined and may not be brought later in a separate action. Permissive counterclaims may be joined but alternatively could be brought later in a separate action.
- Crossclaims are claims against co-parties. A crossclaim must arise out of the same transaction or occurrence that is the subject of the original action or of a counterclaim to be properly joined. Crossclaims are permissive and may also be brought in a separate action.
- A party asserting a claim, counterclaim, crossclaim, or third-party claim may join with it any other claim he has against an opposing party.

Applying the Concepts

Fifteen passengers on a ferry boat incurred damages when the ferry ran aground. Some of the passengers were injured, others had their property damaged or destroyed, and some suffered both property damage and physical injuries. The ferry is owned by Aquatic Transport, Inc. and operated by Marine Pilots, LLC. Assume, under the applicable state law, two defendants whose conduct separately contributed to causing an injury are each liable to the plaintiff for the full damages, but may be sued by each other to share those costs if only one is sued. The passengers wish to bring suit to recover for the physical injuries they sustained in the accident.

1. Must all 15 passengers join together as plaintiffs in a single suit? Why or why not?

2. May all 15 passengers join together as plaintiffs in a single suit? Why or why not?

3. May the plaintiffs involved in the ferry accident join both Aquatic Transport and Marine Pilots as defendants in one action? Why or why not?

4. Assume Marine Pilots and Aquatic Transport have been named as defendants in an action arising out of the ferry accident. Marine Pilots believes that a malfunctioning piece of equipment called a depth finder may have caused the captain to navigate the ship into shallow waters. The depth finder is manufactured by Precision, Inc. What, if anything, can Marine Pilots do to ensure that Precision bears its share of responsibility?

5. Assume that all 15 passengers file a single action against both Aquatic Transport and Marine Pilots. Some passengers assert claims for physical injuries and others assert claims only for damage or destruction to their property. Aquatic Transport and Marine Pilots are concerned that having to decide both personal injury and property damage claims in a single trial may confuse the jury. They are also concerned that the evidence of severe physical injuries offered to prove the personal injury claims, including gruesome photos and medical testimony, may prejudice the jury against them on the claims for damage to and destruction of property. What if anything can Aquatic Transport and Marine Pilots do to avoid this potential for confusion and prejudice?

Civil Procedure in Practice

A married couple on their honeymoon is severely injured in a helicopter crash while on an aerial tour of volcanoes in Hawaii. They file suit against the owner and operator of the crashed helicopter, Hawaiian Helo, LLC, alleging negligence on the part of the pilot. They also file suit against North American Helicopter Company, Inc., the manufacturer of the crashed helicopter, alleging that a defect in the rotors of the helicopter contributed to causing the crash. Assume, under the applicable state law, two defendants whose conduct separately contributed to causing an injury are each liable to the plaintiff for the full damages, but may be sued by each other to share those costs if only one is sued. You represent North American Helicopter Company. The allegedly defective rotors were designed and manufactured by Flight Hardware, LLC.

1. What action might you take, as North American Helicopter's counsel, with respect to Flight Hardware in the honeymooners' suit against your client?

2. Assume Flight Hardware is still not a party to the action. Your client informs you that it is in a $20 million dispute over a parts supply contract with Flight Hardware. For business reasons, your client may not want to complicate this dispute by asserting a claim related to the helicopter crash against Flight Hardware in the married couple's action. On the other hand, it may want to assert a claim for breach of the parts supply contract in the helicopter crash action. Your client asks you if it must make Flight Hardware a party to the action and assert the claim related to the helicopter crash in the married couple's action, or if it could wait and file it later. Could it make Flight Hardware a party and assert only the breach of the parts supply contract claim? Could it make Flight Hardware a party and assert both claims?

Complex Party Joinder

19

As we saw in the last chapter, who does and does not become a party to a civil action is a matter the Rules leave largely to the plaintiffs and defendants. For the most part, the joinder rules leave a plaintiff free to file suit on his own or join together with others who have a claim arising out of the same events. Plaintiffs decide whom to name as defendants, and have no obligation to name everyone who might be responsible for their harm. The joinder rules allow but do not require a defendant to join a third-party defendant who might be responsible for the claim against the defendant. Although they have broad authority to determine who is and who is not a party to the action, plaintiffs and defendants do not have complete control over party joinder. This chapter addresses procedures that are implicated far less often than the basic party joinder rules from the last chapter, but which can have a major impact on the resolution of the action when they are implicated.

Unlike the procedures discussed in the last chapter, Rule 19 *requires* the joinder of persons as parties under certain circumstances. It requires the joinder of persons who are not parties (i.e., are absentees) but who are so important to a fair adjudication of the dispute that they must be made parties to the suit. Rule 24 allows a nonparty to become a party by intervening, even though the intervenor was not originally joined by either the plaintiff or defendant. In other cases, the basic party and claim joinder rules simply do not adequately address the complex issues involved. Perhaps there are too many claimants to join as plaintiffs in a single

Key Concepts

- When a person is a required party under Rule 19 and what might prevent a court from joining a required party
- Intervention and when a court *must* allow it and *may* allow it
- Interpleader and when a plaintiff may interplead defendants
- The prerequisites for certification of a class action and the three types of class actions under Rule 23

action, and therefore the dispute should be resolved through a class action. The interpleader joinder rule allows a party to avoid multiple suits in order to prevent harm to himself or other claimants to a fund or property the party holds.

A. REQUIRED JOINDER OF PARTIES UNDER RULE 19

Rule 19 governs required joinder of parties. Some persons are so important to a fair resolution of the dispute that Rule 19 requires them to be made parties if it is feasible to do so. Rule 19 refers to such a person as a **required party**. If joinder of the required party is feasible, the court makes the person a party (if the person refuses to join voluntarily). If the joinder of a required party is not feasible, the court must decide either to dismiss the action or continue without the required party. If the court decides it must dismiss the action, the person is considered an indispensable party, because the litigation cannot proceed without him. Rule 19 sets out a three-step process for addressing the required joinder of an absentee. First, the court must determine whether the absentee is a required party under the test in Rule 19(a). Second, if the person is a required party, the court must determine whether joinder is feasible (whether the party can be joined without depriving the court of subject matter or personal jurisdiction). Third, if joinder of the required party is not feasible, the court must determine whether to dismiss the entire action or continue without the absentee.

1. Determining Whether or Not a Person Is a Required Party

Rule 19(a), set out in Exhibit 19.1, requires the court to join a required party if it is feasible. A person is a required party when the person meets the terms of either Rule 19(a)(1)(A) or 19(a)(1)(B). As discussed further below, relatively few persons are required parties as the Rules define this term. Only in fairly specialized circumstances will a court conclude that a nonparty should or must be part of the case.

Courts Cannot Accord Complete Relief to Existing Parties

Rule 19(a)(1)(A) is based on the harm failing to join the absentee will do to existing parties. It provides that a person is a required party if "in that person's absence, the court cannot accord complete relief among existing parties." One important point to understand at the outset: Joint tortfeasors are not required parties. As discussed in the previous chapter, the plaintiff need not join as defendants all the persons who are responsible for his harm. This provision of Rule 19 is implicated when the plaintiff seeks relief from the court that the defendant does not have the authority or ability to provide, even if ordered by the court to do so. For example, in *Focus on the Family v. Pinellas Suncoast Transit Authority*, an evangelical organization filed a civil rights action against a public transit authority to challenge on First Amendment grounds certain content-based

EXHIBIT 19.1   **Rule 19(a)**

(a) Persons Required to Be Joined if Feasible.
  (1) *Required Party.* A person who is subject to service of process and whose joinder will not deprive the court of subject-matter jurisdiction must be joined as a party if:
    (A) in that person's absence, the court cannot accord complete relief among existing parties; or
    (B) that person claims an interest relating to the subject of the action and is so situated that disposing of the action in the person's absence may:
      (i) as a practical matter impair or impede the person's ability to protect the interest; or
      (ii) leave an existing party subject to a substantial risk of incurring double, multiple, or otherwise inconsistent obligations because of the interest.

restrictions on advertisements found in a contract between the transit authority and the company that maintained the bus shelters. The evangelical group alleged that the advertisement restrictions in the contract prevented the group from placing ads in the bus shelters and sought injunctive relief. The evangelical group filed suit only against the transit authority, not the company that maintained the shelter, but the transit authority had no ability to require that any particular ad be displayed on a bus shelter. The company that maintained the shelters had that authority. The court of appeals held that the company was a required party, saying that "because [the transit authority] has no power to affirmatively require [the company maintaining the bus shelters] to run a particular advertisement . . . [the evangelical group] cannot possibly benefit from an injunction requiring the placement of its advertisements on the shelters unless [the company] is made a party to this action." 344 F.3d 1263 (11th Cir. 2003).

The Absentee Has an Interest in the Action and Prejudice Would Result

Rule 19(a)(1)(B) provides that an absentee is a required party if he claims an interest in the subject of the action and disposing of the action without him would either prejudice him or existing parties. Prejudice to the absentee occurs when proceeding without him might as a practical matter impair or impede his ability to protect his interest. Prejudice to existing parties occurs when proceeding without the absentee raises a danger of exposing an existing party to double, multiple, or inconsistent liability. This provision is usually implicated in cases involving disputes as to ownership interests in a limited fund or some other property, such as a security. For example, suppose a divorced husband brings suit to set aside the seizure of his retirement plan in which his ex-wife also has an interest. She is likely a required party because disposition of that action without her might, as a practical matter, impair her interest in the retirement plan. *See, e.g., Kamhi v. Cohen*, 512 F.2d 1051 (2d Cir. 1975). The wife could still file her own action, but as a practical matter, the first decision in the husband's case as to ownership is likely to be the same decision in the wife's case because of *stare decisis*. Or suppose two people claim ownership of the same stock. One of them files suit seeking an injunction requiring the defendant corporation to issue the shares in his name, though doing so may prejudice the interests of the other person claiming ownership in the stock. *See, e.g., Haas v. Jefferson National Bank of Miami Beach*, 442 F.2d 394 (5th Cir. 1971). The other alleged owner can still file a lawsuit, but the second court might tend to side with the first court's decision, a decision made without any input from the second plaintiff/owner.

Proceeding Without the Absentee May Prejudice Existing Parties

Sometimes proceeding without the absentee may subject the defendant corporation to double, multiple, or inconsistent liabilities. The examples above both involved multiple claimants to the same property. Not only can proceeding without the absentee harm the absentee, but it can also harm the defendant. Suppose in the stock dispute example the court in the first case orders the defendant to issue the stock in plaintiff 1's name, but the court in the second case orders the court to issue the stock in plaintiff 2's name. The defendant in this example is faced with complying with irreconcilable orders. Thus, plaintiff 2 would be a required party in the first case and the court would likely order her joinder. Or suppose a husband dies leaving the proceeds of his life insurance policy to his wife, but two different women claim to have been married to him at the time of his death. If the life insurance company is ordered to pay one wife in case 1, it might be ordered to pay the other wife in case 2. The life insurance company is at risk of double liability. Alternatively, both courts might determine that the life insurance company owes the absentee wife, in which case the life insurance company has escaped all liability, which is not possible under the terms of the policy. Instead, the court will likely order joinder of the absentee spouse in the first action in order to avoid double or inconsistent liability on the defendant life insurance company.

2. Determining Whether Joinder Is Feasible

A required party must be joined if joinder is feasible. Joinder is not feasible if joinder will deprive the court of subject matter jurisdiction. Most commonly, this occurs when a case is pending in federal court on diversity grounds. In a diversity case, for example, if the required party is to join the suit as a plaintiff, joinder is not feasible if the required party shares citizenship with any defendant (since adding that person as an additional plaintiff will destroy diversity and thereby deprive the court of subject matter jurisdiction to hear the case).

Lack of personal jurisdiction may also make joinder not feasible. If the required party ought to be a plaintiff, but refuses to join voluntarily, the absentee may be joined only if the court has personal jurisdiction over the required party. Compelling a person to join a suit is an example of the court exercising personal jurisdiction over the required party, and as discussed in Chapters 6 through 10, this power is limited both by statute and by the Due Process Clauses of the Constitution.

3. Dismissing the Action or Continuing Without the Required Party

If a person who is not a party is determined to be a "required party," but joinder of that person is not feasible, the court must decide whether it will dismiss the action altogether or proceed without the party. If the court decides it must dismiss the action, the absentee is considered an **indispensable party** to the action. In determining whether or not to dismiss the action or proceed without the required party, the court will consider the "equity and good conscience" factors set out in Rule 19(b), Exhibit 19.2. In *Torrington Company v. Yost*, the court follows the three-part approach discussed in this section, and applies the equity and good conscience factors in Rule 19.

EXHIBIT 19.2   **Rule 19(b)**

> (b) When Joinder Is Not Feasible. If a person who is required to be joined if feasible cannot be joined, the court must determine whether, in equity and good conscience, the action should proceed among the existing parties or should be dismissed. The factors for the court to consider include:
>   (1) the extent to which a judgment rendered in the person's absence might prejudice that person or the existing parties;
>   (2) the extent to which any prejudice could be lessened or avoided by:
>   (A) protective provisions in the judgment;
>   (B) shaping the relief; or
>   (C) other measures;
>   (3) whether a judgment rendered in the person's absence would be adequate; and
>   (4) whether the plaintiff would have an adequate remedy if the action were dismissed for nonjoinder.

Case Preview

Torrington Company v. Yost

As you read *Torrington Company v. Yost,* consider the following questions:

1. Why is INA a required party under Rule 19(a)?
2. Why is INA's joinder not feasible?
3. Why did the court decide it had to dismiss the case?
4. Does the court's decision mean that Yost will never have to defend the claim Torrington asserted against him in federal district court? If not, where might he have to defend it?

Torrington Company v. Yost
139 F.R.D. 91 (D.S.C. 1991)

ORDER

HERLONG, District Judge.

This is a trade secrets case. From 1982 to 1990, the defendant, Mark Yost ("Yost"), worked for the plaintiff, The Torrington Company ("Torrington"), manufacturing various types of bearings. While at Torrington, Yost signed an agreement not to divulge any secret or confidential information of Torrington. After leaving Torrington, Yost went to work for INA Bearing Company, Inc. ("INA") which produces the same type of bearings as Torrington. On June 4, 1991, Torrington filed suit against Yost seeking, among other things, an injunction limiting Yost's employment at INA for eighteen (18) months, and actual damages from the alleged use of Torrington's trade secrets. Yost moved to dismiss under Rule 19 of the Federal Rules of Civil Procedure for failure to join Yost's new employer, INA, as an indispensable party. Yost contends that INA's absence will prejudice him and impair INA's interests.

The issue before this court is whether INA is an indispensable party to this action under Rule 19. For the reasons set forth below, the court concludes that INA, Yost's new employer, is an indispensable party whose joinder would deny the court of diversity jurisdiction. Therefore, this case must be dismissed.

Fed. R. Civ. P. 19 requires a two-step analysis. The first part of the rule, subdivision (a), identifies the persons who should be joined if feasible. If joinder is not feasible, then subdivision (b) is applied to decide whether the case should be dismissed.

Under subdivision (a), a person should be joined when feasible if nonjoinder would under (a)(1) [Eds. — now (a)(1)(A)] deny complete relief to the parties present, or under (a)(2) [Eds. — now (a)(1)(B)], impair the absent person's interest or prejudice the persons already parties by subjecting them to a risk of multiple or inconsistent obligations.

In the matter *sub judice*, 19(a)(2) [Eds. — now 19(a)(1)(B)] is the pertinent subsection. Clearly subsection (a)(2) applies, and INA should be joined if feasible. INA has an employment contract with Yost, and its interest in his fulfilling that contract would be adversely affected if Torrington were granted an injunction preventing Yost from continuing to work for INA in his current position. In addition, there is a real possibility that if INA were not joined, Yost may be subject to inconsistent obligations. In order to obey a court order enjoining him from working for INA (or enjoining him from working on certain projects at INA), Yost may have to breach his employment contract with INA. Because Yost may be prejudiced if INA is not joined and INA has an interest which may be impaired in its absence, under Rule 19(a) the court is required to join INA as a party if feasible.

The sole basis for federal court jurisdiction in this action is diversity of citizenship. 28 U.S.C. §1332. Both INA and Torrington are Delaware corporations. Joinder of INA would destroy diversity jurisdiction. Therefore, it is not feasible to join INA, and the court must consider Rule 19(b) to determine whether the action should proceed with the parties before it, or should be dismissed.

Rule 19(b) contains four factors which must be considered when deciding whether to dismiss the action: (1) to what extent a judgment rendered in the person's absence may be prejudicial to the person or those already parties; (2) the extent to which, by protective provisions in the judgment, the prejudice can be lessened or avoided; (3) whether a judgment rendered in the person's absence will be adequate; and (4) whether the plaintiff will have an adequate remedy if the action is dismissed for nonjoinder.

The first factor weighs heavily in favor of dismissal. Torrington contends that INA is not an indispensable party and is at most a joint tortfeasor who would not be prejudiced by not being joined. In support of this position, Torrington points to *General Transistor Corp. v. Prawdzik,* 21 F.R.D. 1 (S.D.N.Y. 1957) as a similar case involving trade secrets in which the new employer was not joined, and was held not to be an indispensable party. In *General Transistor,* however, the plaintiff was merely seeking a temporary injunction preventing the individual defendant from "continuing to disclose any secret matter. . . ." 21 F.R.D. at 2. In the case at bar, Torrington is seeking to enjoin Yost from "working or consulting for INA for a period of eighteen (18) months, at any plant which makes thrust bearings or any supplier or subcontractor or tool designer involved with thrust bearings." Torrington is also asking the court to compel Yost "and those in privity with him, and those who became aware of any such injunction: . . . To return to Torrington, all documents, computerized and non-verbal disclosures, and physical embodiments of Torrington's trade secrets and confidential information." The potential impact upon the new employer is significantly greater in the case here than in *General Transistor.* In addition, the risk that Yost would be subjected to inconsistent obligations is significant. As already discussed, if the court limits the type of work Yost may do for INA, Yost may have inconsistent obligations to an order of the court and to INA.

The second factor requires the court to consider the feasibility of protective provisions. The drastic remedy of dismissal need not be invoked if the court can fashion relief so that neither the parties nor the person not joined is prejudiced. Torrington contends that if the court merely enjoins Yost from working at INA plants which manufacture the bearings in question, Yost could still work for INA. There is no evidence before the court, however, that such a protective provision would protect Yost from breaching his employment contract. Even if such a provision protects Yost, it would not protect INA. INA would be limited in the manner in which it could use its employee. There is no reasonable means of protecting Yost and INA from the prejudice they would suffer if INA were not a party.

Third, it is doubtful that any judgment Torrington receives would be adequate if INA were not made a party. Torrington's complaint is replete with references to INA. If Yost has revealed trade secrets to INA as Torrington fears, INA will be able to continue profiting from them if INA is not a party in this action. Even if Torrington is completely successful in this suit, if INA is not a party, INA cannot be prevented from using Torrington's trade secrets information.

Finally, another forum exists for the plaintiff. Torrington will not be left without a remedy if this action is dismissed. Torrington can sue both Yost and INA in state court.

The grounds for dismissal in this case are overwhelming. INA is clearly an indispensable party. Each of the four factors of Rule 19(b) indicates that dismissal is appropriate. If Torrington wishes to continue with this suit, it must do so in state court and join INA. For the foregoing reasons, this case is dismissed pursuant to Rule 19, Fed. R. Civ. P.

IT IS SO ORDERED.

Post-Case Follow-Up

One of Torrington's arguments as to why INA was not a required party under Rule 19 was that INA was merely a joint tortfeasor along with Yost. Generally, joint tortfeasors are not required parties under Rule 19. Even if a plaintiff has reason to believe that more than one person caused his injuries, generally he is free to join some as defendants and not others. INA might have been a joint tortfeasor, but INA was not a required party for that reason. Instead, the court focused on the fact that INA claimed an interest in the dispute and that Yost might be subject to inconsistent obligations if INA was not joined, namely, that he would be put in the position of either complying with the injunction Torrington sought to prevent him from working for INA, or else breaching his employment contract with INA by not working. But how does joining INA resolve that conundrum for Yost? Yost still might be ordered to stop working and thereby breach his employment contract. Perhaps more important than Yost's possible conundrum is the interest INA has in its employee's ability to continue to work for it and the possibility that an injunction prohibiting him from doing so would impair or impede that interest under Rule 19(a)(1)(B)(i). As you continue to study this chapter, consider this question: If INA is concerned about this interest and is aware of the lawsuit, do any of the party joinder rules provide INA a means of protecting that interest?

Torrington Company v. Yost: Real Life Applications

Albert & Guzman, LLP is a law firm that leases from Property Solutions, LLC one floor of office space in a high-rise office tower. Property Solutions does not own the office tower. Instead, it leases the office tower from the owner, Global Property Investments, Inc., and then subleases portions of the tower as office space to subtenants like Albert & Guzman. Albert & Guzman file suit in federal district court against Property Solutions, seeking an injunction requiring Property Solutions to stop automatically turning off all the lights in its offices each weeknight at 8:00 P.M. Property Solutions' lease with Global Property Investments requires it to turn off the lights in the office tower each evening at 8:00 P.M. in order to cut down on energy usage.

1. Property Solutions claims that Global Property Investments is a required party under Rule 19. Is Global Property Investments a required party, and if so, on what ground or grounds in Rule 19(a)?

2. Assume the federal district court agrees with Property Solutions that Global Property Investments is a required party. What should the court do?

3. Albert & Guzman, LLP is a California citizen. Property Solutions, LLC is a citizen of Nevada. Global Property Investments is a citizen of both California and Delaware. How, if at all, does this information affect your answer to question 2?

B. INTERVENTION UNDER RULE 24

As discussed above, Rule 19 (and the doctrine of compulsory joinder) address the situation in which one of the parties to a case (usually the defendant) argues that the case cannot proceed without including someone who is not a part of the case. **Intervention** is a very different concept. Intervention instead is initiated by someone outside the case who wants to become a party, often against the wishes of the existing parties. While someone outside the case can be granted limited rights to comment or file briefs on aspects of the case by becoming an "amicus curiae" (or friend of the court), in order to have full rights to participate as a party, a nonparty must seek to intervene under Rule 24. There are two types of interventions under Rule 24—intervention of right under Rule 24(a) and permissive intervention under Rule 24(b).

1. Intervention of Right

Rule 24(a), set out in Exhibit 19.3, governs intervention of right and provides a right to intervene in two situations. The court *must* allow intervention when: (1) a federal statute grants an unconditional right to intervene, or (2) the person moving to intervene has an interest in the action, and disposition of the action without him will impair his ability to protect that interest.

Federal Statute Granting Unconditional Right to Intervene

The right to intervene as a party is granted, by statute, to the government in certain types of litigation in which the public interest may be particularly at stake. Rule 24(a)(1) provides that a court must allow anyone to intervene who "is given an unconditional right to intervene by federal statute." Perhaps the most important

EXHIBIT 19.3 **Rule 24(a)**

> (a) Intervention of Right. On timely motion, the court must permit anyone to intervene who:
> (1) is given an unconditional right to intervene by a federal statute; or
> (2) claims an interest relating to the property or transaction that is the subject of the action, and is so situated that disposing of the action may as a practical matter impair or impede the movant's ability to protect its interest, unless existing parties adequately represent that interest.

example of a federal statute granting an unconditional right to intervene is 28 U.S.C. §2403. Section 2403 grants the United States an unconditional right to intervene in a federal court action in which the constitutionality of a federal statute affecting the public interest is drawn into question. The statute also grants a state the right to intervene in a federal court action if the constitutionality of one of its statutes affecting the public interest is drawn into question. Another example is the Civil Rights Act of 1964, which grants the U.S. Justice Department the unconditional right to intervene in cases in which plaintiffs allege a deprivation of their rights under the Equal Protection Clause.

The Person Claims an Interest in the Subject of the Action

More commonly, Rule 24(a)(2) grants a party an unconditional right to intervene if the person claims an interest in the action and disposing of the action without the person moving to intervene would "as a practical matter impair or impede the movant's ability to protect its interest, unless existing parties adequately protect that interest." This standard should sound familiar, as it is nearly identical to one of the bases for being a required party under Rule 19. A key difference between an intervenor of right and a person who is a required party under Rule 19 is that the person moving to intervene is actively seeking to become a party to the case, whereas the required party is not, and the court is determining whether the person must be made a party.

To have a right to intervene: (1) the person must claim an interest in the property or transaction that is the subject of the action, (2) disposition of the action might as a practical matter impair the person's ability to protect that interest, (3) the existing parties do not adequately represent that interest, and (4) intervention must be sought in a timely manner. In *Atlantis Development Corp. v. United States*, the United States filed suit against a group of defendants to enjoin their construction activities on a group of reefs off the coast of Florida on the grounds that each reef was either controlled by the United States or protected from construction activities by a federal statute. 379 F.2d 818 (5th Cir. 1967). The Atlantis Development Corporation was not a party to this suit, but moved to intervene. Atlantis had long sought to establish its ownership and control over the islands with various governments so that it could build a resort and casino there. The court of appeals reversed the decision of the district denying intervention and held that under Rule 24, Atlantis had a right to intervene. Atlantis satisfied the first element because it claimed an interest in the property that was the subject of the action: Atlantis claimed it owned the reefs. The third element was also satisfied because both the government and the defendants claimed that they owned or controlled the reefs, not Atlantis. As the court of appeals said, "Atlantis is without a friend in this litigation." As for the second element — that disposition of the action might as a practical matter impair or impede Atlantis' ability to protect its interest in the reefs — the court of appeals made clear that this standard can be met even where the person seeking to intervene will not be bound by the judgment in the action and can still bring a separate suit to establish their rights. The court focused on the practical difficulties the person will face in later litigation if she is not permitted to intervene. The court noted that if the government won the case, Atlantis' claims were "for all practical purposes worthless." While Atlantis would have still been able to litigate the same issue in its own lawsuit if it were not allowed to intervene (since a non-party can't be bound by a judgment), because it would have to litigate the issue in the same court, it would still be affected by the legal precedent set in the first case, even if not technically bound by the judgment. As the court explained, when the first decision by the first court is likely to be as a practical matter the last decision on the issue, this impairs or impedes the movant's ability to protect his interest, and intervention should be permitted.

2. Permissive Intervention

Even if a person does not have a *right* to intervene in a case under Rule 24(a), the court may still choose to permit that person to intervene if the test in Rule 24(b) is met. The standard for permissive intervention is more discretionary. Under Rule 24(b), set out in Exhibit 19.4, a court may allow intervention when either a federal statute grants a conditional right to intervene or when the person seeking to intervene has a claim or defense that shares with the main action common questions of law or fact. It is not entirely clear what statutes grant a conditional right to intervene, but it seems that the United States has at least a conditional right to intervene to assert a tax lien, and employers have the right to intervene in suits under the Fair Labor Standards Act. 7C Charles Alan Wright, Arthur R. Miller & Mary Kay Kane, Federal Practice and Procedure §1910 (3d ed. 2007) (stating that these two examples are amongst a number of federal statutes, which if they "do not grant an unconditional right to intervene, they should be regarded as allowing at least a conditional right of intervention and thus as coming within Rule 24(b)(1)(A)").

A court has broad discretion to grant or deny a motion to intervene under Rule 24(b)(1)(B) on the grounds that movant has a claim or defense that shares a common question of law or fact with the main action. Note that this standard is broader even than the Rule 20 permissive joinder standard for adding plaintiffs and defendants. The intervenor's claim or defense need not arise out of the same transaction or occurrence as the claims by the plaintiffs or against the defendants in the main action. Permissive intervention can be appropriate where the nonparty simply has an interest in litigating the same legal issues that will arise in a factually unrelated case. For example, when a French citizen filed a wrongful termination suit against

EXHIBIT 19.4   Rule 24(b)

(b) Permissive Intervention.
    (1) In General. On timely motion, the court may permit anyone to intervene who:
        (A) is given a conditional right to intervene by a federal statute; or
        (B) has a claim or defense that shares with the main action a common question of law or fact.

his employer, the state of Vermont, challenging as unconstitutional a state statute that authorized the state to terminate the employment of aliens, a Canadian citizen who was terminated at a different time but who questioned the validity of the same statute was allowed to intervene under Rule 24(b)(1)(B). *Teitscheld v. Leopold*, 342 F. Supp. 299 (D. Vt. 1971). Important considerations in ruling on a motion seeking permissive intervention will be to avoid undue delay of the action and prejudice to the other parties, which may result if the nonparty is allowed to intervene. So, in the previous example, the court might permit the Canadian citizen to intervene early on in the litigation, when his addition will not delay resolution of the dispute and is less likely to prejudice other parties, but may deny intervention when it is sought later on, such as when the case is nearing the trial date.

C. INTERPLEADER

Interpleader is a procedural device that allows a person facing competing claims to property in his possession or control to join all the claimants as defendants. For example, a bank that is holding jewelry in a safe deposit box for a depositor that has passed away might have to choose between multiple people who claim to own the jewelry. At first this concept may seem strange — that the plaintiff in an interpleader action is suing those who have claims against the plaintiff. Isn't that backwards? Shouldn't the people with claims file suit as plaintiffs? The problem for the person with the property is that the competing claimants are unlikely to join forces and file a single lawsuit asserting their rights. Remember that Rule 20 would allow them to join together as plaintiffs in a single action, but it does not require them to do so. The problem for the person with the property is that a judgment awarding the property to one claimant is not binding on the claimants who were not parties to that action. The person with the property needs all of the claimants to be parties to a single action so that the judgment in that action is binding on all claimants. Interpleader can achieve this end. There are two alternative ways that a stakeholder can proceed with an interpleader action in federal court: so-called rule interpleader under Rule 22, or a statutory interpleader action under section 1335. These have different requirements, and a stakeholder must choose which procedure is appropriate to use.

1. Rule Interpleader Under Rule 22

Rule 22(a), set out in Exhibit 19.5, provides that a plaintiff may interplead defendants when their claims may expose the plaintiff to "double or multiple liability." Suppose that Amara and Imani both believe that Great Fidelity Insurance Co. owes them the $1 million proceeds of a life insurance policy. Great Fidelity knows that the policy requires it to pay the full proceeds to either Amara or Imani, but it is not sure which of them it must pay. Interpleading both Amara and Imani is proper under Rule 22 because their claims might expose Great Fidelity to double liability;

EXHIBIT 19.5   **Rule 22(a)**

(a) Grounds.
  (1) *By a Plaintiff.* Persons with claims that may expose a plaintiff to double or multiple liability may be joined as defendants and required to interplead. Joinder for interpleader is proper even though:
    (A) the claims of the several claimants, or the titles on which their claims depend, lack a common origin or are adverse and independent rather than identical; or
    (B) the plaintiff denies liability in whole or in part to any or all of the claimants.

i.e., liability to both of them. If Amara files suit against Great Fidelity and judgment is rendered in her favor, the judgment does not shield Great Fidelity from liability to Imani. It might end up having to pay $1 million to both Amara and Imani, which is double the limits of the policy. Using Rule 22, Great Fidelity can interplead both Amara and Imani, and the judgment in the action will be binding on both of them and Great Fidelity will have to pay no more than the $1 million policy limits.

Now suppose instead that Amara files suit against Great Fidelity before it can file its interpleader action. Assume Imani files a motion to intervene in Amara's action. Should the court allow her to intervene under Rule 24? Do you think Great Fidelity would urge the court to grant or deny Imani's motion? Assume Amara files her action against Great Fidelity but that Imani does not move to intervene. Can Great Fidelity join Imani as a third-party defendant under Rule 14? If not, does it have any other options to ensure that both Amara and Imani are parties to the action?

2. Statutory Interpleader: 28 U.S.C. §1335

As noted, interpleader under Rule 22 is not the only basis for interpleading defendants. Congress has provided a statutory basis for interpleader in 28 U.S.C. §1335. Rule 22 makes clear that it and section 1335 are separate remedies. A person filing an interpleader action must choose to proceed under Rule 22, referred to as rule interpleader, or under section 1335, called statutory interpleader. Both rule and statutory interpleader allow a person holding property to join competing claimants as defendants, but there are some key distinctions between them. A separate federal statute authorizes nationwide service on the claimants in an interpleader case brought under section 1335. Thus, the federal court in a statutory interpleader action will not be limited by the personal jurisdiction limits of the state in which it sits (as in the ordinary case), but instead can summon claimants from anywhere in the United States to appear and participate in the action. The statute also allows the federal court to restrain the claimants from bringing any other action in state or federal court related to the property. 28 U.S.C. §2361. The statutory interpleader plaintiff has the option to file a case where the general venue statute, discussed in Chapter 11, says venue is proper; but under 28 U.S.C. §1396, the statutory interpleader plaintiff may also file the suit in any district "where one or more claimants reside." 28 U.S.C. 1396.

Perhaps the most important distinction between rule and statutory interpleader cases is the basis for the court's subject matter jurisdiction. In a rule interpleader action, the case will ordinarily have to satisfy the requirements of 28 U.S.C. §1332, the diversity statute. A statutory interpleader case must meet the jurisdictional requirements of the interpleader statute, 28 U.S.C. §1335. The key differences between the two statutes' jurisdictional requirements are the amounts in controversy and the application of the diversity requirements. As discussed in Chapter 3, the diversity statute requires an amount in controversy in excess of $75,000 and complete diversity of citizenship between the plaintiffs and defendants. In the rule interpleader context, this would mean that the claimants each pled that they were entitled to at least $75,000.01 worth of the disputed property or fund, and the plaintiff cannot share citizenship with any of the claimants he interpleads. The interpleader statute requires the money or property to be worth $500 or more and requires only **minimal diversity of citizenship**. Minimal diversity exists when there is any difference in citizenship amongst the claimants. The citizenship of the plaintiff is not relevant to the existence of jurisdiction under the interpleader statute.

Suppose that a Georgia citizen wants to interplead two Florida citizens who claim they are entitled to a $5 million fund in the plaintiff's possession. The Georgia citizen would not meet the jurisdictional requirements of the interpleader statute. The fund certainly meets the $500 minimum established in the statute, but there is not minimal diversity. There is no difference at all in the citizenship of the claimants. They are both Florida citizens. The case would, however, meet the requirements of the diversity statute because the amount in controversy far exceeds the $75,000 threshold, and there is complete diversity of citizenship because the plaintiff does not share citizenship with either of the claimants. The result in this example is that the Georgia citizen could use rule interpleader but not statutory interpleader.

Now suppose that a Tennessee citizen is an additional claimant to the $5 million fund, and the Georgia citizen wants to interplead the Tennessee citizen along with the two Florida citizens. In this example, there would be both diversity of citizenship jurisdiction, because the plaintiff still does not share citizenship with any defendant, and interpleader jurisdiction under section 1335, because there is some difference in citizenship amongst the claimants. Minimal diversity amongst the claimants is met, even if some of them share citizenship, as long as there is some difference in citizenship amongst them. Here the single Tennessee citizen satisfies the requirement of minimal diversity amongst the claimants. So, the Georgia citizen could use either rule interpleader or statutory interpleader, although he might choose statutory interpleader to take advantage of the nationwide service and the additional venue options available in statutory interpleader cases.

Now imagine that a California citizen wants to interplead a Georgia citizen and a citizen of California based on their competing claims to a $50,000 fund. The Californian could only use statutory interpleader in this example. The amount in controversy requirement in the diversity statute is not met, and complete diversity is lacking because the plaintiff shares citizenship with one of the claimants. However, the interpleader statute requires only that the property or fund have a value of $500 or more and some difference in citizenship amongst the claimants. Here the fund is worth $50,000 and the claimants are citizens of different states. The citizenship of the plaintiff is irrelevant to the existence of jurisdiction under the interpleader statute.

As these examples demonstrate, the availability of interpleader by rule was adopted expressly in order to supplement the interpleader statute and make interpleader available as a procedure in federal courts, even if the interpleader statute was not satisfied where the case would otherwise meet the general limits on federal civil actions.

D. CLASS ACTIONS

Another specialized procedure authorized by the Federal Rules is known as a "class action." Class actions can involve legal issues that affect hundreds, thousands, or even millions of people. A class action is a different and unique proceeding that allows the court to issue judgments that will bind persons not participating directly in the case, but who are instead being represented by the parties who are litigating. Because of the key due process issues raised by this procedure, class actions require fairly extensive procedural protections to ensure that the class members are being properly represented and that the case is one for which a class action procedure is appropriate.

Rule 23 allows plaintiffs to bring suit as a **class action** on behalf of other similarly situated persons under certain circumstances. A class action allows the resolution of claims that plaintiffs might not find worth pursuing individually or in small groups. Suppose the battery in your $500 laptop overheats and ruins the laptop. You would understandably be quite upset about the loss of your laptop and all the files on it, but it would cost you far more than $500 to bring suit to recover for your loss. For most persons, there is a $400 fee just to file a civil action in federal court, and you still have to pay an attorney to handle the case. But if you could bring suit on behalf of all 25,000 people who had the same problem with the same laptop, your suit would seek no less than $12.5 million in damages and make economic sense. Bringing this suit as a class action might also allow the defendant to resolve all the claims in a single action, rather than in many different actions filed around the country.

Class actions are not the preferred method of resolving all disputes that involve a class of similarly situated persons. The judgment in the class action may bind members of the class, even though they were not joined as plaintiffs and even if they were not actually aware of the action. Thus, class actions raise due process concerns and stand as an exception to the rule that a person is not bound by a judgment in action to which the person was not a party. Class actions raise a number of concerns that Rule 23 requires the representatives to address before a class action is certified. Is the class really large enough to justify a single class action, rather than allowing each member of the class to seek a remedy in his or her own action? Are the claims of the members of the class truly so similar that a class action is the most efficient way to resolve them? Will the representative plaintiffs adequately represent the interests of class members who are largely unknown to them? A court's decision to allow a suit to proceed as a class action turns on these and other considerations.

1. The Prerequisites of a Class Action

The life cycle of a class action begins when one or more members of a class files suit and seeks an order from the court certifying the case as a class action allowing the plaintiffs to represent all members of the class. The representatives will propose a class definition that describes those who would be members of the class. As a threshold matter, the defined class must satisfy the requirements of Rule 23(a). Rule 23(a), shown in Exhibit 19.6, sets out the prerequisites for certification of a class action. Satisfying the requirements of Rule 23(a) is necessary but not sufficient to warrant certification. The case must also fit within one of the types of class actions described in Rule 23(b). Rule 23(a) is but the first hurdle the case must clear in order to proceed as a class action. To clear this initial hurdle, the case must satisfy Rule 23(a)'s numerosity, commonality, typicality, and adequate representation requirements.

EXHIBIT 19.6 **Rule 23(a)**

> (a) Prerequisites. One or more members of a class may sue or be sued as representative parties on behalf of all members only if:
>   (1) the class is so numerous that joinder of all members is impracticable;
>   (2) there are questions of law or fact common to the class;
>   (3) the claims or defenses of the representative parties are typical of the claims or defenses of the class; and
>   (4) the representative parties will fairly and adequately protect the interests of the class.

The Numerosity Requirement

Rule 23(a)(1) requires that "the class is so numerous that joinder of all members is impracticable." This requirement in Rule 23(a)(1) is known as the numerosity requirement. If the plaintiffs are the only members of the class or if the other members can be easily joined, the numerosity requirement is not met. There is no bright line rule for the number of class members needed to satisfy the numerosity requirement, and this determination is within the trial court's discretion. A class with only 25 members has satisfied the requirement, *Philadelphia Electric Co. v. Anaconda Am. Brass Co.*, 43 F.R.D. 452 (U.S.D.C. D. Pa. 1968), and courts have refused to certify cases involving hundreds of class members. *See, e.g., Minersville Coal Co. v. Anthracite Export Ass'n*, 55 F.R.D. 426 (U.S.D.C. D. Pa. 1971) (refusing to certify a class of 330 members). Though no bright line rule exists, a good rule of thumb is that 100 or more members of a class will typically satisfy the numerosity requirement. The key though is that the commonality requirement is met when joinder of all members of the class is impracticable. Can the class members even find each other in order to collaborate in a lawsuit? All 200 1Ls at Harvard University are less likely to satisfy the numerosity requirement than all 100 passengers on Flight 237, because it is easier for the 1Ls to identify each other and collaborate than for the passengers who are, by and large, strangers to each other.

The Commonality Requirement and *Wal-Mart Stores, Inc. v. Dukes*

Rule 23(a)(2) requires that there be "common questions of law or fact to the class." Rule 23(a)(2) sets out what is known as the commonality requirement. The language does not require that all questions of law or fact be common to the class, but only that at least two or more questions of law or fact are common to the class. Some courts have given little consideration to the commonality requirement, particularly in light of the fact that commonality seems to be subsumed within the more stringent requirements in Rule 23(b).

However, the Supreme Court may have raised the bar for satisfying the commonality requirement in *Wal-Mart Stores, Inc. v. Dukes*. 564 U.S. 338 (2011). *Dukes* involved a class of 1.5 million current and former female employees of Wal-Mart for sex discrimination under Title VII. The Court held that it was not enough that there were common questions — that they each claimed sex discrimination and were employees of Wal-Mart — in a case involving thousands of employment decision across the country by various supervisors, some female and some male. Instead, the key to the commonality requirement "'is not the raising of common "questions"—even in droves—but, rather the capacity of a classwide proceeding to generate common answers apt to drive the resolution of the litigation.'" *Id.* (quoting Nagareda, *Class Certification in the Age of Aggregate Proof*, 84 N.Y.U. L. Rev. 97, 132 (2009)). The Court explained further:

> Quite obviously, the mere claim by employees of the same company that they have suffered a Title VII injury, or even a disparate-impact Title VII injury, gives no cause to

---

Wal-Mart Stores, Inc. v. Dukes: A "Momentous Decision"

Business groups praised the Supreme Court's reversal of the decision to certify a class of more than 1.5 million current and former female employees of Wal-Mart who alleged sex discrimination in violation of Title VII, but labor and consuming groups criticized it. One lawyer for the United States Chamber of Commerce said it was "without a doubt the most important class action case in more than a decade." Both sides agreed it was "a momentous decision." Although Wal-Mart was a workplace discrimination case, it affects other types of cases as well because it narrowed the definition of what constitutes a common issue or issues warranting class certification. The Supreme Court did not decide whether or not Wal-Mart did in fact discriminate against its female employees, but the opinion makes clear that a court may consider the merits of the plaintiffs' claim in making the certification decision and in particular in determining whether the commonality requirement is met.

Adam Liptak, *Justices Rule for Wal-Mart in Class-Action Bias Case*, N.Y. Times, June 20, 2011.

believe that all their claims can productively be litigated at once. Their claims must depend upon a common contention — for example, the assertion of discriminatory bias on the part of the same supervisor. That common contention, moreover, must be of such a nature that it is capable of classwide resolution — which means that determination of its truth or falsity will resolve an issue that is central to the validity of each one of the claims in one stroke.

Dukes seems to raise the bar for commonality because it required not just any common question of law or fact, but a contention that all members of the class make that is central to the validity of their claims.

The Typicality Requirement

Rule 23(a)(3) requires that the claims of the representative parties be typical of the claims of the class. The typicality requirement goes beyond commonality, requiring a comparison of the claims of the representatives with those of the class members. The representatives' claims need not be identical to those of the class members, but typicality may be lacking when there are legal and factual issues involved in the representatives' claims that are different or absent from those of the class members' claims. For example, when the representatives have an actual injury that the class members only have a risk of developing, typicality may be lacking. *See, e.g., Ball v. Union Carbide Corp.*, 385 F.3d 713 (6th Cir. 2004) (typicality requirement lacking when representatives had developed thyroid cancer allegedly due to exposure to nuclear facilities, while class members included those with an alleged risk of developing cancer). Conversely, when the class is defined to include persons who have suffered a particular injury, but no representative has suffered that injury, typicality may be lacking. *See, e.g., Valentino v. Carter-Wallace, Inc.*, 97 F.3d 1227 (9th Cir. 1996) (typicality lacking where "[n]o named plaintiff has experienced aplastic anemia as a result of taking the drug, even though this condition is one of the most serious of the alleged adverse consequences").

Adequate Representation

Rule 23(a)(4) requires the representative parties to "fairly and adequately protect the interests of the class." This requires both the class counsel and the class representatives to be adequate. Rule 23(g) requires the court to appoint class counsel by considering the counsel's knowledge of the case, experience with class actions and other complex litigation, knowledge of the applicable law, the resources at their disposal, and any other pertinent matters. The representatives must also be adequate. If the representatives do not understand the nature of their claims or are not conscientious and diligent in prosecuting the case, they are not adequate. Also, the adequate representation element is lacking when the representatives may have interests adverse to those of the class members. For example, in *Hansberry v. Lee*, the representative sought to enforce a racially restrictive covenant on behalf of a class of landowners. 311 U.S. 32 (1940). The covenant provided that no part of the affected land could be "sold, leased to or permitted to be occupied by any person of the colored race." *Id.* at 37. In *Hansberry*, the representative did not adequately represent the interests of the class, because a number of the class members sought to resist enforcement of the covenant.

Case Preview

In re Teflon Products Liability Litigation

As you read *In re Teflon Products*, consider the following questions:

1. What are the "implicit requirements" of Rule 23(a)?
2. How does the court address the commonality requirement? Do you think the proposed classes in this case meet the commonality standard the Supreme Court set forth in the *Dukes* case?
3. Why is the typicality requirement not met in this case?
4. Why is the adequate representation requirement also not met?

In re Teflon Products Liability Litigation
254 F.R.D. 354 (S.D. Iowa 2008)

ORDER

RONALD E. LONGSTAFF, Senior District Judge.

The Court has before it plaintiffs' motion for class certification, filed August 4, 2008. Defendant E.I. DuPont De Nemours & Company ("DuPont") resisted the motion on September 2, 2008, and plaintiffs filed a reply memorandum on October 6, 2008. The Court held a hearing on October 14 and 15, 2008, and the motion is fully submitted.

I. BACKGROUND

In the present MDL proceeding, plaintiffs seek certification of twenty-three classes of persons who acquired cookware coated with DuPont's "Teflon®" product. Plaintiffs allege that in producing and marketing its Teflon® and unbranded, non-stick cookware coatings ("NSCC"), DuPont made false, misleading and deceptive representations regarding the safety of its product. They also claim that DuPont knew or should have known about potential risks attendant in using cookware containing its coating, and failed to disclose this information to consumers.

The following relevant facts are accepted as true as alleged in the Corrected Unified Class Action Complaint ("the Complaint"). *See, e.g., Bishop v. Comm. on Prof. Ethics,* 686 F.2d 1278, 1288 (8th Cir. 1982) (in evaluating a motion for class certification, the court "accepts as true" the *substantive* facts as alleged in the complaint). Scientists in DuPont's Jackson Laboratory invented Teflon® in 1938. DuPont first began selling Teflon commercially in 1946, and the product became a popular component of cookware in the 1960s. To date, billions of cookware products coated with Teflon have been sold world-wide.

Various studies have shown that DuPont's NSCC can decompose at temperatures within the realm of "normal use," potentially releasing a synthetic chemical known as perfluorooctanoic acid ("PFOA"). Exposure to PFOA, which also is referred to as ammonium perfluorooctanoate ("APFO"), or ("C–8"), may cause a flu-like condition known as "polymer fume fever."

In addition, blood sample data obtained by the Environmental Protection Agency ("EPA") caused the Agency to conclude that PFOA has the ability to cross the human placenta, potentially leading to birth defects. . . .

DuPont has been aware of potential health hazards from the use of NSCC since the 1950s or 1960s, but has represented to consumers that its product is completely safe. In fact, as of April 25, 2006, DuPont continued to represent on its website that Teflon® products are safe for their intended consumer use. DuPont has never disclosed the symptoms of polymer fume fever directly to consumers, nor has it suggested to consumers that there are any potential health risks from the use of its NSCC.

It is important to note that none of the proposed class representatives alleges that he or she has been injured from the use of DuPont NSCC. Rather, in each of the purported class actions, plaintiffs seek recovery solely for economic damage. . . .

[Eds. — Plaintiffs' proposed class definition included three subclasses for the various state-wide class actions proposed. Subclass 1 was defined as owners of cookware branded with certain DuPont trade names. Subclass 2 included owners of both DuPont branded cookware and non-DuPont branded cookware that contained the non-stick coating. Subclass 3 was any purchaser, though not necessarily a current possessor, of cookware that contained the non-stick coating that did not fit within subclasses 1 or 2.]

The independent class actions set forth a number of causes of action, including: breach of express warranty, breach of implied warranty, declaratory judgment, injunction, failure to warn, false advertising, fraudulent concealment, negligent misrepresentation, negligence, strict liability, statutory unfair and deceptive trade practices, and unjust enrichment/restitution. The actual claims pled in each complaint vary, based on the laws of the particular jurisdiction at issue.

Plaintiffs claim entitlement to a variety of remedies as redress for DuPont's allegedly wrongful conduct. These remedies include:

1) creation of a fund for independent scientific researchers to further investigate the potential for adverse health effects from the use of products containing DuPont's non-stick coating;

2) a requirement that DuPont discontinue manufacturing, selling and/or distributing cookware containing the non-stick coating, and/or to compel DuPont to stop making misstatements, misrepresentations and or omissions regarding the safety of its product;

3) to require DuPont to replace and/or exchange all existing cookware containing DuPont non-stick coating possessed by class members with non-hazardous cookware, or to provide the cash equivalent;

4) equitable relief, including rescission and restitution; and

5) a requirement that DuPont provide an appropriate warning label or other disclosure on cookware made with or containing DuPont non-stick coating.

II. APPLICABLE LAW AND DISCUSSION

A. *Rule 23 Prerequisites*

As set forth above, plaintiffs move to certify twenty-three state-wide classes asserting various statutory and common law causes of action against DuPont. The law governing certification is set forth under Rule 23(a) of the Federal Rules of Civil Procedure. This Rule states as follows:

> (a) **Prerequisites to a Class Action.** One or more members of a class may sue or be sued as representative parties on behalf of all only if (1) the class is so numerous that joinder of all members is impracticable, (2) there are questions of law or fact common to the class, (3) the claims or defenses of the representative parties are typical of the claims or defenses of the class, and (4) the representative parties will fairly and adequately protect the interests of the class.

Fed. R. Civ. P. 23(a). The burden is on the party seeking certification to satisfy each of the above factors. . . . In evaluating a motion for certification, the court must "accept [ ] as true" the *substantive* facts as alleged in the complaint, but must also look beyond the pleadings to evidence submitted by the parties in order to ensure specific prerequisites have been satisfied. . . .

B. *Implicit Requirements*

In addition to the above factors, numerous courts also have recognized two "implicit" prerequisites: 1) that the class definition is drafted to ensure that membership is "capable of ascertainment under some objective standard"; and 2) that all class representatives are in fact members of the proposed class. . . .

Because the class definition is at the heart of any decision on certification, the Court will begin its analysis by considering these "implicit" factors.

1. Sufficiency of Class Definition

A well-crafted class definition must ensure that the Court can determine objectively who is in the class, and therefore, bound by the ultimate ruling. . . . The Court should not be required to resort to speculation . . . in order to identify class members. . . .

As set forth above, plaintiffs' revised class definition is divided into three sub-classes. Unfortunately for plaintiffs, however, the newly-created sub-classes do little to ease the Court's concerns regarding ascertainability. Each sub-class is addressed in turn, below.

a. *Sub-Class One*

Sub-class one covers individuals who purchased NSCC labeled with the Teflon®, Autograph®, or Silverstone® trademarks, and who "continue to possess the cookware, cookware packaging, or other documentation of the cookware." . . .

Few proposed representatives have been able to meet this definition. As illustrated by the "Cookware Summary" in Defendant's Exhibit 9, plaintiffs produced documentation identifying the cookware for less than 8% of the items submitted for consideration. Defendant's Ex. 9 at 2. Packaging, literature and/or labels were available for only 5.6% of the items collected. *Id.* Furthermore, the proposed representatives did not know the date or state of purchase for 22.2 and 32.4% percent of the items, respectively.

Accordingly, the proposed representative's own testimony, coupled with the cookware item itself, were the only evidence available to establish membership in sub-class one in the vast majority of cases. Neither have been shown to be particularly reliable.

For example, proposed Texas sub-class one representative Kimberly Cowart testified in her deposition that she did not know whether the pan upon which she bases her claims against DuPont in fact has a Teflon® non-stick coating, but simply *believes* it must be Teflon® "[b]ecause when I purchased the pan, I would have only purchased it if it had said Teflon®." Defendant's Ex. 11, Cowart Dep. at 103–04. She testified further that she did not recall purchasing her pan, did not remember anything about the packaging that came with the pan, and knew only that she purchased it "more than five years ago." *Id.* at 104–05.

Similar to Ms. Cowart, proposed New York sub-class one representative Gary Frechter believed his pan to be a Teflon®-coated product because: "It is older than the rest, and I thought it was Teflon® because [my wife and I] looked for Teflon® products." Defendant's Ex. 11, Frechter Dep. at 113. When questioned further, however, Mr. Frechter indicated he could not ensure his pan actually contained a non-stick coating, and could not identify the place or even decade of purchase. . . .

b. Sub-Class Two

Sub-class two includes purchasers of certain NSCC that was not necessarily sold with a DuPont trademark, but was sold under a brand name believed to contain Teflon® coating during the time-frame at issue. Ex. D to Plaintiffs' Post–Hearing Mem. at 1. During the hearing, plaintiffs contend that they and/or DuPont can establish with relative certainty which brands of cookware were made with DuPont non-stick coating during certain time periods, and that those brands are incorporated into the definition of sub-class two. DuPont vigorously disputes the reliability of the third-party manufacturer records, however. Furthermore, deposition testimony of various cookware manufacturers' representatives shows that it is virtually impossible to identify a brand of non-stick coating based on a visual examination of the item of cookware. Defendant's Ex. 14A, Bradshaw Dep. at 52–53; Defendant's Ex. 14E, Kaur Dep. at 156. Lastly, membership in this class necessarily requires a plaintiff to pinpoint the date on which he or she purchased the item of cookware. As demonstrated in DuPont's Cookware Summary, the proposed class representatives were unable to recall this information almost one-fourth of the time. Defendant's Ex. 9 at 2.

c. Sub-Class Three

Lastly, sub-class three includes: "All purchasers or owners of cookware coated with DuPont non-stick coating who do not qualify as members of Sub-Class 1 or 2."

Ex. D to Plaintiffs' Post–Hearing Mem. at 1. This "catch-all" sub-class theoretically includes anyone who *believes* he or she has *ever* owned or purchased an item of cookware containing DuPont nonstick coating, regardless of whether an objective basis exists to support that belief. Notably, an individual does not even need to possess the pan to assert a claim under this sub-class.

Proposed Illinois sub-class 3 representative Paula Bardwell is illustrative of these individuals. Ms. Bardwell conceded in her deposition that she did not know either the specific type of non-stick coating used on any of her three pieces of cookware or the date(s) on which she purchased the cookware. Nor did she have the original packaging to ensure the non-stick coating was manufactured by DuPont. Defendant's Ex. 11, Bardwell (IL) Dep. at 145–46. In fact, when questioned further by defense counsel, Ms. Bardwell admitted she was unsure whether she in fact purchased the cookware in the State of Illinois. *Id.*

d. *Conclusion Regarding Sufficiency of Definition*

In short, too many infirmities exist in the present class definitions to ensure the Court can determine objectively who is in the class, without resort to speculation .... [M]any class representatives mistakenly believe their product contained Teflon® coating — even when they were informed the particular brand of cookware at issue never used Teflon®....

In their reply memorandum, plaintiffs argue that at this stage, they do not need to show that each class member ultimately will be able to prove his or her membership; rather, the Court need only ensure that the appropriate criteria exists to *evaluate* membership " 'when the time comes.' " ... Unfortunately for plaintiffs, this argument necessarily depends upon the availability of better evidence to establish membership at a later stage of the proceeding. No such additional evidence will be produced in the present case. Rather, even after a lengthy discovery period, during which each proposed representative was thoroughly deposed, many individuals themselves are unable to ascertain whether they belong in a particular sub-class. Neither the Court nor DuPont is in any better position to do so....

Accordingly, the Court finds that the revised definition submitted by plaintiffs fails to provide an objective basis to determine several facts significant to establishing membership: 1) whether the cookware item in fact contains DuPont non-stick coating; 2) whether the item was purchased or obtained in some other manner; and 3) if purchased, whether the item was purchased in the state at issue within the applicable statute of limitations period. Without a clear basis for determining this information, plaintiffs' class definition necessarily fails.

2. Whether Proposed Representatives Satisfy Definition

The second "implicit requirement" of Rule 23 is that each proposed representative is in fact a member of the proposed class, or, in this case, sub-class. As outlined above, however, the fact the vast majority of plaintiffs must rely on memory to establish crucial facts will prevent the parties and the Court from ever being able to establish membership with objective certainty. Without such an assurance, the Court cannot in good conscience grant certification.

C. *Requirements of Rule 23(a)*

Even assuming the class definition had been drafted to ensure that membership is "objectively ascertainable," and that at least one viable class representative exists for each of the sub-classes put forth by plaintiffs, plaintiffs must nevertheless satisfy all four prerequisites listed in Rule 23(a).

1. Numerosity

Rule 23(a)(1) requires that the "class be so numerous that joinder of all members is impracticable." Fed. R. Civ. P. 23(a)(1). The Eighth Circuit has not adopted any "rigid rules regarding the necessary size of classes." *Emanuel v. Marsh,* 828 F.2d 438, 444 (8th Cir. 1987), *rev'd on other grounds,* 487 U.S. 1229, 108 S. Ct. 2891, 101 L. Ed. 2d 925 (1988). Rather, a reviewing court must consider such factors as "the number of persons in the proposed class, the type of action at issue, the monetary value of the individual claims and the inconvenience of trying each case individually." *Liles,* 231 F.R.D. at 573 (citing *Paxton v. Union Nat'l Bank,* 688 F.2d 552, 559 (8th Cir. 1982)).

In the present case, DuPont does not appear to contest the issue of numerosity, and the Court is satisfied that the number of potential claimants in each state-wide class is sufficiently large as to satisfy this Rule 23(a) prerequisite.

2. Commonality

The second express prerequisite is that each class member's claims contain "questions of law and fact common to the class." Fed. R. Civ. P. 23(a)(2). To establish "commonality" for purposes of this subsection, it is not necessary to demonstrate that *every* question of law or fact is common to each member of the class. *Paxton,* 688 F.2d at 561. Rather, the issues linking the class members must be "substantially related" to resolution of the case. *Id.; see also DeBoer v. Mellon Mortgage Co.,* 64 F.3d 1171, 1174 (8th Cir. 1995) (quoting *Paxton*).

Plaintiffs have alleged several legal and factual issues they contend are common to all potential class members. *See* Plaintiffs' Mem. at 31–32. Principal among these issues are: 1) Whether DuPont knew or should have known that the release of chemical substances during the normal, ordinary and foreseeable use of cookware coated with its non-stick coating posed potential risk to human health; 2) whether DuPont knowingly made false, public representations regarding the safety of its NSCC; 3) whether the class representatives' claims are sufficiently similar to the claims of prospective class members; 4) whether DuPont's failure to disclose was uniform across the class; 5) whether equitable relief, in whole or in part, is an appropriate remedy for DuPont's wrongful behavior; and 6) whether a warning label or other appropriate disclosure should be affixed to all pots and pans made with DuPont's NSCC.

Short of conceding the commonality requirement, DuPont argues that plaintiffs are nevertheless unable to show that the common questions predominate over the individual issues, as required under Rule 23(b)(3). For purposes of this motion only, the Court will assume plaintiffs have satisfied the relatively minimal commonality requirement under Rule 23(a)(2), and will focus instead on the predominance requirement, below. . . .

3. Typicality

Dupont also challenges plaintiffs' ability to establish "typicality." To satisfy this requirement, the proponent of certification must show that the "claims or defenses of the representative parties are typical of the claims or defenses of the class." Fed. R. Civ. P. 23(a)(3). In general, typicality is established if the claims of all members arise from a single event or share the same legal theory. *Paxton*, 688 F.2d at 561–62. If the legal theories of the representative plaintiffs are the same or similar to those of the class, slight differences in fact will not defeat certification. *Alpern v. UtiliCorp United, Inc.*, 84 F.3d 1525, 1540 (8th Cir. 1996).

In the present case, plaintiffs appear to build the majority of their claims around particular statements made and/or marketing practices employed by DuPont regarding its NSCC products. According to plaintiffs, the fact that each cause of action derives from a common practice or course of conduct on the part of DuPont renders the claims made by a representative plaintiff typical of the claims of all class members.

This Court does not agree. "The presence of a common legal theory does not establish typicality when proof of a violation requires individualized inquiry." *Elizabeth M. v. Montenez*, 458 F.3d 779, 787 (8th Cir. 2006) (citing *Parke v. First Reliance Stnd. Life Ins. Co.*, 368 F.3d 999, 1004–05 (8th Cir. 2004)). "[I]n situations where claims turn on individual facts, no economy is achieved, and the typicality requirement cannot be met." *Mahoney*, 204 F.R.D. at 154 (citing *Guillory v. American Tobacco Co.*, No. 97 C 8641, 2001 WL 290603, at *5 (N.D. Ill. Mar. 20, 2001)) (finding typicality requirement not satisfied where claims inconsistent from one plaintiff to another).

As noted by DuPont, the alleged misstatements and/or falsities cited by plaintiffs span a forty-plus-year period, across a wide variety of advertising and promotional media. Each plaintiff was exposed to different representations, at different time periods. Because reliance is a key element of plaintiffs' claim for negligent misrepresentation, and is necessary for recovery under the consumer fraud statutes in many jurisdictions, an individualized inquiry must be conducted not only to pinpoint the representation(s) at issue, but also to determine the extent to which each plaintiff relied upon the particular representation(s). Accordingly, DuPont claims that any common questions that may exist do not predominate over the individual issues.

Based on the variety of circumstances under which each proposed plaintiff undoubtedly purchased and proceeded to use his or her NSCC, as well as the varying degrees to which each plaintiff became educated about NSCC prior to purchase, this Court is inclined to agree with DuPont's position on this issue. For example, the exposure to and reliance on DuPont's allegedly false statements regarding the safety of nonstick cookware is a common element of many of plaintiffs' claims. Due to the widespread nature of DuPont's advertising over the years, however, determining the precise statements each plaintiff heard can only be accomplished through individualized inquiry. . . .

Perhaps more importantly, even if class members were exposed to the same representation, advertisement, or omission, the Court cannot presume that each member responded to the representation or omission in an identical fashion. In *Mahoney*, this Court found typicality not satisfied upon evidence that some plaintiffs "may have started smoking and continued to smoke even if full disclosures had been made." *Mahoney,* 204 F.R.D. at 154. In the present case, deposition testimony submitted by DuPont shows that although some proposed class representatives who became informed of potential health risks from NSCC stopped using the cookware, others exposed to similar information not only continued to use their existing cookware, but purchased new non-stick cookware. . . .

The Court acknowledges that a number of states maintain consumer fraud or protection statutes that do not require reliance for recovery. In these jurisdictions, however, individualized inquiry remains necessary to identify the alleged representation at issue, and the date on which the representation was made. For example, taking as true the allegations pled in plaintiffs' master complaint, DuPont was not made aware of potential toxic effects of PFOA until 1981. Complaint at 13–14. It can hardly be said that any advertisements or claims of safety made by DuPont before that date were fraudulent or misleading. If a particular plaintiff, such as Ms. Casper of Massachusetts, purchased her cookware item before 1981, her claims could not be considered "typical" of the class, because she could not have been exposed to fraudulent or false advertising. The Court therefore concludes that plaintiffs have failed to establish the typicality requirement set forth under Federal Rule of Civil Procedure 23(a)(3).

4. Adequacy of Representation

The fourth express requirement under Rule 23(a) is that "the representative parties will fairly and adequately protect the interests of the class." Fed. R. Civ. P. 23(a)(4). Two factors are relevant to this inquiry: 1) whether the named representatives and their counsel are willing and competent to pursue the litigation; and 2) whether the interests of the representative plaintiffs are antagonistic to the interests of others in the class. *See, e.g., Hervey v. City of Little Rock,* 787 F.2d 1223, 1230 (8th Cir. 1986); *Paxton,* 688 F.2d at 562–63.

With regard to the first factor, the Court finds that plaintiffs have retained competent counsel who appear well-versed in class action litigation. Although several of the individual plaintiffs could benefit from further research into the nature and background of their claims, the Court is confident each will continue to pursue the litigation to the best of his or her ability. The fighting issue is whether the interests of the putative class members are sufficiently similar to those of the class such that it is "unlikely that their goals and viewpoints will diverge." *Carson P. ex rel. Foreman v. Heineman,* 240 F.R.D. 456, 509 (D. Neb. 2007).

DuPont contends that plaintiffs' decision to relinquish possible claims for personal injury, products liability or medical monitoring effectively has resulted in "claim-splitting," and prevents the representative plaintiffs from adequately representing the full interests of absent class members. *See, e.g., Thompson v. Am. Tobacco Co.,* 189 F.R.D. 544, 550 (D. Minn. 1999) (finding that "the named Plaintiffs' efforts to reserve personal injury and damage claims may, in fact, jeopardize the class members' rights to bring such claims in a subsequent case"). . . .

Among other requirements, " 'a claim is barred by res judicata if it arises out of the same nucleus of operative facts as the prior claim.' " *Yankton Sioux Tribe v. United*

States Dept. of Health & Human Servs., 533 F.3d 634, 641 (8th Cir. 2008) (quoting *Lane v. Peterson,* 899 F.2d 737, 742 (8th Cir. 1990)). As noted by DuPont, the fact that plaintiffs included claims for medical monitoring in their original complaints suggests that the claims *could have* been brought in the present litigation. [Eds. — The doctrine of *res judicata* prohibits "claim-splitting," and so the representative plaintiffs' decision to drop personal injury claims may bar the class members from later bringing those claims in separate actions.] . . .

Assuming, as it must, that DuPont's NSCC poses a genuine risk of injury to consumers, this Court, like *Thompson,* believes that any *possibility* that a subsequent court could determine that claims for personal injury and medical monitoring were barred by *res judicata* prevents the named plaintiffs' interests from being fully aligned with those of the class. *Thompson,* 189 F.R.D. at 551. The Court therefore concludes plaintiffs are unable to establish the "adequacy of representation" requirement set forth in Rule 23(a)(4). . . .

Post-Case Follow-Up

The court determined that the proposed classes don't meet the implicit requirements of Rule 23(a). Note the importance the court places on the proposed definition of the subclasses. The court was not satisfied that it could ascertain who was a member of the class or whether or not the representatives even fell within the definition of the proposed class. Without an ascertainable class there is no reason to determine whether the proposed class meets the requirements of Rule 23(a). As you continue to read about class actions, consider the problems an inability to identify the members of the class might cause.

In re Teflon Products Liability Litigation: Real Life Applications

Consider the following proposed class actions. Which of Rule 23(a)'s requirements might they have trouble satisfying?

1. Frio Fun Times, Inc. develops and operates rural resorts. It wants to dam a river running along property it owns and plans to develop as a resort in order to create a small lake for its guests to enjoy on the upstream side of the river. Earl owns land upstream from the proposed dam that will be six feet below the surface of the newly created lake. He files suit to enjoin Frio Fun Times from creating the dam. He seeks to have his suit certified as a class action on behalf of all 50 landowners whose land will be flooded by the new lake.

2. Ezekiel files suit against Sheetrock Products, Inc., alleging that he developed a deadly form of cancer called mesothelioma while he worked as a plasterer over the last 40 years. Ezekiel alleges that his mesothelioma is due to exposure to

Sheetrock's products that contained asbestos, a known cause of both mesothelioma and a less-severe disease called asbestosis. Ezekiel's proposed class definition includes "individuals who have been exposed to Sheetrock's products and have developed asbestosis." Persons with asbestosis may develop mesothelioma but can live for many years or even decades after developing it, while mesothelioma is a terminal illness.

2. Types of Class Actions

Satisfying Rule 23(a)'s prerequisites is not sufficient for class certification. The proposed class action must also fit into one of the three types of class actions in Rule 23(b).

The Prejudice Class

Rule 23(b)(1), set out in Exhibit 19.7, permits certification of a class action when Rule 23(a)'s requirements are met and when prosecuting separate actions would prejudice either the class members or the opposing party. The purpose of Rule 23(b)(1) is similar to that of Rule 19. While Rule 19 requires joinder of the absentee who is a required party, Rule 23(b)(1) makes the absentees members of a class who will be bound by the judgment in the class action.

Rule 23(b)(1)(A) permits certification of a class when separate actions would create a risk of "establishing incompatible standards of conduct" for the party opposing the class. This sort of class action is proper where separate actions might place the party opposing the class action in the position of having to comply with conflicting orders from multiple courts — i.e., to comply with one order is to violate another. In *Krueger v. Ameriprise Financial*, Inc., 401(k) retirement plan participants sought class certification in a suit against the plan provider, alleging that it had selected poor performing, higher-cost funds than other available options and had failed to properly negotiate or seek competitive bidding in order to achieve lower

EXHIBIT 19.7   **Rule 23(b)(1)**

A class action may be maintained if Rule 23(a) is satisfied and if:

(1) prosecuting separate actions by or against individual class members would create a risk of:

(A) inconsistent or varying adjudications with respect to individual class members that would establish incompatible standards of conduct for the party opposing the class; or

(B) adjudications with respect to individual class members that, as a practical matter, would be dispositive of the interests of the other members not parties to the individual adjudications or would substantially impair or impede their ability to protect their interests;

record-keeping fees. The court granted the motion for class certification under Rule 23(b)(1), explaining the difficulty of administering a single retirement plan under different, and potentially inconsistent, legal rulings if no class action is allowed:

> The Court finds that class certification in this case is properly granted . . . class certification under this subdivision is appropriate when "[o]ne person may have rights against, or be under duties toward, numerous persons constituting a class, and be so positioned that conflicting or varying adjudications in lawsuits with individual members of the class might establish incompatible standards to govern his conduct." Fed. R. Civ. P. 23(b), Advisory Committee notes (1966 Amendment). As Plaintiffs have noted, Defendants owe duties toward the Plan. Therefore, contrary to Defendants' assertions, separate lawsuits by various individual Plan participants to vindicate the rights of the Plan could establish incompatible standards to govern Defendants' conduct, such as computation of varying "reasonable" record-keeping fees for the Plan, a requirement that Defendants engage in competitive bidding for Plan record-keeping services, determinations of differing "prudent alternatives" against which to measure the proprietary investments, or an order that Defendants be removed as fiduciaries.

Krueger v. Ameriprise Fin., Inc., 304 F.R.D. 559, 576-77 (D. Minn. 2014).

Importantly, a prejudice class is typically not appropriate when separate actions result in merely *different* results, rather than incompatible results. For example, if a manufacturer faces product liability suits brought by numerous customers injured by a given product, the manufacturer may win some cases and lose others, even if the proof offered is identical. These results might seem inconsistent, but they are not incompatible (it simply means that the manufacturer will have to pay damages to some plaintiffs and not to others). The Sixth Circuit Court of Appeals explained this distinction in *Pipefitters Local 636 Insurance Fund v. Blue Cross Blue Shield of Michigan*:

> Rule 23(b)(1)(A) allows for class certification when "prosecuting separate actions by or against individual class members would create a risk of . . . inconsistent or varying adjudications with respect to individual class members that would establish incompatible standards of conduct for the party opposing the class. . . ." A class action is appropriate under this subsection when "the party is obliged by law to treat the members of the class alike," for example when the class touches upon how a utility company interacts with its customers or how the government imposes a tax. See Amchem, 521 U.S. at 614, 117 S. Ct. 2231 (citation omitted). Certification is not appropriate simply because "some plaintiffs may be successful in their suits against a defendant while others may not." In re Bendectin Prod. Liab. Litig., 749 F.2d 300, 305 (6th Cir. 1984) (citations omitted); see also 7AA Wright, Miller, & Kane, supra, §1773 (3d ed. 2010) (explaining that the rule "requires more than a risk that separate judgments would oblige the opposing party to pay damages to some class members and not to others or to pay them different amounts").

Pipefitters Local 636 Ins. Fund v. Blue Cross Blue Shield of Michigan, 654 F.3d 618, 632-33 (6th Cir. 2011).

While Rule 23(b)(1)(A) addresses prejudice to the party opposing certification, Rule 23(b)(1)(B) addresses prejudice to the class members if separate actions are prosecuted rather than a class action. A Rule 23(b)(1)(B) class is appropriate when separate actions by some members of the class "would be dispositive of the interests of the other members not parties to the individual adjudications of the class who were not parties to the separate actions or would substantially impair or impede their ability to protect their interests." The most common class under Rule 23(b)(1)(B) is what is known as the "limited fund" class. A limited fund class is appropriate when the class members have claims to a fund that is not sufficient to satisfy all claims. Suppose 300 people injured by exposure to asbestos have claims averaging $1 million per person against the bankrupt manufacturer of the asbestos, and all that is left to satisfy their claims is $50 million worth of insurance proceeds. The first approximately 50 individual actions would exhaust the fund, leaving the other 250 injured persons without an opportunity to protect their interests. A limited fund class action under Rule 23(b)(1)(B) could ensure that all 300 people have an opportunity to access the fund. The court can determine a fair method of apportioning the fund. Few if any of the class members would get $1 million, but all of them would have an opportunity to get some portion of the $50 million fund.

Class Actions for Injunctive or Declaratory Relief

Rule 23(b)(2), set out in Exhibit 19.8, permits certification of a class when "the party opposing the class has acted or refused to act on grounds that apply generally to the class, so that final injunctive relief or corresponding declaratory relief is appropriate respecting the class as a whole." This type of class action allows the court to determine the propriety of behavior affecting the class in a single action. This type of class action is sometimes called a "Civil Rights" class action, because most cases involve civil or constitutional rights. The *Wal-Mart Stores, Inc. v. Dukes* case, for example, involved class action certification under Rule 23(b)(2) in a Title VII sex discrimination case. Rule 23(b)(2) has also been used to vindicate equal protection, First Amendment, Fourth Amendment, and other rights. Although it may be possible to recover money damages in this type of class action, the remedies available to class members are generally limited to injunctive and declaratory relief. The purpose of this type of class action is to allow the court to provide relief "respecting the class as whole," rather than determine individual claims for damages.

The Damages Class

Rule 23(b)(3), set out in Exhibit 19.9, permits certification when the predominance and superiority requirements are met. The predominance requirement is met when

---

EXHIBIT 19.8 **Rule 23(b)(2)**

A class action may be maintained if Rule 23(a) is satisfied and if:

* * *

(2) the party opposing the class has acted or refused to act on grounds that apply generally to the class, so that final injunctive relief or corresponding declaratory relief is appropriate respecting the class as a whole. . . .

EXHIBIT 19.9 **Rule 23(b)(3)**

A class action may be maintained if Rule 23(a) is satisfied and if:

* * *

(3) the court finds that the questions of law or fact common to class members predominate over any questions affecting only individual members, and that a class action is superior to other available methods for fairly and efficiently adjudicating the controversy. The matters pertinent to these findings include:

(A) the class members' interests in individually controlling the prosecution or defense of separate actions;

(B) the extent and nature of any litigation concerning the controversy already begun by or against class members;

(C) the desirability or undesirability of concentrating the litigation of the claims in the particular forum; and

(D) the likely difficulties in managing a class action.

the questions common to all class members predominate over the individual questions. The superiority requirement is met when the class action is superior to other methods of resolving the dispute. This type of class action is often used for mass tort disputes, such as the one at issue in *In re Teflon Products Liability Litigation*. The court also addressed Rule 23(b)(3) requirements in *Teflon*, even though it had decided that the 23(a) requirements were not met. Recall that in *Teflon* the representatives sought certification of a number of classes consisting of just about anyone who had ever purchased cookware with a certain DuPont non-stick coating. The court spent very little time discussing the commonality requirement under Rule 23(a), and DuPont barely contested commonality. The predominance requirement, however, is far more stringent:

> To evaluate predominance, the district court must examine the type of evidence needed to establish a plaintiff's case. . . .

> If, to make a prima facie showing on a given question, the members of a proposed class must present evidence that varies from member to member, then it is an individual question for purposes of Rule 23(b)(3); if the same evidence will suffice for each member to make a prima facie showing, then it becomes a common question. . . .

> In the present case, plaintiffs have presented the Court with very little guidance as to how they intend to prove the elements of each claim. Instead, plaintiffs assert that the lack of any claim for personal injury will allow damages to be demonstrated on a class-wide, rather than individual, basis, and that this fact is somehow sufficient to establish predominance.

> This Court does not agree. As discussed above in the context of ascertainability, the only common factor binding together all of the present plaintiffs is use of non-stick coated cookware. The fact each class represents a particular state or geographic region does not ensure the purported members of that class used the same brand of cookware, purchased or otherwise obtained their cookware during the same general time period and within the same state or jurisdiction, witnessed the same media advertisements

and promotional materials, and/or used their cookware with the same frequency and at the same degree of heat. In order to recover, each plaintiff may be required to show that he or she purchased NSCC manufactured by DuPont within the time period allowed under the applicable statute of limitations. Each of these issues will require an individualized inquiry, which the Court believes will render each class action unmanageable.

Teflon, 254 F.R.D. at 369-70.

The court was also unpersuaded that the class action was the superior vehicle for resolving the dispute:

The second test under Rule 23(b)(3) is whether the "class action is superior to other available methods for the fair and efficient adjudication of the controversy." Fed. R. Civ. P. 23(b)(3). In evaluating superiority, the Court must consider four non-exclusive factors:

(A) the interest of members of the class in individually controlling the prosecution or defense of separate actions; (B) the extent and nature of any litigation concerning the controversy already commenced by or against members of the class; (C) the desirability or undesirability of concentrating the litigation of the claims in the particular forum; (D) the difficulties likely to be encountered in the management of a class action. Fed. R. Civ. P. 23(b)(3).

In arguing against the class action approach, DuPont again cites to the myriad of issues that must be resolved on an individual basis. Throughout these proceedings, DuPont has made it abundantly clear that it has no plans to relinquish its right to cross-examination and individual proof of injury. See, e.g., In re Ford Motor Co. Vehicle Paint Litig., 182 F.R.D. 214, 221 (E.D. La. 1998) (plaintiffs' proposal to prove causation through individual affidavits submitted to special master rejected as "one-sided procedure [which] would amount to an end-run around defendant's right to cross-examine individual plaintiffs"). DuPont thus contends that the failure of plaintiffs' counsel to propose a trial plan to help resolve these issues renders the class action approach unmanageable.

Plaintiffs attempt to downplay the manageability concerns by arguing that without the class action vehicle, very few plaintiffs would have the motivation or financial resources to proceed with individual litigation. According to plaintiffs, membership in a class is many individuals' best chance of achieving some form of recovery, albeit a de minimus recovery. See, e.g., Mace v. Van Ru Credit Corp., 109 F.3d 338, 344 (7th Cir. 1997) (possibility of de minimus recovery should not bar class action where, absent class certification, a potential plaintiff class is unlikely to "be aware of her rights, willing to subject herself to all the burdens of suing and able to find an attorney willing to take her case").

Accepting as true the premise that non-stick cookware coatings have the potential to cause serious physical injury, the Court must nevertheless reject plaintiffs' argument. As discussed with regard to adequacy of representation, above, the representative plaintiffs' decision to reserve from this litigation any claims for personal injury or medical monitoring might prevent a participating class member from recovering on either claim in the future. Such a possibility — coupled with the immense manageability issues presented by the inherent, ubiquitous nature of the product and the overly-inclusive class definitions — prevents this Court from finding a class approach superior to individual litigation.

Id. at 370-72.

So what type of action could be certified as a damages class under Rule 23(b)(3)? In such actions, a variety of individual issues could prevent the common questions from predominating. For example, in a nationwide class, different states' laws are likely to require proof of different elements of the claims and defenses or different remedies. Note that this is one of the reasons that the representatives in *Teflon* sought certification of a number of state-wide classes; hoping that each class would be governed by a single state's law, to therefore avoid those individual issues within each state-wide class. Some cases present a predominating legal question, such as the validity of a patent or the legality of a particular action on the part of the defendant. But when would defendants, unlike DuPont, be willing to relinquish the requirement of individual proof of causation and damages and allow, as mentioned in *Teflon*, proof by affidavit? Perhaps defendants would be willing to accept such proof in a case in which liability is the key disputed issue and damages can be relatively easily assessed for each class member by resorting to a mathematical formula.

Notice to Members of the Class

As previously discussed, the judgment in a class action binds all members of the class. The class action procedure is an exception to the due process requirement that a person must be a party to an action in order to be bound by its judgment. But the class action procedure is not an exception to the due process requirement of notice to the class members. For Rule 23(b)(1) and (b)(2) class actions—the prejudice and Civil Rights class actions—Rule 23(c)(2)(A) provides that the court "may direct appropriate notice" to the members of the class. Note the word "may." Notice to the class is not required in such actions, but may be provided. Because members of these types of classes are not permitted to opt out of the class, the notice serves only to allow them to intervene in the action if they so choose or allow them to monitor the action.

Rule 23(c)(2)(B) *requires* notice to class members in Rule 23(b)(3) damages class actions. Notice is critical in these class actions because the members have the option to "opt out" of the class action. If they choose not to opt out, they will be bound by the judgment. Rule 23(c)(3)(B) requires the "best notice that is practicable under the circumstances," and requires "individual notice to all members who can be identified through reasonable effort." Notice by mail to those members who can be identified is typical, and notice by publication will be used to notify those who can't be identified.

The notice must describe in "plain, easily understood language" the nature of the action, the claims, issues, and defenses, and provide the definition of the class. The notice must also inform members that they may enter an appearance in the action and opt out of the class if they so choose, in which case they will not be bound by the judgment. It must also state that if they choose not to opt out, they will be bound by the judgment.

Settlement and Voluntary Dismissal of Class Actions

A class action may be settled or dismissed only with the court's approval. The court must also direct notice of the settlement or dismissal to all class members who would be bound by a settlement. For settlements of damages class actions under Rule 23(b)(3), the court may refuse to approve a settlement unless the class members are provided a second opportunity to opt out of the class. Exhibit 19.10 is an example of such a notice to class members.

EXHIBIT 19.10   Sample Class Action Notice

Legal Notice   Legal Notice

Legal Notice
TO HOLDERS OF
CITIBANK CREDIT CARDS
Read This Notice Carefully.   A Class Action Lawsuit May Affect Your Rights.

A settlement has been proposed in a class action lawsuit relating to credit cards issued by Citibank (South Dakota), N.A. ("Citibank"). This notice is only a summary. A detailed notice of the settlement and your rights is available at http://www.casenosacv06571.com.

Description of Litigation. Plaintiff alleges that Citibank imposed increased interest rates due to delinquency or default without giving prior notice. Citibank has denied all allegations of wrongdoing and liability. The Court has not ruled on the merits of Plaintiff's claims or Citibank's defenses.

Who Is Included? You are a member of the settlement class if, between May 5, 2002 and May 24, 2010, you had a credit card account with Citibank (South Dakota), N.A., or its predecessor Citibank USA, National Association, and you paid periodic finance charges that were assessed from the beginning of a billing period in which the periodic rate was increased as a result of a default or delinquency that occurred before August 20, 2009.

Settlement Payments. Citibank has agreed to establish a settlement fund of $10 million. Members of the settlement class who timely submit a valid claim form will receive a check for the lesser of $18 or an equal share of the settlement fund after payment of settlement costs, including certain administration costs and attorneys' fees and costs to class counsel. Plaintiff will request that the Court award $2.5 million in attorneys' fees and costs to class counsel and $5,000 to Plaintiff Laura Hoffman for her services as class representative. Any amounts left over will be paid to charity. Under certain circumstances, interest may be paid on certain of these amounts.

How Do I Make A Claim? To be entitled to a payment from the settlement fund, you must mail in a claim form by February 11, 2011. Claim forms are available at http://www.casenosacv06571.com or by writing to: Hoffman Claim Form, PO Box 44007, Jacksonville, FL 32231-4007.

Other Options. If you don't want to be legally bound by the settlement, you must request exclusion by November 8, 2010, or you will not be able to sue about the legal claims in this case. If you request exclusion, the court will exclude you from the class and you will not get money from this settlement. If you stay in the settlement, you may object to it by November 8, 2010. The detailed notice explains how to exclude yourself or object. If you remain a member of the settlement class, you will be bound by any judgment entered whether or not it is favorable to the settlement class.

The Court will hold a hearing in this case (Hoffman v. Citibank (South Dakota), N.A. SACV 06-571 AJG (MLGx)) to consider whether to approve the settlement on **December 13, 2010 at 10:00 a.m.** before the Honorable Andrew J. Guilford, Courtroom 10D, Ronald Reagan Federal Building and U.S. Courthouse, 411 West Fourth Street, Santa Ana, California 92701-4516. The detailed notice explains what to do if you want to appear at the hearing. Requests to appear must be made by November 8, 2010. For more information, write to class counsel: Barry L. Kramer, Law Offices of Barry L. Kramer, 12428 Promontory Road, Los Angeles, California 90049 or send an email to kramerlaw@aol.com. You may also enter an appearance through your own attorney if you desire.

DO NOT CALL OR WRITE TO THE COURT OR THE CLERK OF THE COURT. DO NOT CONTACT CITIBANK ABOUT THE SETTLEMENT. TELEPHONE REPRESENTATIVES ARE NOT AUTHORIZED TO CHANGE THE TERMS OF THE SETTLEMENT OR THIS NOTICE.

Dated: May 24, 2010 /s/ Andrew J. Guilford, United States District Court Judge

---

3. Subject Matter Jurisdiction over Class Actions

It is probably clear to you that class actions are quite different from most cases you experience in the first year of law school, or any year of law school for that matter. Nevertheless, they are not so different that they escape the requirement that the federal district court must have subject matter jurisdiction over the case. If the class seeks a federal right to relief, the court will have federal question jurisdiction over the class action. Jurisdiction over class actions asserting state law claims, however, is a bit more complicated. The Class Action Fairness Act in 28 U.S.C. §1332(d) allows federal courts to exercise subject matter jurisdiction over class actions based on minimal diversity and an amount in controversy in excess of $5 million. Thus, if the total value of all members' claims exceeds $5 million, and if any class member has a citizenship different from any defendant, the class action can be filed in federal court or, if filed in state court, removed to federal court. The district court may decline, and under certain circumstances must decline, to exercise subject matter jurisdiction over a class action based on some fairly complicated provisions in §1332(d)(3) and (4) that present essentially local, rather than national, controversies.

Chapter Summary

- Required parties are those whose absence may cause harm to them or existing parties. A required party must be joined if feasible. If joinder is not feasible due to lack of personal jurisdiction or subject matter jurisdiction, the court must apply the equity and good conscience factors to determine if it will continue without the required party or dismiss the action.
- A court *must* permit a person to intervene in an action if the person is granted an unconditional right to intervene by federal statute, or if the person has an interest in the action and disposition of the action may impair or impede that interest. A court *may* allow permissive intervention if a statute grants the person a conditional right to intervene, or if the person's claim or defense shares a common question of law or fact with the main action.
- Interpleader is a procedural device that allows a person facing competing claims to property in his possession or control to join all the claimants as defendants.
- Plaintiffs may file suit as representatives of a class of similarly situated persons if Rule 23(a)'s prerequisites of numerosity, commonality, typicality, and adequate representation are met and the class action fits one of the three types of class actions authorized by Rule 23(b).

Applying the Concepts

Dave's property is damaged, along with hundreds of other nearby properties, when an oil and gas drilling rig releases thousands of gallons of saltwater and other liquid waste used in oil and gas production. Dave files suit in federal district court against the company that was operating the drilling rig, A+ Drilling.

1. A+ Drilling takes the position that a defect in the rig caused the release of the salt and wastewater and that, therefore, the manufacturer of the drilling rig must be joined as a party to the suit. Is A+ Drilling correct? Why or why not?

2. Hector's property is also adjacent to the property on which A+ was drilling and was also damaged by the release of saltwater. One month after Dave filed his suit, Hector files a motion to intervene in Dave's suit. Must the court grant the motion? May the court grant the motion? Why or why not?

3. Dave moves to have his case certified as a class action wherein he would bring claims for property damage on behalf of all of the several hundred landowners whose property was harmed by the release of the salt and wastewater. The class would seek money damages for the diminution of value of the property and the cost to remediate the contamination. Dave's attorney is an experienced litigator but he has never before handled this kind of case. County property records identify the owners of the affected properties. All of the properties and the rig were located in Texas. Some properties had damage only to their soil and vegetation, while others also sustained damage to improvements upon the property. Some properties had thousands of gallons of salt and wastewater reach them while others had far less. How should the court rule on the motion and why? If the court were to certify a class action, is notice to the class members required, and if so, how might the court provide that notice?

Civil Procedure in Practice

Ten years ago, Albert purchased from Great Southern Insurance a $1 million life insurance policy insuring his own life. When he dies, he leaves behind his wife of 30 years, Mika, and their two adult children, Ivan and Maria. After Albert's death, his family finds two different wills executed by Albert and the $1 million insurance policy. One of Albert's wills purports to give the $1 million life insurance proceeds to his daughter Maria. The other will purports to give the proceeds to his son Ivan. On the insurance policy, Albert lists his widow Mika as the beneficiary of the policy. Mika, Ivan, and Maria have all separately contacted Great Southern Insurance in writing claiming that they are entitled to the $1 million. You represent Great Southern Insurance and have been tasked with resolving the competing claims to the $1 million proceeds.

1. Mika, Ivan, and Maria have not yet filed a lawsuit against Great Southern Insurance. What are the dangers to your client of choosing between them in the absence of a judgment telling you which one to pay? What action might you take to ensure that your client is protected from these dangers? Assume Great Southern is a citizen of Delaware and that Mika and Ivan are also citizens of Delaware, but that Maria is a citizen of New York. How do these facts, if at all, affect how you will proceed?

2. Now assume Maria files suit against Great Southern Insurance claiming she is entitled to the $1 million. Ivan and Mika seek to intervene in the lawsuit as

plaintiffs on the ground that they are the ones who should be awarded the proceeds. What position do you take on behalf of Great Southern Insurance as to their intervention? Do you think the court will permit their intervention, and if not, what position would you then take to protect your client from the dangers you identified in question 1?

20

Joinder and Supplemental Jurisdiction

In Chapters 2 and 3, we talked about the federal district court's original subject matter jurisdiction over diversity and federal question cases. If a federal district court does not have original jurisdiction, it will dismiss the case, or if removed to federal court, remand the case to the state court where it was filed. Understanding federal question and diversity jurisdiction is a good starting point for a simple federal civil case, such as when the plaintiff sues one defendant and asserts a single claim. In Chapters 18 and 19, however, we learned that additional claims and parties may be added to the action the plaintiff filed. Parties may assert counterclaims and crossclaims. A party defending a claim may implead and assert claims against third-party defendants. A nonparty may seek to intervene in order to assert a claim. Under Rule 18, parties asserting one of these claims may also assert any other claim they have against an opposing party. The foundational concept for this chapter is that the federal district court must have subject matter jurisdiction over every single claim asserted in the action. Even if the court has original jurisdiction over the action the plaintiff filed, the court must also have jurisdiction over additional claims that are joined later. The federal district court may have federal question or diversity jurisdiction over these additional claims. If it does not, it may still be able to exercise what is called **supplemental jurisdiction**. Supplemental jurisdiction allows a federal district court to exercise jurisdiction over most (but not all) additional claims that are factually related to the action over which it has original jurisdiction. This chapter addresses subject matter jurisdiction over these additional claims with an emphasis on supplemental jurisdiction.

Key Concepts

- The federal district court must have subject matter jurisdiction over every claim asserted in the case
- The general rule for exercising supplemental jurisdiction
- The exception to the general rule for exercising supplemental jurisdiction in diversity cases
- When the federal district court may decline to exercise supplemental jurisdiction

A. UNDERSTANDING THE ISSUE

It bears repeating: The federal district court must have subject matter jurisdiction over each and every claim asserted in the case — every claim, counterclaim, cross-claim, or third-party claim. That is, each claim must have its own jurisdictional basis. Suppose Jenna and Roberto are in a car wreck in Texarkana, Texas and both are injured. Each blames the other for causing the accident. Jenna, a Texas citizen, files a $100,000 personal injury suit in federal district court alleging negligence against Roberto, a citizen of Arkansas. The case looks like this.

Jenna (TX) ——————→ Roberto (AR)
$100,000

Jenna's action does not arise under federal law, because she is asserting a state law cause of action for negligence. But the district court has diversity of citizenship jurisdiction. The amount in controversy exceeds $75,000, and there is complete diversity of citizenship because Jenna and Roberto are citizens of different states. After appearing in the action, Roberto asserts a $200,000 counterclaim alleging negligence against Jenna for the personal injuries he sustained in the action. Now the case looks like this.

$200,000
←——————
Jenna (TX) ——————→ Roberto (AR)
$100,000

First, recognize that the federal court must have subject matter jurisdiction over Roberto's counterclaim in order to adjudicate it. Here, the court has diversity jurisdiction over the counterclaim. Jenna and Roberto are citizens of different states, and the amount in controversy for his claim is $200,000, which exceeds the $75,000 threshold. But suppose instead that Roberto sought only $50,000 in damages on his counterclaim. Now the case looks like this.

$50,000
←——————
Jenna (TX) ——————→ Roberto (AR)
$100,000

The court would not have diversity jurisdiction over the counterclaim, because the amount in controversy requirement is not met. Roberto's $50,000 claim does not exceed the $75,000 jurisdictional threshold. There's no federal question jurisdiction over his state law negligence claim either. However, not allowing the federal court to decide the claim does not seem to make sense, since it would be better to litigate in one case the degree of fault and the injuries that each driver claims from the same accident, regardless of the specific damages figure Roberto places on his claim.

Consider another example. Suppose Cedric files suit in federal district court against his former employer, Paladin, LLP, for terminating his employment based on his race. He asserts both a federal Title VII claim and state law claims for workplace racial discrimination. Both Cedric and Paladin are citizens of New Mexico; so, there is no diversity jurisdiction. The court would have federal question jurisdiction over the Title VII causes of action, but the state causes of action for workplace discrimination do not "arise under" federal law. Again, however, it would seem to make more sense to litigate all of Cedric's related claims in a single civil action.

How should the civil justice system handle counterclaims like Roberto's and state law claims like Cedric's that are asserted along with federal law claims? Three possibilities come to mind. Let's see how they would work for Roberto's counterclaim. One, we could require Roberto to litigate his counterclaim in state court while Jenna proceeds on her claim against Roberto in federal court. Of course, requiring two civil actions in separate court systems involving the same two parties and arising out of a single event is not the most efficient use of judicial or party resources. Moreover, the state and federal courts may reach inconsistent results. The state court might find the accident was Jenna's fault and the federal court might find it was Roberto's. A second possibility is to require litigation of the entire action, including Roberto's counterclaim, in state court. State courts of general jurisdiction certainly have the authority to adjudicate both Jenna's and Roberto's claims. The problem with this approach is that it would severely curtail the number of diversity actions that would remain in federal court. In a case like Jenna's, it would also enable a defendant to defeat the plaintiff's choice of a federal forum simply by asserting a counterclaim over which the court did not have original jurisdiction. Each time a claim was asserted in a diversity case over which the federal courts did not have original jurisdiction, the entire action would have to be litigated in state court. In Cedric's case, Cedric would have to choose between a federal forum and pressing his state law claims. He could have one or the other but not both, since he could assert both claims only by filing the case in state court.

The third approach is the one Congress has actually authorized federal courts to take. Under 28 U.S.C. §1367, a federal court may exercise supplemental jurisdiction over claims like Roberto's and Cedric's when they are factually related to the claims over which it has original jurisdiction. The supplemental jurisdiction statute ordinarily avoids the inefficiencies of involving both state and federal courts in the dispute, and does not undermine the federal court's ability to resolve diversity of citizenship or federal question cases.

B. THE GENERAL RULE FOR EXERCISING SUPPLEMENTAL JURISDICTION

Permitting federal courts to exercise supplemental jurisdiction reflects the striking of a balance between the inefficiency of involving both state and federal courts in a single dispute and undermining the federal court's ability to resolve diversity and federal question cases. To strike this balance, Congress has authorized supplemental jurisdiction only over claims that are factually related to those that fall within the court's original jurisdiction; e.g., its diversity or federal question jurisdiction. So, the court looks first at whether or not there is a claim in the case over which it has original diversity or federal question jurisdiction (i.e., is there something to supplement?) and then it looks at whether the additional claims are sufficiently factually related to those claims that it may exercise supplemental jurisdiction over them.

1. There Must Be Something to Supplement

Note that the statute allows a federal district court to exercise supplemental jurisdiction only in an action "of which the district courts have original jurisdiction." This language makes clear that supplemental jurisdiction is just that: supplemental. It may be used only to supplement the court's original jurisdiction. A party cannot file an action in or remove a case to federal court unless the court has original jurisdiction over some claim in the action. Suppose a Florida citizen files a negligence action against another Florida citizen in federal district court. The court should dismiss the case because it has neither diversity of citizenship nor federal question jurisdiction over the action, and supplemental jurisdiction cannot help the plaintiff escape this result.

2. The Common Nucleus of Operative Fact Standard

Section 1367(a) also permits supplemental jurisdiction when the "other claims are so related to claims in the action within such original jurisdiction that they form part of the same case or controversy." This means that a court may exercise supplemental jurisdiction when the claims over which it is exercising supplemental jurisdiction and the claim in the action over which it has original jurisdiction "derive from a common nucleus of operative fact." *United Mine Workers of America v. Gibbs*, 383 U.S. 715 (1966).

Consider Roberto's $50,000 counterclaim against Jenna. Jenna filed suit seeking damages for injuries she sustained in a car wreck with Roberto. The court has diversity of citizenship jurisdiction over the action she filed because Jenna is a Texan asserting a $100,000 claim against Roberto, a citizen of Arkansas. Roberto's counterclaim is for injuries he sustained in the same car wreck, but does not meet the amount in controversy requirement in the diversity statute. However, because Jenna's action and his claim derive from a common nucleus of operative fact — the car wreck — the court can exercise supplemental jurisdiction over Roberto's claim.

Now consider Cedric's workplace discrimination action. The court has federal question jurisdiction over his Title VII claim but not over his state law claims. However, because both the federal question and state law claims derive from the termination of his employment allegedly due to race, the court can exercise supplemental jurisdiction over his state law claims.

In *United Mine Workers of America v. Gibbs*, a decision that predates the supplemental jurisdiction statute, the court addressed a situation not unlike our Title VII example. Gibbs was hired as a mine superintendent and provided a contract to haul coal out of the mine during a union strike against the mine. After the strike ended, Gibbs lost his job as the superintendent and was never able to haul any coal under his contract. He also alleged that the union took action to ensure that others in the coal mining industry did not hire him. Gibbs asserted both a federal law claim under section 303 of the Labor Management Relations Act and a number of factually related Tennessee common law claims against the union. Although federal question jurisdiction existed over the federal claim, there was no basis for original jurisdiction over the Tennessee common law claims. The court held that it could exercise what was at the time called pendent jurisdiction (now called supplemental jurisdiction). Writing for the majority, Justice Brennan set forth the contours of what would become the general rule in the supplemental jurisdiction statute:

> Pendent jurisdiction, in the sense of judicial power, exists whenever there is a claim "arising under (the) Constitution, the Laws of the United States, and Treaties made, or which shall be made, under their Authority . . . ," U.S. Const., Art. III, s 2, and the relationship between that claim and the state claim permits the conclusion that the entire action before the court comprises but one constitutional "case." The federal claim must have substance sufficient to confer subject matter jurisdiction on the court. *Levering & Garrigues Co. v. Morrin*, 289 U.S. 103, 53 S. Ct. 549, 77 L. Ed. 1062. The state and federal claims must derive from a common nucleus of operative fact. But if, considered without regard to their federal or state character, a plaintiff's claims are such that he would ordinarily be expected to try them all in one judicial proceeding, then, assuming substantiality of the federal issues, there is power in federal courts to hear the whole.

383 U.S. 715, 725 (1996).

The effect of the Court's holding in *Gibbs*, now codified in 28 U.S.C. §1367(a), is that a federal court can exercise subject matter jurisdiction over state law claims between non-diverse citizens so long as they are factually related to a claim over which the court has original jurisdiction. Recall that Congress cannot authorize a court to exercise jurisdiction beyond what is allowed by Article III, and Article III does not provide federal courts judicial power over state law claims between citizens of the same state. It's easy to see the practical benefits of the Court's reasoning in *Gibbs*, but how is the holding constitutional? Remember that Article III, Section 2 speaks in terms of the "cases and controversies" over which federal courts may exercise judicial power. The Constitution does not refer to jurisdiction over "claims" or "causes of action." The Court's reasoning is that when there is a basis for original jurisdiction, Article III, Section 2 allows the court to exercise jurisdiction over the "case," which includes all claims derived from a common nucleus of operative fact, even if the court does not have original jurisdiction over all of those claims.

Just how broad is this "common nucleus of operative fact" standard? This standard is clearly met when the claims arise out of the same transaction or occurrence. Recognize that as a practical matter this means that a federal district court may well have supplemental jurisdiction over compulsory counterclaims and crossclaims because, by definition, these claims arise out of the same transaction or occurrence as other claims over which the court must have original jurisdiction. But the common nucleus of operative fact test is broader than the same transaction or occurrence standard. Claims may derive from a common nucleus of operative fact even if they don't arise from the same transaction or occurrence. While the Supreme Court has not fully fleshed out the contours of this standard, one court of appeals has said that the common nucleus of operative facts test is satisfied when there is a "loose factual connection between the claims." *Ammerman v. Sween*, 54 F.3d 423 (7th Cir. 1995) (citing 13D Charles Alan Wright, Arthur R. Miller, Edward H. Cooper & Richard D. Freer, Federal Practice and Procedure §3567.1 (3d ed. 2008 & Supp. 2017)). One practical impact of this standard is that a federal court can exercise supplemental jurisdiction over compulsory counterclaims and *some* permissive counterclaims, which by definition do not arise out of the same transaction or occurrence as the claim against the counterclaimant. Suppose Ciara files a civil action in federal district court against her former employer, All-Tech, Inc., alleging that All-Tech terminated her employment because she is African-American, in violation of Title VII of the federal Civil Rights Act. Her allegations focus on a one-month period at the end of her employment during which she claims that All-Tech instituted a policy of demoting or terminating the employment of minority employees. The court clearly has federal question jurisdiction over Ciara's claim because she asserts a federal cause of action. Suppose that All-Tech then asserts a counterclaim for the state law tort of conversion, alleging that Ciara took $50,000 worth of office equipment and supplies from All-Tech over the course of her five years of employment, and All-Tech also alleges that Ciara's theft of office supplies and equipment is the true reason it terminated her employment. While All-Tech's counterclaim may not arise out of the same transaction or occurrence — Ciara's claim is based on events during a one-month period and All-Tech's is based on conduct over a five-year period — the court would probably have supplemental jurisdiction because there is a "loose factual connection between the two claims," which both involve Ciara's employment and the reason she may have been fired.

C. THE EXCEPTION TO THE GENERAL RULE IN DIVERSITY CASES

The general rule for exercising supplemental jurisdiction in diversity cases is the same as it is in federal question cases — a court may exercise supplemental jurisdiction over other claims that derive from a common nucleus of operative facts as a claim that falls under the court's original jurisdiction. However, as *Owen Equipment and Erection Co. v. Kroger* demonstrates, the court's exercise of supplemental jurisdiction in diversity cases is subject to an additional limitation that is now codified in 28 U.S.C. §1367(b).

Case Preview

Owen Equipment and Erection Co. v. Kroger

As you read *Owen Equipment and Erection Co. v. Kroger*, consider the following questions:

1. Why does the court have original jurisdiction?
2. Does Kroger's claim against Owen satisfy the "common nucleus of operative fact" standard from *Gibbs*?

3. What does the court see as the problem with exercising supplemental jurisdiction over Kroger's claim against Owen?

4. Although the court doesn't address this issue in detail, why did the court have jurisdiction over OPPD's claim against Owen?

NOTE: *Owen* is a pre-28 U.S.C. §1367 case. The opinion uses the term "ancillary jurisdiction." Today, section 1367 uses the term "supplemental jurisdiction" for both "pendent jurisdiction" in *Gibbs* and "ancillary jurisdiction" in *Owen*.

Owen Equipment and Erection Co. v. Kroger
437 U.S. 365 (1978)

Mr. Justice STEWART delivered the opinion of the Court.

In an action in which federal jurisdiction is based on diversity of citizenship, may the plaintiff assert a claim against a third-party defendant when there is no independent basis for federal jurisdiction over that claim? The Court of Appeals for the Eighth Circuit held in this case that such a claim is within the ancillary jurisdiction of the federal courts. We granted certiorari, 434 U.S. 1008, 98 S. Ct. 715, 54 L. Ed. 2d 749, because this decision conflicts with several recent decisions of other Courts of Appeals.

"The Brethren"

Justice Potter Stewart authored the majority opinion in *Owen*. He served as an associate justice on the Supreme Court from 1958 until his retirement in 1981, and was considered a moderate and a "swing vote." In *Jacobellis v. Ohio*, a case involving the definition of "pornography," he famously wrote in his concurring opinion "I know it when I see it. . . ." In 1975, Bob Woodward, the Pulitzer prize winning journalist of Watergate-investigation fame, and Scott Armstrong wrote a book providing a behind the-scenes look at the Supreme Court during Earl Warren's tenure as Chief Justice. Eventually, Bob Woodward revealed that Potter Stewart was his secret source on the Court for the book. The title of Woodward and Armstrong's book was "The Brethren," an apt title for a book about the (at the time) all-male Supreme Court. Ironically, Sandra Day O'Connor, the first woman on the Supreme Court, took Stewart's seat upon his retirement.

I

On January 18, 1972, James Kroger was electrocuted when the boom of a steel crane next to which he was walking came too close to a high-tension electric power line. The respondent (his widow, who is the administratrix of his estate) filed a wrongful-death action in the United States District Court for the District of Nebraska against the Omaha Public Power District (OPPD). Her complaint alleged that OPPD's negligent construction, maintenance, and operation of the power line had caused Kroger's death. Federal jurisdiction was based on diversity of citizenship, since the respondent was a citizen of Iowa and OPPD was a Nebraska corporation.

OPPD then filed a third-party complaint pursuant to Fed. Rule Civ. Proc. 14(a) against the petitioner, Owen Equipment and Erection Co. (Owen), alleging that the crane was owned and operated by Owen, and that Owen's negligence had been the proximate cause of Kroger's death. OPPD later moved for summary judgment on the respondent's complaint against it. While this motion was pending, the respondent was granted leave to file an amended complaint naming Owen as an additional defendant. Thereafter, the District Court granted OPPD's motion for summary judgment in an unreported opinion. The case thus went to trial between the respondent and the petitioner alone.

The respondent's amended complaint alleged that Owen was "a Nebraska corporation with its principal place of business in Nebraska." Owen's answer admitted that it was "a corporation organized and existing under the laws of the State of Nebraska," and denied every other allegation of the complaint. On the third day of trial, however, it was disclosed that the petitioner's principal place of business was in Iowa, not Nebraska,[5] and that the petitioner and the respondent were thus both citizens of Iowa. The petitioner then moved to dismiss the complaint for lack of jurisdiction. The District Court reserved decision on the motion, and the jury thereafter returned a verdict in favor of the respondent. In an unreported opinion issued after the trial, the District Court denied the petitioner's motion to dismiss the complaint.

The judgment was affirmed on appeal. 558 F.2d 417. The Court of Appeals held that under this Court's decision in *Mine Workers v. Gibbs*, 383 U.S. 715, 86 S. Ct. 1130, 16 L. Ed. 2d 218, the District Court had jurisdictional power, in its discretion, to adjudicate the respondent's claim against the petitioner because that claim arose from the "core of 'operative facts' giving rise to both [respondent's] claim against OPPD and OPPD's claim against Owen." 558 F.2d at 424. It further held that the District Court had properly exercised its discretion in proceeding to decide the case even after summary judgment had been granted to OPPD, because the petitioner had concealed its Iowa citizenship from the respondent. Rehearing en banc was denied by an equally divided court. 558 F.2d 417.

II

It is undisputed that there was no independent basis of federal jurisdiction over the respondent's state-law tort action against the petitioner, since both are citizens of Iowa. And although Fed. Rule Civ. Proc. 14(a) permits a plaintiff to assert a claim against a third-party defendant, . . . it does not purport to say whether or not such a claim requires an independent basis of federal jurisdiction. Indeed, it could not determine that question, since it is axiomatic that the Federal Rules of Civil Procedure do not create or withdraw federal jurisdiction.

In affirming the District Court's judgment, the Court of Appeals relied upon the doctrine of ancillary jurisdiction, whose contours it believed were defined by this Court's holding in *Mine Workers v. Gibbs, supra.* The *Gibbs* case differed from this one in that it involved pendent jurisdiction, which concerns the resolution of a plaintiff's federal- and state-law claims against a single defendant in one action. By contrast, in this case there was no claim based upon substantive federal law, but rather state-law tort claims against two different defendants. Nonetheless, the Court of Appeals was correct in perceiving that *Gibbs* and this case are two species of the same generic problem: Under what circumstances may a federal court hear and decide a state-law claim arising between citizens of the same State? But we believe that the Court of Appeals failed to understand the scope of the doctrine of the *Gibbs* case.

* * *

---

[5]The problem apparently was one of geography. Although the Missouri River generally marks the boundary between Iowa and Nebraska, Carter Lake, Iowa, where the accident occurred and where Owen had its main office, lies west of the river, adjacent to Omaha, Neb. Apparently the river once avulsed at one of its bends, cutting Carter Lake off from the rest of Iowa.

It is apparent that *Gibbs* delineated the constitutional limits of federal judicial power. But even if it be assumed that the District Court in the present case had constitutional power to decide the respondent's lawsuit against the petitioner, it does not follow that the decision of the Court of Appeals was correct. Constitutional power is merely the first hurdle that must be overcome in determining that a federal court has jurisdiction over a particular controversy. For the jurisdiction of the federal courts is limited not only by the provisions of Art. III of the Constitution, but also by Acts of Congress. *Palmore v. United States*, 411 U.S. 389, 401, 93 S. Ct. 1670, 1678, 36 L. Ed. 2d 342; *Lockerty v. Phillips*, 319 U.S. 182, 187, 63 S. Ct. 1019, 1022, 87 L. Ed. 1339; *Kline v. Burke Constr. Co.*, 260 U.S. 226, 234, 43 S. Ct. 79, 82, 67 L. Ed. 226; *Cary v. Curtis*, 3 How. 236, 245, 11 L. Ed. 576.

* * *

III

The relevant statute in this case, 28 U.S.C. §1332(a)(1), confers upon federal courts jurisdiction over "civil actions where the matter in controversy exceeds the sum or value of $10,000 . . . and is between . . . citizens of different States." This statute and its predecessors have consistently been held to require complete diversity of citizenship. That is, diversity jurisdiction does not exist unless *each* defendant is a citizen of a different State from *each* plaintiff. Over the years Congress has repeatedly re-enacted or amended the statute conferring diversity jurisdiction, leaving intact this rule of complete diversity. Whatever may have been the original purposes of diversity-of-citizenship jurisdiction, this subsequent history clearly demonstrates a congressional mandate that diversity jurisdiction is not to be available when any plaintiff is a citizen of the same State as any defendant. . . .

Thus it is clear that the respondent could not originally have brought suit in federal court naming Owen and OPPD as codefendants, since citizens of Iowa would have been on both sides of the litigation. Yet the identical lawsuit resulted when she amended her complaint. Complete diversity was destroyed just as surely as if she had sued Owen initially. In either situation, in the plain language of the statute, the "matter in controversy" could not be "between . . . citizens of different States."

It is a fundamental precept that federal courts are courts of limited jurisdiction. The limits upon federal jurisdiction, whether imposed by the Constitution or by Congress, must be neither disregarded nor evaded. Yet under the reasoning of the Court of Appeals in this case, a plaintiff could defeat the statutory requirement of complete diversity by the simple expedient of suing only those defendants who were of diverse citizenship and waiting for them to implead nondiverse defendants.[17] If,

---

[17]This is not an unlikely hypothesis, since a defendant in a tort suit such as this one would surely try to limit his liability by impleading any joint tortfeasors for indemnity or contribution. Some commentators have suggested that the possible abuse of third-party practice could be dealt with under 28 U.S.C. §1359, which forbids collusive attempts to create federal jurisdiction. See, *e. g.,* 3 J. Moore, Federal Practice ¶14.27[1], p. 14–571 (2d ed. 1974); 6 C. Wright & A. Miller, Federal Practice and Procedure §1444, pp. 231–232 (1971); Note, Rule 14 Claims and Ancillary Jurisdiction, 57 Va. L. Rev. 265, 274–275 (1971). . . . But there is nothing necessarily collusive about a plaintiff's selectively suing only those tortfeasors of diverse citizenship, or about the named defendants' desire to implead joint tortfeasors. Nonetheless, the requirement of complete diversity would be eviscerated by such a course of events.

as the Court of Appeals thought, a "common nucleus of operative fact" were the only requirement for ancillary jurisdiction in a diversity case, there would be no principled reason why the respondent in this case could not have joined her cause of action against Owen in her original complaint as ancillary to her claim against OPPD. Congress' requirement of complete diversity would thus have been evaded completely.

It is true, as the Court of Appeals noted, that the exercise of ancillary jurisdiction over nonfederal* claims has often been upheld in situations involving impleader, cross-claims or counterclaims. But in determining whether jurisdiction over a nonfederal claim exists, the context in which the nonfederal claim is asserted is crucial. See *Aldinger v. Howard*, 427 U.S., at 14, 96 S. Ct., at 2420. And the claim here arises in a setting quite different from the kinds of nonfederal claims that have been viewed in other cases as falling within the ancillary jurisdiction of the federal courts.

First, the nonfederal claim in this case was simply not ancillary to the federal one in the same sense that, for example, the impleader by a defendant of a third-party defendant always is. A third-party complaint depends at least in part upon the resolution of the primary lawsuit. . . . Its relation to the original complaint is thus not mere factual similarity but logical dependence. Cf. *Moore v. New York Cotton Exchange*, 270 U.S. 593, 610, 46 S. Ct. 367, 371, 70 L. Ed. 750. The respondent's claim against the petitioner, however, was entirely separate from her original claim against OPPD, since the petitioner's liability to her depended not at all upon whether or not OPPD was also liable. Far from being an ancillary and dependent claim, it was a new and independent one.

Second, the nonfederal claim here was asserted by the plaintiff, who voluntarily chose to bring suit upon a state-law claim in a federal court. By contrast, ancillary jurisdiction typically involves claims by a defending party haled into court against his will, or by another person whose rights might be irretrievably lost unless he could assert them in an ongoing action in a federal court. A plaintiff cannot complain if ancillary jurisdiction does not encompass all of his possible claims in a case such as this one, since it is he who has chosen the federal rather than the state forum and must thus accept its limitations. "[T]he efficiency plaintiff seeks so avidly is available without question in the state courts." *Kenrose Mfg. Co. v. Fred Whitaker Co.*, 512 F.2d 890, 894 (CA4).

It is not unreasonable to assume that, in generally requiring complete diversity, Congress did not intend to confine the jurisdiction of federal courts so inflexibly that they are unable to protect legal rights or effectively to resolve an entire, logically entwined lawsuit. Those practical needs are the basis of the doctrine of ancillary jurisdiction. But neither the convenience of litigants nor considerations of judicial economy can suffice to justify extension of the doctrine of ancillary jurisdiction to a plaintiff's cause of action against a citizen of the same State in a diversity case. Congress has established the basic rule that diversity jurisdiction exists under 28 U.S.C. §1332 only when there is complete diversity of citizenship. "The policy of the statute

---

* Eds. — The Court explained: "As used in this opinion, the term 'nonfederal claim' means one as to which there is no independent basis for federal jurisdiction. Conversely, a 'federal claim' means one as to which an independent basis for federal jurisdiction exists."

calls for its strict construction." *Healy v. Ratta*, 292 U.S. 263, 270, 54 S. Ct. 700, 703, 78 L. Ed. 1248; *Indianapolis v. Chase Nat. Bank*, 314 U.S. 63, 76, 62 S.Ct. 15, 20, 86 L. Ed. 47; *Thomson v. Gaskill*, 315 U.S. 442, 446, 62 S. Ct. 673, 675, 86 L. Ed. 951; *Snyder v. Harris*, 394 U.S., at 340, 89 S. Ct., at 1058. To allow the requirement of complete diversity to be circumvented as it was in this case would simply flout the congressional command.

Accordingly, the judgment of the Court of Appeals is reversed.

It is so ordered.

Post-Case Follow-Up

28 U.S.C. §1332 requires *complete* diversity of citizenship. If the plaintiff could simply sue diverse defendants and await impleader of other non-diverse tortfeasors before asserting a claim against them, the complete diversity requirement would be rendered meaningless. Thus, the Court draws a sharp distinction between the *Gibbs* and *Owen* cases. Central to the Court's decision not to exercise supplemental jurisdiction was the fact that the claim at issue was a claim by a plaintiff against a non-diverse party.

Congress codified the limitation set out in *Owen* in 28 U.S.C. §1367(b). Even if the "common nucleus of operative fact" standard is met, there is no supplemental jurisdiction in a case in which the court's original jurisdiction is based solely on diversity of citizenship (1) "over claims by plaintiffs against persons made parties under Rules 14, 19, 20, or 24" or (2) "over claims by persons proposed to be joined as plaintiffs under Rule 19 . . . or seeking to intervene as plaintiffs under Rule 24. . . . " There is a simpler way to state the exception in 1367(b). The exception prohibits district courts from exercising supplemental jurisdiction over the claims of plaintiffs against co-citizens in a diversity case. This means that 1367(b) does not prohibit supplemental jurisdiction over the claims of defendants or third-party defendants, whether asserted as counterclaims, crossclaims, or third-party claims.

Owen Equipment and Erection Co. v. Kroger: Real Life Applications

1. A citizen of Texas files suit in federal district court against a citizen of Nebraska alleging negligence and seeking personal injury damages of $100,000. The Nebraska defendant impleads a Nebraska company seeking contribution for the plaintiff's injuries in an amount not less than $80,000. Does the court have subject matter jurisdiction over the claims asserted in this action, including the third-party claim? Why or why not?

2. Plaintiff, a citizen of Texas, files suit for wrongful death arising out of a car wreck alleging no less than $3 million in damages against two defendants. One of the defendants manufactured the decedent's vehicle and the other defendant manufactured the tires on the decedent's vehicle. Both defendants are Michigan citizens. The car manufacturer defendant asserts a crossclaim against the tire

manufacturer defendant for breach of a contract to supply tires to the car manufacturer. The tires that are the subject of the breach of contract are not the tires on the decedent's vehicle. Does the court have subject matter jurisdiction over the claims asserted in this action, including the third-party claim? Why or why not?

3. Plaintiff and defendant are both citizens of California. Plaintiff pleads two causes of action — sex discrimination in violation of the federal Title VII workplace discrimination act and negligence for a car wreck plaintiff had with defendant. Does the court have subject matter jurisdiction over the claims asserted in this action? Why or why not?

1. Intervening and Required Plaintiffs

Section 1367(b) provides that there is no supplemental jurisdiction over the claims of plaintiffs in a diversity case. Most persons become plaintiffs by commencing the action by filing a complaint in federal court or by filing the initial pleading in state court. However, as we saw in Chapter 19, some persons may be allowed to intervene as plaintiffs or may be joined as plaintiffs because they are required parties. Section 1367(b) provides that there is no supplemental jurisdiction in a diversity case "over claims by persons proposed to be joined as plaintiffs under Rule 19" or over claims by persons "seeking to intervene as plaintiffs under Rule 24." So, regardless of how one becomes a plaintiff, there is no supplemental jurisdiction over the claims of a plaintiff in a diversity case.

Suppose a Texas citizen and an Oklahoma citizen file a $1 million breach of contract action against an Oklahoma citizen in federal district court. The federal district court should dismiss this action for lack of subject matter jurisdiction. The case does not present a federal question, and there is no diversity of citizenship jurisdiction because one of the plaintiffs and the defendant are both Oklahoma citizens, even though the amount in controversy is met. We reach this conclusion using the basic concepts of original jurisdiction covered in Chapters 2 and 3. But suppose instead that the Texas citizen filed the $1 million breach of contract action against the Oklahoma citizen, without joining the Oklahoma plaintiff. Then, the Oklahoma plaintiff moves to intervene (under Rule 24) as a plaintiff in the action. There is still no diversity of citizenship jurisdiction, because the Oklahoman seeking to intervene shares citizenship with the defendant, and there is no supplemental jurisdiction over the claim of a person seeking to intervene as a plaintiff in a diversity case. The court would deny the motion to intervene. Section 1367(b) thus prevents the plaintiffs from achieving through intervention what they could not achieve by joining together as plaintiffs in the first place. We would reach the same result if, instead of seeking to intervene, the Oklahoma citizen was proposed to be joined under Rule 19 as a required plaintiff. The court could not exercise supplemental jurisdiction over the claim and would not join the Oklahoma citizen as a plaintiff.

2. Supplemental Jurisdiction and the Amount in Controversy Requirement

Section 1367(b) prohibits the exercise of supplemental jurisdiction in diversity cases over the claims of plaintiffs *against a co-citizen*. So, a court can exercise supplemental jurisdiction in a diversity case over the claim of a plaintiff against a party who does not have the same citizenship as the plaintiff. The practical effect of this caveat is that 1367(b) does not necessarily prohibit supplemental jurisdiction over a claim by a plaintiff that does not independently meet the amount in controversy requirement in 28 U.S.C. §1332. Still, there must be a basis for original jurisdiction in order to ever exercise supplemental jurisdiction; so, at least one of the plaintiffs must independently meet the amount in controversy requirement. This issue comes up in diversity cases when: (1) there are two or more plaintiffs, (2) at least one of the plaintiffs independently meets the amount in controversy requirement, and (3) at least one of them does not.

Suppose Marla, a citizen of Montana, and Olivier, a citizen of Idaho, file a breach of contract suit against Consolidators, Inc., a citizen of New Mexico. Both Marla and Olivier are suing for breach of the same contract. Marla's claim is for $100,000 and Olivier's claim is for only $50,000. The case looks like this:

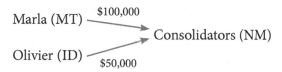

For diversity jurisdiction to exist for each of the claims, each plaintiff must independently meet the amount in controversy requirement. Olivier does not independently meet the amount in controversy requirement. However, a court may exercise supplemental jurisdiction over Olivier's claim. In *Exxon v. Allapattah Services*, the Supreme Court held:

> It follows from this conclusion that the threshold requirement of §1367(a) is satisfied in cases, like those now before us, where some, but not all, of the plaintiffs in a diversity action allege a sufficient amount in controversy. We hold that §1367 by its plain text . . . authorized supplemental jurisdiction over all claims by diverse parties arising out of the same Article III case or controversy, subject only to enumerated exceptions not applicable in the cases now before us.

545 U.S. 546, 565-67 (2005).

So the court can exercise supplemental jurisdiction over Olivier's claim because, although his claim does not meet the amount in controversy requirement, Marla's does, and his claim forms part of the same case or controversy (e.g., arises from a common nucleus of operative fact) as Marla's. The exception in 1367(b) does not prohibit exercising supplemental jurisdiction because, as interpreted in *Exxon*, it only prohibits the exercise of supplemental jurisdiction over the claims of plaintiffs against co-citizens in a diversity case. Notice that Olivier and Consolidators are not co-citizens. If, however, Olivier and Consolidators did share citizenship, the court could not exercise diversity or supplemental jurisdiction over the claim.

D. DECLINING TO EXERCISE SUPPLEMENTAL JURISDICTION

Unlike other types of subject matter jurisdiction, like federal question or diversity of citizenship jurisdiction, supplemental jurisdiction comes with a big caveat: If the court can otherwise exercise supplemental jurisdiction under 28 U.S.C. §1367, a court may nevertheless in its discretion decline to exercise supplemental jurisdiction under the circumstances set out in 1367(c). Subsection 1367(c) provides:

(c) The district courts may decline to exercise supplemental jurisdiction over a claim under subsection (a) if —

(1) the claim raises a novel or complex issue of State law,

(2) the claim substantially predominates over the claim or claims over which the district court has original jurisdiction,

(3) the district court has dismissed all claims over which it has original jurisdiction, or

(4) in exceptional circumstances, there are other compelling reasons for declining jurisdiction.

So courts may decline to exercise supplemental jurisdiction over a state law claim that raises complex or novel issues of state law because state courts, who have the final say over what state law is, are better suited to resolve these issues. A federal court may also decline to exercise supplemental jurisdiction over a state law claim that will raise the predominate issues in the case. Perhaps the most important provision is 1367(c)(3), which states that a district court may refuse to continue to exercise supplemental jurisdiction when it has dismissed the claims over which it has original jurisdiction. In *Gibbs*, the Supreme Court was more categorical than the statute, saying, "Certainly, if the federal claims are dismissed before trial, even though not insubstantial in a jurisdictional sense, the state claims should be dismissed as well." *United Mine Workers of America v. Gibbs*, 383 U.S. 715, 726 (1966). A court may also decline to exercise supplemental jurisdiction in "exceptional circumstances" when there are other "compelling reasons" to decline jurisdiction. The meaning of this language in 1367(c)(4) is likely informed by the Supreme Court's opinion in *Gibbs*, in which the Court said:

That power need not be exercised in every case in which it is found to exist. It has consistently been recognized that pendent jurisdiction is a doctrine of discretion, not of plaintiff's right. Its justification lies in considerations of judicial economy, convenience and fairness to litigants; if these are not present a federal court should hesitate to exercise jurisdiction over state claims, even though bound to apply state law to them .... [T]here may be reasons independent of jurisdictional considerations, such as the likelihood of jury confusion in treating divergent legal theories of relief, that would justify separating state and federal claims for trial, Fed. Rule Civ. Proc. 42(b). If so, jurisdiction should ordinarily be refused.

Thus, if it is inefficient, unfair, or confusing to try the state law claims along with the claims over which the court has original jurisdiction, 1367(b)(4) provides a basis for declining to exercise supplemental jurisdiction. For this reason, a party will always first seek another source of jurisdiction for a claim (such as diversity) before resorting to using supplemental jurisdiction as the sole basis for adding a state law claim to a federal case.

Chapter Summary

■ A federal district court must have subject matter jurisdiction over each of the claims asserted in the action, including every claim, counterclaim, crossclaim, or third-party claim.

■ A court may have original federal question or diversity of citizenship jurisdiction over the additional claims asserted in the action. If it does not have such jurisdiction over these claims, it might be able to exercise supplemental jurisdiction over these additional claims.

■ When the court has original jurisdiction over some claim in the original action filed by the plaintiff, but not over another claim asserted in the action, the court may as a general rule exercise supplemental jurisdiction over the additional claim so long as the claim forms part of the same case or controversy as the claim or claims over which the court has original jurisdiction. The same case or controversy standard is met when the claims arise out of a common nucleus of operative fact.

■ Even if the general rule for exercising supplemental jurisdiction is met, a court may not exercise supplemental jurisdiction in a diversity case over the claim of a plaintiff, including an intervening or required plaintiff under Rule 19, against a co-citizen.

■ A court may in its discretion decline to exercise supplemental jurisdiction when: the state law claim raises complex or novel issues of state law, or predominates over the claims over which the court has original jurisdiction; the court has dismissed all the claims over which it has original jurisdiction; or when concerns of inefficiency, confusion, or unfairness are raised by trying the claims together.

Applying the Concepts

1. A New York citizen files a $1 million negligence action in federal district court against two defendants, one of whom is a California citizen and the other is a citizen of Oklahoma. The court has diversity of citizenship jurisdiction over the action. The Californian asserts a $250,000 crossclaim against the Oklahoman. Does the court have subject matter jurisdiction over the crossclaim? Why or why not?

2. A Texan files an action against a citizen of North Dakota and another citizen of Texas in federal district court, alleging breach of a contract for the sale of goods

and damages in excess of $5 million. The defendant Texan moves to dismiss the action for lack of subject matter jurisdiction. The plaintiff argues that the court has diversity of citizenship jurisdiction over his claim against the North Dakota defendant and supplemental jurisdiction over his claim against the Texas defendant, because both claims form part of the same case or controversy as he is suing them both for breach of the same contract. Under section 1367, how should the court rule on the motion to dismiss and why?

3. A Minnesota citizen files suit against his former employer, also a citizen of Minnesota, in federal district court alleging that his employment was terminated because of his age. The plaintiff had been one of the defendant's salespersons. He asserts causes of action for age discrimination under both the Federal Age Discrimination in Employment Act and under the Minnesota Human Rights Act.

   a. Does the federal district court have subject matter jurisdiction over this action, including both claims? Why or why not?
   b. Now assume that the plaintiff signed a noncompetition agreement with the defendant, his former employer, in which the plaintiff agreed not to compete with the defendant by using his list of potential customers to sell products similar to those sold by the defendant. The defendant asserts a counterclaim against the plaintiff for breach of this agreement, alleging that since his employment with the defendant ended, the plaintiff has been using his customer list to sell products similar to those sold by the defendant. Does the court have subject matter jurisdiction over this claim? Why or why not?
   c. Assume that the district court dismisses the plaintiff's Age Discrimination and Employment Act cause of action 12 months before trial for failure to state a claim. What action might the federal district court take with respect to the Minnesota Human Rights Act cause of action? If that action is taken, who, if anyone, could then decide that cause of action?

4. Rogelio, a citizen of Arizona, files a negligence action against Toasters, Inc., alleging that a toaster he purchased from Toasters caught fire in his home causing him injuries and over $500,000 in medical bills alone. Toasters, Inc. is a citizen of Arkansas and Delaware. Toasters impleads Hot Stuff, Inc., a citizen of both Delaware and Arizona, alleging that Hot Stuff, the manufacturer of the heating element in the Toaster oven, may be responsible for at least part of Rogelio's claim.

   a. Does the district court have subject matter jurisdiction over the third-party claim by Toasters against Hot Stuff? Why or why not?
   b. Assume Rogelio asserts a $1 million claim against Hot Stuff alleging that Hot Stuff's negligent design of the heating element caused his injuries. Does the district court have subject matter jurisdiction over Rogelio's claim against Hot Stuff? Why or why not?

Civil Procedure in Practice

Ingrid and Pom both purchased securities through a financial services firm, Capstone, LLC, based upon Capstone's representation that any income from or capital gain on the security was not subject to federal tax. Ingrid and Pom filed suit in federal district court against Capstone alleging misrepresentation and fraud after being forced to pay federal taxes on income from the securities. Ingrid was born in Maine and has lived there all her life. Pom is a citizen of Thailand but has been admitted to the United States as a permanent legal resident alien and has lived in Massachusetts for five years. Capstone is a limited liability company organized under the law of Delaware with its principal place of business in Boston, Massachusetts. Its sole member is a man named Howard, a U.S. citizen domiciled in Vermont. In their complaint, Ingrid claims $100,000 in damages based on what she had to pay in federal income taxes, but Pom's tax liability was less than Ingrid's; so, he claims only $60,000 in damages. You are the law clerk to the federal district judge assigned to this case.

1. Your judge wants you to tell her whether or not she has subject matter jurisdiction over Ingrid and Pom's action against Capstone and to support your answer with the necessary analysis.

2. Shortly after filing an answer to Ingrid and Pom's complaint, Capstone has a third-party complaint served on Trebuchet, Inc., the company that issued the securities at issue, alleging that Trebuchet misrepresented to Capstone the tax benefits of the securities and is therefore liable to Capstone for Ingrid and Pom's claim against Capstone, totally $160,000. Trebuchet is a corporation organized under the law of Delaware with its principal place of business in New York. Your judge wants to know if she has subject matter jurisdiction over this third-party claim and why or why not.

3. After Trebuchet appears in the action, Ingrid and Pom amend their complaint to assert claims against Trebuchet for fraud and misrepresentation regarding the tax benefits of the securities they purchased through Capstone. Can your judge exercise subject matter jurisdiction over these claims? Why or why not?

Pretrial and Trial

Disposition Without Trial

Not all civil actions result in trials. In fact, the vast majority do not. Most civil actions are disposed of pretrial. We have already addressed a number of different grounds for disposing of a civil action pretrial. A default judgment disposes of a case because the defendant failed to appear and defend. A case may be dismissed because the plaintiff failed to state a claim. Or because the court lacks subject matter or personal jurisdiction, or is not a proper venue. Or because the defendant was not properly served. Or because an indispensable party has not been joined. Sometimes the plaintiff simply does not wish to continue prosecuting his action, at least not in the forum he initially chose. One common method of disposing of a case pretrial not yet discussed is through the plaintiff's **voluntary dismissal** of the action. A plaintiff may voluntarily dismiss the action for a variety of reasons, perhaps most commonly because the parties have reached a settlement and further proceedings are unnecessary and, indeed, disallowed by the settlement agreement. A court may dismiss a case without the plaintiff's consent when the plaintiff has failed to diligently prosecute the case. Even if a plaintiff wishes to proceed to trial, a trial is not always necessary. Trials resolve factual disputes. If there are no factual disputes, or if the factual disputes that exist do not affect the judgment the court should render, a trial is unnecessary. In such cases, the court may grant **summary judgment** pretrial. A motion for summary judgment is appropriately granted when the evidence does not raise a genuine dispute as to a material fact. This chapter

Key Concepts

- When a plaintiff may voluntarily dismiss a case without a court order
- The difference between dismissals with and without prejudice
- When a court may involuntarily dismiss the plaintiff's action
- When there is "no genuine dispute as to any material fact," and why summary judgment is appropriate when no such dispute exists
- How to properly make and support a motion for summary judgment based on which party bears the burden of persuasion at trial on the issue
- How to properly respond to a motion for summary judgment

focuses on both of these types of pretrial dispositions of actions — voluntary dismissals and summary judgment.

A. VOLUNTARY DISMISSAL

Federal Rule 41 addresses the circumstances in which a plaintiff may voluntarily dismiss the action he filed. Your first thought is likely, "Why would a plaintiff want to voluntarily dismiss his action?" This is a good question. After all, the plaintiff went through the trouble of selecting the forum, drafting a complaint, and getting the defendant or defendants served with process. There are many reasons a plaintiff may seek dismissal of his action. He may think better of his initial choice of forum and decide that starting over in a different forum is to his advantage. He may decide he needs additional time to investigate his case, or that his case no longer appears to have merit. Perhaps the parties have reached a settlement of their dispute and the plaintiff no longer needs to pursue the action. Whatever the reason, how a plaintiff secures a dismissal of the action depends upon how, if at all, the defendant has responded to the complaint.

1. Notice Dismissals

A plaintiff has a right under certain circumstances to unilaterally dismiss his action. Under Rule 41(a)(1)(A)(i), set out in Exhibit 21.1, a plaintiff may dismiss an action without a court order simply by filing a notice of dismissal, but he may do this only before the defendant files either an answer or a motion for summary judgment. Once the defendant files either an answer or a motion for summary judgment, the plaintiff must obtain a court order or the agreement of all the parties to dismiss the action. Note that the plaintiff files a *notice* of dismissal. The plaintiff isn't asking anyone's permission to dismiss the case. He is not making a motion, and neither a court order nor the permission of the other parties is required. The plaintiff is simply notifying the court and the other parties that he has unilaterally dismissed his action. This type of dismissal is sometimes called a **notice dismissal**.

EXHIBIT 21.1 Rule 41(a)(1)(A)(i)

(a) Voluntary Dismissal.
    (1) By the Plaintiff.
        (A) Without a Court Order. Subject to Rules 23(e), 23.1(c), 23.2, and 66 and any applicable federal statute, the plaintiff may dismiss an action without a court order by filing:
            (i) a notice of dismissal before the opposing party serves either an answer or a motion for summary judgment. . . .

Limitations on Notice Dismissals

Defendant Files an Answer or Motion for Summary Judgment

Once a defendant files an answer or a motion for summary judgment, the plaintiff may no longer unilaterally dismiss the action by filing a notice of dismissal. Instead, he will have to obtain a court order or secure the permission of the other parties. An answer filed in either state or federal court precludes a notice dismissal. Suppose the plaintiff filed his action in state court. The defendant served an answer in state court before removing the case to federal court. The plaintiff may not unilaterally dismiss the federal court action because the defendant has filed an answer, which precludes a notice dismissal even though the answer was filed and served in state court. On the other hand, a motion to dismiss under Rule 12(b) does not constitute an answer or a motion for summary judgment, and therefore does not preclude a notice dismissal by the plaintiff. Plaintiffs often use this feature of Rule 41 to select a different forum.

Suppose a defendant's first Rule 12 response to the plaintiff's complaint is to file a Rule 12(b)(3) motion to dismiss for improper venue. The plaintiff could dismiss his action simply by filing a notice of dismissal with the federal court. The plaintiff can then file his action in a different venue, perhaps escaping venue litigation altogether. Plaintiffs may also use a notice dismissal to avoid litigating in federal court after removal. Suppose Tonya, a citizen of Texas, is severely injured on a waterslide at a water park operated by Aqua-Fun, LLC, a citizen of Delaware and Florida. Aqua-Fun leases the property on which the water park is located from the property's owner, Nationwide Property, Inc., a citizen of Texas. Tonya files suit in Texas state court against only Aqua-Fun, seeking millions of dollars in damages. Before filing an answer in Texas state court, Aqua-Fun files a notice of removal on diversity of citizenship grounds in the proper federal district court. Tonya believes she has a better chance of success in state court. So Tonya files a notice of dismissal with the federal district court before Nationwide files an answer. Then she files another action in Texas state court, this time naming both Aqua-Fun and Nationwide Property as defendants. Because Nationwide and Tonya are both Texas citizens (and because Nationwide is a citizen of the forum state), Tonya's second action is not removable to federal court.

Although Rule 41 doesn't prevent this sort of gamesmanship regarding the forum, the Rule is not completely silent as to its effects. When a plaintiff refiles a claim she previously dismissed under Rule 41, Rule 41(d) allows the court to order the plaintiff to pay the defendant all or some part of the costs of the previous action. The costs that a court may in its discretion award include attorneys' fees incurred by the defendant in the first action.

Moreover, Rule 41 limits the gamesmanship. The second time a plaintiff dismisses her case, the dismissal is **with prejudice** — meaning it cannot be refiled again. Why place a limit on when and how often a plaintiff can file a notice of dismissal? Wouldn't the defendant always be pleased when a plaintiff wants to dismiss the action against him? The answer is no. The defendant knows that the dismissal of one action is likely only a prelude to the filing of another action against him based on the same event. Without limitations, the plaintiff could dismiss his action when the court's rulings early on are unfavorable to him. As discussed in Chapter 24, a judgment will preclude a plaintiff from relitigating claims and issues decided against him in an earlier action, but if the plaintiff dismisses before the court renders its judgment, these earlier decisions will not be binding on the court in the later action. Without limitations on notice dismissals, a plaintiff could file action after action until he finally finds a court willing to rule in his favor on key issues. Such an approach to notice dismissals leads to both conflicting results and a waste of judicial and party resources.

Before a Motion for Summary Judgment?

Rule 41(a)(1)(A)(i) permits a notice dismissal only before the defendant files either an answer or a motion for summary judgment. The Rule's reference to a motion for summary judgment may strike you as odd, because it assumes that a motion for summary judgment may be filed before an answer, and, as discussed in Chapter 15, only motions to dismiss under Rules 12(b)(1)-(7) may be filed pre-answer. When would a defendant file a motion for summary judgment before filing an answer? The answer to this question lies in the 12(b)(6) motion to dismiss for failure to state a claim. A 12(b)(6) motion asks for a dismissal based on the allegations in the complaint, but sometimes the movant supports his motion to dismiss with matters outside the complaint (e.g., with evidence). So, the motion is *titled* a motion to dismiss for failure to state a claim, but it more closely resembles a motion for summary judgment. In this situation, Rule 12(d) instructs the court to either exclude the evidence and treat the motion as one to dismiss for failure to state a claim, or to treat it as a motion for summary judgment and allow the plaintiff to respond appropriately. So Rule 12(d) gives the court the ability to treat a Rule 12(b)(6) motion as one for summary judgment. Since this motion can be made before the defendant answers, if the court treats it as a motion for summary judgment, the plaintiff is no longer able to unilaterally dismiss his action under Rule 41, even though the defendant has not filed an answer.

Class Actions and Receivers

Rule 41(a)(1)(A) makes notice dismissals subject to the limitations in Rules 23(e), 23.1, 23.2, and 66. These other Federal Rules prohibit a plaintiff from unilaterally dismissing a class action, a shareholder or member derivative action, or a case in which a receiver has been appointed. Class actions were discussed in Chapter 19, but derivative actions and receivers may be unfamiliar to you. A **derivative action** is one in which the shareholders of a corporation or the members of an unincorporated association bring suit on behalf of the corporation or association because the officers and directors of the entity are unwilling to authorize the corporation or association to pursue the action. The shareholders or members derive their claim from the entity — hence, the term derivative action. A **receiver** is someone who has been appointed to be responsible for the property of another person, normally because the person is unable to pay all of his debts and obligations. A plaintiff may not unilaterally dismiss derivative actions or cases in which a receiver has been appointed. In such cases, the plaintiff must obtain a court order to dismiss the action even when the defendant has not yet filed an answer or a motion for summary judgment.

Effect of a Notice Dismissal

Under Rule 41(a)(1)(B), shown in Exhibit 21.2, a notice dismissal is **without prejudice to refiling**. Without prejudice to refiling means that the dismissal will not preclude the plaintiff from refiling the action later in the same or another court. For example, in our water park accident case, Tonya's notice of dismissal is without prejudice; so, she is able to file a second action based on the same event. However, a plaintiff may dismiss an action only one time without prejudice. If the plaintiff has already dismissed any state or federal court action based on or including the same claim, a second dismissal will be with prejudice, meaning the dismissal will preclude later litigation of the claim. Suppose Aqua-Fun and Nationwide remove Tonya's second action, alleging that Nationwide is fraudulently joined, and Tonya files a second notice of dismissal. This second notice of dismissal is an adjudication on the merits and precludes further litigation of the claim in either state or federal court.

[handwritten margin note: what happens if π dismisses + then a court dismisses?]

2. A Stipulation of Dismissal

Under Rule 41(a)(1)(A)(ii), a plaintiff may obtain a dismissal by securing the agreement of all parties who have appeared in the action. A stipulation of dismissal is another means of obtaining a dismissal without a court order. You may be wondering why all the parties would agree that a case should be dismissed. Most commonly, a stipulation of dismissal follows settlement. When the parties settle a claim, they enter into a settlement agreement. The settlement agreement is a contract that sets out the terms of the settlement — typically that the plaintiff will forever give up his claim in exchange for a specified amount of money — but a settlement agreement does not dispose of the legal action pending in federal court. To do that, the parties can file a stipulation of dismissal. A stipulation of dismissal is without prejudice unless the stipulation says otherwise. A defendant who has just paid money to resolve the dispute will likely insist that the dismissal be with prejudice in order to ensure that the plaintiff does not file another action based on the same event again.

EXHIBIT 21.2   **Rule 41(a)(1)(B)**

(B) Effect. Unless the notice or stipulation states otherwise, the dismissal is without prejudice. But if the plaintiff previously dismissed any federal- or state-court action based on or including the same claim, a notice of dismissal operates as an adjudication on the merits.

3. Dismissal with Court Order

Once the defendant has served an answer or a motion for summary judgment, a plaintiff must obtain a court order to have the action dismissed. In other words, the plaintiff no longer has a *right* to dismiss. Instead, the district court has broad discretion to grant or deny the dismissal. The key consideration is whether or not permitting dismissal will cause prejudice to the defendant. The more time that has passed and the more resources that have been expended since the filing of the lawsuit, the more likely dismissal will be denied. A court may, however, grant a dismissal even if the plaintiff may obtain some sort of tactical advantage, such as obtaining new evidence or a more favorable forum. A dismissal of this sort is without prejudice unless the order states otherwise.

4. Effect of Dismissal on Counterclaims

Under Rule 41(a)(2), if the defendant has asserted a counterclaim against the plaintiff before the plaintiff files his motion to dismiss, the defendant may prevent dismissal simply by objecting. However, the court may dismiss the plaintiff's claim over the objection of the defendant if the court allows the counterclaim to remain pending. The court dismisses the plaintiff's claim but proceeds to adjudicate the counterclaim. Thus, a plaintiff cannot avoid litigating a counterclaim simply by moving to dismiss his action under Rule 41. This provision in Rule 41(a)(2) is made subject to dismissals without court order under Rule 41(a)(1). The effect is that the defendant and plaintiff may stipulate dismissal of the plaintiff's action despite the pendency of a counterclaim and without a court order. Rule 41(a)(2) does not intersect with the plaintiff's ability to unilaterally dismiss under Rule 41(a)(1)(A)(i). A defendant asserts a counterclaim in his answer, the filing of which precludes a plaintiff from unilaterally dismissing his action anyway.

B. INVOLUNTARY DISMISSAL

Rule 41(b) allows a court to dismiss a case when a plaintiff "fails to prosecute or to comply with these rules or a court order." Dismissal on this ground makes sense. The plaintiff has sued the defendant claiming he is entitled to a remedy based on some sort of wrongdoing by the defendant. This claim leaves the defendant uncertain as to what his obligations are and how, if at all, he can proceed with his normal affairs. Litigation is also almost always quite stressful for the litigants. It only makes sense to require the plaintiff to pursue his claim with reasonable diligence. Failure to do so must, at some point, result in dismissal of the action.

It is important to distinguish dismissals under Rule 41(b) from voluntary dismissals under Rule 41(a). Under Rule 41(a), a plaintiff wants the case dismissed for some reason. Under Rule 41(b), presumably the plaintiff does not want the case dismissed, because he has not sought a voluntary dismissal. Instead, the court is dismissing the case because the plaintiff has been dilatory in pursuing his claim or has failed to comply with his obligations under the Rules or a court order. It is also important to distinguish the role of Rule 41(b) from other rules authorizing dismissals. As previously discussed, Rule 12 authorizes dismissal of an action on a variety of grounds, including lack of subject matter or personal jurisdiction and for failure to join an indispensable party, among others. Rule 37(b) authorizes dismissal of an action for failure to comply with a discovery order. Rule 4(m) authorizes a court to dismiss an action when a plaintiff fails to serve the defendant with process within 90 days of filing the complaint or within some other time specified by the court.

So what does Rule 41(b) do that is different from the many other rules that authorize dismissals under various circumstances? The principal work of Rule 41(b) is to allow dismissal when the plaintiff fails to diligently prosecute his case. For example, dismissal is appropriate under Rule 41(b) when the plaintiff repeatedly misses pretrial deadlines without notification or justification (*see, e.g., Sanders v. Union Pacific R.R. Co.*, 154 F.3d 1037 (9th Cir. 1998)), and, perhaps most commonly, when the plaintiff fails to appear for trial, particularly when the plaintiff has asked for continuances of previous trial settings. *See, e.g., Dorsey v. Scott Wetzel Services, Inc.*, 84 F.3d 170 (5th Cir. 1996).

A dismissal under Rule 41(b) is with prejudice to refiling, unless the order of dismissal states otherwise. A trial court has broad discretion to dismiss an action under Rule 41(b) either with or without prejudice. The trial court's decision to dismiss a case under Rule 41(b) with prejudice is likely to be affirmed on appeal if the plaintiff repeatedly missed deadlines imposed by the Rules or court orders or repeatedly rescheduled the trial setting and has no adequate justification for the delay, such as serious illness or ongoing settlement negotiations.

> ### Do Clients Suffer for Their Attorneys' Errors?
>
> Rule 41(b) allows a court to dismiss an action due to the plaintiff's failure to prosecute his action diligently. Of course, often the plaintiff has nothing to do with this lack of diligence. It's the plaintiff's attorney who is at fault. And you have probably noticed by now that there are all sorts of mistakes an attorney can make that can harm the interests of the client, even when the client played no role in the mistake. Is it right to allow a client to suffer for the mistakes of his attorney? The Supreme Court addressed this question in *Link v. Wabash R.R. Co.*, a case that was dismissed by the trial court when the plaintiff's attorney failed to appear at a pretrial conference. The court explained that the client "voluntarily chose this attorney as his representative in the action, and he cannot now avoid the consequences of the acts or omissions of this freely selected agent." 370 U.S. 626, 633-34 (1962). To hold otherwise would be to upset "our system of representative litigation." *Id.* at 634. So the client suffers for the mistakes of his lawyer. At least temporarily. When an attorney's actions or omissions harm his client, the client may have a claim for legal malpractice against the attorney. The malpractice suit will seek to shift the costs of the harm from the client to the attorney. The *Link* case drives home the point that representing a client as an attorney is a profound responsibility.

C. SUMMARY JUDGMENT

Rule 56 governs summary judgment in federal court. A motion for summary judgment is a pretrial motion seeking judgment as a matter of law because there is no "genuine dispute as to any material fact." If the motion is granted, the movant will have won without having endured the time, expense, and uncertainty of trial. Summary judgment also provides the court an opportunity to save its own time and effort by eliminating claims and defenses that lack evidentiary support.

1. The Role of Judge and Jury at Trial

Understanding summary judgment requires an understanding of the different roles the judge and jury play. At trial, the judge determines the legal issues, such as whether prospective jurors are qualified to serve, the admissibility of evidence, and the content of jury instructions. The jury decides disputed, material fact issues. Did the defendant run the red light as alleged by the plaintiff? Breach the contract? Terminate the plaintiff's employment due to her race? If there are no disputed fact issues, the jury has no role to play and the court can grant judgment as a matter of law.

2. Genuine Dispute as to a Material Fact

Rule 56(a), set out in Exhibit 21.3, provides that the court may grant summary judgment only if there is no genuine dispute as to any material fact. In making this determination, the court looks to the evidence on the issue, but it does so only to determine if there is a triable issue of fact. It does not resolve conflicts in the evidence or make credibility determinations. And it must draw all reasonable inferences in favor of the nonmovant. If the evidence supports inferences both in favor of the movant and the nonmovant, the court must assume the inference that favors the nonmovant is true.

The disputed fact issue must be material to avoid summary judgment. Disputed but immaterial fact issues will not preclude summary judgment. The substantive law determines what fact issues are material. If the disputed fact issue could not change the verdict regardless of how it is resolved, it is not material. Suppose that

EXHIBIT 21.3   **Rule 56(a)**

(a) Motion for Summary Judgment or Partial Summary Judgment. A party may move for summary judgment, identifying each claim or defense—or the part of each claim or defense—on which summary judgment is sought. The court shall grant summary judgment if the movant shows that there is no genuine dispute as to any material fact and the movant is entitled to judgment as a matter of law. The court should state on the record the reasons for granting or denying the motion.

the law requires the plaintiff to prove elements A, B, C, and D in order to recover. If there is no genuine dispute as *one* of these elements, a genuine dispute as to one or more of the others will not preclude summary judgment. Suppose there is no genuine dispute as to element A. The fact that there is a genuine dispute as to element D will not prevent summary judgment. This is true because, regardless of how element D is resolved, the evidence will not support a verdict for the plaintiff, because he must prove *all* the elements.

3. Supporting a Motion for Summary Judgment; Summary Judgment Evidence

A motion for summary judgment must state the grounds for the motion. A party cannot move for summary judgment saying only "there is no genuine dispute as to any material fact." Instead, the motion must identify the material fact issue or issues as to which there is no genuine dispute. A movant may (and sometimes must) support its motion with evidence. Under Rule 56(c), summary judgment evidence includes depositions, admissions, responses to interrogatories, affidavits, and sworn declarations. Other evidence, such as documents and photos, may be brought to the court's attention by being included as exhibits to depositions, affidavits, or sworn declarations. Affidavits and sworn declarations must be based on the affiant's or declarant's personal knowledge. Inadmissible hearsay and speculation will not be considered at summary judgment. The evidence must also be admissible at trial in order to be considered at summary judgment. You will learn more about what evidence is considered admissible in your Evidence class. The point to remember here is that the court will not consider at summary judgment evidence that the jury would not be able to hear at trial. The court will not consider live testimony or exhibits offered at any summary judgment hearing.

The evidence, if any, necessary to support a summary judgment motion depends upon the grounds for summary judgment. If the motion seeks judgment based on a claim or defense on which the movant bears the burden of proof at trial, the supporting evidence will have to conclusively establish each element of the claim or defense. This makes sense. The movant will have to prove all elements at trial in order to support a verdict on his own claim or defense. Why would the court grant summary judgment pretrial without conclusive proof of all elements? If, on the other hand, the motion seeks judgment on the nonmovant's claim or defense, he may support his motion with evidence negating an essential element of the claim or defense, or alternatively he may simply point out that the nonmovant lacks any evidence of an essential element of the claim or defense. This too makes sense, because the nonmovant has to prove all the elements of his claim or defense at trial, and a lack of evidence on any element or evidence conclusively negating any element precludes a verdict in his favor.

4. Making a Proper Motion for Summary Judgment

A defendant must properly make and support a motion for summary judgment to obtain judgment as a matter of law. In <u>fact, if the motion is not properly made</u>, it <u>must be denied even if the nonmovant fails to respond or responds inadequately</u>. *Celotex Corp. v. Catrett* addresses how to properly make and support a summary judgment motion and how this burden varies depending upon which party carries the burden of proof at trial.

Case Preview

Celotex Corp. v. Catrett

Celotex Corp. v. Catrett was decided under an earlier version of Rule 56. The former version of the Rule is not substantively, materially different than the current Rule, but the Rule has been restyled in order to improve clarity since the *Celotex* decision. As a result, some of the provisions referenced in the Court's opinion are now set out in different subdivisions of the current Rule. Where necessary, an editorial comment in brackets will point you to the current provision of the Rule. As you read *Celotex*, consider the following:

1. Catrett alleged several different theories of liability. What is the fact issue as to which there is no genuine dispute according to Celotex, and why does it dispose of all of Catrett's theories?
2. When will pointing out an absence of evidence constitute a properly made motion for summary judgment? When is more required, and what more is required under those circumstances?
3. What other option did Celotex have for properly supporting its motion for summary judgment?

Celotex Corp. v. Catrett
477 U.S. 317 (1986)

Justice REHNQUIST delivered the opinion of the Court.

The United States District Court for the District of Columbia granted the motion of petitioner Celotex Corporation for summary judgment against respondent Catrett because the latter was unable to produce evidence in support of her allegation in her wrongful-death complaint that the decedent had been exposed to petitioner's asbestos products. A divided panel of the Court of Appeals for the District of Columbia Circuit reversed, however, holding that petitioner's failure to support its motion with evidence tending to *negate* such exposure precluded the entry of summary judgment in its favor. *Catrett v. Johns-Manville Sales Corp.*, 244 U.S. App.

D.C. 160, 756 F.2d 181 (1985). This view conflicted with that of the Third Circuit in *In re Japanese Electronic Products,* 723 F.2d 238 (1983), rev'd on other grounds *sub nom. Matsushita Electric Industrial Co. v. Zenith Radio Corp.,* 475 U.S. 574, 106 S. Ct. 1348, 89 L. Ed. 2d 538 (1986). We granted certiorari to resolve the conflict, 474 U.S. 944, 106 S. Ct. 342, 88 L. Ed. 2d 285 (1985), and now reverse the decision of the District of Columbia Circuit.

Respondent commenced this lawsuit in September 1980, alleging that the death in 1979 of her husband, Louis H. Catrett, resulted from his exposure to products containing asbestos manufactured or distributed by 15 named corporations. Respondent's complaint sounded in negligence, breach of warranty, and strict liability. Two of the defendants filed motions challenging the District Court's *in personam* jurisdiction, and the remaining 13, including petitioner, filed motions for summary judgment. Petitioner's motion, which was first filed in September 1981, argued that summary judgment was proper because respondent had "failed to produce evidence that any [Celotex] product . . . was the proximate cause of the injuries alleged within the jurisdictional limits of [the District] Court." In particular, petitioner noted that respondent had failed to identify, in answering interrogatories specifically requesting such information, any witnesses who could testify about the decedent's exposure to petitioner's asbestos products. In response to petitioner's summary judgment motion, respondent then produced three documents which she claimed "demonstrate that there is a genuine material factual dispute" as to whether the decedent had ever been exposed to petitioner's asbestos products. The three documents included a transcript of a deposition of the decedent, a letter from an official of one of the decedent's former employers whom petitioner planned to call as a trial witness, and a letter from an insurance company to respondent's attorney, all tending to establish that the decedent had been exposed to petitioner's asbestos products in Chicago during 1970–1971. Petitioner, in turn, argued that the three documents were inadmissible hearsay and thus could not be considered in opposition to the summary judgment motion.

In July 1982, almost two years after the commencement of the lawsuit, the District Court granted all of the motions filed by the various defendants. The court explained that it was granting petitioner's summary judgment motion because "there [was] no showing that the plaintiff was exposed to the defendant Celotex's product in the District of Columbia or elsewhere within the statutory period." . . . Respondent appealed only the grant of summary judgment in favor of petitioner, and a divided panel of the District of Columbia Circuit reversed. The majority of the Court of Appeals held that petitioner's summary judgment motion was rendered "fatally defective" by the fact that petitioner "made no effort to adduce *any* evidence, in the form of affidavits or otherwise, to support its motion." . . . The majority therefore declined to consider petitioner's argument that none of the evidence produced by respondent in opposition to the motion for summary judgment would have been admissible at trial . . .

We think that the position taken by the majority of the Court of Appeals is inconsistent with the standard for summary judgment set forth in Rule 56(c) of the Federal Rules of Civil Procedure. Under Rule 56(c), summary judgment is proper "if the pleadings, depositions, answers to interrogatories, and admissions on file, together with the affidavits, if any, show that there is no genuine issue as to any material fact and that the moving party is entitled to a judgment as a matter of law." In our view, the plain language of Rule 56(c) mandates the entry of summary judgment, after adequate time for discovery and upon motion, against a party who fails to make a showing sufficient to establish the existence of an element essential to that party's case, and on which that party will bear the burden of proof at trial. In such a situation, there can be "no genuine issue as to any material fact," since a complete failure of proof concerning an essential element of the nonmoving party's case necessarily renders all other facts immaterial. The moving party is "entitled to a judgment as a matter of law" because the nonmoving party has failed to make a sufficient showing on an essential element of her case with respect to which she has the burden of proof. "[T]h[e] standard [for granting summary judgment] mirrors the standard for a directed verdict under Federal Rule of Civil Procedure 50(a). . . ." *Anderson v. Liberty Lobby, Inc.,* 477 U.S. 242, 250, 106 S. Ct. 2505, 2511, 91 L. Ed. 2d 202 (1986).

Of course, a party seeking summary judgment always bears the initial responsibility of informing the district court of the basis for its motion, and identifying those portions of "the pleadings, depositions, answers to interrogatories, and admissions on file, together with the affidavits, if any," which it believes demonstrate the absence of a genuine issue of material fact. But unlike the Court of Appeals, we find no express or implied requirement in Rule 56 that the moving party support its motion with affidavits or other similar materials *negating* the opponent's claim. On the contrary, Rule 56(c), which refers to "the affidavits, *if any*" (emphasis added), suggests the absence of such a requirement. And if there were any doubt about the meaning of Rule 56(c) in this regard, such doubt is clearly removed by Rules 56(a) and (b), which provide that claimants and defendants, respectively, may move for summary judgment "*with or without supporting affidavits*" (emphasis added). [Eds. — The language in the current version of Rule 56 is different than what is quoted here, but it provides that a party may support its motion by "showing that the materials cited do not establish . . . the presence of a genuine dispute, or that an adverse party cannot produce admissible evidence to support the fact."] The import of these subsections is that, regardless of whether the moving party accompanies its summary judgment motion with affidavits, the motion may, and should, be granted so long as whatever is before the district court demonstrates that the standard for the entry of summary judgment, as set forth in Rule 56(c), is satisfied. One of the principal purposes of the summary judgment rule is to isolate and dispose of factually unsupported claims or defenses, and we think it should be interpreted in a way that allows it to accomplish this purpose.

Respondent argues, however, that Rule 56(e), by its terms, places on the nonmoving party the burden of coming forward with rebuttal affidavits, or other specified kinds of materials, only in response to a motion for summary judgment "made and supported as provided in this rule." According to respondent's argument, since petitioner did not "support" its motion with affidavits, summary judgment was improper in this case. But as we have already explained, a motion for summary judgment may be made pursuant to Rule 56 "with or without supporting affidavits." In cases like the instant one, where the nonmoving party will bear the burden of proof at trial on a dispositive issue, a summary judgment motion may properly be made in reliance solely on the "pleadings, depositions, answers to interrogatories, and admissions on file." Such a motion, whether or not accompanied by affidavits, will be "made and supported as provided in this rule," and Rule 56(e) therefore requires the nonmoving party to go beyond the pleadings and by her own affidavits, or by the "depositions, answers to interrogatories, and admissions on file," designate "specific facts showing that there is a genuine issue for trial."

We do not mean that the nonmoving party must produce evidence in a form that would be admissible at trial in order to avoid summary judgment. Obviously, Rule 56 does not require the nonmoving party to depose her own witnesses. Rule 56(e) permits a proper summary judgment motion to be opposed by any of the kinds of evidentiary materials listed in Rule 56(c), except the mere pleadings themselves, and it is from this list that one would normally expect the nonmoving party to make the showing to which we have referred.

* * *

The last two sentences of Rule 56(e) were added . . . to disapprove a line of cases allowing a party opposing summary judgment to resist a properly made motion by reference only to its pleadings . . . these two sentences were not intended to *reduce* the burden of the moving party, it is also obvious that they were not adopted to *add to* that burden. Yet that is exactly the result which the reasoning of the Court of Appeals would produce; in effect, an amendment to Rule 56(e) designed to *facilitate* the granting of motions for summary judgment would be interpreted to make it *more difficult* to grant such motions. Nothing in the two sentences themselves requires this result, for the reasons we have previously indicated, and we now put to rest any inference that they do so.

Our conclusion is bolstered by the fact that district courts are widely acknowledged to possess the power to enter summary judgments *sua sponte,* so long as the losing party was on notice that she had to come forward with all of her evidence. . . . It would surely defy common sense to hold that the District Court could have entered summary judgment *sua sponte* in favor of petitioner in the instant case, but that petitioner's filing of a motion requesting such a disposition precluded the District Court from ordering it.

Respondent commenced this action in September 1980, and petitioner's motion was filed in September 1981. The parties had conducted discovery, and no serious claim can be made that respondent was in any sense "railroaded" by a premature motion for summary judgment. Any potential problem with such premature motions can be adequately dealt with under Rule 56(f), which allows a summary judgment motion to be denied, or the hearing on the motion to be continued, if the nonmoving party has not had an opportunity to make full discovery. [Eds. — The current version of the Rule provided in Rule 56(d) permits the court to defer consideration of the motion if the nonmovant specifies reasons why it cannot present facts "essential to justify its opposition."]

In this Court, respondent's brief and oral argument have been devoted as much to the proposition that an adequate showing of exposure to petitioner's asbestos products was made as to the proposition that no such showing should have been required. But the Court of Appeals declined to address either the adequacy of the showing made by respondent in opposition to petitioner's motion for summary judgment, or the question whether such a showing, if reduced to admissible evidence, would be sufficient to carry respondent's burden of proof at trial. We think the Court of Appeals with its superior knowledge of local law is better suited than we are to make these determinations in the first instance.

The Federal Rules of Civil Procedure have for almost 50 years authorized motions for summary judgment upon proper showings of the lack of a genuine, triable issue of material fact. Summary judgment procedure is properly regarded not as a disfavored procedural shortcut, but rather as an integral part of the Federal Rules as a whole, which are designed "to secure the just, speedy and inexpensive determination of every action." Fed. Rule Civ. Proc. 1; see Schwarzer, Summary Judgment Under the Federal Rules: Defining Genuine Issues of Material Fact, 99 F.R.D. 465, 467 (1984). Before the shift to "notice pleading" accomplished by the Federal Rules, motions to dismiss a complaint or to strike a defense were the principal tools by which factually insufficient claims or defenses could be isolated and prevented from going to trial with the attendant unwarranted consumption of public and private resources. But with the advent of "notice pleading," the motion to dismiss seldom fulfills this function any more, and its place has been taken by the motion for summary judgment. Rule 56 must be construed with due regard not only for the rights of persons asserting claims and defenses that are adequately based in fact to have those claims and defenses tried to a jury, but also for the rights of persons opposing such claims and defenses to demonstrate in the manner provided by the Rule, prior to trial, that the claims and defenses have no factual basis.

The judgment of the Court of Appeals is accordingly reversed, and the case is remanded for further proceedings consistent with this opinion.

It is so ordered.

Justice BRENNAN, with whom THE CHIEF JUSTICE and Justice BLACKMUN join, dissenting.

This case requires the Court to determine whether Celotex satisfied its initial burden of production in moving for summary judgment on the ground that the plaintiff lacked evidence to establish an essential element of her case at trial. I do not disagree with the Court's legal analysis. The Court clearly rejects the ruling of the Court of Appeals that the defendant must provide affirmative evidence disproving the plaintiff's case. Beyond this, however, the Court has not clearly explained what is required of a moving party seeking summary judgment on the ground that the nonmoving party cannot prove its case. This lack of clarity is unfortunate: district courts must routinely decide summary judgment motions, and the Court's opinion will very likely create confusion. For this reason, even if I agreed with the Court's result, I would have written separately to explain more clearly the law in this area. However, because I believe that Celotex did not meet its burden of production under Federal Rule of Civil Procedure 56, I respectfully dissent from the Court's judgment.

I

Summary judgment is appropriate where the Court is satisfied "that there is no genuine issue as to any material fact and that the moving party is entitled to a judgment as a matter of law." Fed. Rule Civ. Proc. 56(c). The burden of establishing the nonexistence of a "genuine issue" is on the party moving for summary judgment. . . . This burden has two distinct components: an initial burden of production, which shifts to the nonmoving party if satisfied by the moving party; and an ultimate burden of persuasion, which always remains on the moving party. See 10A Wright, Miller & Kane §2727. The court need not decide whether the moving party has satisfied its ultimate burden of persuasion unless and until the Court finds that the moving party has discharged its initial burden of production. . . .

The burden of production imposed by Rule 56 requires the moving party to make a prima facie showing that it is entitled to summary judgment. 10A Wright, Miller & Kane §2727. The manner in which this showing can be made depends upon which party will bear the burden of persuasion on the challenged claim at trial. If the *moving* party will bear the burden of persuasion at trial, that party must support its motion with credible evidence — using any of the materials specified in Rule 56(c) — that would entitle it to a directed verdict if not controverted at trial. *Ibid.* Such an affirmative showing shifts the burden of production to the party opposing the motion and requires that party either to produce evidentiary materials that demonstrate the existence of a "genuine issue" for trial or to submit an affidavit requesting additional time for discovery. . . .

If the burden of persuasion at trial would be on the *non-moving* party, the party moving for summary judgment may satisfy Rule 56's burden of production in either of two ways. First, the moving party may submit affirmative evidence that negates an essential element of the nonmoving party's claim. Second, the moving party may demonstrate to the Court that the nonmoving party's evidence is insufficient to establish an essential element of the nonmoving party's claim. See 10A Wright, Miller & Kane §2727, pp. 130-131; Louis, Federal Summary Judgment Doctrine: A Critical Analysis, 83 Yale L.J. 745, 750 (1974) (hereinafter Louis). If the nonmoving party cannot muster sufficient evidence to make out its claim, a trial would be useless and the moving party is entitled to summary judgment as a matter of law. . . .

Where the moving party adopts this second option and seeks summary judgment on the ground that the nonmoving party — who will bear the burden of persuasion at trial — has no evidence, the mechanics of discharging Rule 56's burden of production are somewhat trickier. Plainly, a conclusory assertion that the nonmoving party has no evidence is insufficient. . . . Such a "burden" of production is no burden at all and would simply permit summary judgment procedure to be converted into a tool for harassment. See Louis 750-751. Rather, as the Court confirms, a party who moves for summary judgment on the ground that the nonmoving party has no evidence must affirmatively show the absence of evidence in the record. *Ante,* at 2553. This may require the moving party to depose the nonmoving party's witnesses or to establish the inadequacy of documentary evidence. If there is literally no evidence in the record, the moving party may demonstrate this by reviewing for the court the admissions, interrogatories, and other exchanges between the parties that are in the record. Either way, however, the moving party must affirmatively demonstrate that there is no evidence in the record to support a judgment for the nonmoving party.

If the moving party has not fully discharged this initial burden of production, its motion for summary judgment must be denied, and the Court need not consider whether the moving party has met its ultimate burden of persuasion. Accordingly, the nonmoving party may defeat a motion for summary judgment that asserts that the nonmoving party has no evidence by calling the Court's attention to supporting evidence already in the record that was overlooked or ignored by the moving party. In that event, the moving party must respond by making an attempt to demonstrate the inadequacy of this evidence, for it is only by attacking all the record evidence allegedly supporting the nonmoving party that a party seeking summary judgment satisfies Rule 56's burden of production. Thus, if the record disclosed that the moving party had overlooked a witness who would provide relevant testimony for the nonmoving party at trial, the Court could not find that the moving party had discharged its initial burden of production unless the moving party sought to demonstrate the inadequacy of this witness' testimony. Absent such a demonstration, summary judgment would have to be denied on the ground that the moving party had failed to meet its burden of production under Rule 56.

* * *

II

I do not read the Court's opinion to say anything inconsistent with or different than the preceding discussion. My disagreement with the Court concerns the application of these principles to the facts of this case.

Defendant Celotex sought summary judgment on the ground that plaintiff had "failed to produce" any evidence that her decedent had ever been exposed to Celotex asbestos. . . . Celotex supported this motion with a two-page "Statement of Material Facts as to Which There is No Genuine Issue" and a three-page "Memorandum of Points and Authorities" which asserted that the plaintiff had failed to identify any evidence in responding to two sets of interrogatories propounded by Celotex and that therefore the record was "totally devoid" of evidence to support plaintiff's claim. See *id.,* at 171–176.

Approximately three months earlier, Celotex had filed an essentially identical motion. Plaintiff responded to this earlier motion by producing three pieces of evidence which she claimed "[a]t the very least . . . demonstrate that there is a genuine factual dispute for trial," *id.,* at 143: (1) a letter from an insurance representative of another defendant describing asbestos products to which plaintiff's decedent had been exposed, *id.,* at 160; (2) a letter from T.R. Hoff, a former supervisor of decedent, describing asbestos products to which decedent had been exposed, *id.,* at 162; and (3) a copy of decedent's deposition from earlier workmen's compensation proceedings, *id.,* at 164. Plaintiff also apparently indicated at that time that she intended to call Mr. Hoff as a witness at trial. . . .

Post-Case Follow-Up

What a movant must do to properly support a summary judgment motion turns on who bears the burden of proof on the issue at trial. Where the nonmovant bears the burden of proof, as was the case in *Celotex*, it is enough for the movant simply to point to materials demonstrating an absence of evidence supporting the issue. This showing alone does not require the court to grant summary judgment, but it does require the nonmovant to respond with evidence that will be admissible at trial showing a genuine dispute as to the issue. This type of summary judgment motion is referred to as a "no-evidence" or "absence of evidence" motion. Notice that the court points out that Catrett was not being "railroaded" by the motion, because there had been plenty of time for discovery of such evidence. If insufficient time to uncover the evidence had not passed, the nonmovant could have requested a continuance, and the court ought to have deferred decision on the motion. Alternatively, Celotex could have supported its motion with evidence that affirmatively disproved that Catrett was exposed to asbestos. Table 21.1 summarizes how to properly support a summary judgment motion.

TABLE 21.1 **Properly Supporting a Motion for Summary Judgment**

Motion seeks judgment on . . .	Supporting Evidence	Illustration
The movant's own claim or defense	The motion must be supported with evidence (or admissions) establishing all elements of the claim or defense.	Movant seeks judgment on his own affirmative defense consisting of elements A, B, C, and D. The supporting evidence must establish elements A, B, C, *and* D. Movant seeks judgment on his own claim, consisting of elements E, F, and G. The motion must be supported with evidence establishing elements E, F, *and* G.
The nonmovant's claim or defense	The motion may either: (1) be supported by evidence that negates an essential element of the nonmovant's claim or defense; or (2) simply point out the absence of evidence of an element of the claim or defense.	Movant seeks judgment on the nonmovant's claim, consisting of elements A, B, C, and D. The supporting evidence need only negate element A, B, C, *or* D. **-Or-** Simply point out the lack of evidence supporting elements A, B, C, *or* D.

Celotex Corp. v. Catrett: Real Life Applications

1. Tonya and Melania are in a car wreck. Tonya's federal court complaint alleges that Melania was negligent by running a red light at the intersection where the wreck occurred. After discovery is completed, Melania moves for summary judgment. Her motion states that "there is no genuine dispute as to the breach element of Tonya's negligence claim." The motion is not supported with any evidence, but it specifically points out that none of the witnesses deposed and none of the responses to discovery provide evidence that Melania ran the red light. Has Melania properly supported her motion? What, if anything, must Tonya do in response to the motion?

2. Alberto files suit in federal district court against Enviro-Tech, Inc. Enviro-Tech moves for summary judgment on its statute of limitations defense. Its motion states that "there is no genuine dispute as to the limitations defense, and Alberto has no evidence that he filed his lawsuit in a timely fashion." How should the court rule on Enviro-Tech's motion?

5. The Movant's Initial Burden of Production

As Justice Brennan explained, the summary judgment movant must make a proper motion for summary judgment by meeting his initial burden of production. What the movant must do to carry this initial burden depends upon who carries the burden of proof on the issue at trial. If the movant's motion fails to carry this burden, the motion should be denied, even if the nonmovant fails to respond or fails to respond properly. Although not a perfect analogy, thinking of a tennis match might help. The server in a tennis match has to hit the ball over the net. If he doesn't, the returner doesn't have to do anything to win the point. He doesn't even need to be standing on the court to win it. Similarly, the movant has to hit the ball over the net by carrying his initial burden of production. If he doesn't, the motion should be denied, regardless of what the nonmovant does or doesn't do. Here's one of the ways in which the tennis match analogy breaks down: The trial court doesn't ensure that the movant has hit the ball over the net before requiring a response from the nonmovant. So, even if the movant has failed to make a proper motion for summary judgment, the nonmovant should respond anyway. But the first point in the response ought to be that the movant has failed to carry his initial burden of production. Subsequent points in the response should attempt to raise a genuine issue of material fact just in case in the court disagrees with the first point.

6. Responding to a Motion for Summary Judgment

The nonmovant must respond to a proper summary judgment motion with evidence that raises a genuine dispute as to the issues attacked in the motion. When does evidence raise a genuine dispute as to a material fact? Clearly a genuine dispute does not exist when the plaintiff is unable to respond with any evidence to support its existence. It's also important to understand that the plaintiff's evidence does not have to conclusively establish the existence of the fact. Instead, the question is whether the evidence is such that a reasonable jury *could* conclude that the fact is true. The *Tolan v. Cotton* case is an example of how this determination is made.

Case Preview

Tolan v. Cotton

As you read *Tolan v. Cotton*, consider the following:

1. What determines which facts are material?
2. What is a trial court to do at the summary judgment phase when the evidence supports reasonable inferences both for and against the nonmovant?
3. What should the trial court do when resolution of the fact issue requires a determination of witness credibility?

Tolan v. Cotton
134 S. Ct. 1861 (2014)

PER CURIAM.

During the early morning hours of New Year's Eve, 2008, police sergeant Jeffrey Cotton fired three bullets at Robert Tolan; one of those bullets hit its target and punctured Tolan's right lung. At the time of the shooting, Tolan was unarmed on his parents' front porch about 15 to 20 feet away from Cotton. Tolan sued, alleging that Cotton had exercised excessive force in violation of the Fourth Amendment. The District Court granted summary judgment to Cotton, and the Fifth Circuit affirmed, reasoning that regardless of whether Cotton used excessive force, he was entitled to qualified immunity because he did not violate any clearly established right. 713 F.3d 299 (2013). In articulating the factual context of the case, the Fifth Circuit failed to adhere to the axiom that in ruling on a motion for summary judgment, "[t]he evidence of the nonmovant is to be believed, and all justifiable inferences are to be drawn in his favor." *Anderson v. Liberty Lobby, Inc.*, 477 U.S. 242, 255, 106 S. Ct. 2505, 91 L. Ed. 2d 202 (1986). For that reason, we vacate its decision and remand the case for further proceedings consistent with this opinion.

I

A

The following facts, which we view in the light most favorable to Tolan, are taken from the record evidence and the opinions below. At around 2:00 on the morning of December 31, 2008, John Edwards, a police officer, was on patrol in Bellaire, Texas, when he noticed a black Nissan sport utility vehicle turning quickly onto a residential street. The officer watched the vehicle park on the side of the street in front of a house. Two men exited: Tolan and his cousin, Anthony Cooper.

Edwards attempted to enter the license plate number of the vehicle into a computer in his squad car. But he keyed an incorrect character; instead of entering plate number 696BGK, he entered 695BGK. That incorrect number matched a stolen vehicle of the same color and make. This match caused the squad car's computer to send an automatic message to other police units, informing them that Edwards had found a stolen vehicle.

Edwards exited his cruiser, drew his service pistol and ordered Tolan and Cooper to the ground. He accused Tolan and Cooper of having stolen the car. Cooper responded, "That's not true." . . . And Tolan explained, "That's my car." . . . Tolan then complied with the officer's demand to lie face-down on the home's front porch.

As it turned out, Tolan and Cooper were at the home where Tolan lived with his parents. Hearing the commotion, Tolan's parents exited the front door in their pajamas. In an attempt to keep the misunderstanding from escalating into something more, Tolan's father instructed Cooper to lie down, and instructed Tolan and Cooper to say nothing. Tolan and Cooper then remained facedown.

Edwards told Tolan's parents that he believed Tolan and Cooper had stolen the vehicle. In response, Tolan's father identified Tolan as his son, and Tolan's mother explained that the vehicle belonged to the family and that no crime had been committed. Tolan's father explained, with his hands in the air, "[T]his is my nephew. This is my son. We live here. This is my house." . . . Tolan's mother similarly offered, "[S]ir this is a big mistake. This car is not stolen. . . . That's our car." . . .

While Tolan and Cooper continued to lie on the ground in silence, Edwards radioed for assistance. Shortly thereafter, Sergeant Jeffrey Cotton arrived on the scene and drew his pistol. Edwards told Cotton that Cooper and Tolan had exited a stolen vehicle. Tolan's mother reiterated that she and her husband owned both the car Tolan had been driving and the home where these events were unfolding. Cotton then ordered her to stand against the family's garage door. In response to Cotton's order, Tolan's mother asked, "[A]re you kidding me? We've lived her[e] 15 years. We've never had anything like this happen before." . . .

The parties disagree as to what happened next. Tolan's mother and Cooper testified during Cotton's criminal trial[1] that Cotton grabbed her arm and slammed her against the garage door with such force that she fell to the ground. . . . Tolan similarly testified that Cotton pushed his mother against the garage door. . . . In addition, Tolan offered testimony from his mother and photographic evidence to demonstrate that Cotton used enough force to leave bruises on her arms and back that lasted for days. . . . By contrast, Cotton testified in his deposition that when he was escorting the mother to the garage, she flipped her arm up and told him to get his hands off her. . . . He also testified that he did not know whether he left bruises but believed that he had not. . . .

---

[1] The events described here led to Cotton's criminal indictment in Harris County, Texas, for aggravated assault by a public servant. 713 F.3d 299, 303 (C.A.5 2013). He was acquitted. *Ibid.* The testimony of Tolan's mother during Cotton's trial is a part of the record in this civil action. . . .

The parties also dispute the manner in which Tolan responded. Tolan testified in his deposition and during the criminal trial that upon seeing his mother being pushed . . . he rose to his knees. . . . Edwards and Cotton testified that Tolan rose to his feet. . . .

Both parties agree that Tolan then exclaimed, from roughly 15 to 20 feet away . . . "[G]et your fucking hands off my mom." . . . The parties also agree that Cotton then drew his pistol and fired three shots at Tolan. Tolan and his mother testified that these shots came with no verbal warning. . . . One of the bullets entered Tolan's chest, collapsing his right lung and piercing his liver. While Tolan survived, he suffered a life-altering injury that disrupted his budding professional baseball career and causes him to experience pain on a daily basis.

B

In May 2009, Cooper, Tolan, and Tolan's parents filed this suit in the Southern District of Texas, alleging claims under Rev. Stat. §1979, 42 U.S.C. §1983. Tolan claimed, among other things, that Cotton had used excessive force against him in violation of the Fourth Amendment.[2] After discovery, Cotton moved for summary judgment, arguing that the doctrine of qualified immunity barred the suit. That doctrine immunizes government officials from damages suits unless their conduct has violated a clearly established right.

The District Court granted summary judgment to Cotton. 854 F. Supp. 2d 444 (S.D. Tex. 2012). It reasoned that Cotton's use of force was not unreasonable and therefore did not violate the Fourth Amendment. *Id.*, at 477–478. The Fifth Circuit affirmed, but on a different basis. 713 F.3d 299. It declined to decide whether Cotton's actions violated the Fourth Amendment. Instead, it held that even if Cotton's conduct did violate the Fourth Amendment, Cotton was entitled to qualified immunity because he did not violate a clearly established right. *Id.*, at 306.

In reaching this conclusion, the Fifth Circuit began by noting that at the time Cotton shot Tolan, "it was . . . clearly established that an officer had the right to use deadly force if that officer harbored an objective and reasonable belief that a suspect presented an 'immediate threat to [his] safety.'" *Id.*, at 306 (quoting *Deville v. Marcantel,* 567 F.3d 156, 167 (C.A.5 2009)). The Court of Appeals reasoned that Tolan failed to overcome the qualified-immunity bar because "an objectively-reasonable officer in Sergeant Cotton's position could have . . . believed" that Tolan "presented an 'immediate threat to the safety of the officers.'" 713 F.3d, at 307. In support of this conclusion, the court relied on the following facts: the front porch had been "dimly-lit"; Tolan's mother had "refus[ed] orders to remain quiet and calm"; and Tolan's words had amounted to a "verba[l] threa[t]." *Ibid.* Most critically, the court also relied on the purported fact that Tolan was "moving to intervene in" Cotton's handling of his mother, *id.*, at 305, and that Cotton therefore could reasonably have

---

[2]The complaint also alleged that the officers' actions violated the Equal Protection Clause to the extent they were motivated by Tolan's and Cooper's race. 854 F. Supp. 444, 465 (S.D. Tex. 2012). In addition, the complaint alleged that Cotton used excessive force against Tolan's mother. *Id.*, at 468. Those claims, which were dismissed, *id.*, at 465, 470, are not before this Court.

feared for his life, *id.,* at 307. Accordingly, the court held, Cotton did not violate clearly established law in shooting Tolan.

The Fifth Circuit denied rehearing en banc. 538 Fed. Appx. 374 (2013). Three judges voted to grant rehearing. Judge Dennis filed a dissent, contending that the panel opinion "fail[ed] to address evidence that, when viewed in the light most favorable to the plaintiff, creates genuine issues of material fact as to whether an objective officer in Cotton's position could have reasonably and objectively believed that [Tolan] posed an immediate, significant threat of substantial injury to him." *Id.,* at 377.

II

A

In resolving questions of qualified immunity at summary judgment, courts engage in a two-pronged inquiry. The first asks whether the facts, "[t]aken in the light most favorable to the party asserting the injury, . . . show the officer's conduct violated a [federal] right[.]" *Saucier v. Katz,* 533 U.S. 194, 201, 121 S. Ct. 2151, 150 L. Ed. 2d 272 (2001). When a plaintiff alleges excessive force during an investigation or arrest, the federal right at issue is the Fourth Amendment right against unreasonable seizures. *Graham v. Connor,* 490 U.S. 386, 394, 109 S. Ct. 1865, 104 L. Ed. 2d 443 (1989). The inquiry into whether this right was violated requires a balancing of " 'the nature and quality of the intrusion on the individual's Fourth Amendment interests against the importance of the governmental interests alleged to justify the intrusion.' " *Tennessee v. Garner,* 471 U.S. 1, 8, 105 S. Ct. 1694, 85 L. Ed. 2d 1 (1985); see *Graham, supra,* at 396, 109 S. Ct. 1865.

The second prong of the qualified-immunity analysis asks whether the right in question was "clearly established" at the time of the violation. *Hope v. Pelzer,* 536 U.S. 730, 739, 122 S. Ct. 2508, 153 L. Ed. 2d 666 (2002). Governmental actors are "shielded from liability for civil damages if their actions did not violate 'clearly established statutory or constitutional rights of which a reasonable person would have known.' " *Ibid.* "[T]he salient question . . . is whether the state of the law" at the time of an incident provided "fair warning" to the defendants "that their alleged [conduct] was unconstitutional." *Id.,* at 741, 122 S. Ct. 2508.

Courts have discretion to decide the order in which to engage these two prongs. *Pearson v. Callahan,* 555 U.S. 223, 236, 129 S. Ct. 808, 172 L. Ed. 2d 565 (2009). But under either prong, courts may not resolve genuine disputes of fact in favor of the party seeking summary judgment. See *Brosseau v. Haugen,* 543 U.S. 194, 195, n. 2, 125 S. Ct. 596, 160 L. Ed. 2d 583 (2004) (*per curiam*); *Saucier, supra,* at 201, 121 S. Ct. 2151; *Hope, supra,* at 733, n. 1, 122 S. Ct. 2508. This is not a rule specific to qualified immunity; it is simply an application of the more general rule that a "judge's function" at summary judgment is not "to weigh the evidence and determine the truth of the matter but to determine whether there is a genuine issue for trial." *Anderson,* 477 U.S., at 249, 106 S. Ct. 2505. Summary judgment is appropriate only if "the movant shows that there is no genuine issue as to any material fact and the movant is entitled to judgment as a matter of law." Fed. Rule Civ. Proc. 56(a). In making that determination, a court must view the evidence "in the light most favorable to the opposing party." *Adickes v. S.H. Kress & Co.,* 398 U.S. 144, 157, 90 S. Ct. 1598, 26 L. Ed. 2d 142 (1970); see also *Anderson, supra,* at 255, 106 S. Ct. 2505

Our qualified-immunity cases illustrate the importance of drawing inferences in favor of the nonmovant, even when, as here, a court decides only the clearly-established prong of the standard. In cases alleging unreasonable searches or seizures, we have instructed that courts should define the "clearly established" right at issue on the basis of the "specific context of the case." *Saucier, supra,* at 201, 121 S. Ct. 2151; see also *Anderson v. Creighton,* 483 U.S. 635, 640–641, 107 S. Ct. 3034, 97 L. Ed. 2d 523 (1987). Accordingly, courts must take care not to define a case's "context" in a manner that imports genuinely disputed factual propositions. See *Brosseau, supra,* at 195, 198, 125 S. Ct. 596 (inquiring as to whether conduct violated clearly established law " 'in light of the specific context of the case' " and construing "facts . . . in a light most favorable to" the nonmovant).

B

In holding that Cotton's actions did not violate clearly established law, the Fifth Circuit failed to view the evidence at summary judgment in the light most favorable to Tolan with respect to the central facts of this case. By failing to credit evidence that contradicted some of its key factual conclusions, the court improperly "weigh[ed] the evidence" and resolved disputed issues in favor of the moving party, *Anderson,* 477 U.S., at 249, 106 S. Ct. 2505.

First, the court relied on its view that at the time of the shooting, the Tolans' front porch was "dimly-lit." 713 F.3d, at 307. The court appears to have drawn this assessment from Cotton's statements in a deposition that when he fired at Tolan, the porch was " 'fairly dark,' " and lit by a gas lamp that was " 'decorative.' " *Id.,* at 302. In his own deposition, however, Tolan's father was asked whether the gas lamp was in fact "more decorative than illuminating." Record 1552. He said that it was not. *Ibid.* Moreover, Tolan stated in his deposition that two floodlights shone on the driveway during the incident, *id.,* at 2496, and Cotton acknowledged that there were two motion-activated lights in front of the house. *Id.,* at 1034. And Tolan confirmed that at the time of the shooting, he was "not in darkness." *Id.,* at 2498–2499.

Second, the Fifth Circuit stated that Tolan's mother "refus[ed] orders to remain quiet and calm," thereby "compound[ing]" Cotton's belief that Tolan "presented an immediate threat to the safety of the officers." 713 F.3d, at 307 (internal quotation marks omitted). But here, too, the court did not credit directly contradictory evidence. Although the parties agree that Tolan's mother repeatedly informed officers that Tolan was her son, that she lived in the home in front of which he had parked, and that the vehicle he had been driving belonged to her and her husband, there is a dispute as to how calmly she provided this information. Cotton stated during his deposition that Tolan's mother was "very agitated" when she spoke to the officers. . . . By contrast, Tolan's mother testified at Cotton's criminal trial that she was neither "aggravated" nor "agitated." . . .

Third, the Court concluded that Tolan was "shouting," 713 F.3d, at 306, 308, and "verbally threatening" the officer, *id.,* at 307, in the moments before the shooting. The court noted, and the parties agree, that while Cotton was grabbing the arm of his mother, Tolan told Cotton, "[G]et your fucking hands off my mom." Record 1928.

But Tolan testified that he "was not screaming." *Id.,* at 2544. And a jury could reasonably infer that his words, in context, did not amount to a statement of intent to inflict harm. Cf. *United States v. White,* 258 F.3d 374, 383 (C.A.5 2001) ("A threat imports '[a] communicated intent to inflict physical or other harm'" (quoting Black's Law Dictionary 1480 (6th ed. 1990))); *Morris v. Noe,* 672 F.3d 1185, 1196 (C.A.10 2012) (inferring that the words "Why was you talking to Mama that way" did not constitute an "overt threa[t]"). Tolan's mother testified in Cotton's criminal trial that he slammed her against a garage door with enough force to cause bruising that lasted for days. Record 2078–2079. A jury could well have concluded that a reasonable officer would have heard Tolan's words not as a threat, but as a son's plea not to continue any assault of his mother.

Fourth, the Fifth Circuit inferred that at the time of the shooting, Tolan was "moving to intervene in Sergeant Cotton's" interaction with his mother. 713 F.3d, at 305; see also *id.,* at 308 (characterizing Tolan's behavior as "abruptly attempting to approach Sergeant Cotton," thereby "inflam[ing] an already tense situation"). The court appears to have credited Edwards' account that at the time of the shooting, Tolan was on both feet "[i]n a crouch" or a "charging position" looking as if he was going to move forward. . . . Tolan testified at trial, however, that he was on his knees when Cotton shot him . . . a fact corroborated by his mother. . . . Tolan also testified in his deposition that he "wasn't going anywhere," . . . and emphasized that he did not "jump up." . . .

Considered together, these facts lead to the inescapable conclusion that the court below credited the evidence of the party seeking summary judgment and failed properly to acknowledge key evidence offered by the party opposing that motion. And while "this Court is not equipped to correct every perceived error coming from the lower federal courts," *Boag v. MacDougall,* 454 U.S. 364, 366, 102 S. Ct. 700, 70 L. Ed. 2d 551 (1982) (O'Connor, J., concurring), we intervene here because the opinion below reflects a clear misapprehension of summary judgment standards in light of our precedents. . . .

The witnesses on both sides come to this case with their own perceptions, recollections, and even potential biases. It is in part for that reason that genuine disputes are generally resolved by juries in our adversarial system. By weighing the evidence and reaching factual inferences contrary to Tolan's competent evidence, the court below neglected to adhere to the fundamental principle that at the summary judgment stage, reasonable inferences should be drawn in favor of the nonmoving party.

Applying that principle here, the court should have acknowledged and credited Tolan's evidence with regard to the lighting, his mother's demeanor, whether he shouted words that were an overt threat, and his positioning during the shooting. This is not to say, of course, that these are the only facts that the Fifth Circuit should consider, or that no other facts might contribute to the reasonableness of the officer's actions as a matter of law. Nor do we express a view as to whether Cotton's actions violated clearly established law. We instead vacate the Fifth Circuit's judgment so that the court can determine whether, when Tolan's evidence is properly credited and factual inferences are reasonably drawn in his favor, Cotton's actions violated clearly established law.

* * *

It is so ordered.

Post-Case Follow-Up

All inferences at summary judgment must be drawn in favor of the nonmovant. At trial this rule goes out the window. The jury will draw the inference either in favor of the movant or the nonmovant. It's the job of the jury to determine disputed issues, such as the lighting conditions and whether Tolan was threatening and preparing to charge Cooper. This determination comes down to the credibility of the witnesses. Will the jury believe Tolan and his parents or the officers? Such credibility determinations should not be made by the court at the summary judgment phase.

But what if the event had been recorded on a nearby security camera and the video clearly shows that Tolan stood and charged Cooper before the shots were fired? Does Tolan's evidence that he had merely risen to his knees at the time the shots were fired still raise a genuine dispute? Is the court still in the position of having to make a credibility determination in order to resolve the motion? The Supreme Court's decision in *Scott v. Harris* helps answer these questions. 550 U.S. 372 (2007). In *Scott*, the key issue was whether the plaintiff's efforts to escape police in his car endangered human life such that a police officer's use of deadly force (ramming his cruiser into the plaintiff's vehicle) was reasonable. The plaintiff's and the defendant officer's testimony as to how the plaintiff was driving differed substantially. The Court acknowledged that when a plaintiff's and defendant's description of events differ, the court must ordinarily deny summary judgment and allow the jury to resolve the credibility issue. However, in *Scott*, the events had been captured on video and the video "utterly discredited" the plaintiff's version of events, and, therefore, summary judgment was appropriately granted in favor of the defendant.

Tolan v. Cotton: The Rest of the Story

Tolan agreed to settle his case on the eve of trial for just $110,000 after six years of litigation, including a trip to the Supreme Court, and Cotton and the Bellaire Police Department admitted to no wrongdoing. The amount of the settlement almost certainly did not cover even the costs of litigating Tolan's case.

Following the settlement, the Tolan family said they were just ready to move on with their lives, but their "diminishing prospects at trial" probably played a role as well. Key to their decision to settle the case may have been the district judge's decision to exclude a number of the plaintiff's witnesses expected to testify as to Tolan's prospects as a professional baseball player. Tolan's proposed witnesses included famous baseball players Ken Griffey Junior and Ken Griffey Senior. Without witness testimony supporting the proposition that his injuries caused him to lose millions of dollars from a professional baseball career, the value of his claim dropped dramatically.

Michael Barajas, *Robbie Tolan's Police Brutality Case Might Be Precedent-Setting — But So What?*, Houston Press, September 16, 2015.

Tolan v. Cotton: Real Life Applications

1. Plaintiff's complaint alleges that Defendant breached their written contract. Plaintiff claims that he paid Defendant $150,000 to purchase equipment, but Defendant never delivered the equipment. Defendant moves for summary

judgment, pointing out that Plaintiff has no evidence that Defendant failed to deliver the equipment, and therefore no genuine dispute exists on the issue of the breach element of Plaintiff's claim. Plaintiff's response points to the allegations in his complaint, which were denied by Defendant, that Defendant failed to deliver the equipment as agreed in the contract. Plaintiff also provides the check along with a supporting affidavit showing that Plaintiff gave Defendant a check for $150,000 and Defendant cashed it. How should the court rule on the motion?

2. Marty sues Patricia for trespassing on his rural Texas ranch. Patricia moves for summary judgment and supports her motion with the affidavits of two hunters who happened to be nearby and do not know either Patricia or Marty. The hunters both state that they are familiar with the location of Marty's property line, were present near the ranch on the day of the alleged trespass, and state that Patricia did not enter on Marty's property. Marty responds to the motion with the deposition of Liz, who was also present near the ranch on the day of the alleged trespass, is familiar with the location of Marty's property line, and testified that Patricia walked onto Marty's property. In her deposition, Liz also admits that she was not wearing her glasses and had consumed three beers before she says she witnessed Patricia enter the property. How should the court rule on Patricia's motion?

3. Rodney files suit against Freshway Groceries, Inc., alleging that Rodney slipped and fell on a banana peel left on the floor of a Freshway Groceries grocery store due to the negligence of one of its employees. Freshway Groceries asserts that Rodney was contributorily negligent, which under the governing substantive law would preclude Rodney from recovering. Freshway Groceries moves for summary judgment on contributory negligence grounds and supports its motion with the allegation of contributory negligence in its answer, stating: "Rodney has no evidence that he acted reasonably in keeping a lookout for possible dangers in the grocery store." Rodney fails to respond at all to the motion. How should the court rule on the motion?

7. Partial Summary Judgment

Rule 56(a) permits a party to move for partial summary judgment. A defendant against whom multiple claims are asserted may, for example, move for summary judgment as to fewer than all of them. Also, a defendant may move for summary judgment on part of a claim or defense. In such a case, Rule 56(g) permits the court to treat the fact as established in the case, while a trial will determine the disputed elements of the claim or defense.

Chapter Summary

- A plaintiff has a right to dismiss his action by filing a notice of dismissal at any time before the defendant files an answer or a motion for summary judgment.
- A plaintiff may dismiss his action without a court order by filing a stipulation of dismissal signed by all parties who have appeared in the action.
- In the absence of a stipulation and after the defendant has filed an answer or a motion for summary judgment, a court order is required to dismiss the action.
- Voluntary dismissals are without prejudice to refiling the action unless the notice, stipulation, or order states it is with prejudice.
- The district court may grant summary judgment when there is no genuine dispute as to any material fact.
- When moving for summary judgment on a claim or defense on which the movant bears the burden of persuasion (i.e., burden of proof) at trial, the movant must support his motion with evidence establishing all elements of the claim or defense.
- When moving for summary judgment on a claim or defense on which the non-movant bears the burden of persuasion at trial, the movant may either support his motion with evidence negating the existence of an essential element or demonstrate the absence of evidence supporting the essential element.
- The nonmovant must support his response with evidence raising a genuine dispute as to a material fact.
- The court must indulge all reasonable inferences from the summary judgment evidence in favor of the nonmovant. The court does not make credibility determinations at the summary judgment stage.

Applying the Concepts

1. Tori files a breach of contract action against Blackfriars, LLC in federal court. Blackfriars responds to Tori's complaint by filing a motion to dismiss for lack of personal jurisdiction under Rule 12(b)(2). Tori has limited resources and does not want to spend time or money litigating personal jurisdiction, particularly when she knows there is another forum in which Blackfriars is subject to personal jurisdiction. What option is available to Tori to pave the way for bringing suit in the other forum?

2. Roderick's complaint alleges that his former employer, Castle Investments, Inc., fired him because of his race in violation of Title VII of the federal Civil Rights Act. Castle Investments files an answer denying many of the material allegations

in Roderick's complaint, and the answer also asserts the defense of failure to join an indispensable party, Watchtower, LLC. Roderick does not believe that Watchtower can be made a party to the dispute, but now wants to pursue the action in a different forum in which he can make both Castle Investments and Watchtower defendants. Roderick files a notice of dismissal of his action with the federal court. What is the effect of Roderick's notice of dismissal? How might Roderick achieve his goal of securing a dismissal of his action?

3. Emory files suit in federal court against Parliament, Inc. Emory has rescheduled the trial twice. Emory fails to attend the pretrial conference for the third trial setting and provides no explanation for his absence. What motion should Parliament make and how is the court likely to rule?

Civil Procedure in Practice

Zhang files suit in federal district court against Alison. Zhang and Alison were in a car accident, and Zhang's complaint alleges that Alison's negligence in driving her car proximately caused him bodily injuries. In particular, Zhang alleges that Alison ran a red light and collided with Zhang as he entered the intersection from the cross street. Alison's answer denies that she was negligent and also alleges the affirmative defense of contributory negligence; i.e., that Zhang's own negligence caused his injuries. Under the applicable law, the plaintiff's contributory negligence is an absolute bar to recovery. You are the federal district judge assigned to this case.

1. Alison moves for summary judgment based on her contributory negligence defense. Her motion states that there is no genuine dispute as to any element of the defense and that Zhang was contributorily negligent as a matter of law. Alison supports her motion by pointing out that Zhang's answers to interrogatories fail to demonstrate that he drove his car as a reasonably prudent person would on the occasion in question. Zhang fails to respond to the motion for summary judgment. How do you rule on the motion and why?

2. Alison makes a second motion for summary judgment on the grounds that there is no genuine issue of material fact as to her own negligence because she did not run the red light as Zhang alleges, and therefore she is entitled to judgment as a matter of law on Zhang's negligence claim against her. She supports her motion with the affidavits of two witnesses to the accident, both of whom swear they had a clear view of the traffic light as Alison entered the intersection, and that the light for Alison was green.

   a. Zhang fails to respond to the motion. How should you rule on the motion and why?
   b. How might Zhang respond to the motion such that it would require you to deny it?

c. Now suppose Zhang files a response to the motion but fails to support it with any evidence. However, at the hearing on the motion, Zhang asks you to consider the live testimony of an eyewitness to the collision who will support Zhang's account of Alison running the red light. The eyewitness is in the courtroom and prepared to testify. Do you allow the testimony of the eyewitness and consider it in ruling on Alison's motion?

22

Trial and Judgment as a Matter of Law

Trials are conducted to determine disputed fact issues arising as part of the parties' claims or defenses. Sometimes a judge determines these disputed fact issues, and sometimes a jury does. A **bench trial** is a trial by a judge. A **jury trial** is a trial by a jury. A party is not always entitled to a trial by jury. The Seventh Amendment to the U.S. Constitution governs the scope of a party's right to trial by jury in federal court. Upon proper demand for a jury trial, a party may have a jury trial on issues of fact that fall within the Seventh Amendment's scope. If the issue does not fall within the Seventh Amendment's scope, or if a proper demand for a jury trial is not made, the judge will determine the issues in a bench trial. This chapter addresses the scope of the right to trial by jury, the composition and selection of the jury in such trials, and the jury trial process.

Even if a jury trial is conducted, the court may grant judgment as a matter of law under Rule 50 either during or after a jury trial when the evidence presented at trial would not allow a reasonable jury to reach a contrary verdict. Judgment as a matter of law is similar to summary judgment, discussed in Chapter 21, except that the court's determination is based on the evidence at trial rather than evidence presented pretrial in summary judgment motions and responses. Alternatively, the court may grant a new trial based on any error committed during trial.

Key Concepts

- The issues that are properly tried to a jury and those that are tried to a judge
- The rules for the composition and selection of a jury—including challenges for cause and peremptory strikes—and juror qualifications, excuses, and exemptions
- How a case is presented to a jury from opening statement to jury argument
- Special Verdicts, General Verdicts, and General Verdicts with Special Interrogatories
- The standard for granting judgment as a matter of law, and when such motions are properly made
- The grounds for and function of a motion for new trial

A. TRIAL

At trial, the fact-finder resolves factual disputes pertinent to a determination of the claims and defenses in the case. This section addresses a number of questions. What kinds of fact issues are determined in a trial, and what kinds are not? Who is the fact-finder at trial, a judge or a jury? In a jury trial, how is the jury selected, and how is the case presented to the jury? When, if ever, can the court grant judgment or a new trial despite a jury's contrary verdict?

1. Triable Issues of Fact

Trials are conducted to resolve disputed fact issues that are part of the parties' claims or defenses — but not all fact issues that arise during litigation are resolved with a trial. In other words, trials are conducted to determine if the elements of the parties' claims or defenses are more likely true than not. For example, in a negligence case, did the defendant breach the standard of care? In a breach of contract case, what were the terms of the contract, and did the defendant breach any of them? In a workplace racial discrimination case, did the defendant fire the plaintiff because of his race? Was the plaintiff contributorily negligent? The court will conduct a trial to determine these issues of fact because they are part of the parties' claims or defenses. These kinds of issues are sometimes called **triable issues of fact**.

But consider the many other fact issues that might arise during litigation. In what state is the plaintiff domiciled? Where is the corporate defendant's principal place of business? The answers to these questions won't determine the merits of the plaintiff's claim or the defendant's defense, but they could determine whether or not the court has diversity of citizenship jurisdiction. What is the defendant's connection to the forum state? This answer might determine whether or not the court has personal jurisdiction. Even during trial, the admissibility of evidence often turns on the existence of certain facts. The judge resolves these kinds of fact issues based upon evidence and arguments supplied by the attorneys. A trial is not conducted to determine these kinds of issues. Put another way, these are fact issues, but they are not *triable* issues of fact.

2. The Right to Trial by Jury in Federal Court

Who ought to resolve the triable issues of fact — a judge (in a bench trial) or a jury (in a jury trial)? In federal court, the Seventh Amendment to the U.S. Constitution, set out in Exhibit 22.1, is the starting point for answering this question. The Seventh Amendment preserves the right to trial by jury in federal court in suits at common law (at least where the "value in controversy exceeds twenty dollars," which isn't usually a problem). The scope of the Seventh Amendment right to trial by jury is more limited than it may appear. First, the Seventh Amendment preserves the right to jury trial only in federal court. A right to civil jury trial exists in state courts, but

EXHIBIT 22.1   **Seventh Amendment to the U.S. Constitution**

> In suits at common law, where the value in controversy shall exceed twenty dollars, the right of trial by jury shall be preserved, and no fact tried by a jury, shall be otherwise reexamined in any Court of the United States, than according to the rules of the common law.

the right is guaranteed by state laws, not the Seventh Amendment. Moreover, the Seventh Amendment provides only that the right to jury trial "is preserved." The Seventh Amendment is not creating a new right. Instead, it is preserving the right to jury trial that existed when the amendment was adopted in 1791. Historically, a party bringing an equitable action — typically one seeking equitable relief such as injunctions, accountings, and specific performance — brought that claim in a court of equity and had no right to a jury trial. A suit seeking a legal remedy — typically money damages — was brought in a court of law where the parties had a right to a jury trial.

Actions were characterized as equitable in nature for a couple of reasons. First, equitable relief was available when the plaintiff had no adequate legal remedy because he would suffer "irreparable harm" if he had to await or depend only upon a legal remedy. For example, money damages alone will not provide an adequate remedy to Burger King® against a person operating without permission a restaurant that is called Burger King, with an identical Burger King menu, because an award of money will not stop the person from operating the restaurant. The equitable remedy of injunctive relief is necessary to remedy the problem. Second, some cases were considered too complex to be decided by juries, particularly because most jurors in the eighteenth century and earlier were illiterate, and were therefore categorized as equitable in nature. Class actions, shareholder derivative actions, interpleader actions, and their analog predecessor actions were equitable actions.

Given this history, the scope of the Seventh Amendment right to a jury trial may seem fairly simple, at least on the surface. If the plaintiff seeks only equitable relief or brings an action considered equitable in the eighteenth century, he has no Seventh Amendment right to a jury trial. If his claim is one for money damages and was considered a legal action, he does. The complexity arises principally as a result of the fact that parties may and often do seek both equitable and legal remedies in a single action. All federal district courts can hear both equitable and legal claims. We do not divide federal courts into courts of law and courts of equity. Moreover, the joinder rules allow parties to assert both legal and equitable claims in a single action. If the plaintiff seeks both an injunction and money damages, does the judge or jury decide the disputed fact issues? If the plaintiff seeks only injunctive relief but the defendant counterclaims for money damages, does the judge or jury decide the counterclaim? And who decides disputed fact issues that are common to both the equitable and legal claims? The Supreme Court's opinion in *Beacon Theatres, Inc. v. Westover*, 359 U.S. 500 (1959), sheds light on these issues.

In *Beacon Theatres*, Fox West Coast Theatres operated a movie theatre in the San Bernardino, California area and exhibited films under contracts with its distributors. The contracts granted Fox the exclusive right to distribute first-run films for a certain period of time in the San Bernardino area. Beacon Theatres began exhibiting first-run films despite the exclusive right in Fox's contract with the distributors because Beacon believed the exclusive right provision violated federal antitrust laws. Fox filed suit against Beacon Theatres seeking declaratory relief; i.e., a declaration that its contractual right to be the exclusive exhibitor of first-run films did not violate the antitrust laws. Fox also sought an injunction to prevent Beacon Theatres from exhibiting first-run films. Beacon counterclaimed for damages under the antitrust laws and demanded a jury trial. Fox's claim for injunctive relief was one "traditionally cognizable in equity," while the counterclaim was for money damages, a legal remedy. Complicating matters was the fact that some of the disputed fact issues were common to both the claim for injunctive relief and the counterclaim for damages. The district court refused to grant a jury trial to Beacon Theatres and the court of appeals refused the writ of mandamus that sought to overturn the district court's decision. The court of appeals reasoned that because Fox's claim was for injunctive relief, the judge could determine all issues related to the propriety of granting injunctive relief, even if those issues were also relevant to the legal rights involved in the case. In other words, the judge's determination of the equitable rights might limit or eliminate a party's right to a jury trial. The Supreme Court disagreed with the court of appeals' approach:

> The basis of injunctive relief in the federal courts has always been irreparable harm and inadequacy of legal remedies. At least as much is required to justify a trial court in using its discretion under the Federal Rules to allow claims of equitable origins to be tried ahead of legal ones, since this has the same effect as an equitable injunction of the legal claims.

> * * *

> Viewed in this manner, the use of discretion by the trial court under Rule 42(b) to deprive Beacon of a full jury trial on its counterclaim . . . as well as on Fox's plea for declaratory relief, cannot be justified. Under the Federal Rules the same court may try both legal and equitable causes in the same action. . . . Thus any defenses, equitable or legal, Fox may have to charges of antitrust violations can be raised either in its suit for declaratory relief or in answer to Beacon's counterclaim. On proper showing, harassment by threats of other suits, or other suits actually brought, involving the issues being tried in this case, could be temporarily enjoined pending the outcome of this litigation. Whatever permanent injunctive relief Fox might be entitled to on the basis of the decision in this case could, of course, be given by the court after the jury renders its verdict. In this way the issues between these parties could be settled in one suit giving Beacon a full jury trial of every antitrust issue. . . . By contrast, the holding of the court below while granting Fox no additional protection unless the avoidance of jury trial be considered as such, would compel Beacon to split his antitrust case, trying part to a judge and part to a jury. Such a result, which involves the postponement and subordination of Fox's own legal claim for declaratory relief as well as of the counterclaim which Beacon was compelled by the Federal Rules to bring is not permissible.

* * *

As this Court said in Scott v. Neely, 140 U.S. 106, 109-110, 11 S. Ct. 712, 714, 35 L. Ed. 358: "In the Federal courts this (jury) right cannot be dispensed with, except by the assent of the parties entitled to it; nor can it be impaired by any blending with a claim, properly cognizable at law, of a demand for equitable relief in aid of the legal action, or during its pendency." This long-standing principle of equity dictates that only under the most imperative circumstances, circumstances which in view of the flexible procedures of the Federal Rules we cannot now anticipate, can the right to a jury trial of legal issues be lost through prior determination of equitable claims.

Beacon Theatres, Inc. v. Westover, 359 U.S. 500, 506-10 (1959).

Beacon Theatres sheds considerable light on what the Seventh Amendment requires when both legal and equitable claims are asserted in the action. First, issues common to both claims must be tried to a jury. Second, issues unique to the legal claim must also be tried to a jury. Finally, the jury trial to determine these issues should precede the court's determination of any issues unique to the equitable claims.

Even after *Beacon Theatres,* questions remained about the scope of the Seventh Amendment right to trial by jury. Both the legal and equitable claims in *Beacon Theatres* turned on a central, common question: Did Fox's exclusive right to exhibit first-run films violate federal antitrust laws? If not, then Fox's injunction should have been granted. If so, Beacon Theatres should have prevailed on its damages claim. So, a jury trial of this common question would go a long way to resolving both the legal and equitable claims. But what if the legal claim is only "incidental" to a claim for equitable relief? Does the Seventh Amendment still require a jury trial of the legal issues in the case? The Supreme Court addressed this question in *Dairy Queen, Inc. v. Wood.*

Case Preview

Dairy Queen, Inc. v. Wood

As you read *Dairy Queen, Inc. v. Wood,* consider the following questions:

1. Why is the distinction between equitable and legal issues important to the existence and scope of the right to jury trial?
2. If a fact issue is common to both the legal and equitable claims, who decides that issue — the judge or the jury?
3. If a case involves both equitable and legal claims, what does *Dairy Queen* say about when the jury trial should ordinarily occur — before or after the court decides the equitable claims?

Dairy Queen, Inc. v. Wood
369 U.S. 469 1962

Mr. Justice BLACK delivered the opinion of the Court.

The United States District Court for the Eastern District of Pennsylvania granted a motion to strike petitioner's demand for a trial by jury in an action now pending before it on the alternative grounds that either the action was 'purely equitable' or, if not purely equitable, whatever legal issues that were raised were 'incidental' to equitable issues, and, in either case, no right to trial by jury existed. The petitioner then sought mandamus in the Court of Appeals for the Third Circuit to compel the district judge to vacate this order. When that court denied this request without opinion, we granted certiorari because the action of the Court of Appeals seemed inconsistent with protections already clearly recognized for the important constitutional right to trial by jury in our previous decisions.

At the outset, we may dispose of one of the grounds upon which the trial court acted in striking the demand for trial by jury — that based upon the view that the right to trial by jury may be lost as to legal issues where those issues are characterized as 'incidental' to equitable issues — for our previous decisions make it plain that no such rule may be applied in the federal courts. In Scott v. Neely, decided in 1891, this Court held that a court of equity could not even take jurisdiction of a suit 'in which a claim properly cognizable only at law is united in the same pleadings with a claim for equitable relief.' That holding, which was based upon both the historical separation between law and equity and the duty of the Court to insure 'that the right to a trial by a jury in the legal action may be preserved intact,' created considerable inconvenience in that it necessitated two separate trials in the same case whenever that case contained both legal and equitable claims. Consequently, when the procedure in the federal courts was modernized by the adoption of the Federal Rules of Civil Procedure in 1938, it was deemed advisable to abandon that part of the holding of Scott v. Neely which rested upon the separation of law and equity and to permit the joinder of legal and equitable claims in a single action. Thus Rule 18(a) provides that a plaintiff 'may join either as independent or as alternate claims as many claims either legal or equitable or both as he may have against an opposing party.' And Rule 18(b) provides: 'Whenever a claim is one heretofore cognizable only after another claim has been prosecuted to a conclusion, the two claims may be joined in a single action; but the court shall grant relief in that action only in accordance with the relative substantive rights of the parties. In particular, a plaintiff may state a claim for money and a claim to have set aside a conveyance fraudulent as to him, without first having obtained a judgment establishing the claim for money.'

The Federal Rules did not, however, purport to change the basic holding of Scott v. Neely that the right to trial by jury of legal claims must be preserved. Quite the contrary, Rule 38(a) expressly reaffirms that constitutional principle, declaring: 'The right of trial by jury as declared by the Seventh Amendment to the Constitution or as given by a statute of the United States shall be preserved to the parties inviolate.' Nonetheless, after the adoption of the Federal Rules, attempts were made indirectly to undercut that right by having federal courts in which cases involving both legal and equitable claims were filed decide the equitable claim first. The result of this

old rule.

procedure in those cases in which it was followed was that any issue common to both the legal and equitable claims was finally determined by the court and the party seeking trial by jury on the legal claim was deprived of that right as to these common issues. This procedure finally came before us in Beacon Theatres, Inc. v. Westover, a case which, like this one, arose from the denial of a petition for mandamus to compel a district judge to vacate his order striking a demand for trial by jury.

Our decision reversing that case not only emphasizes the responsibility of the Federal Courts of Appeals to grant mandamus where necessary to protect the constitutional right to trial by jury but also limits the issues open for determination here by defining the protection to which that right is entitled in cases involving both legal and equitable claims. The holding in Beacon Theatres was that where both legal and equitable issues are presented in a single case, 'only under the most imperative circumstances, circumstances which in view of the flexible procedures of the Federal Rules we cannot now anticipate, can the right to a jury trial of legal issues be lost through prior determination of equitable claims.' That holding, of course, applies whether the trial judge chooses to characterize the legal issues presented as 'incidental' to equitable issues or not. Consequently, in a case such as this where there cannot even be a contention of such 'imperative circumstances,' Beacon Theatres requires that any legal issues for which a trial by jury is timely and properly demanded be submitted to a jury. There being no question of the timeliness or correctness of the demand involved here, the sole question which we must decide is whether the action now pending before the District Court contains legal issues . . . .

[Eds. — This civil action arose out of a dispute over a licensing agreement to use the trademark "Dairy Queen." Under the agreement, respondent permitted petitioner to use the Dairy Queen trademark in exchange for cash payments. Although the complaint was somewhat ambiguous about the precise relief sought, Respondent sought an injunction ordering petitioner to refrain from using the trademark as well as a money judgment.]

Petitioner's contention, as set forth in its petition for mandamus to the Court of Appeals and reiterated in its briefs before this Court, is that insofar as the complaint requests a money judgment it presents a claim which is unquestionably legal. We agree with that contention. The most natural construction of the respondents' claim for a money judgment would seem to be that it is a claim that they are entitled to recover whatever was owed them under the contract as of the date of its purported termination plus damages for infringement of their trademark since that date. Alternatively, the complaint could be construed to set forth a full claim based upon both of these theories — that is, a claim that the respondents were entitled to recover both the debt due under the contract and damages for trademark infringement for the entire period of the alleged breach including that before the termination of the contract. Or it might possibly be construed to set forth a claim for recovery based completely on either one of these two theories — that is, a claim based solely upon the contract for the entire period both before and after the attempted termination on the theory that the termination, having been ignored, was of no consequence, or a claim based solely upon the charge of infringement on the theory that the contract, having been breached, could not be used as a defense to an infringement action even for the period prior to its termination. We find it unnecessary to resolve this ambiguity in the respondents' complaint because we think it plain that their claim for a money judgment is a claim wholly legal in its nature however the complaint is construed. As an action on a debt allegedly due under a contract, it would be difficult to conceive of an action of a more traditionally legal character. And as an action for damages based upon a charge of trademark infringement, it would be no less subject to cognizance by a court of law.

The respondents' contention that this money claim is 'purely equitable' is based primarily upon the fact that their complaint is cast in terms of an 'accounting,' rather than in terms of an action for 'debt' or 'damages.' But the constitutional right to trial by jury cannot be made to depend upon the choice of words used in the pleadings. The necessary prerequisite to the right to maintain a suit for an equitable accounting, like all other equitable remedies, is, as we pointed out in Beacon Theatres, the absence of an adequate remedy at law. Consequently, in order to maintain such a suit on a cause of action cognizable at law, as this one is, the plaintiff must be able to show that the 'accounts between the parties' are of such a 'complicated nature' that only a court of equity can satisfactorily unravel them. In view of the powers given to District Courts by Federal Rule of Civil Procedure 53(b) to appoint masters to assist the jury in those exceptional cases where the legal issues are too complicated for the jury adequately to handle alone, the burden of such a showing is considerably increased and it will indeed be a rare case in which it can be met. But be that as it may, this is certainly not such a case. A jury, under proper instructions from the court, could readily determine the recovery, if any, to be had here, whether the theory finally settled upon is that of breach of contract, that of trademark infringement, or any combination of the two. The legal remedy cannot be characterized as inadequate merely because the measure of damages may necessitate a look into petitioner's business records.

Nor is the legal claim here rendered 'purely equitable' by the nature of the defenses interposed by petitioner. Petitioner's primary defense to the charge of breach of contract — that is, that the contract was modified by a subsequent oral agreement — presents a purely legal question having nothing whatever to do either with novation, as the district judge suggested, or reformation, as suggested by the respondents here. Such a defense goes to the question of just what, under the law, the contract between the respondents and petitioner is and, in an action to collect a debt for breach of a contract between these parties, petitioner has a right to have the jury determine not only whether the contract has been breached and the extent of the damages if any but also just what the contract is.

We conclude therefore that the district judge erred in refusing to grant petitioner's demand for a trial by jury on the factual issues related to the question of whether there has been a breach of contract. Since these issues are common with those upon which respondents' claim to equitable relief is based, the legal claims involved in the action must be determined prior to any final court determination of respondents' equitable claims. The Court of Appeals should have corrected the error of the district judge by granting the petition for mandamus. The judgment is therefore reversed and the cause remanded for further proceedings consistent with this opinion.

Reversed and remanded.

Post-Case Follow-Up

A party has a right to a jury trial with respect to any element of a legal claim, even if it is also an element of an equitable claim and even if the element is incidental to or seems less important than the elements of the equitable claim. Even when the action is historically equitable in nature, a right to jury trial may exist. The Supreme Court addressed this issue in *Ross v. Bernhard* in the context of a shareholder derivative suit, a historically equitable action in which a shareholder asserts a claim on behalf of the corporation. 396 U.S. 531 (1970). The Court in *Ross* acknowledged that whether or not the shareholder has a right to bring a derivative suit is historically an "equitable matter," but whether or not the corporation would be entitled to relief in the action could be either a legal or equitable matter, depending upon the nature of the claim and the relief sought. The Court held that the shareholder in the derivative suit was entitled to a jury trial on the claim if the corporation would have been entitled to a jury trial. The Court concluded:

> In the instant case we have no doubt that the corporation's claim is, at least in part, a legal one. The relief sought is money damages. There are allegations in the complaint of a breach of fiduciary duty, but there are also allegations of ordinary breach of contract and gross negligence. The corporation, had it sued on its own behalf, would have been entitled to a jury's determination, at a minimum, of its damages against its broker under the brokerage contract and of its rights against its own directors because of their negligence.

396 U.S. at 542-43.

Thus, the right to jury trial exists as to legal issues even in an historically equitable action. Under *Ross*, jury trials of legal issues must also occur in other traditionally equitable actions, such as interpleader and class actions. If there is a single theme that emerges from *Beacon Theatres*, *Dairy Queen*, and *Ross*, it may be that district courts should err on the side of permitting jury trials of disputed fact issues when doubt exists as to whether or not the issue is legal or equitable in nature.

Dairy Queen, Inc. v. Wood: Real Life Applications

1. A plaintiff class of landowners seeks only injunctive relief to prevent the construction of a dam on a river, whose construction will cause flooding of their property, and demand a jury trial. The defendants move to strike the jury demand. How should the court rule?

2. Suppose the plaintiff class in question 1 also seeks money damages for devaluation of their property. How should the court rule on the defendants' motion to strike? Should all fact issues be determined by the court? All by the jury? Or some by the court and some by the jury? If the latter, in what order should these issues be tried?

EXHIBIT 22.2 **Rule 38(a)-(d)**

> (a) Right Preserved. The right of trial by jury as declared by the Seventh Amendment to the Constitution — or as provided by a federal statute — is preserved to the parties inviolate.
>
> (b) Demand. On any issue triable of right by a jury, a party may demand a jury trial by:
>
> (1) serving the other parties with a written demand — which may be included in a pleading — no later than 14 days after the last pleading directed to the issue is served; and
>
> (2) filing the demand in accordance with Rule 5(d).
>
> (c) Specifying Issues. In its demand, a party may specify the issues that it wishes to have tried by a jury; otherwise, it is considered to have demanded a jury trial on all the issues so triable. If the party has demanded a jury trial on only some issues, any other party may — within 14 days after being served with the demand or within a shorter time ordered by the court — serve a demand for a jury trial on any other or all factual issues triable by jury.
>
> (d) Waiver; Withdrawal. A party waives a jury trial unless its demand is properly served and filed. A proper demand may be withdrawn only if the parties consent.

3. Demand for Jury Trial

Rule 38(a), set out in Exhibit 22.2, provides that the Seventh Amendment right to jury trial and any right to jury trial provided by federal statute is "preserved inviolate." However, under Rule 38, a party waives his right to jury trial if he does not properly file and serve a written demand for a jury trial. Any party may demand a jury trial as to any issue "triable of right by jury." This demand must be made within 14 days of the last pleading directed to the issue triable by jury. If multiple issues are triable by jury, a party may demand a jury trial as to only some of the issues by specifying the issues on which it seeks a jury trial. A demand that does not so specify is treated as a demand for jury trial on all issues as to which there is a right to trial by jury. Once a jury trial is demanded by any party, it may not be withdrawn without the consent of the other parties. Suppose the plaintiff files and serves a demand for jury trial and, although the defendant also wants a jury trial, the defendant does not make his own demand for jury trial. The defendant does not need to file his own demand to ensure a jury trial, because the plaintiff's demand may not be withdrawn without his consent. Suppose the plaintiff files a negligence action against the defendant but specifies in the demand that he seeks a jury trial only as to the amount of damages, not as to liability; i.e., the court will determine liability. The defendant may, within 14 days of the filing of the plaintiff's demand, file his own demand for trial by jury of the liability issues.

4. The Composition and Selection of the Jury

If a jury is to determine fact issues against one side or the other, it obviously makes sense to require jurors who aren't biased or prejudiced against one side or the other.

Other rules establishing exemptions and excuses from jury service prevent service from unduly burdening the lives of certain people. It is worth recognizing that ordinary citizens are *summoned* to jury service, not invited, and the court may impose consequences on individuals who refuse to answer a jury summons. A jury trial requires the federal government to disrupt its citizens' work and family lives. The rules for the composition and selection of the jury attempt to strike a balance between the need for a fair and impartial jury and the burdens of jury service.

Size of the Jury; Unanimity

Under Rule 48, set out in Exhibit 22.3, the jury must consist of at least 6 members and no more than 12. A verdict may only be returned by a jury of at least six members. For this reason, a federal district court will nearly always begin a civil trial with more than six jurors so that, if the court excuses one or more jurors (e.g., if a juror falls ill), there are still at least six jurors remaining who may return a verdict. If the jury falls below six members, the court must declare a mistrial. Regardless of the size of the jury, the verdict must be unanimous, unless all the parties agree otherwise. This unanimity rule in federal court is different than the requirement in most state courts, which often permit non-unanimous verdicts.

Juror Qualifications, Exemptions, and Excuses

The qualifications for and exemptions from jury service are set out in the Jury Selection and Service Act. 28 U.S.C. §1861 *et seq.* (1968). A person is not qualified to serve as a juror unless he is a U.S. citizen over the age of 18, has lived in the judicial district for at least a year, speaks English, reads and writes English well enough to fill out the juror questionnaire, and has not been convicted of a felony and does not have a pending felony charge. 28 U.S.C. §1865. Certain persons meeting these requirements are nevertheless exempted from jury service, including members of the armed services on active duty, members of fire and police departments, as well as many local, state, and federal governmental officials. 28 U.S.C. §1863(b)(6). These categories of persons may not serve as jurors, even if they want to. Each district is required to have a plan for selecting jurors, and this plan may permit

EXHIBIT 22.3   Rule 48

(a) Number of Jurors. A jury must begin with at least 6 and no more than 12 members, and each juror must participate in the verdict unless excused under Rule 47(c).

(b) Verdict. Unless the parties stipulate otherwise, the verdict must be unanimous and must be returned by a jury of at least 6 members.

(c) Polling. After a verdict is returned but before the jury is discharged, the court must on a party's request, or may on its own, poll the jurors individually. If the poll reveals a lack of unanimity or lack of assent by the number of jurors that the parties stipulated to, the court may direct the jury to deliberate further or may order a new trial.

certain persons to be excused from jury service upon request (i.e., they may serve if they wish but are not required to). Common categories of persons who may seek to be excused from jury service include people over age 70, teachers, persons who have recently already served as jurors, doctors and nurses, and business owners in a "one-person" business. *See, e.g., McCall v. Shields Associates, Inc.*, 617 F. Supp. 244, 246 n.1 (1985) (holding that the D.C. District's plan for selecting jurors that excused these categories of persons did not violate the Federal Jury Selection and Service Act).

Voir Dire: *Seeking a Fair and Impartial Jury*

The clerk of the court summons people for jury service. You may have even received such a summons. Assuming the jurors are qualified and not exempt from jury service, whether or not a person summoned actually serves on a particular jury is determined through a process called *voir dire* or, simply, jury selection. The panel of potential jurors is called the **venire**. During *voir dire*, the court and the attorneys ask questions of the venire, and the parties are permitted to eliminate members of the venire based on their answers to the questions. Typically, *voir dire* occurs immediately before opening statements. The purpose of *voir dire* is to impanel an impartial jury by eliminating jurors who are biased or prejudiced against one side or the other. A party may **challenge for cause** (or "for favor") any juror who has revealed a bias or prejudice against that party. For example, a juror may be related to or employed by a party or one of the attorneys. If the court grants the challenge, the juror is said to have been dismissed for cause. A party has an unlimited number of challenges for cause.

In addition, each party has three peremptory strikes. 28 U.S.C. §1870. Plaintiffs and defendants with similar interests may be treated as a single party and forced to share the three peremptory strikes. *Id.* Historically, a party could use a peremptory strike to eliminate a juror for any reason or for no reason. Today, however, a party may not strike a juror on the basis of race or gender. If a party believes his opponent has struck a juror on the basis of race or gender he may make what is called a *Batson* **challenge**, named after the Supreme Court case that held that exercising strikes in a racially discriminatory manner violates the litigant's constitutional rights to trial by a jury of his peers. The Supreme Court extended this right to racially unbiased jury selection in civil cases in *Edmonson v. Leesville Concrete Co., Inc.*, and included gender as an impermissible basis for excluding a potential juror in *J.E.B. v. Alabama ex rel. T.B.* If the challenge to the peremptory strike is granted during jury selection, the juror struck on the basis of race or gender will be placed on the jury.

5. Overview of a Jury Trial

We've addressed how a jury is selected; now let's address how the case is presented to the jury during trial. Each phase of the trial, from opening statement to closing argument, plays an important role in helping the jury reach its verdict.

Opening Statement

After *voir dire*, the court swears in the 6 to 12 people who will serve as jurors in the case. Subject to resolving any final pretrial motions, the trial begins with the parties' opening statements. The purpose of an **opening statement** is to provide the jury with an overview of the issues in the case and the evidence they will hear. Despite the official purpose of the opening statement, attorneys are already attempting to persuade the jury, but their ability to do so during opening statement is limited in important ways. First, what the attorneys say in opening statement is not evidence. If the attorney mentions a fact in opening statement but fails to offer testimony or other evidence to support it during trial, the jury has heard no evidence of the fact and may not conclude that it is true. This makes sense, because the lawyer is not a witness in the case. He has no personal knowledge of the events and is not under oath. The jury should decide the case based on the testimony of witnesses who perceived the events and who swore or affirmed to tell the truth. Second, the lawyers are not permitted to argue their cases in opening statement. An argumentative objection will ordinarily be sustained when the attorney draws inferences from the evidence, particularly when the attorney states the conclusion with a raised voice or an impassioned tone. An attorney is ordinarily permitted to say something like "you will hear eye-witness testimony that the defendant was weaving in his lane in the moments before the car wreck," but ordinarily he will not be able to say, "and that means the defendant was negligent!" This stands in contrast to closing argument, wherein attorneys may argue their case by drawing inferences from the facts, and are typically granted a wider rhetorical latitude in terms of tone and volume. But even though closing argument permits attorneys greater latitude to argue — for example, that the defendant was negligent — what attorneys say is still not evidence.

Case-in-Chief

A **case-in-chief** is the evidence a party presents "between the time the party calls the first witness and the time the party rests." Black's Law Dictionary (Bryan A. Garner ed., 9th ed. 2009). During its case-in-chief, a party may call witnesses to the stand and ask them questions on direct examination. As with opening statements, what the lawyers say (e.g., the lawyer's question to a witness) is not evidence. The party may also offer documentary and physical evidence in accordance with the rules of evidence. Opposing parties are permitted to cross-examine the witnesses in order to, among other things, test the witnesses' credibility. In its case-in-chief, the party must offer evidence supporting all elements of its claims or defenses. Failure to do so before resting the case-in-chief may be grounds for the court to refuse to submit the claim or defense to the jury for its determination (as discussed more fully in the "Judgment as a Matter of Law" section later in this chapter). Of course, during its case-in-chief the party is attempting to persuade the jury that the elements of its claims or defenses are actually true, not just supported by some evidence.

Who presents his case-in-chief first? Your answer was probably the plaintiff, and ordinarily this is correct. But not always. The party with the burden "on the whole case" presents his case-in-chief first. This party also gives the first opening statement. The party with the burden on the whole case is the party who *must* have an affirmative finding (a "yes" answer) from the jury on at least one question in order to prevail. In most cases, the plaintiff has this burden. Having the burden on the whole case doesn't mean the party has the burden on every question the jury will answer. Consider a case in which the court charges the jury with answering both a question about the defendant's negligence and a question about the defendant's affirmative defense of contributory negligence. The defendant bears the burden to prove contributory negligence while the plaintiff bears the burden on negligence. The defendant does not, however, have the burden on the whole case, because he does not require a "yes" answer to the affirmative defense question to prevail. He would prevail if the jury answers "no" to the affirmative defense question and "no" to the negligence question. The plaintiff in this example must have a "yes" answer to the negligence question to prevail, and therefore he bears the burden on the whole case. On rare occasions, the defendant will have the burden on the whole case. For example, if the only issue for the jury to decide is one on which the defendant bears the burden of proof, the defendant will bear the burden on the whole case. The defendant will give the first opening statement and present his case-in-chief first. Suppose the plaintiff is the beneficiary of a life insurance policy and files suit against the defendant for failing to pay the proceeds on the policy. The defendant acknowledges that it issued a valid policy of life insurance to the insured but refuses to pay the proceeds, citing an exclusion in the policy for death by suicide. The only issue in the case is whether or not the insured committed suicide, and the defendant bears the burden to prove the policy exclusion. In this case, the defendant will bear the burden on the whole case.

Rebuttal Cases

Typically, the plaintiff will put on a **rebuttal case** after the defendant rests his case-in-chief. In the rebuttal case, the plaintiff is attempting to rebut and contradict the evidence offered by the defendant. If the plaintiff puts on a rebuttal case, the defendant is then also permitted to put on a rebuttal case. Once all sides have finished putting on their evidence, the parties close the evidence. The parties close the evidence by saying something to the effect of "we close our case." At the close of all the evidence, the parties' closing arguments and the court's charge to the jury follow.

Jury Argument

Jury argument, sometimes called closing argument or closing statement, is the parties' final opportunity to persuade the jury. Again, what the attorneys say is not evidence. In argument, the attorneys are discussing the evidence the jury has heard and what it says about how the jury should answer the questions in the verdict form the court provides. The attorneys may not discuss matters that were not admitted into evidence, but unlike in opening statement, the attorneys may draw inferences from the facts. In other words, they may argue their cases.

6. Verdict and Judgment

After the parties close the evidence, and usually after final jury argument, the court charges the jury. The court's **charge to the jury** is a question or series of questions along with written instructions and definitions to help the jury answer the questions. The jury answers the questions in writing on a document called the verdict form. The jury's answers to these questions on the form together make up the jury's **verdict**. The questions typically ask about the plaintiff's claims and any affirmative defenses. For example, in a case in which the plaintiff claims her employer fired her because of her race, the court might ask the jury a question like this:

Question 1

　　Has plaintiff proved that she would not have had her employment terminated in the absence of — in other words, but for — her race?

　　Answer "Yes" or "No"

　　――――――――――――――

　　The court will also ask questions about any affirmative defenses. For example, in a race discrimination case under the federal Title VII act, the defendant has what is called a "mixed-motives" affirmative defense. This defense allows the defendant to prevail if it would have made the same decision even if it had not considered the plaintiff's race. The court's question to the jury on this affirmative defense would look something like this:

Question 2

　　Has the defendant proved that it would have made the same decision to terminate the plaintiff's employment even if it had not considered her race?

　　Answer "Yes" or "No"

　　――――――――――――――

　　The jury decides only disputed issues of fact. It does not decide legal issues. Instead, jurors must follow the law as provided to them in the court's instructions that accompany the questions in the charge. For example, the court will instruct the jury on the appropriate burden of proof and what it means. The jury, for example, may be asked if the defendant was negligent, but the court will provide the jury with an instruction on what must be proven before the jury may answer "yes" to the

Criticism of the General Verdict

Civil jury trials raise questions and concerns in the minds of some. Did the jury consider all of the evidence? Did it follow or ignore the judge's instructions on the law? As Judge Frank of the Second Circuit Court of Appeals explained nearly 70 years ago in *Skidmore v. Baltimore & O.R. Co.*, 167 F.2d 54 (2d Cir. 1948), perceived defects in civil jury trials are exacerbated by general verdicts:

> [W]hen a jury returns an ordinary general verdict, it usually has the power utterly to ignore what the judge instructs it concerning the substantive legal rules, a power which, because generally it cannot be controlled, is indistinguishable for all practical purposes, from a "right." Practically, then, for all we may say about the jury's duty when it renders a verdict, we now do have the very conditions which we were warned would result if the jury had the right to decide legal propositions: cases are often decided "according to what the jury suppose the law is or ought to be"; the "law," when juries sit, is "as fluctuating and uncertain as the diverse opinion and different juries in regard to it"; and often jurors are "not only judges but legislatures as well." Indeed, some devotees of the jury system praise it precisely because, they say, juries, by means of general verdicts, can and often do nullify those substantive legal rules they dislike, thus becoming ad hoc ephemeral (un-elected) legislatures (a state of affairs singularly neglected by most writers on jurisprudence, who would do well to modify their ideas

question of whether the defendant was negligent. For example, the court might instruct the jury that negligence means "the failure to use ordinary care." Tex. Pattern Jury Charges, General Negligence, PJC 2.1, State Bar of Texas (2014). In addition, the court's charge will provide definitions of terms of art within the rule, such as "ordinary care" and "proximate cause." Following the instruction above on negligence, the court might define ordinary care as "that degree of care that would be used by a person of ordinary prudence under the same or similar circumstances." *Id.* The court can also define scientific or other technical terms relevant to the case and with which the jury may be unfamiliar.

Special and General Verdicts

Rule 49 allows a court to require the jury to return either a special or a general verdict with special interrogatories. The questions above are examples of a **special verdict**. They ask the jury to resolve specific issues of fact. A special verdict does not ask the jury if it has decided the plaintiff or defendant should win. Instead, the court determines who ought to have judgment entered in their favor based on the jury's answers to questions about specific claims and defenses. A **general verdict**, on the other hand, simply asks the jury to determine who ought to win and the amount of damages, if any. General verdicts are rare in civil cases today. A general verdict makes it difficult if not impossible to determine if the jury properly considered the key disputed issues in the case, or if the jury was overwhelmed by an emotional appeal or sympathy for one side or the other. Rule 49(b) authorizes a general verdict followed by special interrogatories. This allows the jury the opportunity to state clearly who it thinks ought to win, but also helps ensure that the jury has considered the key issues in the case. The jury will answer a general verdict question like this one:

_____ We the jury find in favor of the plaintiff and assess his damages at _____ dollars.

_____ We the jury find in favor of the defendant.

This general verdict will be followed by special interrogatories, which are questions like those found in a special verdict form, about key disputed issues in the case.

Judgment on a Jury Verdict (Court and Judge)

The jury's **verdict** is its answers to the questions on the verdict form. A favorable verdict is a key moment in the

by recognizing what might be called "jurisprudence").

Do the special and general verdicts with special interrogatories contemplated by Rule 49 alleviate the concerns Judge Frank raised?

litigation, but what the parties want most is a favorable judgment. In particular, the party who won the trial wants judgment on the jury verdict. If the jury returns a general verdict, Rule 58(b) requires the clerk of the court to promptly prepare, sign, and enter judgment on the jury verdict without awaiting direction from the court. So judgment on a general verdict is a ministerial act the clerk performs as a matter of course. Court intervention is not necessary to determine for whom the judgment should be entered, because a general verdict is straightforward and clear to anyone who is entitled to judgment. If instead the jury has returned a special verdict or a general verdict with answers to special interrogatories, Rule 54(b) requires the court promptly to approve the form of the judgment, after which the clerk will enter it. This makes sense, because the court's legal expertise may be required to determine for whom judgment should be entered based on the jury's answers to special interrogatories.

B. JUDGMENT AS A MATTER OF LAW

Just because a case goes to a jury trial does not mean a party must have a favorable verdict to win a favorable judgment. Rule 50 permits a court to grant judgment as a matter of law when a reasonable jury could not return a contrary verdict. A court may grant judgment as a matter of law either before the case is submitted to the jury or after verdict and judgment. Under Rule 50, the party who lost the jury verdict can still win a judgment in his favor.

1. The Standard for Granting Judgment as a Matter of Law

Rule 50 allows the federal district court to grant **judgment as a matter of law** (i.e., judgment without a finding of fact by the jury) against a party when "a reasonable jury would not have a legally sufficient basis" to find for the party. Judgment as a matter of law under Rule 50 is similar to summary judgment discussed in Chapter 21, except that it is based on the evidence presented (or not) by the parties at trial rather than the evidence produced pretrial in support of or in response to a motion for summary judgment. Judgment as a matter of law is most frequently granted when either (1) the plaintiff has failed to produce evidence supporting an essential element of his claim, or (2) the defendant has conclusively established all elements of a defense that precludes recovery. The *Simblest v. Maynard* case addresses this standard in greater detail.

Case Preview

Simblest v. Maynard

It is important to understand that in *Simblest v. Maynard*, the governing substantive law at the time provided that a plaintiff whose own negligence contributed in any way to his injury could not recover, even if the defendant was also negligent. The key issue in *Simblest*, therefore, was whether or not, given the law of contributory negligence at the time, the evidence was legally sufficient to permit a verdict for the plaintiff. As you read *Simblest*, consider the following questions:

1. For whom did the jury return a verdict?
2. What standard does the court set out for overturning such verdicts upon motion for judgment as a matter of law (what the court calls a judgment "n.o.v.," which stands for *non obstante veredicto* — a/k/a judgment notwithstanding the verdict)?
3. What did the traffic laws of Vermont require the plaintiff to do as he approached the intersection, and what did the evidence establish that he did (or didn't do)?
4. Why doesn't the plaintiff's own testimony preclude judgment as a matter of law against him?

Simblest v. Maynard
427 F.2d 1 (2d Cir. 1970)

TIMBERS, District Judge:

We have before us another instance of Vermont justice — this time at the hands of a federal trial judge who, correctly applying the law, set aside a $17,125 plaintiff's verdict and entered judgment n.o.v. [Eds. — Today, we would say the trial court granted a "renewed motion for judgment as a matter of law," the terminology that replaced the terms "directed verdict" and "judgement n.o.v."] for defendant, Rule 50(b), Fed. R. Civ. P., in a diversity negligence action arising out of an intersection collision between a passenger vehicle driven by plaintiff and a fire engine driven by defendant in Burlington, Vermont, during the electric power blackout which left most of New England in darkness on the night of November 9, 1965. We affirm.

I.

Plaintiff, a citizen and resident of New Hampshire, was 66 years of age at the time of the accident. He was a distributor of reference books and had been in Burlington on business for three days prior to the accident. He was an experienced driver, having driven an average of some 54,000 miles per year since 1922. He was thoroughly familiar with the intersection in question. His eyesight was excellent and his hearing was very good.

Defendant, a citizen of Vermont, had resided in Burlington for 44 years. He had been a full time fireman with the Burlington Fire Department for 17 years. He was assigned to and regularly drove the 500-gallon pumper which he was driving at the time of the accident. He was thoroughly familiar with the intersection in question.

The accident occurred at the intersection of Main Street (U.S. Route 2), which runs generally east and west, and South Willard Street (U.S. Routes 2 and 7), which runs generally north and south. The neighborhood . . . is partly business, partly residential. At approximately the center of the intersection there was an overhead electrical traffic control signal designed to exhibit the usual red and green lights.

At the time of the accident, approximately 5:27 P.M., it was dark, traffic was light and the weather was clear. Plaintiff was driving his 1964 Chrysler station wagon in a westerly direction on Main Street, approaching the intersection. Defendant was driving the fire engine, in response to a fire alarm, in a southerly direction on South Willard Street, also approaching the intersection.

Plaintiff testified that the traffic light was green in his favor as he approached and entered the intersection; but that when he had driven part way through the intersection the power failure extinguished all lights within his range of view, including the traffic light. All other witnesses, for both plaintiff and defendant, testified that the power failure occurred at least 10 to 15 minutes prior to the accident; and there was no evidence, except plaintiff's testimony, that the traffic light was operating at the time of the accident.

Plaintiff also testified that his speed was 12 to 15 miles per hour as he approached the intersection. He did not look to his right before he entered the intersection; after looking to his left, to the front and to the rear (presumably through a rear view mirror), he looked to his right for the first time when he was one-half to three-quarters of the way through the intersection and then for the first time saw the fire engine within 12 feet of him. He testified that he did not hear the fire engine's siren or see the flashing lights or any other lights on the fire engine.

Plaintiff further testified that his view to the north (his right) as he entered the intersection was obstructed by various objects, including traffic signs, trees on Main Street and a Chamber of Commerce information booth on Main Street east of the intersection. All of the evidence, including the photographs of the intersection, demonstrates that, despite some obstruction of plaintiff's view to the north, he could have seen the approaching fire engine if he had looked between the obstructions and if he had looked to the north after he passed the information booth. One of plaintiff's own witnesses, Kathleen Burgess, testified that 'maybe five to ten seconds previous to when he was struck he might have seen the fire truck,' referring to the interval of time after plaintiff passed the information booth until the collision.

Defendant testified that, accompanied by Captain Fortin in the front seat, he drove the fire engine from the Mansfield Avenue Fire Station, seven and one-half blocks away from the scene of the accident, in the direction of the fire on Maple Street. While driving in a southerly direction on South Willard Street and approaching the intersection with Main Street, the following warning devices were in operation on the fire engine: the penetrator making a wailing sound; the usual fire siren; a flashing red light attached to the dome of the fire engine; two red lights on either side of the cab; and the usual headlights. Defendant saw plaintiff's car east of the information booth and next saw it as it entered the intersection. Defendant testified that he was traveling 20 to 25 miles per hour as he approached the intersection; he slowed down, applied his brakes and turned the fire engine to his right, in a westerly direction, in an attempt to avoid the collision. He estimated that he was traveling 15 to 20 miles per hour at the time of impact. A police investigation found a 15 foot skid mark made by the fire engine but no skid marks made by plaintiff's car.

The fire engine struck plaintiff's car on the right side, in the area of the fender and front door. Plaintiff's head struck the post on the left side of his car, causing him to lose consciousness for about a minute. He claims that this injury aggravated a chronic pre-existing degenerative arthritic condition of the spine.

Other witnesses who virtually bracketed the intersection from different vantage points were called. Frank Valz, called by plaintiff, was looking out a window in a building on the northeast corner of the intersection; he saw the fire engine when it was a block north of the intersection; he heard its siren and saw its flashing red lights. Kathleen Burgess, another of plaintiff's witnesses (referred to above), was driving in a northerly direction on South Willard Street, just south of the intersection; seeing the fire engine when it was a block north of the intersection, she pulled over to the curb and stopped; she saw its flashing lights, but did not hear its siren. Holland Smith and Irene Longe, both called by defendant, were in the building at the southwest corner of the intersection; as the fire engine approached the intersection, they each heard its warning signals and saw its flashing lights in operation.

Defendant's motions for a directed verdict at the close of plaintiff's case and at the close of all the evidence having been denied and the jury having returned a plaintiff's verdict, defendant moved to set aside the verdict and the judgment entered thereon and for entry of judgment n.o.v. in accordance with his motion for a directed verdict. Chief Judge Leddy filed a written opinion granting defendant's motion.

On appeal plaintiff urges that the district court erred in granting defendant's motion for judgment n.o.v. or, in the alternative, in declining to charge the jury on the doctrine of last clear chance. We affirm both rulings of the district court.

II.

In determining whether the motion for judgment n.o.v. should have been granted, a threshold question is presented as to the correct standard to be applied. This standard has been expressed in various ways. Simply stated, it is whether the evidence is such that, without weighing the credibility of the witnesses or otherwise considering the weight of the evidence, there can be but one conclusion as to the verdict that reasonable men could have reached. See, e.g., Brady v. Southern Railway Company, 320 U.S. 476, 479-80 (1943); O'Connor v. Pennsylvania Railroad Company, 308 F.2d 911, 914-15 (2 Cir. 1962). See also 5 Moore's Federal Practice P50.02(1), at 2320-23 (2d ed. 1968); Wright, Law of Federal Courts §95, at 425 (2d ed. 1970). On a motion for judgment n.o.v., the evidence must be viewed in the light most favorable to the party against whom the motion is made and he must be given the benefit of all reasonable inferences which may be drawn in his favor from that evidence. O'Connor v. Pennsylvania Railroad Company, supra, at 914-15; 5 Moore, supra, at 2325; Wright, supra, at 425.

* * *

Our careful review of the record in the instant case leaves us with the firm conviction that . . . plaintiff was contributorily negligent as a matter of law; and that Chief Judge Leddy correctly set aside the verdict and entered judgment for defendant n.o.v. . . .

In our view . . . the critical issue in the case is whether the fire engine was sounding a siren or displaying a red light as it approached the intersection immediately before the collision. Upon this critical issue, Chief Judge Leddy accurately and succinctly summarized the evidence as follows:

'All witnesses to the accident, except the plaintiff, testified that the fire truck was sounding a siren or displaying a flashing red light. All of the witnesses except Miss Burgess and the plaintiff testified that the fire truck was sounding its siren and displaying a flashing red light.'

The reason such evidence is critical is that under Vermont law . . . upon the approach of a fire department vehicle which is sounding a siren or displaying a red light, or both, all other vehicles are required to pull over to the right lane of traffic and come to a complete stop until the emergency vehicle has passed. Since the emergency provision of this statute supersedes the general right of way statute regarding intersections controlled by traffic lights . . . the lone testimony of plaintiff that the traffic light was green in his favor as he approached and entered the intersection is of no moment. And since the emergency provision of 23 V.S.A. §1033 becomes operative if either the siren is sounding or a red light is displayed on an approaching fire engine, we focus upon plaintiff's own testimony that he did not see the fire engine's flashing light, all other witnesses having testified that the red light was flashing.

As stated above, plaintiff testified that he first saw the fire engine when he was one-half to three-quarters of the way through the intersection and when the fire engine was within 12 feet of his car. At the speed at which the fire engine was traveling, plaintiff had approximately one-third of a second in which to observe the fire engine prior to the collision. Accepting plaintiff's testimony that his eyesight was excellent, and assuming that the fire engine's flashing red light was revolving as rapidly as 60 revolutions per minute, plaintiff's one-third of a second observation does not support an inference that the light was not operating, much less does it constitute competent direct evidence to that effect. Opportunity to observe is a necessary ingredient of the competency of eyewitness evidence. Plaintiff's opportunity to observe, accepting his own testimony, simply was too short for his testimony on the operation of the light to be of any probative value whatsoever.

Plaintiff's testimony that he did not see the fire engine's flashing red light, in the teeth of the proven physical facts, we hold is tantamount to no proof at all on that issue. O'Connor v. Pennsylvania Railroad Company, supra, at 915. As one commentator has put it, ' . . . the question of the total absence of proof quickly merges into the question whether the proof adduced is so insignificant as to be treated as the equivalent of the absence of proof.' 5 Moore, supra, at 2320. If plaintiff had testified that he had not looked to his right at all, he of course would have been guilty of contributory negligence as a matter of law. We hold that his testimony in fact was the equivalent of his saying that he did not look at all.

Chief Judge Leddy concluded that plaintiff was guilty of contributory negligence as a matter of law; accordingly, he set aside the verdict and entered judgment n.o.v. for defendant. We agree.

* * *

Affirmed.

Post-Case Follow-Up

The ruling on a motion for judgment as a matter of law is based on a comparison of the controlling substantive law and the evidence presented at trial. Judgment as a matter of law on a claim or defense is appropriate when the evidence does not permit a favorable jury finding on an issue necessary to prevail on that claim or defense. The plaintiff in *Simblest* had to have a favorable jury finding on the contributory negligence defense; i.e., he needed a "no" answer, because a "yes" answer to the contributory negligence question was an absolute bar to recovery under the controlling law. The evidence conclusively established that the answer should be "yes" to that question, and so judgment as a matter of law was granted.

Consider another example. Suppose the plaintiff's negligence claim is based on the allegation that the defendant ran a red light and collided with plaintiff's car. To prevail on this claim, the law of negligence requires the plaintiff to prove, among other things, that the defendant breached the standard of care for operating a car by running the red light. If the plaintiff fails to offer any evidence that the defendant ran the red light, no reasonable jury could conclude that the defendant was negligent. In other words, the evidence is legally insufficient to support a finding of negligence, and judgment as a matter of law in the defendant's favor is appropriate. To avoid this result, the plaintiff in this example needs to offer some evidence that the defendant ran the red light. Doing so avoids judgment as a matter of law, even if the defendant has offered evidence that he didn't run the red light. In a jury trial, the jury resolves conflicting evidence on material issues, not the judge. Judgment as a matter of law against a plaintiff is appropriate when there is no evidence of an issue he must prove in order to recover (i.e., a material element of his claim), or when the evidence conclusively establishes a matter (i.e., a defense) that precludes recovery.

Simblest v. Maynard: Real Life Applications

Suppose the plaintiff's complaint alleges only negligence. The controlling law of negligence requires the plaintiff to prove: (1) that the defendant owed a duty to the plaintiff and (2) breached that duty, (3) that the breach of duty was the cause of harm to the plaintiff, and (4) that the harm caused is legally compensable. The defendant's answer denies the negligence allegations, and also asserts the affirmative defense of release based upon allegations that the plaintiff had released his negligence claim as part of an earlier settlement. To prevail on the release defense, the defendant must prove: (1) the existence of a valid release agreement between plaintiff and defendant, and (2) that the plaintiff's negligence claim falls within the scope of the release.

1. At trial, the plaintiff offers evidence of all the necessary elements of his negligence claim, except he offers no evidence of causation. The defendant fails to offer evidence proving the existence of a valid release agreement. The defendant moves for judgment as a matter of law. How should the court rule?

2. Plaintiff offers evidence supporting all the elements of his negligence claim that would allow reasonable jurors to find in his favor on those elements. The defendant offers evidence that he did not breach any duty to the plaintiff. The only evidence on the release defense is that the plaintiff and defendant entered into a valid agreement and that the negligence claim falls within its scope. The defendant moves for judgment as a matter of law. How should the court rule and why?

3. Plaintiff offers evidence in support of all the elements of his negligence claim from which a reasonable juror could find in plaintiff's favor on the issue. The defendant offers evidence from which a reasonable juror could conclude that he did not breach any duty to the plaintiff. As to the release defense, there is evidence both that the defense was valid and evidence that it was not. The defendant moves for judgment as a matter of law. How should the court rule?

---

2. When to Make a Rule 50 Motion: Making and Renewing Motions for Judgment as a Matter of Law

Rule 50(a), set out in Exhibit 22.4, provides that a motion for judgment as a matter of law "may be made at any time before the case is submitted to the jury." Rule 50(a)(1) provides that a motion for judgment as a matter of law is appropriate after "a party has been fully heard on an issue during trial. . . ." Taking these two provisions of the rule together, a party may make a motion for judgment as a matter of law as early as when his opponent rests his case, but no later than before the case is submitted to the jury. Motions for judgment as a matter of law typically are made when one's opponent rests, when all parties rest, or when all parties have closed their cases (i.e., when rebuttal cases have concluded). Lawyers and judges sometimes refer to this motion as a motion for directed verdict. Rather than awaiting the jury's answers to a question or questions, the court is directing a certain verdict, and thus obviating the need for the trial to continue.

If the court does not grant the motion for judgment as a matter of law, Rule 50(b), set out in Exhibit 22.5, provides that "the court is considered to have submitted the action to the jury subject to the court's later deciding the legal questions

EXHIBIT 22.4 **Rule 50(a)**

(a) Judgment as a Matter of Law.

(1) In General. If a party has been fully heard on an issue during a jury trial and the court finds that a reasonable jury would not have a legally sufficient evidentiary basis to find for the party on that issue, the court may:

(A) resolve the issue against the party; and

(B) grant a motion for judgment as a matter of law against the party on a claim or defense that, under the controlling law, can be maintained or defeated only with a favorable finding on that issue.

(2) Motion. A motion for judgment as a matter of law may be made at any time before the case is submitted to the jury. The motion must specify the judgment sought and the law and facts that entitle the movant to the judgment.

decided by the motion." A party may then renew its motion for judgment as a matter of law after verdict and even up to 28 days after judgment. As described above, this motion is sometimes called a motion for judgment notwithstanding the verdict or, if you prefer Latin, a motion for judgment *non obstante veredicto*. This name describes what the motion seeks — a judgment contrary to what the verdict supports; i.e., a judgment in favor of the "loser" in the verdict.

Importantly, a party may not make a renewed motion for judgment as a matter of law after verdict or judgment if it did not make a motion for judgment as a matter of law before submission of the case to the jury. Put simply, a party may not renew a motion it never made in the first place.

District courts will often deny a motion for judgment as a matter of law, even if the court thinks the evidence only supports a single verdict. Suppose the defendant moves for judgment as a matter of law before the case is submitted to the jury on the ground that the plaintiff failed to offer any evidence to prove the breach element of his negligence claim. The court may very well deny this motion, even if it thinks there

EXHIBIT 22.5 **Rule 50(b)**

(b) Renewing the Motion After Trial; Alternative Motion for a New Trial. If the court does not grant a motion for judgment as a matter of law made under Rule 50(a), the court is considered to have submitted the action to the jury subject to the court's later deciding the legal questions raised by the motion. No later than 28 days after the entry of judgment — or if the motion addresses a jury issue not decided by a verdict, no later than 28 days after the jury was discharged — the movant may file a renewed motion for judgment as a matter of law and may include an alternative or joint request for a new trial under Rule 59. In ruling on the renewed motion, the court may:

(1) allow judgment on the verdict, if the jury returned a verdict;

(2) order a new trial; or

(3) direct the entry of judgment as a matter of law.

is no evidence of breach. This may sound odd, but there are two principal reasons the court will deny or delay ruling. First, the trial court may want to give the jury the chance to get it right and, in this example, return a verdict for the defendant. After all, if the jury gets it wrong, the judge can always grant the renewed motion after verdict.

Second, granting the renewed motion instead may ultimately save the court and the parties a lot of time. If the judge grants a motion for judgment as a matter of law before submission of the case to the jury and that decision is reversed on appeal, the appellate court will remand the case for a new trial. In our example this would mean that the appellate court decided, contrary to the district court, that there was some evidence from which a reasonable jury *could* conclude the defendant breached his duty. Remand is necessary, however, because the jury was never given an opportunity to actually reach that conclusion. We know the jury *could* decide the defendant was negligent, but would it actually do so? We would need a new trial to know the answer.

If, on the other hand, the trial court allows the case to proceed to verdict and then grants a *renewed* motion for judgment as a matter of law, the appellate court will reverse and render judgment if it disagrees with the trial court's ruling. Thus, the case is at an end whether or not the trial court properly granted the renewed motion. No new trial is necessary. In our example, this would mean that the jury returned a verdict for the plaintiff; then the trial court granted the defendant's renewed motion for judgment as a matter of law and rendered judgment for the defendant (despite the verdict for the plaintiff); and then the appellate court concluded that there was some evidence from which a reasonable jury could conclude that the defendant breached his duty and was negligent. Since the jury has already rendered a verdict based on legally sufficient evidence for the plaintiff, the appellate court can simply render judgment for the plaintiff, rather than remanding for a new trial. This saves considerable time, money, and effort for all involved.

3. Determinations as a Matter of Law

Even if there is legally insufficient evidence of an important issue, judgment as a matter of law is not always appropriate. Under the Federal Rules, as a general rule a judgment is an order or decree that concludes the entire case. The court's determination that there is legally insufficient evidence to support a finding on a particular issue may or may not conclude the entire case. Rule 50(a)(1)(A) provides that when there is legally insufficient evidence to find for a party on an issue, the court may "resolve the issue against the party." Rule 50(a)(1)(B) allows the court to go further and grant judgment as a matter of law if the party cannot prevail without a favorable finding on that issue. These two provisions of Rule 50 set out a two-step analysis. First, is there legally insufficient evidence to support a favorable finding on an issue? If so, the court can find against the party on the issue. Second, the court needs to determine if this finding concludes the entire case, or only part of it. In other words, the court determines whether or not the finding warrants judgment as a matter of law against the party. Sometimes a party may be able to prevail despite the court's adverse finding on an issue, in which case judgment as a matter of law would be inappropriate.

Suppose a plaintiff brings a product liability suit against the manufacturer of his automobile alleging that a defect in the brakes of the car caused him bodily injuries. Further suppose that the plaintiff's complaint alleges two different causes of action — negligence and strict product liability. The jury should return a verdict for the plaintiff if he proves the elements of either cause of action. These two causes of action share some common elements. They both require proof that the brakes were defective and that this defect caused the plaintiff's injuries. The negligence cause of action, however, requires proof of an additional element — that the defect resulted from the defendant's breach of the standard of care for manufacturing or designing the product. Now suppose at trial that the plaintiff presents evidence of defect, causation, and injury but fails to present any evidence that the defendant breached the standard of care. Many trial lawyers keep a checklist of the elements of their causes of action and defenses to ensure that they have offered legally sufficient evidence for each element. In our example, a legal sufficiency checklist for the elements of these two causes of action at the close of the evidence would look like this:

Negligence	Strict Liability
× Breach	
√ Defect	√ Defect
√ Causation	√ Causation
√ Injury	√ Injury

There is legally insufficient evidence on the issue of breach, so the plaintiff cannot prevail on the negligence cause of action. But the jury could return a verdict for the plaintiff on the strict liability cause of action, and judgment on the verdict would be for the plaintiff. In this example, the court could not grant judgment as a matter of law against the plaintiff (he might still prevail), but the court could find against the plaintiff on the issue of breach and refuse to submit a negligence question to the jury. If the court did submit the question to the jury and the jury found for the plaintiff on the negligence question, the court could determine as a matter of law that the defendant was not negligent and ignore the jury's answer to the question. It would then render judgment based on the jury's answers to the remaining questions.

Now consider a variation on this example. Suppose the plaintiff failed to present any evidence that the defect in the brakes of his car was a cause of his injuries. Now our legal sufficiency checklist would look like this:

Negligence	Strict Liability
√ Breach	
√ Defect	√ Defect
× Causation	× Causation
√ Injury	√ Injury

Here, upon motion for judgment as a matter of law (or renewed motion), the court should find that there is legally insufficient evidence on the issue of causation. Furthermore, because both causes of action share this element, the jury cannot properly return a verdict for the plaintiff on either the negligence or strict liability theory, and judgment as a matter of law against the plaintiff is appropriate.

C. MOTION FOR NEW TRIAL

After verdict, or even after judgment, a trial court may grant the losing party a new trial. A new trial is a do-over. For fans of golf, it's akin to a mulligan. The party who won the verdict and judgment the first time might win the second trial too. Then again, the losing party might win the second time around. Rule 59(b) provides that a motion for new trial must be filed within 28 days of entry of judgment. This section discusses when a party might make a motion for new trial and why a court might grant it.

1. A New Trial as an Alternative to Judgment as a Matter of Law

Under Rule 50(b)(2), when the losing party makes its renewed motion for judgment as a matter of law, the trial court has the authority to grant a new trial instead. Thus, the grounds for a new trial are often the same as the grounds for a renewed motion for judgment as a matter of law — that the evidence is legally insufficient to support a contrary judgment. A trial court may prefer to grant a new trial, because a new trial is a less drastic action. Granting the renewed motion for judgment as a matter of law takes a favorable judgment away from one party and gives it to an opposing party. In contrast, if a new trial is granted, the same party might win again. Because a court might prefer to grant a new trial rather than judgment as a matter of law, the party renewing its motion for judgment as a matter of law will often request, in the alternative, a new trial. The movant is saying: "If you won't take the judgment from my opponent and give it to me, at least give us a new trial." The new trial doesn't guarantee a win for the movant, but it avoids, or at least delays, a loss. Of course, what's good for the goose is good for the gander. The party against whom judgment as a matter of law has been rendered may request a new trial within 28 days of the entry of judgment.

2. A Motion for New Trial in Lieu of a Motion for Judgment as a Matter of Law

A motion for new trial may be made on legal sufficiency grounds in lieu of a renewed motion for judgment as a matter of law because the party failed to move for judgment as a matter of law before the case was submitted to the jury. Recall that a party may not renew a motion for judgment as a matter of law unless the party made a motion for judgment as a matter of law before the case was submitted to the jury. In other words, a party cannot renew a motion it never made in the first place. Failure to move for judgment as a matter of law before the case is submitted to the jury waives the right to judgment as a matter of law post-verdict. In this situation, the party who lost at trial can no longer have judgment granted in his favor on the grounds that the evidence is legally insufficient to support the judgment, but he can still get the next best thing — a new trial.

3. A Motion for New Trial Based on Other Errors

Up to this point, we have discussed motions for new trial that are made on legal insufficiency grounds either as an alternative to or a substitute for a renewed motion for judgment as a matter of law. Legal insufficiency is only one of many grounds for granting a new trial. Rule 59 does not attempt to set out the grounds for granting a new trial, because they are too numerous to list. The trial court has broad discretion to grant a new trial based on almost any error during trial, but new trials are nevertheless fairly rare. Rule 59 permits a new trial "for any reason for which a new trial has heretofore been granted in an action at law in federal court"; so the attorney seeking a new trial must research the case law to see if his ground for a new trial is one that fits that definition. As examples, a new trial may be granted because: (1) the jury's finding(s), although supported by *some* evidence, is against "the great weight of the evidence"; (2) there is an error in the admission or an exclusion of evidence; (3) there is an error in the instructions provided to the jury; (4) the damage award is excessive or inadequate; (5) an improper jury argument occurs; (6) new evidence is introduced; and (7) juror or attorney misconduct occurs.

These are just examples. A new trial may be granted based on almost any error, but generally two things must also be true: (1) the party seeking the new trial must have made a timely and proper objection to the error during trial, and (2) the error must be harmful. Suppose the motion for new trial is based upon the admission of evidence that ought to have been excluded. If the new trial movant did not object to the evidence at the time it was offered, the trial court will not grant a new trial, even if the evidence should have been excluded had there been a timely objection. Even if there was a timely objection, the trial court will not grant a new trial unless the error was harmful. A harmful error is one that affects a party's "substantial rights." If the error did not affect the outcome of the case (i.e., it did not result in an improper judgment), the error is not harmful. Suppose that in our example there was a timely objection to the erroneously admitted evidence, but there was also a great deal of other properly admitted evidence that proves the same proposition. This error was not harmful, because it almost certainly did not affect the outcome.

4. Remittitur and Additur

One ground for a new trial is that the jury's damages award is too high or too low. Specifically, a court may grant a new trial when the jury's damages award "shocks the conscience." Suppose for example in a personal injury case the jury awards $6 million in damages when the only injury the plaintiff proved was a sprained ankle. The trial court may find the jury award "shocks the conscience" and award and grant a new trial on this basis. In addition to a new trial, the court has another tool at its disposal in this scenario — **remittitur**. Remittitur grants a new trial if the plaintiff refuses to accept a judgment for a lesser amount than the verdict. In our sprained ankle example, remittitur would allow the judge to put the plaintiff to a decision: Either accept a lower amount (say, for example, $100,000) or there will be a new trial, in which the plaintiff may wind up getting less than $100,000, or nothing at all. **Additur** is the mirror image of remittitur. If the jury's damages award is so low that it shocks the conscience, the judge may grant a new trial unless the defendant agrees to a higher damages award. Importantly, although additur may be allowed in state court, it is not permitted in federal court, because it violates the Seventh Amendment right to a jury trial.

Chapter Summary

- Trials are conducted to resolve triable issues of fact, not all factual disputes that arise during the course of litigation. Triable issues are those factual disputes that are part of the parties' claims and defenses.
- A party has a right to a jury trial with respect to any element of a legal claim, even if it is also an element of an equitable claim and even if the element is incidental to or seems less important than the elements of the equitable claim.
- Judgment as a matter of law on a claim or defense is appropriate when the evidence does not permit a favorable jury finding on an issue necessary to prevail on that claim or defense; i.e., the evidence is legally insufficient to support a contrary verdict. Typically, judgment as a matter of law is granted when a plaintiff has no evidence of an issue he must prove in order to recover (i.e., a necessary element of his claim), or when the evidence conclusively establishes a matter (i.e., a defense) that precludes recovery.
- A motion for judgment as a matter of law must be made before the case is submitted to the jury. If denied, the movant may make a renewed motion for judgment as a matter of law after verdict or even after judgment.
- A trial court may order a new trial after verdict or even after judgment based on almost any error committed during trial. Often a new trial is ordered as an alternative to granting judgment as a matter of law.

Applying the Concepts

1. Does a right to a jury trial exist in these scenarios? Why or why not?

   a. As to the amount of damages plaintiff incurred as a result of defendant's breach of a contract he had with plaintiff, and/or as to whether or not the defendant breached any term of the contract?

> **b.** As to whether the plaintiff is domiciled in the Southern or the Western District of Texas for purposes of determining if venue is proper?
>
> **c.** As to an action seeking only an injunction preventing the defendant from constructing a cell phone tower that will obstruct the ocean view from plaintiff's property?
>
> **d.** As to a breach of contract action by the plaintiff against the defendant seeking only specific performance of the contract, and/or as to the defendant's counterclaim seeking money damages for breach of the same contract?

2. Assume that a motion for judgment as a matter of law was timely made and denied in each of the cases below. Should the court grant a renewed motion for judgment as a matter of law?

> **a.** Plaintiff brings a product liability action against defendant. Plaintiff alleges that he developed cancer as a result of exposure to Defendant's asbestos-containing products. The jury finds for Plaintiff and awards $2.5 million in damages. The evidence at trial established that Plaintiff was exposed to asbestos and that this exposure caused Plaintiff's cancer, but there was no evidence that Plaintiff was ever exposed to the asbestos in Defendant's products.
>
> **b.** Plaintiff brings an age discrimination lawsuit against her former employer under the federal Age Discrimination and Employment Act (ADEA). To prevail under the ADEA, the employee must prove that her employer committed an adverse employment action (e.g., demotion or termination) because of the employee's age at a time when the employee was over the age of 40. The evidence at trial conclusively established that Defendant fired Plaintiff because of her age and that plaintiff was 39 years old when she was fired. The jury returns a verdict for Plaintiff.
>
> **c.** Plaintiff's suit against Defendant alleges that a defect in the heating element in an industrial clothes dryer manufactured and designed by Defendant caused the dryer to catch fire, which in turn caused severe damage to Plaintiff's facility. Plaintiff brings suit for damages claiming both negligence in the design of the dryer and breach of an express warranty by Defendant that the dryer posed no fire hazard. The jury found for Plaintiff on both the warranty and negligence theories. At trial, Plaintiff offered no evidence Defendant expressly warranted that the dryer was not a fire hazard. As to the defective design claim, Plaintiff offered evidence that the dryer was defectively designed and that this defect caused the fire, but Defendant also offered evidence that the fire was the result of misuse of the product by Plaintiff rather than a defect in the dryer.
>
> **d.** In a negligence action, the jury answers "yes" to the question about Defendant's negligence and "no" to the question about whether or not Plaintiff's negligence claim was barred by the governing two-year statute of limitations. The evidence at trial conclusively establishes both that Defendant was negligent and that Plaintiff did not commence his action within the governing two-year limitations period.

3. The federal district court begins a trial with a jury of seven. During the course of the trial, the court excuses one juror because he has fallen gravely ill and dismisses another because the court discovers he is not a citizen of the United States. After the second juror is dismissed, the defendant moves for a mistrial. How should the court rule and why?

Civil Procedure in Practice

Hot Burger, Inc. is a nationwide fast food restaurant chain. Hot Burger authorizes franchisees to purchase and operate Hot Burger restaurant franchises and provides training, advertising, recipes, and licenses to use Hot Burger trademarked logos and designs in exchange for a franchise fee from the owner. Omar owns a Hot Burger franchise but is nine months in arrears on his franchise payments to Hot Burger. Hot Burger files suit for breach of the franchise agreement, seeking both the nine months of unpaid franchise fees and an injunction prohibiting Omar from continuing to operate his restaurant as a Hot Burger. You represent Hot Burger in its suit against Omar.

1. Omar files and serves a timely demand for a jury trial on the breach of contract claim for the unpaid franchise fees. Omar unilaterally withdraws his jury demand. Hot Burger wants a jury trial on this claim but did not file a demand. Should the trial court conduct a jury trial on this claim? Why or why not?

2. Omar moves the court to try the claim for an injunction before trying the claim for money damages. Hot Burger wants the claim for money damages tried first. Which claim should be tried first and should it be tried to a judge or a jury?

3. The jury returns a verdict for Hot Burger and awards it the nine months of unpaid franchise fees. Omar moves for judgment as a matter of law for the first time after the clerk enters judgment on the verdict in favor of Hot Burger. What argument do you make in response to Omar's motion?

Appealing the Trial Court's Decision

23

Appealing the Trial Court's Decisions

In this chapter we will explain when you may appeal a trial court's decision to an appellate court, what issues the appellate court is likely to consider, and how an appellate court will decide, in a general manner, whether the trial court made a significant mistake, and if so, what the remedy should be. This last issue is one better-suited to an appellate procedure class. However, a good trial lawyer must understand when a decision is appealable, how to preserve error so that the appellate court will consider the argument that the trial court made a mistake, and whether the appellate court is likely to determine whether or not the trial court made a mistake worth correcting.

Trials are rare. Many disputes never become lawsuits. Many lawsuits never reach the trial stage. Even fewer cases result in an appeal. The federal system — and most state systems — allow an appeal as a matter of right to an appellate court designated to review the decisions of the trial court. Even so, few cases ever make it to a decision by an appellate court, and the issues the appellate court decides are usually few in number — especially compared to the number of decisions a trial court makes over the course of a lawsuit. All of this may seem strange because most of how the law is taught, particularly in the first year of law school, is via reading, understanding, and synthesizing the law from appellate opinions. Hopefully this gives you some perspective on the role of appellate cases in a class focused on the rules that apply in federal trial courts.

Key Concepts

- The "final judgment rule" and its exceptions
- How to "preserve error" so an appellate court will consider your argument that the trial court made an error
- How, generally, an appellate court will analyze whether the trial court made an error that is worth correcting

A. WHEN TO APPEAL: THE FINALITY RULE

Courts make numerous decisions in the course of a lawsuit. A complete list of possible court rulings a party may disagree with and want to appeal would be impossible to list. Some examples, however, would include a court's decision to grant a motion to dismiss, to permit or refuse discovery into a matter, ruling on a motion for summary judgment, and admitting or excluding evidence at trial. If the parties could appeal each ruling they disagreed with in a piecemeal fashion, litigation would be less efficient, more expensive, and take longer than it already does.

    The general rule is that the trial court's decisions cannot be reviewed on appeal unless and until the trial court has entered a **final judgment** that ends the case in the trial court. Put simply, a judgment is final if there is nothing left for the trial court to decide. That means that all claims by all parties have been fully resolved and the court has signed a document called a final judgment. Like any rule, there are exceptions, explained both in the following case and in more detail after the case. However, the following case is intended to illustrate the concept of the final judgment rule — the most important rule for determining when a court's decision may be appealed. Exhibit 23.1 is the statute requiring trial court judgments to be final before an appeal is available.

EXHIBIT 23.1   **28 U.S.C. §1291 Final Decisions of District Courts**

>   The courts of appeals . . . shall have jurisdiction of appeals from all final decisions of the district courts of the United States. . . .

Case Preview

Liberty Mutual Insurance Co. v. Wetzel

As you read *Liberty Mutual Insurance Co. v. Wetzel*, consider the following questions:

1. Was the trial court's judgment final? Did it recite that it was? Was that sufficient to make the judgment final and appealable?
2. Did the parties raise the issue of whether the judgment was final on their own?
3. Did the Court discuss any exceptions to the final judgment rule?

Liberty Mutual Insurance Co. v. Wetzel
424 U.S. 737 (1976)

Opinion

Mr. Justice REHNQUIST delivered the opinion of the Court.

Respondents filed a complaint in the United States District Court for the Western District of Pennsylvania in which they asserted that petitioner's employee insurance benefits and maternity leave regulations discriminated against women in violation of Title VII of the Civil Rights Act of 1964. . . . The District Court ruled in favor of respondents on the issue of petitioner's liability under that Act, and petitioner appealed to the Court of Appeals for the Third Circuit. That court held that it had jurisdiction of petitioner's appeal under 28 U.S.C. §1291, and proceeded to affirm on the merits the judgment of the District Court. We [also] heard argument on the merits. Though neither party has questioned the jurisdiction of the Court of Appeals to entertain the appeal, we are obligated to do so on our own motion if a question thereto exists. Because we conclude that the District Court's order was not appealable to the Court of Appeals, we vacate the judgment of the Court of appeals with instructions to dismiss petitioner's appeal from the order of the District Court.

Respondents' complaint, after alleging jurisdiction and facts deemed pertinent to their claim, prayed for a judgment against petitioner embodying the following relief: "(a) requiring that defendant establish non-discriminatory hiring, payment, opportunity, and promotional plans and programs; (b) enjoining the continuance by defendant of the illegal acts and practices alleged herein; (c) requiring that defendant pay over to plaintiffs and to the members of the class the damages sustained by plaintiffs and the members of the class by reason of defendant's illegal acts and practices, including adjusted backpay, with interest, and an additional equal amount as liquidated damages, and exemplary damages; (d) requiring that defendant pay to plaintiffs and to the members of the class the costs of this suit and a reasonable attorneys' fee, with interest; and (e) such other and further relief as the Court deems appropriate." After extensive discovery, respondents moved for partial summary judgment only as to the issue of liability. Fed. R. Civ. Proc. 56(c). The District Court . . . finding no issues of material fact in dispute, entered an order to the effect that petitioner's pregnancy-related policies violated Title VII of the Civil Rights Act of 1964. It also ruled that Liberty Mutual's hiring and promotion policies violated Title VII. . . .

[The Court quoted the trial court's order, which stated:]

"In its Order the court stated it would enjoin the continuance of practices which the court found to be in violation of Title VII. The Plaintiffs were invited to submit the form of the injunction order and the Defendant has filed Notice of Appeal and asked for stay of any injunctive order. Under these circumstances the court will withhold the issuance of the injunctive order and amend the Order previously issued under the provisions of Fed. R. Civ. P. 54(b), as follows:

"And now this 20th day of February, 1974, it is directed that final judgment be entered in favor of Plaintiffs that Defendant's policy of requiring female employees to return to work within three months of delivery of a child or be terminated is in violation of the provisions of Title VII of the Civil Rights Act of 1964; that Defendant's policy of denying disability income protection plan benefits to female employees for disabilities related to pregnancies or childbirth are [sic] in violation of Title VII of the Civil Rights Act of 1964 and that it is expressly directed that Judgment be entered for the Plaintiffs upon these claims of Plaintiffs' Complaint; there being no just reason for delay."

It is obvious from the District Court's order that respondents, although having received a favorable ruling on the issue of petitioner's liability to them, received none of the relief which they expressly prayed for in the portion of their complaint set forth above. They requested an injunction, but did not get one; they requested damages, but were not awarded any; they requested attorneys' fees, but received none. . . .

The District Court and the Court of Appeals apparently took the view that because the District Court made the recital required by Fed. R. Civ. Proc. 54(b) that final judgment be entered on the issue of liability, and that there was no just reason for delay, the orders thereby became appealable as a final decision pursuant to 28 U.S.C. §1291. We cannot agree with this application of the Rule and statute in question.

Rule 54(b) "does not apply to a single claim action. . . . It is limited expressly to multiple claims actions in which 'one or more but less than all' of the multiple claims have been finally decided and are found otherwise to be ready for appeal." Sears, Roebuck & Co. v. Mackey, 351 U.S. 427 (1956). Here, however, respondents set forth but a single claim: that petitioner's employee insurance benefits and maternity leave regulations discriminated against its women employees in violation of Title VII of the Civil Rights Act of 1964. They prayed for several different types of relief in the event that they sustained the allegations of their complaint, see Fed. R. Civ. Proc. 8(a)(3), but their complaint advanced a single legal theory which was applied to only one set of facts. Thus, despite the fact that the District Court undoubtedly made the findings required under the Rule had it been applicable, those findings do not in a case such as this make the order appealable pursuant to 28 U.S.C. §1291.

[Eds. — Interlocutory refers to a court's decision during the course of a case that does not finally resolve the case.]

We turn to consider whether the District Court's order might have been appealed by petitioner to the Court of Appeals under any other theory. The order, viewed apart from its discussion of Rule 54(b), constitutes a grant of partial summary judgment limited to the issue of petitioner's liability. Such judgments are by their terms interlocutory, see Fed. R. Civ. Proc. 56(c), and where assessment of damages or awarding of other relief remains to be resolved have never been considered to be "final" within the meaning of 28 U.S.C. §1291. . . . Thus the only possible authorization for an appeal from the District Court's order would be pursuant to the provisions of 28 U.S.C. §1292.

If the District Court had granted injunctive relief but had not ruled on respondents' other requests for relief, this interlocutory order would have been appealable under §1292(a)(1). But, as noted above, the court did not issue an injunction. It might be argued that the order of the District Court, insofar as it failed to include the injunctive relief requested by respondents, is an interlocutory order refusing an injunction within the meaning of §1292(a)(1). But even if this would have allowed respondents to then obtain review in the Court of Appeals, there was no denial of any injunction sought by Petitioner and it could not avail itself of that grant of jurisdiction.

Nor was this order appealable pursuant to 28 U.S.C. §1292(b). Although the District Court's findings made with a view to satisfying Rule 54(b) might be viewed as substantial compliance with the certification requirement of that section, there is no showing in this record that petitioner made application to the Court of Appeals within the 10 days therein specified. And that court's holding that its jurisdiction was pursuant to §1291 makes it clear that it thought itself obliged to consider on the merits petitioner's appeal. There can be no assurance that had the other requirements of §1292(b) been complied with, the Court of Appeals would have exercised its discretion to entertain the interlocutory appeal.

Were we to sustain the procedure followed here, we would condone a practice whereby a district court in virtually any case before it might render an interlocutory decision on the question of liability of the defendant, and the defendant would thereupon be permitted to appeal to the court of appeals without satisfying any of the requirements that Congress carefully set forth. We believe that Congress, in enacting present §§1291 and 1292 of Title 28, has been well aware of the dangers of an overly rigid insistence upon a "final decision" for appeal in every case, and has in those sections made ample provision for appeal of orders which are not "final" so as to alleviate any possible hardship. We would twist the fabric of the statute more than it will bear if we were to agree that the District Court's order of February 20, 1974, was appealable to the Court of Appeals.

The judgment of the Court of Appeals is therefore vacated, and the case is remanded with instructions to dismiss the petitioner's appeal.

It is so ordered.

Post-Case Follow-Up

Liberty Mutual Insurance Co. v. Wetzel

The trial court's judgment was not an appealable final judgment; it was final as to liability, but not the remedy. The Court discussed in detail the topic of our next section — exceptions to the final judgment rule. How many exceptions did you see the Court discuss?

Why would it be so bad to allow appeals like the one in this case? What would happen if the court of appeals simply decided the appeal on the merits? What would be the harm? Can you think of reasons why the final judgment rule is the general rule — even though there are a number of exceptions that allow parties to have appellate courts review trial courts' interlocutory orders?

Are there certain types of orders that should be immediately appealable, even if the court's decision is not a final decision ending the case?

Liberty Mutual Insurance Co. v. Wetzel: Real Life Applications

1. A buyer purchased a custom motorcycle from a custom motorcycle dealership and sued both the salesman and the dealership. The buyer claimed that the salesman guaranteed the motorcycle would be worth at least $30,000, but when the buyer had it appraised, he learned that it was worth more no more than $15,000. The salesman crossclaimed against the motorcycle dealership, alleging that if the salesman is found liable, the dealership should pay all or part of the damages award against him, because the dealership told the salesman to lie about the value of the motorcycle. After trial, the jury returned a verdict that the salesman was liable for fraud and the buyer was entitled to damages of $15,000. The court entered judgment on the jury's verdict and recited that it was a final judgment, but did not mention the dealership. Is this judgment appealable under the final judgment rule? Why or why not?

2. A swimmer sued a pool slide manufacturer for making a defective slide after the swimmer was paralyzed while using the slide. The pool slide manufacturer believes it did not actually make the slide; rather, the slide was a counterfeit. The slide manufacturer moves to sever the issue of whether it manufactured the slide from the other issues in the case, such as whether the slide was defective or the plaintiff's damages. The court severed the issue of who manufactured the slide, and the jury decided that the manufacturer did manufacture it. The trial court then set a trial date for the jury to decide whether the slide was defective and the amount, if any, of the plaintiff's damages. May the slide manufacturer immediately appeal the jury's decision that the manufacturer made the slide at issue? Why or why not?

3. A plaintiff sued a defendant who claimed he had no connection to the forum state. The defendant moved to dismiss the complaint on the grounds that the court lacked personal jurisdiction over him. The court denied the plaintiff's motion. May the defendant appeal the denial of his personal jurisdiction motion now? Why or why not?

---

1. When to Appeal Final Judgments: The Deadline

The Federal Rules of *Appellate* Procedure govern the deadline to file a notice of appeal of a final judgment. Specifically, Rule 4 of the appellate rules requires an appellant to file his notice of appeal with the district clerk within 30 days after the judgment or order appealed from is entered. *See* Fed. R. App. P. 4(a)(1)(A). Post-trial motions under Federal Rules of Civil Procedure 50(b) or 59 will postpone the 30-day deadline until the court has ruled on such motions. Fed. R. App. P. 4(a)(4)(A). The district court can even extend the deadline if a party so requests, but the party must show excusable neglect or good cause.

2. Exceptions to the Final Judgment Rule

Like any rule, there are exceptions. There are several ways to have an appellate court review a trial court's **interlocutory** decision or order. But beware: Many if not most of these exceptions are narrow, constantly changing, and typically disfavored by courts of appeals.

Review of Interlocutory Injunctions

Recall *Liberty Mut. Ins. Co. v. Wetzel*. The plaintiff sought both monetary relief and injunctive relief. If the court had granted or denied the plaintiff's request for injunctive relief, the appellate court would have had appellate jurisdiction under §1292(a), even if the **injunction** was just to preserve the status quo while the court decided the rest of the case — particularly whether the defendant was liable and whether any damages should have been awarded. *See* Exhibit 23.2. Why would the law allow review of such orders? Put simply, injunctions are court orders to do or refrain from doing something. Given the fact that trials can be lengthy, such a court order could end up being very costly to the party enjoined. A party may have to expend considerable resources to comply with the court's order. On the other hand, if the court fails to enter such an order, unique property or valuable assets that should be used to satisfy a judgment may be lost, or the court may lose its ability to provide an adequate remedy to the plaintiff.

EXHIBIT 23.2   **28 U.S.C. §1292(a)**

> [T]he courts of appeals shall have jurisdiction of appeals from:
>   (1) Interlocutory orders of the district courts of the United States . . . granting, continuing, modifying, refusing or dissolving injunctions, or refusing to dissolve or modify injunctions. . . .

Review of Certified Questions

A trial court can transform a decision ordinarily not yet reviewable by the court of appeals by making a three-point certification: (1) the order must involve a controlling question of law, (2) there is substantial ground for difference of opinion on the question, and (3) an immediate appeal of the order may materially advance the termination of the litigation. *See* Exhibit 23.3. If the court does so, act quickly; you have only ten days to take advantage of the opportunity for the court of appeals to answer the certified question. Even then, the court of appeals has wide discretion to answer or refuse to answer the certified question.

    This exception is rarely used and even more rarely granted. The three-point certification is difficult to meet and both the trial court and the appellate court

EXHIBIT 23.3   **28 U.S.C. §1292(b)**

When a district judge, in making in a civil action an order not otherwise appealable under this section, shall be of the opinion that such order involves a controlling question of law as to which there is substantial ground for difference of opinion and that an immediate appeal from the order may materially advance the ultimate termination of the litigation, he shall so state in writing in such order. The Court of Appeals which would have jurisdiction of an appeal of such action may thereupon, in its discretion, permit an appeal to be taken from such order, if application is made to it within ten days after the entry of the order. . . .

must agree to permit the interlocutory appeal. As a result, only a tiny fraction of a percent of interlocutory orders are certified in the first place, and less than half of those were decided on the merits. *See* Charles Alan Wright, *Law of Federal Courts* §102 (5th ed. 1994); Michael E. Solimine, *Revitalizing Interlocutory Appeals in the Federal Courts*, 58 Geo. Wash. L. Rev. 1165, 1174 (1990).

Final by Fiat: Rule 54(b) — Multiple Parties or Multiple Claims

If a case involves multiple claims or multiple parties, the court can turn an otherwise interlocutory judgment into an appealable judgment. Suppose a factory worker who was exposed to asbestos and is now ill sued 200 companies that allegedly used asbestos in the products he worked with over his long career. One defendant company moved for summary judgment on the grounds that it had stopped using asbestos in its products ten years before the plaintiff began working in the factory. The court finds no dispute of material fact on that issue and grants the product manufacturer summary judgment. Notice that this order by the court does not meet the definition of a final judgment, because it does not dispose of all parties and all claims. The case will continue with respect to the claims against the other defendants. However, Rule 54(b) allows the court to issue an order creating a final judgment as to the claims or parties it has disposed of. *See* Exhibit 23.4. Under Rule 54(b), the product manufacturer could request that the court enter a final judgment in its favor so that the summary judgment becomes immediately appealable, so long as the court's summary judgment order disposes of all claims against this single party in the multi-party action. Now consider *Liberty Mut. Ins. Co. v. Wetzel* again. The trial court used the required language — it recited in the judgment that it

EXHIBIT 23.4   **Fed. R. Civ. P. 54(b) Judgment on Multiple Claims or Involving Multiple Parties**

When an action presents more than one claim for relief—whether as a claim, counterclaim, crossclaim, or third-party claim—or when multiple parties are involved, the court may direct entry of a final judgment as to one or more, but fewer than all, claims or parties only if the court expressly determines that there is no just reason for delay.

was final and that "there is no just reason for delay." Why was the order not immediately appealable under Rule 54(b)? Should it have been?

Class Actions: Do You Have One?

Another Federal Rule of Civil Procedure, Rule 23(f), potentially renders a specific interlocutory decision appealable — the court's ruling on a motion to certify a class action. *See* Exhibit 23.5. As you learned in Chapter 21, some lawsuits involve so many potential plaintiffs that the typical joinder rules are insufficient. For example, imagine a lawsuit in which all purchasers of mass-produced items, such as a smartphone or a certain diesel-powered vehicle, wanted to join together to sue the defendant and prove their case. It may be much more economical for some of the claimants to bring the action as a class action on behalf of all similarly situated persons, particularly if their complaints about the phone or car are similar, as litigating hundreds or even thousands of cases around the country would be inefficient. As Chapter 21 explained, however, there are many requirements plaintiffs must establish before a lawsuit can proceed as a class action. The trial court's ruling on the motion to certify the class action determines the fundamental nature of the action. Denying the motion may make the case quite small, with only a few plaintiffs alleging modest damages. Granting the motion might mean the action is of national significance, with enormous amounts of money at stake. Recognize, however, that whether the court grants or denies the motion to certify, its order is not a final judgment. Whether the trial court decides that the case should proceed as a class action or not, the court still has work to do on the case, because it has not disposed of all parties and all claims. However, because of the great significance of the court's ruling on the motion to certify, this decision may be immediately appealed. Note the specific requirements for a court of appeals to review a trial court's request to certify a class action lawsuit. First, the language of the rule — it uses the word "may" — makes the appeal discretionary with the court of appeals. Second, procedurally, you must petition the *circuit clerk* (the clerk of the court of appeals — not the trial court) for permission to appeal. Finally, you must act quickly. You must file your petition within 14 days after the trial court enters an order certifying or refusing to certify the lawsuit as a class action.

EXHIBIT 23.5 **Fed. R. Civ. P. 23(f) Appeals**

> A court of appeals may permit an appeal from an order granting or denying class-action certification under this rule if a petition for permission to appeal is filed with the circuit clerk within 14 days after the order is entered. An appeal does not stay proceedings in the district court unless the district judge or the court of appeals so orders.

The Collateral Order Doctrine

The court of appeals also has the authority to review the trial court's interlocutory decisions on **collateral orders**. To be a collateral order: (1) the court's decision on a discrete issue must conclusively determine the disputed question, (2) the decision must resolve an important question completely separate from the merits of the action, and (3) the decision must be effectively unreviewable from a final judgment. What counts as a collateral order is narrow and evolving. For example, a typical interlocutory order that used to qualify as an appealable collateral order is a court's discovery order requiring a party to produce to her opponent privileged documents that are claimed to be privileged. *See United States v. Philip Morris, Inc.*, 314 F.3d 612, 617-22 (D.C. Cir. 2002). This sort of order seems to meet all three requirements: The court's order finally determined that the documents were not privileged (otherwise, they would not be discoverable); privileges are certainly important questions, and it is arguable that whether the documents were privileged had nothing to do with whether the plaintiff's claims had merit; and the decision would be effectively unreviewable on appeal. The appellate court cannot unring the bell. Once disclosed, the privilege — the secrecy — is destroyed, and simply ordering the documents returned is not an adequate remedy for the privilege holder. However, in *Mohawk Indus. v. Carpenter*, the Court came to the opposite conclusion, holding that "piecemeal appeals of all adverse attorney-client [privilege] rulings would unduly delay [the trial court] and needlessly burden the Court of Appeals." 558 U.S. 100, 112 (2009).

Some orders still qualify as appealable collateral orders. For example, in *Cohen v. Beneficial Indus. Loan Corp.*, the court of appeals reviewed the trial court's order requiring the plaintiffs to post a $125,000 bond before they could proceed with their shareholders' derivative suit. 337 U.S. 541 (1949). The Court held this met all three prongs. Do you agree? Why is a decision like this effectively unreviewable on appeal — especially when compared to the privileged documents example?

A few other examples remain. Courts have found immediately appealable decisions where a court: (1) denied a governmental official's motion to dismiss on the grounds of qualified immunity while performing discretionary duties, (2) denied a nonparty's motion to intervene as of right, (3) placed gag orders on the press, and, perhaps most famously, (4) denied President Nixon's absolute immunity from suit. This is not a comprehensive list, but the Court refers to appealable collateral orders as a "small class." Examples that do not qualify as appealable collateral orders include decisions: (1) denying a motion to dismiss based on a forum-selection clause, (2) denying that an extradited person is immune from civil process, (3) denying a motion to dismiss on *forum non conveniens* grounds, and (4) denying a motion claiming immunity from suit for certain government employees.

The Writ of Mandamus

Another exception to final judgment appellate review is the **writ of mandamus**. Congress has retained this ancient remedy, often referred to as one of the extraordinary writs due to its rare nature. Although there are many different types of extraordinary writs (writs of prohibition, writs of quo warranto, etc.), the writ that allows the court of appeals to review interlocutory decisions that constitute alleged abuses of authority is the writ of mandamus, codified in the All Writs Act, 28 U.S.C. §1651(a). A writ of mandamus is an appropriate vehicle to have the court of appeals review a trial court's interlocutory decision provided that the petitioner can show:

(1) some special risk of irreparable harm from the decision, and (2) a clear entitlement to the relief requested.

Courts of appeals have permitted review by writ of mandamus, for example, for claims of clear error by a trial judge in ordering disclosure of materials protected by the attorney-client privilege (note how this differs from the decision on the same issue under the collateral order doctrine in *Mohawk* in the previous section), assigning an entire case to a special master who is *not* an Article III judge over the parties' objections, and refusing to recuse herself on nonfrivolous grounds of conflict of interest or bias. There is also a narrow exception where a writ of mandamus is appropriate to guide the lower courts on a recurring and important question of case management, sometimes called "advisory" or "supervisory" mandamus. *See Schlagenhauf v. Holder*, 379 U.S. 104 (1964) (issuing writ of mandamus to instruct the trial court in the construction and proper application of its authority to order physical examinations under Rule 35, addressing a recurring issue of discovery in the district courts).

Just Say No

The Supreme Court in *Mohawk Indus., Inc. v. Carpenter* also explained that counsel has a "last resort" option — to defy the trial court's allegedly erroneous order and see if the court's sanction is appealable. If the trial court issues a sanction severe enough, counsel may be able to appeal the sanction and thereby challenge the reason for it. A court might order a "death penalty" sanction that effectively terminates the litigation (e.g., striking all of the defiant party's pleadings). That could end the litigation and result in an appealable final judgment. As the *Mohawk* Court explained, another possibility is that the party defying the order could be held in contempt, which can sometimes be immediately appealable:

> Another long-recognized option is for a party to defy a disclosure order and incur court-imposed sanctions. . . . [W]hen the circumstances warrant it, a district court may hold a noncomplying party in contempt. The party can then appeal directly from that ruling, at least when the contempt citation can be characterized as a criminal punishment.

However unattractive, these are options. They are risky, both in terms of alienating the judge whose order you disobey and in finding out you were wrong after all, potentially harming your client's position and subjecting you to monetary consequences or even jail. For advocates who believe strongly that they are right and the court is unquestionably wrong on a crucially important issue, defying an interlocutory order to provoke a sanction in order to make the underlying decision immediately reviewable on appeal is an option. Just remember to pack a toothbrush.

Mohawk Indus., Inc. v. Carpenter: A Summary

Although *Mohawk Indus., Inc. v. Carpenter* deals primarily with the collateral order doctrine, it does provide a nice summary of some of the key features of the major exceptions to the final judgment rule:

In the present case, the Court of Appeals concluded that the District Court's privilege-waiver order satisfied the first two conditions of the collateral order doctrine — conclusiveness and separateness — but not the third — effective unreviewability. Because we agree with the Court of Appeals that collateral order appeals are not necessary to ensure effective review of orders adverse to the attorney-client privilege, we do not decide whether the other Cohen requirements are met.

Mohawk does not dispute that "we have generally denied review of pretrial discovery orders." . . . We routinely require litigants to wait until after final judgment to vindicate valuable rights, including rights central to our adversarial system. [Eds. — Citing cases holding that (1) an order disqualifying counsel in a civil case did not qualify for immediate appeal under the collateral order doctrine, (2) reaching the same result in a criminal case, notwithstanding the Sixth Amendment rights at stake] . . . . In our estimation, postjudgment appeals generally suffice to protect the rights of litigants and ensure the vitality of the attorney-client privilege. . . .

[W]ere attorneys and clients to reflect upon their appellate options, they would find that litigants confronted with a particularly injurious or novel privilege ruling have several potential avenues of review apart from collateral order appeal. First, a party may ask the district court to certify, and the court of appeals to accept, an interlocutory appeal pursuant to 28 U.S.C. §1292(b). The preconditions for §1292(b) review — "a controlling question of law," the prompt resolution of which "may materially advance the ultimate termination of the litigation" — are most likely to be satisfied when a privilege ruling involves a new legal question or is of special consequence, and district courts should not hesitate to certify an interlocutory appeal in such cases. Second, in extraordinary circumstances — i.e., when a disclosure order "amount[s] to a judicial usurpation of power or a clear abuse of discretion," or otherwise works a manifest injustice — a party may petition the court of appeals for a writ of mandamus. . . . While these discretionary review mechanisms do not provide relief in every case, they serve as useful "safety valve[s]" for promptly correcting serious errors.

Mohawk Indus., Inc. v. Carpenter, 558 U.S. 100, 107-12 (2009). Thus, the final judgment rule has several exceptions — rarely granted, however — that allow a party to appeal an adverse interlocutory trial court decision.

B. WHAT TO APPEAL: PRESERVING ERROR FOR APPELLATE RELIEF

The court of appeals will not review a trial court's allegedly erroneous decision unless you appropriately **preserve error**. Preserving error requires attention to detail. At its essence, however, are four steps: (1) you must clearly request the trial court to take some action; (2) the trial court must give you a definitive, adverse ruling on your request that appears on the record; (3) you must adequately inform the court of appeals about your complaint in your written brief(s); and (4) the adverse ruling must be sufficiently harmful to warrant a remedy. In other words, you first have to give the trial court the chance to give you what you want. Only if it refuses and you make your record (i.e., the court's decision appears in the transcript), do you have any reason (or ability) to appeal that decision. Next, the court of appeals will not wade through the record — sometimes consisting of many thousands of pages — to figure out if the trial court made a mistake. It is your job as an advocate to clearly point to the error in your brief and the record, and to persuasively explain why the decision is an error in the first place. Finally, not all errors are worth fixing. The error must constitute a reversible error. The court of appeals must be convinced that the error was sufficiently prejudicial to your case that you should prevail on appeal and be given an appropriate remedy, such as another chance to try the case or even having the court of appeals immediately render judgment in your favor. Many trial court errors, however, are simply not considered harmful enough to warrant reversing the trial court's decision.

This last point — that even an error by the trial court may not be a reversible error — has important implications when considered with the final judgment rule. Many of a court's decisions are effectively insulated from review by the appellate court. For example, suppose the court ruled that the losing party was not entitled to a document it sought in discovery. Even if the appellate court agrees that the document should have been produced to the losing party, the appellate court must be convinced that not having that document caused harm severe enough to reverse the case and send it back to the trial court. Many trial court decisions (as the section on standards of review describes below) are subject to review by an abuse of discretion standard. In other words, the trial court is given wide latitude to make a decision either way on arguable matters. As a result, the party appealing the trial court's decision has an uphill battle even establishing that the court made an error in the first place. In addition, appellate courts require a brief that explain what errors the trial court made and why they should be remedied. The briefs have page limits. An appealing party must often make difficult decisions about *what* to appeal. Knowing that some errors are easier to prove than others means that parties will often choose to argue only certain alleged errors; thus, many alleged trial court errors will never be reviewed by an appellate court.

Like the final judgment rule, there are exceptions:

> First, an appellate court will consider an issue not raised in the district court if it involves a pure question of law, and if refusal to consider it would result in a miscarriage of justice. Second, the rule may be relaxed where the appellant raises an objection to an order which he had no opportunity to raise at the district court level. Third, the rule does not bar consideration by the appellate court in the first instance where the interest of substantial justice is at stake. Fourth, a federal appellate court is justified in resolving an issue not passed on below . . . where the proper resolution is beyond any doubt. Finally, it may be appropriate to consider an issue first raised on appeal if that issue presents significant questions of general impact or of great public concern.

Narey v. Dean, 32 F.3d 1521, 1526-27 (11th Cir. 1994) (footnotes and internal citations omitted).

The exception that seems the most ill-defined, the third exception noted above, is often referred to as the **plain error rule**. Also like the final judgment rule, these exceptions are narrow and rarely successful.

Case Preview

MacArthur v. University of Texas Health Center at Tyler

As you read the case, consider the following questions:

1. The plaintiff argued to the court of appeals that the trial court should not have dismissed her Title VII retaliation claim. She included it in her notice of appeal and brief to the court of appeals, and the court listened to her oral argument. So why did the court of appeals refuse to consider and rule on her claim of error in dismissing that claim?

2. The plaintiff also argued that the trial court should not have dismissed her sex discrimination and First Amendment retaliation claims. The court of appeals found that she "effectively" raised challenges to both decisions in her notice of appeal. Why would the court of appeals not consider and rule on these challenges either?

MacArthur v. University of Texas Health Center at Tyler
45 F.3d 890 (5th Cir. 1995)

E. GRADY JOLLY, Circuit Judge. . . .

[Eds. — Plaintiff MacArthur asserted five claims related to her employment against the defendants: (1) retaliation against her for exercising her First Amendment rights, (2) sex discrimination, (3) intentional infliction of emotional distress, (4) violation of equal protection, and (5) retaliation under Title VII for exercising her rights.

Plaintiff eventually presented only the first three claims to the jury, which returned a verdict for her only on the third claim, intentional infliction of emotional distress.

The district court entered judgment for $65,000 on that claim and dismissed the rest. After the trial court denied MacArthur's motion for new trial, she filed a timely notice of appeal challenging the dismissal of her other four claims. An individual defendant, Painter, cross-appealed, attacking the judgment against him on the intentional infliction of emotional distress claim.]

We now turn to examine the underlying judgment to determine what claims and issues are before us — especially focusing on MacArthur's Title VII retaliation claim. The procedural facts concerning this claim are simple. MacArthur pleaded in her complaint a cause of action for retaliation under Title VII, together with First Amendment retaliation, sex discrimination, intentional infliction of emotional distress, and a violation of the Equal Protection Clause. Each of these claims appeared in the pretrial order. It is clear, however, that MacArthur ultimately argued and presented for the jury's determination only three claims: the First Amendment retaliation claim, the sex discrimination claim, and the intentional infliction of emotional distress claim. In her closing argument, MacArthur argued evidence that she contended supported retaliation generally; she did not refer to retaliation based on Title VII at any point during this argument. It is further clear that the district court did not instruct the jury on Title VII retaliation; the court instructed the jury extensively on the law concerning First Amendment retaliation, as well as on the other two claims, but did not say a single word with respect to Title VII retaliation. At the close of the instructions, when given an opportunity to object, MacArthur did not object to the court's failure to instruct on Title VII retaliation. Neither did she object to the omission of any interrogatory to the jury with respect to her Title VII retaliation claim. Her failure to lodge an objection to these omissions of Title VII retaliation is all the more indicative of her intent to abandon the claim because she specifically objected to the omission of an Equal Protection Clause claim, which the court overruled; in other words, her failure to object was not inadvertent as though she were asleep at the switch. In sum, MacArthur failed to argue this claim, failed to have the jury instructed on this claim and failed to submit this claim for the jury's determination and verdict. Under these circumstances, the jury failed to return any verdict with respect to her Title VII retaliation claim. The court specifically stated in the final judgment "pursuant to the verdict returned by the jury, the Court enters the following judgment." The court then dismissed, with prejudice, all claims against the defendants, except the claim for intentional infliction of emotional distress, with respect to which it entered judgment for MacArthur. Neither in post-trial motions, nor on appeal, does MacArthur raise as error the district court's failure to instruct the jury or submit an interrogatory on Title VII retaliation. Our review of the record, therefore, demonstrates that MacArthur abandoned her Title VII claim and choose [sic] to travel with her First Amendment claim for retaliation based on the exercise of her right to speak freely.

B

In appealing the final judgment, MacArthur effectively raised her claims of sex discrimination and First Amendment retaliation. She also effectively raised in her notice of appeal, the denial of her motion for a partial new trial. She has abandoned each of these claims on appeal, however, by her failure to argue any of these claims to this court — her brief arguing only error with respect to the Title VII retaliation claim. Although some confusion arose between the parties as to whether MacArthur was appealing her sex discrimination claim, MacArthur clarified this point in her reply brief when she stated that the sole issue on appeal was that of retaliation. Throughout her briefs, this claim of retaliation was consistently referred to as "a discrimination/retaliation case." She explained that she used this label "because the anti-retaliatory provision of Title VII refers to retaliation as another prohibited form of discrimination." Furthermore, MacArthur's sole argument for admissibility of the evidence at the center of this appeal is that its exclusion prevented her from proving pretext as required under Title VII. In her briefs, MacArthur does not refer to her First Amendment retaliation claim a single time. In sum, the only conclusion that can be drawn from the foregoing facts is that MacArthur does not appeal her claim that the retaliation at issue was for exercising her First Amendment rights. See Fed. R. App. P. 28(a)(5) [now 28(a)(9)(A)] ("The argument must contain the contentions of the appellant on the issues presented, and the reasons therefor"); *Yohey v. Collins*, 985 F.2d 222, 225 (5th Cir. 1993) (holding that appellant abandoned argument by failing to argue it in body of brief). Instead, on appeal MacArthur apparently made a strategic determination that in retrospect a Title VII retaliation claim was a stronger basis for her sole argument on appeal that the district court erred in excluding comparative evidence to establish disparate treatment.

Thus, in conclusion, we must dismiss this appeal. We do so on the basis that the one claim that she raises — Title VII retaliation — was abandoned at the district court, thus is not embodied in the district court judgment, and consequently is not before this court on appeal. With respect to the claims that were presented to the jury and that are embodied in the district court's final judgment, she has abandoned these claims on appeal by failure to brief and argue. MacArthur's appeal is therefore dismissed. . . . In sum, we dismiss MacArthur's Title VII retaliation claim because she failed to argue or present it to the jury.

[Eds. — The court of appeals also found the evidence insufficient to support the jury's verdict on the intentional infliction of emotional distress claim against one of the individual defendants, Painter. As a result, the defendant Painter won outright; the court refused to hear her appeal, yet heard his cross-appeal and agreed with him that she should not have prevailed on the one claim she prevailed on at the trial court. Thus, the court of appeals rendered judgment for Painter.]

. . . For the foregoing reasons, this appeal is DISMISSED and the judgment of the district court is REVERSED and RENDERED. . . .

Post-Case Follow-Up

This case is a good example of how a good trial lawyer should also think like an appellate lawyer. No one ever said MacArthur's arguments were unpersuasive. Everyone knew what the plaintiff's appeal was about — at least, well enough to explain how her attorney had botched it.

It should make sense that she cannot appeal a claim she abandoned at trial. If you don't even press the claim, then you can't really argue that you should be given a chance to recover on that claim. That should strike you as basic fairness.

What about the claims she "effectively raised" on appeal? Why might MacArthur's counsel have decided not to devote much (if any) time or space in her brief to argue the claims she effectively raised (sex discrimination and First Amendment violation)? Consider your legal writing class. Can you make every argument you want to in your memos and briefs? Can you fully argue every issue as extensively as you want? That raises a question — is this just a situation where the attorney faced constraints similar to the ones you have experienced? Or could this be a case of failure to understand the trial process and the appellate process well enough to protect a client's rights?

MacArthur v. University of Texas Health Center at Tyler: Real Life Applications

1. Your client was hit in a crosswalk while the defendant was texting and driving. The defense counsel calls a witness who intends to testify about your client's criminal history, which you think has nothing to do with this case. When the defense lawyer asks about your client's sexual history, you fail to object. The ex-girlfriend answers the question. The jury eventually returns a verdict in favor of the defendant. The trial court enters a final judgment on the jury's verdict. You suspect the jury disliked your client based on this irrelevant testimony and that is why you lost, even though it seemed pretty obvious that the defendant should be held liable for his negligence. Will the court of appeals consider your claim that the court committed an error by allowing the ex-girlfriend's testimony? Why or why not?

2. Assume the same facts as in question 1. Now assume that when the defense lawyer asked about your client's sexual history, you properly objected based on relevance and the court sustained your objection—the ex-girlfriend was not permitted to testify about your client's sexual history. The jury eventually returns a verdict in favor of the defendant. The trial court enters a final judgment on the jury's verdict. Will the court of appeals consider your claim that the court committed an error by allowing the ex-girlfriend's testimony? Why or why not?

3. Assume the same facts as in question 1. Now assume that when the defense lawyer asked about your client's sexual history, you properly objected based on relevance and the court sustained your objection—the ex-girlfriend was not permitted to testify about your client's sexual history. However, the defense counsel later called the ex-girlfriend's best friend as a witness, who testified without objection about your client's sexual history. The jury eventually returns a verdict in favor of the defendant. The trial court enters a final judgment on the jury's verdict. Will the court of appeals consider your claim that the court committed an error by allowing the ex-girlfriend's testimony? Why or why not?

4. Assume the same facts as in question 1. Your complaint includes two claims against the defendant: a claim of negligence and a claim of intentional conduct—battery—based on the collision between the defendant and your client in the crosswalk. The jury returns a verdict in favor of the defendant on both claims. The trial court enters a final judgment on the jury's verdict. Your notice of appeal informs the court of appeals that the court made errors that require the court to reverse the judgement on both claims—negligence and battery. While writing your brief to the court of appeals, you decide that the evidence of intentional conduct was weak at trial, and you extensively brief the errors you believe the court made with respect to the negligence claim that warrant reversal. You use only a paragraph to argue that the judgment should be reversed for the battery claim. Do you run any risk that the court of appeals will refuse to consider your appeal as to either claim? If so, which one? Why or why not?

C. HOW APPELLATE COURTS DECIDE APPEALS: STANDARDS OF REVIEW

Now that you have learned when to appeal and what you must do before you may appeal a decision, this section focuses on the standard the court of appeals will apply to your claim of error. As we mentioned in the prior section, the court of appeals has to determine whether the court committed an error in the first place, and if so, whether that error was harmful enough to justify a different outcome. How much deference the court of appeals will give to the trial court's decision depends on the nature of the decision. At one end of the spectrum is *de novo* review, where the court appeals gives no deference to the court's decision. This is the standard when the court of appeals is trying to determine whether the trial court made an error of law; for example, the court of appeals might be confronted with an error about what the statute of limitations was, or whether negligent infliction of emotional distress is a claim under the applicable law. At the other end of the spectrum are questions of fact found by a jury. The standard is the familiar judgment as a matter of law standard, where the court asks if any reasonable jury could find that the facts are true. The jury is in the best position to judge the credibility of witnesses, see the trial demonstrations, and hear the arguments. The court of appeals is limited to a dry, paper transcript of what went on, and granting wide deference to jury fact-finding makes sense.

What about the decisions that fall between questions of law and questions of fact? There are no bright lines, though the rules give us guidance and the appellant must state the standard of review that applies to his claim of error in his brief to the court of appeals. Exhibit 23.6 demonstrates how decisions between the extremes can be thought of on a continuum, but it is sometimes difficult to determine exactly where on the continuum of deference a given decision will fall.

EXHIBIT 23.6	**Standards of Review by Type of Issue and Amount of Deference**

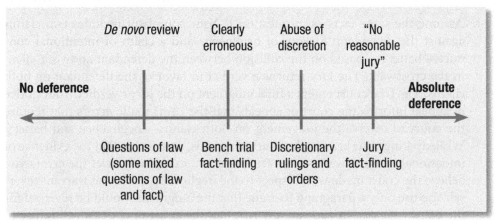

1. *De Novo* Review

It makes sense to review trial courts' decisions on pure questions of law with no deference to the trial court. The court of appeals is in as good a position to determine what the law is, and the court of appeals' decisions are binding on a larger number of courts, promoting greater uniformity in the law. Courts of appeals, however, also sometimes apply *de novo* review to mixed questions of fact and law, such as when "the historical facts are admitted or established, the rule of law is undisputed, and the issue is whether the rule of law *as applied to the established facts* is or is not violated." *Pullman-Standard v. Swint*, 456 U.S. 278, 289-90 n.19 (1982) (emphasis added). A common example is when the facts consist of the defendant's own words. For example, where the defendant's own words are undisputed, do they constitute intentional discrimination or a statement made with actual malice? *See Woods v. Graphic Contractors*, 92 F.2d 1195 (9th Cir. 1991) (intentional discrimination); *Bose Corp. v. Consumers Union of United States, Inc.*, 466 U.S. 485 (1984) (actual malice). There is no clear answer from the Supreme Court on the proper standard of review, and the continuum above is a good guide for determining the proper standard. The more a fact is in dispute or doubt, the more deference the court of appeals should give to mixed questions of law and fact and vice versa.

2. Clearly Erroneous

In a bench trial, the judge wears both hats — deciding the facts and applying the law to the facts. The judge "must find the facts specially and state its conclusions of law separately." Fed. R. Civ. P. 52(a)(1). Even in a jury trial, a judge may make findings of fact to rule on preliminary motions like motions to dismiss for lack of personal jurisdiction, improper venue, and similar non-merits defenses. Rule 52(a)(6) provides that such judicial "[f]indings of fact, whether based on oral or other evidence, must not be set aside unless clearly erroneous, and the reviewing court must give due regard to the trial court's opportunity to judge the witnesses' credibility." The clearly erroneous standard therefore requires a measure of deference to the trial judge. One obvious reason is that the judge has an advantage when judging credibility in making factual determinations based on witness testimony — an advantage the court of appeals does not have from a dry, written transcript.

Although the advantage disappears when the trial judge finds facts using only written evidence, the clearly erroneous standard still applies. *See Anderson v. City of Bessemer City*, 470 U.S. 564 (1985). The Supreme Court explained the clearly erroneous standard of review as follows:

> Although the meaning of the phrase "clearly erroneous" is not immediately apparent, certain general principles governing the exercise of the appellate court's power to overturn findings of a district court may be derived from our cases. The foremost of

these principles, as the Fourth Circuit itself recognized, is that "[a] finding is 'clearly erroneous' when although there is evidence to support it, the reviewing court on the entire evidence is left with the definite and firm conviction that a mistake has been committed." *United States v. United States Gypsum Co.*, 333 U.S. 364, 395 (1948). This standard plainly does not entitle a reviewing court to reverse the finding of the trier of fact simply because it is convinced that it would have decided the case differently. The reviewing court oversteps the bounds of its duty under Rule 52(a) if it undertakes to duplicate the role of the lower court. "In applying the clearly erroneous standard to the findings of a district court sitting without a jury, appellate courts must constantly have in mind that their function is not to decide factual issues de novo." *Zenith Radio Corp. v. Hazeltine Research, Inc.*, 395 U.S. 100, 123 (1969). If the district court's account of the evidence is plausible in light of the record viewed in its entirety, the court of appeals may not reverse it even though convinced that had it been sitting as the trier of fact, it would have weighed the evidence differently. Where there are two permissible views of the evidence, the factfinder's choice between them cannot be clearly erroneous.

This is so even when the district court's findings do not rest on credibility determinations, but are based instead on physical or documentary evidence or inferences from other facts. . . . Rule 52(a) [now 52(a)(6)] "does not make exceptions or purport to exclude certain categories of factual findings from the obligation of a court of appeals to accept a district court's findings unless clearly erroneous." *Pullman-Standard v. Swint*, 456 U.S., at 287. The rationale for deference to the original finder of fact is not limited to the superiority of the trial judge's position to make determinations of credibility.

The trial judge's major role is the determination of fact, and with experience in fulfilling that role comes expertise. Duplication of the trial judge's efforts in the court of appeals would very likely contribute only negligibly to the accuracy of fact determination at a huge cost in diversion of judicial resources. In addition, the parties to a case on appeal have already been forced to concentrate their energies and resources on persuading the trial judge that their account of the facts is the correct one; requiring them to persuade three more judges at the appellate level is requiring too much. As the Court has stated in a different context, the trial on the merits should be "the 'main event' . . . rather than a 'tryout on the road.'" *Wainwright v. Sykes*, 433 U.S. 72, 90 (1977). For these reasons, review of factual findings under the clearly-erroneous standard — with its deference to the trier of fact — is the rule, not the exception.

Anderson, 470 U.S. at 573-75.

3. Abuse of Discretion

During the course of litigation, the court makes many decisions. The court will decide scheduling issues, discovery and disputes regarding discovery, and how to manage the case as a whole — including how much time to allow for trial, what evidence is admissible or not, and whether to order a new trial. For example, in *Beeck v. Aquaslide 'N' Dive Corp.*, 562 F.2d 837 (8th Cir. 1977), the trial judge allowed the defendant to amend its answer shortly before trial and bifurcated the issues of liability and damages, both of which seriously prejudiced the plaintiff and likely cost him the case. Even so, these decisions were within the trial court's discretion. A trial court's discretion is difficult to define. It involves "multifarious, fleeting, special, narrow facts that utterly resist generalization." *Pierce v. Underwood*, 487 U.S. 552, 560-62 (1988). When the issue on appeal involves case management or scheduling, the court of appeals gives the trial court wide latitude. A court of appeals will give less latitude to a trial court that enters a default judgment, because the result is severe for the defaulting party.

A trial court's decisions on motions for new trial depend on the circumstances. If the trial court denies a motion for new trial where the jury has returned a verdict, the trial court gets the deference owed under the new trial standard as well as the deference owed to jury determinations. On the other hand, if the court grants such a motion, the court receives less deference, because it overturns the jury's verdict.

4. Reasonable Jury

In reviewing a jury's decisions in its verdict, the appellate court uses the familiar standard from motions for judgment as a matter of law. Could any reasonable jury have returned this verdict based on the evidence in the record? This is the most deferential standard and is required by the Seventh Amendment's right to trial by jury.

Chapter Summary

- The general rule that a judgment must be final, disposing of all claims by all parties, before it is appealable is codified in 28 U.S.C. §1291 and in most state rules.
- The final judgment rule has many exceptions, however. 28 U.S.C. §1292 authorizes the appeal of non-final interlocutory orders that affect injunctive relief, as well as questions that are certified for immediate appeal by the trial court and accepted for appeal by the court of appeals.
- In multi-party and/or multi-claim cases, Rule 54(b) authorizes the trial court to direct entry of a final judgment as to one or more claims or parties, provided the court tracks the language of the Rule. Similarly, if a court certifies or refuses to certify a class action, Rule 23 makes that order immediately appealable.
- The collateral order doctrine treats as final a decision that is collateral to the merits, presents an important and unresolved question, conclusively decides the disputed question, and is effectively unreviewable on appeal from a final judgment. The last of these — the "review it now because review after final judgment is too late" component is key.
- The All Writs Act, 28 U.S.C. §1651(a), authorizes a party to petition a court of appeals for a writ of mandamus directed to the trial court to do its duty or abide by its jurisdiction. It is an extraordinary remedy requiring a showing both of a special risk of harm and a clear entitlement to relief, usually based on the trial court's usurpation or abdication of authority.
- A party may also obtain immediate appellate review of certain rulings by disobeying them and waiting for the court to impose sanctions. Sanctions that

dismiss the case in its entirety (a/k/a "death penalty" sanctions) or certain sanctions such as contempt of court may render the underlying decision reviewable.

■ A claim of error is reviewable only if it was prejudicial to the appellant, preserved in the lower court by timely objection or request (except for plain error), and presented to the appeals court by proper briefing and argument.

■ A party may make any argument on appeal that is supported by the record to affirm a judgment, but the party must formally appeal or cross-appeal to change a judgment.

■ The standard of review expresses how much deference the court of appeals should pay the decision-maker below. Questions of law are reviewed "de novo" (anew), as are some of mixed questions of law and fact. Questions of fact found by the trial judge are reviewed for clear error under the clearly erroneous standard, even when the fact-finding was based only on documentary evidence.

■ Jury verdicts challenged for insufficiency of the evidence are reviewed by the appellate court under the same standard the district court uses to rule on original and renewed motions for judgment as a matter of law: whether a reasonable jury could have reached the verdict. Most other decisions by the trial court, including the vast majority of decisions made managing the case and the trial, are reviewed for abuse of discretion.

Applying the Concepts

1. A married man sues a foreign car manufacturer for a design defect after his seatback broke on impact. The car manufacturer files a motion to dismiss for failure to state a claim upon which relief could be granted and for lack of personal jurisdiction, because it is a foreign company and sells its cars in the forum state through an independent distributor. The plaintiff based personal jurisdiction over the defendant on the fact that the manufacturer had contacts via the stream of commerce. The court denies the motion to dismiss for lack of personal jurisdiction, but takes the motion to dismiss for failure to state a claim under advisement. Can you immediately appeal either of the trial court's actions? Why or why not?

2. Assume the same facts from question 1. Five days after the court denies the motion to dismiss for lack of personal jurisdiction, the plaintiff requests the court to certify the order under section 1292(b). The court does so and states that the court is of the opinion that the order involves a controlling question of personal jurisdiction law as to which there is substantial ground for difference of opinion, and that an immediate appeal from the order may materially advance the ultimate termination of the litigation. Can the plaintiff immediately appeal the trial court's order? Why or why not?

3. Assume that the plaintiff in question 1 tries his case to a jury. The jury hears three weeks of evidence, deliberates for two days, and returns a verdict in favor

of the defendant. Can the plaintiff appeal now? Why or why not? If so, what standard of review is the court likely to apply to an alleged error in admitting evidence that the plaintiff had been previously cited for reckless driving? If not, what steps must the plaintiff have taken and take in the future so that the court of appeals can hear the appeal?

4. Assume that the plaintiff from question 1 is at trial. The defense calls the plaintiff's wife to testify against him and anticipates she will testify that he is a reckless driver. As a married couple, they each have a privilege to refuse to testify against the other. His counsel objects to the wife testifying and the court overrules the objection, requiring her to testify. Is the court's ruling reviewable by the collateral order doctrine or mandamus? Why or why not?

5. Assume the same facts from question 4. However, when the plaintiff's counsel objects, the judge does not sustain or overrule the objection. He merely says "move along" and the wife does not testify. On appeal, the defendant wants to claim the court's ruling disallowing the wife to testify was error. Will the court of appeals consider the defendant's claim of error? Why or why not?

6. Assume the same facts as in question 1, except the defendant manufacturer also moves to dismiss based on limitations because the injury occurred more than two years ago. The court grants the motion to dismiss on limitations and enters a final judgment. On appeal, the plaintiff argues that the applicable statute of limitations is four years, not two. What is the standard of review a court of appeals would use to determine this appeal, and what kind of question is it? Explain your answer.

Civil Procedure in Practice

You represent an employer in an employment discrimination case brought as a class action by all female employees of your client. The court certifies the class and the action proceeds. After several months of discovery, you file a motion for summary judgment and the court grants the motion, holding that there is no genuine issue of material fact and the employer is entitled to judgment as a matter of law. What must the plaintiffs do to appeal the court's decision? Can you appeal the court's decision to certify the employees as a class? Assuming the court will hear the class certification cross-appeal, what standard of review is it likely to apply to the court's decision to certify the class? What sort of questions are involved in certifying a class? What standard of review is the court of appeals likely to apply to the trial court's ruling on the motion for summary judgment? Is it likely to apply the same standard to all aspects of the summary judgment order? Why or why not? Which standards could apply?

Precluding
Further Litigation

Precluding Further Litigation

24

In this chapter we will explain the effect of a court's decisions in one case on other litigation. Put simply, when — if ever — do you get more than one bite at the litigation apple? When we talk about precluding further litigation, we are referring to two related — but separate — concepts. Both concepts, however, are affirmative defenses, explicitly listed in Rule 8(c).

The first concept is known by its Latin name, ***res judicata***, or more simply, **claim preclusion**. If you try your claim and lose, can you file the same claim against the same defendant and try that claim again? If you try your claim and lose, but did not join it with a related claim that is based on essentially the same underlying facts, should you be able to file the related claim against the same defendant and try the omitted claim? Generally, the answer is no. This should seem fair. If you sought relief from the court for a certain set of circumstances against a defendant and failed to prove your case, the justice system gave you your chance. You had your bite at the apple. However, claim preclusion is not always quite that simple. As you will learn below, what counts as the "same claim," what counts as actually losing on that claim, and exactly who can claim the benefit of claim preclusion sometimes present difficult problems.

The second concept also goes by two names: **collateral estoppel**, or more simply, **issue preclusion**. What if the court makes a decision on a discrete *issue* in a lawsuit (something smaller than the entire claim), such as whether a will was valid, whether two people were lawfully married, whether someone owns property, or some similar decision? Should another court decide the same issue again? Once again, the answer is generally no.

Before we launch into the two doctrines, a practical tip: When a fact pattern or other question involves or

Key Concepts

- "Res judicata," or claim preclusion
- "Collateral estoppel," or issue preclusion
- When the doctrines of claim or issue preclusion will prevent a party from relitigating claims or issues in another lawsuit

specifically asks about multiple lawsuits, you probably have a question asking you to apply claim or issue preclusion.

A. *RES JUDICATA* OR CLAIM PRECLUSION

Before a party can use claim preclusion as a defense, the party must prove three elements:

> First, the claim must be the same as one that was litigated in a previous case. Second, the previously litigated claim must have resulted in a valid, final judgment on the merits. And third, the parties who litigated the previous claim must typically be the same parties who are litigating the current claim.

Federated Department Stores, Inc. v. Moitie, 452 U.S. 394, 399 (1981).

1. The Same Claim

This element sounds simple. However, what constitutes the same claim for claim preclusion purposes is not as simple as it seems. The following case demonstrates how this first element of claim preclusion is much broader than you might imagine.

Case Preview

River Park, Inc. v. City of Highland Park

As you read the case, consider the following questions:

1. What were the claims in the first case? What were the names or labels of the claims?
2. What motion did the defendant file? Who prevailed on that motion?
3. What were the claims in the second case? Did any of them have the same name or label as the claims in the first action?
4. Does it matter what label a claim is known by before claim preclusion can apply?

River Park, Inc. v. City of Highland Park
703 N.E.2d 883 (Ill. 1998)

Opinion

Justice McMorrow delivered the opinion of the court:

This case arises from the efforts of plaintiffs River Park, Inc., Spatz & Company, and Country Club Estates, Ltd., to develop a parcel of real estate located within defendant City of Highland Park. After defendant failed to approve their plan to develop the property and their request for rezoning, plaintiffs sought relief under 42 U.S.C. §1983 (1994) by filing a complaint against defendant in federal court. Following the dismissal of their federal cause of action, plaintiffs asserted various violations of state law in an amended complaint filed against defendant in the circuit court of Lake County. The circuit court dismissed this complaint pursuant to defendant's motion to dismiss. . . . The circuit court found that . . . the dismissal of plaintiffs' federal complaint barred their state claims under the doctrine of *res judicata*. . . . The appellate court affirmed the circuit court's dismissal of plaintiffs' claim for tortious interference with business expectancy, but reversed its decision to dismiss plaintiffs' claims for breach of implied contract and abuse of governmental power and remanded the cause for further proceedings on these counts. 295 Ill. App. 3d 90, 229 Ill. Dec. 596, 692 N.E.2d 369. We granted defendant's petition for leave to appeal. 166 Ill. 2d R. 315. We reverse in part the judgment of the appellate court on the basis that plaintiffs' state claims were barred by the doctrine of *res judicata*.

* * *

River Park, Inc. (River Park), had an ownership interest in a 162–acre piece of land in the City of Highland Park known as the Highland Park Country Club (Country Club). Plaintiff Spatz & Company (Spatz) was a builder and had purchased the capital stock of River Park. Spatz's purchase of the capital stock was financed in part by a loan from La Salle National Bank of Chicago (La Salle). The loan was secured by a mortgage on the Country Club property. Plaintiff Country Club Estates (CCE) was a limited partnership and purchased a portion of the Country Club property from River Park in 1991.

In July 1988, Spatz petitioned defendant on behalf of River Park to obtain approval for its plans to develop the Country Club property. In the petition, Spatz requested that defendant change the zoning classification of one portion of this property from R–1 to R–4. The petition also included a request for approval of a planned residential development on the property.

Between April 1988 and October 1989, Spatz appeared at numerous hearings before the City of Highland Park plan commission. While Spatz's petition was pending before the commission, a city council member, Raymond Geraci, formed a citizen's group named "Save the Open Space," the purpose of which was to encourage defendant to purchase the property in order to prevent Spatz's planned development.

What Is a Restatement?

Throughout this case and the remainder of the chapter, you will see references to the Restatement of Judgments. What is a **Restatement**?

A Restatement is "[o]ne of several influential treatises published by the American Law Institute describing the law in a given area and guiding its development. The Restatements use a distinctive format of black-letter rules, official comments, illustrations, and reporter's notes. Although the Restatements are frequently cited in cases and commentary, a Restatement provision is not binding on a court unless it has been officially adopted as the law by that jurisdiction's highest court." RESTATEMENT, BLACK'S LAW DICTIONARY (Bryan A. Garner ed., 10th ed. 2014).

Both claim and issue preclusion rely heavily on case law that has been assembled into a Restatement. Restatements cover many areas of the law, including many typical first-year classes such Torts, Contracts, and Property. Restatements are often highly influential on courts, and sometimes become binding law any time a court adopts a Restatement's phrasing of a test or rule.

Geraci also proposed at city council meetings that defendant purchase the property in order to prevent Spatz's development. Without Spatz's knowledge, the city council ordered studies to assess the economic feasibility of defendant's purchase of the property.

On November 14, 1989, the commission approved the zoning change Spatz had proposed. The commission also approved the planned development, with certain modifications. On November 22, 1989, the commission provided the city council with an unconditional recommendation for approval of the zoning change and the planned development.

Between November 1989 and January 22, 1990, Spatz appeared before the city council three times to discuss the commission's recommendation. During this time, the city council received the results of the feasibility studies in executive session. The city council did not, however, communicate to Spatz that it was interested in purchasing the property. On January 22, 1990, the city council adopted the commission's zoning recommendation and approved the preliminary development plan.

For Spatz to obtain final approval, defendant's zoning ordinance required it to provide the commission and the city council with final engineering plans and a final development plan that conformed with the preliminary plan. In addition, Spatz was required by defendant's zoning ordinance to obtain the city engineer's verification that the engineering plans complied with applicable statutes and ordinances. According to the ordinance, if a developer failed to receive the city engineer's approval of the engineering plans within one year of preliminary plat approval, the development plan would be deemed withdrawn.

In April 1990, Spatz submitted the final engineering plans to the city engineering department. The city engineer refused Spatz's requests to review or discuss the plans until October 5, 1990. At that time, defendant's engineers and Spatz's engineers agreed that, with certain modifications and corrections, 95% of the engineering plans were complete and satisfied all of defendant's requirements. Defendant's engineers agreed to review the remaining 5% of the plans by December 1, 1990, and provide criteria for completion of those plans.

Spatz made the necessary corrections for the 95% of the plans already reviewed by defendant's engineers, but the city engineer refused to review either the corrected plans or the other 5% by the December 1 deadline. Spatz requested that its rezoning petition be placed on the city council agenda so that Spatz could obtain the council's approval of its plans prior to January 22, 1991, the date on which the engineering review period would expire. Based on the city engineer's failure to act on the plans, however, the city council refused Spatz's request to place the petition on its agenda.

Defendant was aware of Spatz's and River Park's financing arrangement with La Salle and was advised by their attorney that, without approval of the final development plans by January 22, 1991, La Salle would foreclose its mortgage on the Country Club property. On January 22, 1991, the city council withdrew its preliminary approval of the plans and informed Spatz that, in order to have the zoning of the Country Club property changed, it would be required to start the commission review process from the beginning.

As a result of defendant's failure to approve the final development plans, River Park was forced to declare bankruptcy. As part of the bankruptcy reorganization plan, River Park entered into an agreement to sell 34 acres of the Country Club property to CCE. In March 1991, River Park, Spatz, and CCE filed a new petition with defendant, in which they requested R–4 zoning only for the 34-acre parcel purchased by CCE. Again, plaintiffs participated in public hearings on the petition before the commission. The transcript of these hearings was delivered to the commission on June 29, 1992. Under defendant's zoning ordinance, the commission had 45 days from this date to vote on the petition.

In June 1992, La Salle instituted foreclosure proceedings on the Country Club property. Plaintiffs entered into an agreement with La Salle whereby they would continue to pursue rezoning and would have the right to redeem the property if their efforts were successful. Defendant was aware of this arrangement with La Salle. Without plaintiffs' knowledge, however, defendant negotiated with La Salle for the purchase of the mortgaged property while the second petition for rezoning was pending.

On July 21, 1992, the commission adopted a resolution requiring plaintiffs to submit proof of their ownership of the subject property by August 11, 1992. The resolution further provided that the commission would deem the petition withdrawn if it did not receive plaintiffs' evidence of title by this date. Plaintiffs challenged the commission's authority to require them to provide evidence of ownership. Nevertheless, they notified the commission that they had requested proof of title from La Salle but would be unable to obtain this documentation by August 11, 1992. The commission refused to grant plaintiffs an extension of time. When plaintiffs attempted to present proof of ownership at a later commission meeting, the commission informed plaintiffs that their petition had been deemed withdrawn and that they would be required to once again start the rezoning process from the beginning.

Subsequently, defendant purchased the Country Club property from La Salle for $10 million, a price far below the market value of the property. According to plaintiffs' information and belief, defendant sold or attempted to sell substantial portions of this property to others for residential development.

Based on these alleged events, on February 23, 1993, plaintiffs filed a two-count complaint against defendant in the United States District Court for the Northern District of Illinois. In this complaint, plaintiffs asserted that defendant was liable pursuant to 42 U.S.C. §1983 (1994) for depriving them of their property rights without due process of law in violation of the United States Constitution. According to plaintiffs, they had a legal entitlement to approval of their engineering plans and to the rezoning they requested. They alleged that defendant's failure to act on the plans and vote on their second petition deprived them of this property right without due process of law. The complaint alleged no claims under state law.

Defendant filed a motion to dismiss plaintiffs' federal complaint for lack of subject matter jurisdiction and for failure to state a claim upon which relief can be granted. See Fed. R. Civ. P. 12(b)(1), (6). On July 22, 1993, the district court issued a written order in which it found that plaintiffs had failed to allege a violation of due process. The court therefore granted defendant's motion and dismissed plaintiffs' complaint with prejudice. On April 25, 1994, the United States Court of Appeals for the Seventh Circuit affirmed the dismissal of plaintiffs' federal complaint.

Having failed in their attempt to obtain a remedy for defendant's actions in federal court, plaintiffs filed a six-count complaint against defendant in the circuit court of Lake County on November 21, 1994. On March 15, 1995, they filed an amended complaint, which added a seventh count. The theories of relief asserted in plaintiffs' amended complaint were based on state law and included, *inter alia,* (1) tortious interference with business expectancy, (2) breach of implied contract, and (3) abuse of governmental power. In the tortious interference with business expectancy count of the amended complaint, plaintiffs alleged that they had a reasonable expectation of entering into profitable sale and development contracts and that defendant had intentionally interfered with this expectancy by delaying the rezoning and plat approval process in order to acquire the property at a price less than market value. With respect to their claim for breach of implied contract, plaintiffs alleged that, by accepting the fee they paid for processing their zoning petition, defendant entered into an implied contract to process this petition in good faith. They alleged that defendant breached this agreement by prolonging the zoning process, by failing to review the engineering plans within a reasonable period of time, and by deeming their application withdrawn. In the abuse of power count of their amended complaint, plaintiffs alleged that, by forcing them into bankruptcy and foreclosure in order to acquire their land at a reduced price, defendant abused its power under the Illinois Constitution to acquire private property for public use in exchange for just compensation. In each of these counts, plaintiffs requested damages of $25 million. They requested an additional $25 million in punitive damages for their abuse of governmental power claim.

Defendant filed a motion . . . to dismiss plaintiffs' amended complaint in its entirety for failure to state a claim. The circuit court granted defendant's motion and dismissed all counts of plaintiffs' complaint with prejudice.

On appeal, the appellate court affirmed the circuit court's dismissal of all but three of the counts included in plaintiffs' amended complaint. The appellate court found that the circuit court had erred in dismissing the counts of plaintiffs' complaint involving tortious interference with business expectancy, breach of implied contract, and abuse of governmental power. The court remanded the cause for further proceedings on these counts. . . .

On remand, defendant moved to dismiss the remaining three counts of plaintiffs' amended complaint. Defendant requested that these claims be dismissed . . . on the basis that (1) plaintiffs' claims were barred under the doctrine of *res judicata* by the dismissal of plaintiffs' federal complaint. . . . The circuit court granted this motion and dismissed plaintiffs' complaint with prejudice.

* * *

Under the doctrine of *res judicata,* a final judgment on the merits rendered by a court of competent jurisdiction acts as a bar to a subsequent suit between the parties involving the same cause of action. The bar extends to what was actually decided in the first action, as well as those matters that could have been decided in that suit. For the doctrine of *res judicata* to apply, the following three requirements must be satisfied: (1) there was a final judgment on the merits rendered by a court of competent jurisdiction, (2) there is an identity of cause of action, and (3) there is an identity of parties or their privies.

In the case before us, the parties do not dispute that plaintiffs' federal and state suits involve an identity of parties. They do, however, disagree with respect to the existence of the other two prerequisites to the application of the *res judicata* doctrine. According to defendant, the federal court dismissed plaintiffs' complaint for failure to state a claim, which operated as a final adjudication on the merits. In addition, defendant contends that the causes of action asserted in plaintiffs' federal and state complaints are the same because they arose out of the same core of operative facts. Defendant notes that both actions were based on its alleged wrongful refusal to act on or approve plaintiffs' plan to develop the Country Club property, resulting in foreclosure and the plaintiffs' loss of this property.

By contrast, plaintiffs argue that the dismissal of their federal complaint was based in part on a lack of subject matter jurisdiction and was, therefore, not a decision on the merits. They also dispute defendant's assertion that their federal and state suits involved the same cause of action. Plaintiffs argue that their section 1983 action required "proof of facts (*i.e.,* a federally protected property interest and violation of due process) which are not necessary" to sustain their state claims for breach of implied contract and abuse of governmental power. Since the evidence necessary to prove their state and federal claims is different, plaintiffs maintain that these suits do not constitute the same cause of action.

To determine whether the doctrine of *res judicata* applies in this case, our initial inquiry is whether the dismissal of plaintiffs' federal complaint was a final judgment on the merits. . . . [I]t is clear that the dismissal of a complaint for failure to state a claim is an adjudication on the merits . . . , while the dismissal of a complaint for lack of subject matter jurisdiction is not considered a decision on the merits of that complaint. The same is true under federal law.

Neither party challenges these principles. Instead, they disagree with respect to the basis of the federal court's dismissal of plaintiffs' complaint. Defendant argues that the federal court dismissed the complaint for failure to state a claim, while plaintiffs maintain that the dismissal was for failure to state a claim *and* lack of subject matter jurisdiction. Our review of the text of the decisions issued by the federal district and appellate courts convinces us that defendant's interpretation is the correct one.

Thus, the language of the district court's opinion does not permit the conclusion that the jurisdictional issue raised in defendant's motion to dismiss served as a basis for the court's decision to dismiss plaintiffs' complaint. Rather, its dismissal was plainly based on the insufficiency of the allegations of the complaint.

* * *

Having found that two of the three elements for the applicability of the *res judicata* doctrine are present in this case, we turn to a discussion of the third requirement: identity of cause of action. . . . Illinois courts have adopted two tests for determining whether causes of action are the same for purposes of *res judicata*. Under the "same evidence" test, a second suit is barred "if the evidence needed to sustain the second suit would have sustained the first, or if the same facts were essential to maintain both actions." [citations omitted] The "transactional" test provides that " ' "the assertion of different kinds or theories of relief still constitutes a single cause of action if a single group of operative facts give rise to the assertion of relief." ' " [citations omitted]

* * *

Based on these arguments by the parties, we find it appropriate in this case to address whether the transactional or same evidence test should be applied in cases involving issues of *res judicata*.

[Eds. — The court engages in an extended discussion of the two competing tests.]

* * *

Our adoption of the transactional test *in lieu* of the same evidence test is consistent with the approach proposed in the Restatement (Second) of Judgments, as well as the trend of decisions in other jurisdictions. In 1982, the Restatement abandoned the same evidence test in favor of the transactional test. The current version of the Restatement advances the transactional test:

"Dimensions of 'Claim' for Purposes of Merger or Bar — General Rule Concerning 'Splitting'

(1) When a valid and final judgment rendered in an action extinguishes the plaintiff's claim pursuant to the rules of merger or bar . . . , the claim extinguished includes all rights of the plaintiff to remedies against the defendant with respect to all or any part of the transaction, or series of connected transactions, out of which the action arose.

(2) What factual grouping constitutes a 'transaction', and what groupings constitute a 'series', are to be determined pragmatically, giving weight to such considerations as whether the facts are related in time, space, origin, or motivation, whether they form a convenient trial unit, and whether their treatment as a unit conforms to the parties' expectations or business understanding or usage."

Restatement (Second) of Judgments §24, at 196 (1982).

* * *

Like the Restatement, a majority of federal courts, as well as numerous courts in other states, have applied a transactional analysis when determining whether there is an identity of cause of action for purposes of *res judicata*. Our decision in this case that the transactional test should control is in accordance with these authorities, as well as this court's existing recognition of this analysis.

We now turn to an application of the transactional test to the case before us. Under this test, we find that plaintiffs' claims for breach of implied contract and abuse of governmental power are the same cause of action as the section 1983 claim alleged in their federal complaint. Plaintiffs' federal and state claims are the same cause of action for purposes of *res judicata* because they arise from the same core of operative facts. Like their section 1983 action, plaintiffs' state law claims are based on defendant's alleged refusals to timely process and approve their rezoning petition in an effort to deprive plaintiffs of their rightful use of their property. Plaintiffs themselves concede in their brief that "both the federal action and the present state action in the case at bar arise out of the processing of the plaintiffs' applications for plan approval by the defendant and both actions seek damages for the wrongful acts of the defendants in processing those applications."

Perhaps the most telling indication of identity of cause of action in this case, however, is the parallels between the factual allegations of plaintiffs' state complaint and their federal complaint. In support of their section 1983 claim, plaintiffs alleged, *inter alia,* that (1) they had received preliminary approval of their zoning request and development plan, (2) as a result of the city engineer's refusal to act on the engineering plans they submitted, defendant withdrew its preliminary approval, (3) the withdrawal of this approval resulted in LaSalle's foreclosure on the property, (4) defendant was without authority to demand proof of plaintiffs' ownership of the property and failed to give plaintiffs a reasonable time to provide this information, (5) plaintiffs were entitled to the zoning approval they requested, and (6) defendant's refusals to properly process plaintiffs' request for rezoning were intended to prevent plaintiffs' development of the Country Club property so that defendant could purchase the property itself at a reduced price. As our previous description of the facts contained in plaintiffs' state complaint demonstrates, the facts on which they base their claim for relief under state law are virtually identical to the facts on which their federal claim was based.

In arguing that their federal and state claims are not the same causes of action, plaintiffs rely on differences in the theories of relief asserted in these suits. This is contrary to the principles of the transactional analysis, which we have explained before and reaffirm in this case.

* * *

In the case before us, our review of the pleadings convinces us that there is no material difference between plaintiffs' federal and state causes of action. Plaintiffs' assertion of state law claims for breach of implied contract and abuse of governmental power after their section 1983 action was dismissed was merely a "substitution of labels." . . . We hold that the breach of implied contract and abuse of governmental power claims contained in the amended complaint plaintiffs filed in state court are the same cause of action as the section 1983 claim alleged in plaintiffs' federal complaint. Accordingly, the three requirements for the application of the doctrine of *res judicata* are satisfied in this case.

* * *

The judgment of the appellate court is affirmed in part and reversed in part, and the judgment of the circuit court, dismissing plaintiffs' complaint, is affirmed.

It is so ordered.

Post-Case Follow-Up

The doctrine of claim preclusion bars relitigating claims. This case adopted a standard for determining whether the claim to be relitigated is the same claim as the one already litigated: the **transactional test**. The underlying, or "group of operational facts," are key. What was the case about? What were the plaintiffs unhappy about? It is easy to make the complaints, claims, or causes of action sound different. Do not get caught up in labels, titles, or names of claims or causes of action. It's the facts that matter. What happened that caused the plaintiffs to sue? If the second lawsuit is based on essentially the same set of facts, then it does not matter whether the causes of action have different names. The doctrine of claim preclusion bars both the claims that were brought in the earlier action and any claim that *could have been brought* arising out of the same set of facts.

Does it seem fair that the defendants prevailed on a motion to dismiss, and that the motion precludes the later litigation? Should claim preclusion apply when the plaintiff never got an opportunity to prove his case on the merits? What do you think?

River Park, Inc. v. City of Highland Park: *Real Life Applications*

1. A cement truck struck a car from behind at a stoplight. The driver of the car sued the cement truck driver and the company that employed the cement truck driver for his bodily injuries and prevailed.

   a. Suppose the driver of the car later sues the cement truck driver for damage to his car. Can the cement truck driver use claim preclusion to preclude the second suit against him? Why or why not?

   b. Now suppose the same cement truck delivered cement to the driver's house because the driver was having renovations done to his driveway. The cement that was delivered was of poor quality and cracked prematurely. Could the driver bring a lawsuit against the cement company for breach of contract? Why or why not?

2. A landlord sued his tenant for failing to pay rent for January to March. The landlord won at trial and the tenant paid the landlord the judgment the landlord had won. The landlord decided to give the tenant a second chance and allow the tenant to continue to live at the property under the same lease. Two years later, the tenant fell behind on rent again and the landlord sued the tenant for the unpaid rent. Can the tenant use claim preclusion to prevail in the second lawsuit over unpaid rent? Why or why not?

---

2. Valid Final Judgment on the Merits

Claim preclusion not only requires that the claim be the same, but also that the claim be part of a valid, final judgment on the merits. This breaks down into three sub-elements or questions: (1) What does it mean for a judgment to be valid? (2) What is a final judgment? and (3) What is a judgment on the merits? The answer to these questions may surprise you.

As you will learn below, each portion of this requirement has a sort of *Through the Looking Glass* quality: What do words really mean? A valid final judgment on the merits doesn't actually have to be "valid" (e.g., the issuing court may have lacked subject matter jurisdiction over the claim), the judgment may not be completely final (e.g., the judgment might be on appeal), and the judgment may not seem to be on the merits (e.g., a dismissal based on the statute of limitations).

What Is a Valid Judgment?

What work does the word "valid" do? Not much. The most important point to understand is that even if the court "got it wrong," the judgment still has preclusive effect. Recall from Chapter 23 that a final judgment is final when it disposes of all claims and parties; i.e., there is nothing left for the court to decide. This is true even if the judgment is on appeal. This illustrates a key point. If a litigant is dissatisfied with the court's judgment, the litigant's remedy is by appeal via the appellate chain, *not* by collateral attack in a different proceeding or court system. To put a finer point on it, even if the court truly lacks personal jurisdiction, or even subject matter jurisdiction, the judgment is still "valid" for claim preclusion purposes.

Do not confuse a rare permissible collateral attack for an invalid judgment. The signature example is where a defendant fails to respond to a lawsuit in a court that lacks personal jurisdiction over him; the prevailing party may win by default, but must still enforce and satisfy the judgment. When the prevailing party files a second suit in the state in which the defendant has assets available to satisfy the judgment, the defendant/judgment debtor may resist enforcement of the judgment on the grounds that the judgment is void because it was rendered by a court that lacked personal jurisdiction. This attack on the judgment is a permissible collateral attack. This is a risky and rare tactic, however, because failing to contest personal jurisdiction in the first action means a defendant has waived *all* defenses on the merits as well as other objections in the first lawsuit. In other words, you had better be sure the first court lacks personal jurisdiction over your client before you advise this course of action.

You may also be surprised to learn that a final judgment from a court lacking subject matter jurisdiction can have preclusive effect. Only in rare circumstances would a second court question the subject matter jurisdiction of the first court that rendered the final judgment that precludes further litigation. Courts and commentators have recognized that claim preclusion should apply unless the first court manifestly abused its authority, or the court's decision to enter the judgment would "substantially infringe the authority of another tribunal." *See, e.g.,* Restatement (Second) of Judgments §12 cmt. d (1982); *see also Travelers Indem. Co. v. Bailey,* 557 U.S. 137, 153 & n.6 (2009) (citing the Restatement in a similar context); *Chicot County Drainage Dist. v. Baxter State Bank,* 308 U.S. 371, 376-77 (1940); David L. Shapiro, *Civil Procedure: Preclusion in Civil Actions* 25-29 (2001).

Remember, however, that the lawsuit is unlikely to result in a judgment at all if anyone learns the court lacks subject matter jurisdiction. Recall also that the court can raise its lack of subject matter jurisdiction on its own and sometimes judges and parties may not realize the court lacks subject matter jurisdiction until the case is on appeal. If such a situation presented itself, the court would likely hold that claim preclusion does not apply because there is no valid judgment *on the merits*—the last element required for claim preclusion as described below. *See Federated Dep't Stores, Inc. v. Moitie,* 452 U.S. 394, 398 (1981). Again, the important point is that the "valid judgment" element of claim preclusion is rarely the proper vehicle for arguing a final judgment in a prior lawsuit should not be given preclusive effect in a second lawsuit. The court would likely see that as an impermissible collateral attack on a judgment.

What Is a Final Judgment?

A final judgment is one disposing of all parties and all claims. This should sound familiar. It is the same definition from Chapter 23 regarding when a judgment is final for appellate purposes. A judgment does not have claim preclusive effect until it is "final." For example, a summary judgment that rules the plaintiff has no evidence of his breach of contract claim, yet has produced evidence raising a genuine dispute of fact on his fraud claim that should be resolved by a jury is not a final judgment. Recall, however, that a judgment can be "final" even if it is being appealed. Once again, the requirement for a "final judgment" is not as simple as it may sound at first blush.

What Is a Judgment on the Merits?

Finally, once more, what the doctrine of claim preclusion considers to be "on the merits" may surprise you. Certainly, if a case goes to trial and ends with a jury verdict, or, in a bench trial, the court makes findings of fact and conclusions of law and enters a final judgment on the court's own findings and conclusions — that is a judgment on the merits. Like the definition of a claim, however, what qualifies as a judgment on the merits is more expansive than this simple example. Summary judgments, judgments as a matter of law, and even (depending on the court) default judgments all qualify. Motions to dismiss that are granted on grounds similar to those in the *River Park, Inc.* case above qualify too. What kind of motions to dismiss would *not* be on the merits? Examples of motions to dismiss that have nothing to do with the merits include dismissals for lack of subject matter jurisdiction, personal jurisdiction, improper notice, or improper venue. One example of a common problem is dismissals based on the expiration of the statute of limitations. If your case is dismissed for missing the limitations deadline, does that mean that if you find a different state with a longer limitations period you are precluded from refiling your claims there? The answer is probably yes, you are precluded. Rule 41(b) suggests that such dismissals are on the merits and would preclude further litigation not only in the same court, but also in any court in the country. This is the general trend in the law. However, this rule is not absolute and you must check the law of the jurisdiction you are in for the case in which preclusion is sought to see if the general rule holds.

3. The Same Parties, or Parties in Privity

If the claim is part of a valid, final judgment between the same parties, it has preclusive effect on further litigation. What if you read the judgment and it appears that the parties are not the same? First, a person could simply agree to be bound by the court's judgment in an action to which he is not a party. This might be useful in a "test" case, where multiple plaintiffs or multiple defendants decide to try a case involving fewer than all plaintiffs or all defendants and agree to be bound by the result. Second, a person who was not a party to the judgment may be bound because of his relationship to someone who *is* bound by the judgment. This is called **privity** — a relationship between two parties with sufficiently similar interests in the same transaction, proceeding, or property. There are many examples of a party in privity with someone who is bound by a judgment. Those who own property can be bound by a judgment related to that property that a prior owner was a party to. Someone who was not a party but was adequately represented in the litigation may also be bound. For example, class action suits, suits brought by guardians, or suits brought by a person's representative or agent may bind a nonparty to the judgment. Finally, some suits — by their very nature — bind nonparties. Bankruptcy, probate, and *quo warranto* **suits** (suits brought on behalf of the public at large) all can result in judgments that bind people who were not a party to the judgment. *See generally Taylor v. Sturgell*, 553 U.S. 880 (2008).

4. Exceptions to Claim Preclusion

There are six recognized exceptions to claim preclusion, even if all the elements are satisfied:

(a) The parties have agreed in terms or in effect that the plaintiff may split his claim, or the defendant has acquiesced therein; or

(b) The court in the first action has expressly reserved the plaintiff's right to maintain the second action; or

(c) The plaintiff was unable to rely on a certain theory of the case or to seek a certain remedy or form of relief in the first action because of the limitations on the subject matter jurisdiction of the courts or restrictions on their authority to entertain multiple theories or demands for multiple remedies or forms of relief in a single action, and the plaintiff desires in the second action to rely on that theory or to seek that remedy or form of relief; or

(d) The judgment in the first action was plainly inconsistent with the fair and equitable implementation of a statutory or constitutional scheme, or it is the sense of the scheme that the plaintiff should be permitted to split his claim; or

(e) For reasons of substantive policy in a case involving a continuing or recurrent wrong, the plaintiff is given an option to sue once for the total harm, both past and prospective, or to sue from time to time for the damages incurred to the date of suit, and chooses the latter course; or

(f) It is clearly and convincingly shown that the policies favoring preclusion of a second action are overcome for an extraordinary reason, such as the apparent invalidity of a continuing restraint or condition having a vital relation to personal liberty or the failure of the prior litigation to yield a coherent disposition of the controversy.

Restatement (Second) of Judgments §26(1) (1982).

Some concrete examples illustrate the discretionary nature of this doctrine. Examples (a) and (b) are straightforward. Because claim preclusion is intended to prevent duplicative litigation primarily as a protection for the parties and the system, if the parties agree or the court expressly states in the judgment that claim preclusion should not apply, those agreements and court orders are usually given effect. *Id.* at cmts. a & b.

A simple example of (c) comes up with courts of limited jurisdiction. For example, a small claims court may only be able to entertain claims with an amount in controversy of $10,000. If a plaintiff sued a defendant for a breach of contract case worth $7,000, he could not sue the defendant in the same small claims action for a fraud claim worth $12,000 — even if the breach of contract and fraud claims were based on the same underlying facts. Similarly, some courts can entertain only eviction proceedings or other equitable relief and cannot award monetary damages. If so, it may be unfair to preclude the plaintiff from seeking monetary relief in a second court that does have the authority to award him money damages. Another example comes up with respect to personal jurisdiction. The plaintiff may have been able to obtain specific personal jurisdiction over the defendant because the defendant committed a wrong in the forum state, giving the defendant a sufficient connection to the forum and the litigation. If, however, the claim to be precluded does not arise out of that same wrong, it may be unfair to prevent the plaintiff from pursuing that claim in a court that would have personal jurisdiction over the defendant and that particular claim. *Id.* at cmt. c. Examples d-f illustrate the discretionary nature of the doctrine. These subsections invite policy arguments as to why, even though the elements of claim preclusion are met, the court should refuse to apply claim preclusion. *See id.* at cmts. d-j.

B. COLLATERAL ESTOPPEL OR ISSUE PRECLUSION

Rather than preclude an entire claim, a party may want to avoid having to retry a specific issue. Many issues come up during litigation. If the party wants the benefit of a court's prior decision on a particular issue because the decision was favorable, the party may be able to invoke collateral estoppel — issue preclusion.

> When an issue of fact or law is actually litigated and determined by a valid and final judgment, and the determination is essential to the judgment, the determination is conclusive in a subsequent action between the parties, whether on the same or a different claim.

Restatement (Second) of Judgments §27. The first element a party must prove to rely on issue preclusion is that the two issues are the same.

1. The Same Issue

The following case illustrates what the same issue is for claim preclusion purposes.

Case Preview

In re Porter

As you read the case, consider the following questions:

1. What is the claim that the defendant is trying to extinguish in the bankruptcy process? Why doesn't claim preclusion apply in this case?

2. What issues were determined in the first lawsuit? How do we know how they were determined?

3. Whose burden is it to plead and prove issue preclusion?

In re Porter
539 F.3d 889 (8th Cir. 2008)

Opinion

MELLOY, Circuit Judge.

Michael Allen Porter filed for bankruptcy under Chapter 7 of the Bankruptcy Code. Holly Sells filed an adversary complaint against Porter, seeking to bar the discharge of a judgment debt that she had obtained against him in an employment retaliation case. The bankruptcy court gave collateral estoppel effect to the judgment, finding that the jury in the retaliation case necessarily found that Porter willfully and maliciously injured Sells. Accordingly, the bankruptcy court excepted the judgment debt from discharge under 11 U.S.C. §523(a)(6). The Bankruptcy Appellate Panel affirmed, and Porter appealed. We affirm.

I.

Holly Sells sued Mr. Speedy Car Care Center, John Huffer, Porter, and PorJohn Enterprises, LLC for sexual harassment, retaliation, and constructive discharge under Title VII and the Arkansas Civil Rights Act. Huffer and Porter were the owners of Mr. Speedy Car Care Center, a partnership. Sells alleged that Huffer sexually harassed her and that Huffer and Porter retaliated against her after she reported the sexual harassment to her supervisor and to Porter.

[Eds. — The court described in graphic detail the evidence from the trial showing that Huffer had sexually harassed Sells. The court also noted that Sells had repeatedly complained to her direct supervisor and Porter, who was her employer and owned the business. Porter insisted that she sign a document admitting her interactions with Huffer were consensual. Sells refused and eventually resigned.]

The jury found against Mr. Speedy Car Center, Huffer, and Porter, and awarded $360,000 in damages to Sells. Based on the jury instructions and findings, we know the following. The jury found that Huffer sexually harassed Sells, which required the jury to find: (1) she was subjected to sexual advances, sexually graphic and lewd comments, and inappropriate physical touching by Huffer; (2) such conduct was unwelcome; (3) such conduct was based on Sells's sex and made her working conditions intolerable; (4) either the defendants took adverse action against Sells with the intent of forcing her to quit, or her resignation was a reasonably foreseeable result of their actions; and (5) Sells's rejection of or failure to submit to such conduct was a motivating factor in the defendants taking adverse action against Sells. The jury also found that the defendants retaliated against Sells, which required the jury to find: (1) Sells complained to defendants that Huffer harassed her on the basis of her sex; (2) the defendants took adverse action against Sells; and (3) Sells's complaint of sexual harassment was a motivating factor in the defendants' actions.

The jury awarded Sells punitive damages in addition to actual damages. The jury necessarily found that the defendants acted "with malice or reckless indifference" to Sells's right not to be sexually harassed or subject to retaliation. The instructions provided that the defendants acted with malice or reckless indifference if they "knew that the sexual harassment of [Sells] and/or constructive discharge of [Sells] was in violation of the law prohibiting sexual harassment and retaliation, or acted with reckless disregard of that law."

Porter then filed for bankruptcy under Chapter 7, and Sells filed an adversary complaint against him claiming that the damages award was excepted from discharge under §523(a)(6). The bankruptcy court gave collateral estoppel effect to the judgment, finding that the jury in the underlying case necessarily found that Porter willfully and maliciously injured Sells, and accordingly, that the judgment was nondischargeable under §523(a)(6). The Bankruptcy Appellate Panel affirmed. Porter appeals, arguing that the record from the district court does not support a finding that the judgment is excepted from discharge under §523(a)(6).

II.

* * *

Section 523(a) exempts certain debts from discharge in bankruptcy. It states: "A discharge under section 727 . . . of this title does not discharge an individual debtor from any debt . . . for willful and malicious injury by the debtor to another entity or to the property of another entity. . . ." §523(a)(6). Willful and malicious are two distinct requirements that Sells must prove by a preponderance of the evidence. The Supreme Court has made clear "debts arising from recklessly or negligently inflicted injuries do not fall within the compass of §523(a)(6)." *Kawaauhau v. Geiger*, 523 U.S. 57, 64 (1998). . . . "[N]ondischargeability takes a deliberate or intentional injury, not merely a deliberate or intentional act that leads to injury." *Geiger*, 523 U.S. at 61. . . . A willful injury is "a deliberate or intentional invasion of the legal rights of another, because the word 'injury' usually connotes legal injury . . . in the technical sense." *Geiger v. Kawaauhau (In re Geiger)*, 113 F.3d 848, 852 (8th Cir. 1997), *aff'd*, 523 U.S. at 57. Further, the debtor need not intend the consequences of his conduct to cause a willful injury. *In re Patch*, 526 F.3d at 1180. It is enough "[i]f the debtor knows that the consequences are certain, or substantially certain, to result from his conduct." *Id*. Maliciousness is conduct "targeted at the creditor . . . at least in the sense that the conduct is certain or almost certain to cause . . . harm." *Siemer v. Nangle (In re Nangle)*, 274 F.3d 481, 484 (8th Cir. 2001). . . .

The collateral estoppel doctrine applies in bankruptcy proceedings brought under §523(a)(6). *Hobson Mould Works, Inc. v. Madsen (In re Madsen)*, 195 F.3d 988, 989 (8th Cir. 1999). In the Eighth Circuit, the party asserting collateral estoppel must prove:

> (1) the party sought to be precluded in the second suit must have been a party, or in privity with a party, to the original lawsuit; (2) the issue sought to be precluded must be the same as the issue involved in the prior action; (3) the issue sought to be precluded must have been actually litigated in the prior action; (4) the issue sought to

be precluded must have been determined by a valid and final judgment; and (5) the determination in the prior action must have been essential to the prior judgment.

Robinette v. Jones, 476 F.3d 585, 589 (8th Cir. 2007) (quotation omitted).

Porter argues the bankruptcy court improperly applied collateral estoppel to Sells's judgment in determining whether the debt was non-dischargeable under §523(a)(6). Porter argues that the judgment does not prove that Sells suffered an injury, that Porter caused such injury, or that such injury was willful or malicious. Porter's primary focus is on the argument that the jury in the underlying retaliation case did not make a finding that any injury was the result of willful and malicious conduct by Porter. He argues that issue was not actually litigated and therefore collateral estoppel cannot support a finding of non-dischargeability. We disagree.

We focus only on Porter's actions because §523(a)(6) reads "willful and malicious injury by the debtor." The jury found that Porter, as one of the defendants, took adverse action and retaliated against Sells. In so finding, the jury had to have believed Sells's testimony that Porter threatened her with termination if she did not sign the memo. She faced the choice of stating that Huffer did not sexually harass her, admitting complicity in the activity, and working in an environment where sexual harassment was permitted, or losing her job. She faced an injury either way — loss of the legal right to be free from sexual harassment or an adverse employment action. Accordingly, the jury necessarily found that Porter injured Sells.

The jury also necessarily found that Porter willfully injured Sells. The jury found that Sells's allegations of harassment motivated Porter to take adverse action against her. Forcing Sells to choose between giving up a potential harassment claim and working in a harassment-filled environment or losing her job was a deliberate and intentional injury. Porter left Sells no other alternative.

The jury necessarily found that Porter maliciously injured Sells. Porter's memo and threat were targeted specifically to Sells and were certain to cause her harm. Porter wrote untruthful statements in the memo to retaliate for her complaints and tried to force her recantation of those complaints by a threat. The memo stated: "Based on information provided by both of you in discussions with me, it appears that if anything did happen, any fault would have to be attributed to you both. It appears there was a mutual understanding and agreement between the two of you that this was on a consensual basis." Those statements directly contradict Sells's complaints to Porter about Huffer's harassment. Further, Porter testified that he did not know the truth regarding Sells's allegations against Huffer when he wrote the memo and that he knew Huffer had put his arm around Sells and pinched her buttocks without her consent.

The facts accepted by the jury belie Porter's argument that he was trying to resolve the problem in good faith. He knew she would be harmed, and she was the only target of his unjustifiable and inexcusable actions. Cf. *Johnson v. Miera (In re Miera)*, 926 F.2d 741, 744 (8th Cir. 1991) (affirming summary judgment under the collateral estoppel doctrine and concluding that the state court judgment of battery against the debtor "implicitly contained a finding of malice" because the debtor kissed the creditor, despite knowing that the kiss was unwelcome and would harm the creditor); *Jones v. Svreck (In re Jones)*, 300 B.R. 133, 140 (B.A.P. 1st Cir. 2003) (affirming summary judgment under the collateral estoppel doctrine as "malice is inherent" in the sexual harassment finding); *Dorer v. Moberg (In re Moberg)*, 156 B.R. 810, 814

(Bankr. D. Minn. 1993) (holding that the debtor willfully and maliciously injured the creditor by having sex with the creditor while knowing that the creditor did not want to have sex). The dearth of case law regarding judgment debts from retaliation cases in the context of §523(a)(6) does not concern us. Sufficient case law exists that excepts from discharge judgment debts from sexual harassment cases, and here, Porter retaliated after Sells alleged sexual harassment. Although Porter did not harass Sells, he compounded her problems by first condoning Huffer's actions and then retaliating against her. Porter's actions were willful and malicious under §523(a)(6).

* * *

We affirm the judgment of the Bankruptcy Appellate Panel.
It is so ordered.

Post-Case Follow-Up

Recall who is invoking issue preclusion here. Suppose this was not a bankruptcy proceeding, where Porter was trying to extinguish the judgment debt he owed Sells by virtue of having lost the employment discrimination suit Sells brought against him. Instead, suppose Sells has already won her lawsuit and Porter later brings suit against Sells for breaching her employment contract while she worked for him at the car care center by refusing to sign the memo and later failing to show up for work. Porter would actually have two problems. First, his breach of contract claim would almost certainly qualify as a compulsory counterclaim under Rule 13 as you learned in Chapter 18. Use it or lose it. Second, a court would likely decide that the breach of contract claim was the same claim as the employment discrimination claim. It arose from the same set of underlying facts, Sells has obtained a valid final judgment against Porter, and we have exactly the same two parties in the second suit. Sells would likely invoke Rule 13 and issue preclusion in such a lawsuit. But that is not what is happening here.

Porter is trying to rid himself of this debt by filing for bankruptcy protection. Bankruptcy is generally intended to give debtors a fresh start from their debts and other liabilities. Sells, however, is on the attack, trying to make sure Porter remains liable to her. Her weapon is a part of the bankruptcy code that provides that some debts cannot be discharged. One such type of nondischargeable debt is one incurred via a judgment for "willful and malicious injury." Sells proved Porter's actions were willful and malicious in her employment lawsuit against him, so why should she have to prove it again to the bankruptcy court?

She didn't have to. Was the jury expressly asked in Sells' initial lawsuit whether Porter acted willfully and maliciously? No. But the evidence is in the record. The court found that the nature of her claim, the evidence required to prove it, and the fact that she prevailed on her claim necessarily meant that the jury believed Porter had retaliated against her in a willful and malicious way for reporting her harassment. Do you see any danger in allowing issue preclusion when there is no express finding of fact on the issue to be precluded?

In re Porter: Real Life Applications

1. Tamika wants to paint the interior of her new apartment. When she calls her landlord Stanley to ask whether he would pay for it or whether she must pay for it, Stanley tells her she is forbidden by the lease to paint her apartment at all. Tamika consults a lawyer who reads the lease and tells her she does have the right to paint the apartment, as long she bears all the expenses of painting. When Stanley learned that Tamika painted the apartment, he sued her, claiming the lease prevents her from painting the apartment. The judge agreed with Tamika, however, and held that she could paint the apartment. Next year, Tamika repainted again and the landlord sued her again, claiming the same provision of the lease prevents her from painting. Does claim preclusion apply? Why or why not? Does issue preclusion apply? Why or why not?

2. Jordan divorced Marta and Jordan wants to get remarried. Jordan's fiancée, Jennifer, wants Jordan to have his marriage to Marta annulled so that it will be as if Jordan had never been married before. Jordan sues Marta for an annulment. Does claim preclusion apply? Why or why not? Does issue preclusion apply? Why or why not?

3. An employee claims he developed back problems at work from lifting heavy objects and sued his employer for personal injuries. At trial, the jury was asked in a special verdict form whether the employee suffered back injuries proximately caused by his employment. In a general verdict form, the jury found the employer liable. The employer transferred the employee to a light duty job and the employee sued the employer for retaliating against him for filing the first lawsuit. If the employer wants to use the employee's back injuries as a legitimate reason to have transferred the employee to light duty in defending the lawsuit, can the employer rely on issue preclusion to prevent the employee from litigating whether or not he had a back injury? Why or why not?

2. The Issue Must Have Been Actually Litigated with a Full and Fair Opportunity for the Parties to Make Their Case

Unlike claim preclusion, where a claim may be precluded that was never even alleged in a prior lawsuit, let alone actually decided, issue preclusion requires an actual decision. (Recall that the plaintiffs in *River Park, Inc.* did get a decision on their federal section 1983 action, but never got a chance to litigate their state law claims.) In the *In re Porter* case above, this is an easy question. The issue of whether Porter willfully and maliciously retaliated against Sells for reporting her sexual harassment was a central issue in the case. It was so central that the bankruptcy court found there was no way Sells could have prevailed if she had not proven Porter acted willfully and maliciously, as defined in her original harassment case and the bankruptcy exception. As long as Porter had the opportunity to put on evidence that he was not acting willfully or maliciously, then he had a full and fair opportunity to be heard.

An issue can have preclusive effect even when it is not part of a judgment as a result of a trial. Motions to dismiss for failure to state a claim, summary judgment, judgment on the pleadings, directed verdict, judgment as a matter of law, or judgment notwithstanding the verdict can all qualify. "When an issue is properly raised, by the pleadings or otherwise, and is submitted for determination, and is determined, the issue is actually litigated." Restatement (Second) of Judgments §27, cmt. d.

3. The Issue Must Have Been Essential to the Judgment

As we said at the beginning of the issue preclusion section, many issues come up at trial. As we just saw, sometimes it can be difficult for the party or the court to determine whether the issue was actually decided at all. If there is no express finding on the issue, the court may have to wade through the evidentiary records. When the court in *In re Porter* searched through the record for the evidence necessary to the final judgment, the court was looking for logical necessity; i.e., the plaintiff could not have prevailed without having prevailed on these issues. "Necessary to the judgment," however, is also concerned with *legal* necessity. Was the issue decided legally necessary for the prevailing party to win on the subject issue? If the court actually decides an issue, but the judgment would have come out the same way anyway, then the issue was not essential to the judgment.

For example, imagine you buy a used car. The car breaks down repeatedly and you quit making payments. When the dealer sues you, you defend on the grounds that (1) the contract was void because the seller lied to you to fraudulently induce you to enter into the contract, (2) the contract failed for lack of consideration because the car was not sufficient consideration for your payments, and (3) the seller breached an implied warranty that the car was merchantable. You and the seller both move for summary judgment. The court holds that the contract is valid because you were not fraudulently induced, nor does the contract fail for lack of consideration. However, the court also holds that the seller breached the contract by failing to comply with the applicable warranty term. After the court entered a final judgment on the cross motions for summary judgment, the seller pays you damages and fixes your car. Six months later, the seller sues you again, claiming that you failed to make payments on time and seeking repossession of the car. You defend on the grounds that you were fraudulently induced into the contract and that it fails for lack of consideration. Are your two defenses the same issue from the prior trial? Yes. Did the court actually decide them? Yes. Did the court enter a valid, final judgment on the merits? Yes. Was either issue essential to the court's finding that the seller breached the contract? No. Why not?

You as the buyer did not prevail on summary judgment because the contract was enforceable. You won in spite of these findings. If you disagreed with the court, you alone could not have appealed the erroneous decisions, because you prevailed. The court's decisions on these two contract defenses (fraudulent inducement and failure of consideration) were not legally necessary to the result. You would have won even if the court had not decided either issue. As a result, the court will have to retry these two issues, even though they were actually decided in the prior action. This may seem like a waste of time, but this should highlight the discretionary nature of the doctrine.

4. The Same Parties, or Parties in Privity

For *mutual* issue preclusion, not only must the issue be the same, but the parties must be the same. (We deal with non-mutual issue preclusion in the next section.) However, even with respect to mutual issue preclusion, there is an exception. What if the parties in the two actions seem related, but not identical? If a party was in privity with a party who seeks to preclude from litigating an issue, then — despite not actually being a formal party to the prior litigation — that party in privity may be bound by the determination.

The most common example of two parties in privity is an insurer who has a contract with an insured. This scenario often plays out when a person is in involved in an accident and the insurance company steps in to defend the person covered by insurance. For example, two parties may litigate a tort claim and the defendant is covered by insurance. If the defendant is found liable in the first suit, the defendant's insurer may be bound by the earlier determination that the defendant is liable. Even though the insurer was not a party, it is so closely identified with the defendant (often insurance policies have provisions requiring the insurer to hire a lawyer for the defendant to defend the claim in the first lawsuit) that the insurer is bound by the judgment of liability against its insured — the defendant from the first lawsuit. If a second lawsuit between the insured and the insurer raises the issue of whether the defendant was liable to the plaintiff in the first lawsuit, the insurer is likely to be collaterally estopped from trying that issue. The first court decided liability. The insurance company will likely be stuck with that decision if the other requirements of issue preclusion are satisfied because the insurer and insured likely had sufficiently similar interests in the outcome of the case to be considered in privity.

C. NON-MUTUAL DEFENSIVE ISSUE PRECLUSION

So far, we have discussed scenarios in which the same parties litigated an issue to conclusion, only for the same issue to come up in a later lawsuit between them. However, issue preclusion is not limited to cases in which the parties are identical. In addition to the privity example above, parties may sometimes use issue preclusion as a defense against a person who was not a party to the original lawsuit.

The Supreme Court has explicitly approved of **defensive non-mutual issue preclusion.** Non-mutual is self-explanatory — the parties are not the same. But what makes issue preclusion "defensive"? The typical fact pattern involves a *plaintiff* who has tried a lawsuit and lost on a particular issue. Then, the same plaintiff sues a different defendant — one who was not a party to the first lawsuit. The different defendant wants to use the plaintiff's prior loss against him — defensively. A typical case would look like Exhibit 24.1 below:

EXHIBIT 24.1   "Defensive" Non-Mutual Issue Preclusion

Suit #1: P v. D1
P loses on a particular issue.

Suit #2: P v. D2
D2 pleads collateral estoppel. P should be precluded from relitigating the issue on which he lost in **Suit #1**, even though D2 was not a party to **Suit #1**.

In *Blonder-Tongue Laboratories v. University of Illinois Foundation*, the University of Illinois Foundation sued Blonder-Tongue Laboratories for infringing its patent on an antenna. Blonder-Tongue claimed that the University's patent was invalid. The Foundation had previously sued Wineguard, a different laboratory, for manufacturing an antenna that infringed on the University's patent. However, the court found that the University's patent was invalid and entered judgment in Wineguard's favor.

When the University later sued Blonder-Tongue for infringing the same patent, Blonder-Tongue asserted issue preclusion as a defense. Blonder-Tongue claimed that a prior court had already ruled that the University's patent was invalid in the case against Wineguard, so the University should be precluded from relitigating whether the patent was valid. The Supreme Court approved this use of issue preclusion by someone who was not a party to the first lawsuit against someone who was. 402 U.S. 313 (1971).

The Court applied the elements of issue preclusion, but was careful to examine one element in particular — whether the party to be precluded had a full and fair opportunity to litigate the issue in the prior litigation:

> In any lawsuit where a defendant, because of the mutuality principle, is forced to present a complete defense on the merits to a claim which the plaintiff has fully litigated and lost in a prior action, there is an arguable misallocation of resources. To the extent the defendant in the second suit may not win by asserting, without contradiction, that the plaintiff had fully and fairly, but unsuccessfully, litigated the same claim in the prior suit, the defendant's time and money are diverted from alternative uses — productive or otherwise — to relitigation of a decided issue. And, still assuming that the issue was resolved correctly in the first suit, there is reason to be concerned about the plaintiff's allocation of resources. Permitting repeated litigation of the same issue as long as the supply of unrelated defendants holds out reflects either the aura of the gaming table or "a lack of discipline and of disinterestedness on the part of the lower courts, hardly a worthy or wise basis for fashioning rules of procedure." Kerotest Mfg. Co. v. C-O-Two Co., 342 U.S. 180, 185 (1952). Although neither judges, the parties, nor the adversary system performs perfectly in all cases, the requirement of determining whether the party against whom an estoppel is asserted had a full and fair opportunity to litigate is a most significant safeguard.

Blonder-Tongue, 402 U.S. at 329.

The Court could have found that the University didn't have the same incentive or the same opportunity to put on evidence or decided that the University did not have a "full and fair" opportunity to litigate whether the patent was valid. That was not the case here.

Consider the opposite result in the first lawsuit. What if the University had sued Wineguard for patent infringement and prevailed? What if the University even had an express finding that the patent was valid? Can it now take its win and use it against other defendants? Suppose the University takes the judgment from the first case and uses it to sue Blonder-Tongue for patent infringement. If Blonder-Tongue defends on the basis that the patent is invalid, can the University use the prior judgment to preclude Blonder-Tongue from disputing whether the patent is valid? No. Why?

In the case described above, *the University* was the party to be precluded and it had its day in court. Here, Blonder-Tongue, the party to be precluded, has not. As a matter of fundamental due process, Blonder-Tongue should and will get an opportunity to prove the patent was invalid. Issue preclusion should not bar Blonder-Tongue under this second scenario.

D. NON-MUTUAL OFFENSIVE ISSUE PRECLUSION

As we have explained, defensive non-mutual issue preclusion usually involves a defendant trying to avoid liability by using issue preclusion as a defense. By contrast, **offensive non-mutual issue preclusion** typically involves plaintiffs trying to use findings from prior cases offensively; i.e., to help the plaintiff prove his later case by claiming some issue has already been litigated in his favor. Such claims resemble Exhibit 24.2 below:

EXHIBIT 24.2   **"Offensive" Non-Mutual Issue Preclusion**

Suit #1: P1 v. D
D loses on a particular issue.

Suit #2: P2 v. D
P2 pleads collateral estoppel. D should be precluded from litigating the issue on which he lost in **Suit #1**, even though P2 was not a party to **Suit #1**.

Case Preview

Parklane Hosiery Co., Inc. v. Shore

As you read the following case, consider the following questions:

1. What is the issue that was decided in the first case? Is it the same issue to be decided in the second case?

2. Why would the Court be concerned with allowing non-mutual issue preclusion offensively?

3. Did the Court approve the use of non-mutual offensive collateral estoppel?

4. Which suit was filed first? Which suit proceeded to judgment first?

Parklane Hosiery Co., Inc. v. Shore
439 U.S. 322 (1979)

Opinion

Mr. Justice STEWART delivered the opinion of the Court.

This case presents the question whether a party who has had issues of fact adjudicated adversely to it in an equitable action may be collaterally estopped from relitigating the same issues before a jury in a subsequent legal action brought against it by a new party.

The respondent brought this stockholder's class action against the petitioners in a Federal District Court. The complaint alleged that the petitioners, Parklane Hosiery Co., Inc. (Parklane), and 13 of its officers, directors, and stockholders, had issued a materially false and misleading proxy statement in connection with a merger. The proxy statement, according to the complaint, [violated] . . . Securities Exchange Act of 1934 . . . as well as various rules and regulations promulgated by the Securities and Exchange Commission (SEC). The complaint sought damages, rescission of the merger, and recovery of costs.

Before this action came to trial, the SEC filed suit against the same defendants in the Federal District Court, alleging that the proxy statement that had been issued by Parklane was materially false and misleading in essentially the same respects as those that had been alleged in the respondent's complaint. Injunctive relief was requested. After a 4-day trial, the District Court found that the proxy statement was materially false and misleading in the respects alleged, and entered a declaratory judgment to that effect. . . .

The respondent in the present case then moved for partial summary judgment against the petitioners, asserting that the petitioners were collaterally estopped from relitigating the issues that had been resolved against them in the action brought by the SEC. The District Court denied the motion on the ground that such an application of collateral estoppel would deny the petitioners their Seventh Amendment right to a jury trial. The Court of Appeals for the Second Circuit reversed, holding that a party who has had issues of fact determined against him after a full and fair opportunity to litigate in a nonjury trial is collaterally estopped from obtaining a subsequent jury trial of these same issues of fact.

I

The threshold question to be considered is whether . . . the petitioners can be precluded from relitigating facts resolved adversely to them in a prior equitable proceeding with another party under the general law of collateral estoppel. Specifically, we must determine whether a litigant who was not a party to a prior judgment may nevertheless use that judgment "offensively" to prevent a defendant from relitigating issues resolved in the earlier proceeding.

A

Collateral estoppel, like the related doctrine of res judicata, has the dual purpose of protecting litigants from the burden of relitigating an identical issue with the same party or his privy and of promoting judicial economy by preventing needless litigation. Until relatively recently, however, the scope of collateral estoppel was limited by the doctrine of mutuality of parties.

* * *

By failing to recognize the obvious difference in position between a party who has never litigated an issue and one who has fully litigated and lost, the mutuality requirement was criticized almost from its inception. Recognizing the validity of this criticism, the Court in Blonder-Tongue Laboratories, Inc. v. University of Illinois Foundation, supra, abandoned the mutuality requirement, at least in cases where a patentee seeks to relitigate the validity of a patent after a federal court in a previous lawsuit has already declared it invalid.

* * *

B

The Blonder-Tongue case involved defensive use of collateral estoppel — a plaintiff was estopped from asserting a claim that the plaintiff had previously litigated and lost against another defendant. The present case, by contrast, involves offensive use of collateral estoppel — a plaintiff is seeking to estop a defendant from relitigating the issues which the defendant previously litigated and lost against another plaintiff. In both the offensive and defensive use situations, the party against whom estoppel is asserted has litigated and lost in an earlier action. Nevertheless, several reasons have been advanced why the two situations should be treated differently.

First, offensive use of collateral estoppel does not promote judicial economy in the same manner as defensive use does. Defensive use of collateral estoppel precludes a plaintiff from relitigating identical issues by merely "switching adversaries." Bernhard v. Bank of America Nat. Trust & Savings Assn., 19 Cal. 2d, at 813, 122 P.2d, at 895. Thus defensive collateral estoppel gives a plaintiff a strong incentive to join all potential defendants in the first action if possible. Offensive use of collateral estoppel, on the other hand, creates precisely the opposite incentive. Since a plaintiff will be able to rely on a previous judgment against a defendant but will not be bound by that judgment if the defendant wins, the plaintiff has every incentive to adopt a "wait and see" attitude, in the hope that the first action by another plaintiff will result in a favorable judgment. Thus offensive use of collateral estoppel will likely increase rather than decrease the total amount of litigation, since potential plaintiffs will have everything to gain and nothing to lose by not intervening in the first action.

A second argument against offensive use of collateral estoppel is that it may be unfair to a defendant. If a defendant in the first action is sued for small or nominal damages, he may have little incentive to defend vigorously, particularly if future suits are not foreseeable. The Evergreens v. Nunan, 141 F.2d 927, 929 (CA2); cf. Berner v. British Commonwealth Pac. Airlines, 346 F.2d 532 (CA2) (application of offensive collateral estoppel denied where defendant did not appeal an adverse judgment awarding damages of $35,000 and defendant was later sued for over $7 million). Allowing offensive collateral estoppel may also be unfair to a defendant if the judgment relied upon as a basis for the estoppel is itself inconsistent with one or more previous judgments in favor of the defendant. Still another situation where it might be unfair to apply offensive estoppel is where the second action affords the defendant procedural opportunities unavailable in the first action that could readily cause a different result.

C

We have concluded that the preferable approach for dealing with these problems in the federal courts is not to preclude the use of offensive collateral estoppel, but to grant trial courts broad discretion to determine when it should be applied. The general rule should be that in cases where a plaintiff could easily have joined in the earlier action or where, either for the reasons discussed above or for other reasons, the application of offensive estoppel would be unfair to a defendant, a trial judge should not allow the use of offensive collateral estoppel.

In the present case, however, none of the circumstances that might justify reluctance to allow the offensive use of collateral estoppel is present. The application of offensive collateral estoppel will not here reward a private plaintiff who could have joined in the previous action, since the respondent probably could not have joined in the injunctive action brought by the SEC even had he so desired. Similarly, there is no unfairness to the petitioners in applying offensive collateral estoppel in this case. First, in light of the serious allegations made in the SEC's complaint against the petitioners, as well as the foreseeability of subsequent private suits that typically follow a successful Government judgment, the petitioners had every incentive to litigate the SEC lawsuit fully and vigorously. Second, the judgment in the SEC action was not inconsistent with any previous decision. Finally, there will in the respondent's action be no procedural opportunities available to the petitioners that were unavailable in the first action of a kind that might be likely to cause a different result.

We conclude, therefore, that none of the considerations that would justify a refusal to allow the use of offensive collateral estoppel is present in this case. Since the petitioners received a "full and fair" opportunity to litigate their claims in the SEC action, the contemporary law of collateral estoppel leads inescapably to the conclusion that the petitioners are collaterally estopped from relitigating the question of whether the proxy statement was materially false and misleading.

* * *

The judgment of the Court of Appeals is affirmed.

Post-Case Follow-Up

Even when the issues were the same (is the proxy false and misleading?), the Court expressed several concerns. Much of the rationale justifying preclusion doctrines consists of efficiency and consistency. There is no need to decide something more than once (which conserves everyone's resources), and if there is no second decision, there is no risk of inconsistent decisions (which preserves faith in the judicial process). Here, those rationales may break down. An incident with many potential plaintiffs actually promotes a "wait and see" attitude. Rather than joining together and sinking or swimming as a group, a person has an incentive to let someone be the test case. If the first plaintiff wins, then other plaintiffs are likely to follow, using the favorable judgment to estop the defendant. If the first plaintiff (or, for that matter, the next dozen or more) loses, the next potential plaintiff knows he is not bound as a matter of due process and still may take his bite at the apple. If it appears to the court that this is the case, a court is less likely to grant the "wait and see" plaintiff(s) the ability to use offensive non-mutual collateral estoppel.

The second matter of concern comes down to ability and incentive. As with defensive non-mutual collateral estoppel, the court is concerned about whether some procedural hurdle, evidentiary matter, or the fact that not much was at stake in the first suit resulted in the defendant either being unable or unwilling to defend the issue in the same manner as it would in the second lawsuit.

The Court left these issues to lower courts to decide. The Court said such use of collateral estoppel is permitted, but lower courts should focus particularly on whether the defendant had a full and fair opportunity to litigate the issue.

Remember also due process. The Court would not have even entertained the use of non-mutual collateral estoppel unless this were true: "In both the offensive and defensive use situations, the party against whom estoppel is asserted has litigated and lost in an earlier action." *Parklane*, 439 U.S. at 333.

Once again, consider the opposite scenario. What if the SEC had lost and Parklane had prevailed on whether its proxy statement was false and misleading? Could Parklane, judgment in hand, return to the still-pending case against it by Shore and estop Shore from proving the proxy statement was false and misleading? No. Why? Due process will give Shore a bite at the apple. Shore may only get one bite, but at least it gets one bite. Shore never had its day in court.

Parklane Hosiery Co., Inc. v. Shore: Real Life Applications

1. A buyer purchased a boat from a seller and the seller said the boat was seaworthy. After the buyer took the boat out on the lake, the boat promptly sank because the hull was riddled with holes. The buyer sued the seller and won. The buyer now wants to use the judgment in his case against the seller in a second lawsuit against the boat manufacturer, claiming its hulls decay prematurely due to a defective design. Can the buyer preclude the manufacturer from litigating whether its hulls are defective? Why or why not?

2. A train derailed, injuring over 100 people. The potential plaintiffs decide not to join in a single action. Instead, each plaintiff files his or her own case against the railroad. The first five cases result in defense verdicts, premised on the fact that the railroad was not negligent. If a sixth plaintiff decides to sue, can the railroad use the findings from any of the first five cases to preclude the sixth plaintiff from suing for negligence? Why or why not?

3. Suppose the same train derailment from question 2. Now, however, the first plaintiff prevailed in his negligence suit against the railroad, but sued in a jurisdiction that limits railroads' liability using a damages cap of $50,000. A second plaintiff sues the railroad in a different jurisdiction with no damages cap for $1 million. Can the plaintiff use the finding from the first case to preclude the railroad from litigating negligence? Why or why not?

E. WHOSE PRECLUSION LAW APPLIES?

As you will learn in the next chapter, courts sometimes have to determine what law to apply. A federal court may be required to apply state law or federal law. And if state law applies, the court may have to determine which state's laws apply. This situation comes up in state court as well — sometimes a state court determines that it must apply the law of another state. Indeed, some disputes become so complicated that a court may have to apply the law of a foreign nation, and may apply the laws of more than one jurisdiction in a single case!

Although most jurisdictions have similar rules regarding when claim and issue preclusion apply to preclude further litigation, you may have to consider what specific preclusion law applies. Fortunately, the rule is simple to state, though not always easy to apply. The preclusion law of the jurisdiction that rendered the judgment or made the decision to be given preclusive effect is the law that applies. For example, if you are sued in a Kentucky state court and wish to use claim preclusion as an affirmative defense when you are sued a second time, this time in Tennessee, Kentucky's law on claim preclusion will determine whether the Kentucky judgment will have preclusive effect — even in a Tennessee court. The next chapter will introduce this topic; however, many law schools offer an entire course on the concept of "choice of law" or "conflicts of law," where it becomes necessary to determine what law the court must apply.

Chapter Summary

- Claim preclusion prevents claimants from relitigating claims that they fully litigated or should have litigated in a previous case.
- Claim preclusion requires three elements: (1) the claim must be the same in both cases; (2) the claim that provides preclusive effect must be part of a valid,

final judgment; and (3) the parties in both cases must be the same or the one in privity.

- Courts tend to look at the underlying facts of the claim to determine whether the claim is the "same claim" or not.

- Courts consider a judgment final for claim preclusion purposes when the trial court has disposed of all claims and all parties, even though the judgment may be on appeal.

- A judgment on the merits includes most dispositions; some exceptions are when the case is dismissed for lack of personal jurisdiction, subject matter jurisdiction, service-related issues, and venue.

- Issue preclusion, or collateral estoppel, bars a party from relitigating an issue that a court has already decided.

- Issue preclusion requires five elements: (1) the issue must be the same in both lawsuits, (2) the issue was actually litigated, (3) the party sought to be precluded in the second lawsuit had a full and fair opportunity to litigate the issue, (4) the issue was actually decided, and (5) the issue was essential to the court's decision.

- Issue preclusion usually requires the same parties. However, non-mutual issue preclusion is available both defensively and offensively. In both cases, particularly in an offensive use of issue preclusion, the court will scrutinize whether the party to be precluded had a full and fair opportunity to litigate the issue on which he lost.

Applying the Concepts

1. Domingo, from Texas, sued John, from Oklahoma, in Texas federal court, claiming that John's livestock had wandered onto Domingo's property, which borders John's, and destroyed crops he was growing. Two weeks later, John sued Domingo in federal court in Oklahoma for a declaratory judgment that the property line between the two properties includes the areas on which John's livestock allegedly wandered. Both cases are still ongoing. Does claim or issue preclusion apply? Why or why not?

2. Assume the same facts from question 1, except now the Oklahoma federal suit goes to trial first and results in a judgment that John's property line does not include the area of the alleged trespass by John's livestock. Can Domingo use the judgment from the Oklahoma suit to preclude John from raising the defense regarding the property line? What doctrine or doctrines would he use and why?

3. Assume the same facts from question 2. Can Domingo use claim preclusion to prevail in the Texas federal suit? Why or why not?

4. Assume the same facts from question 1, except the Texas federal suit goes to trial first and results in a judgment that John's livestock trespassed onto Domingo's land. Can Domingo use claim preclusion to prevail in the Texas federal suit? Why or why not?

Civil Procedure in Practice

1. New clients approach you. They claim they are the grandparents of a child whose father recently died. You learn that their son was not married to the mother when their grandchild was born. But their son had sued the mother, claiming that he was the biological father of her child. After a trial at which the court considered DNA evidence establishing that the man was the father, the court entered a final judgment declaring the man to be the father. Six months later, the father died. The mother refuses to let the alleged grandparents see the child. Now the father's parents want to sue the mother for visitation of the child. Your research uncovered a statute that allows grandparents a right to visitation if the alleged grandparents are related to the child by blood or marriage and if such visitation would be in the best interest of the child. Can the alleged grandparents use the judgment in the first suit to help them establish that they are entitled to visitation in the second suit? Why or why not?

2. Employee #1 sued her male employer for sexual harassment, claiming the speech that the employer gave at a company meeting, broadcast as a video webcast, included several derogatory remarks about women. Employee #1, who heard the speech at her workplace in Texas, sued the employer in a Texas court under Texas law even though she was not demoted or fired. Texas law caps damages for any sexual harassment claim at $25,000.00, and grants employers a presumption that no harassment occurred unless the employee was also demoted or fired. After a short trial, the jury found in favor of Employee #1 and awarded her $5,000 in damages. The court entered a final judgment on the jury's verdict.

   Employee #2 heard the same speech and works for the same employer at a branch office in California. Employee #2 was fired shortly after the speech. Employee #2 comes to you and wants to sue her employer in a California court for sexual harassment. California has no damages cap. Your law partner took Employee #2's case and thinks that the employer will be precluded from arguing that the speech was not sexually harassing. Your law partner wants you to tell him what the employer's best argument would be in response so he can deal with those arguments when they come. How would you advise your law partner about the employee's best counterargument that you are likely to get in response?

3. Patient #1 had hip replacement surgery using a new hip made by Hip Co. Hip Co.'s new hip has been installed in several hundred people. Unfortunately, the new hip had a design defect that caused it to fracture when used on anyone weighing more than 100 pounds. Patient #1's hip fractured and he filed suit against Hip Co. in Texas state court for a design defect in the hip. As soon as Hip Co. learned about the defect, it recalled all of its products. Texas evidence law does not allow evidence of the recall as evidence of a defect. Texas law also caps noneconomic damages at $250,000. Patient #1 was 72 years old and retired; thus

he had low economic damages. Patient #1 prevailed at trial. The jury found the replacement hip was defective and awarded Patient #1 $50,000, all in noneconomic damages. The judge entered a final judgment on the jury's verdict.

Patient #2, who also had hip replacement surgery using a new hip made by Hip Co., is your new client. After doing some research, you learn about Patient #1's similar lawsuit. You also learn that you have subject matter jurisdiction to file in federal court in Oklahoma. Finally, you learn that Oklahoma has no damages cap and the Federal Rules of Evidence would likely allow evidence of the recall to prove the hip was defective. What argument would you make to the Oklahoma federal court to allow your client, Patient #2, to preclude Hip Co. from litigating whether its hip is defective? Are there any counterarguments Hip Co. may make in response? If so, what are they?

The *Erie* Problem

25

The *Erie* Problem: The Law to Be Applied in Federal Court

This chapter addresses this question: Does a federal court apply state or federal law in a diversity case? You have probably already noticed that federal courts often apply state law. You've read cases where federal courts resolve state law claims, for example. Federal courts routinely apply state law. This fact shouldn't be all that surprising given the federal nature of the American government and the co-existing court systems in which the federal government shares judicial power with the states. In large part, this chapter is about helping you transition from a tacit understanding of this fact to a more focused knowledge of when and why federal courts must apply state law.

A federal court's choice between state and federal law is called the *Erie* Problem, named for the seminal Supreme Court case on the issue, *Erie Railroad Co. v. Tompkins*. Whether the federal court applies state or federal law is important, because the choice could change the outcome of the case. The application of one principle may favor the plaintiff, while application of the other may favor the defendant. But the importance of *Erie* goes beyond simply who wins or loses. *Erie* and its progeny say something important, not only about what law federal courts must apply, but also about the nature of federal law itself and its relationship to state law in a federal system of government.

Key Concepts

- The Rules of Decision Act's principle for determining whose law applies in federal court
- The Supreme Court's interpretation of "state law" in *Swift v. Tyson*, and the forum shopping problem this caused
- The Supreme Court's reinterpretation of state law in the RDA when it overruled *Swift v. Tyson* in *Erie Railroad Co. v. Tompkins*
- The Rules Enabling Act and the applicability of the Federal Rules of Civil Procedure
- The outcome determinative test as described *Hanna v. Plumer*

A. THE *ERIE* PROBLEM: THE LAW TO BE APPLIED IN FEDERAL COURT

The federal structure of our government creates the need to decide whether state or federal law applies in federal court. Often, it is clear what law applies. If the claim is a federal question claim, brought in federal court, the claim is governed by federal law, and the Federal Rules of Civil Procedure will govern how the dispute is resolved. It probably comes as no surprise that federal law governs a federal question claim, but diversity of citizenship cases are more complicated.

Suppose the plaintiff files a breach of contract action against the defendant based on the allegation that the defendant failed to deliver $100,000 worth of goods the plaintiff purchased. Think about the kinds of law a court would need to resolve this dispute. First, the court would need substantive contract law to supply the elements of the claim as well as any defenses the defendant might have to the contract claim. The court would also need rules of civil procedure to govern how the dispute would be litigated. The court may need to apply evidence rules to make decisions about the breach of contract claim. The court would also need judge-made procedural practices that find their origins in case law, as well as local rules of court that govern matters as basic as the permissible length of motions and briefs, and acceptable font types and sizes.

Now suppose this breach of contract action is filed in a Texas state court. The law to be applied to each of these kinds of issues would probably not come as any surprise. State contract law (probably Texas contract law) will supply the elements of the claim and any defenses; the Texas Rules of Civil Procedure and Evidence will govern; and any uncodified, judge-made state procedural practices will apply. As you learned in Chapters 2-5 on subject matter jurisdiction, federal and state courts often have concurrent subject matter jurisdiction over cases, and some cases that start in state court can be removed to federal court. When the basis for subject matter jurisdiction is diversity of citizenship subject matter jurisdiction, the question arises: To what extent will federal law supplant state law when cases such as this one are filed in or removed to federal court on diversity grounds?

Frankly, courts know the answer to this question, as shown in Exhibit 25.1, better than they know *why*. If our example breach of contract action is filed in or removed to federal court, state contract law will supply the elements of the claims and defenses; the Federal Rules of Civil Procedure and Evidence, not state rules, will ordinarily govern; and federal judge-made procedural practices, including the local rules of the federal venue, will often — though not always — apply. A helpful rule of thumb is that a federal court sitting in diversity will apply state substantive law and federal procedural law. Although helpful, this rule of thumb is just that — a rule of thumb — and not always accurate. Sometimes federal procedural law gives way to state law in federal court. Though we've used a breach of contract action as the example here, we would come to the same result in almost every type of diversity case, including tort actions, property disputes, and other claims created by state law. We turn our attention now to *why* these are ordinarily the answers to the question of what law is to be applied in a federal court diversity action.

EXHIBIT 25.1 A Comparison of the Laws Ordinarily Applied in Diversity Actions in State and Federal Court

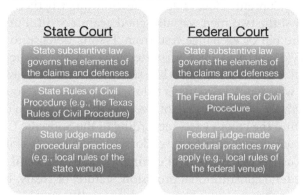

State Court	Federal Court
State substantive law governs the elements of the claims and defenses	State substantive law governs the elements of the claims and defenses
State Rules of Civil Procedure (e.g., the Texas Rules of Civil Procedure)	The Federal Rules of Civil Procedure
State judge-made procedural practices (e.g., local rules of the state venue)	Federal judge-made procedural practices *may* apply (e.g., local rules of the federal venue)

1. State Laws as the Rules of Decision

Since starting law school (or perhaps before) you have probably heard of the analytical process called IRAC (Issue-Rule-Application-Conclusion) or some variation of it, such as CRAC (Conclusion-Rule-Application-Conclusion) or CREAC (Conclusion-Rule-Explanation-Application-Conclusion). These approaches to legal problem solving all have something in common—they reflect the fact that solving a legal problem requires identification of the legal rule that governs the issue to be resolved. Sometimes both a state law and a federal law purport to resolve the same issue differently. The question is this: When faced with this situation, does a federal court sitting in diversity choose the state or federal law to resolve the issue?

The Rules of Decision Act (RDA), 28 U.S.C. §1652, set out in Exhibit 25.2, attempts to answer this question. The RDA seems like a simple decree: Apply state law unless there is a conflicting federal constitutional provision, treaty, or statute. Unfortunately, the Supreme Court has not always regarded the RDA as being as simple as it may seem. Consider the Supreme Court case of *Swift v. Tyson*, 42 U.S. 1 (1842). Swift filed a diversity action in federal court in New York against Tyson seeking payment on a commercial instrument called a bill of exchange. The bill of exchange amounted to an agreement by Tyson to pay two other men approximately $1500 in exchange for real property the two men claimed they owned. It turned out that the two men did not actually own the property. Tyson believed, therefore, that he was under no obligation to pay the $1500 plus accrued interest under the bill of exchange. Swift entered the picture because he acquired the right to be paid under the bill of exchange. Swift filed suit against Tyson for payment.

EXHIBIT 25.2 28 U.S.C. §1652 State Laws as Rules of Decision

The laws of the several states, except where the Constitution or treaties of the United States or Acts of Congress otherwise require or provide, shall be regarded as rules of decision in civil actions in the courts of the United States, in cases where they apply.

The law seemed clear that Tyson would not owe the two men any money under the bill of exchange, because they had failed to transfer title to the property. The key legal issue for the Supreme Court's determination was whether or not the defense Tyson had against the two men was also good against Swift. Put another way, did Swift acquire the bill of exchange free from Tyson's defense to payment against the two men? Two legal principles purported to resolve this issue differently — one state, one federal. The rule in New York as set down in the case law of the New York Supreme Court was that the two men's failure to transfer title would provide Tyson a defense to payment against Swift. However, the general rule on this point of commercial law around the country was, according to the Supreme Court, that Tyson's defense was not good against a remote endorsee like Swift. This kind of general rule became known as the federal general common law. The federal general common law was not a federal constitutional provision, statute, or treaty. Instead, it was the Supreme Court's pronouncement of what the majority rule is or ought to be and what federal courts must apply. Perhaps the closest analog we have to the federal general common law today is found in the restatements on various subjects, such as the restatements of contracts and torts. If you're wondering why you haven't heard already of the federal general common law in one of your other courses, (spoiler alert) it doesn't exist anymore. Exhibit 25.3 below may help you better understand the choice of law issue presented in *Swift*.

The Supreme Court looked to an earlier version of the modern RDA to answer the question. The RDA would seem to require application of the New York state common law rule that permitted Tyson to raise the defense against Swift. The RDA required the application of state law (seemingly like the New York common law rule at issue in *Swift*), unless the contrary federal rule was a federal constitutional provision, treaty, or statute. The federal general common law rule was certainly none of those things. Thus, New York's state law would apply.

EXHIBIT 25.3   **Changing the Outcome**

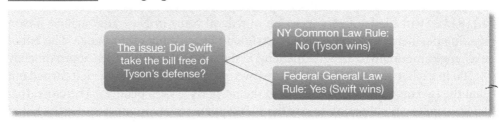

Despite what the language of the RDA seemed to require, the Supreme Court in *Swift* applied the federal general common law principle in lieu of the New York common law rule. The Supreme Court interpreted the RDA to exclude a state's case law from the phrase "laws of the several states." In other words, the Supreme Court determined that state common law, even the pronouncements of a state supreme court, were not considered "state law" at all under the RDA. This meant that a federal court would be bound to apply a state statute or state constitutional provision *so long as it did not conflict* with the federal Constitution or statutes. However, a federal court would not be bound by a state common law rule found only in a state court opinion. Instead, in that circumstance, federal courts were free to pronounce and apply their own federal general common law.

The *Swift* decision invited forum shopping. In many cities, the federal court and state court buildings may be mere blocks away from each other — yet *Swift* provided the opportunity to drastically change the ultimate outcome by filing in a federal court just down the street and thereby changing the governing law. This is an example of forum shopping that the law ordinarily tries to discourage. This forum shopping helped inspire the Supreme Court to overturn *Swift*'s central holding in perhaps the most famous Civil Procedure case the Court has yet decided: *Erie Railroad Co. v. Tompkins.*

Case Preview

Erie Railroad Co. v. Tompkins

As you read *Erie Railroad Co. v. Tompkins,* consider these questions:

1. How did the Court change the way federal courts decide choice of law questions?
2. What are the main reasons the Court departed from the rule announced in *Swift*?
3. Did the Court hold that the Rules of Decision Act was unconstitutional?
4. Why is Justice Reed's opinion merely a concurrence? In other words, in what respect does he seem to disagree, at least in part, with the majority opinion's reasoning?

Erie Railroad Co. v. Tompkins
304 U.S. 64 (1938)

Mr. Justice BRANDEIS delivered the opinion of the Court.

[Eds. — The plaintiff, Mr. Tompkins, was walking along a path parallel to the rail line when something struck him. He claimed that a door swung open on one of the railway cars, causing him to lose an arm. He sued in federal court in New York based on diversity jurisdiction, because he was a Pennsylvania citizen and the railroad was incorporated and had its principal place of business in New York. The railroad moved to dismiss Mr. Tompkin's complaint on the grounds that it owed him no duty of care because he was a trespasser. Under Pennsylvania common law where Mr. Tompkins was injured, the railroad owed no duty to a trespasser like Mr. Tomkins. However, under federal common law, Mr. Tomkins would not be considered a trespasser and the railroad would have to defend on the merits as to whether it exercised its applicable duty of care. The trial court followed *Swift* and applied federal common law. The railroad defended on the merits and lost. The jury awarded Tomkins nearly half a million dollars in today's money and the railroad appealed and lost again. The railroad then petitioned the Supreme Court for certiorari. The opinion that follows ushered in a revolution in choice of law.]

The question for decision is whether the oft-challenged doctrine of *Swift v. Tyson* shall now be disapproved.

* * *

Because of the importance of the question whether the federal court was free to disregard the alleged rule of the Pennsylvania common law, we granted certiorari.

First. Swift v. Tyson, 16 Pet. 1, 18, 10 L. Ed. 865, held that federal courts exercising jurisdiction on the ground of diversity of citizenship need not, in matters of general jurisprudence, apply the unwritten law of the state as declared by its highest court; that they are free to exercise an independent judgment as to what the common law of the state is — or should be. . . .

Doubt was repeatedly expressed as to the correctness of the construction given section 34, and as to the soundness of the rule which it introduced. But it was the more recent research of a competent scholar, who examined the original document, which established that the construction given to it by the Court was erroneous; and that the purpose of the section was merely to make certain that, in all matters except those in which some federal law is controlling, the federal courts exercising jurisdiction in diversity of citizenship cases would apply as their rules of decision the law of the state, unwritten as well as written.

Criticism of the doctrine became widespread after the decision of Black & White Taxicab & Transfer Co. v. Brown & Yellow Taxicab & Transfer Co., 276 U.S. 518. There, Brown &Yellow, a Kentucky corporation owned by Kentuckians, and the Louisville & Nashville Railroad, also a Kentucky corporation, wished that the former should have the exclusive privilege of soliciting passenger and baggage transportation at the Bowling Green, Ky., Railroad station; and that the Black & White, a competing Kentucky corporation, should be prevented from interfering with that privilege. Knowing that such a contract would be void under the common law of Kentucky, it was arranged that the Brown & Yellow reincorporate under the law of Tennessee, and that the contract with the railroad should be executed there. The suit was then brought by the Tennessee corporation in the federal court for Western Kentucky to enjoin competition by the Black & White; an injunction issued by the District Court was sustained by the Court of Appeals; and this Court, citing many decisions in which the doctrine of Swift v. Tyson had been applied, affirmed the decree.

Second. Experience in applying the doctrine of Swift v. Tyson, had revealed its defects, political and social; and the benefits expected to flow from the rule did not accrue. Persistence of state courts in their own opinions on questions of common law prevented uniformity; and the impossibility of discovering a satisfactory line of demarcation between the province of general law and that of local law developed a new well of uncertainties.

On the other hand, the mischievous results of the doctrine had become apparent. Diversity of citizenship jurisdiction was conferred in order to prevent apprehended discrimination in state courts against those not citizens of the state. Swift v. Tyson introduced grave discrimination by noncitizens against citizens. It made rights enjoyed under the unwritten 'general law' vary according to whether enforcement was sought in the state or in the federal court; and the privilege of selecting the court in which the right should be determined was conferred upon the noncitizen. Thus, the doctrine rendered impossible equal protection of the law. In attempting to promote uniformity of law throughout the United States, the doctrine had prevented uniformity in the administration of the law of the state.

The discrimination resulting became in practice far-reaching. This resulted in part from the broad province accorded to the so-called 'general law' as to which federal courts exercised an independent judgment. In addition to questions of purely commercial law, 'general law' was held to include the obligations under contracts entered into and to be performed within the state, the extent to which a carrier operating within a state may stipulate for exemption from liability for his own negligence or that of his employee; the liability for torts committed within the state upon persons resident or property located there, even where the question of liability depended upon the scope of a property right conferred by the state; and the right to exemplary or punitive damages. Furthermore, state decisions construing local deeds, mineral conveyances, and even devises of real estate, were disregarded.

In part the discrimination resulted from the wide range of persons held entitled to avail themselves of the federal rule by resort to the diversity of citizenship jurisdiction. Through this jurisdiction individual citizens willing to remove from their own [*did this happen?*] state and become citizens of another might avail themselves of the federal rule. And, without even change of residence, a corporate citizen of the state could avail itself of the federal rule by reincorporating under the laws of another state, as was done in the Taxicab Case.

The injustice and confusion incident to the doctrine of Swift v. Tyson have been repeatedly urged as reasons for abolishing or limiting diversity of citizenship jurisdiction. Other legislative relief has been proposed. If only a question of statutory construction were involved, we should not be prepared to abandon a doctrine so widely applied throughout nearly a century. But the unconstitutionality of the course pursued has now been made clear, and compels us to do so.

Third. Except in matters governed by the Federal Constitution or by acts of Congress, the law to be applied in any case is the law of the state. And whether the law of the state shall be declared by its Legislature in a statute or by its highest court in a decision is not a matter of federal concern. There is no federal general common law. Congress has no power to declare substantive rules of common law applicable in a state whether they be local in their nature or 'general,' be they commercial law or a part of the law of torts. And no clause in the Constitution purports to confer such a power upon the federal courts.

Thus the doctrine of Swift v. Tyson is, as Mr. Justice Holmes said [in his dissent in *Black & White Taxicab & Transfer Co. v. Brown & Yellow Taxicab & Transfer Co.*], 'an unconstitutional assumption of powers by the Courts of the United States which no lapse of time or respectable array of opinion should make us hesitate to correct.' In disapproving that doctrine we do not hold unconstitutional section 34 of the Federal Judiciary Act of 1789 or any other act of Congress. We merely declare that in applying the doctrine this Court and the lower courts have invaded rights which in our opinion are reserved by the Constitution to the several states. . . .

As we hold this was error, the judgment is <u>reversed</u> and the case <u>remanded</u> to it for further proceedings in conformity with our opinion.

Reversed.

Mr. Justice REED (concurring in part).

I concur in the conclusion reached in this case, in the disapproval of the doctrine of Swift v. Tyson, and in the reasoning of the majority opinion, except in so far as it relies upon the unconstitutionality of the 'course pursued' by the federal courts.

* * *

The 'unconstitutional' course referred to in the majority opinion is apparently the ruling in Swift v. Tyson that the supposed omission of Congress to legislate as to the effect of decisions leaves federal courts free to interpret general law for themselves. I am not at all sure whether, in the absence of federal statutory direction, federal courts would be compelled to follow state decisions. There was sufficient doubt about the matter in 1789 to induce the first Congress to legislate. No former opinions of this Court have passed upon it. . . . If the opinion commits this Court to the position that the Congress is without power to declare what rules of substantive law shall govern the federal courts, that conclusion also seems questionable. The line between procedural and substantive law is hazy, but no one doubts federal power over procedure. The Judiciary Article, 3, and the 'necessary and proper' clause of article 1, §8, may fully authorize legislation, such as this section of the Judiciary Act.

* * *

There is no occasion to discuss further the range or soundness of these few phrases of the opinion. It is sufficient now to call attention to them and express my own non-acquiescence.

Post-Case Follow-Up

Why would a state court pronouncement on what the law is be any different than a state legislature's pronouncement, signed by the governor? *Swift* reflects a school of thought that believed law existed independent from the judges who applied it, while *Erie* <u>reflects an example of legal realism</u>. *Erie* rejected the outdated notion that all judges creating common law through their opinions were all moving toward some universal, external, and preexisting law rather than making law. The Court clearly stated: "There is no federal general common law." Justice Oliver Wendell Holmes, who dissented in *Swift*, famously said: "The life of the law has not been logic; it has been experience." He rejected the idea that all judges were simply trying to uncover a "correct" principle and were equally qualified to do so. The *Erie* decision adopted Justice Holmes' reasoning and put state court opinions on equal footing with state statutes. This is part of the meaning of the court's declaration: "There is no federal general common law."

Although *Erie* did not declare the RDA itself unconstitutional, it did declare that *Swift*'s application of the RDA was unconstitutional in its unequal treatment of state court opinions and statutes. In short, the Constitution, as a matter of equal protection of the laws, compelled federal courts to treat people equally regardless of the nature of the law. Why should a litigant be able to completely change the outcome by merely, in some cases, walking a few blocks down the street and suing in federal court instead of state court?

Think carefully about Justice Reed's concurring opinion. Note that he makes a distinction between substance and procedure. This distinction has become a key part of choice of law that survives today. Consider that both *Erie* and the Federal Rules of Civil Procedure came out in 1938. What would be the implications if the Court had held that the RDA did not permit the federal government to create and use procedural rules in federal courts?

Erie Railroad Co. v. Tompkins: Real Life Applications

An employee who is a citizen of Nevada sued his former employer, another citizen of Nevada, for employment discrimination in federal court in Nevada. The federal Age Discrimination in Employment Act (ADEA) requires that a plaintiff be older than 40 years of age at the time of the adverse employment decision before he or she can maintain an ADEA cause of action. Nevada state law has a similar common law, judge-created age discrimination claim that has no minimum age requirement; rather, the Nevada law considers whether the employee was replaced by a younger employee.

1. Suppose the employee sued the former employer only under the ADEA. Must the employee be older than 40 before he can maintain his claim against his former employer? Why or why not? Would the result have been any different under *Swift*? Why or why not?

2. Now suppose the employee sued the former employer under both the ADEA and the similar Nevada common law claim in federal district court in Nevada. What law must the court apply? Does it matter which claim is at issue? Would the result have been any different under *Swift*? Why or why not?

3. Suppose the employee sued the former employer under both the ADEA and the similar Nevada common law claim in *Nevada state court*. What law must the court apply? Does it matter which claim is at issue? Would the result have been any different before or after *Erie*? Why or why not?

2. What Is State Law?

After *Erie*, many fundamental questions remained. One question is simply how to determine what state law is. If there is a recent state supreme court opinion on point, then the court can easily determine what state law it must apply. But this is not always the case. State statutes may be vague or ambiguous without any judicial clarification; state courts (particularly in larger jurisdictions with many courts of appeals) may come to conflicting judgments on the meaning of state law; the state court of last resort may not have opined on the issue; or the state court of last resort may have decided the issue long ago, but would probably decide the issue differently today. Simply stated, even if the federal court knows it must apply state law, the federal court may not be able to easily find out what state law actually "is." In this situation, the federal court can either make a guess about what it is or ask the state supreme court to answer the question.

The Erie *Guess*

The Court has clarified this problem over time by giving federal courts flexibility to make an "***Erie* guess**." The court should ask itself: How would the state's highest court decide this issue if presented with it today? *See Comm'r v. Bosch*, 387 U.S. 456 (1967). As a practical matter, federal courts should and do follow state intermediate appellate court opinions, but this predictive approach is still the method the court uses to resolve the question of what state law is. *See id.* (a federal court should follow intermediate court precedents unless convinced the state's highest court would rule otherwise).

For example, suppose in a diversity case based on the tort of negligence that the court (or, more likely, the court's law clerk) conducts research and finds a state supreme court case about a defense to negligence called contributory negligence. Under this doctrine, if the plaintiff caused or contributed to any part of his own harm, the plaintiff would be barred from recovering anything — even if the defendant is largely responsible for causing the harm. The case is nearly 100 years old but has never been overruled. Further research reveals that several lower state court decisions have criticized the rule as being overly harsh. The lower courts describe the doctrine as drastic and bad policy, as it would discourage plaintiffs with worthy claims from pursuing them because a defendant could simply convince the fact-finder that the plaintiff contributed to his own harm in even the slightest manner and completely escape liability. Thus, the plaintiff would recover nothing, even though a better rule might be to simply reduce the plaintiff's recovery by the amount of his own fault. After conducting all of its research, if the federal court truly believes that the state supreme court, if faced with the question today, would overrule its own precedent and abolish or modify the contributory negligence defense, the federal court is making an *Erie* guess and should apply the law accordingly. Ironically, the federal trial court would then be applying a different law than a state trial court in the same state would apply, because the state trial courts would still be bound by the rule as announced by the state supreme court and the intermediate court in its appellate chain, despite any criticism. This is a result *Erie* was intended to avoid, but is theoretically possible. As a practical matter, however, federal courts are unlikely to ignore state supreme court precedent, even if seemingly outdated and unpopular among lower courts.

Certified Questions

Another method many states have to permit a federal court to determine the content of a state's law is called a certified question. If the federal court cannot find the answer, and the court of last resort of the state has the final word on what state law is, then why not just ask that court what the law is? While this seems like an elegant way to resolve a problem, certification is rarely used. Accepting a certified question is often discretionary with the state supreme court at issue, and the procedure varies from state to state. Compare Exhibit 25.4 with Exhibit 25.5. If you are a law clerk to a federal district judge, can you see any difference between these two rules that may affect whether certifying an uncertain question of Texas law to the Supreme Court of Texas is a viable option, versus certifying a question of Massachusetts law to the Massachusetts Supreme Judicial Court?

EXHIBIT 25.4   **Texas Rule of Appellate Procedure 58.1. Certification**

The Supreme Court of Texas may answer questions of law certified to it by any federal appellate court if the certifying court is presented with determinative questions of Texas law having no controlling Supreme Court precedent. The Supreme Court may decline to answer the questions certified to it.

EXHIBIT 25.5   **Massachusetts Supreme Judicial Court Rule 1:03: Uniform Certification of Questions of Law**

Section 1. Authority to Answer Certain Questions of Law.

This court may answer questions of law certified to it by the Supreme Court of the United States, a Court of Appeals of the United States, or of the District of Columbia, or a United States District Court, or the highest appellate court of any other State when requested by the certifying court if there are involved in any proceeding before it questions of law of this State which may be determinative of the cause then pending in the certifying court and as to which it appears to the certifying court there is no controlling precedent in the decisions of this court.

3. *Erie* and Supplemental Jurisdiction

In diversity cases, federal courts adjudicate state law claims. Federal courts also adjudicate state law claims when they exercise supplemental jurisdiction. The RDA, *Erie*, and its progeny require federal courts to apply state substantive law when exercising supplemental jurisdiction. The principles we've discussed as applying in diversity cases also apply when the court is exercising supplemental jurisdiction.

4. Federal Common Law Still Exists

Do not read this statement from *Erie* too broadly: "There is no federal general common law." There is no *general* federal common law that applies in diversity or supplemental jurisdiction cases — cases where federal law does not apply the rule of decision. *Erie*, however, did not purport to take away federal courts' authority to interpret, fill in gaps, and otherwise make federal law in areas of federal concern. For example, federal courts pronounce binding case law when they interpret any federal law such as the U.S. Constitution, congressional statutes, and federal regulations. Federal courts also fashion federal common law in areas involving special or even exclusive federal concerns, such as resolving disputes between states or resolving tort or contract disputes with the federal government.

B. THE FEDERAL RULES OF CIVIL PROCEDURE VERSUS CONFLICTING STATE LAW

The Federal Rules of Civil Procedure were adopted in the same year *Erie* was decided — 1938. Does the Court's holding in *Erie* mean the Federal Rules can be applied only when they don't conflict with state law? The answer is no. A Federal Rule of Civil Procedure ordinarily will be applied even when it is different than state law on the point. As you'll see, the Supreme Court is fairly confident this is the answer, although it can't quite come to agreement on *why* this is the answer.

1. Framing the Issue: What Are Federal Rules of Civil Procedure?

Let's begin by making sure we understand the issue and the context in which it arises. The conflict we're addressing arises when a federal court confronts an issue that a Federal Rule of Civil Procedure and state law resolve differently. Is the federal court free to apply the Federal Rule of Civil Procedure, or must it apply the state law? Recall that the RDA directs the federal court to apply state law unless there is a conflicting federal statute, treaty, or constitutional provision. A Federal Rule of Civil Procedure is not a statute, constitutional provision, or treaty; so you may believe, because of the wording of the RDA, that state law should ordinarily apply in federal court when it conflicts with a Federal Rule of Civil Procedure. A brief overview of the nature of the Federal Rules of Civil Procedure might help you understand why resolution of this kind of conflict is not as simple as the RDA makes it seem.

The Federal Rules are drafted by an advisory committee appointed by the United States Supreme Court. The Court is authorized to create rules of practice and procedure through this process by a federal act called the Rules Enabling Act (REA), the immediately relevant portions of which are shown in Exhibit 25.6. The REA requires the Rules to be submitted to Congress before they can become law, and they do become law after a certain period of time unless Congress affirmatively

EXHIBIT 25.6   **28 U.S.C. §1652 The Rules Enabling Act**

(a) The Supreme Court shall have the power to prescribe general rules of practice and procedure and rules of evidence for cases in the United States district courts (including proceedings before magistrate judges thereof) and courts of appeals.

(b) Such rules shall not abridge, enlarge or modify any substantive right. All laws in conflict with such rules shall be of no further force or effect after such rules have taken effect.

prevents it. If Congress does nothing, the proposed rules are enacted as Federal Rules of Civil Procedure and govern in federal district courts. This means that each Federal Rule has at least the tacit approval of Congress. The REA also provides that, if a Federal Rule meets its requirements, all other laws in conflict with it are of no further force or effect. Nevertheless, the Supreme Court has struggled with the REA's requirements and with maintaining a consistent rationale for resolving conflicts between a Federal Rule and state law.

2. The *Hanna* Test: Applicability and Validity

The Supreme Court's decision in *Hanna v. Plumer* makes clear that, because of the REA, the analysis for determining whether or not a Federal Rule of Civil Procedure is applied in federal court is different than the "typical, relatively unguided" *Erie* analysis. In *Hanna*, the plaintiff brought suit in federal district court in Massachusetts seeking damages for personal injuries she sustained in a car wreck with a person who was, by the time the lawsuit was filed, deceased; thus, the plaintiff named the executor of the decedent's estate as the defendant. The plaintiff served the executor by leaving a copy of the summons and complaint with the executor's wife at the decedent's residence. Rule 4 of the Federal Rules of Civil Procedure permits process to be served at the defendant's abode upon someone of suitable age and discretion who also resides there. Service of process in *Hanna* complied with this provision, but it did not comply with a Massachusetts statute that required personal, in-hand delivery to the executor in such cases.

The Supreme Court held that Rule 4 controlled the method of service, and therefore service upon the executor's wife at the decedent's home was proper. The *Hanna* Court also set out a two-part test for determining whether or not a Federal Rule applied in lieu of conflicting state law, saying: "When a situation is covered by one of the Federal Rules, the question facing the court is a far cry from the typical, relatively unguided *Erie* Choice: the court has been instructed to apply the Federal Rule, and can refuse to do so only if the Advisory Committee, this Court, and Congress erred in their prima facie judgment that the Rule in question transgresses neither the terms of the Enabling Act nor constitutional restrictions." In short, a federal court must apply the Federal Rule, despite conflicting state law, so long as the Federal Rule is (1) applicable and (2) valid.

Is the Federal Rule Applicable?

The first part of the test from *Hanna* requires that the Rule truly answer the legal question the court must resolve. If the Federal Rule does not answer the question, the court will apply state law. For example, in *Walker v. Armco Steel Corp.*, the Supreme Court had to decide whether Oklahoma law or Federal Rule 3 governed when an action is commenced for purposes of tolling of the statute of limitations. 446 U.S. 740 (1980). In *Walker*, the plaintiff was a carpenter who brought a negligence claim under Oklahoma law against the manufacturer of an allegedly defective nail that had shattered and injured the plaintiff's eye. The applicable Oklahoma statute of limitations required the plaintiff to commence his action within two years of the day the nail shattered and injured his eye. Oklahoma law deemed the action commenced when the plaintiff served process on the defendant. This definition of commencement required the plaintiff to both file his complaint and serve it on the defendant within two years, although Oklahoma provided that service of process could occur beyond two years so long as it occurred within 60 days of filing the complaint. However, the plaintiff did not file and serve his complaint within two years nor did he serve it within 60 days of filing the complaint. The plaintiff urged application of Federal Rule 3, which provides that a civil action is "commenced by filing a complaint with the court." The Court applied Oklahoma law, because it held that Federal Rule 3 simply did not answer the question at issue in the case. The Court explained:

> As has already been noted, we recognized in Hanna that the present case is an instance where "the scope of the Federal Rule [is] not as broad as the losing party urge[s], and therefore, there being no Federal Rule which cover[s] the point in dispute, *Erie* command[s] the enforcement of state law." . . . Rule 3 simply states that "[a] civil action is commenced by filing a complaint with the court." There is no indication that the Rule was intended to toll a state statute of limitations, much less that it purported to displace state tolling rules for purposes of state statutes of limitations. In our view, in diversity actions Rule 3 governs the date from which various timing requirements of the Federal Rules begin to run, but does not affect state statutes of limitations.

Walker, 446 U.S. at 750-51.

Unless there is a "direct collision" between the Federal Rule and state law — i.e., both answer the same question differently — state law will apply. *Id.* at 750. Thus, *Hanna* commands federal district courts to ensure that the Federal Rule and state law truly conflict, avoiding such conflict if possible, before moving on to the next question — whether the Federal Rule is valid.

Is the Federal Rule Valid?

Assuming the Federal Rule answers the question, the court must apply it so long as it is valid. The Federal Rule is valid if it violates neither the Constitution nor the terms of the REA. It may be helpful to understand at the outset that the Supreme Court has never held that a Federal Rule violates either the Constitution or the terms of the REA. A rule certainly could violate the terms of the REA if it does not regulate procedure, because the REA only provides the Supreme Court the power to make rules of practice and procedure.

The REA also contains a more problematic second limitation. The REA provides that a Federal Rule of Civil Procedure cannot abridge, enlarge, or modify any *substantive* right. Does this language mean that a Federal Rule may only be applied in lieu of conflicting state procedural law? Where is the line between state procedural and substantive law?

The most recent Supreme Court case to address this issue, *Shady Grove Orthopedic Associates, P.A. v. Allstate Insurance Co.*, 559 U.S. 393 (2010), resulted in a fractured Court and plurality opinions. *Shady Grove* involved a class action to recover statutory penalties and a conflict between a New York state law that prohibited class actions to recover penalties and Federal Rule 23, which might permit such a class action.

Writing for a group of four Justices, Justice Scalia explained the test he believed should be used to determine if a Federal Rule should be applied in lieu of conflicting state law:

> We have long held that this limitation [in the REA] means that the Rule must "really regulat[e] procedure, — the judicial process for enforcing rights and duties recognized by substantive law and for justly administering remedy and redress for disregard or infraction of them." . . . The test is not whether the rule affects a litigant's substantive rights; most procedural rules do. . . . What matters is what the rule itself regulates: If it governs only "the manner and the means" by which the litigants' rights are "enforced," it is valid; if it alters "the rules of decision by which [the] court will adjudicate [those] rights," it is not.

Shady Grove, 559 U.S. at 407.

To determine if the Federal Rule is valid under the REA, it seems Justice Scalia would ask a single question — does the Rule regulate procedure? If it does, it is to be applied. Because Federal Rule 23 addresses how the federal court processes the claims (as a class action), Justice Scalia believed it regulates procedure, and therefore, should be applied.

Despite the REA's statement that a Federal Rule must not abridge, enlarge, or modify a substantive right, Justice Scalia's opinion seemed unconcerned with whether or not the state law it displaced was substantive or procedural.

> . . . the substantive nature of New York's law, or its substantive purpose, makes no difference. A Federal Rule of Procedure is not valid in some jurisdictions and invalid in others — or valid in some cases and invalid in others — depending upon whether its effect is to frustrate a state substantive law (or a state procedural law enacted for substantive purposes).

Shady Grove, 559 U.S. at 409.

Despite the REA's command that a Federal Rule not "abridge, enlarge, or modify a substantive right," Justice Scalia would apply the Federal Rule so long as it regulates procedure, even if the state law it displaces is substantive. Otherwise, a particular Federal Rule may be applicable in a case where there happens not to be a conflicting state substantive rule and inapplicable in a case where there happens to be a conflicting state substantive law, and the uniformity provided by the Federal Rules would be jeopardized. Scalia writes:

> In sum, it is not the substantive or procedural nature or purpose of the affected state law that matters, but the substantive or procedural nature of the Federal Rule.... [T]he validity of a Federal Rule depends entirely upon whether it regulates procedure.... If it does, it is authorized by [the REA] and is valid in all jurisdictions, with respect to all claims, regardless of its incidental effect upon state-created rights.

Shady Grove, 559 U.S. at 410.

Justice Stevens' concurring opinion sets out a different understanding of the limitation in the REA:

> The Enabling Act requires, *inter alia*, that federal rules "not abridge, enlarge or modify *any* substantive right." 28 U.S.C. §2072(b) (emphasis added). Unlike Justice SCALIA, I believe that an application of a federal rule that effectively abridges, enlarges, or modifies a state-created right or remedy violates this command. Congress may have the constitutional power "to supplant state law" with rules that are "rationally capable of classification as procedure," ... but we should generally presume that it has not done so.... Indeed, the mandate that federal rules "shall not abridge, enlarge or modify any substantive right" evinces the opposite intent, as does Congress' decision to delegate the creation of rules to this Court rather than to a political branch.

Shady Grove, 559 U.S. at 422 (Stevens, concurring).

Although he agrees with Justice Scalia that Federal Rule 23 should apply in this particular case, Justice Stevens does not agree that the application of a Federal Rule is determined solely by looking at whether or not a Federal Rule regulates procedure. If a Federal Rule conflicts with a state substantive rule, then Justice Stevens allows for the possibility that state law must apply in federal court despite its conflict with a Federal Rule of Civil Procedure.

Shady Grove provides only one clear message — when a Federal Rule of Civil Procedure conflicts with a contrary state rule, the Federal Rule ordinarily ought to be applied. Again, the Supreme Court has never held that a Federal Rule violates the terms of the REA. The Court's fractured opinions did not set out a clear analytical framework to guide future cases. So, we know what the answer is ordinarily going to be — the Federal Rule of Civil Procedure applies in federal court in lieu of conflicting state law — but we don't yet understand *why* this is the answer.

C. UNCODIFIED FEDERAL PROCEDURAL PRACTICES VERSUS CONFLICTING STATE LAW

Most *Erie* questions in suits pending in federal court are straightforward. Exhibit 25.7 below summarizes the law to be applied in federal court in diversity and supplemental jurisdiction cases, and should provide some certainty about what law will govern in federal court. However, this section of the chapter addresses the

EXHIBIT 25.7 | **A Summary of State Laws Federal Courts Apply in Diversity Cases**

1. **The Elements of the Claim**
   Examples: the elements (and their definition) of tort, contract, property, and warranty claims.

2. **The Elements of the Defenses**
   Examples: the elements (and their definitions) of contract defenses (e.g., statute of frauds, unconscionability, duress) and tort defenses (e.g., contributory negligence, intervening cause).

3. **The Statute of Limitations**
   Example: the statute of limitations of the state that provides the substantive elements of the claim will govern.

4. **Rules for Tolling the Statute of Limitations**
   Example: state law that supplies the statute of limitations will also define when an action is commenced for purposes of tolling the statute of limitations.

murkiest of all the types of *Erie* Problems — what law does the federal court sitting in diversity apply when the conflict is between an uncodified federal procedural practice and state law?

This type of *Erie* Problem is difficult, because neither the RDA nor the REA resolves it. The RDA tells federal courts to apply state law unless it conflicts with a federal statute, constitutional provision, or treaty, and under the REA, Federal Rules of Civil Procedure ordinarily are applied in lieu of conflicting state law. Taken together, the RDA and REA provide that a federal legal principle codified in the Constitution, United States Code, a federal treaty, or the Federal Rules should apply in lieu of conflicting state law. The corollary to this rule is that state law should apply when there is no conflicting, codified federal law. Does this mean that a federal court sitting in diversity can never apply its uncodified procedural law, such as a common law procedural practice? The answer is not as simple as the RDA and REA might make it seem.

As you know by now, not all federal procedural law is codified. Much of it can be described as judge-made procedural practices that find their origins in federal case law or in the local rules of a particular federal district. The doctrines of laches and *forum non conveniens*, for example, have their origins in federal case law, not in the federal Constitution, statutes, or rules. Local rules of court are decided upon by the judges presiding in the particular district, and govern seemingly mundane matters critical to the day-to-day practice before the court, such as the permissible length of motions and briefs, the deadline to file a response to a motion, and whether or not the parties must meet and confer before seeking relief from the court. The question now is whether or not these judge-made procedural practices apply in lieu of conflicting state law in federal court.

This question is a difficult one in part because *Erie* did not deal with procedural law. The duty of care owed to Mr. Tompkins as he walked near the rail line was clearly a matter of state substantive tort law — there was no issue of a conflict between codified federal law and state law. *Erie* and its progeny are often described as requiring the application of state substantive law and federal procedural law in diversity and supplemental jurisdiction cases, but *Erie* did not attempt to define the elusive difference between a substantive and a procedural law. Recall Justice Reed's concurrence in *Erie*:

> The line between procedural and substantive law is hazy, but _no one doubts federal power over procedure._ The Judiciary Article, 3, and the "necessary and proper" clause of article 1, §8 [authorizing Congress to enact legislation necessary and proper to carry out its enumerated powers], may fully authorize legislation, such as this section of the Judiciary Act.

Erie, 304 U.S. at 91 (emphasis added).

The next term after *Erie* brought the substance/procedure distinction to a head. In *Cities Service Oil Co. v. Dunlap*, the Court was faced with a conflict that seemed procedural in nature, rather than substantive. 308 U.S. 208 (1939). The federal district court had to choose who had the burden of proof in a dispute over title to land. Federal practice would place it on the party who brought the lawsuit (i.e., the plaintiff), while state law would place it on the party challenging who had proper title to the land (here, the defendant). Although the lower court distinguished *Erie* because the burden of proof seemed to be a matter of "practice or procedure" rather than a substantive law, the Supreme Court reversed. The Court was convinced that the matter was so "related to a substantial right" as to who owned the property that the Court held the federal district court must use the state law placing the burden on the party challenging title. Thus, it seemed the Court may also require federal courts to apply state procedural rules that are "bound up" with the applicable state substantive law.

The next prominent case, *Guaranty Trust Co. v. York*, presented a similar substance versus procedure issue. 326 U.S. 99 (1945). The issue was whether the federal court had to apply the state statute of limitations to a claim (resulting in the claim being time-barred) or the federal court's more flexible laches doctrine (making it possible for the claim to proceed). Rather than hold that the statute of limitations was somehow bound up with the state law claim, the Court announced another approach: If following a federal practice would result in a different outcome than if the case were pending in state court, the federal court must follow the state practice. This has come to be known as the "outcome determinative" test. In other words, federal courts should not be an avenue for gamesmanship. The parties should not be afforded a different result just because the state law claim is pending in federal court. Thus, *York* held that the state statute of limitations applied because the result should be the same whether the case is pending in state court or in a federal court based on diversity jurisdiction.

Dunlap, *York*, and other cases that followed them created a new justification for applying arguably procedural state law in federal court. As described above, *Erie* had a constitutional basis to require federal courts to apply state substantive law where no federal law controlled. Cases like *Dunlap* and *York*, however, relied on a policy justification. By focusing on making the result the same in a federal diversity case as in a state court case, these cases and others that followed them seemed to require a federal court to always apply state procedural law in the event of a conflict. After all, applying a different, conflicting rule could always change the outcome of a case.

The next major case to face the substance/procedure distinction and outcome determinative policy applied both approaches. *Byrd v. Blue Ridge Rural Electric Cooperative*, applied both the *Erie/Dunlap* rules, considering whether the state law was substantive (or so bound up with it) and whether applying the Federal Rule would result in changing the outcome. The issue in *Byrd* was who should determine whether the plaintiff was classified as an "employee" of the defendant. The South Carolina state rule left the decision to the judge; the federal practice left such decisions to the jury. The Court first considered whether this question was controlled by *Erie* and *Dunlap* — is this a question of applying state substantive law or state procedural law so "bound up with the definition of the rights and obligations of the parties" that the court must apply it as a constitutional matter? The Court held that who decides employee status was merely a "form and mode" of enforcing state law (i.e., merely procedural), and was not constitutionally compelled. The second part of *Byrd*'s analysis introduced a new consideration: Because the outcome determinative test is a matter of policy, the Court considered not just the effect on the outcome, but also countervailing federal policies. Here, the issue at least touched on the Seventh Amendment's right to trial by jury. The Court ultimately held that uniformity must yield to the broad right to a jury trial, and applied the federal practice where juries decide who qualifies as an employee.

On its face, the result in *Byrd* seemed to hold that some federal practices and procedures could survive and be applied in federal court, even when faced with a conflicting state procedure that could be outcome determinative. However, the circumstances of *Byrd* were also unusual and the holding could be read narrowly. In other words, it drew no bright line between when a state practice is "bound up" with state substantive law as in *York*, and it might take an arguable conflict between a state procedure and an amendment to the Constitution to trump the outcome determinative test from *Dunlap*.

Although *Hanna* dealt with a direct conflict between a Federal Rule of Civil Procedure and state law, it also says something important about the conflict between uncodified federal procedural practices and state law, and the "outcome determinative" test in particular. The *Hanna* Court decided that the outcome determinative test meant something more than "Would the result be different if the court applied the state law rather than the federal law"? Which law applies should be analyzed with the policy behind *Erie* in mind: Minimize the plaintiff's incentive to choose federal court over state court based on which rule would give a significant procedural advantage. This makes sense, because recall that the problem *Swift* caused was that plaintiffs chose federal court over state court to get a result they could not get in state court in the same case. Swift encouraged forum shopping and led to the inequitable administration of laws. *Hanna* noted that the "twin aims" of *Erie* were to eliminate these problems. The Court in *Hanna* did not believe that the manner in which the plaintiff must serve process — either by leaving it with "a person of suitable age and discretion" at the defendant's residence, as permitted by Federal Rule 4, or by personally serving the executor as required by Massachusetts law — would cause a plaintiff to pick one court over another. The difference between the two laws might decide the outcome of the case in a retrospective sense; i.e., looking backwards, the manner of service decided the outcome of the case. But the method of service was not prospectively outcome determinative; i.e., plaintiffs would not choose federal court to get a substituted service rule and, therefore, a result they could not get in state court in the same case.

Without doubt, the conflict between an uncodified federal procedural practice and state law is the murkiest of all the types of *Erie* Problems. So much so, in fact, that it is difficult to predict how the Supreme Court would decide such an issue in the future. But *Hanna* seems to provide the best guidance with its reference to the twin aims of *Erie*: Apply the judge-made federal procedural practice, unless doing so would cause plaintiffs to choose federal court to get a different result than they could on the same case in state court.

Application Exercise

Use *Hanna*'s version of the outcome determinative test to answer the question following the hypothetical below.

> Letitia files a complaint in federal court on diversity grounds naming Noor as a defendant and alleging the tort of conversion based on the allegation that Noor intentionally destroyed Letitia's Ferrari. Letitia files her complaint on the last day before the applicable two-year statute of limitations expires. The clerk of the federal district court rejects the filing of Letitia's complaint and returns it by mail, because Letitia's complaint did not comply with a local rule of the district court that requires all pleadings filed with the court to have two hole punches centered at the top of the document (so that the clerk's office workers can place them into a binder with two brads at the top). Letitia hole-punches the complaint and refiles it two days later. Noor moves for summary judgment on the grounds that Letitia's complaint was not filed within the time required by the applicable statute of limitations. Letitia's response to the motion argues that the complaint was timely filed and that the federal court must apply the state rule, which only requires pleadings to be stapled (as her complaint was upon the initial filing attempt) not hole-punched, because applying the federal local rule would be outcome determinative.

How should the federal district court rule? Explain your answer.

D. A BRIEF WORD ON HORIZONTAL CHOICE OF LAW

The *Erie* Problem is a subset of a larger question, applicable in every court case, state or federal, that is known as "choice of law" or "conflict of laws." The *Erie* Problem is a vertical choice of law issue. A vertical choice of law issue arises when the court is choosing between a federal law and a state law. It makes sense to call this type of issue vertical, because the Supremacy Clause of the U.S. Constitution provides that constitutional provisions and federal statutes are the supreme law of the land, hence federal and state law's "vertical" relationship. In contrast, a horizontal choice of law issue arises when the court is choosing between the law of two or more different co-equal states. Up to this point, you may have assumed that a forum applies its own state law to all issues governed by state law. This assumption is understandable, but it isn't accurate. For example, recall that in *Erie*, Pennsylvania substantive law applied, even though New York was the forum state.

Each state has a body of law for determining what state's substantive law applies in a particular case, called choice of law or conflict of laws rules. Filing suit in a particular forum state (in either state or federal court) does not guarantee application of that state's substantive law. Instead, filing suit in a particular forum only requires application of that forum state's choice of law rule. For example, filing a negligence action in Texas state court or a federal court in Texas does not necessarily mean that Texas negligence law will govern the action, but it does mean that Texas's choice of law rule will be applied to determine what state's negligence law will apply.

Each state is free to develop its own choice of law rules. Perhaps the most common is the "most significant relationship test." Under this test, the court applies the substantive law of the state with the most significant relationship to the dispute. In making this determination, the court considers a variety of factors, including where the injury occurred (or where the contract was formed or to be performed); the domicile, state of organization, or principal place of business of the parties; and the state where the parties' relationship is centered (if any). Like many other states, Texas follows the most significant relationship test. So, in our earlier example, filing a negligence action in Texas state court or in a federal court in Texas does not necessarily require application of Texas negligence law, but it would guarantee application of Texas's most significant relationship test, which would be applied to determine what state's negligence rules should govern the action.

Chapter Summary

- The RDA requires federal courts to apply state law unless there is a conflicting federal constitutional provision, treaty, or statute.
- Under the Supreme Court's decision in *Erie*, the RDA's reference to state law includes state common law. Thus, federal courts are obligated to apply state tort, contract, property, and other substantive law in diversity cases.
- The REA authorizes the Supreme Court to make rules of practice and procedure to govern actions in federal district court.
- *Hanna* requires application of the Federal Rule even if it is different than state law, so long as the Rule is applicable and valid.
- An uncodified federal procedural practice is applied in lieu of conflicting state law, unless its application in federal court would cause plaintiffs to choose federal court over state law to get an outcome they could not get in the same case in state court.

Applying the Concepts

1. Polly brings an action in federal district court against Delvin, alleging that while a passenger in Delvin's car she was injured as a result of Delvin's negligent, gross negligent, and reckless driving. The applicable state law includes a "Guest Statute," which requires a passenger in a vehicle seeking damages from the driver to prove more than simple negligence, but the statute is not clear on what the standard for recovery is. The federal judge finds a United States Supreme Court case holding that the Guest Statute requires proof of gross negligence, but it also finds a case from the state high court whose substantive law applies, holding that the statute requires proof of recklessness. What standard should the federal district court apply? Why?

2. Alvin files a Texas Deceptive Trade Practices Act claim in federal district court against Beta Testing, LLC, alleging that Beta Testing's advertisements were false or misleading. Beta Testing moves to dismiss Alvin's complaint for failure to state a claim, because Alvin's complaint does not state a "plausible claim" as required by Rule 8(a) of the Federal Rules of Civil Procedure. Alvin acknowledges that his complaint does not satisfy Rule 8(a), but argues that it does not need to satisfy this standard because Texas pleading law only requires that he provide "fair notice" of his claim. Should the court apply Rule 8(a) or Texas law to determine the motion? Why?

3. Jorge brings a state law claim for specific performance of a contract in federal district court on diversity grounds against Arrow Industries, Inc. The applicable four-year state statute of limitations bars Jorge's claim, but Jorge's claim may be timely under the federal common law doctrine of laches, which would not bar the claim unless Jorge's delay in bringing his action was unreasonable. Should the federal court apply the state statute of limitations or the doctrine of laches? Why or why not?

Civil Procedure in Practice

A Texas resident sued a German manufacturer of cars for a state law product liability claim in federal court based on diversity of citizenship subject matter jurisdiction. The Texas resident alleged that the car was defective because the manufacturer placed the gas tank in an unreasonably dangerous position, causing the car to catch fire and burn when rear-ended. Both sides researched the law of product liability so that the court can give the jury the proper instructions and questions, allowing the jury to properly decide whether the defendant is liable. You are a law clerk to the federal district judge who is presiding over this case. How would you advise the judge to resolve the questions below?

1. Suppose proximate cause is a necessary element of the product liability claim. Also, suppose that both sides research and find two different definitions for

proximate cause. The plaintiff finds and proposes a definition from federal case law of what constitutes proximate cause. The defendant proposes a definition that conflicts with the Texas Supreme Court's definition of proximate cause. Neither definition appears in any statute. Which definition should the court use in the instructions to the jury? Why?

2. Now assume that both sides have presented all their evidence and rested their cases and the jury has begun to deliberate. Assume that the Seventh Amendment to the U.S. Constitution requires jury verdicts to be unanimous, while the Texas Constitution permits jury verdicts by a simple majority. The jury deliberates for 20 minutes. The foreperson then informs the court security officer that five of the six jurors have agreed on a verdict. However, the sixth juror does not agree with the other five. Is there a conflict between federal and state law under this scenario? Is there a way to avoid the conflict? How would you advise the court to avoid a conflict?

3. Now assume that the jury has deliberated for days and informs the court security officer that the jury is hopelessly deadlocked five-to-one, and the court must decide which constitutional provision to apply. Which provision must the court apply? Why? Does it matter whether the provisions can be classified as procedural? Does it matter whether deciding to apply federal law instead of state law is outcome determinative? Why or why not?

4. Now assume that there is no constitutional provision at issue. Rather, under Federal Rule of Civil Procedure 48, a jury verdict on whether the defendant was liable must be unanimous, while Texas Rule of Civil Procedure 292 requires only five out of six jurors to agree. The jury is still hopelessly deadlocked five-to-one, and the court must decide which law to apply. Which law is the court more likely to apply? Why?

Glossary

Additur.   A trial court order granting a new trial to the plaintiff unless the defendant agrees to an increase in the amount of damages awarded by the jury. The 7th Amendment to the Constitution prohibits additur in federal court. (Ch. 22)

Affirmative Defense.   A defense in confession and avoidance, allowing the defendant to reduce or avoid liability by proving the facts constituting the defense, even if the plaintiff's claim is also established. (Ch. 15)

Alienage Jurisdiction.   The original subject matter jurisdiction that 28 U.S.C. §1332 grants to federal district courts over cases between a citizen or citizens of a state and a citizen or citizens of a foreign state. E.g., a citizen of Spain files suit against a citizen of Texas. (Ch. 3)

Amount in Controversy Requirement.   A requirement that the amount of money at issue in the case exceed a certain threshold in order for a court to have subject matter jurisdiction. Importantly, the amount in controversy must exceed $75,000, exclusive of interest and costs, for a federal district court to have diversity of citizenship jurisdiction under 28 U.S.C. §1332. (Ch. 3)

Answer.   The defendant's responsive pleading to the plaintiff's complaint. (Ch. 1)

Appellate Jurisdiction.   A higher court's judicial power to review the decision of a lower court to determine if any error requires reversal of the judgment. (Ch. 1)

***Batson* Challenge.**   An objection that a potential juror was struck from the venire on the basis of race or gender. (Ch. 22)

Bench Trial.   A trial to the bench (i.e., without a jury) in which the judge determines the disputed fact issues and applies the law to the facts. (Ch. 22)

Case-in-Chief.   The evidence a party presents between the time the party calls his first witness or offers his first exhibit and the time the party rests his case. (Ch. 22)

Challenge for Cause.   An objection to a potential juror on the grounds that the juror has an interest in the outcome of the case or a bias or prejudice against or in favor of a party to the case. (Ch. 22)

Charge to the Jury.   The trial court's instructions and questions to the jury. The jury's answers to the questions in the charge constitute its verdict. (Ch. 22)

Civil Action.   A proceeding brought to resolve a dispute between the litigants based on the breach of some duty the defendant is alleged to owe the plaintiff, rather than one brought to determine whether the defendant is guilty of a crime. (Ch. 1)

Claim Preclusion.   The defense that gives preclusive effect to a final judgment, preventing the same parties or those in privity from relitigating claims that were decided or could have been decided in the prior case, a/k/a *res judicata*. (Ch. 24)

Class Action.   A civil action in which one or more parties represent a class of similarly situated persons who will be bound by the judgment in the action, even though they are not parties to it. (Ch. 19)

Collateral Estoppel.   The defense that a court's prior determination of an issue be given preclusive effect so that the parties or those in privity in another case cannot relitigate the issue, a/k/a issue preclusion. (Ch. 24)

Collateral Orders.   An interlocutory court decision on a discrete issue that would conclusively determine an important, disputed question; the question must be completely separate from the merits of the action, and the decision must be effectively unreviewable from a final judgment. E.g., a court order prohibiting a party who is allowed to intervene in the action as of right and some decisions regarding parties' immunity from suit. (Ch. 23)

Complaint.   The plaintiff's initial pleading that provides the legal and factual basis for his claim. A federal civil action is commenced with the filing of the plaintiff's complaint. (Ch. 1)

Complete Diversity of Citizenship.   A requirement for diversity of citizenship jurisdiction under 28 U.S.C. §1332 that no party on one side of the claim share citizenship with any party on the other side of the claim; i.e., no plaintiff may share citizenship with any defendant. (Ch. 3)

Concurrent Jurisdiction.   More than one court or court system has subject matter jurisdiction over the action; e.g., state and federal courts have concurrent jurisdiction over diversity cases and most federal question cases. (Ch. 1)

Consolidation Order.   An order making multiple civil actions a single civil action. (Ch. 18)

Contribution.   A claim that a party must pay for a portion of the claimant's liability to another party. (Ch. 18)

Counterclaim.   A claim against an opposing party; e.g., the defendant asserted a counterclaim against the plaintiff. (Ch. 3)

Creation Test.   A test for determining the existence of federal question jurisdiction, which provides that a civil action arises under the law that creates the cause of action. (Ch. 4)

Crossclaim.   A claim against a co-party; e.g., the defendant asserted a crossclaim against his co-defendant. (Ch. 18)

Declaratory Judgment Act.   A federal act that authorizes federal courts to declare the rights and relations of a party who seeks such a declaration in cases of "actual controversy." 22 U.S.C. §2201. (Ch. 4)

Declaratory Judgment Action.   An action seeking a declaration of the rights, liabilities, or obligations of the parties. (Ch. 4)

Default. A notation on the docket sheet after a defendant's failure to respond to the plaintiff's complaint that precludes the defendant from filing a Rule 12 response. (Ch. 15)

Default Judgment. A judgment rendered based on the defendant's failure to defend the civil action. (Ch. 1)

Defendant(s). The person against whom a plaintiff seeks judgment in a civil action. The person the plaintiff names in his complaint as having caused or contributed to cause the plaintiff's harm. (Ch. 1)

Deponent. A deposition witness. (Ch. 17)

Derivative Action. An action in which the shareholders of a corporation or the members of an unincorporated association bring suit on behalf of the corporation or association because the officers and directors of the entity are unwilling to authorize the entity to pursue the action. (Ch. 21)

Discretionary Review. The power of a court, ordinarily a court of last resort such as a supreme court, to refuse to hear a case; e.g., the United States Supreme Court may decline to consider an appeal because it is a court of discretionary review. (Ch. 1)

Dismissal. The trial court's rejection of a civil action, which may be with or without prejudice to refiling. (Ch. 21)

Domicile. Under 28 U.S.C. §1332, a U.S. citizen is a citizen of the U.S. state of his or her domicile. An individual is domiciled in the place where the individual resides with the intent to remain indefinitely. (Ch. 3)

***Erie* Guess.** A federal court's determination of how the state's highest court would resolve a question of state law if presented with the question today. (Ch. 25)

Essentially at Home. The standard for where an individual or entity is subject to general personal jurisdiction. (Ch. 8)

Exclusive Jurisdiction. Only one court or court system has subject matter jurisdiction over the case; e.g., state courts may not hear a patent infringement claim because federal courts have exclusive jurisdiction over patent infringement claims. (Ch. 1)

Fact Pleading. A pleading standard, now abandoned in federal court, that required a statement of the facts constituting the cause of action. (Ch. 14)

Federal. Relating to the U.S. Government; e.g., the federal court system. (Ch. 1)

Federal Civil Procedure. The body of law that governs how civil actions are resolved in the federal court system. (Ch. 1)

Final Judgment. A judgment signed by the court disposing of all claims and all parties. (Ch. 23)

Forum Court. The court in which the action is pending. (Ch. 6)

Forum Selection Clause. A term in many contracts that requires any disputes between the parties to the contract to be litigated, if at all, in a particular forum. (Ch. 9)

Forum State.   The state in which the action is pending. (Ch. 6)

Forum State Defendant Rule.   A rule prohibiting removal of a civil action from state to federal court on diversity grounds when any defendant properly joined and served is a citizen of the forum state. 28 U.S.C. §1441(b)(2). (Ch. 5)

Fraudulently Joined.   A term that describes a defendant who was joined based upon fraudulently alleged facts or based upon allegations that do not state a claim for relief against the defendant. (Ch. 5)

General Personal Jurisdiction.   The authority of a court to require the defendant to defend herself against any suit filed in the forum state because the defendant is considered essentially at home in the forum state. (Ch. 7)

General Subject Matter Jurisdiction.   The judicial power to hear any case, without regard to the nature of the claims or parties. Each state court system has a trial court with general subject matter jurisdiction. (Ch. 1)

General Verdict.   A verdict in which the jury states only who wins and, if it is the plaintiff, the amount of damages. (Ch. 22)

Impleader.   The joinder of a third-party defendant. (Ch. 18)

In Rem.   A court's exercise of authority over property located within the forum state for the purposes of determining the status of that property and, as a result, the rights of persons with respect to the property. (Ch. 9)

In-Hand Service.   Personal service; i.e., service of process accomplished by handing the summons and complaint to the party to be served. (Ch. 13)

Indemnification.   A claim that a party is obligated to pay for the claimant's entire liability to another party. (Ch. 18)

Indispensable Party.   A person who is not a party to the action and whose absence requires the court to dismiss the action. (Ch. 19)

Initial Disclosures.   One of the self-executing disclosures under the federal discovery rules that requires parties to disclose all documents, witnesses, and tangible things the party may use to support its claims or defenses even though the other parties have not requested the information. (Ch. 17)

Injunction.   A court order that requires a party to do or refrain from doing something. (Ch. 3)

Interpleader.   A procedural device that allows a person facing competing claims to property in his possession or control to join all the claimants as defendants. (Ch. 19)

Interrogatories to Parties.   A pretrial, written question to another party that the party must answer under oath. (Ch. 17)

Intervention.   A procedural device that allows a person to join a pending action because the person claims an interest in the subject of the action or because the person's claim or the claim against the person shares common questions of law or fact with a claim in the pending action. (Ch. 19)

Issue Preclusion.   The defense that a court's prior determination of an issue be given preclusive effect so that the parties or those in privity in another case cannot relitigate the issue, a/k/a *collateral estoppel*. (Ch. 24)

Joint Hearing.   A hearing that resolves issues common to more than one civil action. (Ch. 18)

Joint Trial.   A trial that resolves disputed fact issues in more than one civil action. (Ch. 18)

Judgment.   A decree or order from which an appeal lies. (Ch. 1)

Judgment as a Matter of Law.   A judgment that is based on a point of law rather than on resolution of disputed fact issues. (Ch. 22)

Judgment on a Jury Verdict.   A judgment that is rendered based on and consistent with a jury verdict. (Ch. 1)

Jury Argument.   An argument that is made by an attorney to the jury about the verdict the jury should reach. (Ch. 22)

Jury Trial.   A trial in which a jury determines the triable issues of fact. (Ch. 22)

Limited Subject Matter Jurisdiction.   Subject matter jurisdiction that is limited in scope by a constitutional provision or statute. (Ch. 1)

Local Rule.   A local rule is a rule of a particular court that supplements the Federal Rules of Civil Procedure over a nonresident defendant. (Ch. 17)

Long Arm Statute.   A statute or rule that authorizes a court to exercise personal jurisdiction. (Ch. 6)

Minimal Diversity of Citizenship.   Any difference in citizenship amongst certain parties; e.g., 28 U.S.C. §1335 requires only minimal diversity of citizenship between claimants to invoke interpleader jurisdiction in a statutory interpleader case; i.e., it requires only that there is some difference in citizenship amongst the claimants. (Ch. 19)

Misidentification.   When the plaintiff names the wrong defendant in the complaint. (Ch. 16)

Misjoinder.   The term that describes the improper joinder of a party or claim. (Ch. 18)

Misnomer.   When the plaintiff served process on the correct defendant but has called him by the wrong name in the complaint; e.g., plaintiff served process on Frank's Store, Inc. but called the defendant Frank's Store, LLC in the complaint. (Ch. 16)

Nerve Center.   The location of a corporation's principal place of business for purposes of determining its citizenship under the diversity statute, 28 U.S.C. §1332. The nerve center is the place from which the high-level officers and managers direct, control, and coordinate the activities of the corporation; ordinarily, this is the corporate headquarters. (Ch. 3)

Notice.   The requirement that a defendant must be informed of the action against him and given the opportunity to defend himself. (Ch. 13)

Notice by Publication.   A method of Notice to the defendant about the pendency of the action against him often published in a newspaper and likely permitted only by court order. (Ch.13)

Notice Dismissal.   A filing that allows a plaintiff to dismiss his action before a defendant answers without a court order and without prejudice to refiling. (Ch. 21)

Notice of Removal.   A federal court filing by which a defendant or defendants remove a case from state to federal court. (Ch. 5)

Notice Pleading.   A pleading standard that requires the pleader only to give opposing parties fair notice of his claim or defense. (Ch. 14)

Opening Statement.   An attorney's statement to the jury that outlines what the attorney believes the evidence at trial will prove. (Ch. 22)

Oral Deposition.   The testimony of a witness (i.e., a deponent) that is given pre-trial, orally, and under oath. (Ch. 17)

Original Jurisdiction.   The judicial authority to hear the case first before another court considers or reviews the case. (Ch. 1)

***Per Curiam* Opinion.**   A judicial opinion that is "by the court" and does not identify a particular judge as the author of the opinion. (Ch. 5)

Personal Jurisdiction.   The court's authority to require a defendant to appear and personally defend himself against a pending lawsuit. (Ch. 6)

Physical or Mental Examination.   A discovery device that, upon court order, allows a party to obtain a medical examination of another party whose physical or mental condition is relevant to the case. (Ch. 17)

Plain Error Rule.   The concept that an appellate court will review a trial court error that affects a party's substantial rights even though the party did not properly preserve error. *See* Fed. R. Civ. P. 61. (Ch. 23)

Plaintiff(s).   A party who files a civil action and seeks a remedy from the court. (Ch. 1)

Plausibility Pleading Standard.   A pleading standard that requires a party seeking affirmative relief to plead facts sufficient to show a plausible claim. *Compare* Notice Pleading. (Ch. 14)

Principal Place of Business.   The place from which the high-level decision-makers such as officers and managers direct, control, and coordinate the activities of the entity; ordinarily, this is the entity's headquarters. (Ch. 3)

Preparation Prejudice.   Prejudice to the non-moving party that justifies refusing to allow a party to amend its pleading. (Ch. 16)

Preserve Error.   The act of requesting the trial court to take some action; receiving a definitive, adverse ruling on your request that appears in the trial record; adequately informing the appellate court why the trial court made an error and why the erroneous adverse ruling is sufficiently harmful to warrant a remedy. (Ch. 23)

Pretrial Disclosures.   One of the self-executing disclosures under the federal discovery rules that requires parties to disclose witness and exhibit lists shortly before trial. (Ch. 17)

Privity.   A connection or relationship between parties who share sufficient interests in the proceeding such that the non-party to the original lawsuit is considered adequately represented in the prior lawsuit and therefore bound by the resolution of the claim or issue in the prior lawsuit. (Ch. 24)

Pro Se.   A status that denotes a party who is unrepresented by legal counsel. (Ch. 14)

Procedure.   A rule or rules that regulate the manner in which a legal proceeding is resolved. (Ch. 1)

Process.   The papers served on a defendant that trigger her obligation to respond to the pending action, which consist of a copy of the summons and complaint. (Ch. 1)

Quasi In Rem.   Jurisdiction over a person based on the person's interest in property located in the forum state. (Ch. 9)

Quo Warranto **Suits.**   A common-law device used to inquire into the authority of one's actions or status. (Ch. 24)

Rebuttal Case.   The portion of a trial in which a party is permitted to present evidence that rebuts the evidence offered by an opposing party. (Ch. 22)

Receiver.   A person who is entrusted with the property of another. (Ch. 21)

Remand.   A federal court order that returns a removed case to the state court from which it was removed. (Ch. 5)

Remittitur.   A trial court order granting a new trial to the defendant unless the plaintiff agrees to a decrease in the amount of damages awarded by the jury. *Compare* Additur. (Ch. 22)

Removal.   Moving a case filed in state court to federal court (Ch. 5)

Removal Venue.   The rule that makes venue in removed cases proper in the federal district and division embracing the location of the state court in which the action was originally filed. (Ch. 5)

Request for Admission.   A discovery request that asks a party to admit or deny the truth of certain alleged facts. (Ch. 17)

Request for Production.   A discovery request that seeks production or inspection of documents, electronically stored information, or tangible things, or inspection or testing of premises or other property. (Ch. 17)

Required Disclosures of Expert Witnesses.   One of the self-executing disclosures under the federal discovery rules that requires parties to disclose the identities and opinions of expert witnesses retained or employed to provide expert testimony in the action. (Ch. 17)

Required Party.   A person the court must join as a party to the action if feasible because the person claims an interest in the action or because the court may not be able to accord complete relief in the person's absence. (Ch. 19)

Res Judicata.   The defense that gives preclusive effect to a Final Judgment, preventing the same parties or parties in privity from relitigating claims that were decided or could have been decided in the prior case, a/k/a claim preclusion. (Ch. 24)

Restatement.   An influential secondary source that describes the law in a given area. A Restatement's description of the law is not binding authority unless and until the language of the Restatement is adopted as law by a particular jurisdiction. (Ch. 24)

Scienter.   A state of mind that encompasses knowledge of wrongdoing or intent to deceive. (Ch. 14)

Service of Process.   The formal procedure by which the defendant is served with the summons and complaint, notifying him that he has been sued, providing basic notice of the claims against him, and informing him of his obligation to respond. (Ch.13)

Settlement Agreement.   A contract that resolves a civil dispute by requiring the claimant to release his claim in exchange for something of value, typically money. (Ch. 1)

***Smith* Exception.**   An exception to the Creation Test that provides that certain state-created causes of action arise under federal law, invoking federal question jurisdiction under 28 U.S.C. §1331. (Ch. 4)

Special Verdict.   A verdict that requires the jury to answer specific questions about the disputed fact issues in the case. (Ch. 22)

Specific Personal Jurisdiction.   The authority of a court to require the defendant to defend herself in the forum court because the defendant had sufficient contacts with the forum state, the suit arises out of or is connected to the defendant's contact(s) with the forum state, and the exercise of jurisdiction over the person of the defendant is fair and reasonable. (Ch. 7)

Spoliation.   The bad faith destruction or alteration of evidence. (Ch. 17)

Stare Decisis.   A principle courts apply to guide their decision by referring to past precedent, which generally requires the court to follow the court's own prior rulings on points of law and those of a higher court within the same court system. (Ch. 1)

Sua Sponte.   A term that means "of its own accord" that is ordinarily used to refer to an issue that was raised by the court, rather than the parties; e.g., none of the parties questioned the court's subject matter jurisdiction, but the court raised the issue *sua sponte*. (Ch. 2)

Subject Matter Jurisdiction.   The judicial power of a court to hear and decide a case. (Ch. 1)

Subpoena.   A writ issued by a court that compels a witness to appear at a particular time and place. (Ch. 17)

Summary Judgment.   A type of pretrial judgment as a matter of law that is rendered because there is no genuine dispute as to any material fact. (Ch. 1)

Summons.   The court document that informs the defendant of her legal obligation to respond to the complaint and the consequences of the failure to do so in a timely manner. (Ch. 13)

Supplemental Jurisdiction.   A type of subject matter jurisdiction that allows a federal district court to exercise jurisdiction over most (but not all) additional claims that are factually related to the action over which it has original jurisdiction. (Ch. 20)

Tag Jurisdiction.   *See* Transient Presence Jurisdiction. (Ch. 9)

Third-Party Defendant.   A party who is joined by a defending party, typically the defendant, on the ground that he must pay at least a share of the defending party's liability. (Ch. 18)

Transfer of Venue.   Moving a case from one federal district court or division thereof to another federal district court or division thereof. (Ch. 12)

Transient Presence Jurisdiction.   Personal jurisdiction based on personal service on an individual nonresident defendant while the defendant is voluntarily present in the forum state resulting in a court properly exercising general personal jurisdiction over the defendant, a/k/a Tag Jurisdiction. (Ch. 9)

Triable Issues of Fact.   A disputed fact issue regarding an element of a party's claim or defense that is resolved by a fact-finder at trial. (Ch. 22)

Unanimity of Consent Rule.   The rule that requires all defendants properly joined and served to consent to the removal of a civil action from state to federal court. (Ch. 5)

Venire.   The panel of potential jurors from which the jury is selected. (Ch. 22)

Venue.   In federal law, a judicial district and division that is a proper location for a lawsuit, often because the forum has an appropriate connection to the lawsuit or the parties. (Ch.11)

Verdict.   The jury's answers to the questions in the court's charge. (Ch. 22)

Voir Dire.   The process of selecting a jury from the panel of prospective jurors (i.e., the venire), a/k/a jury selection. (Ch. 22)

Voluntary Dismissal.   A dismissal that is based on the plaintiff's desire to end the civil action he filed. The plaintiff may unilaterally dismiss his action before the defendant files an answer but afterwards dismissal requires the agreement of the parties or a court order. *See* Notice of Dismissal. (Ch. 21)

Well-Pleaded Complaint Rule.   A rule for determining whether a civil action invokes federal question jurisdiction that requires a federal question to exist on the face of the plaintiff's well-pleaded complaint and in the statement of his cause of action. The rule precludes defenses as well as anticipated responses to defenses from properly invoking federal question jurisdiction, even if mentioned in the plaintiff's complaint. (Ch. 4)

With Prejudice.   The effect of a dismissal that precludes refiling the action. (Ch. 21)

Without Prejudice to Refiling.   The effect of a dismissal that does not preclude refiling the action. (Ch. 21)

Writ of Mandamus.   A vehicle to have an appellate court review an interlocutory decision of a trial court upon a showing that the party seeking appellate relief will suffer some special risk of irreparable harm from the decision, and the party is clearly entitled to the relief requested. (Ch. 23)

Table of Cases

Principal cases are italicized.

Table of Rules

Index